EXPLORING THE INTERNET

Gretchen Marx / Robert T. Grauer

Saint Joseph College   University of Miami

Prentice Hall, Upper Saddle River, New Jersey 07458

Acquisitions editor: Carolyn Henderson
Editorial/production supervisor: Greg Hubit Bookworks
Interior and cover design: Suzanne Behnke
Senior manufacturing supervisor: Paul Smolenski
Editorial assistant: Audrey Regan

©1996 by Prentice Hall, Inc.
A Simon & Schuster Company
Upper Saddle River, New Jersey 07458

All rights reserved. No part of this book may be
reproduced, in any form or by any means,
without permission in writing from the publisher.

Printed in the United States of America
10 9 8 7 6 5 4 3 2 1

ISBN 0-13-504051-5

Prentice Hall International (UK) Limited, *London*
Prentice Hall of Australia Pty. Limited, *Sydney*
Prentice Hall of Canada Inc., *Toronto*
Prentice Hall Hispanoamericano, S.A., *Mexico*
Prentice Hall of India Private Limited, *New Delhi*
Prentice Hall of Japan, Inc., *Tokyo*
Simon & Schuster Asia Pte. Ltd., *Singapore*
Editora Prentice Hall do Brasil, Ltda., *Rio de Janeiro*

To Ben, Barret, Jeremy, and Elliot,
for your constant love, support, and encouragement.
—G. M.

Contents

PREFACE   xi

1

Introduction to the Internet: Welcome to Cyberspace   1

CHAPTER OBJECTIVES   1
OVERVIEW   1
The Internet   2
What You Will Find on the Internet   3
    Sending and Receiving E-Mail   3   Using a Web Browser   5   Gopher and FTP   7   Conversing on the Internet   12   Netiquette, Safe Surfing, and Other Issues   14   Web Publishing with HTML   16
Connecting to the Internet   17
How the Internet Works   20
    The TCP/IP Protocol   21   Internet Architecture Layers   22
    The Domain Name System   24   Internet Addresses   24
Learning by Doing   25
HANDS-ON EXERCISE 1: WELCOME TO CYBERSPACE   26
Summary   30
Key Words and Concepts   31
Multiple Choice   31
Exploring the Internet   33
Practice with the Internet   36
Case Studies   36

2

Global Communication on the Internet: Using E-mail 39

CHAPTER OBJECTIVES 39
OVERVIEW 39

E-mail 40
    The Structure of an E-Mail Message 40   Logins and Security 42   Mailboxes 42

Sending and Receiving E-Mail 44
    E-Mail Using a POP Mail Client 44

Learning by Doing 46

HANDS-ON EXERCISE 1: WELCOME TO E-MAIL WITH PC EUDORA 46

E-Mail with a Unix Mail Program 55

HANDS-ON EXERCISE 2: E-MAIL USING PINE 56

Additional E-Mail Capabilities 60
    Distribution Lists 60   Customizing Your Signature 60   Personal Mail Folders 61

Mailing Lists 62
    Finding Mailing Lists 63   Subscribing to a List 63   Subscription Options 64

HANDS-ON EXERCISE 3: CUSTOMIZING E-MAIL AND SUBSCRIBING TO MAILING LISTS USING A PC MAIL CLIENT 64

HANDS-ON EXERCISE 4: CUSTOMIZING E-MAIL AND SUBSCRIBING TO MAILING LISTS USING PINE 71

Summary 77
Key Words and Concepts 77
Multiple Choice 78
Exploring the Internet 80
Practice with E-Mail 82
Case Studies 84

3

Finding Things on the World Wide Web: Netscape and Lynx 85

CHAPTER OBJECTIVES 85
OVERVIEW 85

The World Wide Web 86
Netscape 88
    The Uniform Resource Locator (URL) 88   Hypertext Transport Protocol (HTTP) 89   Hypertext Markup Language (HTML) 91   Saving and Printing Web Documents 92   Bookmarks 93

Learning by Doing   94
HANDS-ON EXERCISE 1: SURFING THE NET   94
Web Search Engines   100
    Search Rules and Techniques   103   And, Or, and Not   106
Other Browser Capabilities   106
    To Load or Not to Load Images   106   Using E-Mail in Netscape   107
HANDS-ON EXERCISE 2: SEARCHING THE WEB AND USING ADDITIONAL NETSCAPE FEATURES   108
Lynx   114
HANDS-ON EXERCISE 3: USING LYNX ON THE WORLD WIDE WEB   115
Summary   122
Key Words and Concepts   122
Multiple Choice   123
Exploring the Internet   125
Practice with the World Wide Web   127
Case Studies   128

4

Other Internet Tools: Gopher, FTP, Veronica, and Archie   129

CHAPTER OBJECTIVES   129
OVERVIEW   129
Gopher   130
Gophering with a Web Browser   130
Learning by Doing   133
HANDS-ON EXERCISE 1: TUNNELING THROUGH GOPHERSPACE USING A WEB BROWSER   133
Gophering Using Your Shell Account   135
HANDS-ON EXERCISE 2: GOPHERING USING YOUR UNIX SHELL ACCOUNT   135
File Transfer Protocol (FTP)   138
    FTP with a Web Browser   139
HANDS-ON EXERCISE 3: FTP WITH A WEB BROWSER   140
    FTP with a Windows-based FTP Client   142
HANDS-ON EXERCISE 4: FTP WITH A WINDOWS FTP CLIENT   144
    FTP Using the Unix Prompt   146
HANDS-ON EXERCISE 5: FTP FROM THE UNIX PROMPT   148
Searching for Gopher and FTP Files and Directories Using Veronica and Archie   150
Summary   152
Key Words and Concepts   152
Multiple Choice   153
Exploring the Internet   155
Practice with Gopher and FTP   157
Case Studies   159

5

Conversations on the Internet: IRC, WebChat, and Usenet 161

CHAPTER OBJECTIVES   161
OVERVIEW   161

Internet Relay Chat (IRC)   162
   IRC Commands   165
Learning by Doing   166
HANDS-ON EXERCISE 1: IRC CHAT   166
WebChat   173
HANDS-ON EXERCISE 2: USING WEBCHAT   174
Usenet   180
Learning by Doing   185
HANDS-ON EXERCISE 3: USENET   185
Summary   193
Key Words and Concepts   193
Multiple Choice   194
Exploring the Internet   196
Practice with IRC, WebChat, and Usenet   197
Case Studies   198

6

The Internet and Society: Netiquette, Safe Surfing, and Other Issues in Cyberspace 199

CHAPTER OBJECTIVES   199
OVERVIEW   199

Legal Issues   200
   Copyright Infringement   200   Freedom of Speech and the Right to Privacy   200
Social Issues   202
HANDS-ON EXERCISE 1: EXPLORING LEGAL AND SOCIAL ISSUES ON THE INTERNET   205
Security   206
   Encryption and the Clipper Chip   206   Viruses   207   Safeguards   208   Authentication   208
HANDS-ON EXERCISE 2: INTERNET SECURITY AND PRIVACY   209
Netiquette   210
   Do's and Don'ts   210   NetSpeak—The Language of the Internet   211   Smilies and Emoticons   213
The Commercialization of Cyberspace   213
   Commercial Online Network Providers   214   Shopping in Cyberspace   216

HANDS-ON EXERCISE 3: SHOPPING ON THE INTERNET   217
Summary   219
Key Words and Concepts   219
Multiple Choice   219
Exploring the Internet   221
Practice with the Internet   222
Case Studies   223

7

Web Publishing: Creating Home Pages with HTML   225

CHAPTER OBJECTIVES   225
OVERVIEW   225
Introduction to HTML   226
HTML Codes   227
    Titles   227   Headings and Lists   227   Links to URLs and Local Files   230   Linked Documents   230   Links to Bookmarks   232   Other HTML Tags   232   Inserting Images   234
Learning by Doing   237
HANDS-ON EXERCISE 1: ENTERING HTML TAGS IN NOTEPAD   237
Using an HTML Editor   243
HANDS-ON EXERCISE 2: USING MICROSOFT INTERNET ASSISTANT FOR WORD   244
Summary   255
Key Words and Concepts   255
Multiple Choice   255
Exploring the Internet   258
Practice with HTML   259
Case Studies   260

APPENDIX A: REMOTE ACCESS TO THE INTERNET   263
OVERVIEW   263
Dialing In to the Internet   263
    The HyperTerminal Accessory   265   Logging in with SLIP/PPP   266
Using a Commercial Online Provider   267

APPENDIX B: HOT SITES ON THE INTERNET   269

APPENDIX C: INTERNET ACRONYM LIST   277

APPENDIX D: INTERNET GLOSSARY   279

INDEX

Preface

Exploring the Internet is a natural extension of the *Exploring Windows* series for the instructor who may wish to present the Internet in an introductory computer or applications class. Other Internet books, and there are literally hundreds of them, are written as reference books rather than textbooks, and there is a tremendous difference. *Exploring the Internet,* however, is written for the novice and assumes no prior knowledge on the part of the reader. Equally important, it employs the same pedagogy and writing style that is common to all books in our series.

The *Exploring Windows* series features a full line of texts for both the Windows 3.1 and Windows 95 environments. Our most recent titles include: *Exploring Microsoft Word Version 7.0, Exploring Microsoft Excel Version 7.0, Exploring Microsoft Access Version 7.0, Exploring Microsoft PowerPoint Version 7.0,* and *Exploring Windows 95 and Essential Computing Concepts.* We have also created *Exploring Microsoft Office Professional—Volume I* by taking selected chapters from the individual books. And finally, there is *Exploring Microsoft Office Professional—Volume II,* which consists of advanced chapters and appendices from the individual books that are not included in Volume I.

Each book in the *Exploring Windows* series is suitable on a stand-alone basis for any course that teaches a specific application; alternatively, several modules can be bound together for a single course that teaches multiple applications. All of the books possess a common design, pedagogy, and writing style that is appropriate for microcomputer applications courses in both two- and four-year schools.

The *Exploring Windows* series will appeal to students in a variety of disciplines including business, liberal arts, and the sciences. Each book has a consistent presentation that stresses the benefits of the Windows environment, especially the common user interface, multitasking, and the extensive on-line help facility. Students are taught concepts, not just keystrokes or mouse clicks, with hands-on exercises in every chapter providing the necessary practice to master the material.

The *Exploring Windows* series is different from other books, both in its scope as well as in the way in which material is presented. Students learn by doing. Concepts are stressed and memorization is minimized. Shortcuts and other important information are consistently highlighted in the many tips that appear throughout the series. Every chapter contains an average of three directed exercises at the computer, but equally important are the less-structured end-of-chapter problems that not only review the information, but extend it as well. The end-of-chapter material is a distinguishing feature of the entire series, an integral part of the learning process, and a powerful motivational tool for students to learn and explore.

Each book in the *Exploring Windows* series is accompanied by a comprehensive Instructor's Resource Manual with solutions to all exercises, PowerPoint lectures, and student/instructor resource disks. (The Instructor's Resource Manual for the entire series is also available on a single CD-ROM.) Instructors can also use the Prentice Hall Computerized Online Testing System to prepare customized tests for their courses and may obtain Interactive Multimedia courseware as a further supplement. The *Exploring Windows* series is part of the Prentice Hall custom binding program.

FEATURES AND BENEFITS

Exploring the Internet is written for the computer novice and assumes no previous knowledge on the part of the reader. Chapter 1 provides an overview of what the Internet is and explains its many services.

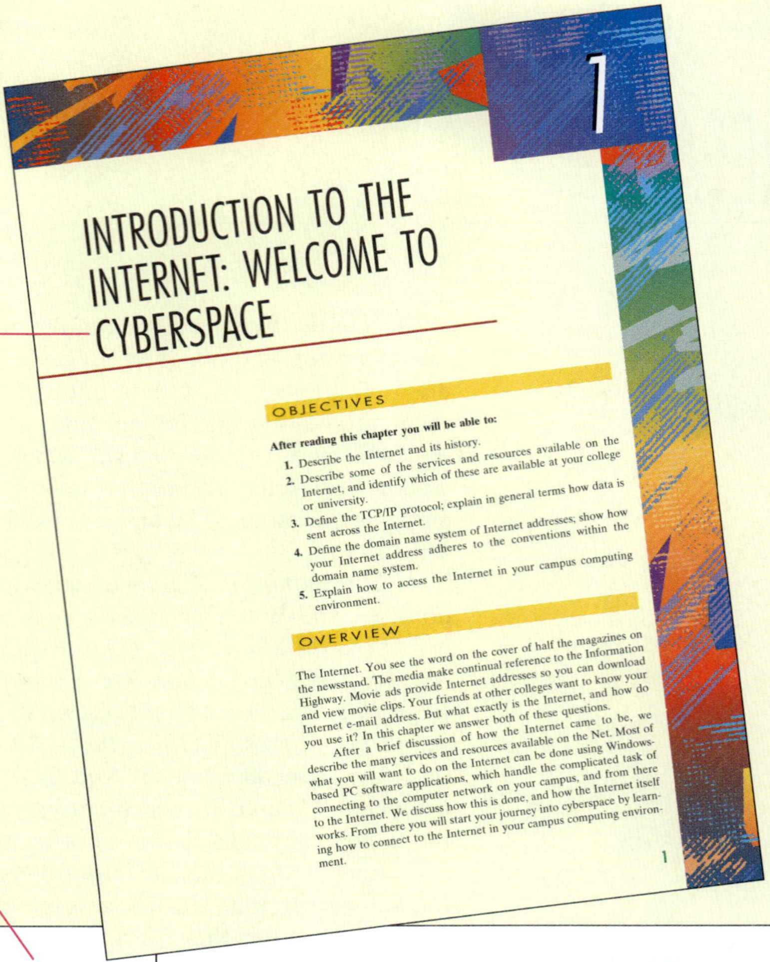

Chapter 2 focuses entirely on e-mail, emphasizing concepts rather than keystrokes. Our examples use both a Windows-based program (PC Eudora) as well as a menu-based Unix program (Pine), but the concepts apply equally well to any e-mail system.

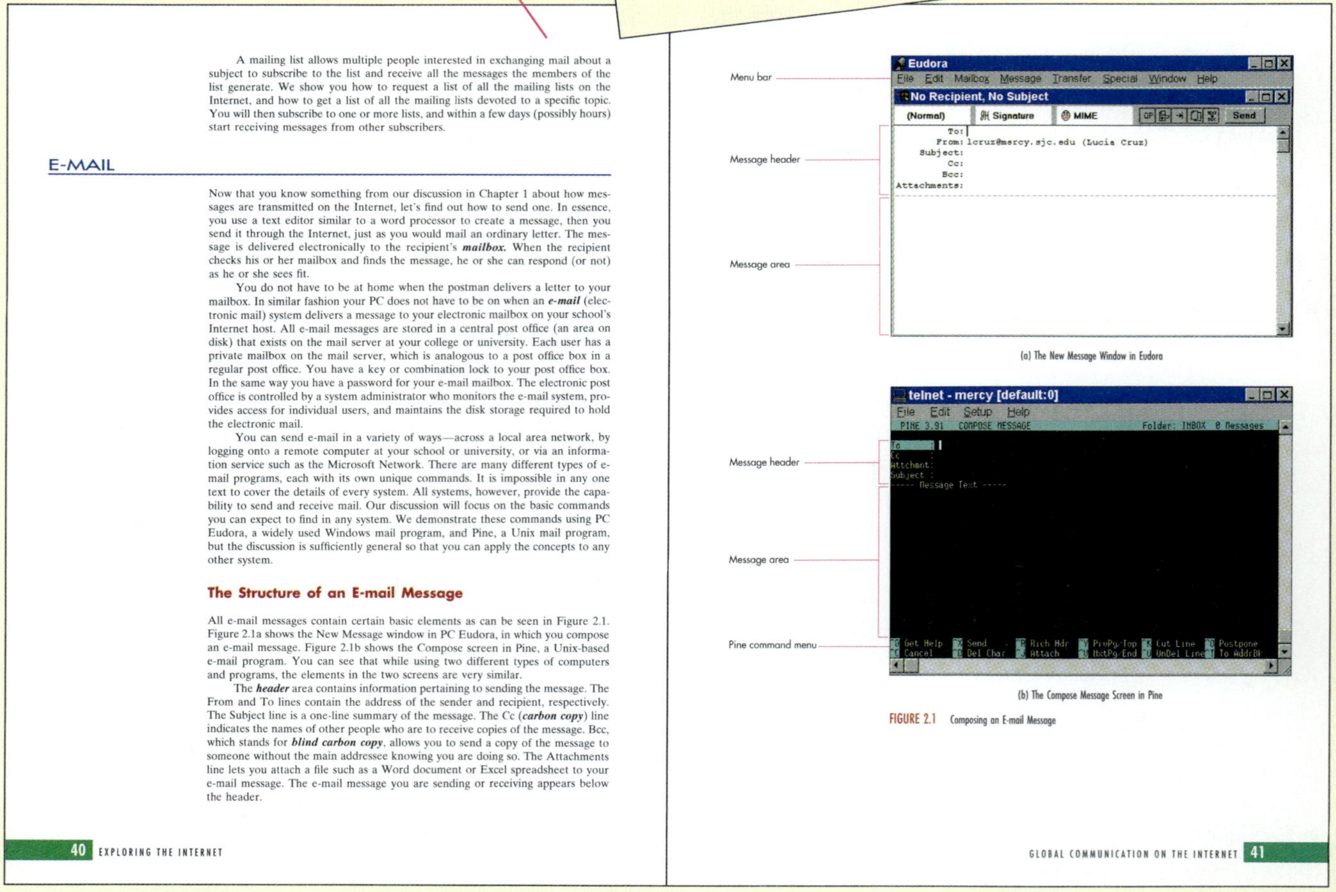

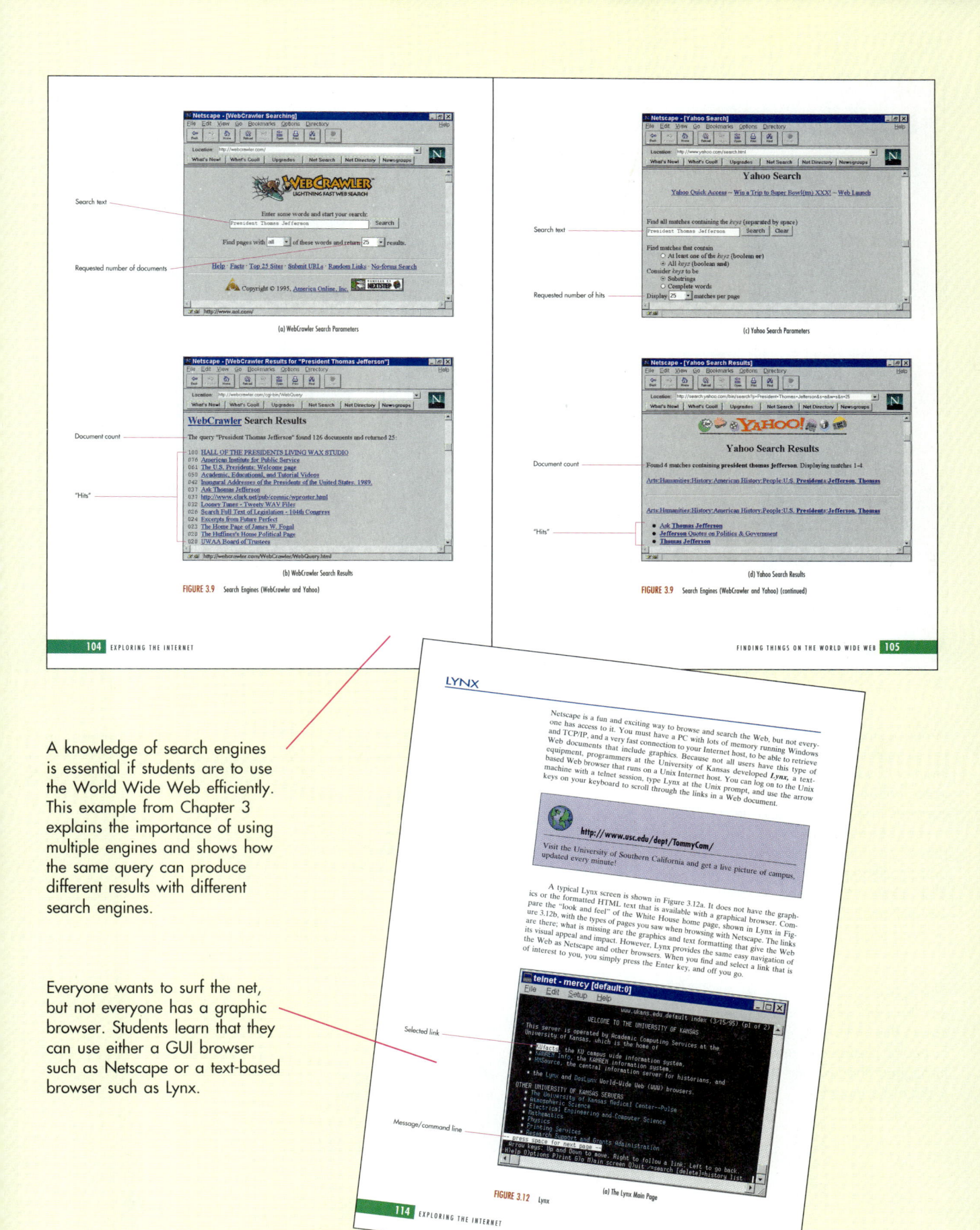

A knowledge of search engines is essential if students are to use the World Wide Web efficiently. This example from Chapter 3 explains the importance of using multiple engines and shows how the same query can produce different results with different search engines.

Everyone wants to surf the net, but not everyone has a graphic browser. Students learn that they can use either a GUI browser such as Netscape or a text-based browser such as Lynx.

PREFACE xiii

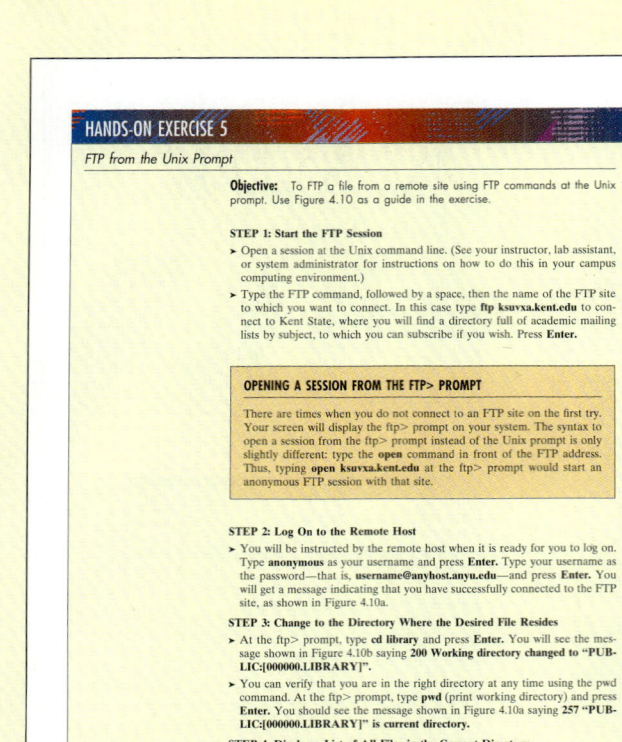

HANDS-ON EXERCISE 5
FTP from the Unix Prompt

Objective: To FTP a file from a remote site using FTP commands at the Unix prompt. Use Figure 4.10 as a guide in the exercise.

STEP 1: Start the FTP Session
- Open a session at the Unix command line. (See your instructor, lab assistant, or system administrator for instructions on how to do this in your campus computing environment.)
- Type the FTP command, followed by a space, then the name of the FTP site to which you want to connect. In this case type **ftp ksuvxa.kent.edu** to connect to Kent State, where you will find a directory full of academic mailing lists by subject, to which you can subscribe if you wish. Press **Enter**.

OPENING A SESSION FROM THE FTP> PROMPT
There are times when you do not connect to an FTP site on the first try. Your screen will display the ftp> prompt on your system. The syntax to open a session from the ftp> prompt instead of the Unix prompt is only slightly different: type the **open** command in front of the FTP address. Thus, typing **open ksuvxa.kent.edu** at the ftp> prompt would start an anonymous FTP session with that site.

STEP 2: Log On to the Remote Host
- You will be instructed by the remote host when it is ready for you to log on. Type **anonymous** as your username and press **Enter**. Type your username as the password—that is, **username@anyhost.anyu.edu**—and press **Enter**. You will get a message indicating that you have successfully connected to the FTP site, as shown in Figure 4.10a.

STEP 3: Change to the Directory Where the Desired File Resides
- At the ftp> prompt, type **cd library** and press **Enter**. You will see the message shown in Figure 4.10b saying **200 Working directory changed to "PUBLIC:[000000.LIBRARY]"**.
- You can verify that you are in the right directory at any time using the pwd command. At the ftp> prompt, type **pwd** (print working directory) and press **Enter**. You should see the message shown in Figure 4.10a saying **257 "PUBLIC:[000000.LIBRARY]" is current directory.**

STEP 4: Display a List of All Files in the Current Directory
- Before you can retrieve the document, you must be sure it is in the current directory. Type **dir** and press **Enter**. You will see the long list of files in the library subdirectory, shown in Figure 4.10b. The file you want to retrieve is the bsn.investments;1 file, which contains a list of mailing lists having to do with investments. (The bsn is for *business*.) (You can scroll up and down in the window to see all the files in the directory.)

(a) Logging In and Changing Directories

(b) The Directory Listing

FIGURE 4.10 Hands-on Exercise 5 (continued)

In-depth tutorials (hands-on exercises) guide the reader in every chapter. Each exercise is illustrated with large, full-color screen captures that are clear and easy to read. Each tutorial is accompanied by numerous tips that present different ways to accomplish a given task, but in a logical and relaxed fashion.

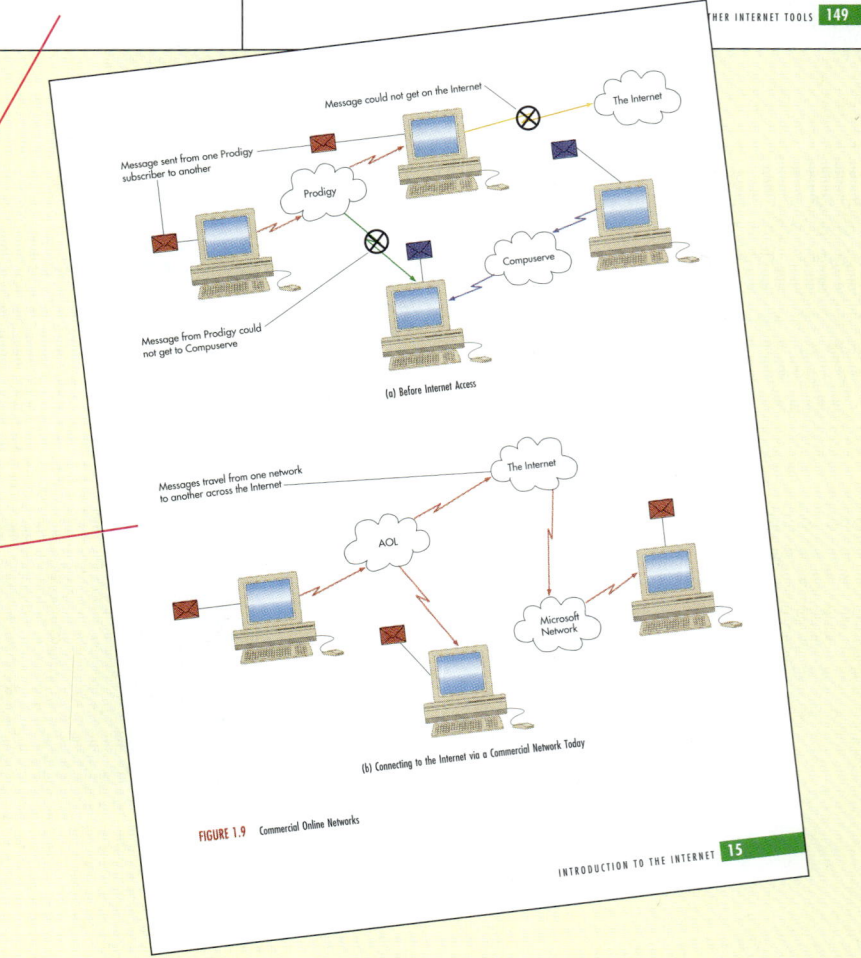

Our text not only provides practical "how to" information but also covers the underlying concepts. Full-color illustrations appear throughout the text and help explain the material.

FIGURE 1.9 Commercial Online Networks

Chapter 7 introduces HTML and shows students how to create a home page. Students learn the meaning of various HTML codes and are shown the benefits of an HTML editor such as the Internet Assistant.

Chapter 6 covers important issues such as the right to privacy and commercialization of the Internet. Students enjoy light-hearted coverage of additional topics such as Netspeak acronyms and smilies.

PUBLISHING ON THE NET: GETTING STARTED WITH HTML

OBJECTIVES

After reading this chapter you will be able to:
1. Define HTML; explain what HTML markup tags are and what they do.
2. Use Notepad to create a home page with bookmarks, ordered and unordered lists, in-line images, and hyperlinks to other Web resources.
3. Add formatting tags to create headings; bold, italicized, and underlined text; horizontal lines; and other design elements.
4. Use an HTML editor to modify your home page.
5. View the source of other HTML documents and copy useful elements to your own page.

OVERVIEW

Hypertext Markup Language (HTML) is the language used to create a Web page. In essence, HTML consists of a set of codes that allows you to format a document for display on the World Wide Web and that marks links to other Web sites. Since the inception of the World Wide Web, millions of people and organizations have created home pages. You can too.

It is easy to learn and use the basic HTML commands. In this chapter you will set up a simple home page that displays your name, a few lines of information about you, and your e-mail address.

This chapter is just a beginning. You can learn more about HTML on the Web, by conducting a search on the keywords *HTML guide* or *HTML primer*. Several excellent primers are available.

Before starting your home page, you should check with your system administrator to determine how he or she wants you to submit your material when it is complete. You also need to find out any site-specific information about using HTML in your campus computing environment.

225

TABLE 6.1	Commonly Used NetSpeak Acronyms
BCNU	Be Seeing You! Ciao! Arrivederci!
BOF	Birds Of a Feather. People interested in the same topic; they flock together.
BTW	By The Way.
FAQ	Frequently Asked Question.
FOF	Friend Of a Friend. A rather distant, and possibly unreliable, source.
FWIW	For What It's Worth
<G>	Grin.
GIGO	Garbage In, Garbage Out. From general computer usage, if your input data is inaccurate, you will not get good results from your program.
HHOK	Ha Ha Only Kidding. Just a joke, man.
HHOS	Ha Ha Only Serious. Whatever was said was funny, but at least half serious too.
IMHO	In My Humble Opinion. If it really was so humble, you wouldn't use this!
IMO	In My Opinion. IMO, this sounds more humble than IMHO.
IWBNI	It Would Be Nice If.
IYFEG	Insert Your Favorite Ethnic Group. Used in humor newsgroups to allow the user to insert whatever ethnic group he/she desires, to avoid offending anyone on the joke list.
LOL	Laughing Out Loud.
LTNS	Long Time No See.
MEGO	My Eyes Glaze Over. Used to indicate being overrun by technical or boring detail.
MOTAS	Member Of The Appropriate Sex.
MOTOS	Member Of The Other Sex.
MOTSS	Member Of The Same Sex.
PMJI	Pardon My Jumping In.
POMKIF	Pounding On My Keyboard In Frustration. Learn how to type!
ROTFL	Rolling On The Floor Laughing. It was that funny, really...or was it?
RTFAQ	Read The Frequently Asked Questions. Read the FAQ archive instead of posting stupid questions to the newsgroup.
RTM	Read The Manual. A polite way of suggesting that you should try to find the information in online Help or a manual before posting the question.
<S>	Smile.
SO	Significant Other.
TIA	Thanks In Advance. Nice to add to the end of an e-mail posting in which you ask for reader response or assistance.
TTFN	TaTa For Now!
WOMBAT	Waste Of Money, Brains, And Time.
WRT	With Respect To.
YMMV	Your Mileage May Vary. You won't necessarily get the same results.

212 EXPLORING THE INTERNET

Smilies and Emoticons

This chapter has raised some very heavy and demanding issues and has warned you about proper behavior. (We are beginning to sound like your Great-Aunt Mildred!) Well, the Net is there to learn on, to explore, to get lost on, then found, to have fun. To ensure the latter, we introduce one of our favorite topics—how to enrich your text with silly symbols, called *emoticons* (emotional icons) by very proper surfers, *smilies* by those of us who just want to have fun.

Since the Internet is currently based primarily on written, not oral, communication, the nuances of inflection, facial expression, and body language are lost on the recipient of your message. Therefore it is important that you relay to the person, particularly the one that you do not know well if at all, the emotional subtext of your message. Newbies often **PUT EVERYTHING IN UPPERCASE**, but this implies you are yelling, and it is not recommended. An alternative is to add an explanatory statement in your text, highlighted in some way: <hehehe>, <giggle>, <just kidding>.

Some people prefer a more graphic approach, and have devised smilies to help broadcast their meaning. Table 6.2 shows some of the more popular and/or clever emoticons, which are created from various combinations of letters and symbols in the character set. (Tip your head to the left, or rotate the book to the right, to decipher their meaning more clearly.) Use them freely, invent your own, and spread cheer and good tidings on the Net.

TABLE 6.2	Smilies and Other Emoticons		
:-) or :)	Smilie face	C=]:-)	I am a chef
;-) or ;)	Winky; just kidding	:X	My lips are sealed
:-(	Oh, so sad	(_)>	Java brew
:'-(	So sad I'm crying	C|_|	A mug of coffee
:'-)	So happy I'm crying	:-&	I'm tongue-tied
>;-)>	Little devil	X-(	That comment killed me
8-()	Dude with shades and mustache	%-)	User has been looking at the screen too long!
8-)	Cool dude with shades	:-o	Surprise!

THE COMMERCIALIZATION OF CYBERSPACE

The topic of commercialization of the Internet has emerged several times throughout this book, and it is an ongoing issue for many long-time Internet gurus. Because the Internet was developed without the involvement of advertisers and major vendors, it should remain a pure, commercial-free zone of communication, goes the argument. That is not a likely prospect, and indeed as we have discussed, many commercial organizations already have Web pages and are advertising all types of products and services on the Internet.

The **backbone**, or main network links between Internet providers around the country, is no longer provided or maintained by either Department of Defense or National Science Foundation funding. Since April 1995 it has been operated by telecommunications companies such as Sprint and MCI. The Internet service providers, which formerly were NSF-funded and located on major campuses such

THE INTERNET AND SOCIETY 213

PREFACE XV

Acknowledgments

We want to thank the many individuals who helped bring this project to fruition. We are especially grateful to our editor at Prentice Hall, Carolyn Henderson, without whom the series would not have been possible. Cecil Yarbrough and Susan Hoffman did an outstanding job in checking the manuscript and proofs for technical accuracy. Suzanne Behnke developed the innovative and attractive design. Phyllis Bregman helped us to go online. Carlotta Eaton of Radford University wrote a superb set of Instructor Manuals, and Grace Walkus and Dave Moles created the associated CD-ROM. Paul Smolenski was senior manufacturing supervisor. Greg Hubit was in charge of production and kept the project on target from beginning to end. Nancy Evans and Deborah Emry, our marketing managers at Prentice Hall, developed the innovative campaigns that made the series a success. Audrey Regan helped in ways too numerous to mention. We also want to acknowledge our reviewers who, through their comments and constructive criticism, greatly improved the *Exploring Windows* series.

Paul E. Aho, Michigan Technological University
Azad H. Azadmanesh, University of Nebraska
Lynne Band, Middlesex Community College
Stuart P. Brian, Holy Family College
Carl M. Briggs, Indiana University School of Business
Kimberly Chambers, Scottsdale Community College
Alok Charturvedi, Purdue University
Jerry Chin, Southwest Missouri State University
Dean Combellick, Scottsdale Community College
Cody Copeland, Johnson County Community College
Larry S. Corman, Fort Lewis College
Janis Cox, Tri-County Technical College
Martin Crossland, Southwest Missouri State University
Paul E. Daurelle, Western Piedmont Community College
David Douglas, University of Arkansas
Carlotta Eaton, Radford University
Raymond Frost, Central Connecticut State University
James Gips, Boston College
Vernon Griffin, Austin Community College
Michael Hassett, Fort Hays State University
Wanda D. Heller, Seminole Community College
Bonnie Homan, San Francisco State University
Ernie Ivey, Polk Community College
Mike Kelly, Community College of Rhode Island
Jane King, Everett Community College
John Lesson, University of Central Florida
David B. Meinert, Southwest Missouri State University
Alan Moltz, Naugatuck Valley Technical Community College
Kim Montney, Kellogg Community College
Josephine F. Morecroft, Virginia Commonwealth University
Evan Noynaert, Missouri University
Kevin Pauli, University of Nebraska
Mary McKenry Percival, University of Miami
Delores Pusins, Hillsborough Community College
Gale E. Rand, College Misericordia
Judith Rice, Santa Fe Community College
David Rinehard, Lansing Community College
Marilyn Salas, Scottsdale Community College
John Shepherd, Duquesne University
Helen Stoloff, Hudson Valley Community College
Mike Thomas, Indiana University School of Business
Suzanne Tomlinson, Iowa State University
Karen Tracey, Central Connecticut State University
Sally Visci, Lorain County Community College
David Weiner, University of San Francisco
Connie Wells, Georgia State University
Wallace John Whistance-Smith, Ryerson Polytechnic University
Jack Zeller, Kirkwood Community College

A final word of thanks to the unnamed students at the University of Miami and Saint Joseph College who make it all worthwhile. And most of all, thanks to you, our readers, for choosing this book. Please feel free to contact us with any comments and suggestions.

Robert T. Grauer
RGRAUER@UMIAMI.MIAMI.EDU
http://www.bus.miami.edu/~rgrauer

Gretchen Marx
gmarx@mercy.sjc.edu
http://www.sjc.edu/~gmarx

INTRODUCTION TO THE INTERNET: WELCOME TO CYBERSPACE

OBJECTIVES

After reading this chapter you will be able to:

1. Describe the Internet and its history.
2. Describe some of the services and resources available on the Internet, and identify which of these are available at your college or university.
3. Define the TCP/IP protocol; explain in general terms how data is sent across the Internet.
4. Define the domain name system of Internet addresses; show how your Internet address adheres to the conventions within the domain name system.
5. Explain how to access the Internet in your campus computing environment.

OVERVIEW

The Internet. You see the word on the cover of half the magazines on the newsstand. The media make continual reference to the Information Highway. Movie ads provide Internet addresses so you can download and view movie clips. Your friends at other colleges want to know your Internet e-mail address. But what exactly is the Internet, and how do you use it? In this chapter we answer both of these questions.

After a brief discussion of how the Internet came to be, we describe the many services and resources available on the Net. Most of what you will want to do on the Internet can be done using Windows-based PC software applications, which handle the complicated task of connecting to the computer network on your campus, and from there to the Internet. We discuss how this is done, and how the Internet itself works. From there you will start your journey into cyberspace by learning how to connect to the Internet in your campus computing environment.

THE INTERNET

The Internet is a network of networks that connects computers across the country and around the world. It grew out of a U.S. Department of Defense (DOD) experimental project begun in 1969 to test the feasibility of a wide area (long distance) computer network over which scientists and military personnel could share messages and data. The network had to work regardless of where the users were or the type of computer they were using. The DOD imposed the additional requirement that the network be able to function with partial outages in times of national emergency, when one or more computers in the network might be down.

The proposed solution was to create a network with no central authority. Each *node* (computer attached to the network) would be equal to all other nodes, with the ability to originate, pass, and receive messages. The path that a particular message took in getting to its destination would be insignificant. Only the final result was important, as the message would be passed from node to node until it arrived at its destination.

The experiment was (to say the least) successful. Known originally as the ***ARPAnet (Advanced Research Projects Agency),*** the original network of four computers has grown exponentially to include millions of computers at virtually every major U.S. university and government agency, and an ever increasing number of private corporations and international sites. To say that the Internet is large is a gross understatement, but by its very nature, it's impossible to determine just how large it really is. At the time this book went to press, a commonly accepted estimate was 36 million users worldwide. Recent figures indicate it is growing at 15% per month, which means it is doubling every seven months!

The Internet, as described, is a network of networks. However, if that was all it were, there would hardly be so much commotion over it. It's what the user can *do* on the Internet that makes it so exciting, rather than the hardware and software of which it is composed. No longer confined to the Pentagon and DOD, the Internet brings a worldwide library of on-line information resources on a seemingly limitless number of topics to anyone connected to it. All you need to access data anywhere on the Internet is a computer connected to it, and a username and password, which you will get from your college or university data center or LAN administrator. (If you are dialing into your campus network or a commercial service provider from a remote computer, you will need special hardware and software, which is described in Appendix A: Remote Access to the Internet.)

What can you do on the Internet? The primary capabilities are information retrieval and worldwide communication, two functions already provided by postal systems, libraries, print media, telephones, television, and other types of long distance media. Three characteristics, when taken together, set the Internet apart from these other information and communication technologies. The first two are the immediacy and global nature of the medium. When you request a document or send an e-mail message, the transmission begins almost instantly. And it doesn't matter if the document or message is coming from across the world or two blocks away.

The other defining characteristic of the Internet is the personal, two-way nature of much of the communication. Television has the capability to send information globally in real time (while events are unfolding). Yet you don't control the content or the timing of the message sent by the television studio. On the Internet users control the services and the content of the messages. You can search for resources of interest to you and request them whenever you want. You can create your own documents to put on the Internet. You can determine what is newsworthy and create information that can be accessed by any other authorized user, anywhere on the globe.

Writing and sending a message to thousands of people around the world at the same time instantly—that's heady stuff. Being able to request a picture of 5th century B.C. antiquities from a museum in Sardinia, and getting it instantly without leaving your chair—that's amazing. Retrieving satellite images of a meteor crashing into Jupiter, *while it is actually happening*—that's awe inspiring!

WHAT YOU WILL FIND ON THE INTERNET

At the time the Internet was created, the primary objective of its developers was to be able to send and receive files from any computer to any other computer on the Net. A second desirable objective was the ability to log into a remote computer as though the user were actually physically attached to it. From there the use of the Internet expanded to *e-mail,* which is the passing of electronic messages through a network. These services required the user to know and understand the sometimes complex syntax of computer commands. The services were generally limited to forwarding files, which meant that graphics, sound, and video resources could not be viewed on the Net. Accounts were available only to government employees and scientists and researchers at major universities. The legislation creating the Internet prohibited the use of the network for commercial purposes.

In the 1970s and '80s membership in the Internet community was expanded to include smaller colleges, international sites, and commercial organizations that were involved in the computer and networking industries. Services were expanded to include the ability to search for documents by using menu-driven programs instead of commands. Eventually graphics files became accessible, and easy-to-use Windows interfaces, which provided point-and-click access, were designed. These resources and programs attracted a flood of new users, so that by the early 1990s the Internet was no longer the exclusive province of computer scientists, physicists, and mathematicians. In addition, commercial access was expanded to include any company that wanted to pay for a site on the Internet.

Anyone with a PC and an Internet connection can travel through **cyberspace,** the term coined to describe the invisible realm of the Internet universe. College students, families, employees of businesses and nonprofit organizations—all are now *surfing* the Net, sending messages, retrieving files, and visiting remote sites to find information. To become an accomplished **Internaut,** or Internet explorer, you will want to try using as many of these services as you have available at your college or university.

Sending and Receiving E-mail

Electronic mail is available in many forms, some of which are limited to internal mail on your campus network. The focus of our discussion will be the tools that let you send and receive e-mail using the Internet. As with many other Internet applications, there are menu-based e-mail services that require the user to know a series of commands to use e-mail. Other e-mail programs run in a Windows environment and provide the user a **graphical user interface (GUI).** (GUIs provide pull-down menus and icons that allow the user to invoke commands by using a mouse and/or keyboard shortcuts.) Figure 1.1 shows the same e-mail message using (a) a menu-based system called Pine, and (b) a Windows-based mail program, PC Eudora.

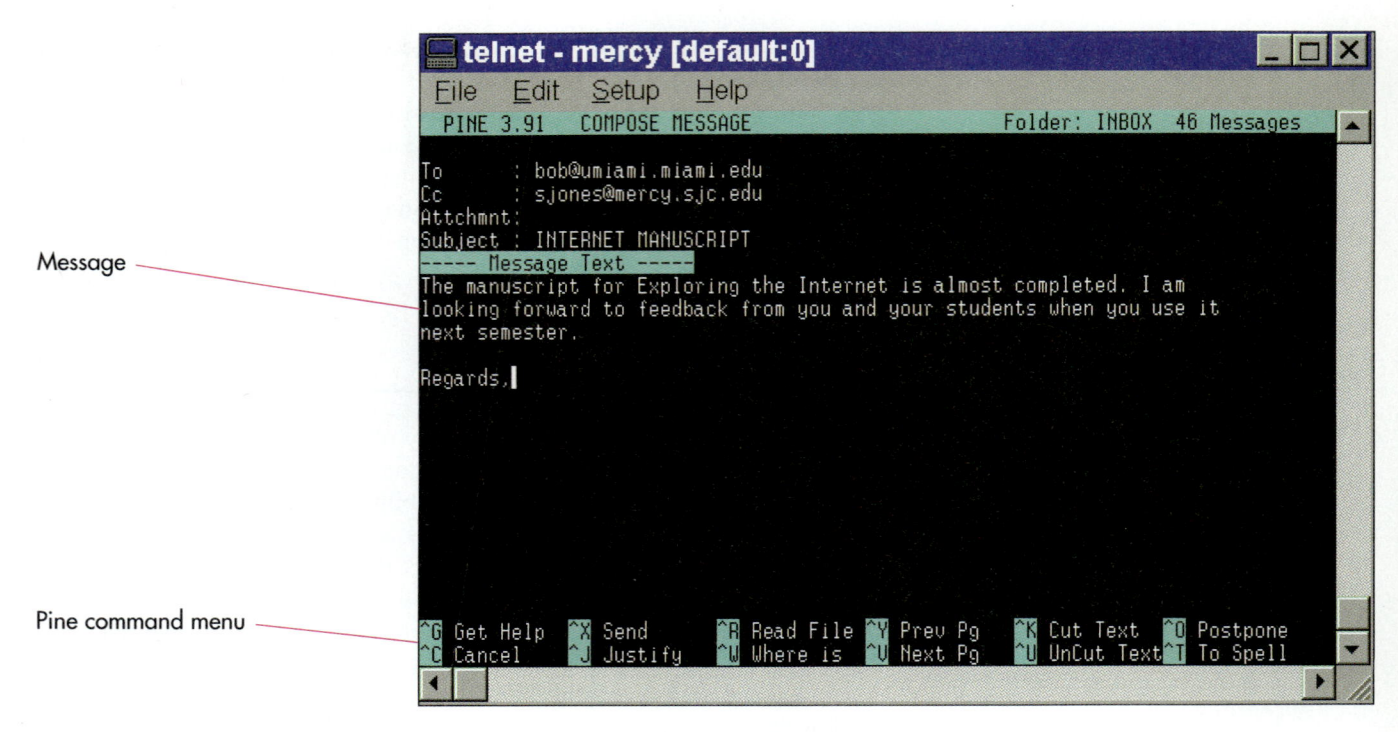

(a) An E-mail Message in Pine

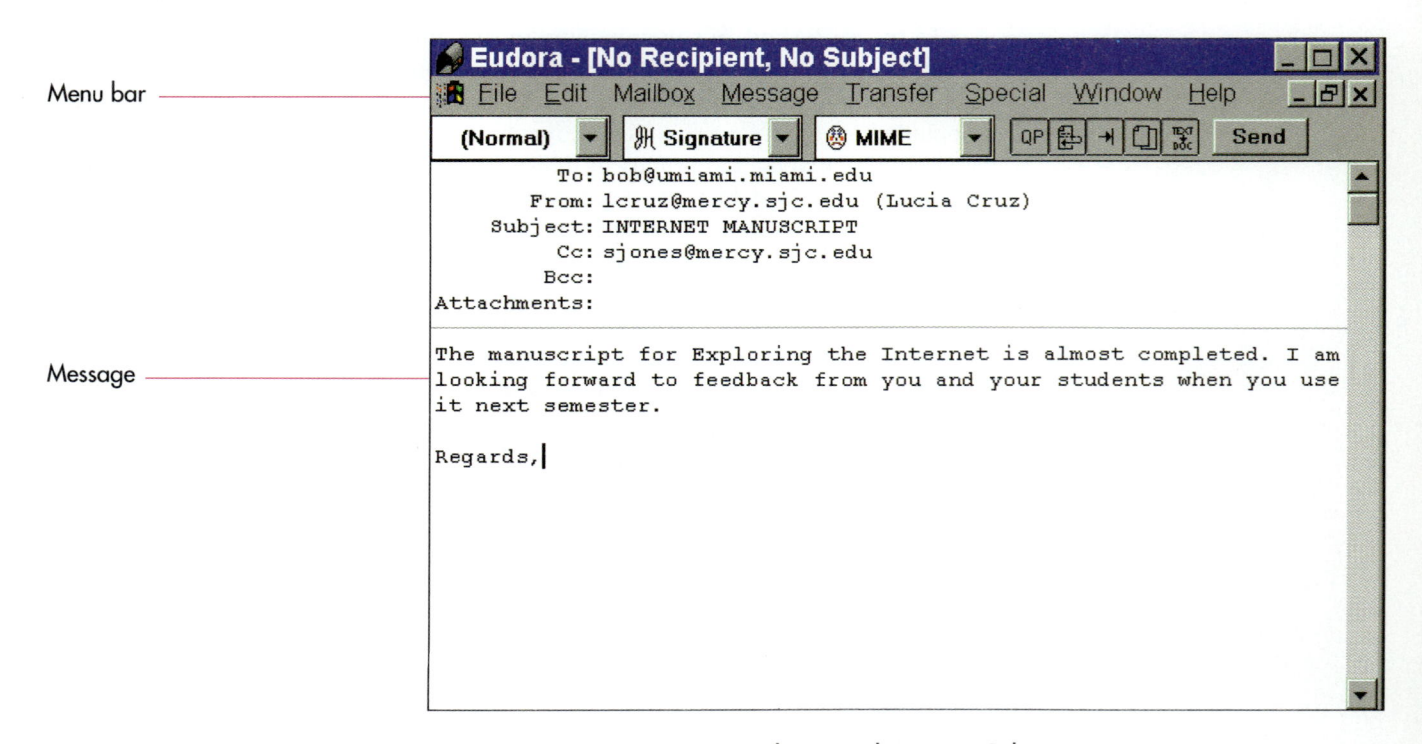

(b) An E-mail Message in Eudora

FIGURE 1.1 E-mail

You will experience both types of e-mail interfaces in Chapter 2, and will perform special e-mail functions such as replying to a message and creating a distribution list to send mail to more than one person. Internet e-mail also lets you sign up to an electronic mailing list on a specific topic, so you can participate in ongoing discussions on that subject with other subscribers around the world. You will learn how to retrieve the global list of the mailing lists so you can choose one, to which you will then subscribe. After subscribing, you can expect to receive lots of mail!

Using a Web Browser

The resources on the Internet are vast and fascinating. You will find yourself wanting to browse through these resources just as you might browse through your local library or bookstore reading a page from a book or magazine here, a chapter there. In the beginning you had to know the correct commands in many different programs to access the resources you wanted. Furthermore, those resources were not cataloged or indexed globally, so you had to search through many different archives to locate the information for which you were looking. In 1991 a new way of organizing Internet resources, called the **World Wide Web,** was developed. The Web, as it is often called, provides a way to locate a file on the Internet, regardless of where it is stored, or what type of resource it is.

You can meander through the Web using a GUI interface called, aptly enough, a ***browser.*** Two of the most widely used Web browsers, **Mosaic** and **Netscape,** are shown in Figures 1.2a and 1.2b, respectively. Since many users do not have access to GUI browsers (primarily because of the extensive hardware requirements), the University of Kansas developed a text-based browser called **Lynx.** Lynx provides much of the functionality of the GUI browsers, but lacks the ability to display graphics. Figure 1.2c shows the Web document found in Figure 1.2b as it appears using Lynx.

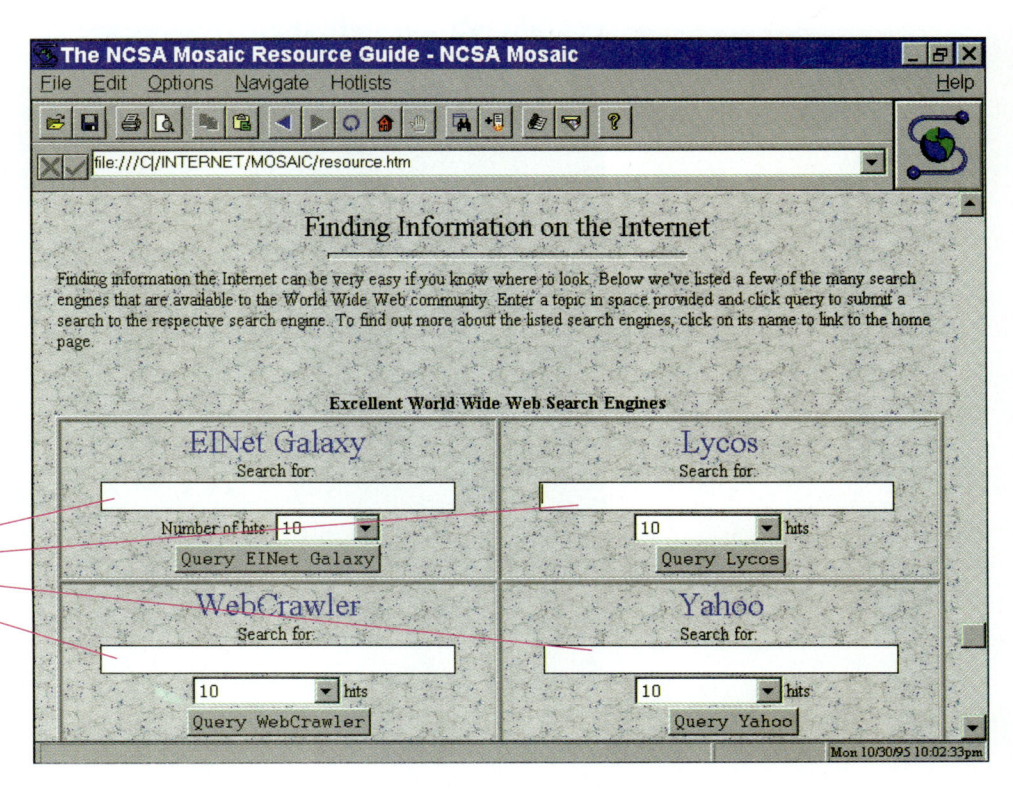

(a) A Mosaic Document

FIGURE 1.2 Web Browsers

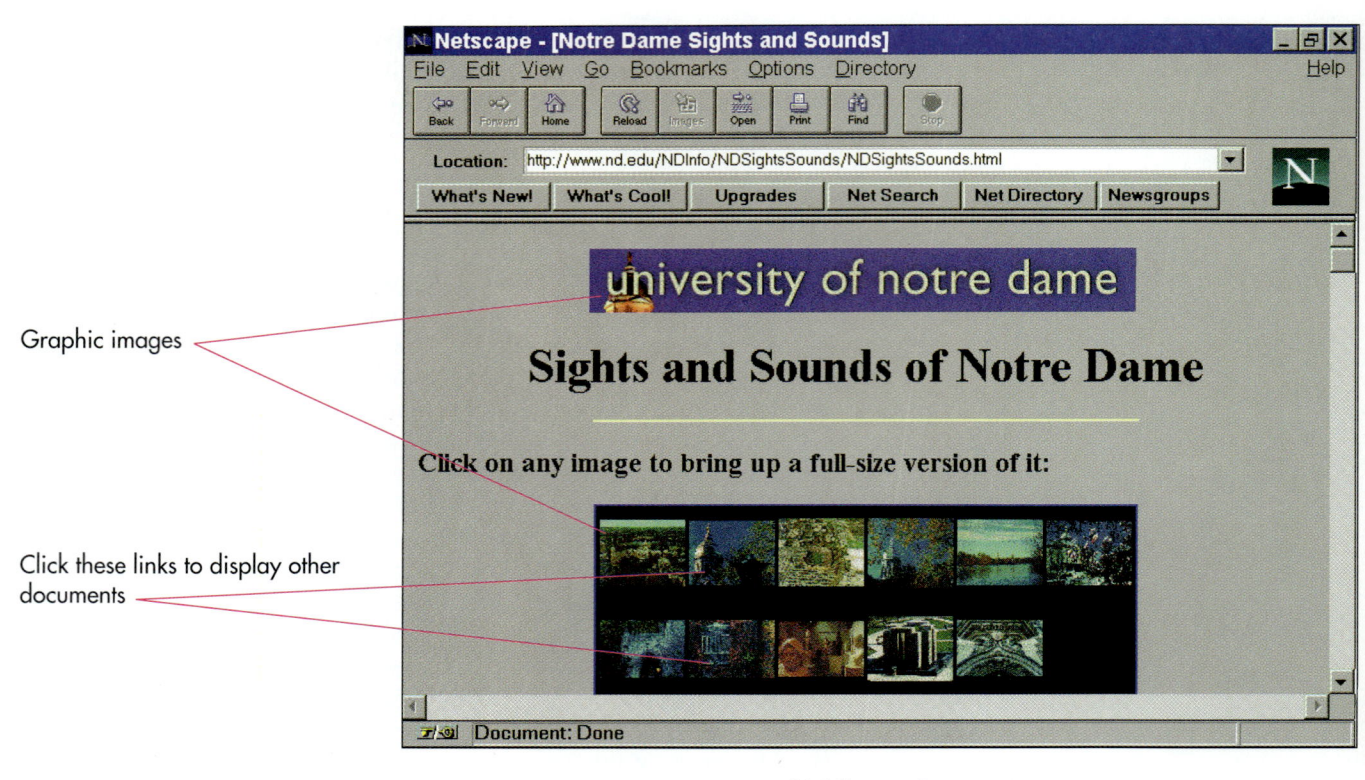

Graphic images

Click these links to display other documents

(b) A Netscape Screen

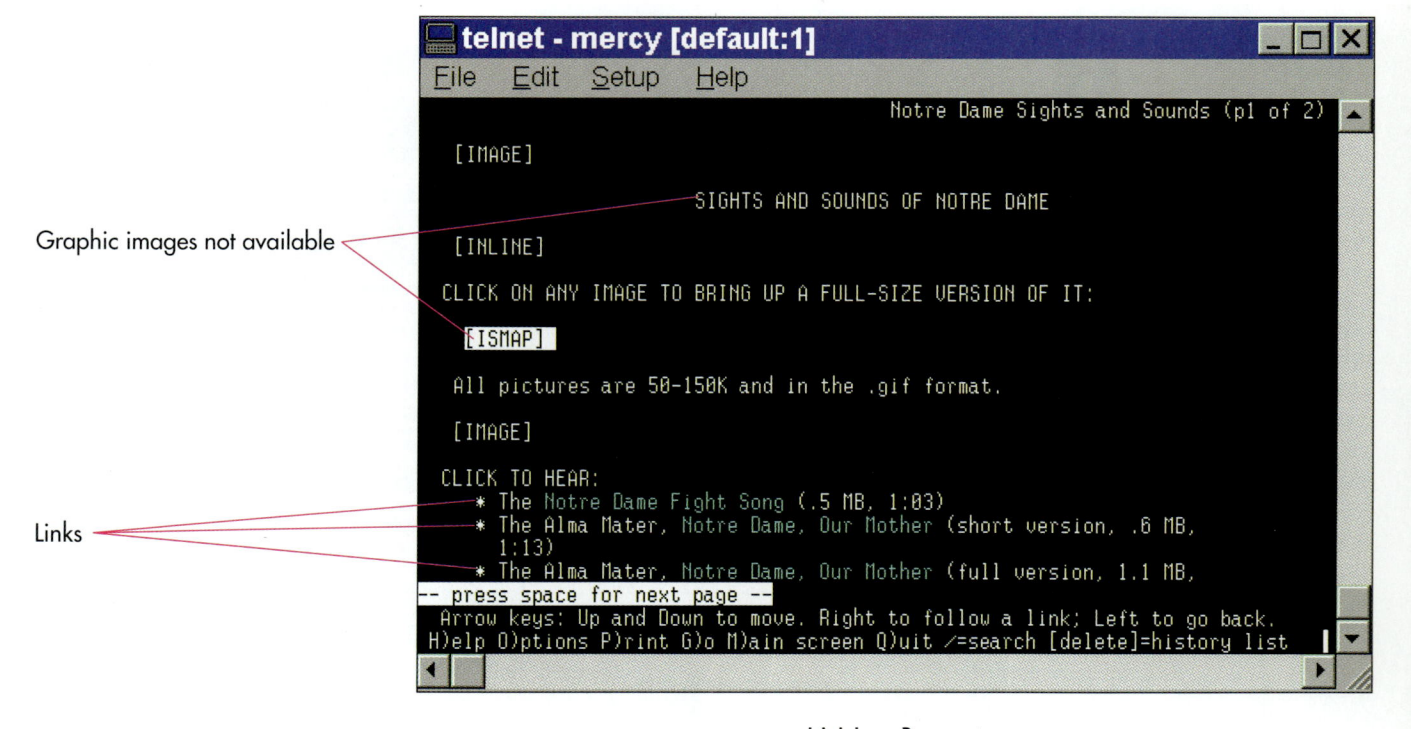

Graphic images not available

Links

(c) A Lynx Document

FIGURE 1.2 Web Browsers (continued)

6 EXPLORING THE INTERNET

Documents created for the World Wide Web contain embedded **links** to other documents. You simply select (click) a link, and your browser will automatically display the associated document, no matter where it is on the Internet. You can browse indefinitely, clicking on link after link. You will find many fascinating tidbits of information and visit many interesting **Web sites** (computers that have a connection to the portion of the Internet that is the World Wide Web).

You will also find that, while fun and interesting, browsing is not a very efficient way of locating specific information. If you are writing a paper on the architecture of European churches for an art history class, for instance, you would probably not do your research by browsing through all of the stacks in the campus library. In similar fashion you would not want to browse the Web at random until you found the pictures of Notre Dame shown in Figure 1.2b.

It is much more efficient to use your browser to link to a special Web search tool called a **search engine.** Using the search engine you can conduct a keyword search of the Web, much as you search a card catalog or online database in the library. The search engine will return abstracts of documents it finds that match the keywords. The abstracts will contain links to the documents themselves, so you can quickly locate the sources you want to read. You will learn to browse and search the World Wide Web using Netscape (or the browser you have at your college or university) and Lynx in Chapter 3.

Gopher and FTP

You can also find interesting resources on the Internet using a menu-based service called **gopher** (as in, if you want something, go "pher" it!). Figure 1.3 shows a gopher menu as it appears in Netscape. In Figure 1.3a you see the highest menu

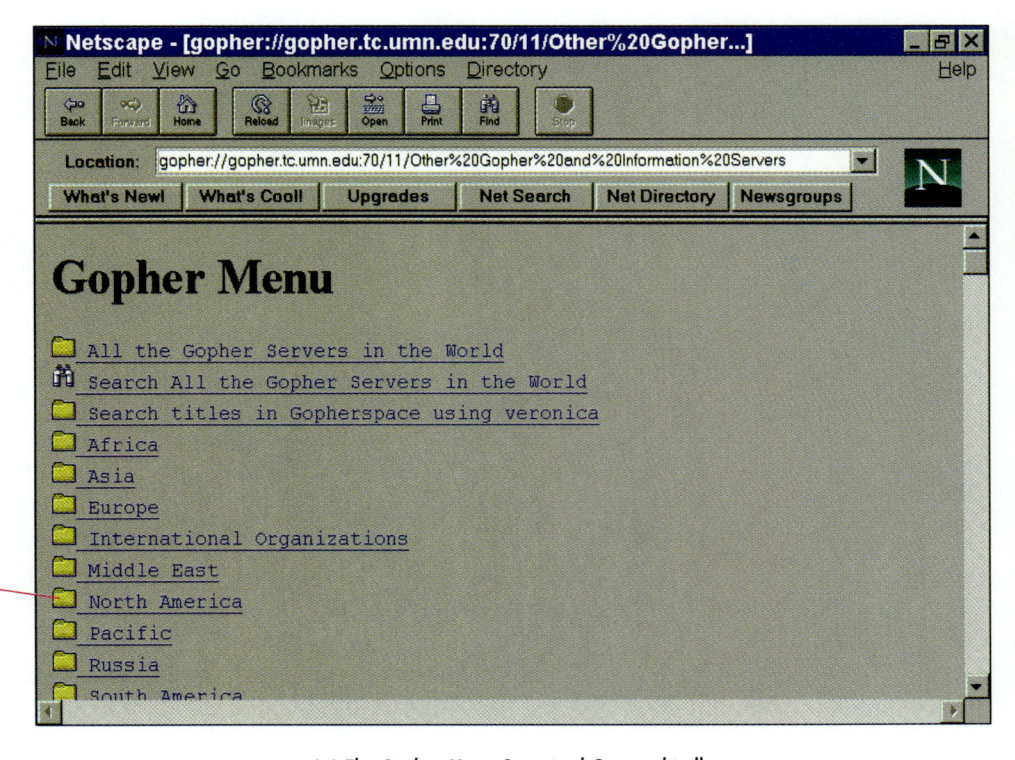

Click here to jump to North America menu

(a) The Gopher Menu Organized Geographically

FIGURE 1.3 Gopher Using Netscape

(b) The North America Gopher Menu

(c) The USA Gopher Menu

FIGURE 1.3 Gopher Using Netscape (continued)

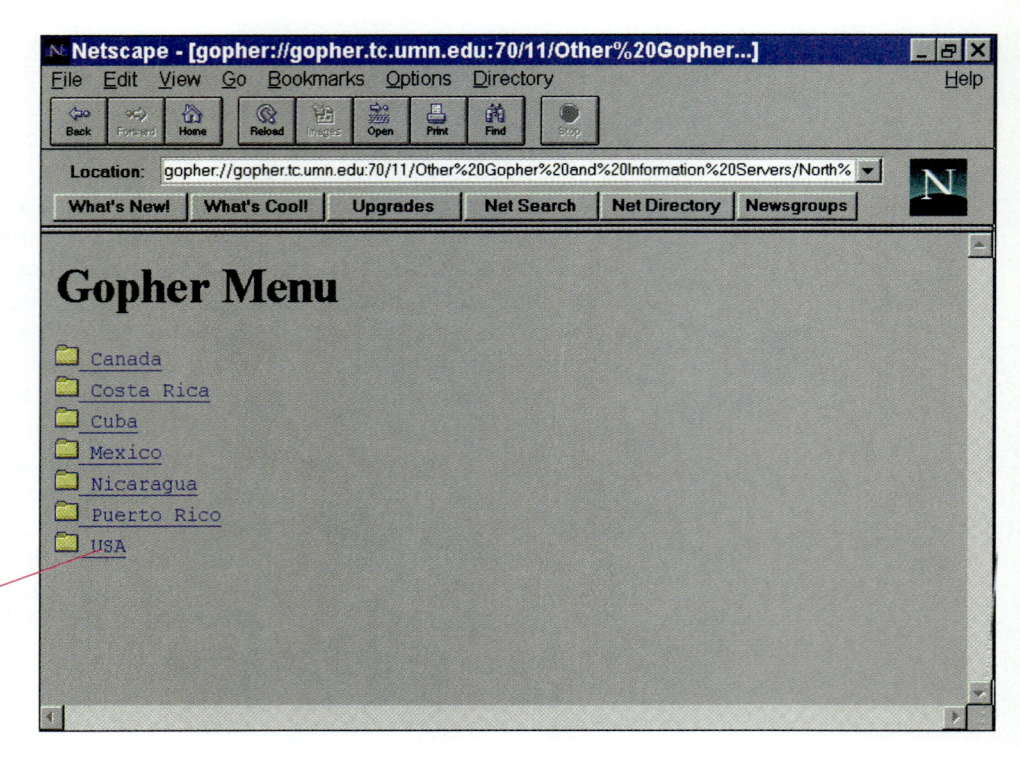

8 EXPLORING THE INTERNET

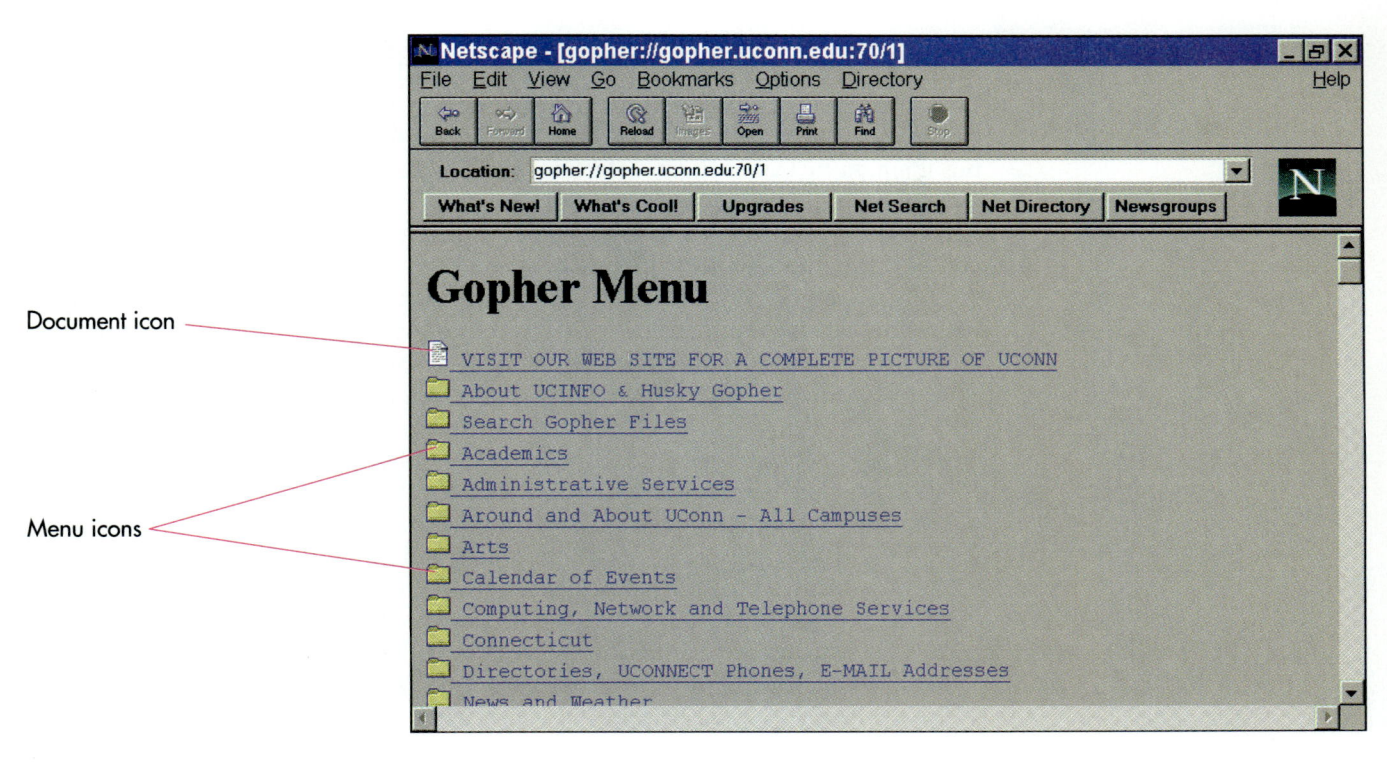

Document icon

Menu icons

Gopher Menu

- VISIT OUR WEB SITE FOR A COMPLETE PICTURE OF UCONN
- About UCINFO & Husky Gopher
- Search Gopher Files
- Academics
- Administrative Services
- Around and About UConn – All Campuses
- Arts
- Calendar of Events
- Computing, Network and Telephone Services
- Connecticut
- Directories, UCONNECT Phones, E-MAIL Addresses
- News and Weather

(d) The UConn Gopher

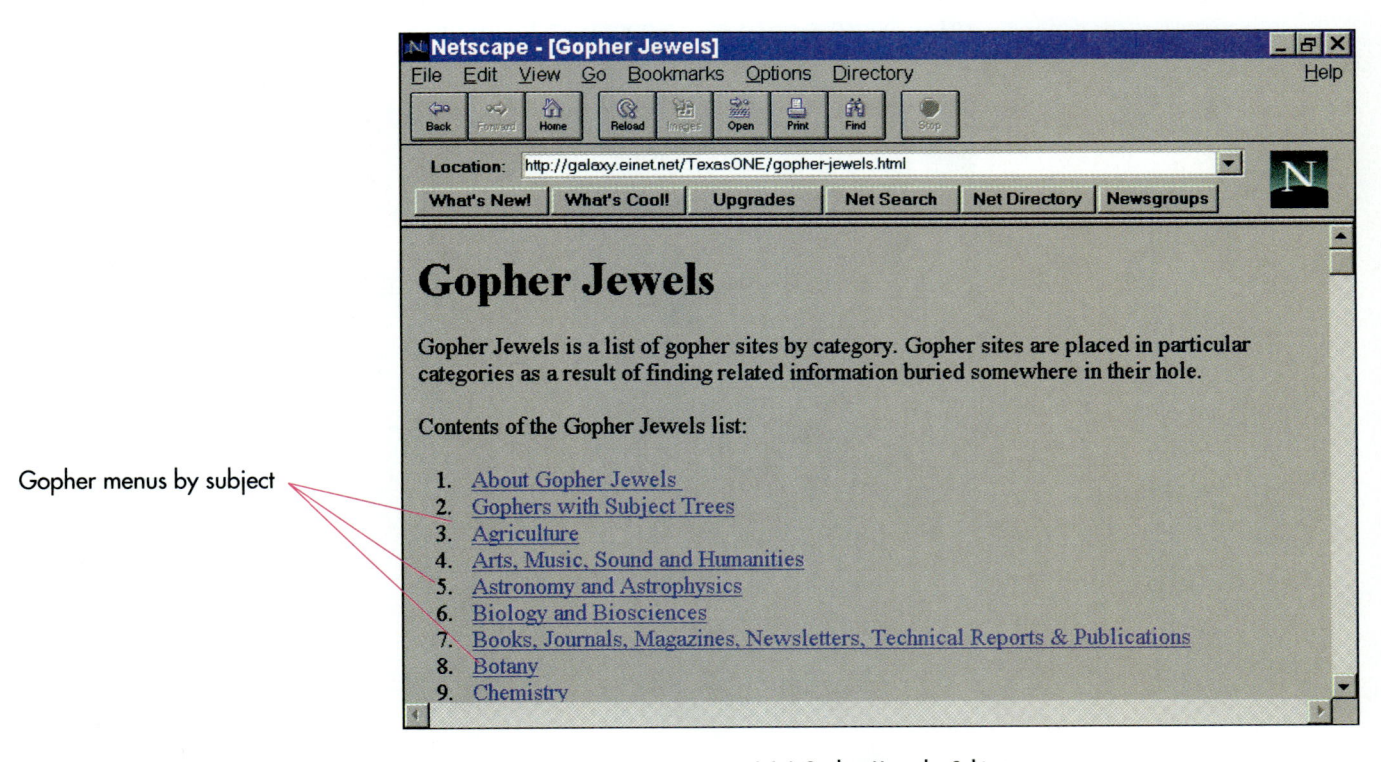

Gopher Jewels

Gopher Jewels is a list of gopher sites by category. Gopher sites are placed in particular categories as a result of finding related information buried somewhere in their hole.

Contents of the Gopher Jewels list:

Gopher menus by subject

1. About Gopher Jewels
2. Gophers with Subject Trees
3. Agriculture
4. Arts, Music, Sound and Humanities
5. Astronomy and Astrophysics
6. Biology and Biosciences
7. Books, Journals, Magazines, Newsletters, Technical Reports & Publications
8. Botany
9. Chemistry

(e) A Gopher Menu by Subject

FIGURE 1.3 Gopher Using Netscape (continued)

INTRODUCTION TO THE INTERNET

on the particular gopher shown, which is organized geographically. If you select North America gophers from this menu, you will see the menu shown in Figure 1.3b, which lists regions in North America. Figure 1.3c shows the USA menu, from which you could select the state of Connecticut, for instance. From the list of all the gophers in Connecticut, selecting the University of Connecticut gopher displays a menu that the computing staff at UConn created and has stored on a computer at their site, shown in Figure 1.3d. You can continue to select menus until you find the information you want.

This method of searching is, of course, quite time consuming, and assumes you know where you want to look for the information. To avoid this problem, other gopher menus are organized by subject, as shown in Figure 1.3e. Fortunately, as you will discover in Chapter 4, almost all gopher resources are indexed and can be found by using the search engines in your browser. You will find this much more efficient than starting at the top of the gopher menu structure.

Some of the documents you find while browsing, searching, and gophering you will simply read on your PC and then go on to something else. At other times you will find files such as software programs and graphic images, which you will not display using a browser, but instead will want to retrieve to use locally on your PC. The browser you use can also perform this function, called ***downloading.*** Many of these files are actually transferred over the Internet by the browser using something called the **File Transfer Protocol (FTP).**

A ***protocol*** is a set of rules by which computers interact; FTP is a protocol that governs how computers exchange files. In Chapter 4 you will retrieve files from an **FTP site,** a computer that archives files, using both your browser and special FTP software. Figure 1.4 shows a list of **FTP files** (files stored at an FTP site), (a) in Netscape, (b) as it appears in the Windows-based FTP program WS_FTP,

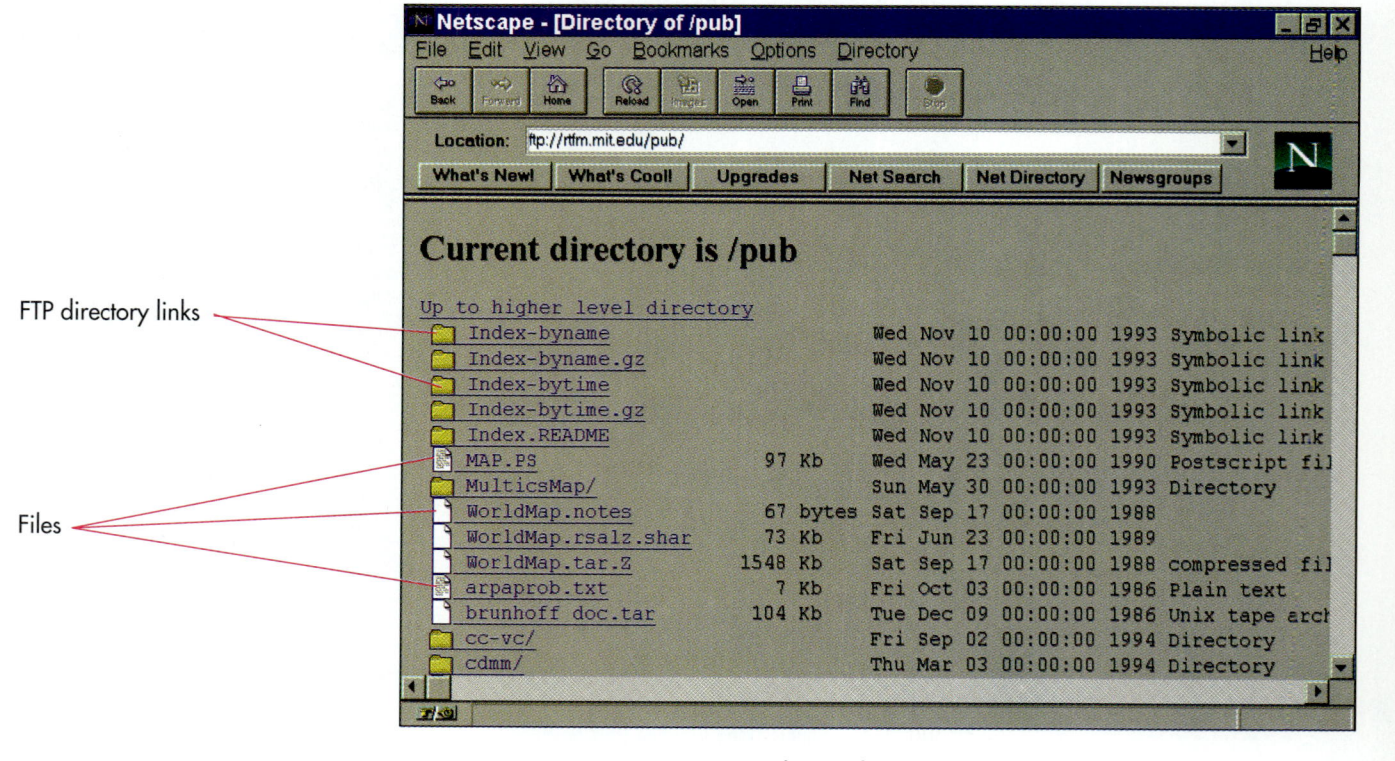

(a) The FTP File List in Netscape

FIGURE 1.4 FTP

EXPLORING THE INTERNET

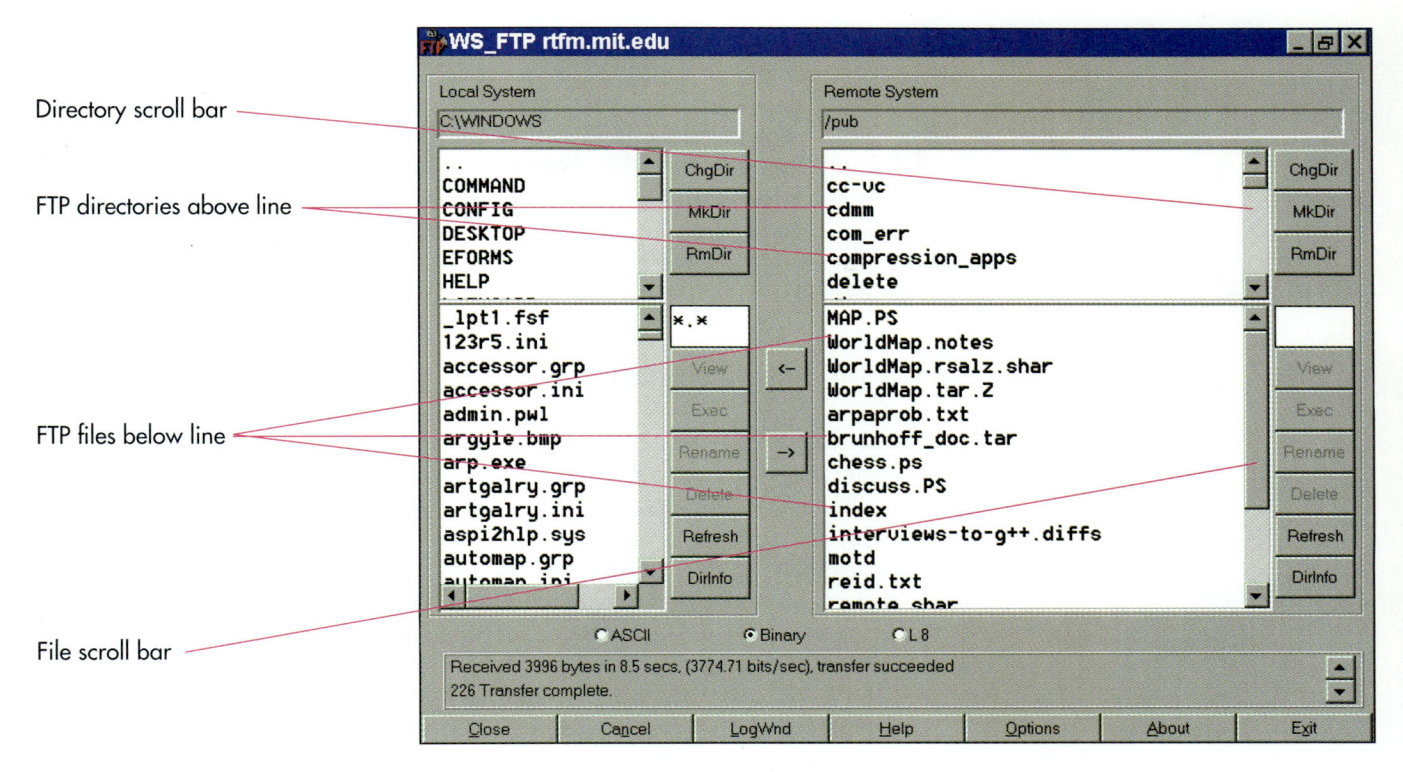

(b) The FTP File List in WS_FTP

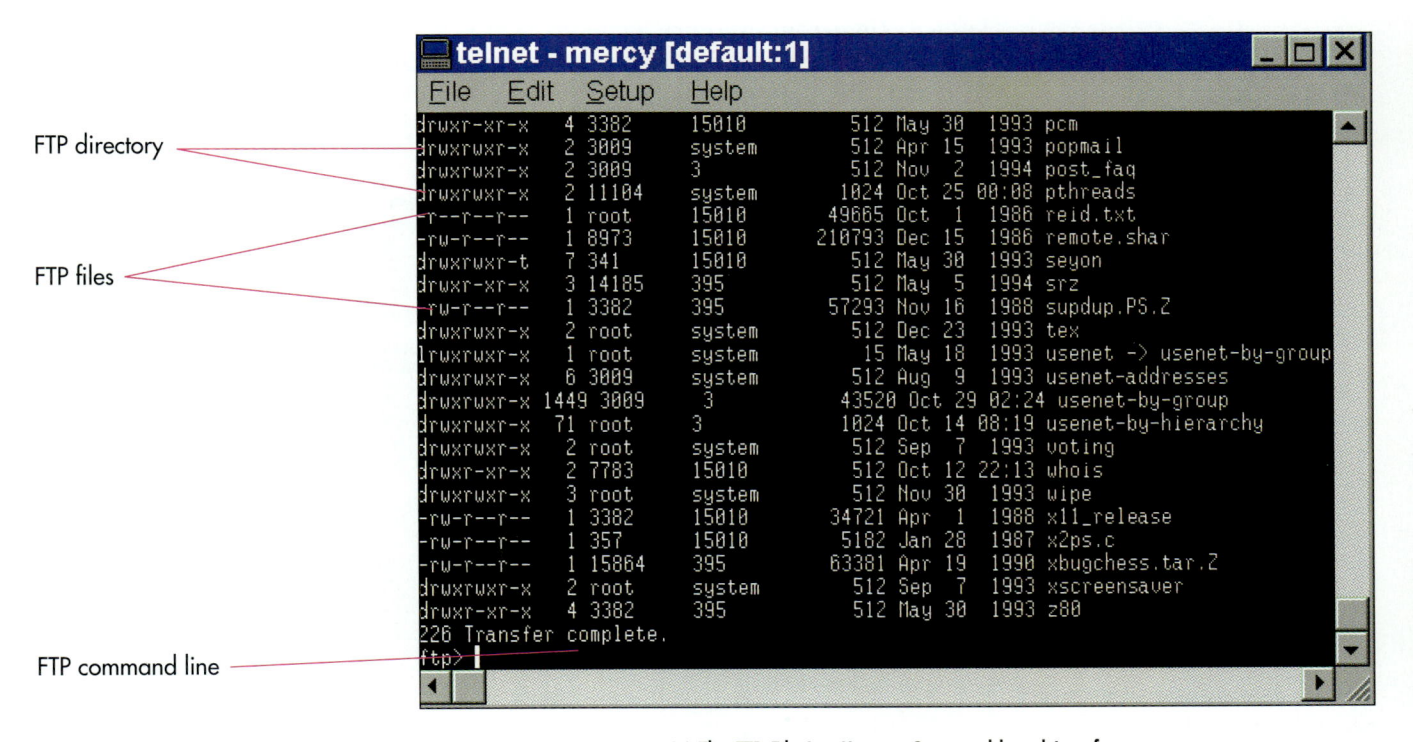

(c) The FTP File List Using a Command-based Interface

FIGURE 1.4   FTP (continued)

INTRODUCTION TO THE INTERNET

and (c) as it appears using a command-based FTP program on the computer that connects your campus to the Internet, your *Internet host.*

As with other services on the Internet, you will find it very time consuming to locate files to download simply by browsing. You can use a Web search engine to locate gopher menus and FTP sites. We also discuss in Chapter 4 how to find these resources by using the special search tools, ***Veronica*** to search ***gopherspace,*** and ***Archie*** to search FTP archives. Figure 1.5 shows a Veronica search using Netscape; Figure 1.6 shows an Archie search using a Windows-based program called WSArchie.

Conversing on the Internet

You already know you can send mail and subscribe to mailing lists on the Internet. You can also instantly communicate with people all over the world by using what are called ***chat*** programs. They allow you to send a typed message to everyone else who is logged in to the same channel at the same time you are. A ***channel*** is like a global conference call, where anyone who picks up the phone and dials a certain number can join an ongoing conversation and hear everything everyone else is saying. The messages everyone is sending are displayed on everyone's monitor as they are received, as shown in Figure 1.7. As long as you are attached to the channel, you will continue to see the messages.

Participating in chat sessions can be fun and interesting, but it can also be an addicting waste of time. Many people prefer to subscribe to mailing lists and get their mail ***offline,*** that is, at a different time than it was sent, when it is convenient for them. Another kind of offline subscription service is provided by Usenet. ***Usenet, newsgroups,*** or ***news,*** as it is also called, allows you to subscribe to one or many discussion groups, which are organized by topic. Subscribers can read and submit, or ***post,*** messages to the group by using a program called a ***newsreader.***

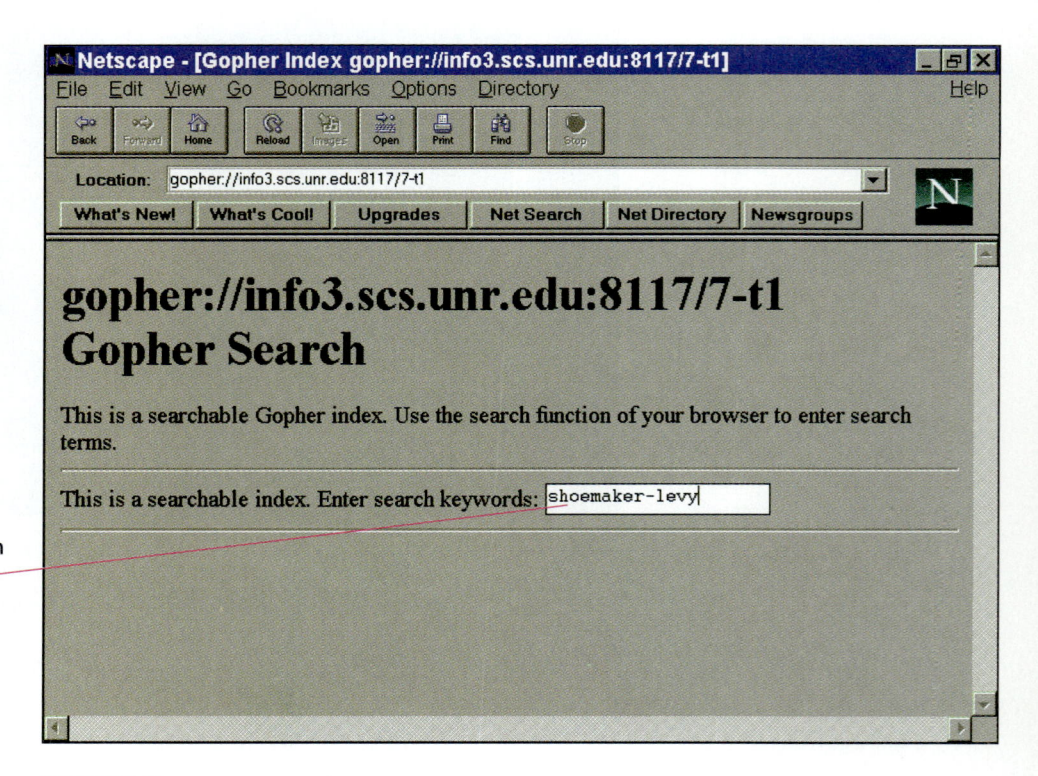

A Veronica search for information about Shoemaker-Levy comet

FIGURE 1.5   A Veronica Search

An Archie search for FTP archives about Shoemaker-Levy comet

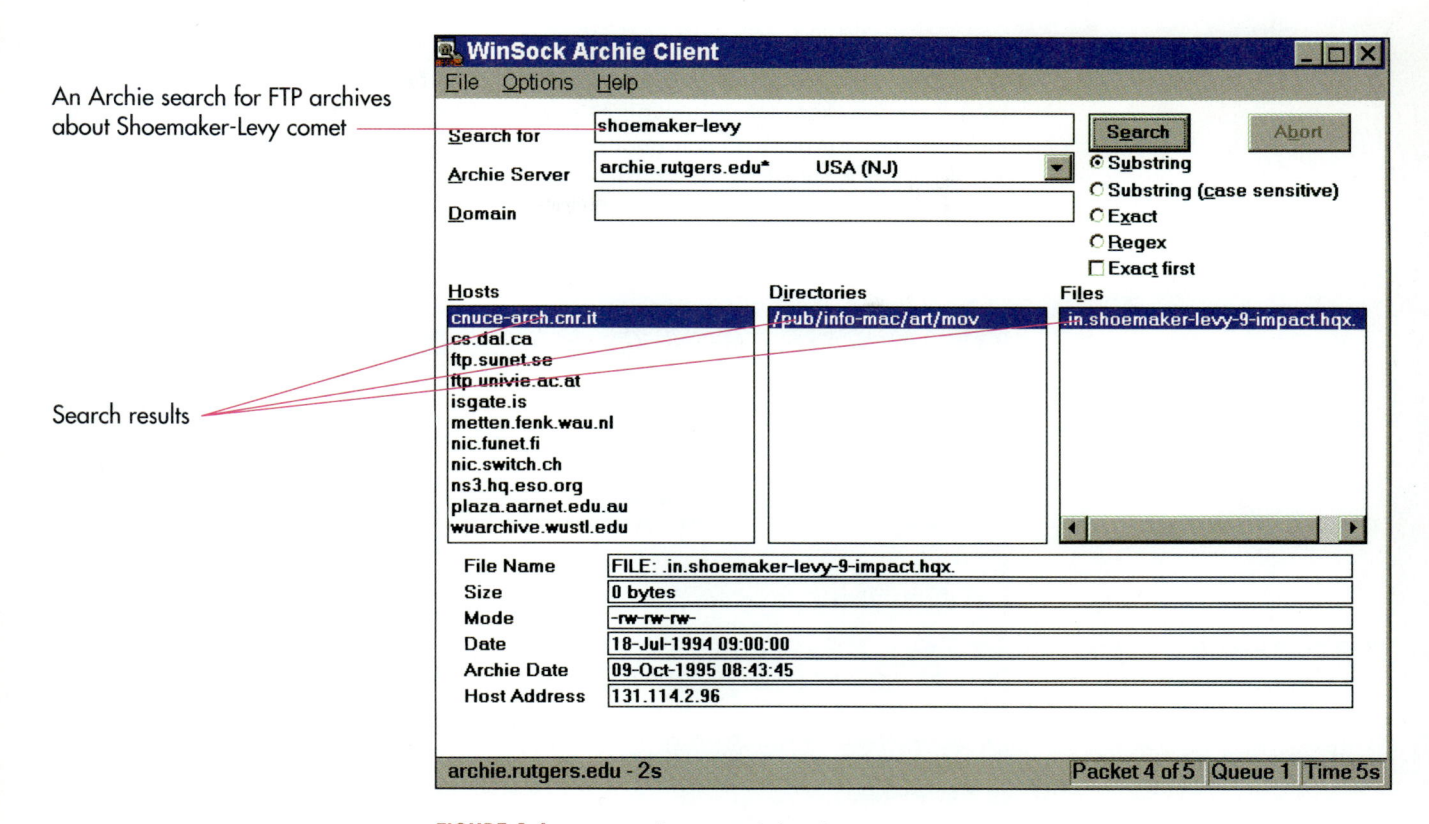

Search results

FIGURE 1.6   Using Archie to Search for Files

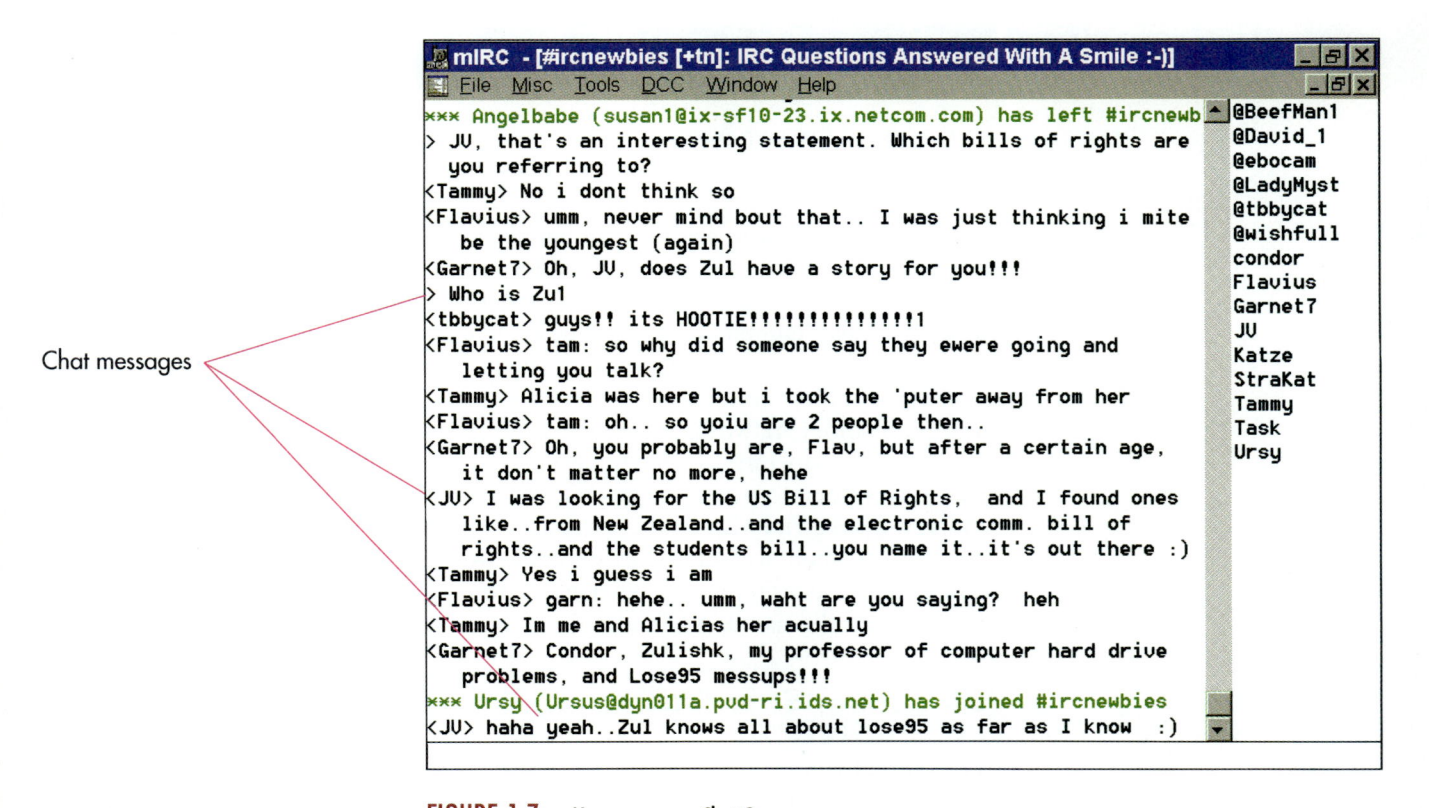

Chat messages

FIGURE 1.7   Messages on a Chat Screen

INTRODUCTION TO THE INTERNET   **13**

The postings are collected and then periodically mailed in batches with all the other newsgroup messages submitted since the last mailing. Since there are over 7,000 newsgroups, you can imagine the number of messages that arrive from all over the world with each mailing! Your computer center may elect to receive all, some, or none of the newsgroups. Figure 1.8 shows a message about Netscape being sent to a newsgroup. You can see that it looks very similar to an e-mail message.

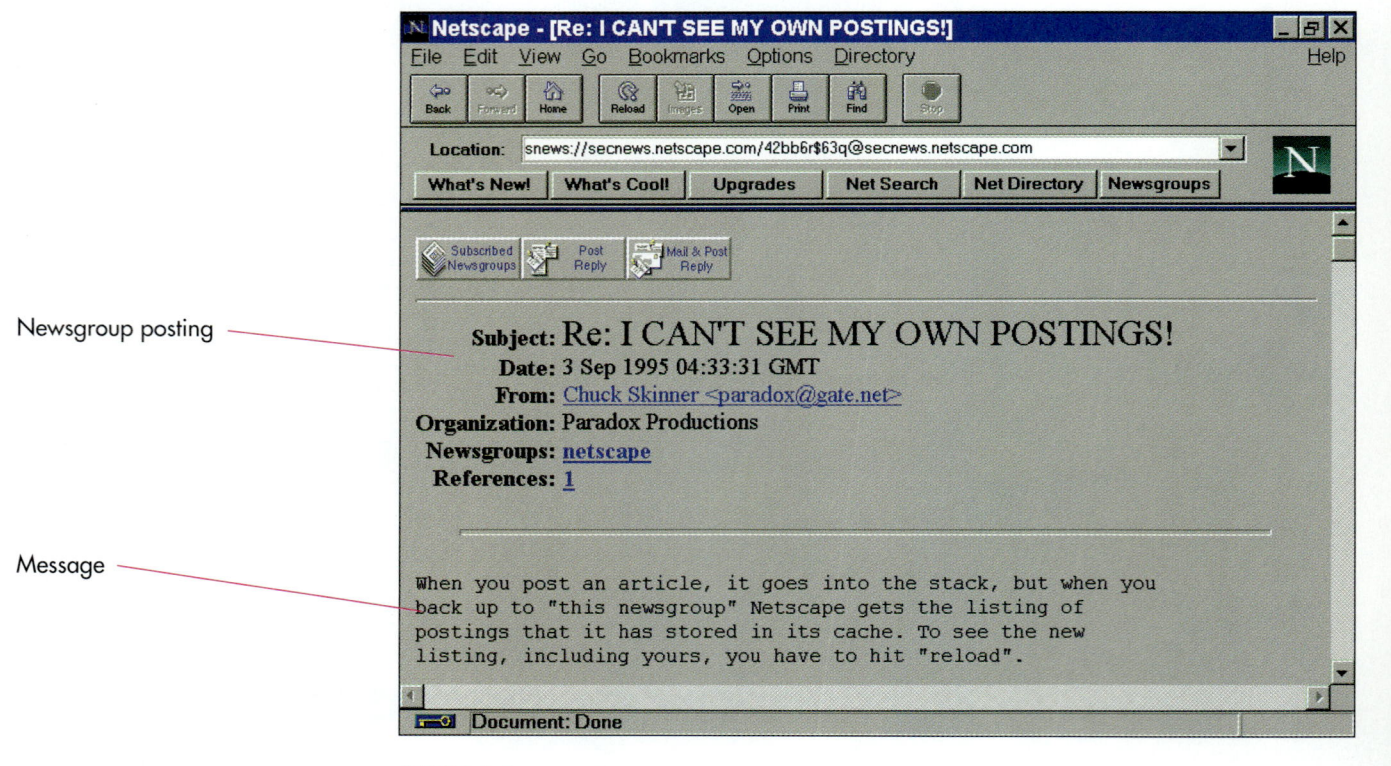

FIGURE 1.8 A Newsgroup Message

Many people who were not affiliated with a college or university were unable until recently to gain access to the Internet. Instead they often subscribed to a commercial service provider such as America Online (AOL), CompuServe, or Prodigy. These companies maintained their own networks, separate from the Internet. A subscriber could participate in a discussion group or send mail to another subscriber on the same network, but could not access the resources of the Internet or other networks, as illustrated in Figure 1.9a.

With the opening of the Internet to commercial providers, the online services have rushed to provide browsing and e-mail capabilities that access the Internet. Now a subscriber on AOL, for example, can send a message to someone with an Internet e-mail account, or to someone using the newly formed Microsoft network, as illustrated in Figure 1.9b. Chat, Usenet, and the services offered by online providers are discussed in Chapter 5.

Netiquette, Safe Surfing, and Other Issues

The Internet is a *virtual* community, that is, one that exists outside the bounds of time and space. People the world over communicate, carry on commerce and research, fall in love, and otherwise conduct the same kinds of human interactions

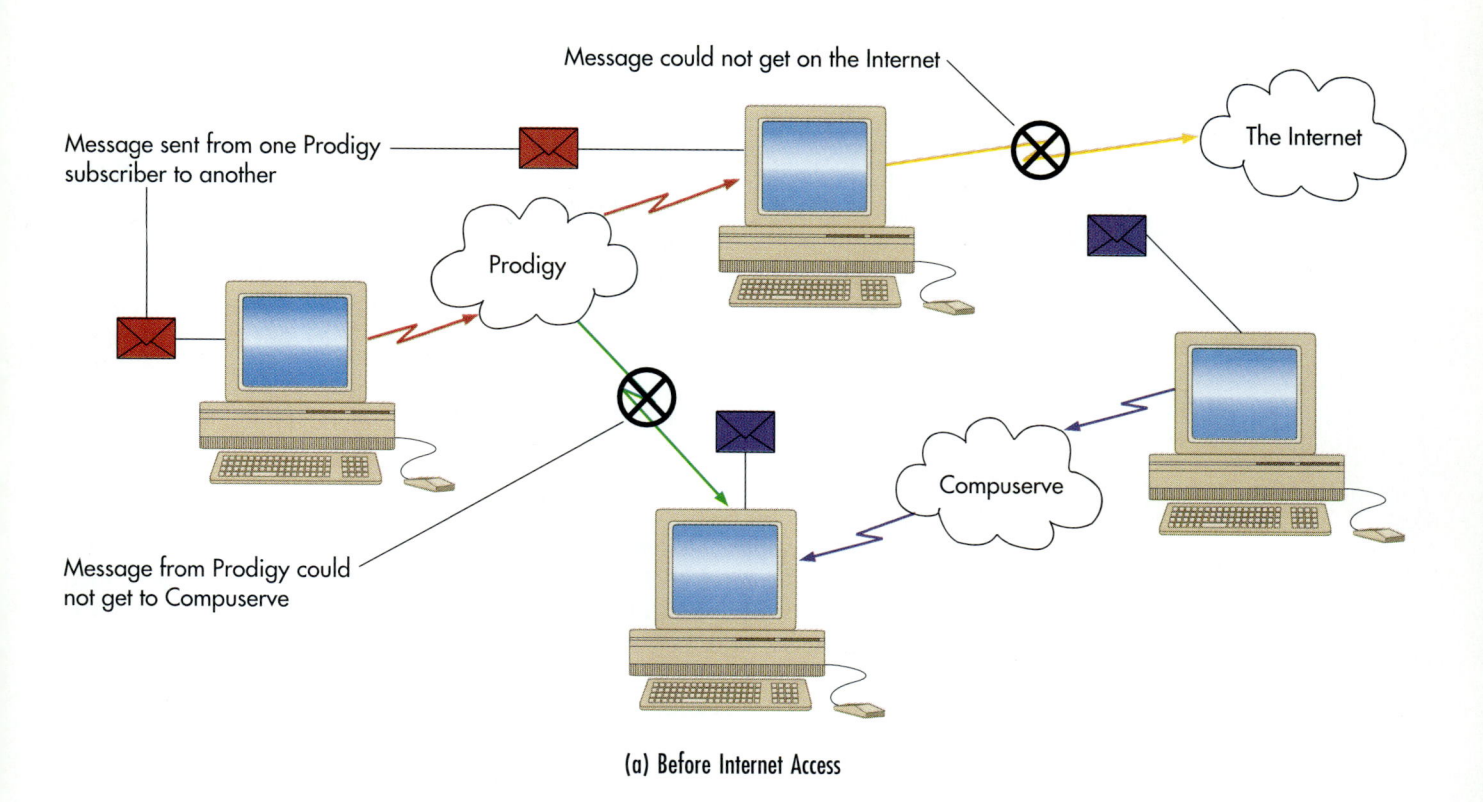

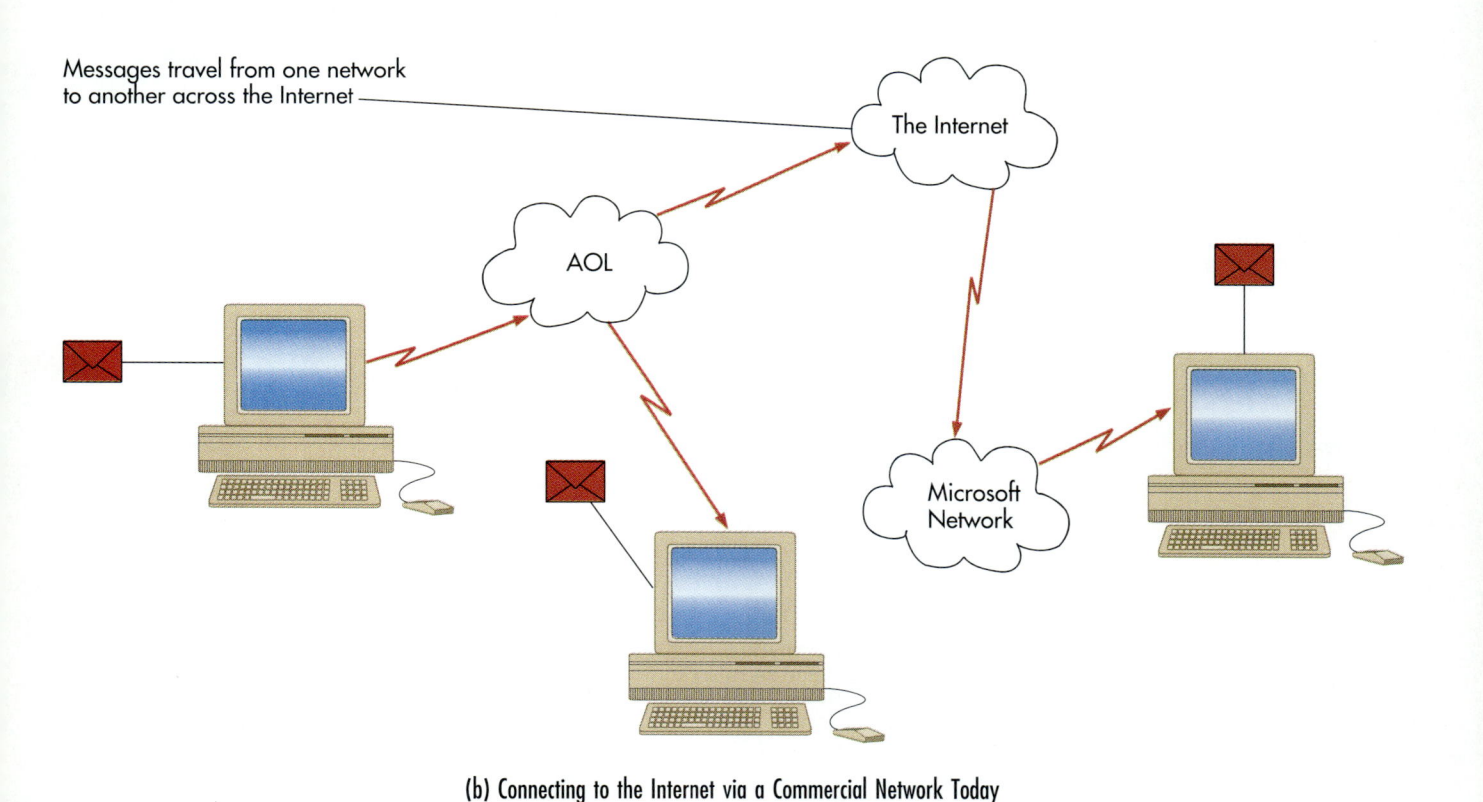

FIGURE 1.9 Commercial Online Networks

over the Net as they would via the telephone or postal systems. Just as in any other community, there are well-intentioned people and those who are con artists and crooks. The overwhelming majority are pleasant and helpful, but you will occasionally come across someone who is downright nasty.

Chapter 6 discusses some of the rules of the road for traveling the ***Information Superhighway.*** We strongly urge you to read it before you find yourself running afoul of the unwritten laws governing its use. While you probably won't get a speeding ticket on the Net, that might be less painful than getting 6,000 pieces of unwanted e-mail in response to your violating some taboo. Ignorance on the Net, as in life, is no excuse.

Web Publishing with HTML

Web documents, as you have seen in the figures in this chapter, contain both text and graphic images. Some contain audio and video clips as well. Web documents are produced using a special language called ***Hypertext Markup Language (HTML),*** which we discuss in Chapter 7. ***Hypertext*** refers to the embedded links we described earlier, which allow you to jump from document to document on the Web. HTML is composed of special ***tags,*** or codes, which you insert in a standard word processing document. A sample HTML page is shown in Figure 1.10. The tags, the codes surrounded by angled brackets (< >), control how the document will appear to a Web browser. You will create your own Web document in Chapter 7.

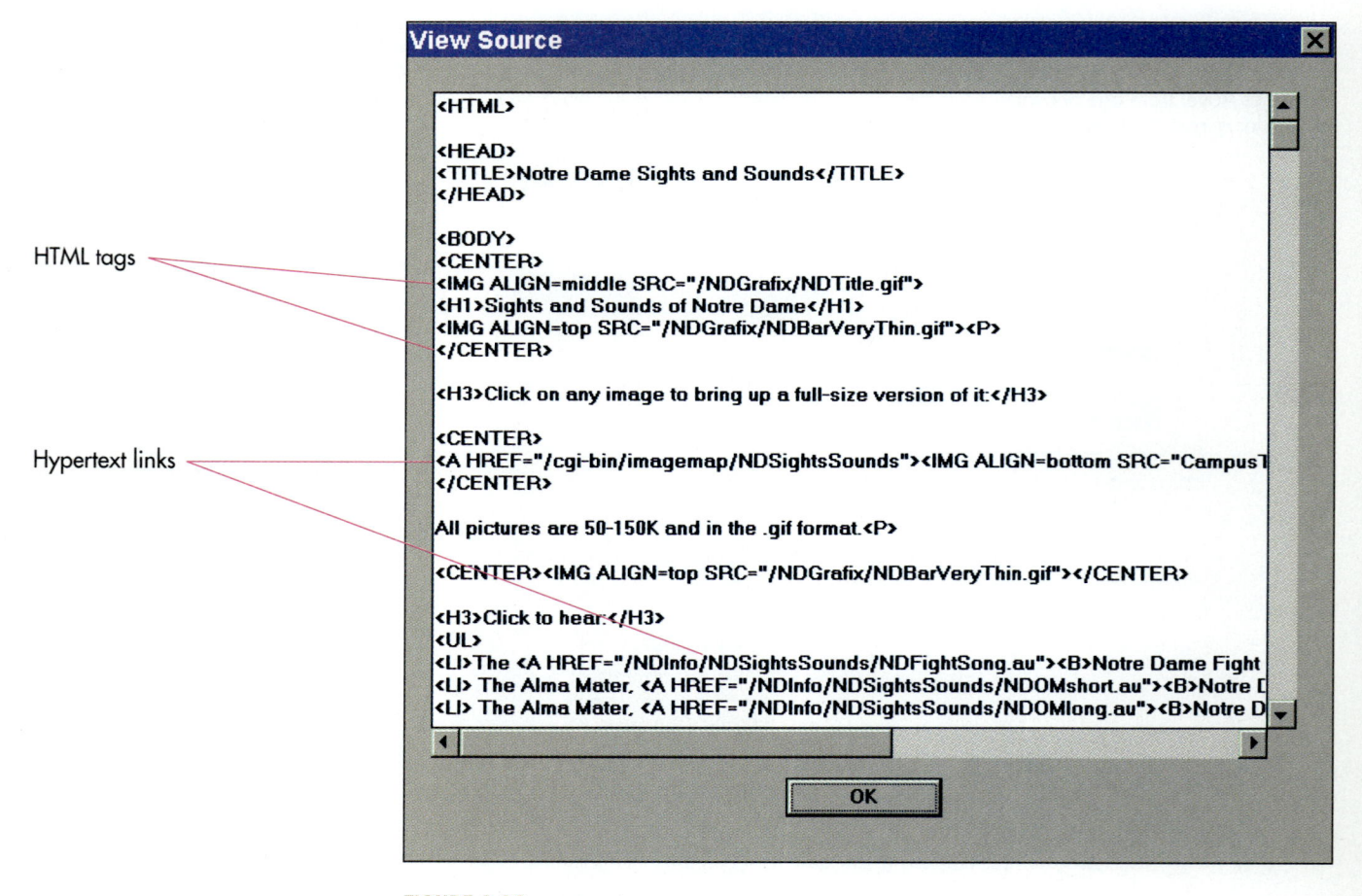

View Source

```
<HTML>

<HEAD>
<TITLE>Notre Dame Sights and Sounds</TITLE>
</HEAD>

<BODY>
<CENTER>
<IMG ALIGN=middle SRC="/NDGrafix/NDTitle.gif">
<H1>Sights and Sounds of Notre Dame</H1>
<IMG ALIGN=top SRC="/NDGrafix/NDBarVeryThin.gif"><P>
</CENTER>

<H3>Click on any image to bring up a full-size version of it:</H3>

<CENTER>
<A HREF="/cgi-bin/imagemap/NDSightsSounds"><IMG ALIGN=bottom SRC="CampusT
</CENTER>

All pictures are 50-150K and in the .gif format.<P>

<CENTER><IMG ALIGN=top SRC="/NDGrafix/NDBarVeryThin.gif"></CENTER>

<H3>Click to hear:</H3>
<UL>
<LI>The <A HREF="/NDInfo/NDSightsSounds/NDFightSong.au"><B>Notre Dame Fight
<LI> The Alma Mater, <A HREF="/NDInfo/NDSightsSounds/NDOMshort.au"><B>Notre D
<LI> The Alma Mater, <A HREF="/NDInfo/NDSightsSounds/NDOMlong.au"><B>Notre D
```

- HTML tags (pointing to `<HTML>`, `<HEAD>`, `<BODY>`, `<CENTER>`)
- Hypertext links (pointing to `<A HREF=...>` lines)

FIGURE 1.10   A Sample HTML Page

CONNECTING TO THE INTERNET

There are several ways of gaining access to the Internet, depending on whether you are using a computer in your campus computer lab or dialing in from home. If you are connecting from your computer center, the PC you use in the lab is most likely connected to a ***local area network (LAN).*** A LAN is a group of computers within close physical proximity to one another, which are connected via special cable to a powerful PC called a ***file server.*** The file server provides a common place to store data and programs, and provides rapid access to those files. The PCs on the network can share the disk storage on the server and can share print resources on the network. Figure 1.11 represents a conceptual view of a LAN consisting of multiple workstations and a laser printer connected to a file server. A ***workstation*** (also known as a client or node) is any PC on which an individual works. Different types of workstations (PCs and Macs, for instance) can be connected to the same network.

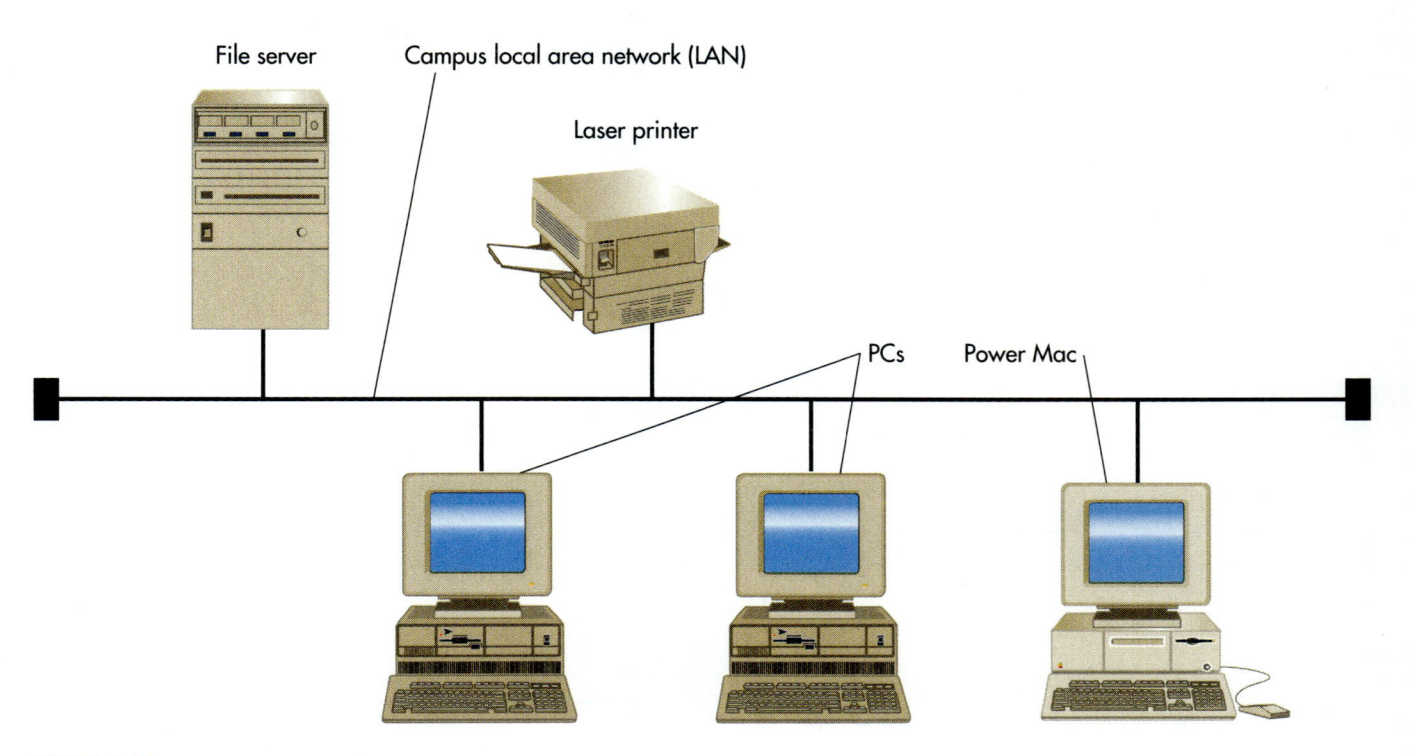

FIGURE 1.11 A Conceptual View of a LAN

The memory and processing requirements for file services and Internet services may compete and degrade performance if they are both on the same computer. It is, therefore, common for the Internet services to reside on a separate file server running a version of the Unix operating system, as shown in Figure 1.12. When you select a link in a Web document, send an e-mail message, or select some other Internet resource, the message sent from your PC includes instructions indicating that it should be handled by the Internet server. Figure 1.12 shows the Internet server being on the same LAN as your computer lab. However, in a computing environment that includes more than one LAN, the Internet server may be in an entirely different location. You may connect to it via a high-speed fiber optic cable, generically called a campus backbone, as shown in Figure 1.13.

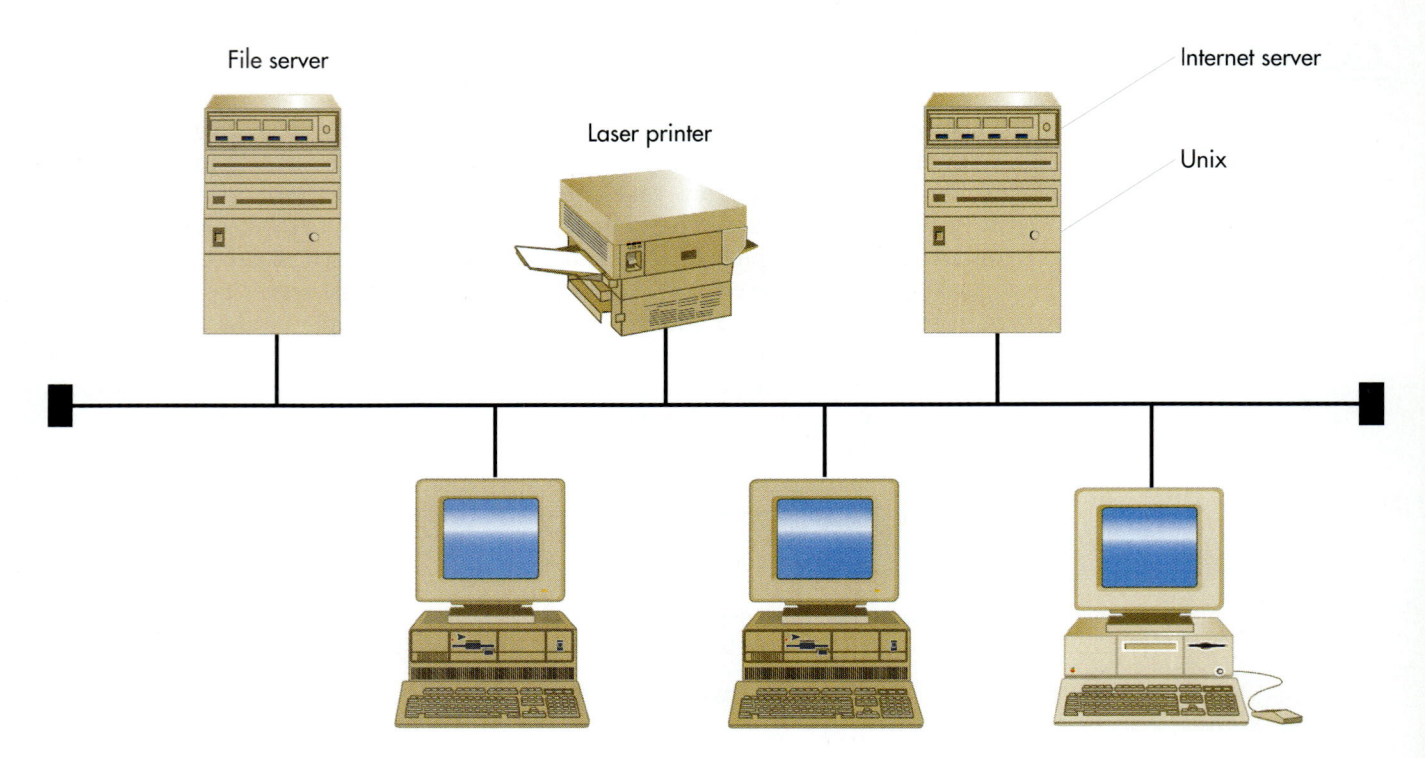

FIGURE 1.12 The Internet Server on the LAN

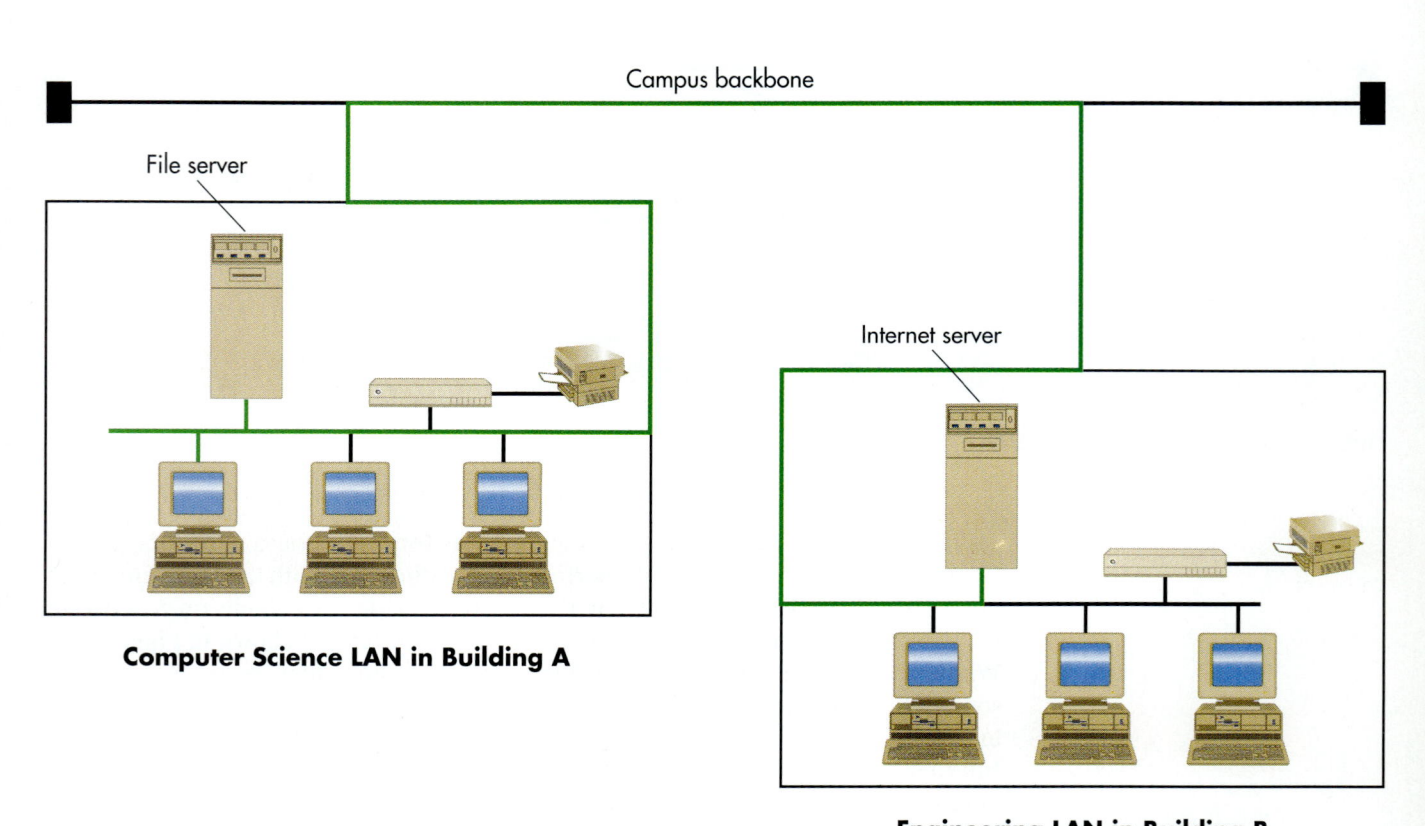

FIGURE 1.13 The Internet Server at Another Location

18 EXPLORING THE INTERNET

TWO FORMS OF ID REQUIRED

If your campus computing environment uses a local area network with both a file server and a Unix Internet server, chances are good that you will have a login ID and password on both machines. This seems a bit confusing; however, it helps ensure system security. When you use word processing, a spreadsheet program, or other general academic software, you will log on to the file server. When you want to send e-mail, you will log on again to the Internet server with your Internet username and password. Check with your LAN administrator, lab assistant, help desk, or instructor for more information about user IDs, usernames, and passwords in your environment.

When you start up an Internet program such as e-mail, you may be using a Windows-based program that runs on your PC. Such a program, called a *client*, passes your request on to the network, where it is picked up by the Internet server and acted upon. On the other hand, particularly if you are dialing into the campus from home, you may run a program on your PC that sets up a terminal session with your Internet server. A *terminal session* is a connection to the Internet server that emulates, or mimics, a terminal directly attached to the computer. (A *terminal* is a device without memory or disk storage that can communicate with a computer via a keyboard and display.) If you are using a terminal session, you will log on to the Internet server with your Internet username, which is generally a different login ID than you used to access the file server. A typical login screen for a terminal session is shown in Figure 1.14. The Unix $ prompt (or % prompt on some systems), indicates that you are communicating with the Internet server and have successfully logged in.

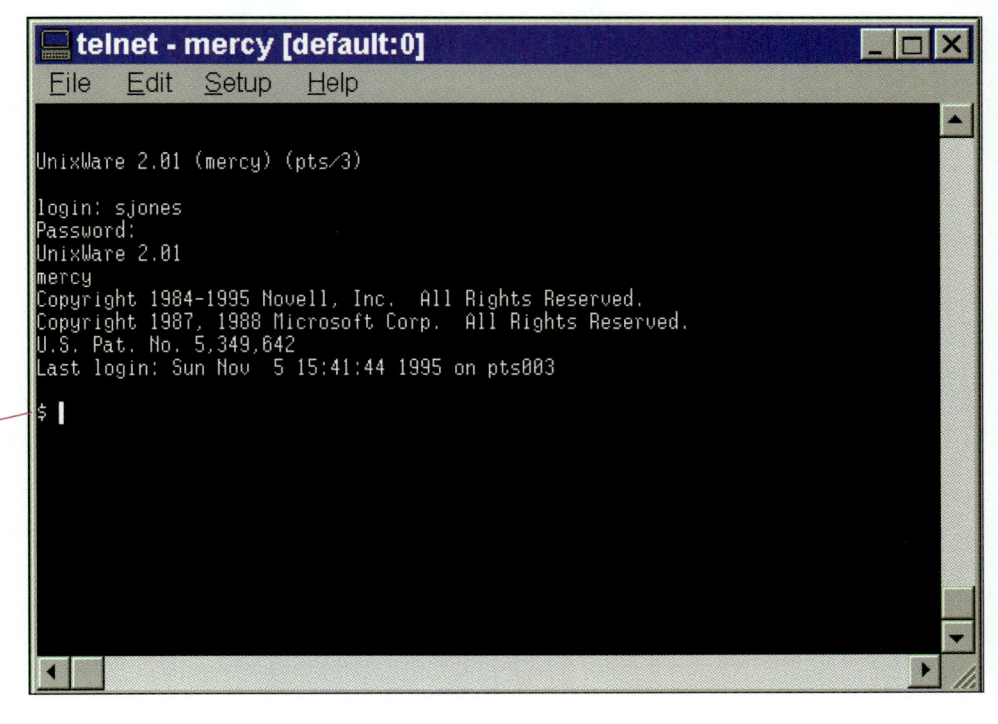

FIGURE 1.14   The Login Prompt for a Telnet Session

INTRODUCTION TO THE INTERNET   **19**

When using a terminal session to log on to a computer on the Internet, called a *telnet session,* or *telnetting,* you will use commands instead of a GUI interface to browse, search, and retrieve Internet resources. You will not be able to use pull-down menus or view the graphics incorporated into most Web documents. For these reasons most people prefer to access the Internet via a GUI interface on their PC. We will return to the topic of telnetting several times, and you will retrieve various Internet resources using the appropriate commands as you complete hands-on exercises in other chapters.

HOW THE INTERNET WORKS

The postal system provides a good analogy of how (but certainly not how fast) information travels across the Internet.[1] (E-mail travels at the speed of light, which is infinitely faster than the air- and land-based transportation to which the post office is limited.) When you mail a letter, you drop it in a mailbox where it is picked up with a lot of other letters and delivered to the local post office. The letters are sorted and sent on their way to a larger post office or substation where the letters are sorted again, until eventually each letter reaches the post office closest to its destination. The local mail carrier at the receiving post office then delivers each letter to its final destination.

There is no direct connection between the origin and destination because it is impossible to connect every pair of cities within the United States. If you were to send a letter from Coral Springs, Florida, to Englewood Cliffs, New Jersey, the letter would not travel directly from Coral Springs to Englewood Cliffs. Instead the postal service would route the letter from one substation to the next, making a new decision at each substation—for example, from Coral Springs, to Miami, to Newark, to Englewood Cliffs.

Each postal substation considers all of the routes it has available to the next substation and makes the best possible decision according to the prevailing conditions. This means that the next time you mail a letter from Coral Springs to Englewood Cliffs, the letter may travel a completely different path. If the mail truck from Coral Springs to Miami has already left or is full to capacity, the letter can be routed through Fort Lauderdale to New York City and then to Englewood Cliffs. It really doesn't matter because your only concern is that the letter arrive at its final destination.

THE INTERNET IS NOT FREE

The fact that there is no "Internet Incorporated" to collect a usage fee has given many people the mistaken idea that the Internet is free. The computers and networks that make up the Internet cost money, and each node (e.g., your college or university) must fund its own network connection through grants, user fees, or tuition.

The Internet works the same way, as data travels across the Internet through several levels of networks until it gets to its destination. E-mail messages arrive at the local post office (the host computer) from a remote PC connected by modem, or from a node on a local area network. The messages then leave the local post

---

[1] Krol, Ed, *The Whole Internet,* O'Reilly and Associates, Inc., Sebastopol, CA, 1992, pp. 24, 26.

office and pass through a special-purpose computer known as a ***router*** that connects the networks on the Internet to one another.

A message may pass through several networks to get to its destination. Each network has its own router that determines how best to move the message closer to its destination, taking into account the traffic on the network. A message passes from one network to the next, until it arrives at the local area network on the other end, from where it can be sent to its final destination. The process is depicted graphically in Figure 1.15.

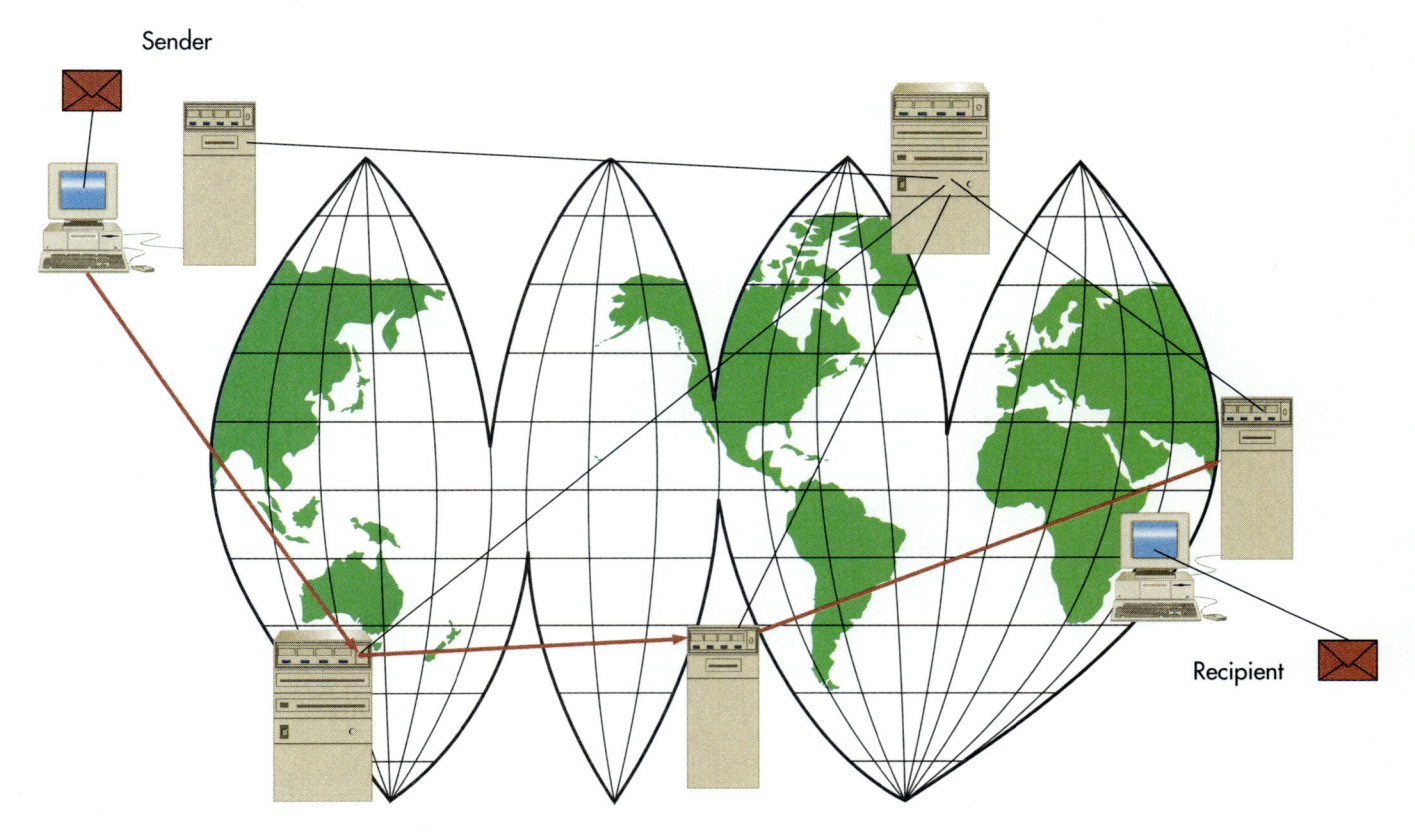

FIGURE 1.15 A Message Travels the Internet

The TCP/IP Protocol

Let's assume that you are working on a research project with a professor at another campus, and that you have several reports the professor must see tomorrow morning. The entire bundle is a stack six inches high. Now, let's pretend that the post office no longer accepts large packages for overnight delivery. One alternative would be to mail the pages individually by placing each page into its own envelope, then trust that all the envelopes would arrive on time, and finally that the professor would be able to reassemble the individual pages. That may sound awkward, but it is a truer picture of how the Internet works.

Information is sent across the Internet in ***packets,*** with each packet limited in size. The rules for creating, addressing, and sending the packets are specified by the ***TCP/IP protocol (Transmission Control Protocol/Internet Protocol)*** that governs the flow of data across the Internet. The TCP portion divides the file that you want to send into pieces, then numbers each piece so that the message can be reconstructed at the other end. The IP portion sends each packet on its way by specifying the address of the sending and receiving computer so that the routers will be able to do their job.

Why, you might ask, are files divided into packets rather than sent in their entirety? When the messages are divided into packets, many different messages may be flowing over the network at the same time. The packets may be routed to best utilize network resources, avoiding busy lines and allowing better load balancing across the network. If one part of the network is down, the packets can still get through on multiple other routes.

A second reason has to do with ensuring that the file arrives correctly. Static or noise on a telephone line is merely annoying to people having a conversation, but devastating when a file (especially a computer program) is transmitted and a byte or two is garbled. The larger the file being sent, the greater the chance that noise will be introduced and that the file will be corrupted. Sending the data in smaller pieces (packets), and verifying that the packets were received correctly, helps ensure the integrity of the data. If one packet is received incorrectly, the entire message does not have to be sent again.

Internet Architecture Layers

The Internet is built in layers that revolve around the TCP/IP protocols, as shown in Figure 1.16. At the sending computer, the **application layer** (with which you interact) creates the message and passes it to the **transport layer** on your computer, where the message is divided into packets. The packets are addressed at the ***Internet layer,*** then sent across the Internet using the **network access layer,** which interacts with the various levels of networks through which the data must travel to get to its destination. The process is reversed at the receiving computer. The Internet layer receives the individual packets from the network access layer, then passes the packets up to the transport layer where they are reassembled and sent to the application layer to display the message.

Each computer communicating with the Internet, whether dialing in or attached on a local area network (LAN), must have the software necessary to accomplish the task of the four layers. TCP/IP protocol drivers, or **stacks** as they are called, must be installed on each computer. Each computer must also have an ***IP address,*** a unique Internet address that identifies the computer as a node on the Internet.

The IP address is like a street address on a letter. Each computer on the Internet has a unique numeric address composed of four numbers, each less than 256, and each separated by a period: 192.25.13.01, for example. Each site on the Internet must apply for a specific block of IP addresses from its Internet provider. Each PC, Mac, router, server, and other device on the network must be assigned an IP address by the network administrator, just as someone in your town has designated a number for every house or building on your street.

The protocols in the lowest level in the architecture, the network access layer, control the sending of messages to devices physically attached to the local

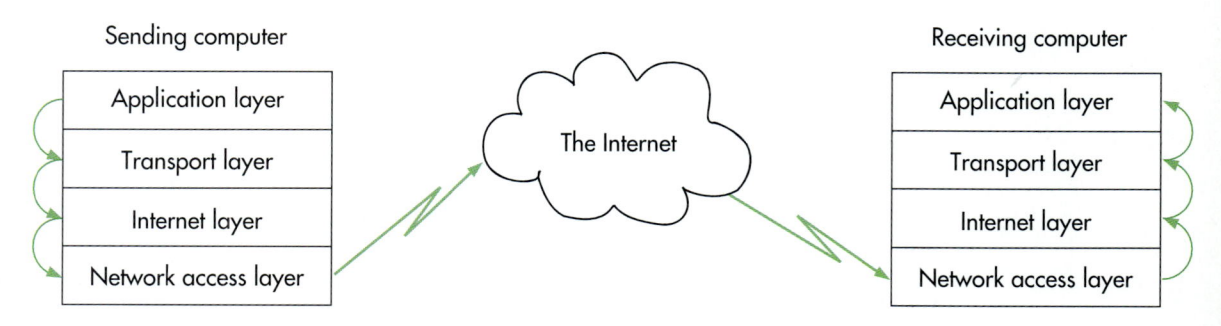

FIGURE 1.16 The Internet Architecture

network. They map the IP address of inbound messages to the actual hardware address of each local workstation on the LAN.

Let's use the more specific example shown in Figure 1.17. Bob, at the University of Miami, composes and sends an e-mail message. The transport layer divides the message into packets and delivers the packets to the Internet layer. The transport layer also keeps track of how many bytes have been sent, and waits to hear back from the receiving end whether the data was transmitted. Since the destination address is not on the local network to which Bob is attached, the Internet layer attaches a **header** (address information) to it and forwards it to the network access layer.

The network access layer, in turn, adds additional header information and sends the message out through the router onto the Internet. From there it is passed to another router, which examines the header and passes the packet on to another router. Each router contains a routing table that determines where (to what network router) to send the message next, based on the IP address of the message. This process continues until the destination router is reached, and the TCP/IP stacks on the receiving host deliver the message. They then send an acknowledgment of receipt to the sending computer. All of this happens in a matter of seconds, in a network that spans the globe!

The protocols that govern each layer are hardware independent, enabling the sender and recipient to use two different types of computers, yet receive the messages without problems. In our diagram we show Bob working on a Windows 95 PC and Gretchen on a Mac. In addition, the networks themselves may be different—that is, use different types of wiring—in which case the Internet layer will change the size of the packets to those required for the specific network.

Think of the post office analogy. Some mail routes are handled by mail truck, others on foot. If the mail carrier is on a walking route, he or she must remove the mail from the plastic mail tub and place it in the mail shoulder bag. Not all of the mail will fit, so some pieces will wait for the carrier to return and load

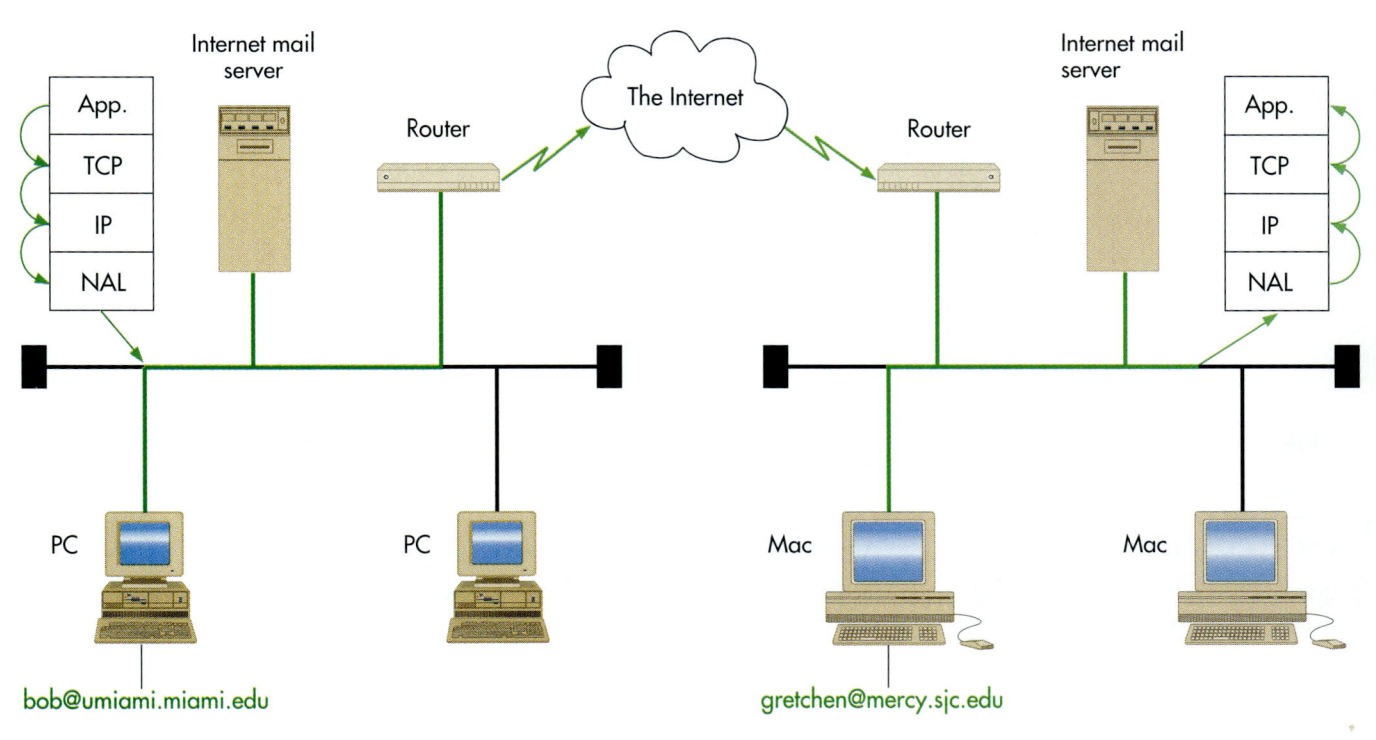

FIGURE 1.17   A Message Is Routed over the Internet

INTRODUCTION TO THE INTERNET   23

up for the second round. In a similar way, some Internet messages must be broken into different size packets for different parts of the physical network. The information about the type of protocols used is contained in the header attached to the packets.

The Internet layer performs additional important functions in the transmission of messages:

- Requesting routers to slow down the traffic when too many messages are being received (flow control)
- Returning error messages to the sender if a message is undeliverable
- Checking remote hosts to determine if they are operational

Similarly, the transport layer has additional responsibilities:

- Notifying the remote host that data is coming
- Keeping track of how many bytes of data have been sent
- Receiving acknowledgments from the receiving host
- Retransmitting the message if no acknowledgment is received
- Delivering data from the Internet layer to the correct application

Fortunately, most, if not all of these functions are transparent to the user. You simply type your message, click Send, and off it goes, aided by all the protocol stacks installed on your system.

The Domain Name System

The *Domain Name System (DNS)* was created to ensure a unique Internet address for every site. The Internet is divided into a series of component networks called *domains* that enable e-mail (and other files) to be sent across the entire network. Each site attached to the Internet belongs to one of the domains. Universities, for example, belong to the EDU domain. Government agencies are in the GOV domain. Commercial organizations (companies) are in the COM domain. Large domains are in turn divided into smaller domains, with each domain responsible for maintaining unique addresses in the next lower-level domain, or subdomain. Table 1.1 lists the six major Internet domains.

Internet Addresses

An *Internet address* or *Fully Qualified Domain Name (FQDN)* consists of the username, the host computer, and the domain (or domains) by which the com-

TABLE 1.1 Internet Domains

Domain	Description	Example Subdomain
edu	Educational institutions	Your college or university
gov	Federal, state, and local government entities	NASA, the CIA, the U.S. Senate, the Library of Congress, the National Archives
mil	Military organizations	U.S. Navy
com	Commercial nodes	Microsoft, Prentice Hall, Prodigy
net	Network service providers	The National Science Foundation's Internet Network Information Center
org	Nonprofit organizations	The Internet Town Hall

puter is connected to the Internet. The domains are listed in importance from right to left; that is, the highest-level domain appears on the end (the extreme right) of the Internet address. (You may find additional information following the highest-level domain. This is the country code, used if the host computer is located outside the U.S.) The @ sign separates the username from the host computer. For example:

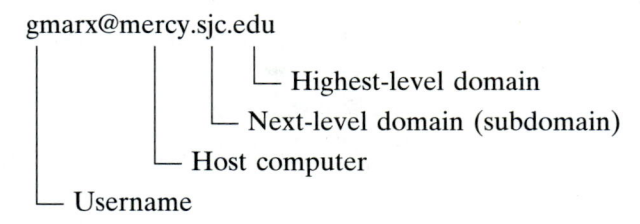

```
gmarx@mercy.sjc.edu
   │      │     │   └── Highest-level domain
   │      │     └────── Next-level domain (subdomain)
   │      └──────────── Host computer
   └─────────────────── Username
```

Each Internet address has an underlying numeric IP address, which the software uses to establish connections between machines. Fortunately, we are generally able to use a name instead of the numeric IP address to send messages.

Since messages are sent from all over the world to all over the world, these names must be translated to IP addresses constantly. That is the purpose of a special program called Domain Name Service (DNS), which runs on your Unix host. If your message contains an Internet address that is unknown to your host, it can look up the numeric IP address by querying the nearest **domain root server,** a special site on the Internet that keeps information about IP addresses in its domain. This is similar to your going to the post office to look up a zip code for a letter you wish to send. You can keep the zip code handy in case you want to send a letter to that address again. In a similar fashion the Internet host can keep in memory the numeric IP address found in any query so it will not have to look it up again the next time a message is sent to that Internet address.

AN ADDRESS TO REMEMBER

An Internet address is easier to remember when you realize that the address consists of the username, the host computer, and the domain (or domains) by which the computer is connected to the Internet. For example, President Clinton's e-mail address is president@whitehouse.gov, where president is the username, whitehouse is the host computer, and gov is the domain. Vice President Gore may be reached at vice-president@whitehouse.gov. (Use lowercase only—addresses are usually case sensitive.)

LEARNING BY DOING

Learning is best accomplished by doing, and so we come to the first of the many hands-on exercises that appear throughout the book. The exercises enable you to apply the concepts you have learned, then extend those concepts to further exploration on your own.

In contrast to subsequent exercises in the book, our first exercise is up to you to complete largely on your own. You will find out about the computing environment on your campus, learn how to apply for and get a user account and password for your LAN, and another for your Internet server, if required. You will log on to your LAN and investigate what Internet tools are available. If possible, you will set up a telnet session to your Unix host, log on, then log out. These simple activities will help you verify the validity of your username or password. There is nothing more frustrating than being several weeks into the semester and still not being able to log on. If you are unable to log on, please seek immediate assistance from your instructor, lab assistant, and/or LAN administrator.

> **THERE'S ALWAYS A REASON**
>
> We would love to tell you that everything will go perfectly, that you will never be frustrated, and that the computer will always perform exactly as you expect. Unfortunately, that is not going to happen, because a computer does what you tell it to do, which is not necessarily what you want it to do. There can be a tremendous difference! There is, however, a logical reason for everything the computer does or does not do; sooner or later you will discover that reason, at which point everything will fall into place.

HANDS-ON EXERCISE 1

Welcome to Cyberspace

Objective: Log on to your campus network. Determine what Windows-based Internet programs you can access on your PC. Open a telnet session with the campus Unix host. Use Figure 1.18 as a guide in the exercise.

STEP 1: Get Your Username and Password
➤ While it may seem self-evident, the first thing you must do before you can proceed with any other exercises in the book is get a username and password. Take some time to familiarize yourself with your campus computing environment. It is much better to answer these questions before you start than the night before a big assignment is due!
- What are the lab hours?
- Is there a help desk? What are its hours?
- Will you need to have your student ID with you to get in?
- How do you get a username and password?
- Do you need two different accounts (one for your academic LAN, one for the Internet)?

➤ Apply for your username(s) and password(s).

STEP 2: Start Netscape (or Another Browser)
➤ If you received more than one user account and password, check with your lab assistant or help desk to determine which one to use to log on to the campus network. Log on now. (Our example uses Windows 95, but it works equally well in Windows 3.1.)
- Check the Windows 95 desktop for any shortcuts to Internet programs, such as the Netscape icon shown in Figure 1.18a, then double click the icon, *or*
- Click **Start** on the taskbar, then click **Programs.** Search the program list for any Internet programs or program groups such as the Internet program group shown in Figure 1.18b. Start Netscape (or another browser) by selecting it from the list of programs.

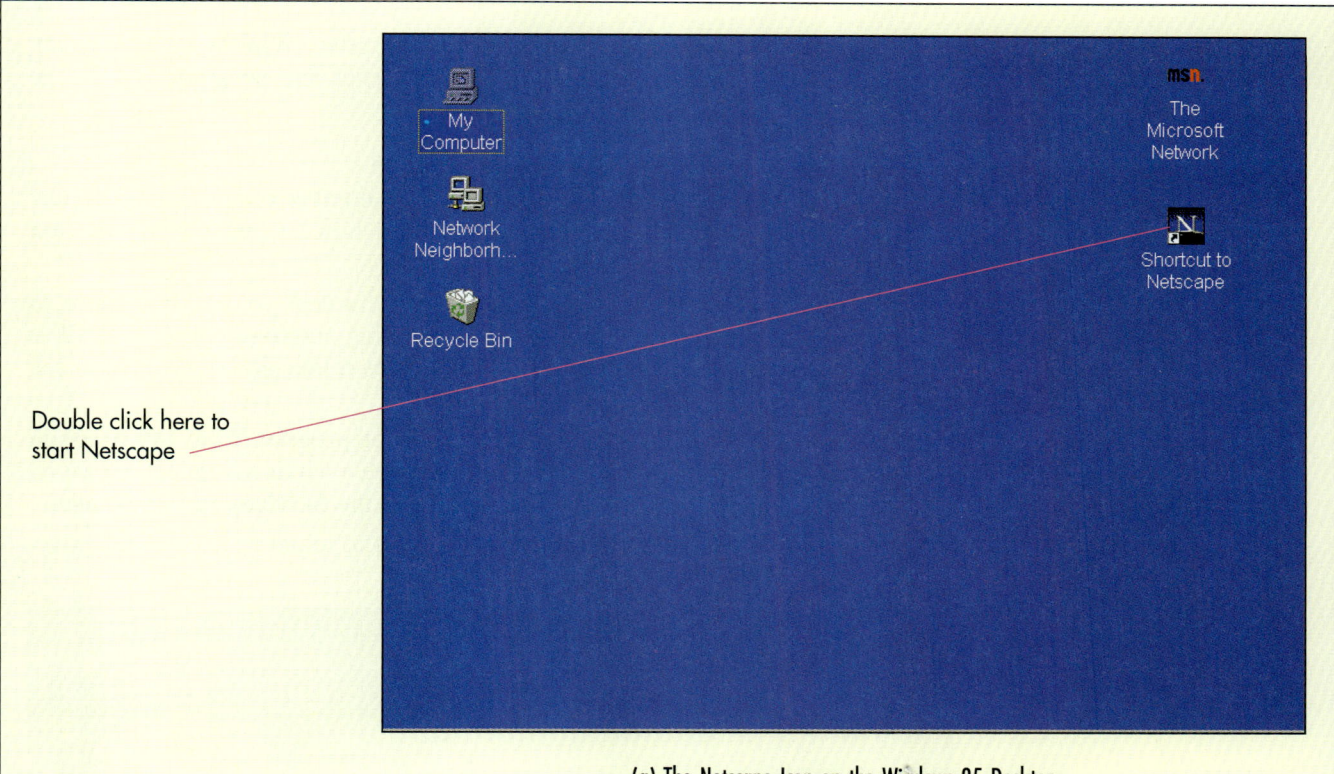

(a) The Netscape Icon on the Windows 95 Desktop

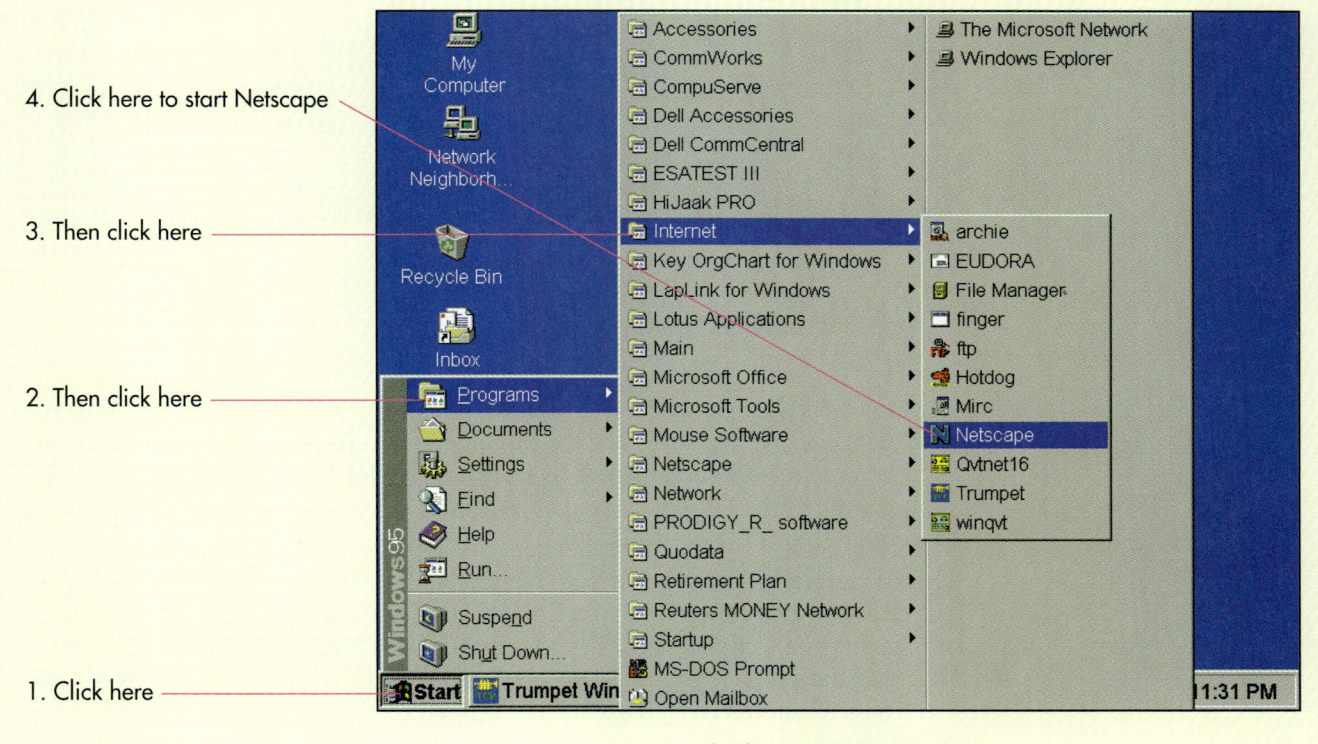

Double click here to start Netscape

4. Click here to start Netscape

3. Then click here

2. Then click here

1. Click here

(b) The Internet Program Group

FIGURE 1.18 Hands-on Exercise 1

- Exit Netscape the same way you exit any other Windows 95 program. Select **Exit** from the **File** menu or double click the **program icon** in the upper-left corner of the screen.

STEP 3: Find Out How to Start a Telnet Session

➤ You will need to get to the Unix prompt for a number of subsequent hands-on exercises. Therefore you will need to know how to start a telnet session and log on to your Unix Internet host.

➤ Check with your instructor, lab assistant, or help desk to determine how to set up a telnet session in your campus computing environment. (WinQVT is a widely used Windows program that provides telnet access. Check to see whether it is available.)

- Select **WinQVT** or other appropriate icon or program from the program list. If you are using WinQVT, you should see a window similar to the one shown in Figure 1.18c. Select **Terminal** from the **Services** pull-down menu.
- Enter the name of the site to which you want to telnet (your campus Inter-

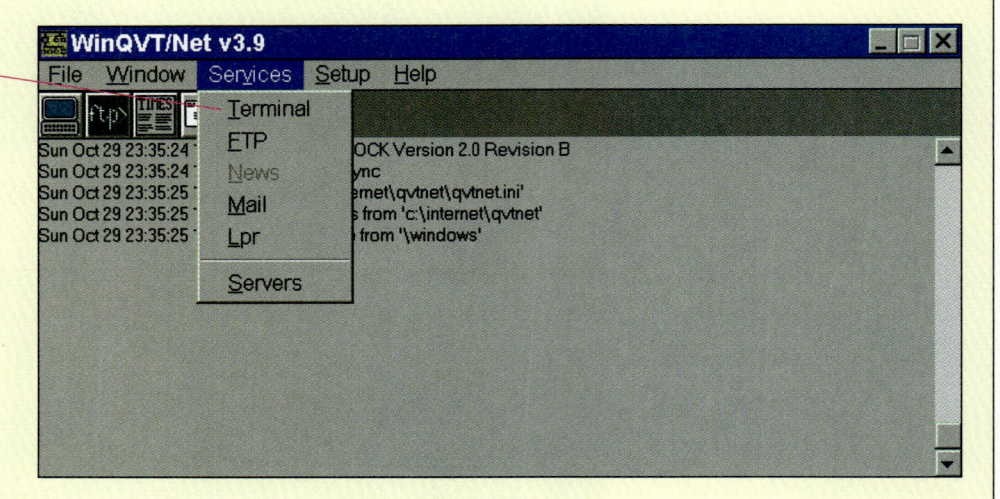

Click here →

(c) The WinQVT Window

FIGURE 1.18 Hands-on Exercise 1 (continued)

net host). Depending on your environment, you may be able to enter the host name only, instead of the Fully Qualified Domain Name (FQDN) (the complete Internet address), as shown in Figure 1.18d. If that doesn't work, try the entire FQDN, as shown in Figure 1.18e, substituting the address of your Internet host. Click **OK.**

- If successful, you will see a window similar to the one shown in Figure 1.18f, which shows the Unix Login: prompt. Type your **login ID** (your username) and press **Enter.** Type your password and press **Enter.** You should see the Unix $ prompt (you may see a % or other symbol). Congratulations! You made it to your Unix account!

➤ Type the command to exit your Unix account. It may be **exit, logoff, log,** or some other command. (See your lab assistant or help desk for assistance.)

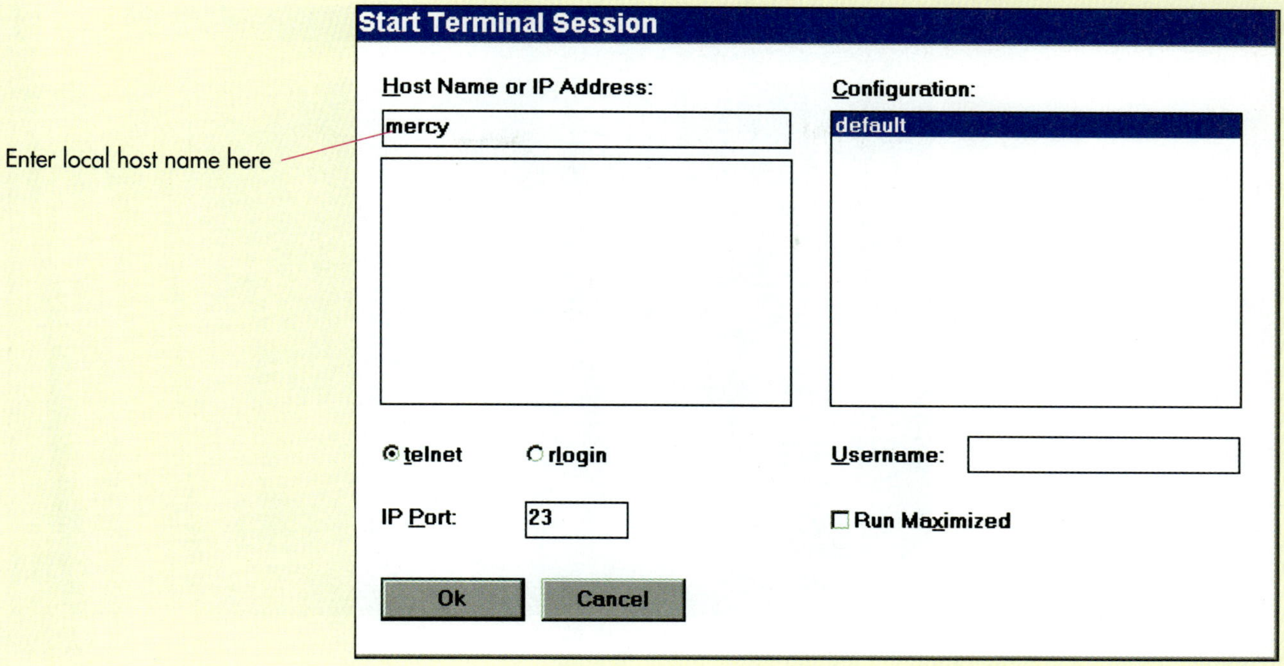

Enter local host name here

(d) Setting Up a Connection Using the Host Name

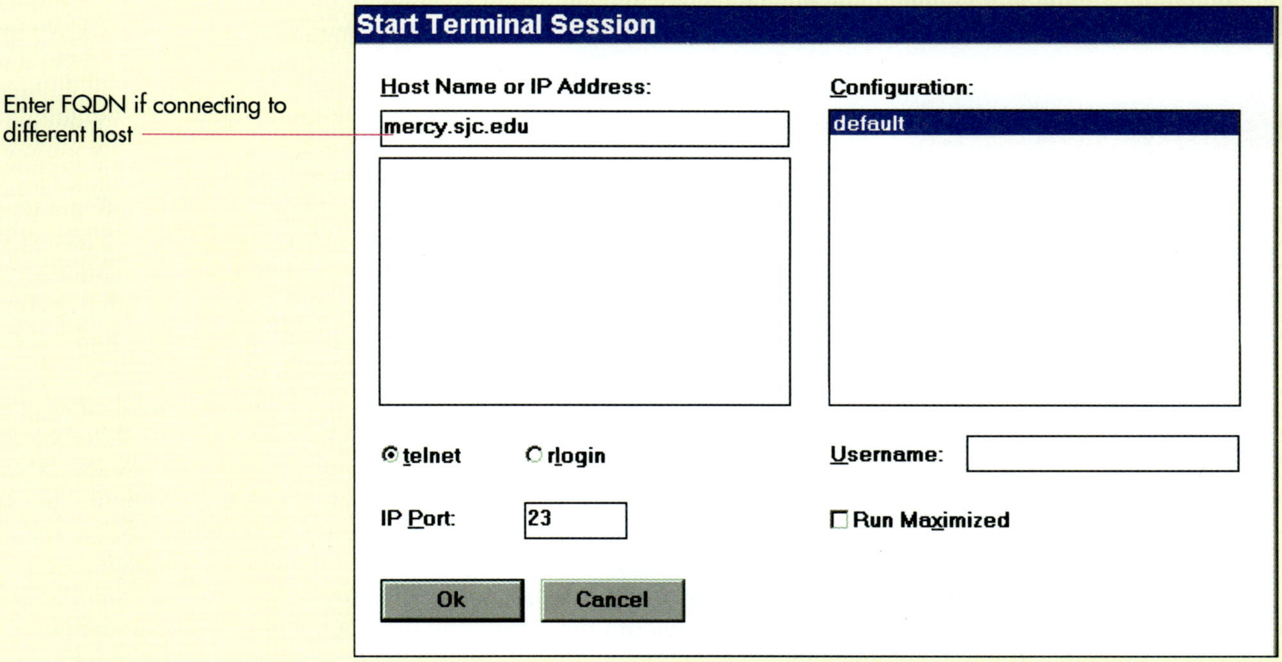

Enter FQDN if connecting to different host

(e) Setting Up a Session Using the Fully Qualified Domain Name

FIGURE 1.18   Hands-on Exercise 1 (continued)

Unix login prompt ──────

[Screenshot: telnet - mercy [default:0] window showing:
UnixWare 2.01 (mercy) (pts/3)
login:]

(f) The Unix Login Prompt

FIGURE 1.18 Hands-on Exercise 1 (continued)

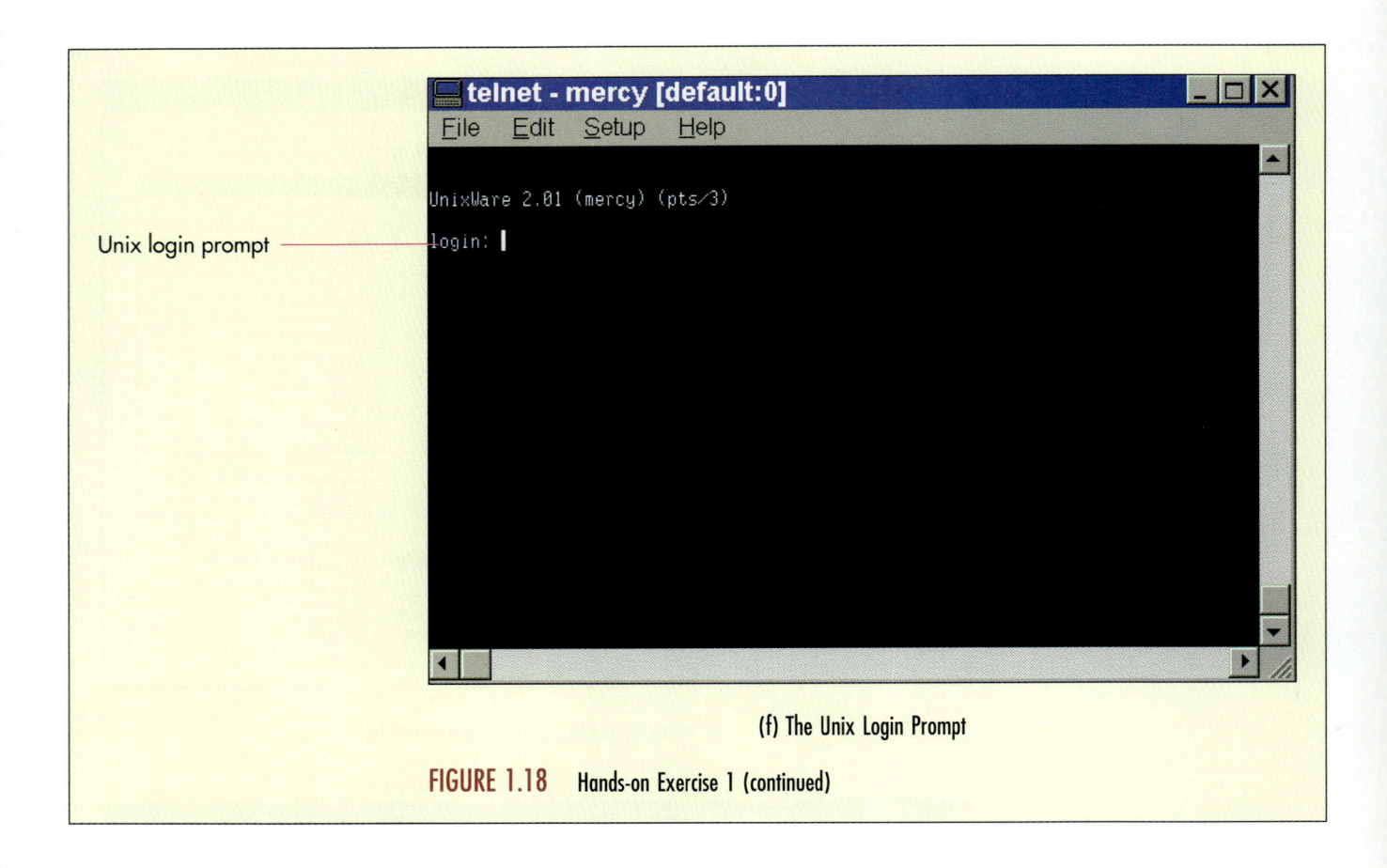

SUMMARY

The Internet is a network of networks that connects computers across the country and around the world. It began as an experimental project in 1969 to test the possibility of creating a network over which scientists and military personnel could share messages and data no matter where they were. Today the Internet includes virtually every major U.S. university, various government agencies, and an ever increasing number of commercial networks around the world.

You can access many resources and services on the Internet. E-mail users send electronic messages instantly around the world. World Wide Web documents let you link from one document to another by using a Web browser. Search engines help you locate Web resources, including HTML documents, gopher menus, and FTP sites. Chat and Usenet are additional resources for online and offline Internet communication, respectively. Some of these resources will be available using Windows-based GUI programs. Others will be accessed from the Unix prompt on your campus Internet host. You will need a username and password to get started.

Each institution that maintains a node on the Internet is responsible for supporting and administering that node. Each individual node pays its own way, and is responsible for providing services such as e-mail to its users.

The Internet works by sending all files and messages in packets. Packets are routed using TCP/IP, the software protocols that govern the flow of data across the Internet. Each computer using the Net must have a TCP/IP stack installed, and must have an IP address. Users generally prefer to use Internet addresses that consist of names as opposed to numbers. The Domain Name Service (DNS) translates Internet addresses into IP addresses. Security is very important on the Internet. Each user is assigned a username and password, which should be protected and changed often.

KEY WORDS AND CONCEPTS

Advanced Research Projects Agency (ARPAnet)
Application Layer
Archie
Browser
Channel
Chat
Client
Cyberspace
Domain
Domain Name System (DNS)
Domain root server
Download
E-mail
File server
File Transfer Protocol (FTP)
FTP site
Fully Qualified Domain Name (FQDN)
Gopher
Gopherspace
Graphical user interface (GUI)
Header
Hypertext
Hypertext Markup Language (HTML)
Information Superhighway
Internaut
Internet address
Internet host
Internet layer
IP address
Link
Local area network (LAN)
Lynx
Mosaic
Netscape
Network access layer
News
Newsgroups
Newsreader
Node
Offline
Packet
Post
Protocol
Router
Search engine
Stack
Surfing
Tag
Telnetting
Telnet session
Terminal
Terminal session
The Internet
Transmission Control Protocol/Internet Protocol (TCP/IP protocol)
Transport Layer
Usenet
Veronica
Virtual
Web site
Workstation
World Wide Web

MULTIPLE CHOICE

1. Which of the following statements about the Internet is true?
    (a) The Internet was started in the 1940s
    (b) The Internet is international in scope
    (c) The Internet is available only to the Department of Defense and large research universities
    (d) The number of Internet users is in the thousands

2. Which of the following is required to access the Internet?
    (a) A user ID
    (b) A password

INTRODUCTION TO THE INTERNET   31

    (c) Both (a) and (b)
    (d) Neither (a) nor (b)

3. Which of the following typically provides a graphical user interface to access the Internet?
    (a) Client software
    (b) A Unix shell account
    (c) A command-line prompt
    (d) All of the above

4. Users from which of the following organizations may access the Internet?
    (a) Government agencies
    (b) Nonprofit organizations
    (c) Commercial organizations
    (d) All of the above

5. Which of the following Internet services provides real-time interaction with other users?
    (a) Chat
    (b) E-mail
    (c) Usenet
    (d) All of the above

6. Which of the following products let(s) you browse the World Wide Web?
    (a) Mosaic
    (b) Netscape
    (c) Both (a) and (b)
    (d) Neither (a) nor (b)

7. E-mail allows you to send messages to:
    (a) Another user on your campus network
    (b) Another user on the Internet
    (c) Both (a) and (b)
    (d) Neither (a) nor (b)

8. Which of the following is the central authority of the Internet?
    (a) The Department of Defense
    (b) The Advanced Research Projects Agency
    (c) Both (a) and (b)
    (d) Neither (a) nor (b)

9. Which of the following is (are) the standard protocol(s) required for a computer to be connected to the Internet?
    (a) Pine
    (b) TCP/IP
    (c) POP
    (d) Windows

10. Which of the following statements about messages on the Internet is true?
    (a) The sending computer must run TCP/IP
    (b) The receiving computer must run TCP/IP

(c) Both (a) and (b)
(d) Neither (a) nor (b)

11. In the Internet address *postmaster@mercy.sjc.edu,* which is the highest level domain?
    (a) Postmaster
    (b) Mercy
    (c) Sjc
    (d) Edu

12. Which of the following will a search engine be able to locate?
    (a) Web documents
    (b) Gopher menus
    (c) FTP files
    (d) All of the above

13. Internet packages are broken into packets to:
    (a) Improve the load balance in the network
    (b) Help ensure the data gets through without error
    (c) Both (a) and (b)
    (d) Neither (a) nor (b)

14. Which of the following allows you to subscribe to a discussion group?
    (a) Usenet
    (b) Mailing lists
    (c) Both (a) and (b)
    (d) Neither (a) nor (b)

15. Which of the following is used to create Web documents?
    (a) Gopher
    (b) HTML
    (c) TCP/IP
    (d) Usenet

ANSWERS

1. b	6. c	11. d
2. c	7. c	12. d
3. a	8. d	13. c
4. d	9. b	14. c
5. a	10. c	15. b

Exploring the Internet

1. Use Figure 1.19 to match each Internet service with its description; a given resource may be used more than once or not at all. Some descriptions may have more than one matching resource.

Resource	Description
a. Netscape	____ Provides a menu-based mail interface
b. Pine	____ Allows text-only browsing on the World Wide Web
c. Eudora	____ Uses TCP/IP to send information over the Internet
d. Lynx	____ Requires a username and password
	____ Uses links to connect with other Web documents
	____ Displays graphic images in documents

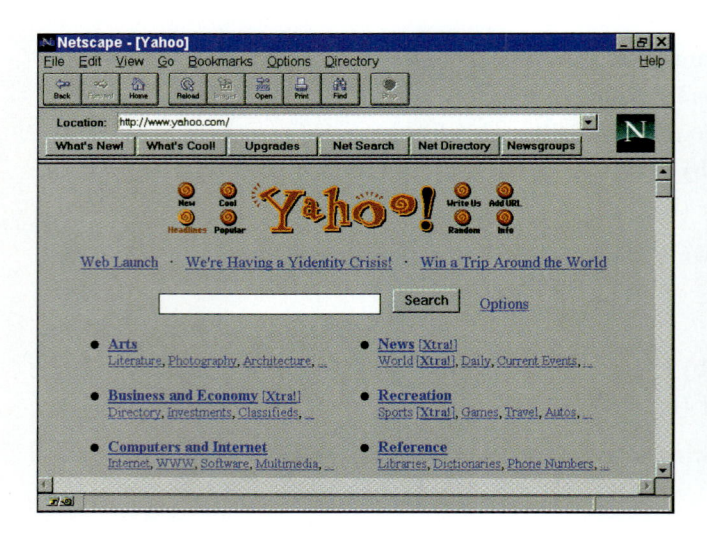

(a) Netscape

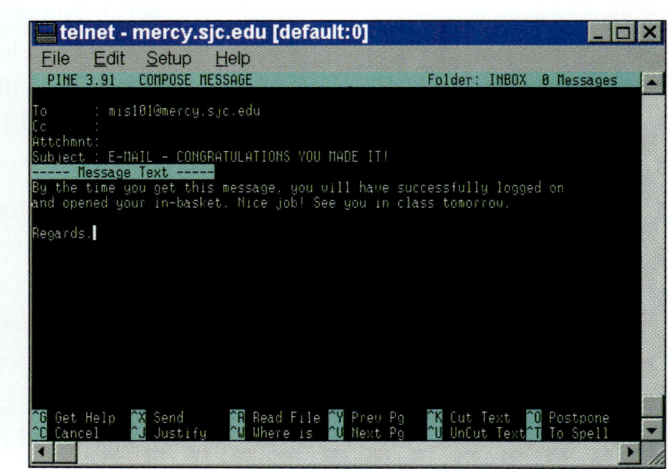

(b) Pine

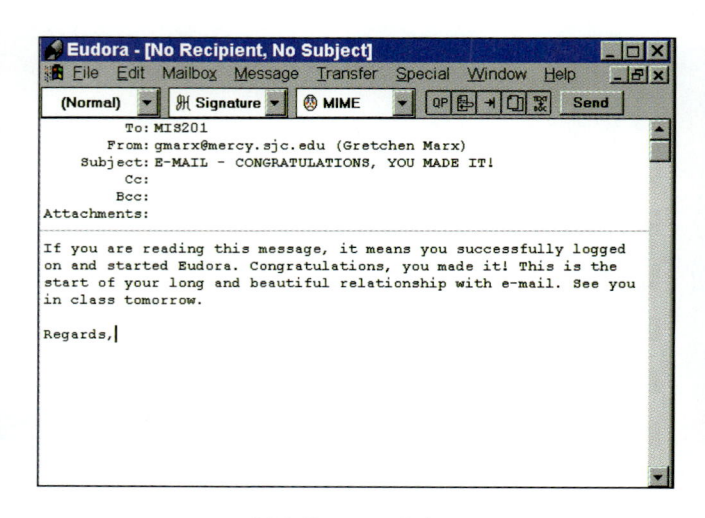

(c) A Message in Eudora

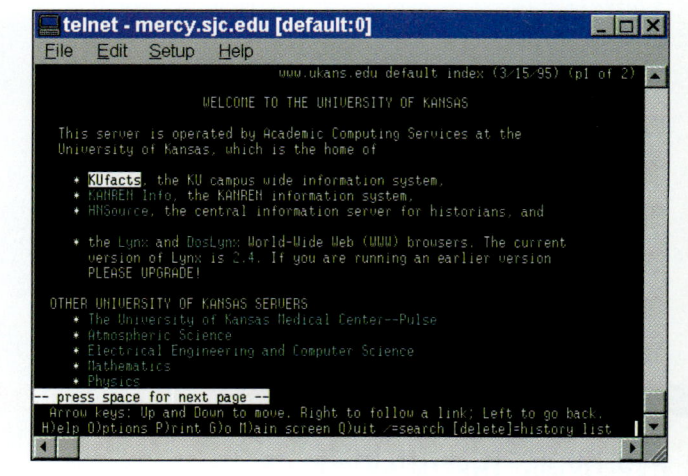

(d) Lynx

FIGURE 1.19   Figure for Exploring the Internet Exercise 1

2. Examine the e-mail message shown in Figure 1.20 and answer the following questions.
   a. What is the sender's host name?
   b. What is the highest-level domain in the sender's Internet address?
   c. What is the sender's username?
   d. What is the recipient's host name?
   e. Can there be another person with the same username as the recipient at the same Internet address?
   f. Can there be another person with the same username as the recipient in the same domain?
   g. To what type of organization does the recipient probably belong? How can you tell?

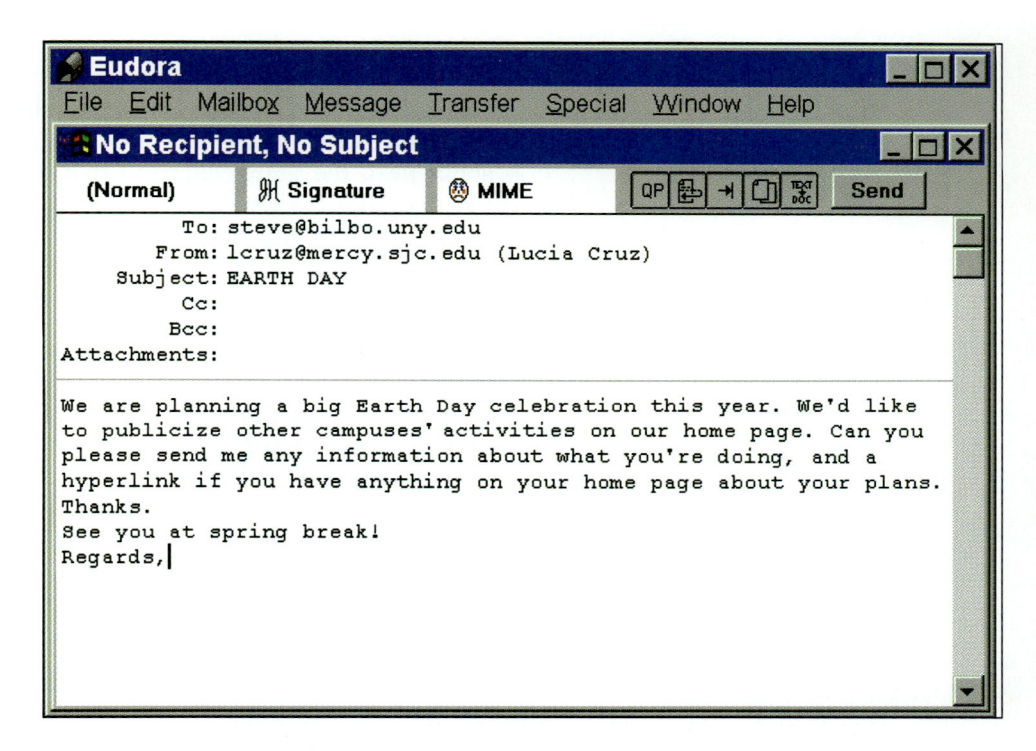

```
To: steve@bilbo.uny.edu
From: lcruz@mercy.sjc.edu (Lucia Cruz)
Subject: EARTH DAY
     Cc:
    Bcc:
Attachments:

We are planning a big Earth Day celebration this year. We'd like
to publicize other campuses' activities on our home page. Can you
please send me any information about what you're doing, and a
hyperlink if you have anything on your home page about your plans.
Thanks.
See you at spring break!
Regards,
```

FIGURE 1.20 Figure for Exploring the Internet Exercise 2

3. Answer the following with respect to the Internet system at your college or university.
   a. Who is allowed access to Internet accounts?
   b. Do you have dial-in access?
   c. What e-mail program do you use?
   d. What is your username?
   e. What is your college or university's domain name?
   f. How often do you have to change passwords?
   g. Where do you go to get help?

4. Answer the following questions with respect to passwords:
   a. What advantage, if any, is there in choosing an eight-character password instead of one with four characters?
   b. What advantage (disadvantage) is there in choosing as a password a word found in the dictionary? Would it be better to use a nonsensical word, such as acissej (Jessica spelled backwards)?
   c. How often should you change your password? Why?

Practice with the Internet

1. **Practice Logging On:** Log on to your campus network, entering the wrong login name or ID. What error message do you get? What happens? Log on again, entering the correct login name or ID, but the wrong password. What happens this time? It is helpful to know what to expect in these situations, so that when you are under time pressure and make these common mistakes, you don't panic and assume something is wrong with your account. (Most computer problems are caused by human error.)

2. **Learn about Unix Help:** It helps to know more about Unix to do some of the things you will want to do on the Internet. Log on to your Unix server. At the Unix prompt type **man,** the Unix command to display the online Help manual. A list of available Unix commands is displayed. To learn more about a particular command, type **man commandname,** substituting the name of the command you want to review. For example, **man pwd,** displays information about **pwd,** the Unix command that displays the name of the current directory. Explore the Unix help manual by pressing the spacebar to move down a page. When you reach the end of the section you are reading you will automatically exit Help. When finished, log out using the Unix command appropriate for your computing environment.

3. **Learn about Unix Talk:** Most Unix systems provide an online dialog feature similar to Chat. With a classmate, go to the computer lab and each log on to your Unix accounts. Find out about the talk command by typing **man talk** at the Unix prompt. In particular, note how to end a talk session. After reading the help topic, type **talk username** at the Unix prompt, substituting the name of your classmate. Type a few messages to each other. Obviously this is not particularly useful if you are both in the same room, but it can be a lifesaver if you are communicating with someone on the other side of the campus. Quit the talk program and log out when finished.

4. **Find Out Who Is Logged On:** In the previous exercise you made arrangements to try the talk program with a classmate. At other times it is convenient to find out who is logged in at the same time you are. Log on and at the Unix prompt type **who.** A list of other users will be displayed. You may set up a talk session with any of them. However, just as you wouldn't randomly dial a phone number and start talking to whomever answered, you shouldn't disturb other users without good reason, and unless you know them.

Case Studies

Your Campus Computing Environment

Working with a friend or two from your class, interview your instructor, lab assistant, help desk specialist, LAN administrator, and anyone else who can provide information about your campus network. Draw a diagram of the network similar to Figure 1.12. Indicate which server or computer provides your Internet connection.

The Net Is Everywhere

Take a trip to a local pharmacy or bookstore that carries many types of magazines. Determine how many have the word *Internet* on the cover, and notice which types of magazines they are. (Are they all computer magazines, or are general-interest publications including articles about the Net?) Read the local paper for a week or two and watch for headlines about the Internet. You may find them on the front page, in the *Living* or *Business* sections, or just about anywhere else. Do a visual search in the periodical room at your campus or town library for references to the Internet. What did you find? Compare notes with classmates and write a brief report on the Internet and the media.

Is a Picture Worth a Thousand Words?

Much has been made of the World Wide Web and its ability to retrieve and display documents with embedded graphics. Review Figure 1.2 and compare the Netscape and Mosaic screens with the Lynx screen. Go back through this chapter and cover the illustrations and screens with a piece of paper, reading just the text. What value do graphics add to these documents?

The Commercialization of the Internet

The original design of the Internet precluded access to it by commercial organizations. That changed in the early 90s, and now it seems as though every company, from the multinational with its headquarters in Bahrain to the mom-and-pop grocery store on the corner, has a Web site. What reasons might the Department of Defense have had for limiting access initially? Why were commercial organizations eventually allowed access? Identify the pros and cons of commercial access to the Internet, and prepare a brief summary of your findings.

GLOBAL COMMUNICATION ON THE INTERNET: USING E-MAIL

OBJECTIVES

After reading this chapter you will be able to:

1. Discuss the general commands that are present in every e-mail system; send and receive an e-mail message.
2. Explain the differences between client- and server-based e-mail programs.
3. Create a distribution list to send the same e-mail message to many people.
4. Create a custom signature and mailbox.
5. Subscribe to an Internet mailing list.

OVERVIEW

Electronic mail (e-mail) is simply a means of sending messages by computer. One of the most widely used Internet services, it has changed the way we communicate. In many ways it is superior to the telephone. You send a message when it is convenient for you. The recipient reads the message when it is convenient for him or her. Neither of you has to be online for the other to access his or her e-mail system. Either of you can obtain a printed copy of the message. You can also use a mailing list capability to send the same message to many people. With very little training or effort, most people can understand the concepts involved with e-mail and learn to use it. And best of all, e-mail is a lot less costly than a long distance phone call.

In this chapter we describe two types of mail programs, Windows-based programs that run on a PC, and menu-based Unix programs. We begin by describing how e-mail is sent, received, and stored on your system. We show you how to send, receive, and reply to messages. We also discuss how to set up a custom mailbox, a distribution list, and a customized signature. Our examples use PC Eudora for Windows and the Unix mail program Pine, but the concepts apply equally well to any e-mail system.

A mailing list allows multiple people interested in exchanging mail about a subject to subscribe to the list and receive all the messages the members of the list generate. We show you how to request a list of all the mailing lists on the Internet, and how to get a list of all the mailing lists devoted to a specific topic. You will then subscribe to one or more lists, and within a few days (possibly hours) start receiving messages from other subscribers.

E-MAIL

Now that you know something from our discussion in Chapter 1 about how messages are transmitted on the Internet, let's find out how to send one. In essence, you use a text editor similar to a word processor to create a message, then you send it through the Internet, just as you would mail an ordinary letter. The message is delivered electronically to the recipient's ***mailbox.*** When the recipient checks his or her mailbox and finds the message, he or she can respond (or not) as he or she sees fit.

You do not have to be at home when the postman delivers a letter to your mailbox. In similar fashion your PC does not have to be on when an ***e-mail*** (electronic mail) system delivers a message to your electronic mailbox on your school's Internet host. All e-mail messages are stored in a central post office (an area on disk) that exists on the mail server at your college or university. Each user has a private mailbox on the mail server, which is analogous to a post office box in a regular post office. You have a key or combination lock to your post office box. In the same way you have a password for your e-mail mailbox. The electronic post office is controlled by a system administrator who monitors the e-mail system, provides access for individual users, and maintains the disk storage required to hold the electronic mail.

You can send e-mail in a variety of ways—across a local area network, by logging onto a remote computer at your school or university, or via an information service such as the Microsoft Network. There are many different types of e-mail programs, each with its own unique commands. It is impossible in any one text to cover the details of every system. All systems, however, provide the capability to send and receive mail. Our discussion will focus on the basic commands you can expect to find in any system. We demonstrate these commands using PC Eudora, a widely used Windows mail program, and Pine, a Unix mail program, but the discussion is sufficiently general so that you can apply the concepts to any other system.

The Structure of an E-mail Message

All e-mail messages contain certain basic elements as can be seen in Figure 2.1. Figure 2.1a shows the New Message window in PC Eudora, in which you compose an e-mail message. Figure 2.1b shows the Compose screen in Pine, a Unix-based e-mail program. You can see that while using two different types of computers and programs, the elements in the two screens are very similar.

The ***header*** area contains information pertaining to sending the message. The From and To lines contain the address of the sender and recipient, respectively. The Subject line is a one-line summary of the message. The Cc (***carbon copy***) line indicates the names of other people who are to receive copies of the message. Bcc, which stands for ***blind carbon copy***, allows you to send a copy of the message to someone without the main addressee knowing you are doing so. The Attachments line lets you attach a file such as a Word document or Excel spreadsheet to your e-mail message. The e-mail message you are sending or receiving appears below the header.

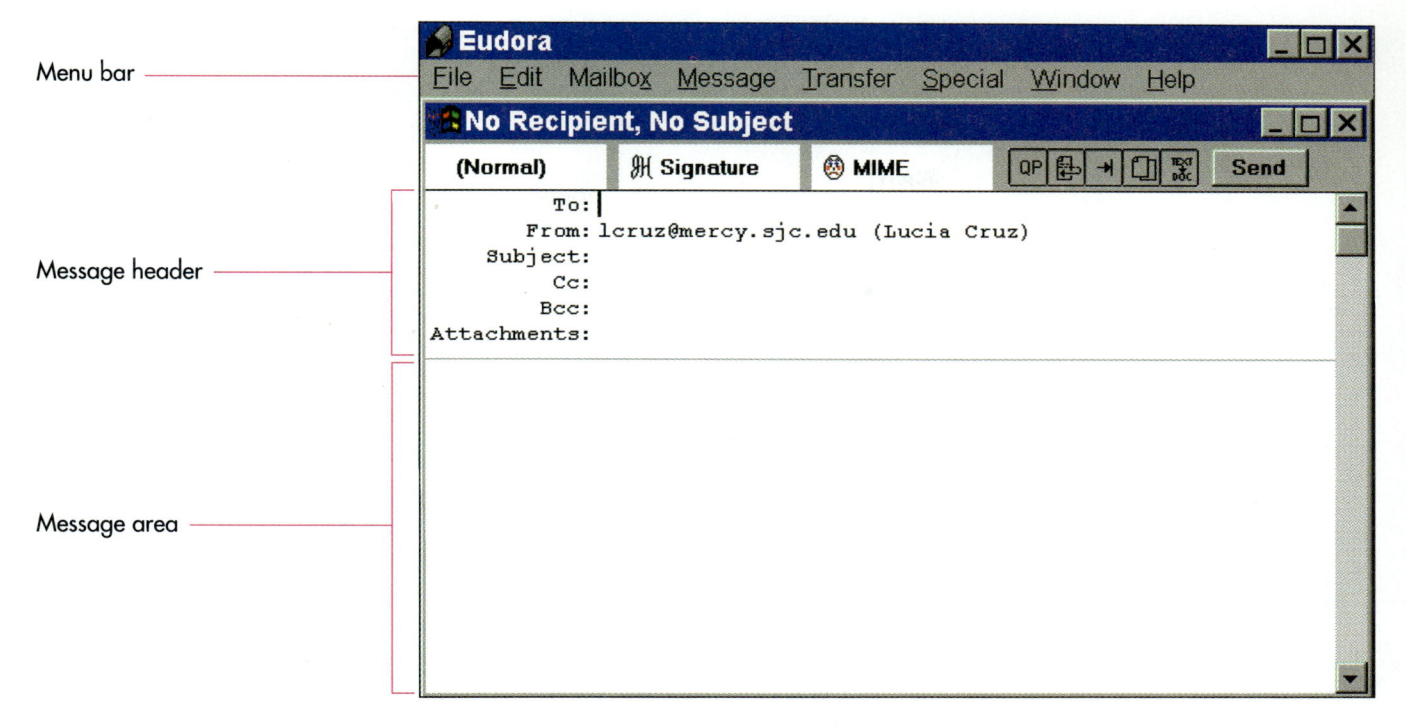

(a) The New Message Window in Eudora

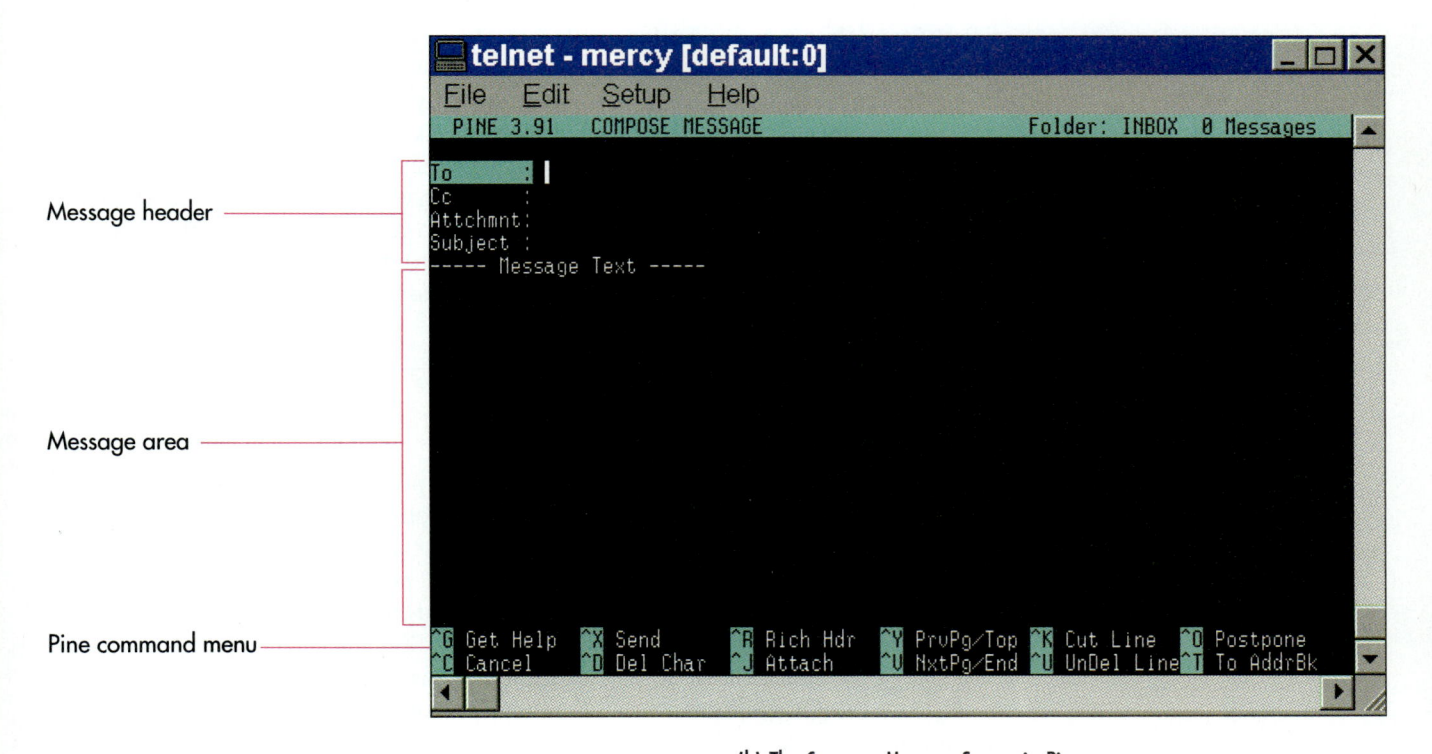

(b) The Compose Message Screen in Pine

FIGURE 2.1   Composing an E-mail Message

GLOBAL COMMUNICATION ON THE INTERNET

E-mail commands are executed by pulling down a menu, by clicking the corresponding icon on the toolbar, or by entering the appropriate command at the prompt in a command-driven system. The following commands (or their equivalent) are found in every system:

Compose: To create a new message
Send: To send a message that you created
Reply: To respond to a message you received
Forward: To send to another person a message you received

These commands are straightforward and will be illustrated in the hands-on exercises that follow.

Logins and Security

All e-mail systems let you send/receive messages to/from anyone on your network or information service. You can also send e-mail to individuals outside the network or information service, provided that they each have an Internet address and that your system has access to the Internet. You will need a userID and password to log on to your system. A *userID* is assigned to you and identifies you to the system. The *password* protects your account from unauthorized use by others. (As discussed in Chapter 1, you may actually have two or more userIDs and passwords, depending on how many systems you access on campus.) Your userID for the e-mail system will be the username you use in your Internet address. If Melissa Boyer is attending AnyU and uses an Internet host in the psychology department called Freud, her e-mail address would be *mboyer@freud.anyu.edu*. She would log on to the Unix system using the userID *mboyer*.

Many people choose passwords that are easy to remember, but what is easy for you is also easy for someone trying to break into your account. Thus, you should choose a password consisting of at least six characters, preferably letters *and* numbers or special characters. Keep the password to yourself and change it periodically. Do your LAN administrator a favor, and remember your password. If every user frequently forgets his or her password, the academic computing staff will have time to do little else but change user passwords!

PROTECT YOUR PASSWORD

Many computer break-ins occur because of a poorly chosen password consisting of only four characters. A hacker's computer is fast and it doesn't get discouraged if its first several attempts at guessing a password are rejected. A four-letter password has fewer than 500,000 combinations, which can be solved in only 30 seconds of computer time. Opting for eight letters increases the number of combinations to more than 200 billion, which makes the hacker's job much more difficult. And if you include numbers in addition to letters, an eight-character password (letters and numbers) has more than 2 trillion combinations! You should also avoid proper names and common words, as a hacker will use a program that goes through the dictionary trying common words until it finds one that allows the hacker in.

Mailboxes

Mail programs keep track of your mail by having default mailboxes, one for incoming messages (generally called the In-box or something similar), and one for outgoing messages (called the Out-box or sent-mail). In Figure 2.2a, the Eudora In-box folder is selected. It contains previously received messages (which the mailbox owner has decided to keep), as well as new messages waiting to be read. A bullet in the first column on the left indicates that the message in that row is

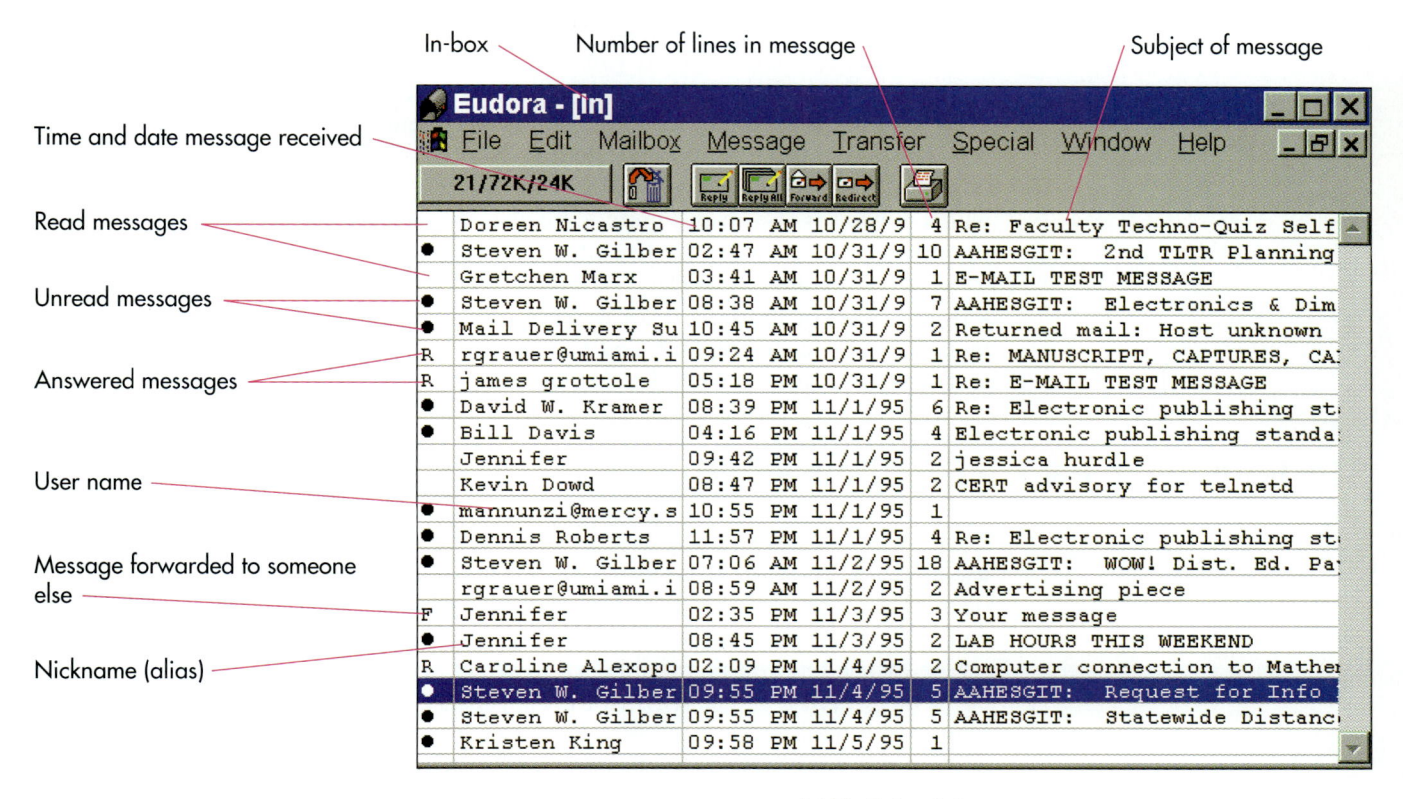

(a) The Eudora In-box

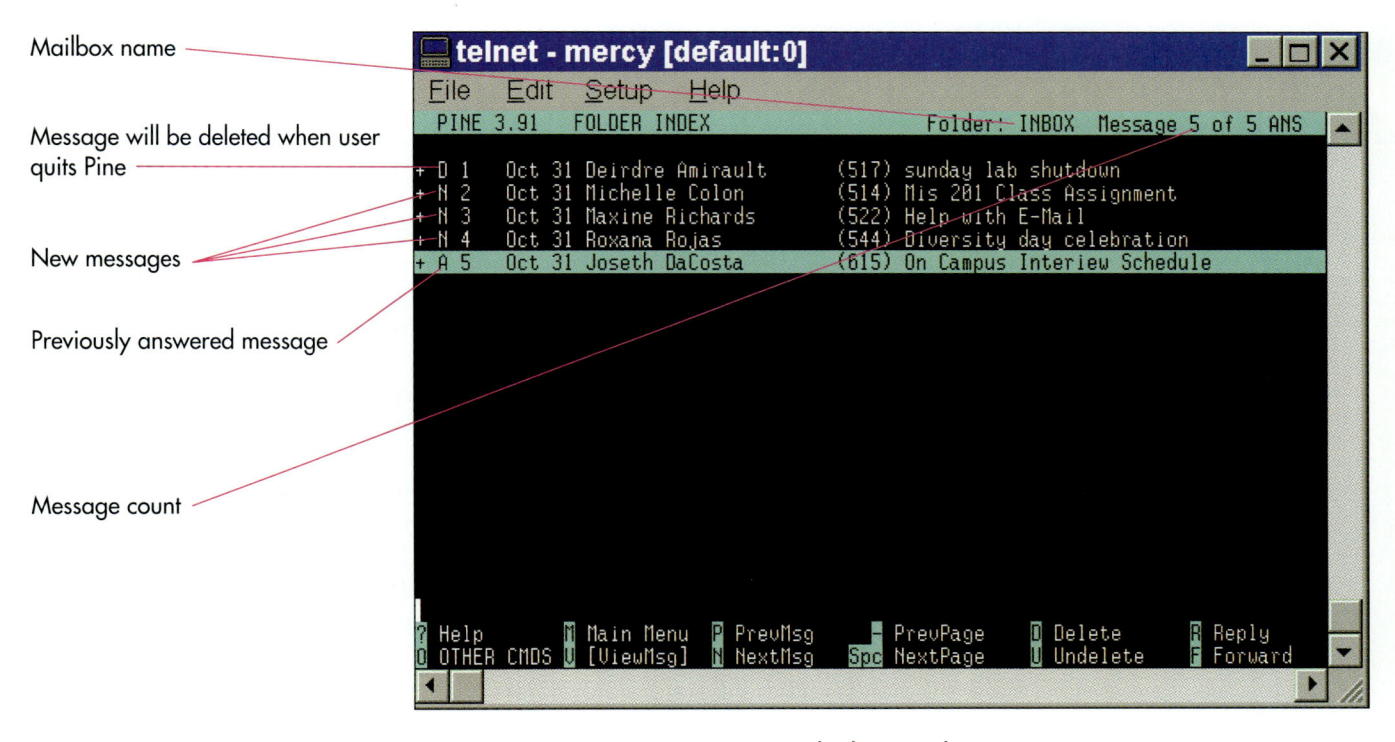

(b) The Pine In-box

FIGURE 2.2   The E-mail In-box

GLOBAL COMMUNICATION ON THE INTERNET   43

unread mail. An "R" indicates the message has been read and replied to. A blank field means the recipient has read the message without responding to it. The second column shows the sender's username or *alias.* (An alias is a nickname that is converted to a username by the e-mail system the sender is using.)

Figure 2.2b shows the INBOX folder in Pine. Messages are numbered and marked according to their status. Messages marked with a "D" will be expunged, or permanently deleted when you exit Pine. Messages marked with an "N" are new, unread messages, with an "A" are those you have read and replied to, with a "+" are those for which you are the sole recipient. Depending on how your system administrator has configured Pine, you may be able to flag a message as important, in which case you will see an asterisk "*" next to it. The *folder index,* which is what is shown in Figure 2.2b, also shows the date the message was sent, the name of the sender, the size of the message, and the subject, if any.

After reading a message you may decide to "throw it away" by moving it to a trash basket or marking it for deletion. When you exit Eudora, messages in the trash basket will be emptied, and the messages in it will be discarded. When you exit Pine, messages marked for deletion will be expunged.

SENDING AND RECEIVING E-MAIL

There is more than one way to send and receive e-mail on the Internet; which you use depends on your campus network environment. By far the easiest way is through the use of a Windows-based *mail client,* or e-mail program, running on your PC. The *client software* presents a graphical user interface (GUI) on the screen, which lets you point and click to select mail options and commands. If you don't have access to client software on your PC, you will access e-mail using a Unix-based mail program such as Pine. (Unix is a multipurpose operating system used in most campus Internet systems.) We will discuss both methods, and present two hands-on e-mail exercises that allow you to use whichever type of interface you have in your campus computing environment.

E-mail with a POP Mail Client

The process of sending and receiving mail using a PC-based mail client is illustrated in Figures 2.3a and 2.3b, respectively. The client software uses a protocol known as the *Post Office Protocol (POP)* to send and receive mail. When you use a POP mail client, your incoming mail is kept on the *mail server,* or Unix-based host, until you connect and request it. The mail client on your PC communicates with the mail server and *downloads* (retrieves) the inbound messages. It places them in a mailbox on your local PC disk drive (or in your personal mail directory on a network drive on a different file server).

You can read the messages when they are downloaded, or, because they are stored locally, you can read them at a later time without being logged on to the mail server. Outbound messages are composed on the PC using the POP mail client, *uploaded* (forwarded) to the Unix mail server, and also stored in your personal mailbox on your PC or network mail directory. The mail server sends the outbound messages through the router to the Internet by using a protocol known as *Simple Mail Transfer Protocol (SMTP).* (Hence the mail server is known as an SMTP server.)

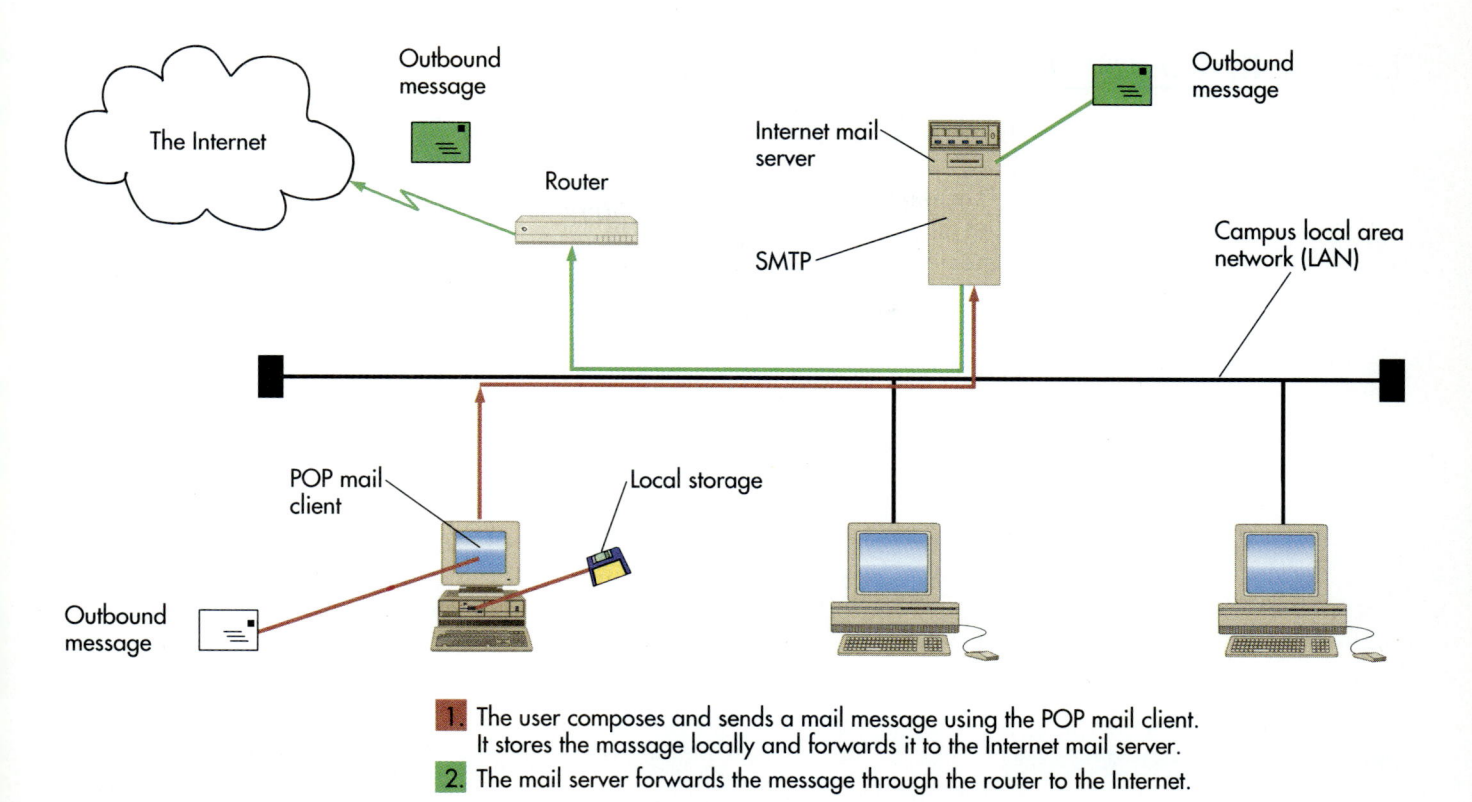

(a) Sending a Message with a POP Mail Client

1. The user composes and sends a mail message using the POP mail client. It stores the massage locally and forwards it to the Internet mail server.
2. The mail server forwards the message through the router to the Internet.

(b) Receiving a Message with a POP Mail Client

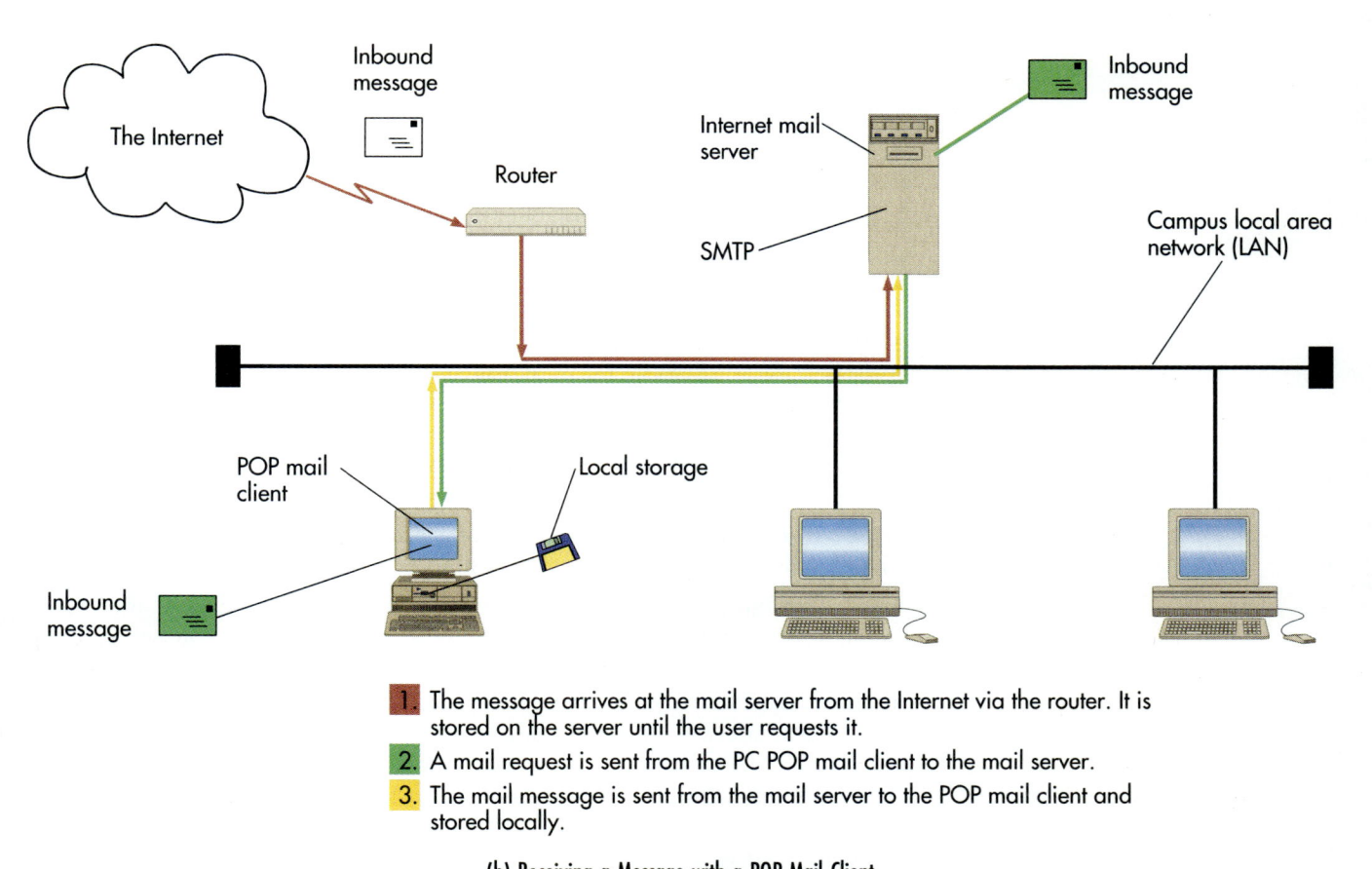

1. The message arrives at the mail server from the Internet via the router. It is stored on the server until the user requests it.
2. A mail request is sent from the PC POP mail client to the mail server.
3. The mail message is sent from the mail server to the POP mail client and stored locally.

FIGURE 2.3 Sending and Receiving E-Mail

GLOBAL COMMUNICATION ON THE INTERNET

LEARNING BY DOING

The following exercise demonstrates the basics of e-mail in the context of PC Eudora. Although the commands in the exercise are specific to Eudora, they are sufficiently general that you should be able to adapt the exercise to any PC-based POP mail client. See your instructor, lab assistant, or help desk for assistance. And remember, the programs used to access the Internet are constantly changing. What you see on your screen may differ (possibly substantially) from the figures that follow.

FIND A PEN PAL

Everyone likes to get mail, especially when using e-mail for the first time. Find a classmate and exchange e-mail addresses so that you can practice sending and receiving mail. Do the following exercise with your partner. Find a pen pal at another school so you can practice sending mail across the Internet.

HANDS-ON EXERCISE 1

Welcome to E-mail with PC Eudora

Objective: Send and receive an e-mail message. The exercise is written for PC Eudora, but it can be done with any e-mail system. Use Figure 2.4 as a guide in the exercise.

STEP 1: Log On

➤ Log on to the local area network that you will use for e-mail.

STEP 2: Configure Your Mail Program

➤ Open the icon on your desktop that contains your Internet tools and start Eudora (or other POP mail client). Before you can use it, you will have to customize Eudora on your PC so it will recognize your username and password. *The instructions provided here give you a general overview of what you need to do to configure Eudora. See your instructor or LAN administrator for specific instructions for your computing environment. You will have to complete the configuration only once. It will be saved for future use.*

- Press the **Esc** key to ignore the password message shown in Figure 2.4a, which is displayed when you start Eudora.

- Select **Configuration** from the **Special** menu shown in Figure 2.4b. The Configuration dialog box shown in Figure 2.4c is displayed. You will enter your POP account (Internet address), real name (First Name, Middle Initial, and Last Name), your SMTP server name (your Unix mail server), and your return address (Internet address) in the dialog box. PC Eudora will use your full name to create an alias, or nickname, for your mail messages. (See your instructor or lab assistant if you are not sure what your username and/or SMTP server name is.) Your dialog box should look similar to Figure 2.4d when complete. Click **OK** when you have finished entering the required fields.

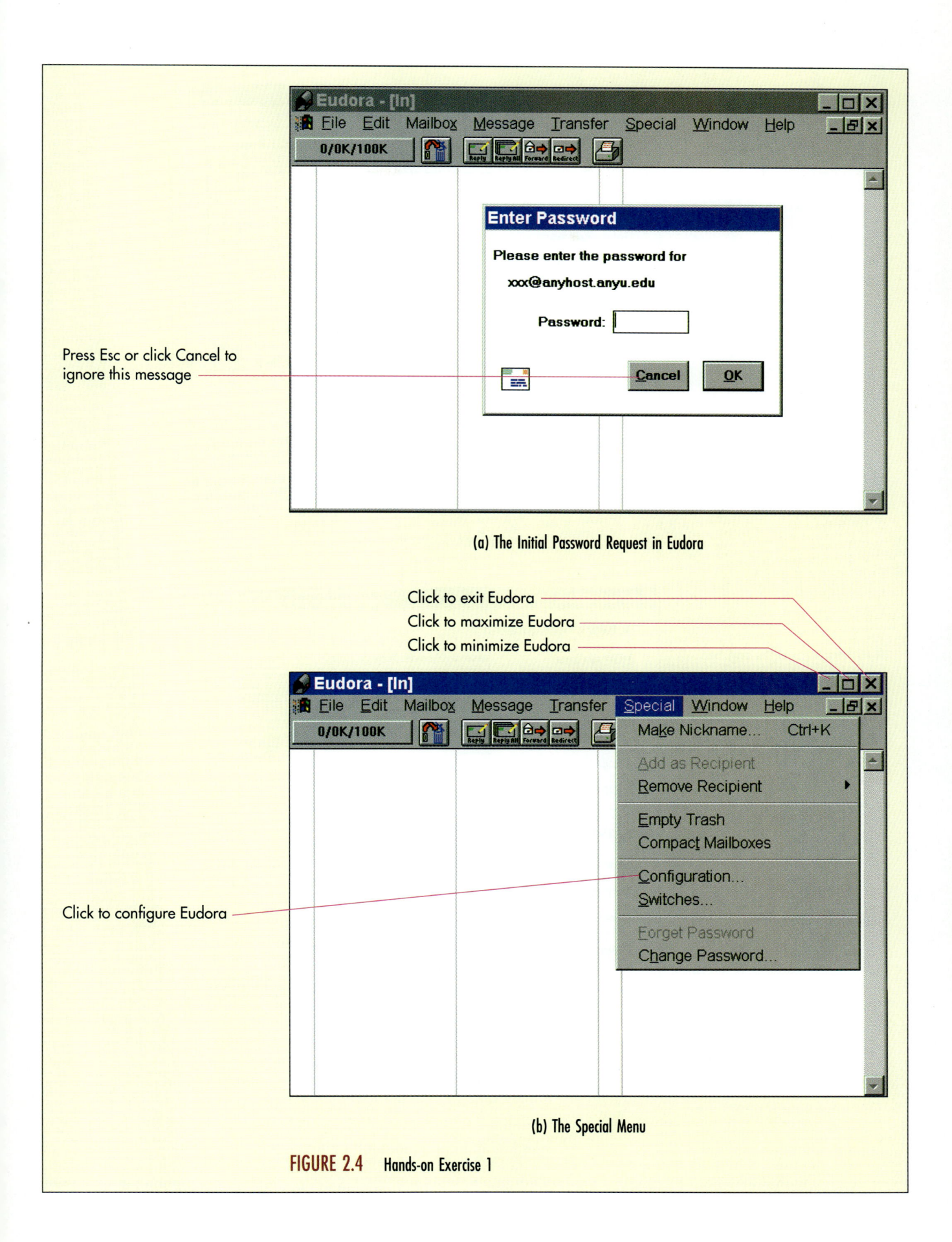

Press Esc or click Cancel to ignore this message

(a) The Initial Password Request in Eudora

Click to exit Eudora
Click to maximize Eudora
Click to minimize Eudora

Click to configure Eudora

(b) The Special Menu

FIGURE 2.4   Hands-on Exercise 1

GLOBAL COMMUNICATION ON THE INTERNET   47

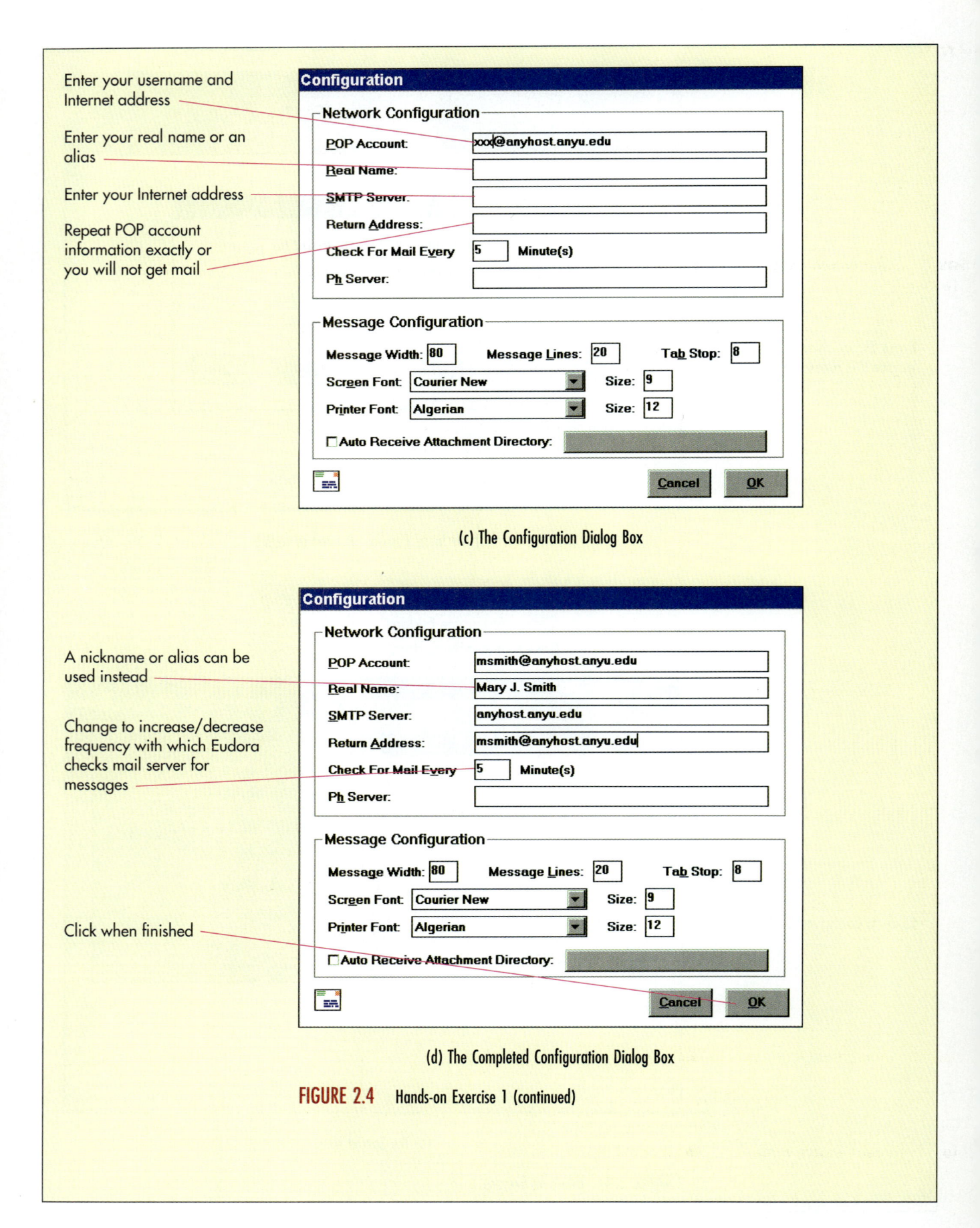

Enter your username and Internet address

Enter your real name or an alias

Enter your Internet address

Repeat POP account information exactly or you will not get mail

(c) The Configuration Dialog Box

A nickname or alias can be used instead

Change to increase/decrease frequency with which Eudora checks mail server for messages

Click when finished

(d) The Completed Configuration Dialog Box

FIGURE 2.4 Hands-on Exercise 1 (continued)

- Select **File** then **Exit,** and leave Eudora; then start it again. (This step is required to update the system with the information you just entered.) This time at the password screen enter your e-mail password, which you should have obtained from your instructor or LAN administrator. *For security reasons, the password is not displayed on the screen as you enter it.*
- Select **Special** then **Change Password,** and enter a new password. You will be asked to enter the new password a second time to verify it. Again, the password is not displayed on the screen as you type it. (Check with your instructor to be certain this is the correct method to change a password in your environment.)

STEP 3: Send a Message

➤ Sending messages in Eudora is simple. Pull down the **Message** menu, click **New Message,** and the New Message window in Figure 2.4e is displayed. You will fill in the username and Internet address of the recipient, send a copy of the message to a second person, and type the message in the message portion of the screen. Your completed message will look similar to Figure 2.4e after you have completed this step.

- The insertion point should be blinking next to To:. Type the Internet address(es) of the person(s) to whom you are sending the message. For instance, if you were sending e-mail to the authors, you would enter **gmarx@mercy.sjc.edu,** or **rgrauer@umiami.miami.edu.** (If you have not

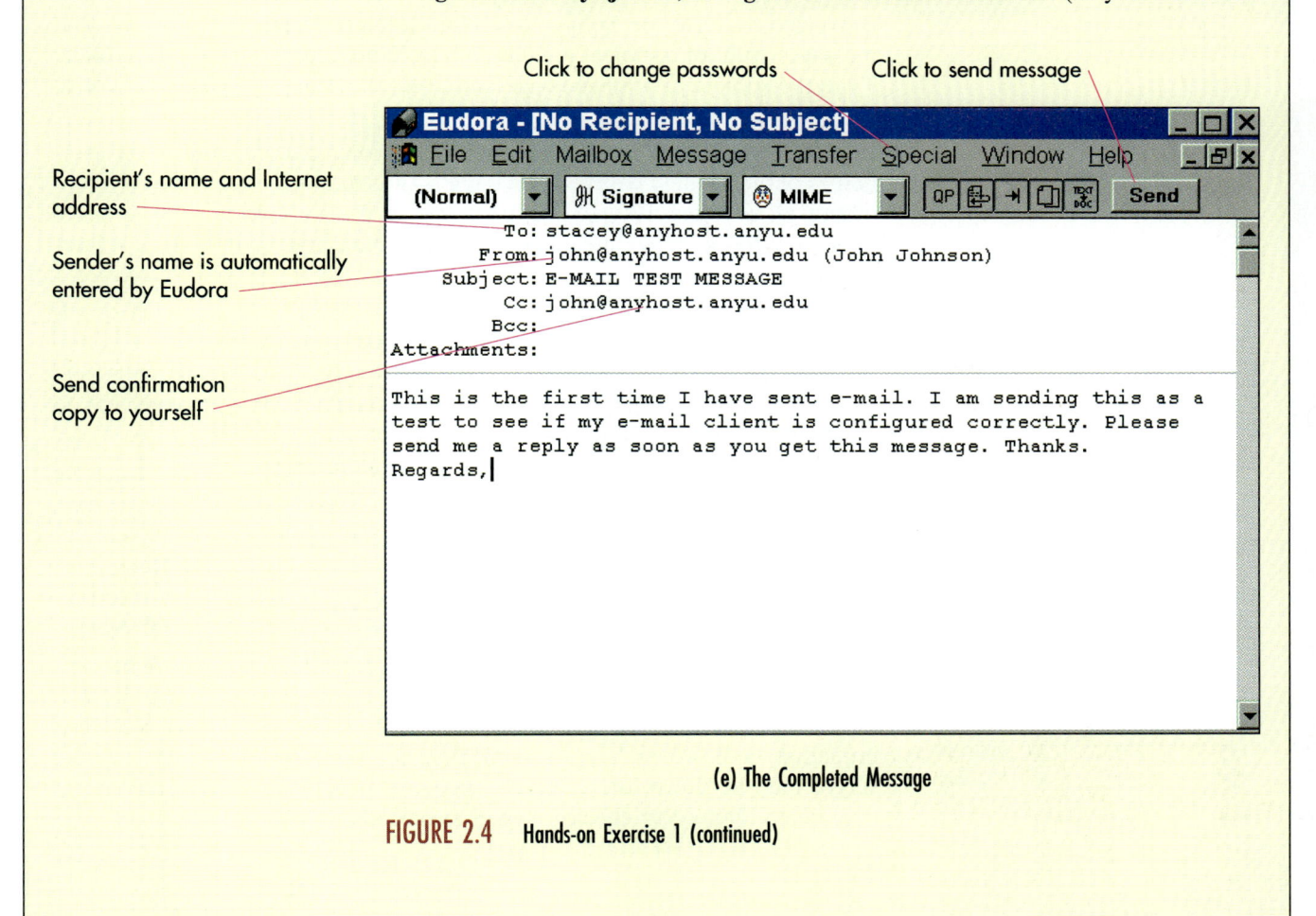

(e) The Completed Message

FIGURE 2.4   Hands-on Exercise 1 (continued)

made arrangements to send a message to a classmate, you can type your own username and Internet address in the To field.) To send the message to more than one person, separate the usernames with a comma. The From address is automatically entered by the system, and should show your Internet address. Usernames and Internet addresses may be case sensitive; use lowercase for both unless instructed otherwise.

> **INTERNET ADDRESSES SIMPLIFIED**
>
> If you are sending e-mail to someone on the same mail server you're on, the message doesn't have to go out to the Internet through the router, the device that provides your school's Internet connection, but can be processed locally. You can simply type the recipient's username, without the host and domain information. For example, if the author and series editor were on the same host, one could simply address the other as gmarx or rgrauer, respectively.

- Press the **Tab** key to move the insertion point (or click in) to the **Subject** line. It is advisable to enter a subject for every message you send (unless instructed to leave the Subject line blank); many e-mail users assume that messages without a subject are "junk mail," and automatically delete them. Type the subject of your message and press the **Tab** key again to move to the **Cc** field.
- If you are going to copy the message to additional people, enter their usernames in the Cc field (for "carbon copy"—now that's old technology!), separated by commas. Enter your **username** in the **Cc** field now so you will get a confirming copy, and so you will have mail in your in-box for a later step.
- Skip the Bcc and Attachments fields for now. The Bcc field, which stands for blind carbon copy, allows you to send a copy of the message to someone without the recipient knowing you are doing so. The Attachments field lets you attach a file such as a Word document or Excel spreadsheet to your e-mail message. You will use this field in an end-of-chapter exercise.
- Press the **Tab** key until the insertion point is blinking in (or click in) the message area. Type your message as you would using any word processor, correcting any mistakes as you go. Many word processing cursor movement keys will work in e-mail messages. For instance, you can use the Backspace and Delete keys to delete left and right, respectively. Move the insertion point one word at a time by using **Ctrl+Right Arrow** or **Ctrl+Left Arrow.**
- When you are satisfied that the message is complete, click the **Send** button at the top of the document window. Your message will arrive at its destination within seconds! (It is possible that the recipient will not receive it immediately, however. The recipient may not be logged on, his or her mail server may be down, there may be network problems, or the mail server may be configured to check for mail at periodic intervals.)

MOVING ABOUT THE EUDORA SCREEN AND EDITING TEXT

You can correct mistakes in Eudora just as you can in other Windows programs. Use the Backspace and Delete keys to remove small amounts of unwanted text. Select larger amounts by using the mouse. Move forward and backward through the fields by pressing Tab and Shift+Tab, respectively. Click in any field you want to change, then delete the appropriate text and reenter.

STEP 4: Read and Print a Mail Message

➤ When you start Eudora and enter your password, the program will check the mail server for new mail, notify you if you have any, and automatically download it and open your in-basket if you do. While you are using Eudora, it will check the mail server for new mail every five minutes (or whatever interval is specified in the configuration information), and notify you if any has arrived. You can also manually check for new mail by selecting Check Mail in the File menu.

- Select **Check Mail** on the **File** menu. Any messages you have received should be displayed in the In-box document window as shown in Figure 2.4f.
- There are three ways to display a message that you want to read.
    1. Press the **Down Arrow** until you select the message you want to read, then press **Enter** to open it;
    2. Click on the message, then press **Enter;** or
    3. Double click the message.
- Use the **PageUp** and **PageDown** keys and scroll bars to scroll through and read the message.
- Print the message by selecting **Print** on the **File** menu.
- When you have finished reading the message, double click the Windows icon at the left of the message window (*not the blue title bar at the top of the screen that says Eudora*), or select **Close** on the **File** menu, as shown in Figure 2.4g.
- You will return to the In-box window. If you have no need to do anything further with the selected message, you can discard it by clicking on the **Trash button** (the blue trash can with the red arrow). The message is stored in the trash can and may be recalled at any time before you end this Eudora session. **Trash** the message now.
- Retrieve the message from the trash by pulling down the **Mailbox** menu, then selecting **Trash,** then clicking on the message you want to retrieve from the trash. Select **In** on the **Transfer** menu, and the message is moved to your in-box. Do this now so the message is available for later use.

Click to check for new mail

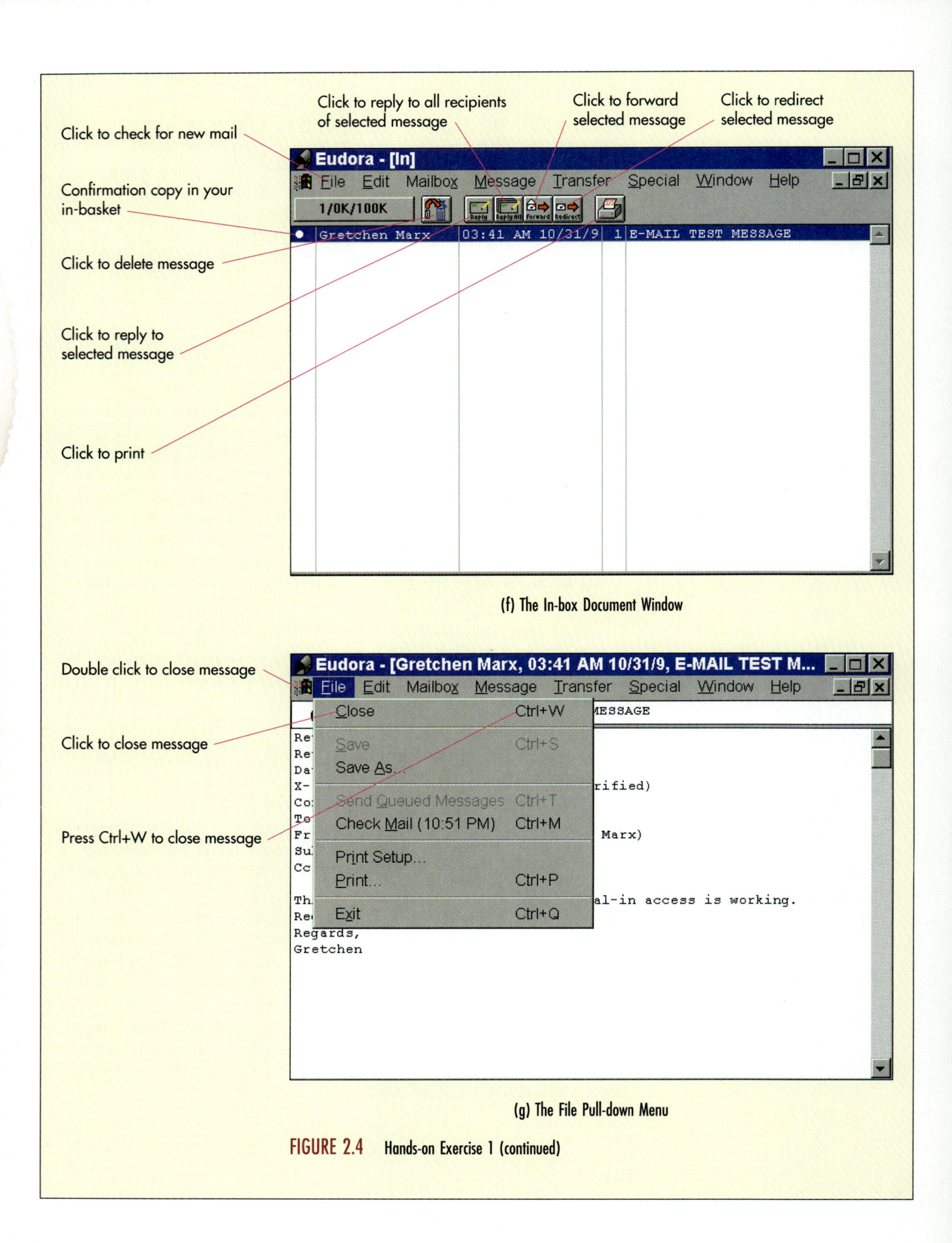

Confirmation copy in your in-basket

Click to delete message

Click to reply to selected message

Click to print

Click to reply to all recipients of selected message

Click to forward selected message

Click to redirect selected message

(f) The In-box Document Window

Double click to close message

Click to close message

Press Ctrl+W to close message

(g) The File Pull-down Menu

FIGURE 2.4 Hands-on Exercise 1 (continued)

52 EXPLORING THE INTERNET

> **REJECTED MAIL**
>
> You will occasionally get returned mail with a message indicating it could not be delivered. There are two common causes of returned mail—the receiving site was down, or you used the wrong username or Internet address.

STEP 5: Reply to a Message

➤ After you have read your e-mail message, you may reply to the sender as shown in Figure 2.4h.

- If your in-box is not visible, select **In** on the **Mailbox** pull-down menu.

- With your in-box on the screen, single click on the e-mail message you want to reply to, then click the **Reply** button. Eudora will display the standard message screen with the To address already filled in with the sender's username, and the From address filled in with your username. The message area of the screen contains the original e-mail message sent to you. Each line of the original message is preceded by a greater than sign (>). This indicates the text was part of the original message.

- Press the **Tab** key several times until the insertion point is blinking at the left edge of the first line of text. You may press the **Enter** key two or three times to give yourself a few blank lines above the original message in which to enter your reply. Press the **Up Arrow** key to move the insertion point back to the first line of the message area, then type your response. (The original text will be included with your message. You may

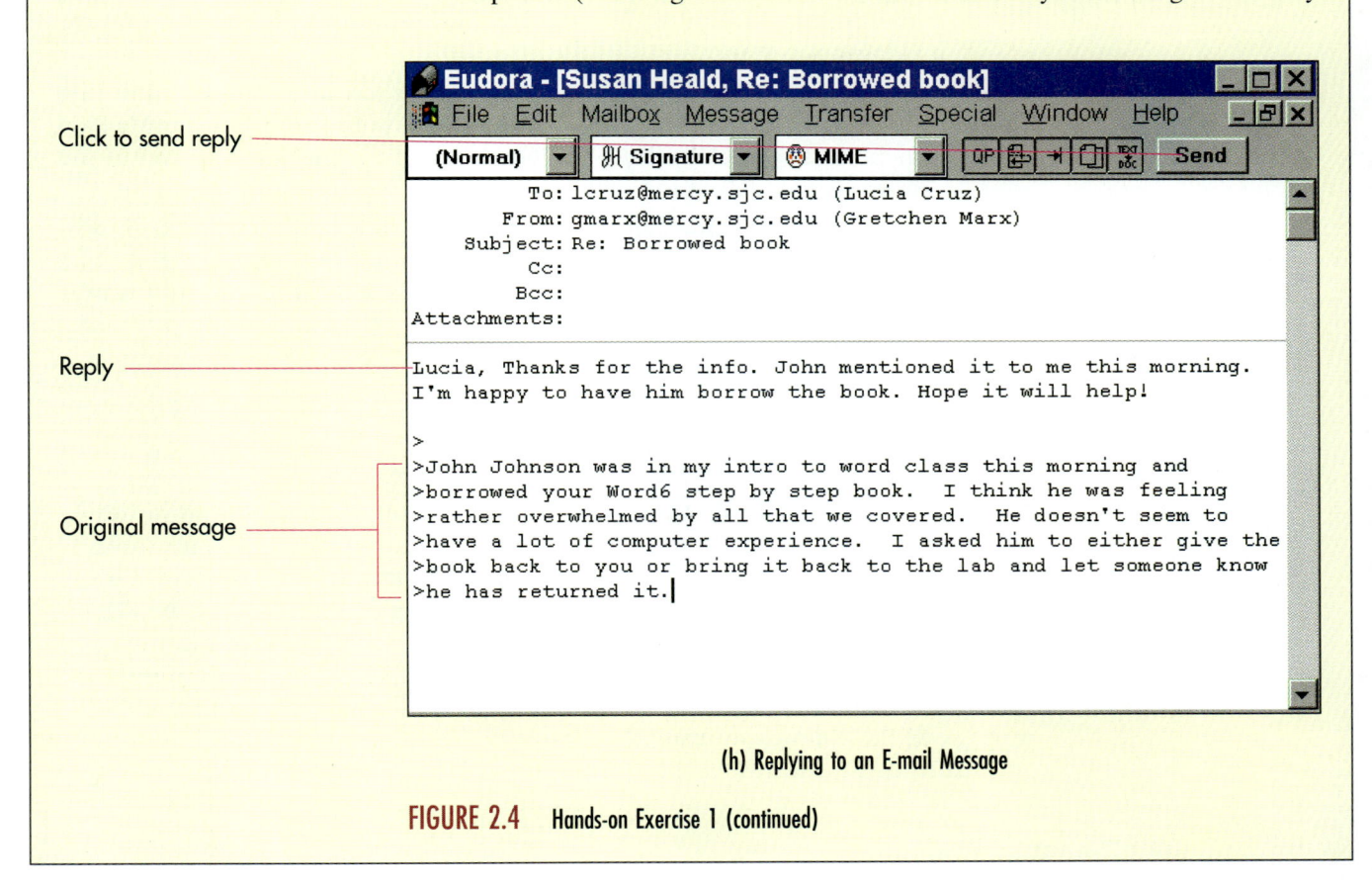

(h) Replying to an E-mail Message

FIGURE 2.4 Hands-on Exercise 1 (continued)

choose to delete all or part of the original text instead. To do so, select the text (click and drag) and press the **Delete** key as you would in any word processor.)
- Click the **Send** button, and off goes your reply. The original message will remain in your in-box until you transfer or trash it. The reply will be in your out-box.

FORWARDING AND REDIRECTING MAIL

You can forward a message to someone else by choosing the Forward button instead of the Reply button. The recipient will see your username in the From field, but will also see the orginal sender information. You can add comments to a forwarded message just as you do to a reply. You can redirect the message to someone else by choosing the Redirect button. The recipient will see the original sender's username in the From field, and you will not add comments to the redirected message. (This is analogous to redirecting U.S. mail that arrives at your house or apartment addressed to a previous occupant—you write a new address on the front and send it on unopened.)

STEP 6: Check Your Mailboxes and Delete Messages

▶ You can review your messages at any time by selecting **Mailbox** from the pull-down menu, then clicking **In** or **Out** as appropriate (In for messages you receive, Out for message you send). Keep your mailbox from overflowing (and from running out of allocated disk space) by deleting messages that are no longer necessary.
- To see both the In and Out mailboxes on the screen at the same time first pull down the **Mailbox** menu and select **In,** then pull down the **Mailbox** menu and select **Out.** Both mailboxes are open, but one is on top of the other so you do not see both.
- Click on the **Window** pull-down menu, then click on **Tile** to see both windows together as shown in Figure 2.4i. Transfer any message from one mailbox to the other by selecting the mailbox name from the **Transfer** menu.

SELECTING MULTIPLE FILES

You can select multiple files from your mailboxes the same way you select multiple lines of text in a Windows application. Click the first file, hold the Shift key, then click the last file in the group you wish to select. You can select multiple nonadjacent files by clicking one file, holding the Ctrl key, then clicking the additional files. Once you have selected a group of files, you can delete them all by clicking the Trash button, or transfer them all to another mailbox by selecting the Transfer menu, then clicking the appropriate mailbox name.

Click to move message from one mailbox to another

Click to delete selected message

Double click to open selected message

(i) The Tiled In- and Out-boxes

FIGURE 2.4 Hands-on Exercise 1 (continued)

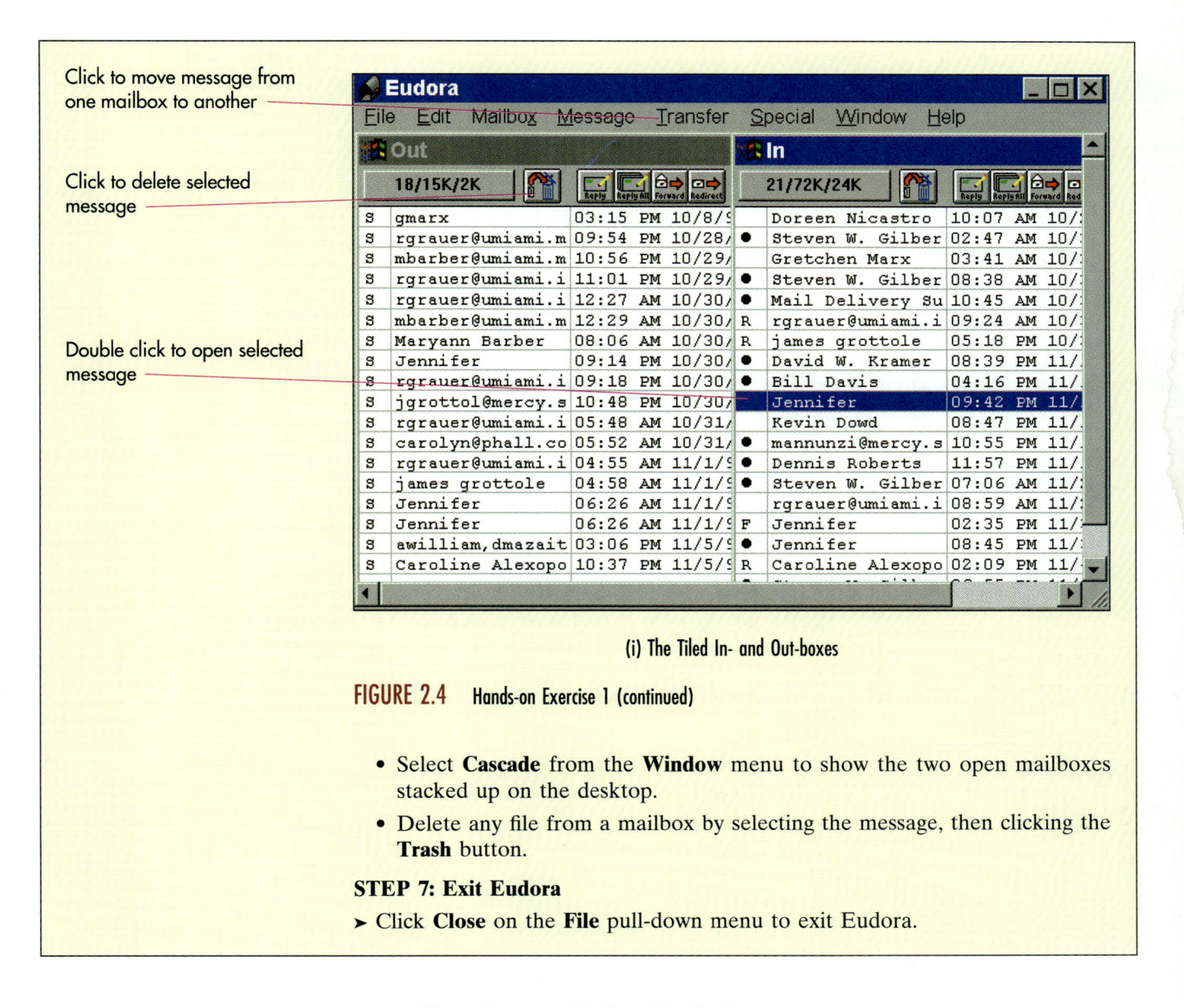

- Select **Cascade** from the **Window** menu to show the two open mailboxes stacked up on the desktop.
- Delete any file from a mailbox by selecting the message, then clicking the **Trash** button.

STEP 7: Exit Eudora

➤ Click **Close** on the **File** pull-down menu to exit Eudora.

E-mail Using a Unix Mail Program

While it is easier to compose and send mail using a Windows-based POP mail client, it involves a fairly complex setup for both you and your college computing staff. Therefore, your college may choose to have you access your e-mail by using a Unix-based *shell account* instead. Unix accounts work with a *command-line interface,* not a graphical user interface, which means you will have to enter commands at the Unix system prompt to retrieve your mail. Typically you will enter a command to start a menu-driven mail program such as Pine, which was illustrated in Chapter 1.

Your incoming messages are not downloaded from the mail server and stored on your PC. Instead, they reside on the mail server, and can be viewed only when you are logged in to your account on the mail server. In the post office analogy this is similar to having a post office box and being required to read your mail at the post office. Using your Unix shell account to access e-mail is illustrated in Figure 2.5. In the following hands-on exercise you will send an e-mail message with Pine, a Unix-based mail program that lets you compose, send, and retrieve mail messages using your mail server.

GLOBAL COMMUNICATION ON THE INTERNET

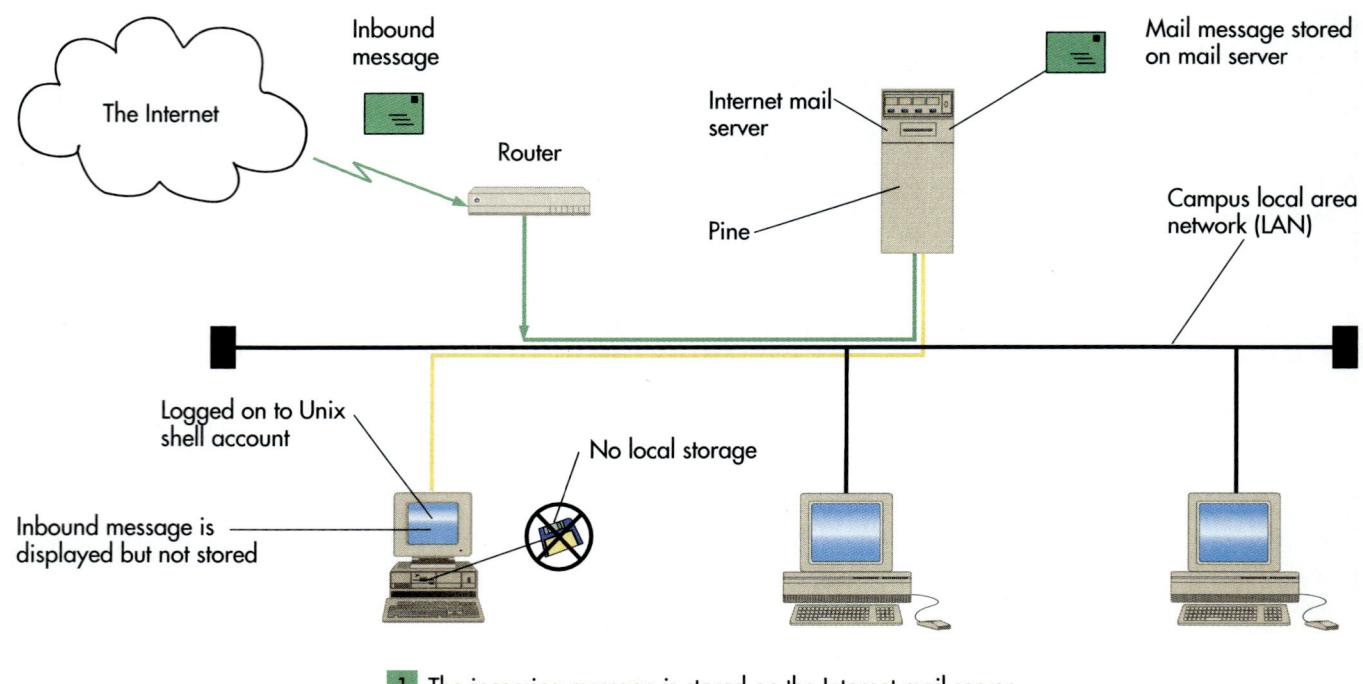

1. The incoming message is stored on the Internet mail server.
2. The user logs on to the mail server, types Pine at the Unix prompt, and reads e-mail messages. Messages are stored on the server, not on the PC.

FIGURE 2.5   Using Your Unix Shell Account and a Menu-Driven Program to Retrieve E-mail

LOST MAIL

If you have a post office box at your local U.S. mail substation, you can go there and get new mail. However, you will not see mail that was delivered to you yesterday, because it is already in a stack on your kitchen counter at home. In a similar way you may be able to dial into your Unix shell account from home and read your new mail by using Pine or other Unix-based mail software. You will not be able to see any old mail that you already retrieved while you were on campus. Don't despair—it is not lost. When you retrieved it, the POP mail client downloaded it from the Internet mail server to your personal mail directory on your campus PC or file server hard drive. You can read it by using your POP mail client when you log on next time you are on campus.

HANDS-ON EXERCISE 2

E-mail Using Pine

Objective: Send and receive an e-mail message using your Unix shell account. The exercise is written for Pine, but is general enough that you can apply the instructions to other menu-driven e-mail software. Use Figure 2.6 as a guide in completing the exercise.

STEP 1: Log On

➤ Log on to the system you will use for e-mail.
- If you are using a local area network at school, you will need an account (userID) and a password, which your instructor or LAN administrator should provide for you. You may need a second account (userID) and password to access your mail server.

STEP 2: Send a Message

➤ At the Unix prompt (see your instructor or LAN administrator for information on how to get to the Unix prompt if you have not already done so), type **Pine** and press **Enter.** You will see the menu interface shown in Figure 2.6a. Notice the menu options across the bottom of the screen. They identify what actions you can take at this point.
- Type the letter **C** to select the Compose Message command. You will see the Compose Message screen shown in Figure 2.6b. Note that there is a new menu at the bottom of the screen. Each option is preceded by the ^ character, which stands for the Ctrl key.
- Fill in the **To** field with the Internet address of the person to whom you are sending mail. (If you have not made arrangements to do this exercise with a classmate, enter your own username and address.)
- Press **Tab** once to go to the Cc field. Enter the Internet address of anyone to whom you want to send a copy. In this case enter your username so you will have a confirmation of the message, and so you will have new mail.
- Press **Tab** twice to move to the Subject field. Type the subject of your message.

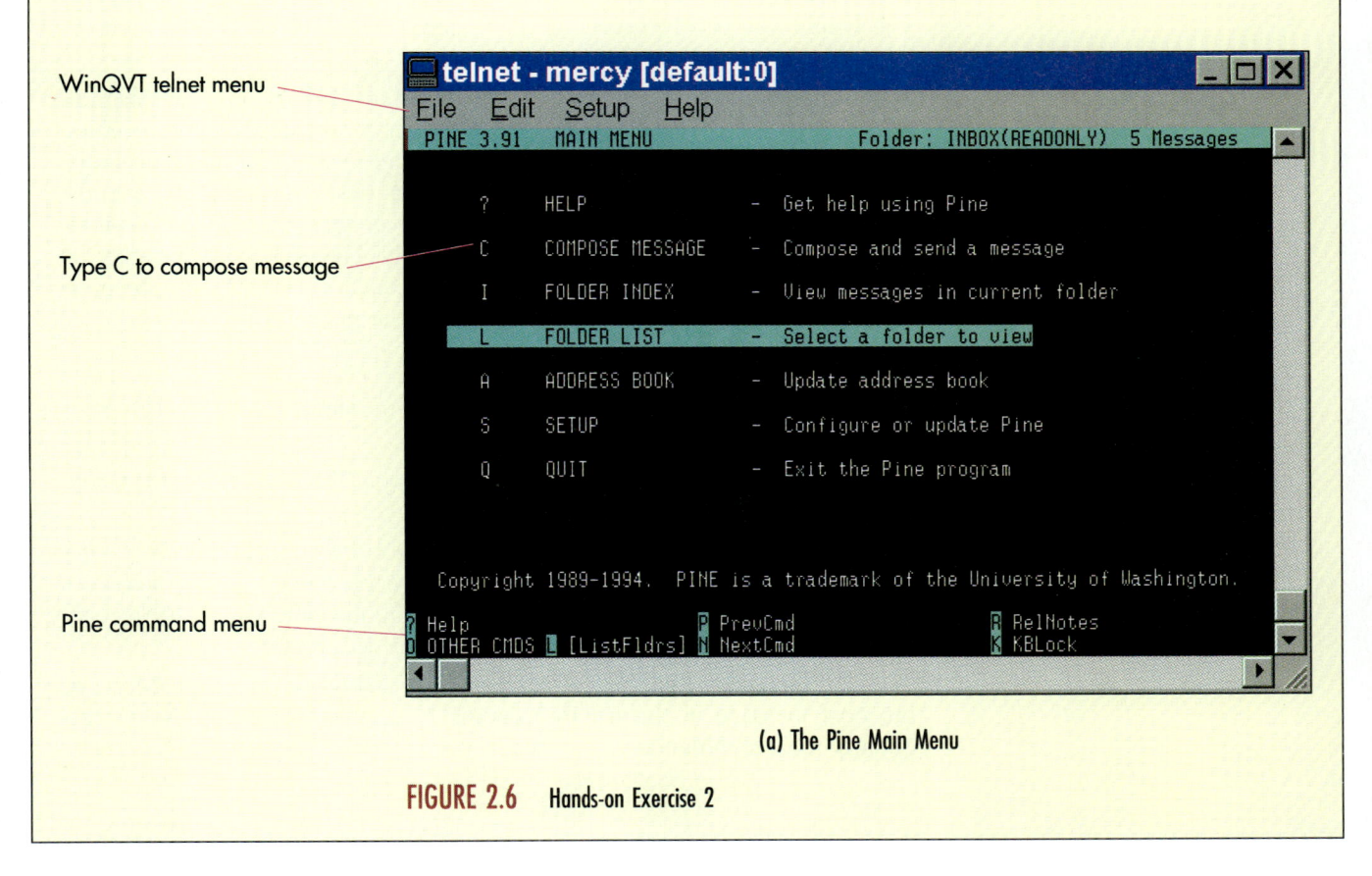

(a) The Pine Main Menu

FIGURE 2.6   Hands-on Exercise 2

Enter recipient's Internet address

Enter message

Command menu has changed

Press Ctrl+X to send message

(b) The Compose Message Screen

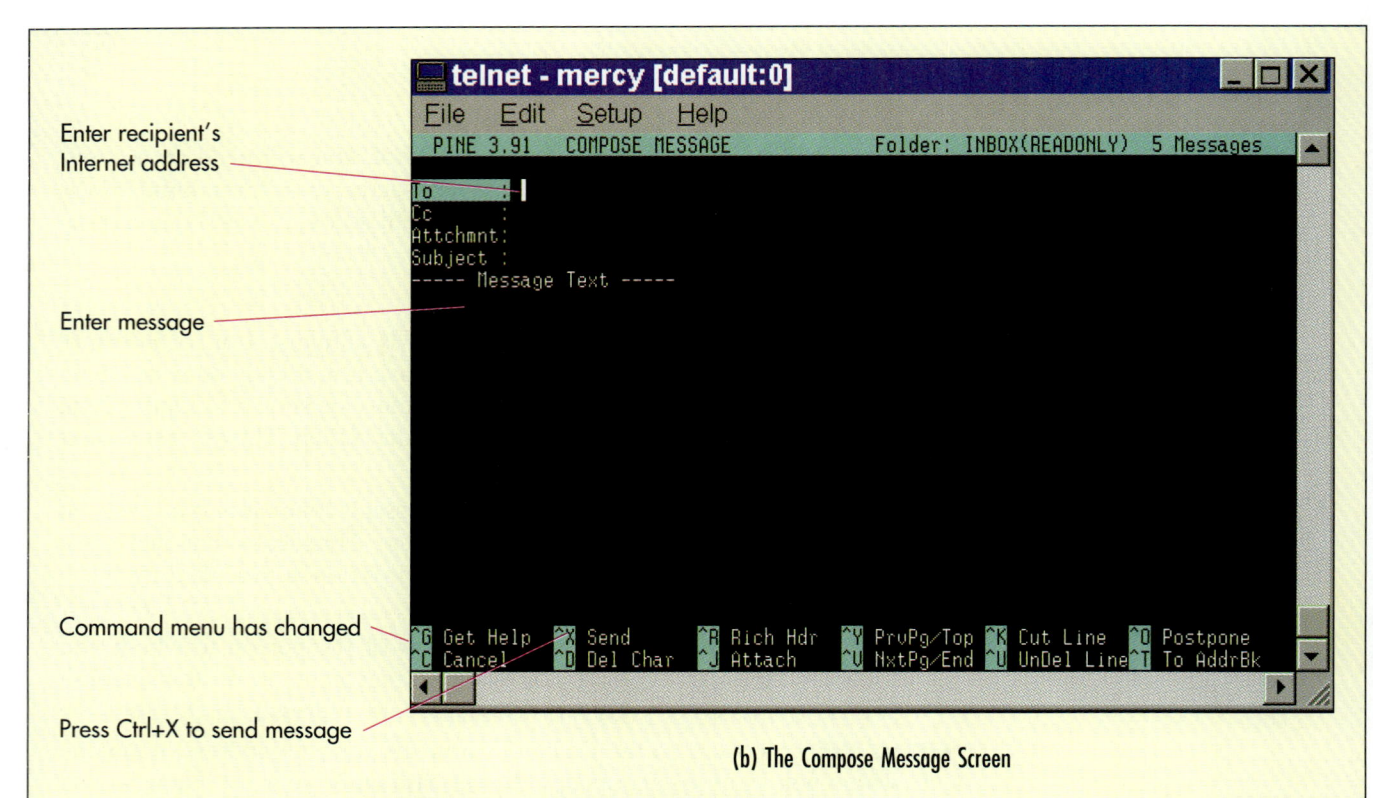

FIGURE 2.6 Hands-on Exercise 2 (continued)

- Press **Tab** again to move to the message area. Type the e-mail message as you would any word processing document, correcting mistakes as you go by using the **Backspace** and/or **Delete** keys.
- When your message is complete, press **Ctrl+X** to send the message, as indicated in the menu at the bottom of the screen. You will get a confirmation request, to which you reply by typing **Y** if you want to send the message, or **N** if you don't. The message will reach its destination within seconds! (While the Internet has the capability to deliver messages almost instantaneously, the recipient may not get it instantly. His or her system may be down, or may be configured to deliver mail once a day.) Once your message has been sent, you will be returned to the main menu.

STEP 3: Read Your Mail

➤ Now that you have sent yourself a message, you should have mail in your mail folder. You will read it now.

- From the main menu, type **I** to view messages in the current folder, which by default is the INBOX folder.
- Your e-mail messages will be displayed as a numbered list similar to the one shown in Figure 2.6c (although you may not have as many messages yet!). Use the arrow keys to scroll down to the message you want to read. When it is selected, press **Enter.** The message will be displayed.
- Move to the second page of a message by pressing the spacebar. Move to the next message in the list by pressing **N** for Next message. Other frequently used commands are shown at the bottom of the screen.

EXPLORING THE INTERNET

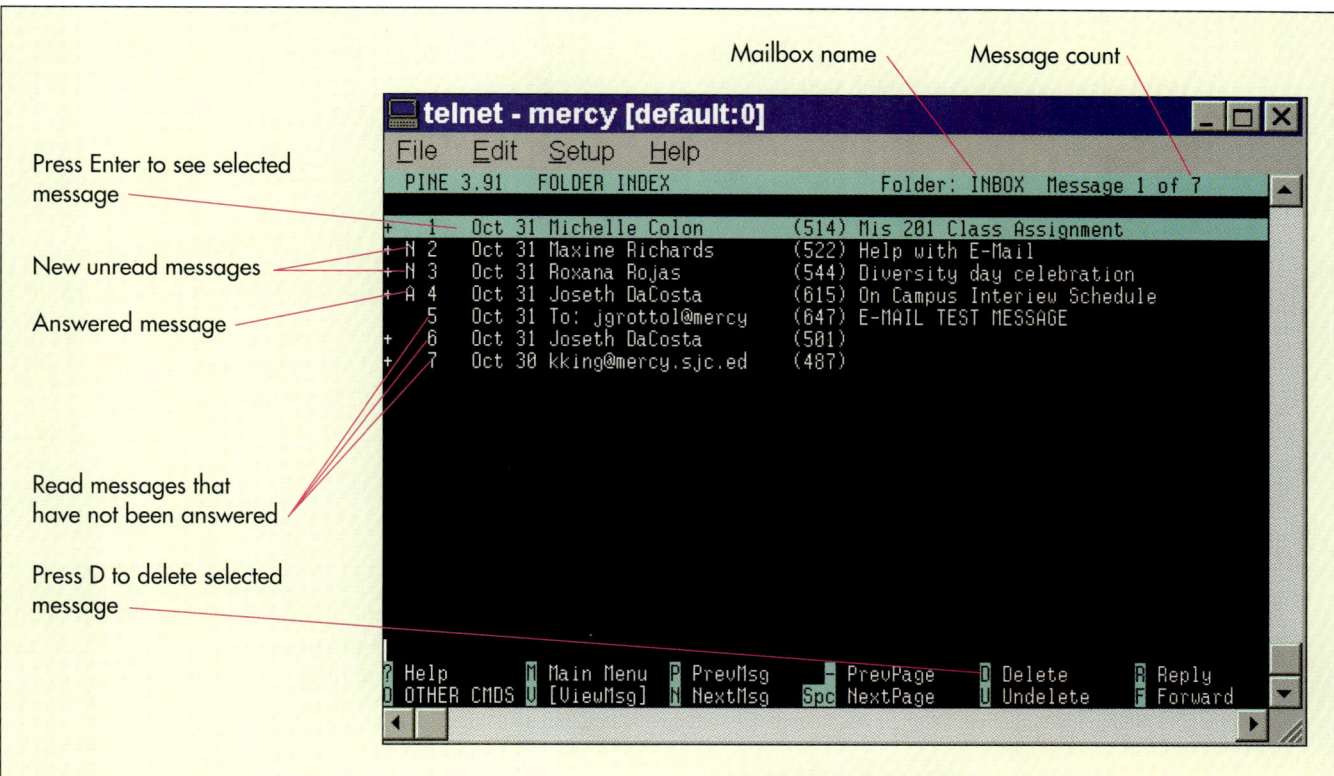

(c) The List of Mail Messages

FIGURE 2.6 Hands-on Exercise 2 (continued)

STEP 4: Reply to a Message

➤ You can send a response to the person who sent you a message.
- If necessary, press **M** to return to the main menu.
- From the main menu, type **I** to select a message in your in-box.
- While reading the message, press the letter **R** to reply. Pine will display a message asking whether you want the text of the original message included in your reply.
- Enter **Y** to include the text, **N** to leave the message area blank. The Reply message screen will be shown (which is the same as the New Message screen), with the To and From fields filled in with the original senders' name and your name, respectively.
- Enter the text of your reply in the message area, and press **Ctrl+X** to send the reply.

STEP 5: Delete a Message

➤ You can delete messages while viewing the folder index.
- Press **M** to return to the main menu if necessary.
- Type **I** to return to the in-box.
- Use the **Up/Down Arrow** keys to select the message you want to delete, then press **D**. The message is marked for deletion, but remains in the folder until you quit Pine. (When you quit, Pine will warn you that it is going to "expunge" deleted messages, that is, permanently delete them, and let you change your mind. If you want the message deleted, respond with a **Y** to

expunge the message. Enter **N** to quit Pine without expunging the marked messages.)

STEP 7: Exit Pine

➤ Getting out of Pine is easy.

- Return to the main menu, if necessary, by pressing the letter **M**.
- Type **Q** to quit. You will see a message asking if you really want to quit.
- Answer by typing **Y**. If you have deleted any messages, you will be warned that they will be expunged.
- Answer **Y** if that is OK, **N** if you don't want deleted messages removed from your In-box. You will be returned to the Unix prompt.

ADDITIONAL E-MAIL CAPABILITIES

Most e-mail programs have additional capabilities beyond sending and receiving mail. You can customize the program to create a distribution list, a personal signature, and multiple folders in which to store your mail.

Distribution Lists

In the exercise you just completed, you composed a message for a specific person. What if you often compose and send the same message to a group of people with whom you frequently correspond? It would be an unfortunate waste of time to type and send the message several times. Instead you can create a ***distribution list,*** or ***nickname list,*** which contains the Internet addresses of all the recipients in the group. You can then send the message once, addressed to the distribution list. The mail program reads the list or nickname and automatically retrieves the e-mail addresses of the recipients from a nickname file, which is set up when you create the list.

Customizing Your Signature

You can create a custom ***signature*** (minus the actual handwriting sample!) that will be placed at the end of each message you send. Some people type their name,

SIGNATURE NETIQUETTE

No one wants to read an endless soliloquy attached to your messages, so keep your signature short, preferably to four or fewer lines. Also, it is not considered good form to use four-letter words, racial slurs, or other unacceptable text in your signature. Such inappropriate use may cause you to lose your computer privileges. Remember, your e-mail is not really private, and has the potential to be read by many people. Use common sense and good manners in all you write.

title, address, telephone, and fax number. Others use a closing, their name, and a short, pithy saying. For example:

> Regards and good surfing,
> Sarah Goodall
> If you think education is expensive, consider the alternative.

Others give themselves colorful nicknames surrounded by simple graphics created from standard keyboard characters. Your signature can be as unique as you are and convey something personal about you.

Personal Mail Folders

Think, for a moment, about how you process your regular mail. You bring it into your house from the mailbox and you read it at your leisure. Some mail will be junk mail, which you will immediately throw away. Other mail will be important and you will want to file it with your important papers. And there may be letters that you will want to share with others in your household, and so you may leave those on the kitchen table to reread at a later time.

After you have been sending and receiving e-mail for some time, and have subscribed to several mailing lists (covered in the next topic), you will discover that you are receiving too much mail to save it all in your in-box. Like the kitchen table, the in-box simply gets too crowded with messages. You can alleviate the mess by setting up different mailboxes, or *folders,* for each type of mail you receive, then transferring messages you want to save to the appropriate mailboxes. Figure 2.7a illustrates these mailboxes as they are implemented in PC Eudora. Figure 2.7b shows Pine folders.

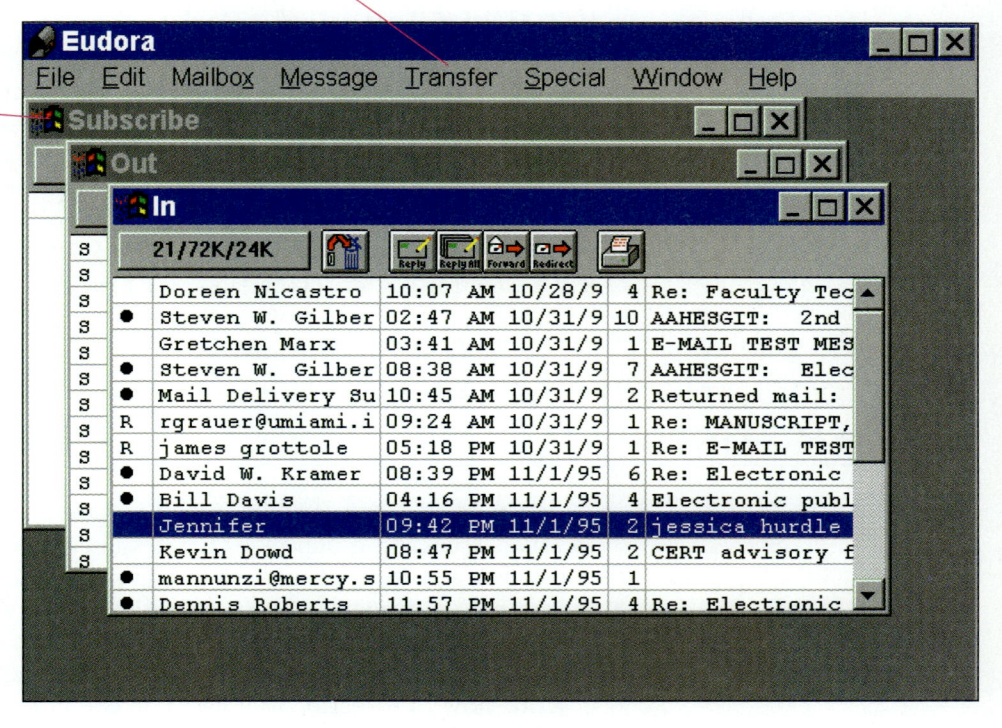

(a) Multiple Mailboxes in Eudora

FIGURE 2.7   E-mail Mailboxes

Message count for selected mailbox

Default mail folders

User-created mail folder

(b) The Folders List in Pine

FIGURE 2.7   E-mail Mailboxes (continued)

ATTACHING FILES

Many e-mail systems provide the capability to attach a file to the message you're sending. Suppose you are assigned a group project, and are working on a section of the final report. You could attach your section to a mail message, and mail it to the rest of your group for their review and comment. Check with your instructor or system administrator to find out if your system has this capability. Also, be advised that, just because you can attach and send a document, this doesn't mean the recipient will receive it correctly!

MAILING LISTS

Access to mailing lists is an important feature of the Internet. A *mailing list* is an Internet discussion group that operates much like a magazine subscription—you find a list on a topic of interest to you and subscribe. You then get all the mail sent to and from people on the subscription list. The big difference between this and a magazine subscription is that you get to help write the news! There are thousands of mailing lists that cover every conceivable topic. In this section we'll describe how to subscribe to a list. You will also want to know how to *suspend* a subscription—while you are on spring break, for instance—and how to unsubscribe. All this is done via e-mail messages.

Participating in mailing lists generally requires that you know two addresses, and send different types of messages to each. The first address is that of the computer that manages the list, usually called a *listserv, listproc,* or *majordomo.* This address is where you will send subscription information, such as your initial request, a suspend request, or an unsubscribe request. This is analogous to the subscription department at a magazine.

The second address is the mail address where you will send your contributions to the discussion on the list. All mail you send to this address will be broadcast to the entire list, so be sure you really want to send the message! Sending a message to the list is analogous to sending a letter to the editor, which will in turn be published for all subscribers to see. Many lists have a *list owner* or *moderator* who reads and rejects messages that do not relate to the general topic discussed by the list.

Be sure you understand the difference between the list and the listserv. Just as you would not send a subscription hold or cancellation notice to every reader of *Time* or *Newsweek,* you should not send an unsubscribe message to the list, but rather to the listserv. You will find that many new users do not understand the difference, and you will receive annoying unsubscribe letters in your e-mail once you are on a list.

ADDING YOUR TWO CENTS

It is a good idea to read the messages being sent to a mailing list for a while before sending one yourself. Known as *lurking,* this allows you to discover the tone and subject matter of the discussions so what you add will be appropriate to the conversation. Some lists are quite friendly and patient with newcomers' "dumb questions." Others have a very low tolerance for new members and the introduction of topics that do not meet the group's approval. Should you send an inappropriate comment or question to one of these lists, your mailbox may be flooded with very derisive replies. Called *flaming,* this can be a very unpleasant experience for the recipient. Be forewarned!

Finding Mailing Lists

There are thousands of mailing lists on the Internet. You can retrieve a (very long) list of mailing lists by sending mail to **listserv@bitnic.educom.edu.** In the message area type **list global** and nothing else. You will receive a message listing thousands of mailing lists. You will have an opportunity to try this in the following hands-on exercise. You can get a list about a specific subject—skiing, for instance—by sending the message **list global/skiing** to the same address.

Subscribing to a List

Once you have found the list to which you want to subscribe, you do so by simply sending an e-mail message to the *list server* requesting that your name be added to the subscription list. The message will generally follow the form *subscribe listname,* where you substitute the name of the list in the message. The listserv software automatically adds your name to the list (and generally sends you a confirmation). You will start receiving e-mail messages from other subscribers within a day or two.

> **DON'T OVERSUBSCRIBE!**
>
> Be careful about subscribing to too many lists—you will find yourself reading hundreds of messages a day if the lists are active. If you don't routinely read your messages and dispose of them, your disk space on your mail server will quickly overflow, and you will have to contact your system administrator to resolve the problem.

Subscription Options

As indicated earlier, you may suspend a subscription so you will remain on the list but not receive mail until you release the suspension. You should do this before going on any school breaks. Many, if not most, lists keep an archive of all messages sent, so you can find out later what happened while your subscription was suspended. Where the archive is and how you can access it is generally described in a message you receive from the list manager when you subscribe. You can turn your mail off temporarily by sending a message in the form *set listname nomail*. To resume receiving mail, you can use the command *set listname mail*. You should, of course, send these messages to the list server, not to the list itself.

You can set your subscription to send you all messages in ***digest*** form. This is particularly useful on a very active list, from which you receive more than 10 to 15 messages per day. The digest option will notify the list server to send all the messages as one file, which reduces the time it takes you to open, read, and dispose of the messages.

When you sign on to a mailing list, the list server keeps a record of your e-mail address (how else would it be able to send you mail?). Anyone subscribing to the list can get a list of all subscribers by sending the list server the command *review listname* (where the actual listname is substituted for *listname*). You can send the message *set listname mail conceal* to the list server to hide your name, and maybe keep Internet "junk mail" out of your mail box.

> **SAVING SUBSCRIPTION INFORMATION**
>
> You should set up a mailbox called SUBSCRIBE or something similar in which to retain the subscription confirmations you will receive after subscribing to mailing lists. The confirmation messages will tell you how to suspend and digest mail, and how to unsubscribe or sign off the lists. If you save all these messages in one SUBSCRIBE or CONFIRM mailbox, you will be able to find them easily at a later time when you want to change a subscription.

HANDS-ON EXERCISE 3

Customizing E-mail and Subscribing to Mailing Lists Using a PC Mail Client

Objective: Create a distribution list (nickname), signature, and mailbox, and subscribe to a mailing list. Use Figure 2.8 as a guide in the exercise.

STEP 1: Create a Distribution/Nickname List

➤ Log on to your system and open Eudora (or other PC mail client).

➤ Select **Window,** then **Nicknames,** then click the **New** button at the bottom of the screen as shown in Figure 2.8a. The New Nickname dialog box shown in Figure 2.8b is displayed. Enter your course number (such as MIS201) in the New Nickname dialog box, then click **OK.**

- The nickname is shown in the Nickname list at the left of the screen. Click in the Address(es) area. Type each recipient's Internet username on a new line in the Address text box. Enter three or four classmates' usernames, as shown in Figure 2.8c.

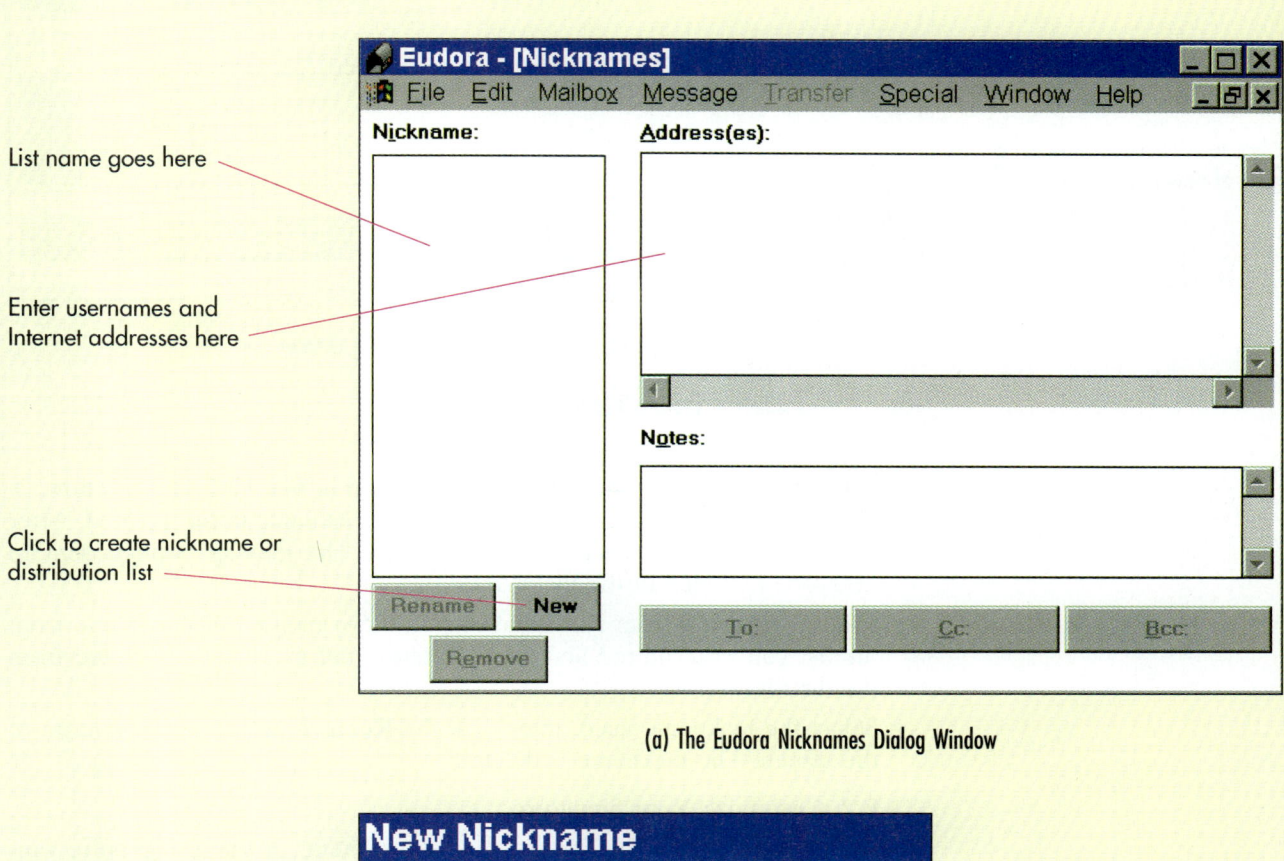

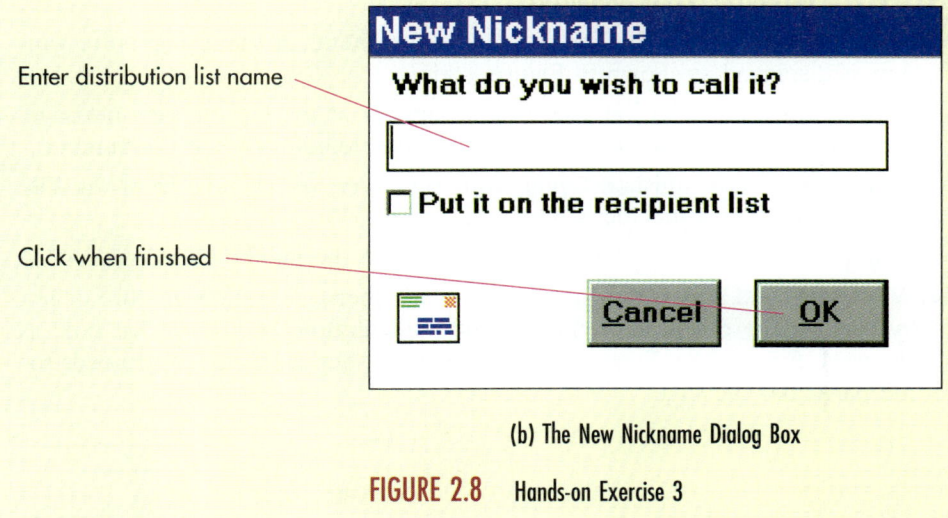

List name goes here

Enter usernames and Internet addresses here

Click to create nickname or distribution list

(a) The Eudora Nicknames Dialog Window

Enter distribution list name

Click when finished

(b) The New Nickname Dialog Box

FIGURE 2.8   Hands-on Exercise 3

GLOBAL COMMUNICATION ON THE INTERNET   **65**

Enter usernames for local recipients

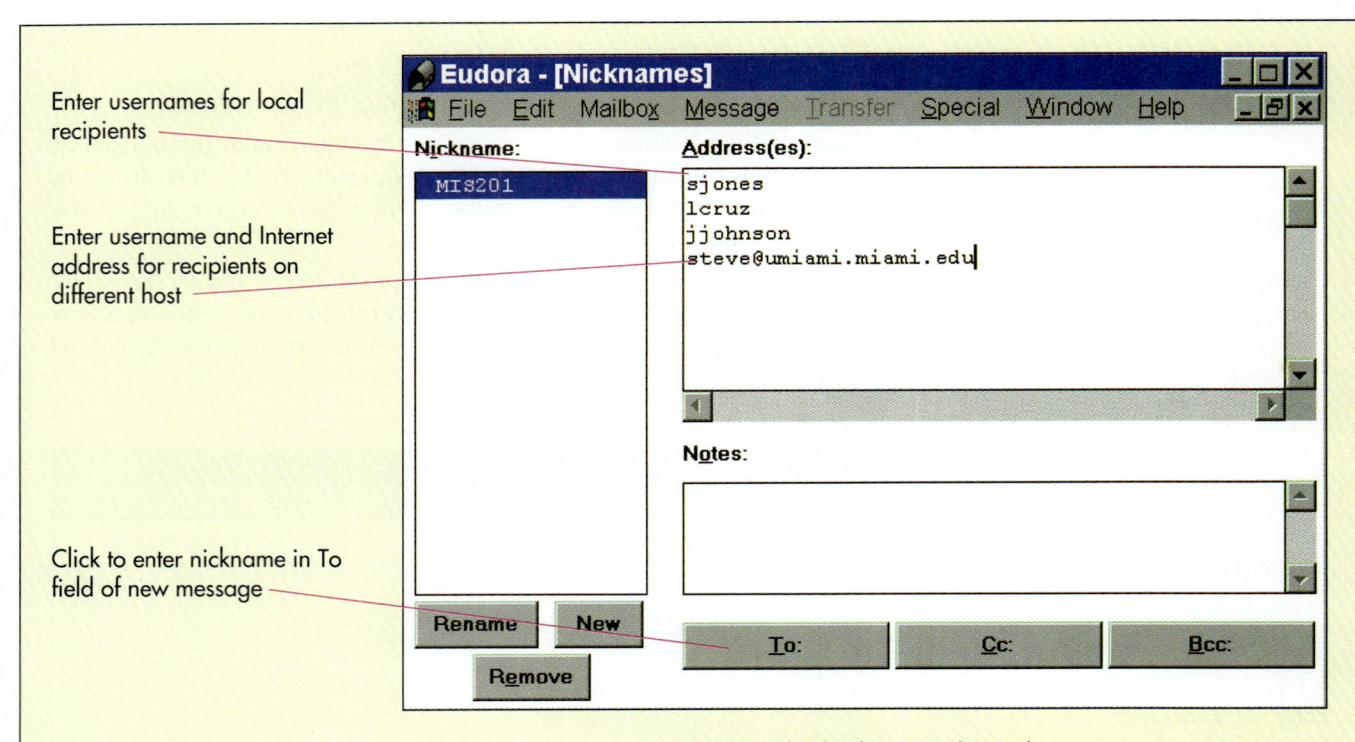

Enter username and Internet address for recipients on different host

Click to enter nickname in To field of new message

(c) The Completed Nicknames Dialog Window

FIGURE 2.8 Hands-on Exercise 3 (continued)

- Select the nickname, then click the **To** button in the Nickname window. A New Message window is displayed, with the nickname in the To field. After typing the message, click the **Send** button. The message will be sent to everyone included in the nickname list.
- Select **Nickname** from the **Window** pull-down menu. Select a name from the list you just entered and press **Delete.** That username is deleted from the distribution list.
- Select the nickname itself, then click the **Remove** button at the bottom of the screen. The nickname is deleted.

STEP 2: Customize Your Signature

➤ Select **Signature** from the **Window** pull-down menu. A blank Signature window is displayed as shown in Figure 2.8d.
- Type in the information you want to appear at the end of each message. Some people type their name, title, address, telephone, and fax number.
- When you have finished typing your signature, select **Save** from the **File** menu. The signature file is updated.
- Select **Close** from the **File** menu to return to the mailbox window.

➤ When you send a message you can select whether to use the signature or not by clicking the down arrow in the Eudora signature drop-down list box, as shown in Figure 2.8e. Select **none** or **Signature,** depending on your needs for the particular message.

66 EXPLORING THE INTERNET

Click to save new signature

Enter your signature here

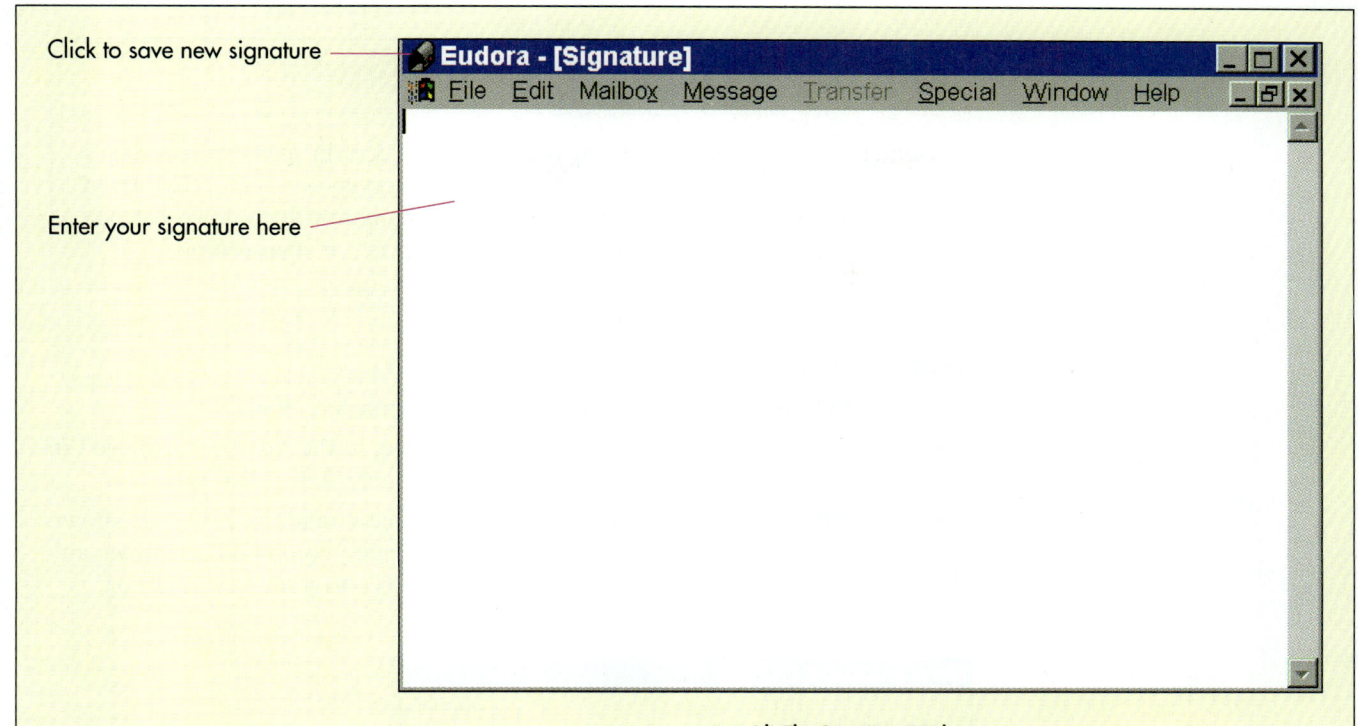

(d) The Signature Window

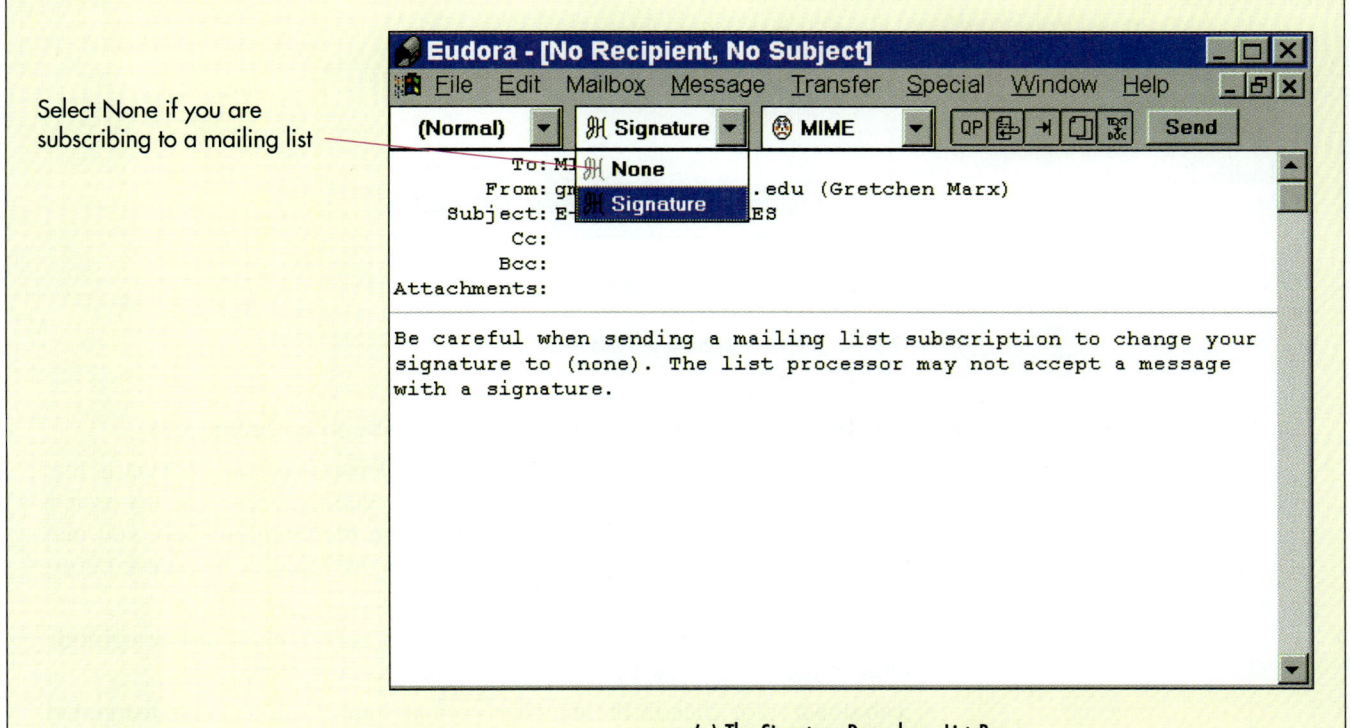

Select None if you are subscribing to a mailing list

(e) The Signature Drop-down List Box

FIGURE 2.8   Hands-on Exercise 3 (continued)

GLOBAL COMMUNICATION ON THE INTERNET   **67**

WATCH THAT SIGNATURE

Commands sent to a list server must follow a certain format. Inserting a signature in your message may cause the list server to reject it. To avoid this problem, be sure to select **None** in the Signature drop-down list box before sending any message to a listserv, listproc, or majordomo.

STEP 3: Create a Mailbox

➤ Select **Mailbox** from the pull-down menus, then select **New.**
  - Enter the name of the new mailbox, **subscribe,** in the text box displayed in the New Mailbox dialog box, as shown in Figure 2.8f. Click **OK.**
  - Select **Mailbox** again. You should see your new mailbox listed, as shown in Figure 2.8g. You can now use the Transfer command to move any selected mail from any of your other mailboxes to your new mailbox.

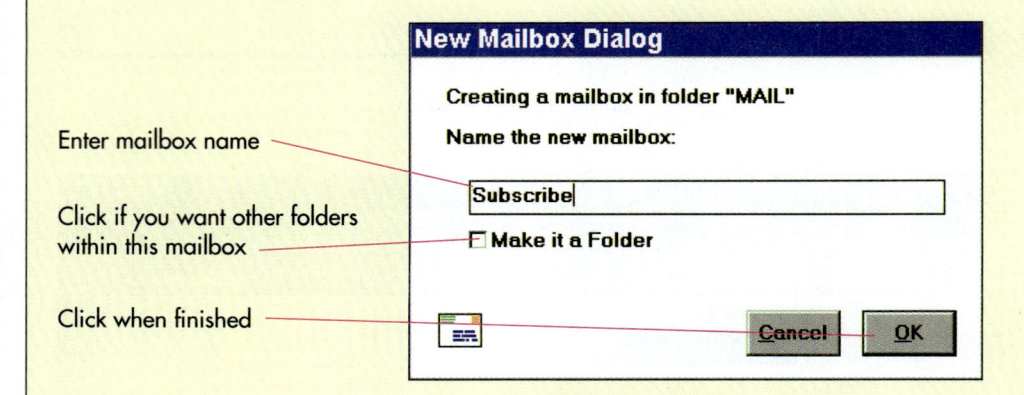

Enter mailbox name

Click if you want other folders within this mailbox

Click when finished

(f) The Completed New Mailbox Dialog Box

FIGURE 2.8   Hands-on Exercise 3 (continued)

STEP 4: Retrieve the "List of Lists" and Subscribe to a Mailing List

➤ Send an e-mail message to retrieve the "list of lists." (Your instructor may choose to have only one or two people in the class retrieve the list as it is quite long. If a copy of it is already available in the computer lab, you may not need to retrieve it at all. Check with your lab assistant or help desk before proceeding.)
  - Select **Message,** then **New** and enter the list server name **listserv@bitnic.educom.edu** in the To field. Leave the Subject line blank.
  - **Tab** down to or click in the message area and enter the message **list global.** Your message should look like that shown in Figure 2.8h when complete.
  - Click **Send.** (Wait for the list to be sent to you before completing this exercise. You may have to wait 24 hours for the list to be returned.)
➤ Check your incoming mail for the returned mail message from Educom, which is an organization formed to promote technology in education. Select the message, then select **File** and **Print** to print the list.
➤ Choose a list to which you want to subscribe.

68   EXPLORING THE INTERNET

Default mailboxes

Custom mailboxes

(g) The Mailbox Pull-down Menu

Click to remove signature

Click to send message

Listserv address

List command

(h) The List Global Message

FIGURE 2.8 Hands-on Exercise 3 (continued)

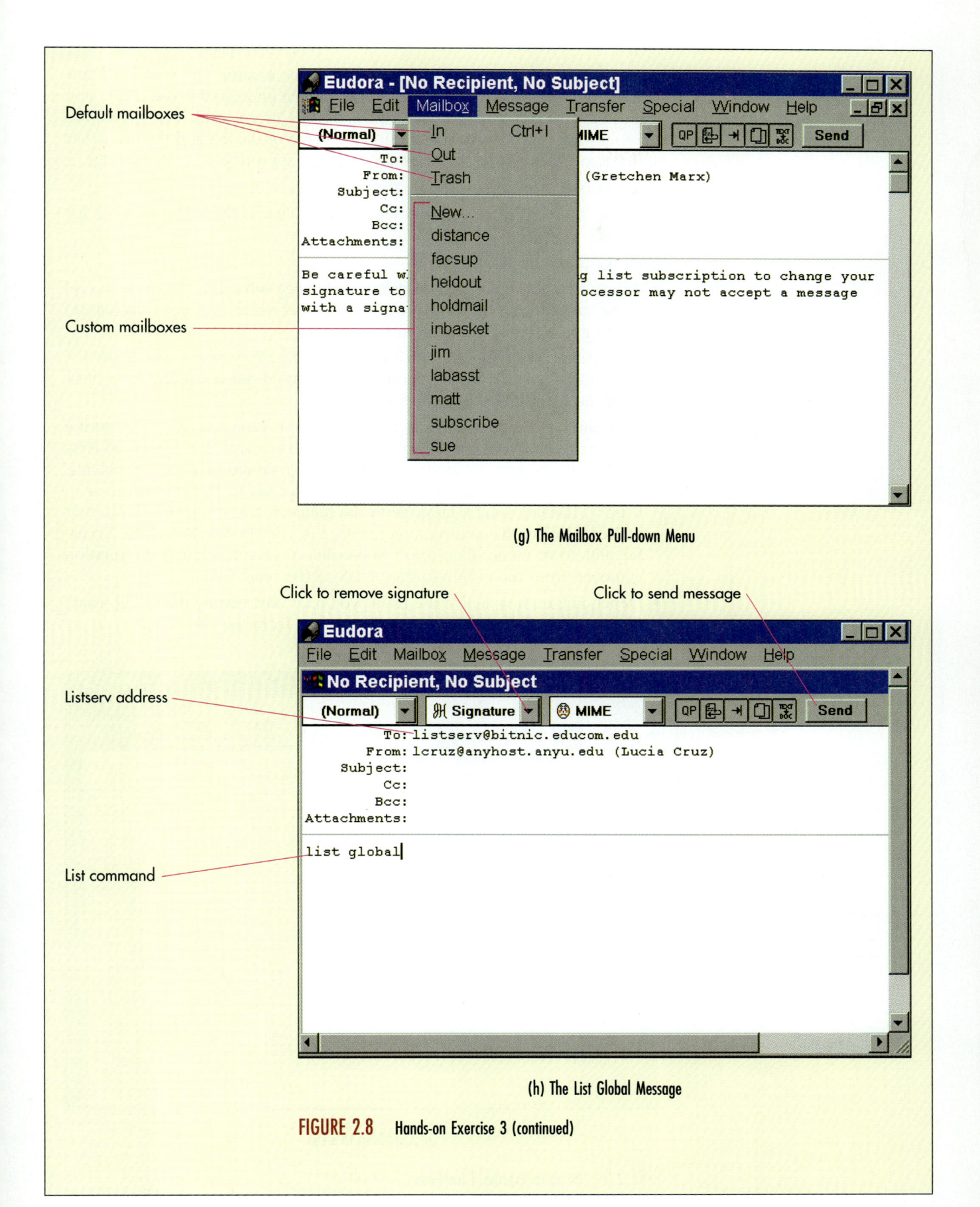

GLOBAL COMMUNICATION ON THE INTERNET

- Subscribe to the list. The following instructions assume you want to know more about biking, and want to find other people interested in the sport. You want to try the bicycling list, *bicycle,* owned by Chris Tanski. You should use the following instructions, substituting the name of the list and the list server address to which you wish to subscribe where appropriate in the message.
  - Select **New Message** from the **Message** menu.
  - In the To field, enter **listproc@list.cren.net.** That is the address of the list server.
  - Leave the Subject field blank.
  - Tab to the message area, and type the message **subscribe bicycle your real name,** substituting the listname and your real name (not your username) where appropriate, as shown in Figure 2.8i.
  - Click **Send.** Your subscription to the list called *bicycle* (or whichever list you subscribed to) will be entered. You should get a confirmation back from the list server within 24 hours.
  - Save the confirmation message. It will explain how you can unsubscribe and/or suspend your mail, and should have the name and e-mail address of the list manager or moderator to write to should you have problems. (Do not send e-mail about problems with the list to the entire list, or to listserv. Instead, send a message to the manager's or moderator's Internet address.) Select the confirmation message in your in-box. Select the **Transfer** pull-down menu, then select **Subscribe.** Your subscription information is moved from the in-box to the SUBSCRIBE mail folder.
  - Depending on how active the list is, you may start getting mail right away. Check within 24 hours to see your messages from the list.

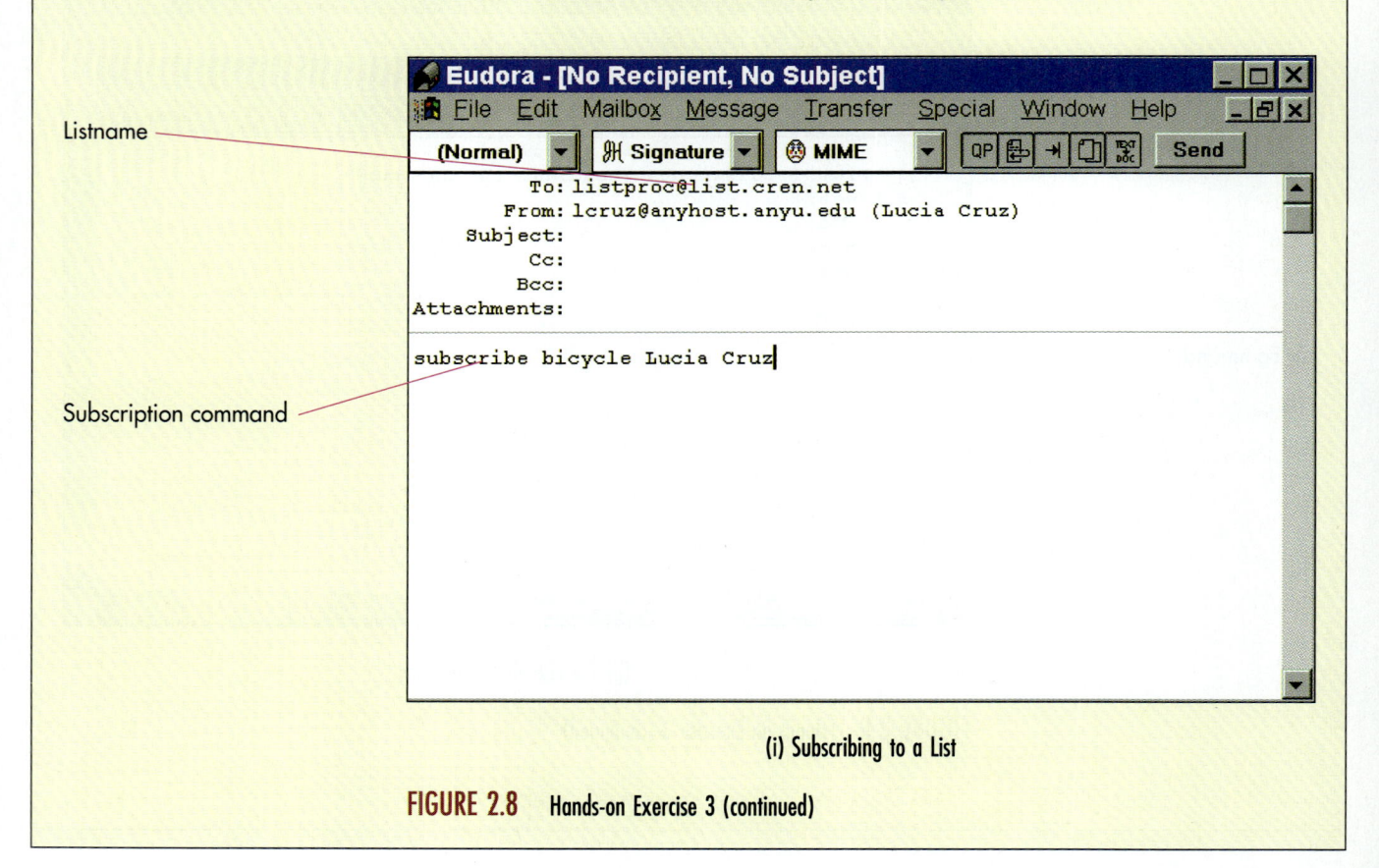

(i) Subscribing to a List

FIGURE 2.8   Hands-on Exercise 3 (continued)

HANDS-ON EXERCISE 4

Customizing E-mail and Subscribing to Mailing Lists Using Pine

Objective: Create a distribution list and folder, and subscribe to a mailing list. Use Figure 2.9 as a guide in the exercise.

STEP 1: Create a Distribution/Nickname List

➤ Log on to your system and type **Pine** at the Unix prompt.

- At the main menu type **A** to update your *address book*. The blank Address Book screen shown in Figure 2.9a is displayed.

- Type **S** to create a distribution list (this and other available commands are shown at the bottom of the screen). A message is displayed at the bottom of the screen requesting the long name/description of the list as shown in Figure 2.9b. Enter a descriptive name for the list, such as **MIS201 Class List** (substitute the course number for your class), and press **Enter**.

- Next enter the list nickname (a one-word abbreviation for the distribution list). This is the name you will later enter in the To field when you send a message to the list. Enter **MIS201** or something similar and press **Enter**.

- You will be prompted to enter the first address in the distribution list as shown in Figure 2.9c. Enter the username of someone in your class, then press **Enter**. (If you are creating a distribution list of people using the same Internet host as you, you can simply enter their usernames. If they are at another site, enter their usernames and Internet addresses.)

- Continue entering usernames and pressing **Enter** until you have entered all the names you want on the distribution list.

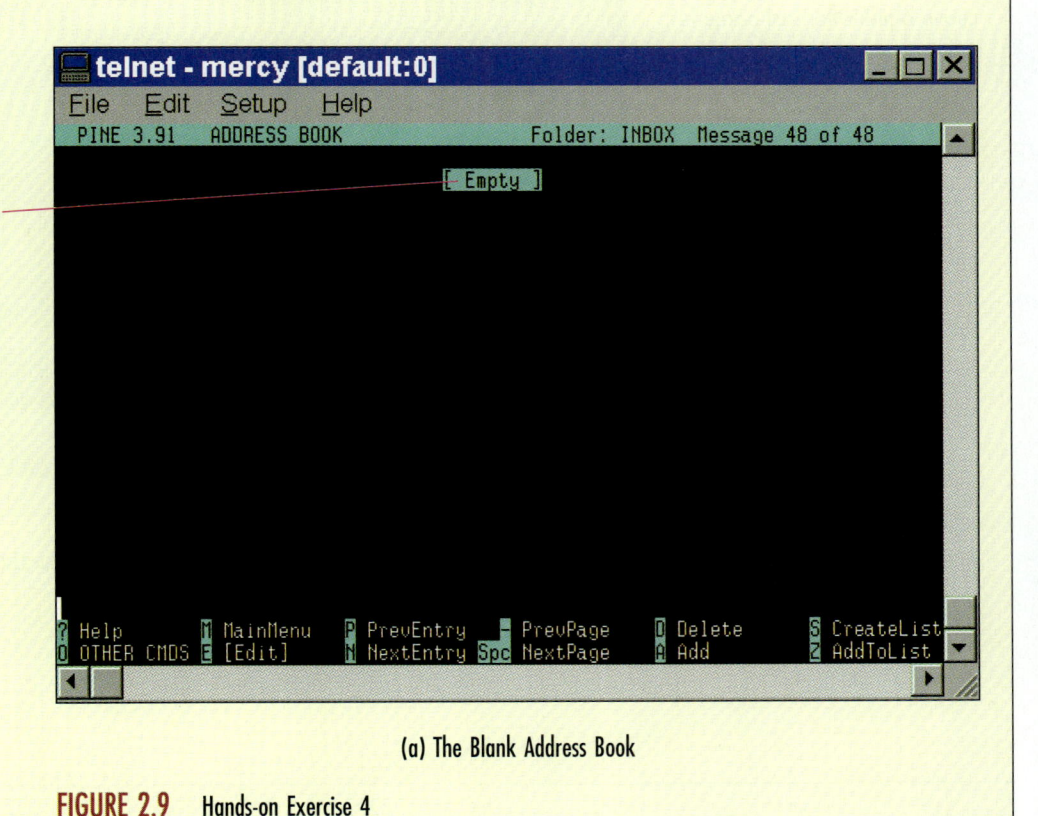

There are no distribution lists

(a) The Blank Address Book

FIGURE 2.9 Hands-on Exercise 4

Enter full name (description) of distribution list

(b) The Long Name/Description Message

Leave blank after last name is entered

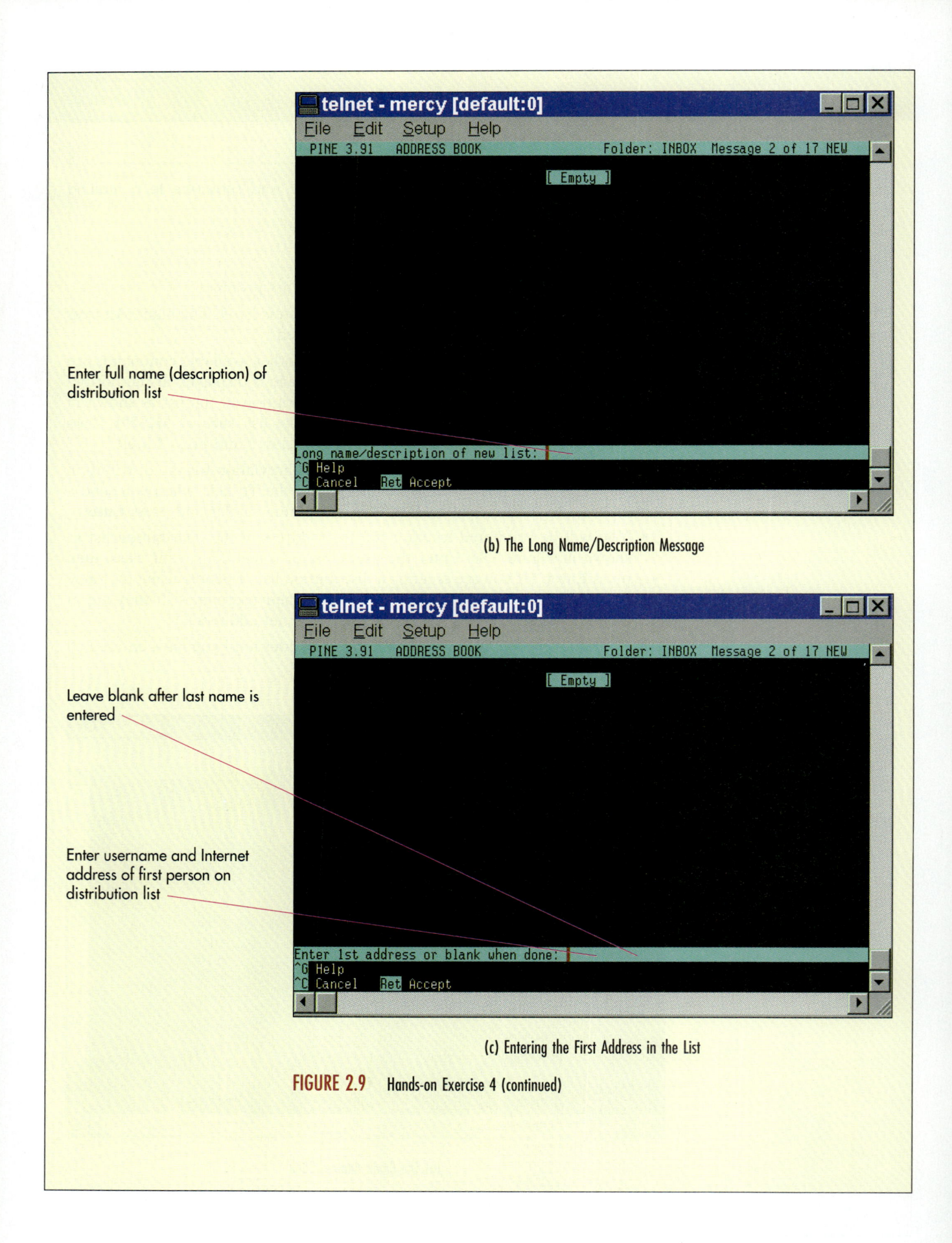

Enter username and Internet address of first person on distribution list

(c) Entering the First Address in the List

FIGURE 2.9 Hands-on Exercise 4 (continued)

- When you have no more names, leave the address line blank and press **Enter** one more time. (The blank address field tells Pine you have reached the end of the list.) A message is displayed briefly, indicating that Pine is updating the address book. You should now see a screen similar to that shown in Figure 2.9d, displaying the distribution list you just created.
- Press **M** to return to the main menu.

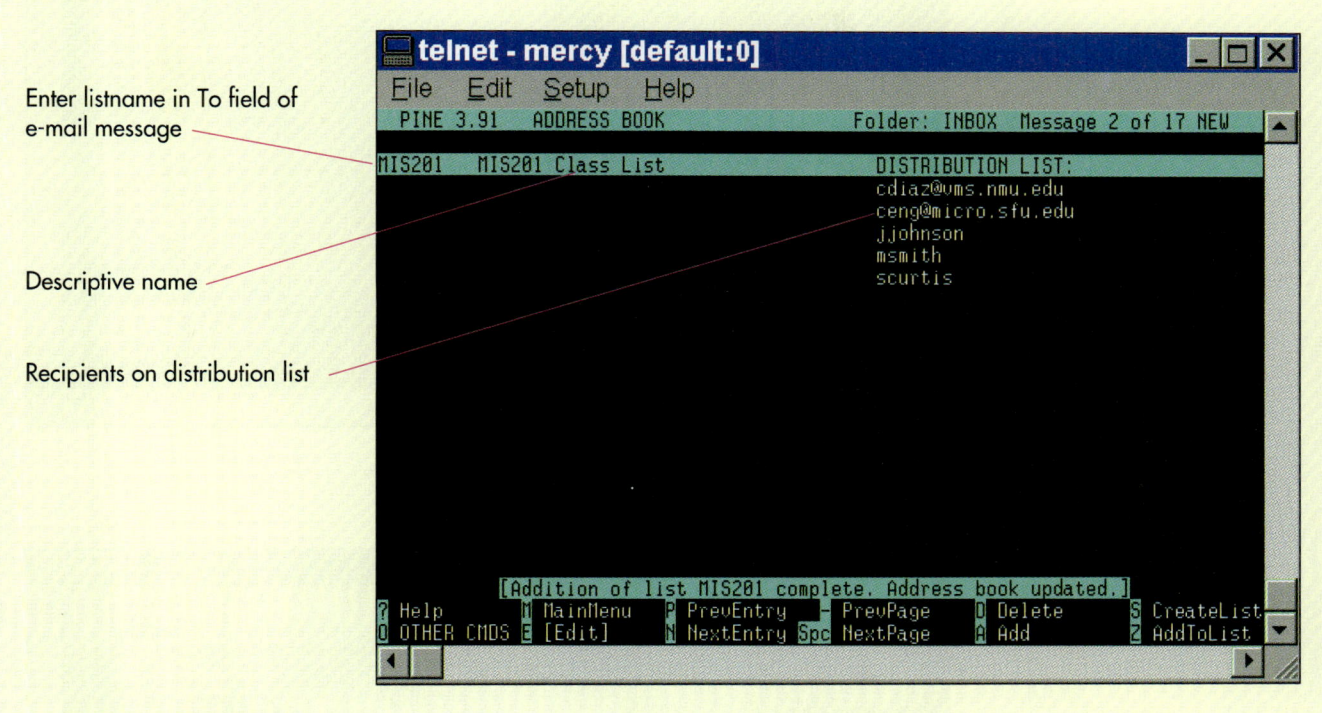

(d) The New Distribution List

FIGURE 2.9   Hands-on Exercise 4 (continued)

STEP 2: Create a New Mail Folder and Move a Message to It

➤ You will want to customize Pine to organize mail messages you want to save indefinitely, as opposed to having them cluttering your in-box.
- At the main menu type **L** to display a list of existing mail folders as shown in Figure 2.9e.
- When you see the list, which by default includes INBOX, sent-mail, and saved-messages, type **A** to add a folder. You will be prompted for the name of the folder you want to add, as shown in Figure 2.9f.
- Type the name of the folder you want to add, **subscribe,** and press **Enter.** You will see the new folder displayed in your folder list.

➤ Press **M** to return to the main menu, then type **I** to see an index of messages in the current folder, which by default is INBOX.

➤ Select a message to transfer to the **SUBSCRIBE** folder. Type **S** to save the message, then enter the name of the folder to save to, **subscribe,** as shown in Figure 2.9g. The message will be marked for deletion in the INBOX, and saved to the new folder.
- Type **M** to return to the main menu.

GLOBAL COMMUNICATION ON THE INTERNET   **73**

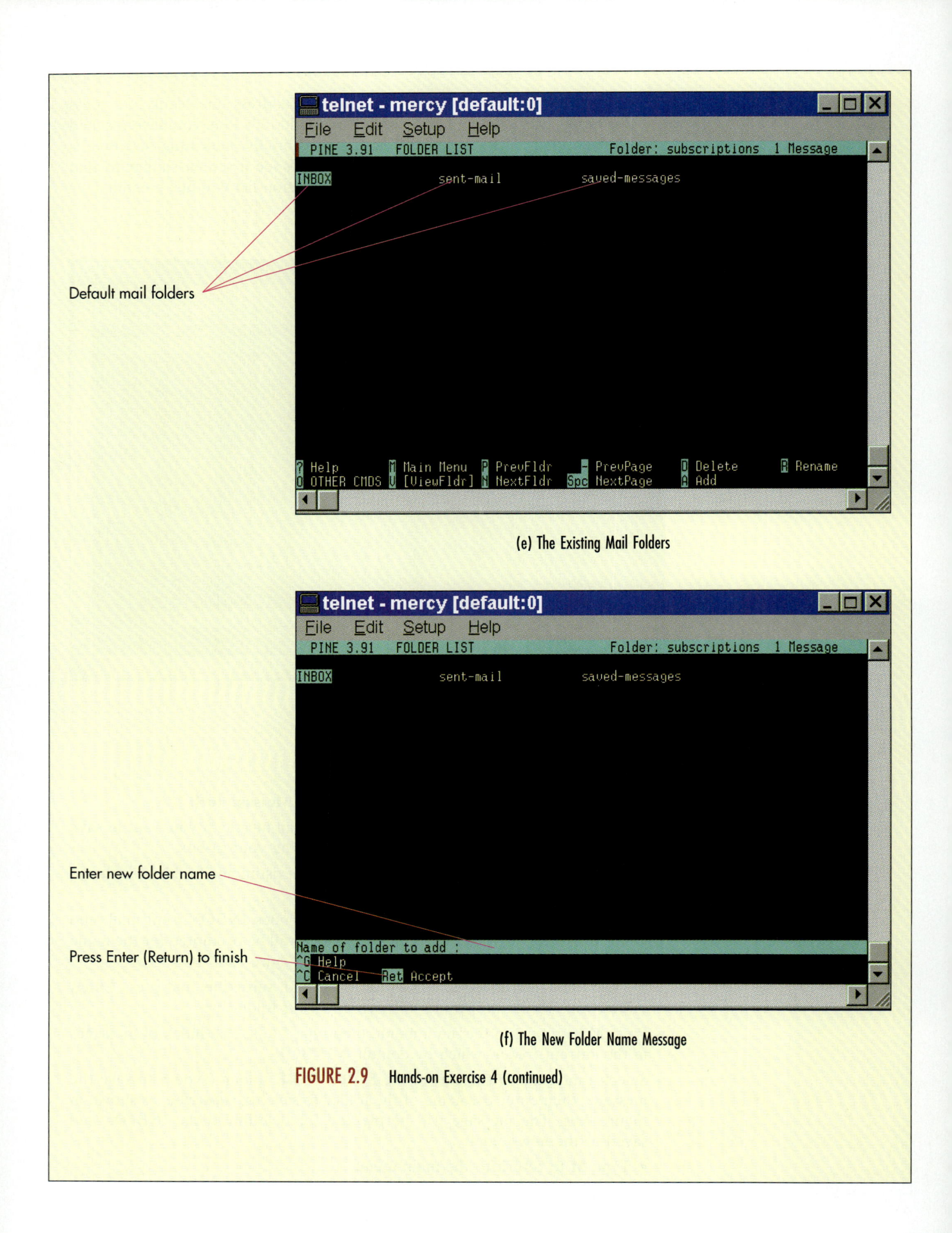

(e) The Existing Mail Folders

(f) The New Folder Name Message

FIGURE 2.9   Hands-on Exercise 4 (continued)

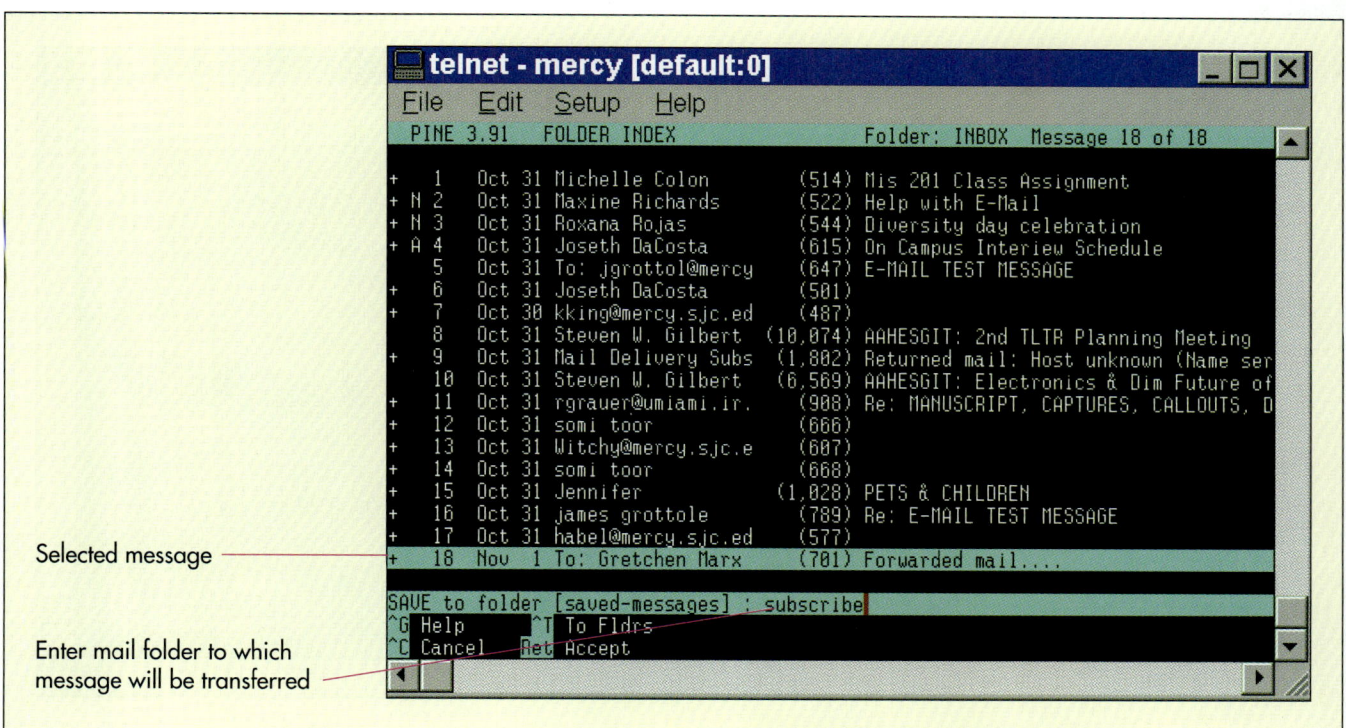

```
 telnet - mercy [default:0]                                    _ □ ×
File   Edit   Setup   Help
 PINE 3.91    FOLDER INDEX              Folder: INBOX  Message 18 of 18

+   1    Oct 31  Michelle Colon      (514) Mis 201 Class Assignment
+ N 2    Oct 31  Maxine Richards     (522) Help with E-Mail
+ N 3    Oct 31  Roxana Rojas        (544) Diversity day celebration
+ A 4    Oct 31  Joseth DaCosta      (615) On Campus Interiew Schedule
    5    Oct 31  To: jgrottol@mercy  (647) E-MAIL TEST MESSAGE
+   6    Oct 31  Joseth DaCosta      (501)
+   7    Oct 30  kking@mercy.sjc.ed  (487)
    8    Oct 31  Steven W. Gilbert (10,074) AAHESGIT: 2nd TLTR Planning Meeting
    9    Oct 31  Mail Delivery Subs (1,802) Returned mail: Host unknown (Name ser
   10    Oct 31  Steven W. Gilbert  (6,569) AAHESGIT: Electronics & Dim Future of
+  11    Oct 31  rgrauer@umiami.ir.  (908) Re: MANUSCRIPT, CAPTURES, CALLOUTS, D
+  12    Oct 31  somi toor           (666)
+  13    Oct 31  Witchy@mercy.sjc.e  (607)
+  14    Oct 31  somi toor           (668)
+  15    Oct 31  Jennifer          (1,028) PETS & CHILDREN
+  16    Oct 31  james grottole      (789) Re: E-MAIL TEST MESSAGE
+  17    Oct 31  habel@mercy.sjc.ed  (577)
+  18    Nov  1  To: Gretchen Marx   (701) Forwarded mail....

SAVE to folder [saved-messages] : subscribe
^G Help          ^T To Fldrs
^C Cancel       Ret Accept
```

Selected message → (points to line 18)

Enter mail folder to which message will be transferred → (points to SAVE prompt)

(g) Saving a Message to a Folder

FIGURE 2.9   Hands-on Exercise 4 (continued)

STEP 3: Retrieve the "List of Lists" and Subscribe to a Mailing List

➤ Send an e-mail message to retrieve the "list of lists." (Your instructor may choose to have only one or two people in the class retrieve the list as it is quite long. If a copy of it is already available in the computer lab, you may not need to retrieve it at all. Check with your lab assistant or help desk before proceeding.)

- Type **C** at the Pine main menu and enter the list server name **listserv@bitnic.educom.edu** in the To field in the message screen. Leave the Subject line blank.
- **Tab** down to the message area and enter the message **list global.** Your message should look like that shown in Figure 2.9h when complete.
- Press **Ctrl+X.** (Wait for the list to be sent to you before completing this exercise. You may have to wait 24 hours for the list to be returned.)

➤ Check your incoming mail for the returned mail message from Educom, which is an organization formed to promote technology in education. Select the message, then select **File** and **Print** to print the list.

➤ Choose a list to which you want to subscribe.

➤ Subscribe to the list. The following instructions assume you want to know more about biking, and want to find other people interested in the sport. You want to try the bicycling list, *bicycle,* owned by Chris Tanski. You should use the following instructions, substituting the name of the list and the list server address to which you wish to subscribe where appropriate in the message.

- Type **C** at the main menu to compose your subscription message.
- In the To field, enter **listproc@list.cren.net.** That is the address of the list server.

Listserv address

Leave subject blank when requesting list

List global command

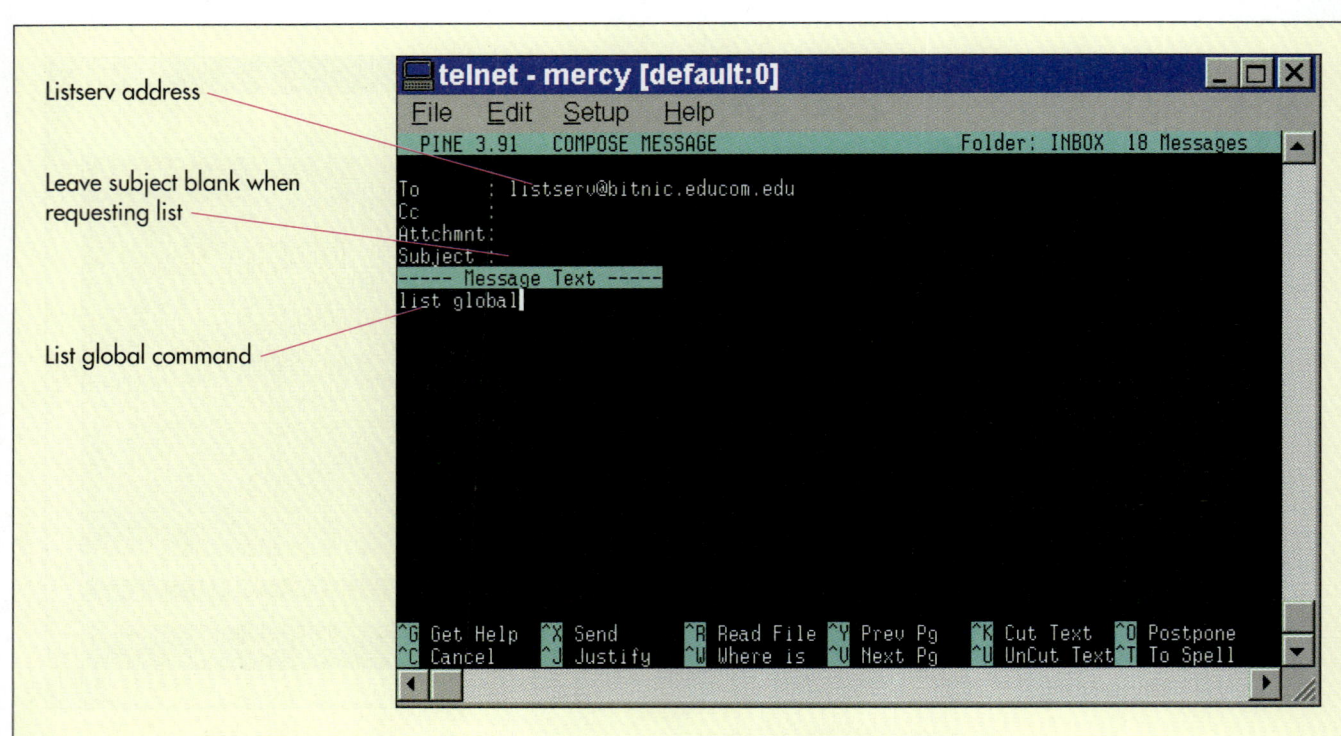

(h) The Completed List Global Message

FIGURE 2.9 Hands-on Exercise 4 (continued)

- Leave the subject field blank.
- Tab to the message area, and type the message **subscribe bicycle your real name,** substituting the listname and your real name (not your username) where appropriate, as shown in Figure 2.9i.
- Type **Ctrl+X.** Your subscription to the list called *bicycle* (or whichever list you subscribed to) will be entered. You should get a confirmation back from the list server within 24 hours.
- Save the confirmation message. It will explain how you can unsubscribe and/or suspend your mail, and should have the name and e-mail address of the list manager or moderator to write to should you have problems. (Do not send e-mail about problems with the list to the entire list, or to listserv. Instead, send a message to the manager's or moderator's Internet address.) Select the confirmation message in your INBOX folder. Type **S** to save the message. When you see a message asking what folder to save to, enter **subscribe,** or whatever name you gave your subscription information folder in the previous step. Your subscription information is copied to the SUBSCRIBE mail folder and marked for deletion in the in-box.
- Depending on how active the list is, you may start getting mail right away. Check within 24 hours to see your messages from the list.

List server

Leave subject field blank when subscribing to list

Press Ctrl+X to send

(i) Subscribing to the Bicyle Mailing List

FIGURE 2.9 Hands-on Exercise 4 (continued)

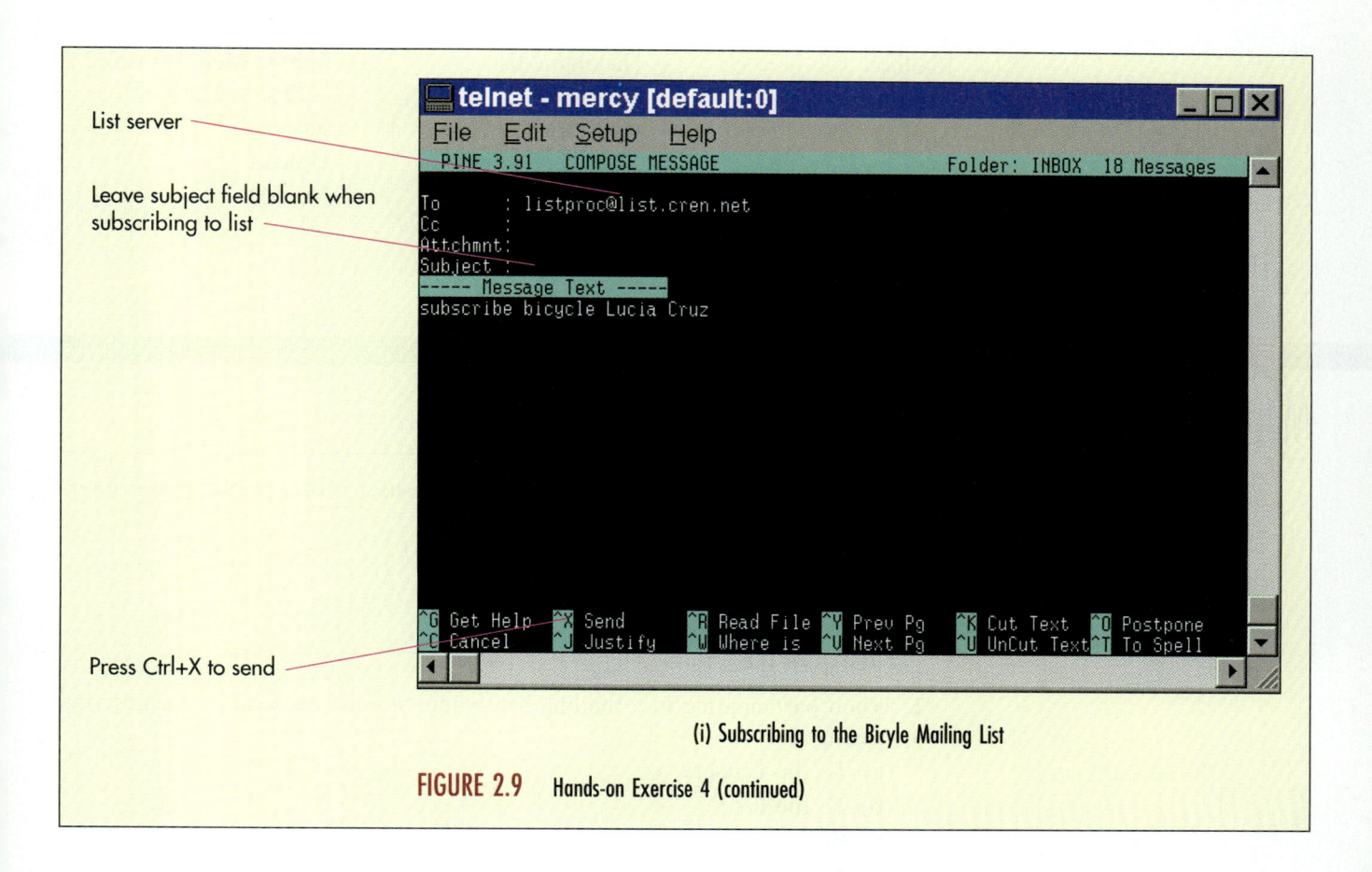

SUMMARY

Using e-mail you can send a message to anyone on the Internet in a matter of seconds (although they, for various reasons, may not immediately receive it). All e-mail systems give you the capability to compose and send messages; to receive, reply to, and forward mail; and to set up custom distribution lists. You can also subscribe to mailing lists, which will automatically send you messages sent by other subscribers to the list. Many people subscribe to mailing lists and correspond about their favorite subjects with other people from all over the world.

How you send and retrieve your mail depends on whether you are using a POP mail client or a Unix mail program. A POP mail client retrieves mail from the Internet server and stores it on your PC or the file server in the computer lab. A Unix mail program leaves the mail on the Internet server. However, both provide the capabilities described above.

KEY WORDS AND CONCEPTS

Alias	Distribution list	Header
Blind carbon copy	Download	List owner
Carbon copy	E-mail	Listproc
Client software	Flaming	Listserv
Command-line interface	Folder	List server
Digest	Folder index	Lurking

GLOBAL COMMUNICATION ON THE INTERNET   77

Mailbox	Nickname list	Simple Mail Transfer
Mail client	Password	Protocol (SMTP)
Mailing list	Post Office Protocol	Suspend
Mail server	(POP)	Upload
Majordomo	Shell account	UserID
Moderator	Signature	

MULTIPLE CHOICE

1. Which of the following typically provides the user with a graphical user interface to access the Internet?
   (a) Client software
   (b) A Unix shell account
   (c) A command-line prompt
   (d) All of the above

2. When participating in a mailing list, where would you send an unsubscribe message?
   (a) To the Listserv
   (b) To the list
   (c) Both (a) and (b)
   (d) Neither (a) nor (b)

3. If you often send messages to the same group of recipients at your college, which of the following should you do?
   (a) Subscribe to a mailing list
   (b) Set up a distribution list
   (c) Both (a) and (b)
   (d) Neither (a) nor (b)

4. Which of the following capabilities is available in most e-mail systems?
   (a) Compose
   (b) Send
   (c) Forward
   (d) All of the above

5. E-mail allows you to send messages to:
   (a) Another user on your local area network
   (b) Another user on the Internet
   (c) Both (a) and (b)
   (d) Neither (a) nor (b)

6. Which of the following downloads your mail to be stored on your local PC when requested?
   (a) Post Office Protocol (POP) software
   (b) Pine
   (c) A Unix mail program
   (d) All of the above

7. Which e-mail program allows you to create a distribution list?
   (a) Pine
   (b) Eudora
   (c) Both (a) and (b)
   (d) Neither (a) nor (b)

8. Which symbol is used in an e-mail address to separate the username from the host computer name?
   (a) *
   (b) @
   (c) .
   (d) #

9. If you use a POP mail client, where is the mail stored while enroute to you?
   (a) On the Unix server
   (b) On local storage on the PC
   (c) Both (a) and (b)
   (d) Neither (a) nor (b)

10. Which of the following statements regarding Internet e-mail programs is true?
    (a) You may move a message from one folder to another
    (b) You may create an alias for your username
    (c) You can define your own distribution lists
    (d) All of the above

11. Which of the following allows you to send an e-mail message to a second person without the first recipient knowing it?
    (a) The To field
    (b) The Cc field
    (c) The Bcc field
    (d) All of the above

12. If you choose to redirect an e-mail message, what happens to it?
    (a) It is automatically sent back to the originator
    (b) It is sent to the new recipient with your username in the From field
    (c) It is sent to the new recipient with the originator's name in the From field
    (d) It goes into the trash folder for deletion at the end of the mail session

13. Which of the following statements regarding Eudora mailboxes is true?
    (a) The user cannot create mailboxes
    (b) Mail transferred to the Trash folder cannot be recalled
    (c) Mailboxes can be viewed only one at a time
    (d) None of the above

14. Which of the following guidelines should be used when creating an e-mail signature?
    (a) Keep the length to a minimum
    (b) Use appropriate verbiage
    (c) Both (a) and (b)
    (d) Neither (a) nor (b)

15. To which of the following mailing list programs would you recommend sending a signature with the Subscribe command?
    (a) Listserv
    (b) Listproc
    (c) Majordomo
    (d) None of the above

ANSWERS

1. a	**6.** a	**11.** c
2. a	**7.** c	**12.** c
3. b	**8.** b	**13.** d
4. d	**9.** c	**14.** c
5. c	**10.** d	**15.** d

Exploring the Internet

1. Using Figure 2.10, match each action with its result; a given action may be used more than once or not at all.

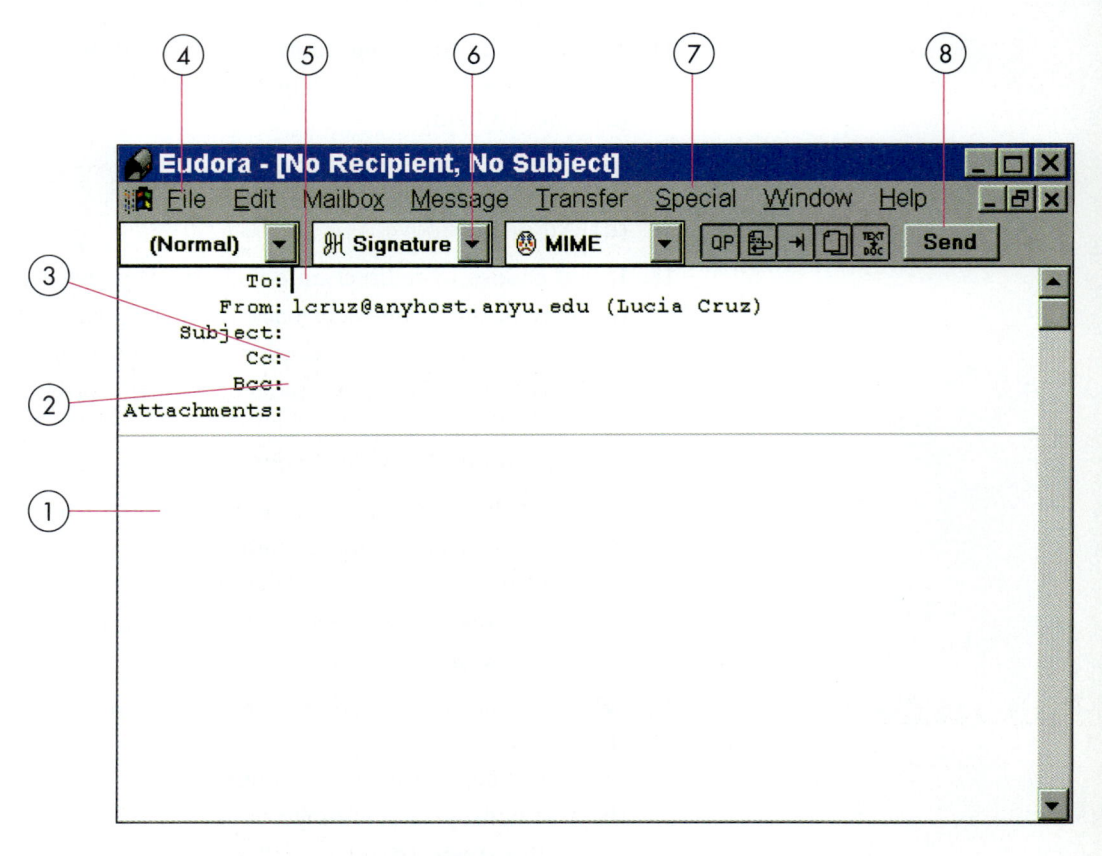

FIGURE 2.10   Figure for Exploring the Internet Exercise 1

Action	Result
a. Click at 1	____ Enter the text of the message
b. Click at 2	____ Change your password
c. Click at 3	____ Send a copy to someone without the addressee's knowledge
d. Click at 4	
e. Click at 5	____ Send a copy; the addressee will know the copy has been sent
f. Click at 6	
g. Click at 7	____ Send the message
h. Click at 8	____ Remove your signature from the message
	____ Check for incoming mail
	____ Enter the recipient's username

2. The messages shown in Figure 2.11 appeared (or could have appeared) in conjunction with one of the hands-on exercises in this chapter. Explain the nature of each message and indicate the necessary corrective action (if any).

(a) Message 1

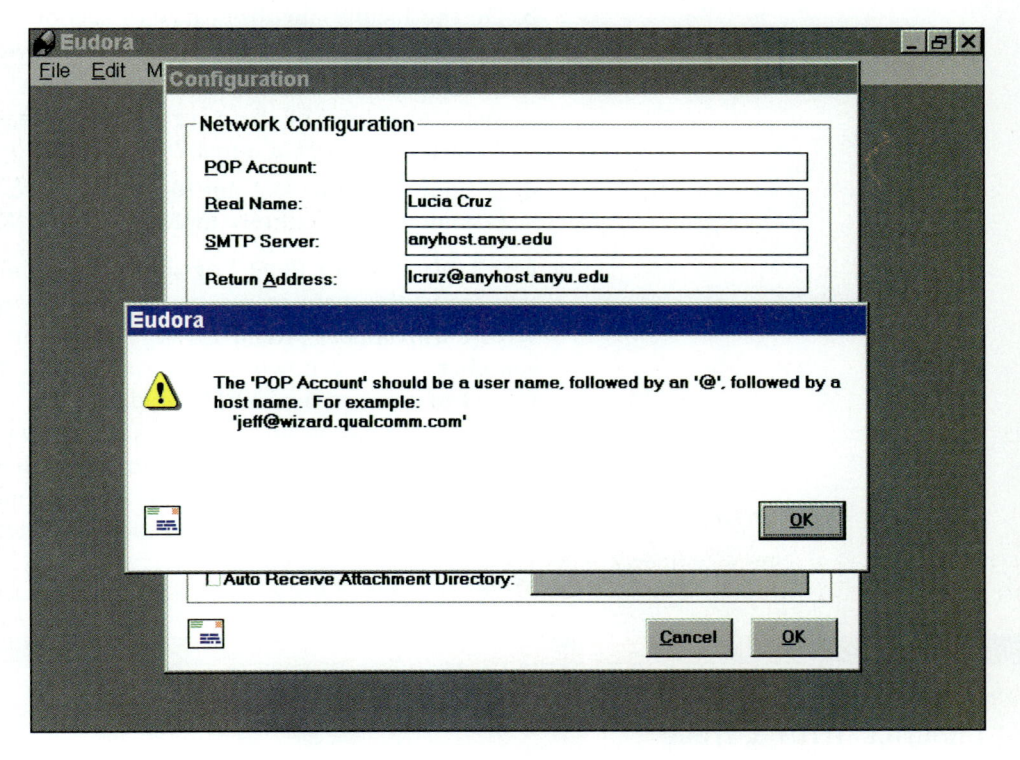

(b) Message 2

FIGURE 2.11   Messages for Exploring the Internet Exercise 2

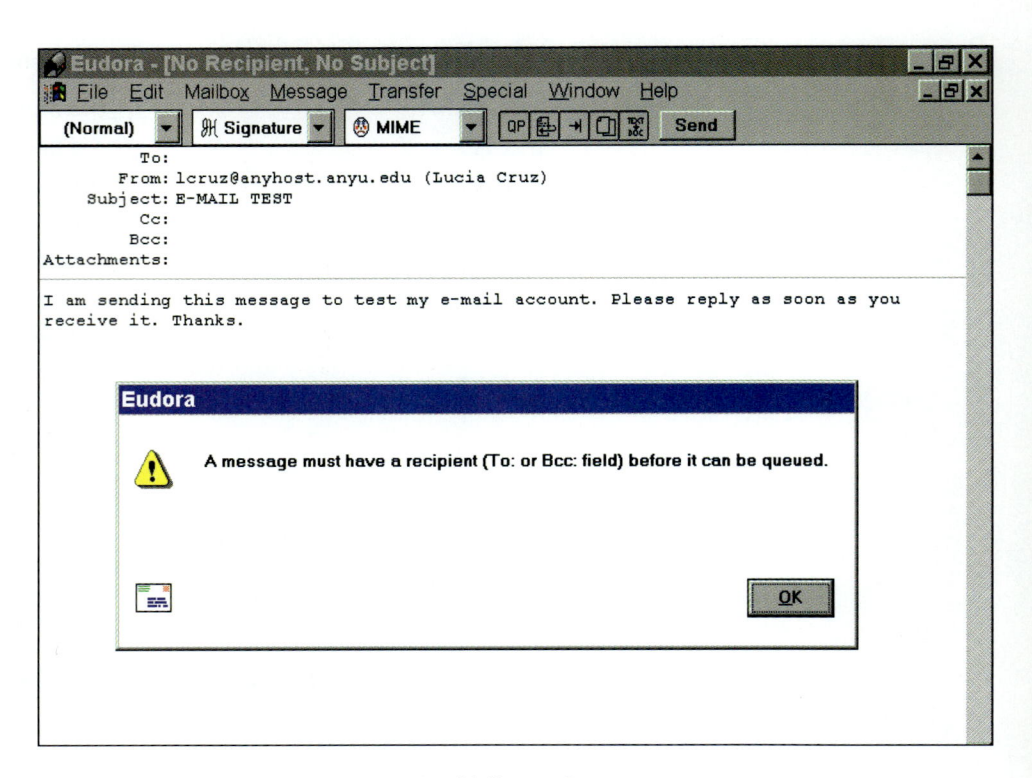

(c) Message 3

FIGURE 2.11   Messages for Exploring the Internet Exercise 2 (continued)

3. Answer the following questions regarding e-mail. Compare your answers to those of your classmates.
    a. What mailing lists, if any, are sponsored by your college or university?
    b. Do the faculty members at your school use e-mail to communicate with (a) each other, (b) colleagues at other institutions, (c) administrators, or (d) students?
    c. What are some of the advantages/disadvantages of communicating with faculty members via e-mail?
    d. Distance learning is a hot topic at many colleges. Could a course be successfully taught entirely through e-mail? Why or why not?

4. Learn More about Pine: Log on to your Unix server and type **Pine.** Once you are at the main menu, type a question mark (**?**). The main Pine Help screen will appear. Read through the overview about Pine, pressing the **spacebar** to move down a screen at a time. Pine Help is context sensitive. Press **I** to move to the INBOX folder index, and press **?** again. This time you will see information about various options in using the index. For instance, you will learn that you can jump to a specific message in the index by pressing the letter **J,** then entering the message number. You can press the **Tab** key to move to the next unread message. Press **E** at any time to exit Help.

PRACTICE WITH E-MAIL

1. Find a Pen Pal: Find a pen pal in the class or at another university and send that person an e-mail message describing how you plan to use the Internet

82   EXPLORING THE INTERNET

this semester. Send a copy of the message to your instructor as proof that you did the exercise.

2. **Subscribe to a Mailing List about the Internet:** Send the message **list global/internet** to the listserv at **listserv@bitnic.educom.edu.** Wait for the reply and then choose a list about the Internet to which to subscribe. For example, you could subscribe to the Scout Report, a weekly update on new and interesting sites and Net developments. To subscribe to the Scout Report, send e-mail to **majordomo@is.internet.nic.** In the message area enter **subscribe scout-report Your Real Name.** When you get your subscription confirmation, transfer it to the **SUBSCRIBE** mailbox you set up in Hands-on Exercise 2.3 or 2.4.

3. **Attach a File:** Eudora, other POP mail programs, and some versions of Pine provide the capability to attach a file to the message you're sending. Suppose you are assigned a group project, and are working on a section of the final report. You could attach your section to a mail message, and mail it to the rest of your group for their review and comment. The following instructions describe how to attach a file in Eudora. See your instructor for attaching files in Pine.

   a. Log on and start Eudora. Select **New Message** from the **Message** menu.
   b. While you are preparing the e-mail message, click on **Attach Document** in the **Message** menu. You will see a dialog box, shown in Figure 2.12a, that requests information about the document you wish to attach to the message. Eudora wants to know on which drive the document is found. First click the **down arrow** next to the drive name, to see a drop-down list box of all the disks attached to your system. Select the disk on which the document is stored.
   c. If your document is in a subdirectory, double click the desired subdirectory in the directories list, and a list of all files in the subdirectory will be displayed at the left of the window.

(a) The Attach Document Dialog Box

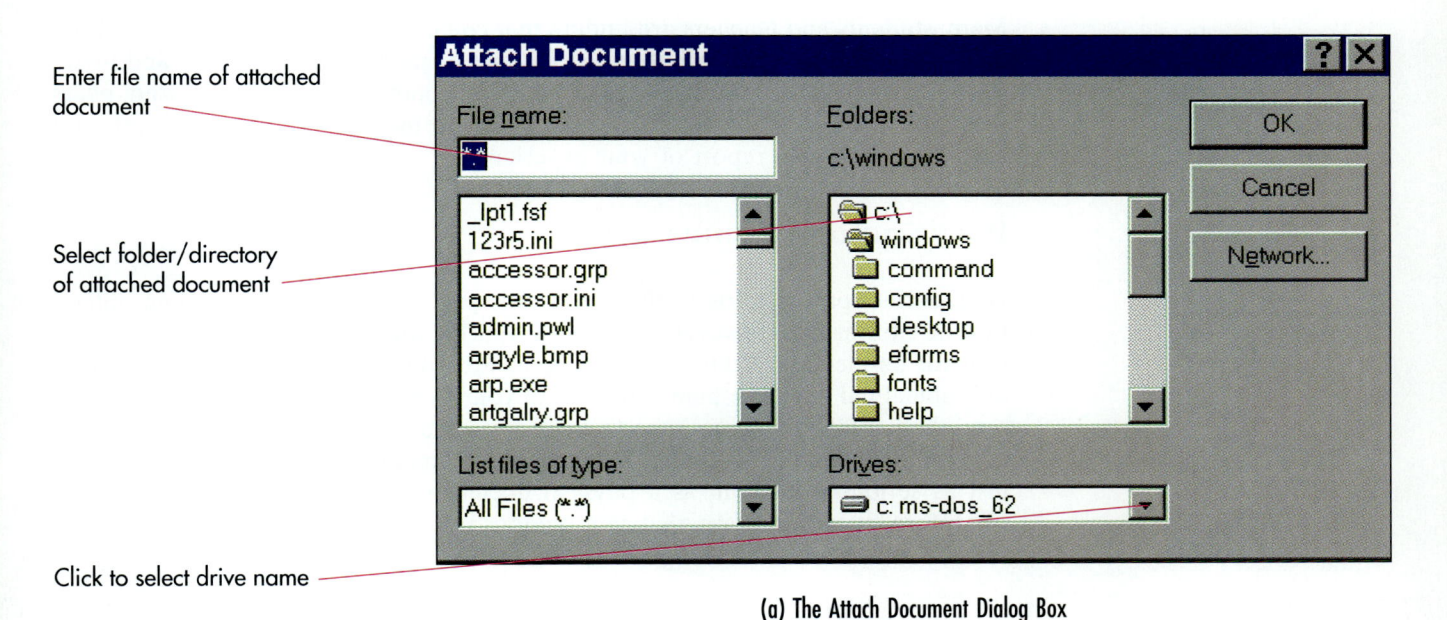

FIGURE 2.12 Figure for Practice Exercise 3

d. Click the file you want to attach, then click **OK.** You will be returned to the mail message window. The Attachments field will contain the name of the file you want to attach.

e. Complete your message, click **Send,** and the document, in its original form, is sent as an attachment with the message.

4. Send a Message to a List: Subscribe to a mailing list that interests you, and read the messages posted to the list for a few weeks. After you have been on a mailing list for a while and feel comfortable with the types of messages being sent to the list, compose a message or a reply to someone else's question or statement. Remember to send the message to the list address, not the listserv.

Case Studies

Finding a List

Assume you want to find a mailing list on a particular subject—Shakespeare, for example. Send a message to **listserv@bitnic.educom.edu** with the command **list global/shakespeare** in the message area. You will receive an e-mail message showing the mailing lists on the topic in which you are interested. Find mailing lists for two or three topics of interest to you and subscribe to them. ***Be sure to send the subscribe message without a signature.*** Save the subscription confirmations in your **SUBSCRIBE** mailbox (set one up if you have not already done so).

Collaborative Learning Using E-mail

Many students and teachers are finding that collaborative learning helps everyone learn better. Set up a distribution list for one or more of your classes, and invite people to join an online study group for the course. How many of your peers respond? Do they know about e-mail? Can you use e-mail for group work and studying? Prepare a report of your experience.

Participatory Democracy

As a citizen, participating in the democratic process is your right, and an obligation of citizenship. However, with the advent of the Internet, you don't have to wait for an election. Your voice can be heard with an immediacy not previously available. Find out the e-mail addresses of your Congressional representatives, and send them e-mail about an issue that concerns you—perhaps legislation regarding government funding of student financial aid. Remember, however, that e-mail is just as serious a medium as a physical document. You will not be anonymous. Therefore, it is important that you compose your thoughts and send a clearly worded, finely crafted message.

Analyzing E-mail Content

Subscribe to a list of interest to you, and read the e-mail daily for a week. Analyze the content of the e-mail for its information-to-noise ratio. How much of the traffic provides useful information, and how much is sent just so the sender can expound to thousands of people? Noise can be a problem everywhere on the Net.

FINDING THINGS ON THE WORLD WIDE WEB: NETSCAPE AND LYNX

3

OBJECTIVES

After reading this chapter you will be able to:

1. Explain the basic terminology of the World Wide Web, and explore the Web using a graphical browser such as Netscape.
2. Describe what a URL is and use one to find a specific Web document or home page.
3. Explain how to navigate through the Web using hypertext and hypermedia links.
4. Create a bookmark for a Web site; save and print a Web document.
5. Use a search engine to find Web resources that match a specific query.
6. Understand the differences between a graphical browser and a text-based browser such as Lynx.

OVERVIEW

The World Wide Web (WWW, W3, or simply the Web) is the newest, hottest tool on the Internet, and what's more, it couldn't be easier to use. The Web is a means of information storage and retrieval that has captivated millions of people and thousands of companies around the globe, and it is critically important that you understand how to make productive use of it. Any document on any Web server, anywhere in the world, is accessible using a Web browser on your PC or Unix server. Learning how to use a Web browser, software that lets you locate and retrieve these documents, is the key to a vast library of millions of references, including audio, video, and graphic files.

In this chapter we show you how to surf the Web using Netscape Navigator, a graphical Web browser that lets you locate text, graphics, video, sound, and other files. You will use hypertext links to jump from document to document and site to site. You will also learn to use Web search engines to conduct directed searches, or queries.

The millions of files and documents available on the Web can also be accessed with a text (rather than graphical) browser. We show you how to use Lynx, a text-based browser that allows those who do not have a GUI client such as Netscape to access the Web and use hypertext links from the Unix prompt.

THE WORLD WIDE WEB

In Chapter 2 we discussed e-mail, and you learned to send and receive messages over the Internet. However, the Internet is much more than a message switching network for e-mail. It connects computers around the globe and lets users access a vast array of text, graphic, audio, video, and programming files from wherever they are connected anywhere in the world.

The original language of the Internet was uninviting to say the least. You needed a variety of esoteric programs (e.g., Telnet, FTP, Archie, Gopher, and so on), which were derived from the Unix operating system. You had to know the precise syntax of those programs. And, even if you were able to get what you wanted, everything was communicated in plain text (graphics and sound were not available).

The **World Wide Web (WWW)** was developed in 1991 at the European Particle Physics Laboratory (CERN) in Switzerland. It introduced a new way to connect the resources on the Internet to one another. The Web is based on the technology of **hypertext** and **hypermedia,** which link computer-based documents in nonlinear fashion. Unlike a traditional document, which is read sequentially from top to bottom, a hypertext document includes links to other documents, which can be viewed (or not) at the reader's discretion. A **link** is a line of text in a hypertext document that contains an embedded Internet address and other information.

When you select a link, it directs a program called a **browser** to connect to the site specified by the link and retrieve the document identified in the link. The first browsers were restricted to text that followed the links from one document to another, even if the documents were on different computers. As users began to create other document types (images, sound, and video), the text browsers evolved naturally into a more powerful GUI tool. These browsers run on your PC, and request services from an Internet host on your campus network. The host is known as the **Web server;** the program that runs on your PC is called the **client.**

Assume, for example, that you are reading a hypertext document about the federal budget deficit. You come to a reference to the Concord Coalition, a nonpartisan organization dedicated to eliminating the deficit. Rather than finishing the original text, you select a link and jump to the Concord Coalition **home page,** or starting point on the Web, shown in Figure 3.1a. From there you tour the site by clicking on any interesting link you see. We clicked on the **Information** link, then followed a few more links to the page shown in Figure 3.1b. You can click the **Back button** at any time to go back to previous pages to follow other links.

Hypermedia is similar in concept to hypertext except that it provides links to graphic, sound, and video files in addition to text files. Hypertext and hypermedia links may be to documents on the same computer or to files stored on another computer somewhere else on the World Wide Web. As the user, you don't need to know or care where the documents are physically located.

Mosaic was the first Windows-based Web browser. Developed at the National Center for Supercomputing Applications at the University of Illinois at Urbana-Champaign, NCSA, it introduced point-and-click navigation to the Web. Today there are many different browsers from which to choose, but all offer the

Links

Click to go back to previous page

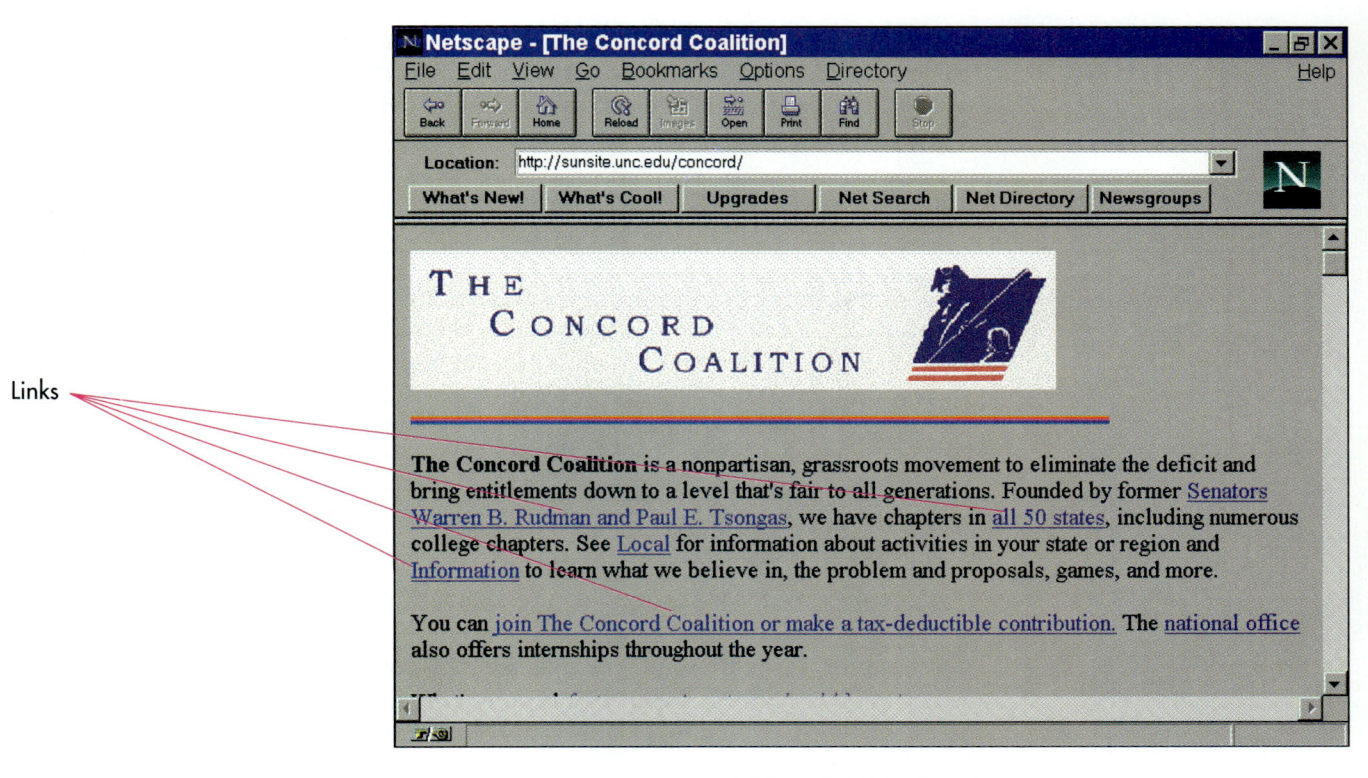

(a) Concord Coalition Home Page

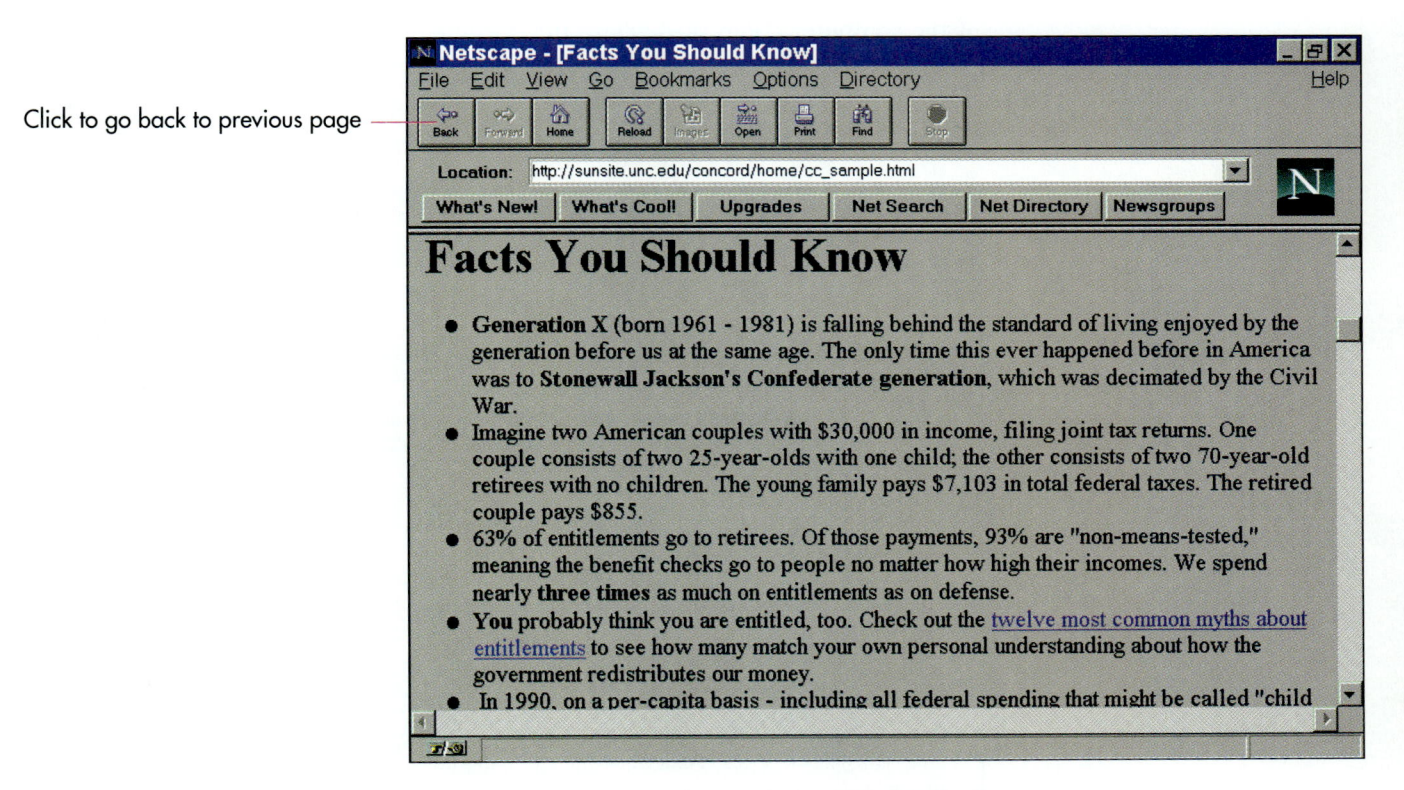

(b) Concord Coalition Fact Page

FIGURE 3.1   The Concord Coalition

FINDING THINGS ON THE WORLD WIDE WEB

same basic capabilities. We have chosen to focus on **Netscape Navigator**, commonly called **Netscape,** a newer and more powerful client than Mosaic and currently the market leader in browser programs. The discussion, however, is sufficiently general to apply to other programs.

NETSCAPE

A Windows-based browser is easy to use because it shares the common user interface and consistent command structure present in every Windows application. Figure 3.2 displays a **Netscape** screen, which contains several familiar elements. These include the title bar, Minimize, Maximize (or Restore), and Close buttons. Commands are executed from pull-down menus or from command buttons that appear under the menu bar. A vertical and/or horizontal scroll bar appears if the entire document is not visible at one time. The title bar displays the name of the document you are currently viewing.

The Uniform Resource Locator (URL)

The location (or address) of the document appears in the **location text box** and is known as a **Uniform Resource Locator** (URL). The URL is the primary means of navigating the Web, as it indicates the **Web site** (computer) from which you have requested a document. Change the URL (we describe how in the next section) and you jump to a different document.

A URL consists of several parts: the method of access, the Internet address of the computer (Web site) where the document is located, the path in the direc-

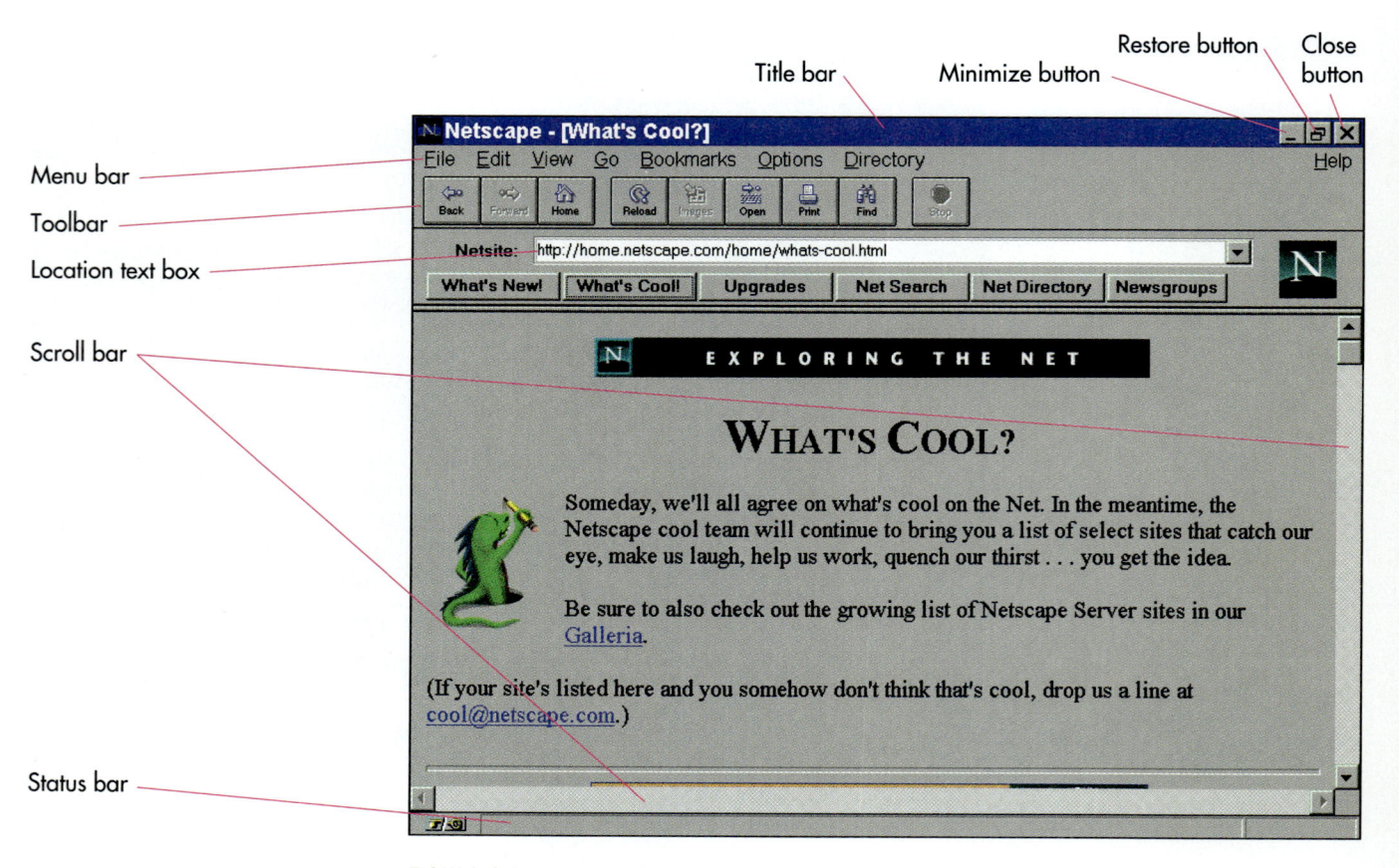

FIGURE 3.2   Netscape Screen

88   EXPLORING THE INTERNET

tory structure on the Web server to that document (if any), and the file name. For example:

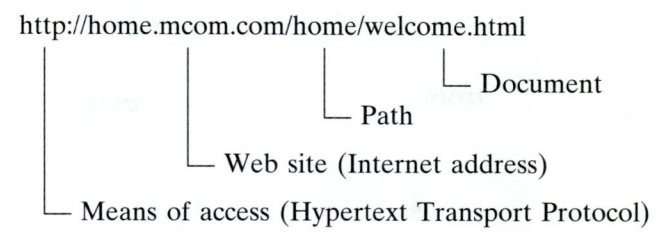

```
http://home.mcom.com/home/welcome.html
     │         │          │       │
     │         │          │       └─ Document
     │         │          └─ Path
     │         └─ Web site (Internet address)
     └─ Means of access (Hypertext Transport Protocol)
```

To go to a particular site, enter its URL through the **Open Location command** in the File menu or type the URL directly in the Location text box, press Enter, and off you go. Once you arrive at a site, click the **hyperlinks** (underlined items) that interest you, which in turn will take you to other documents at that site (or even at a different site). The resources on the Web are connected in such a way that you need not be concerned with where (on which computer) the linked document is located.

Hypertext Transport Protocol (HTTP)

Consider, for example, the hypermedia document in Figure 3.3. We began by choosing a Web site and entering its URL (http://www.yahoo.com), shown in Figure 3.3a. Most of the time, however, you don't even have to enter the URL, because Netscape is constantly suggesting sites to explore. (And those sites may suggest other sites. Yes, it helps to know various sites on the Web, and we suggest several in Appendix D.). The Yahoo site consists of a searchable index of Web resources and is a good starting point for any Web exploration.

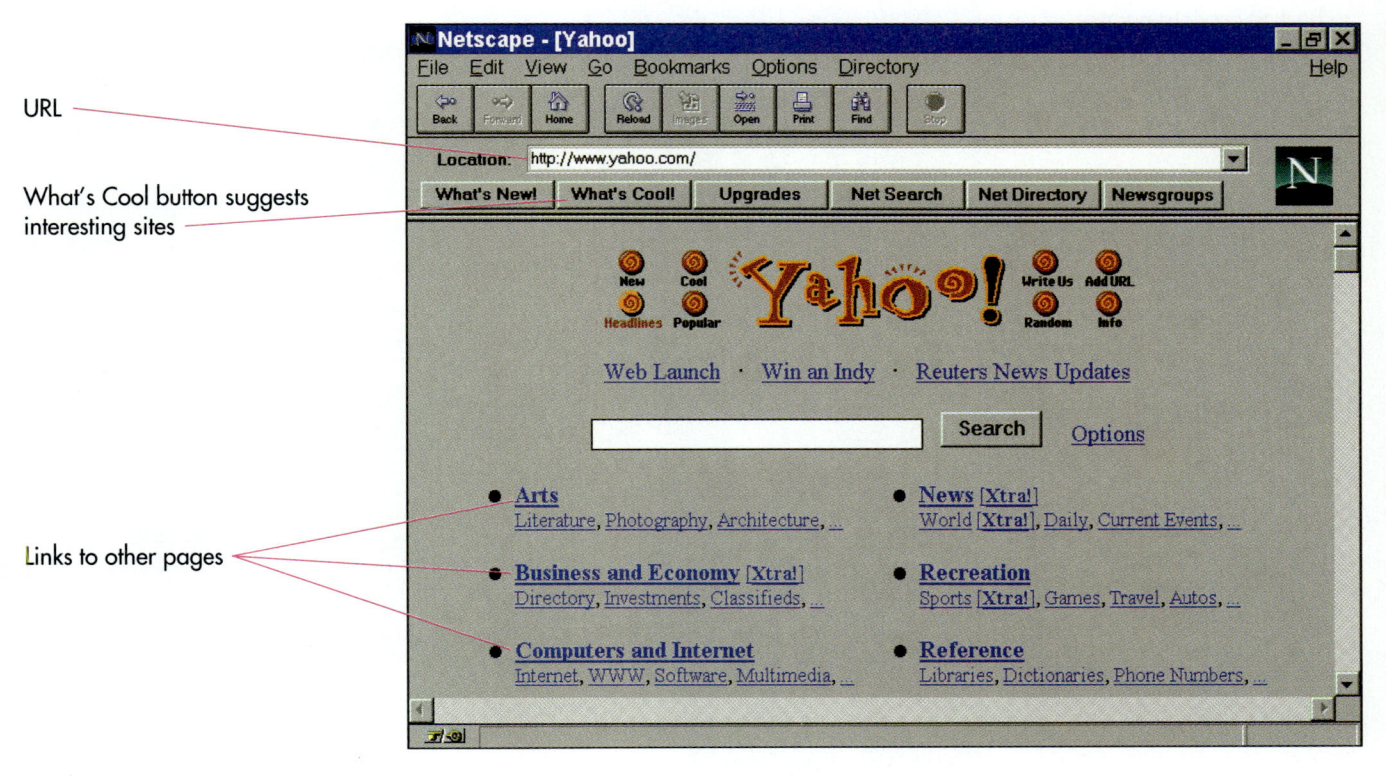

(a) The Yahoo Home Page

FIGURE 3.3 Yahoo

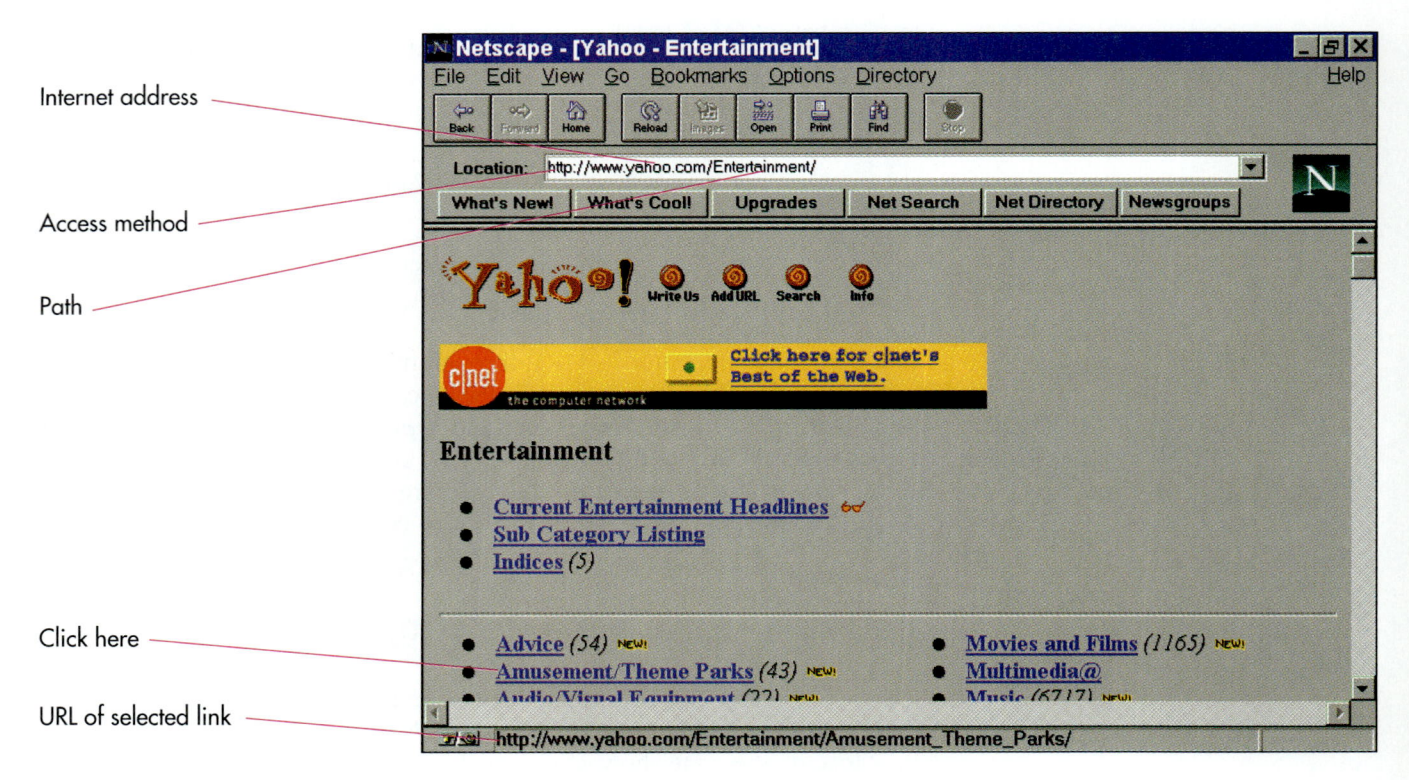

(b) The Yahoo Entertainment Page

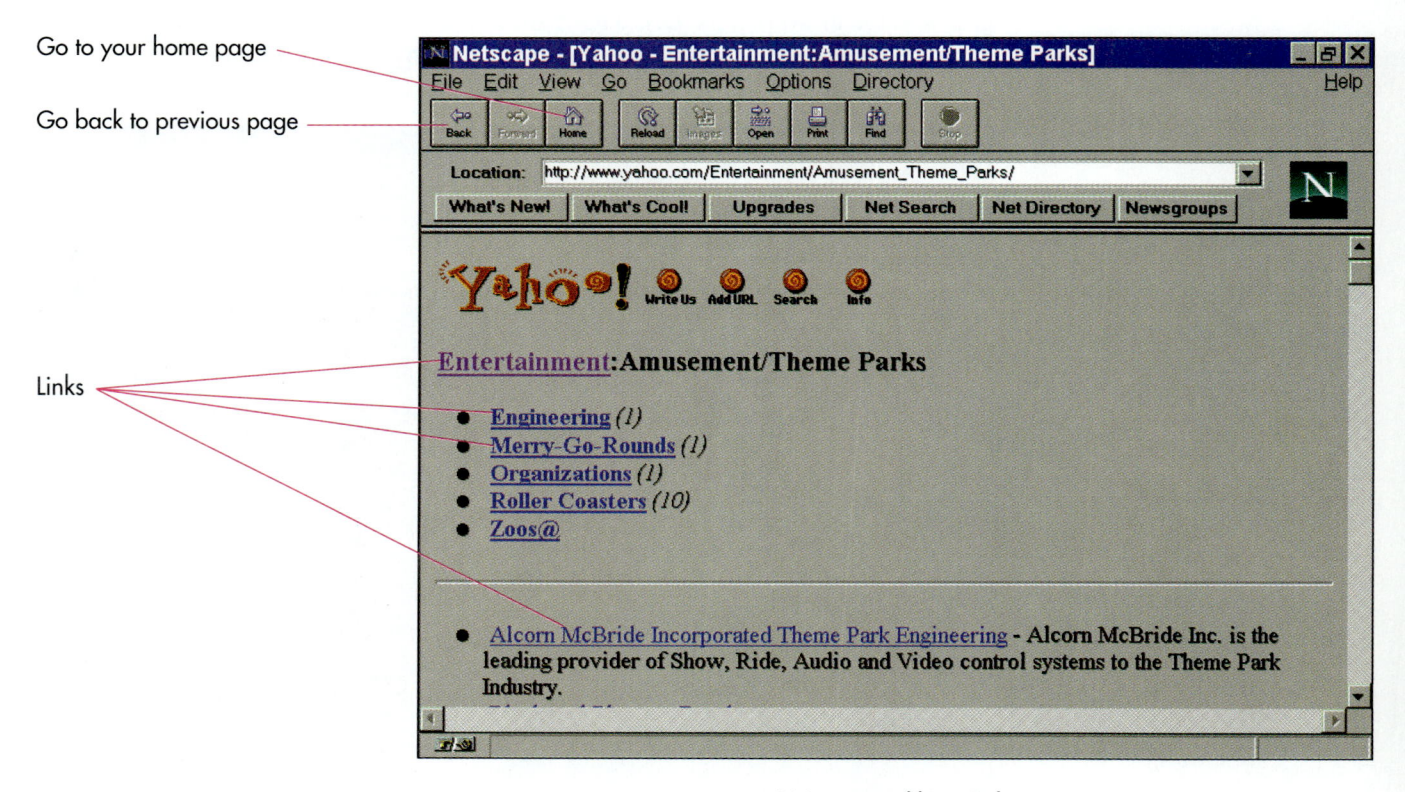

(c) Amusement/Theme Parks

FIGURE 3.3 Yahoo (continued)

90 EXPLORING THE INTERNET

The method of access to retrieve hypertext and hypermedia documents is called **HTTP (Hypertext Transport Protocol).** Therefore the http:// delimiter precedes the Internet address in the URL of all hypertext documents. (Not all documents cataloged on the Web are retrieved using HTTP. You will learn more about other types of Web documents in Chapter 4.)

Once you arrive at a home page (e.g., Figure 3.3a), click any link that interests you. We scrolled down and clicked on **Entertainment,** which took us to the document in Figure 3.3b. (The URL in the location text box changes automatically to reflect the location of the new document.) From there we clicked **Amusement/Theme Parks,** which took us to the document in Figure 3.3c. There is no beginning (other than the starting point or home page) and no end. You simply read a hypermedia document in any way that makes sense to you, jumping to explore whatever topic you want to see next.

The World Wide Web is a "living document" that is constantly changing. The information at many sites is updated daily, and you never know just what you will find. We doubt, for example, that you will see the same list of links if you access the Entertainment home page shown in Figure 3.3b, because new information is always being added.

Your exploration of the World Wide Web is limited only by your imagination. The Netscape What's Cool button suggests several interesting sites and is an excellent place to begin your exploration. Alternatively, you may begin with any of the sites listed in Appendix D.

IT'S STILL UNDER DEVELOPMENT

The World Wide Web is under constant development, so you shouldn't be surprised if it doesn't always work as you expect. There will be times when you will be unable to connect to a specific site because its developer has temporarily taken it offline, or because there are too many other users already at the site. Be patient and try again, or try another site. It is worth the wait!

Hypertext Markup Language (HTML)

Web documents containing hyperlinks are written using **HTML (Hypertext Markup Language),** an easy-to-learn language that controls the formatting of Web documents. An HTML document contains *tags* that describe how to display the text, hyperlinks, and multimedia elements within the document. The letters HTML appear at the end of many URL addresses to indicate that the link points to this type of document.

Figure 3.4 shows the Entertainment home page (found in Figure 3.3b) as it looks in HTML. The various tags, the commands between the angled brackets (< >), determine how the document will be displayed. Heading styles, bulleted and numbered lists, graphics, and many other features that give Web documents their look and feel can be defined by HTML tags.

You will want to learn about HTML to create your own home page if the capability to link one to your college or university's home page is offered at your school. The Web contains many online references to learn more about creating documents using HTML. An end-of-chapter exercise points you in the right direction in cyberspace to find these sites. In addition, Chapter 7 presents an overview of frequently used commands and guides you in setting up a simple home page.

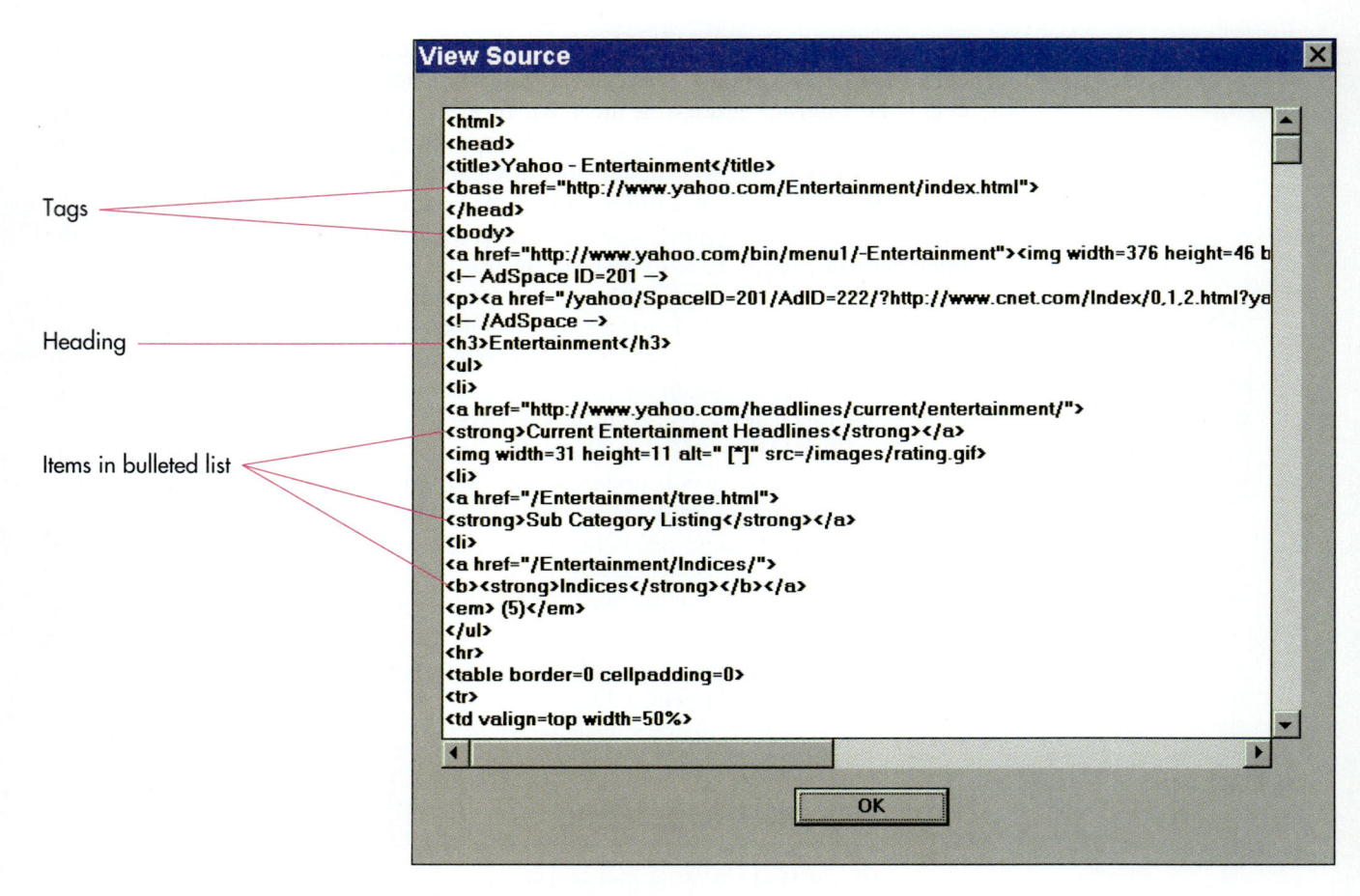

FIGURE 3.4 The Entertainment Page in HTML

Saving and Printing Web Documents

Any document you retrieve from the Web may be printed and/or saved for use at a later time. Printing simply requires you to select the Print command from the File menu as you would in any other Windows application. The Save command is generally the same as in any other Windows application. You can specify the destination drive and directory for the file you are retrieving. However, you may occasionally find documents that are in a format with which Netscape is unfamiliar or cannot display. Netscape will display a message similar to the one shown in Figure 3.5 if you try to save a document that it cannot, for some reason, automatically download to your computer.

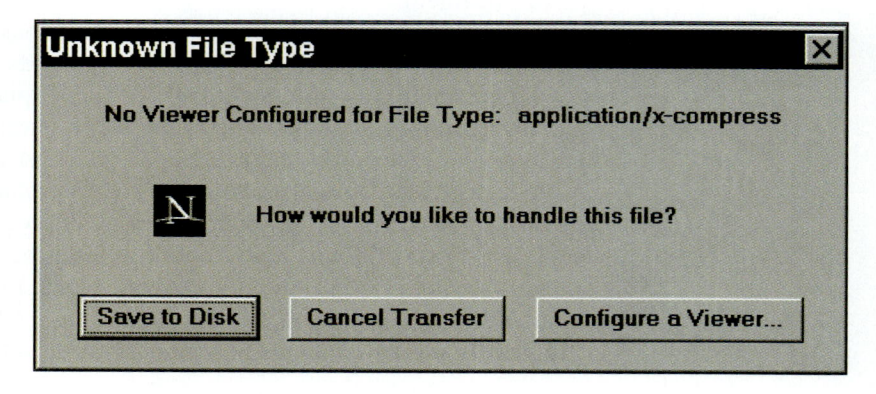

FIGURE 3.5 A Netscape Error Message

92 EXPLORING THE INTERNET

Bookmarks

Suppose you are browsing through a magazine at the library and find an interesting article you don't have time to read. You put the magazine down, then head off to class, intending to come back and finish it later. By the time you really return to the library, you've forgotten where you saw the article. Similarly, while surfing the Net you will find many interesting sites you will want to visit again, but because your travels are done with hyperlinks, it is often difficult to retrace your steps to a specific URL. A **bookmark** lets you store a URL so you can recall it at a later time. Figure 3.6 shows the bookmarks set up on the author's PC. Clicking on a bookmark links you directly to the document. Adding bookmarks, as you will discover in the following hands-on exercise, simply requires a few clicks with the mouse.

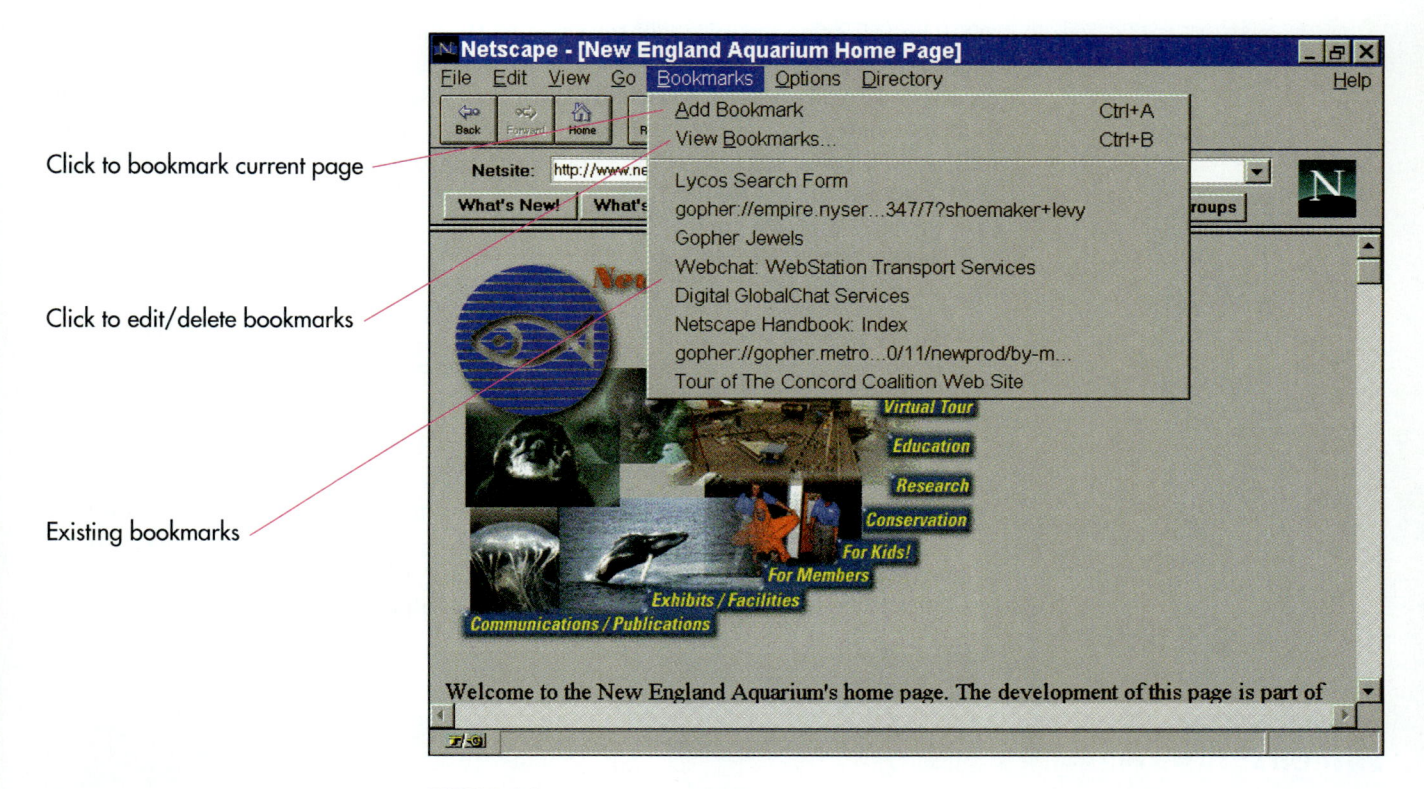

FIGURE 3.6 Netscape Bookmarks

THE NEW NETSCAPE: ALL THIS AND JAVA TOO

By the time you read this book, a new version of Netscape Navigator will be available (but possibly not yet installed at your site). It is projected to have in-line viewers that will allow you to load and run movie, sound, and audio files without requiring additional software (if your PC has suitable hardware). It is also expected to have more sophisticated and powerful HTML capabilities. In addition, the new version will allow you to use Java applets, small applications using Sun Microsystems' new programming language for animated home pages, Java. Visit Netscape's home page, at http://home.netscape.com, for the most current information about the new release.

> **http://www.vcn.com/server/help.html**
>
> Visionary Communications, located in Wyoming, has put up a very complete site with all sorts of introductory information about the Internet and its resources. Spend some time here if you can.

LEARNING BY DOING

The World Wide Web cannot really be appreciated until you experience it yourself. The following exercise will take you to Washington, DC, to explore Congress and learn more about its workings. The exercise is written for Netscape, but it can be applied to Mosaic or any other Windows-based browser. It is the document (and associated URL) that is important rather than the particular browser. We suggest a specific starting point (Thomas, the Congressional home page, named after Thomas Jefferson, the third President of the United States), and a progression through that document. You can, however, start with any other home page, and choose any links you want. Going from one document or link to the next is what "surfing the Net" is all about. Bon voyage!

> ### GETTING READY TO SURF THE NET
>
> Using PC-based clients such as Mosaic and Netscape requires that the browser software be loaded on the PC you are using. Often the software must be customized specifically for your use—to save your bookmarks, for instance. Ask your instructor, lab assistant, or system administrator for the instructions to set up your browser in your campus computing environment.

HANDS-ON EXERCISE 1

Surfing the Net

Objective: To use Netscape Navigator (or another GUI browser) to surf the Net. Use Figure 3.7 as a guide in the exercise.

STEP 1: Load Netscape
- Find the appropriate program group or list that allows you to access your Internet software. (See your instructor or lab assistant for help.)
- Double click the **Netscape icon.** Most computing centers configure Netscape to display the college or university home page at start-up. If this is not the case, you will probably see the Netscape Corporation home page shown in Figure 3.7a when you start Netscape.

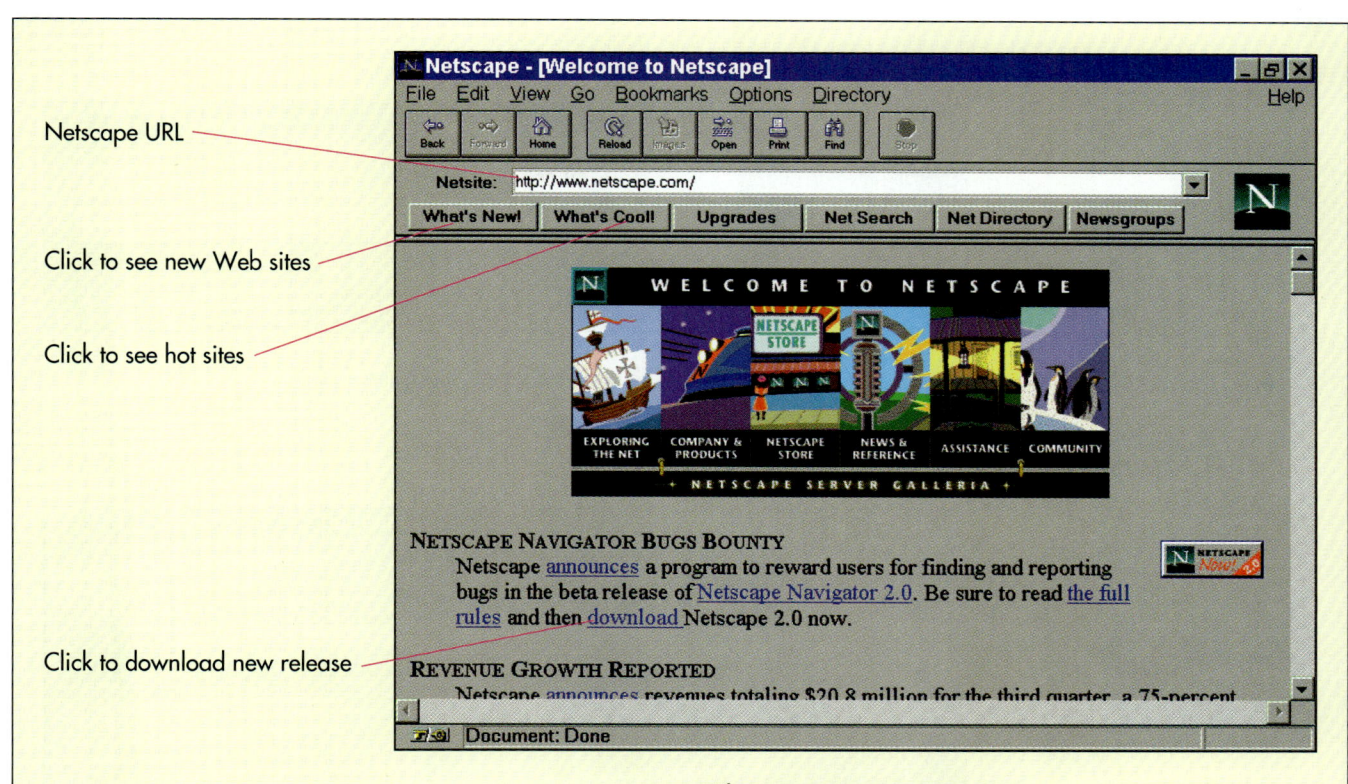

Netscape URL

Click to see new Web sites

Click to see hot sites

Click to download new release

(a) The Netscape Corporation Home Page

FIGURE 3.7 Hands-on Exercise 1

> **WHAT'S COOL**
>
> The What's Cool button is an excellent place to begin. The list of suggested sites changes every day, and you never know what you will find, but the results are always interesting. Click the button and see for yourself.

STEP 2: Visit Congress

➤ Pull down the **File menu.** Click the **Open button.** Type the name of the Web site you want to explore—for example, **http://thomas.loc.gov** as shown in the dialog box in Figure 3.7b. Press **Enter.**

➤ You should see the home page in Figure 3.7c (assuming that it hasn't changed since we did the exercise). If you are unable to get to this site:

- Pull down the **File menu,** click **Open URL,** and re-enter the URL shown in Figure 3.7b. You must type the address exactly as it appears in the figure (case matters). Press **Enter.**

- If you are still unable to get to the site, it may be because it is not available due to technical problems or because there are too many visitors already at the site. Click the **What's Cool button** and select a different site to explore.

➤ Scroll down and click the **hyperlink** to the <u>**hot bills under Congressional consideration this week.**</u>

FINDING THINGS ON THE WORLD WIDE WEB   **95**

Thomas URL

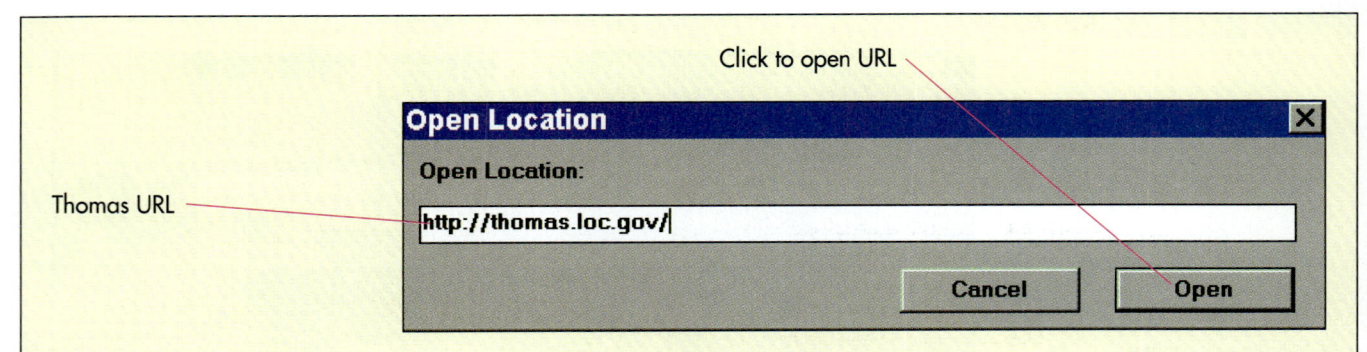

Click to open URL

(b) The Open Location Dialog Box

Click to stop data transfer

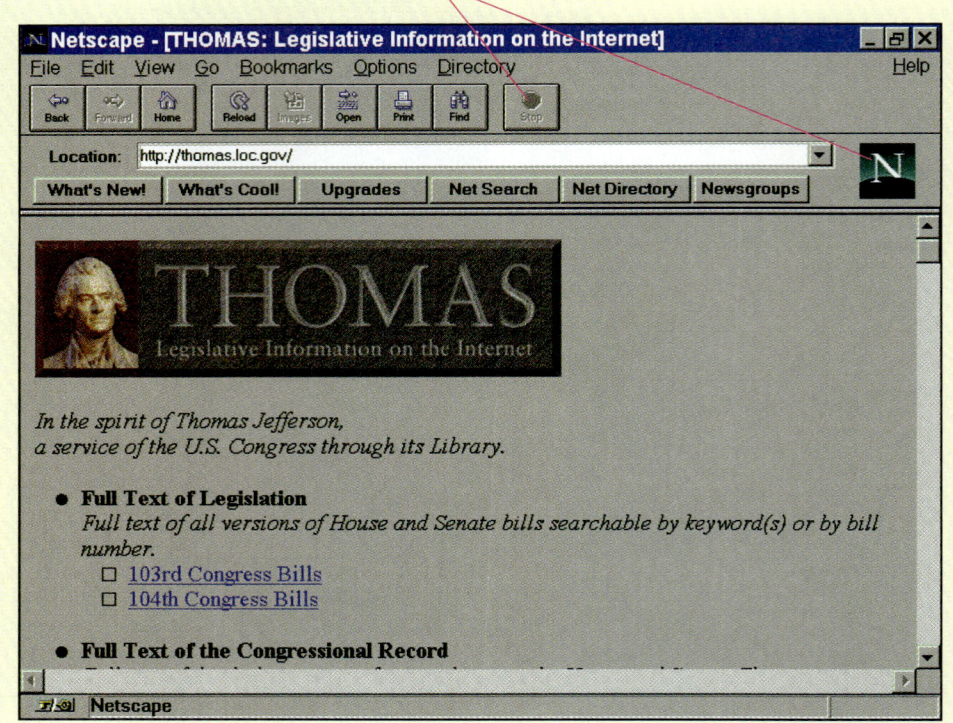

(c) Thomas Jefferson Home Page

FIGURE 3.7   Hands-on Exercise 1 (continued)

THE FLASHING LOGO

The Netscape logo (the capital N) in the upper-right-hand corner of the Netscape window indicates the status of a Netscape search. The icon will be animated when Netscape is connecting to a URL, searching for a document, or otherwise involved in data transfer. The icon will be still otherwise. You can click the logo at any time to cancel a search or data transfer; that is, just click the flashing "N" (or the Stop button), and the data transfer will be terminated.

96   EXPLORING THE INTERNET

STEP 3: Navigate through Thomas

▶ You should see the screen in Figure 3.7d. Continue to browse through the Congressional Web pages by clicking on hyperlinks of interest to you to get a feeling for the information contained at this site. You can get immediate information about what's happening in Washington in a way never before possible by periodically exploring the Congressional site. (Now, what will you do with the information?)

▶ Click the **Back button** to return to the previous screen. Notice that when you go back to a previous site, the links you have already visited are displayed in a different color, to indicate you have visited the site before.

THE SAVE COMMAND

You can save many Web documents as files on your local PC or network drive. Simply click the File Save command, and save as you would any Windows file. (Some files, such as those written for Macs, cannot be saved on a Windows-based PC. Others, particularly compressed files, can be saved, but you cannot use them unless you have the software necessary to uncompress them.)

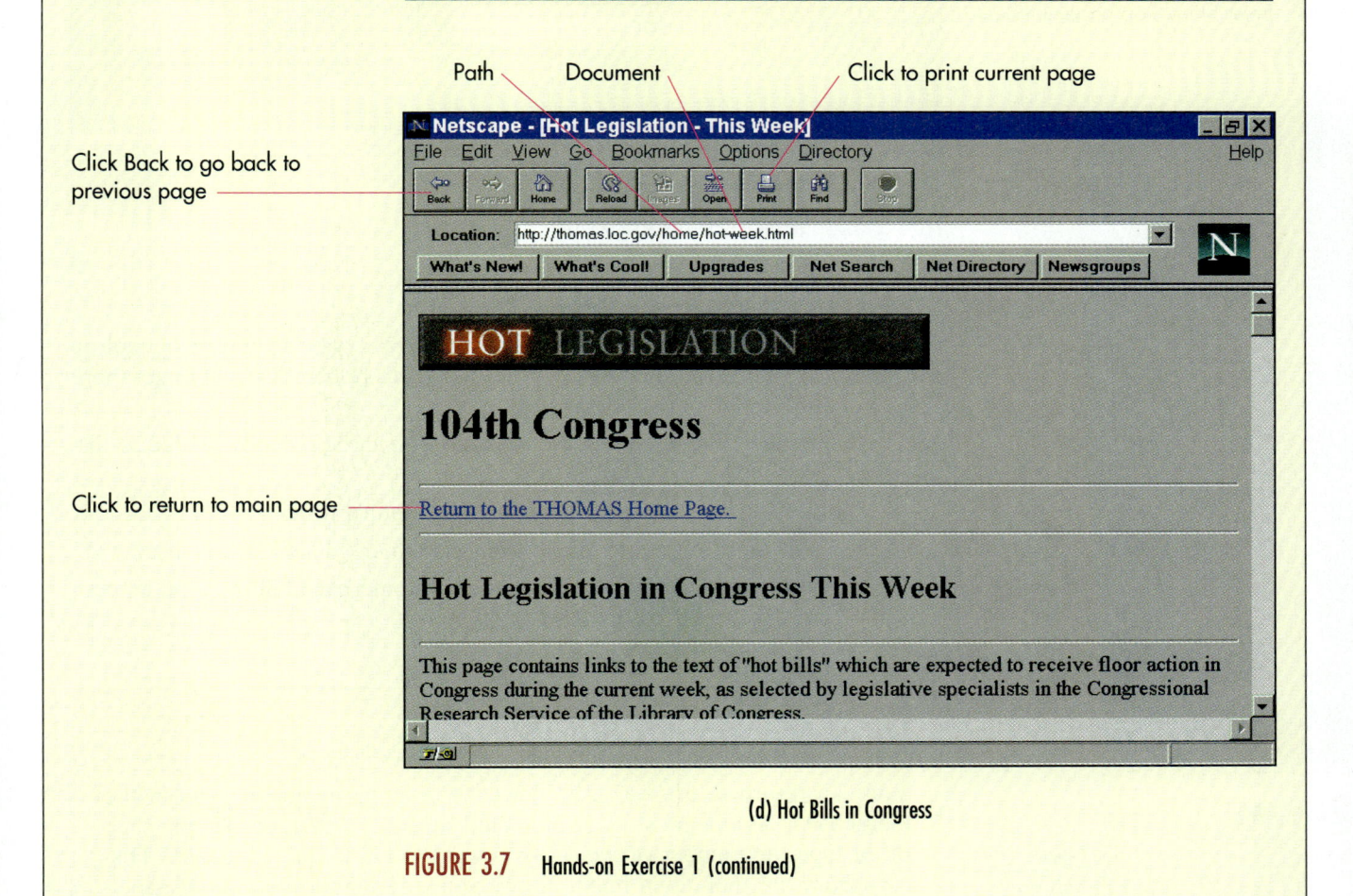

(d) Hot Bills in Congress

FIGURE 3.7 Hands-on Exercise 1 (continued)

STEP 4: Print a Web Page

➤ At any point in your journey through Thomas, pull down the **File menu.** Click **Print** to display the dialog box in Figure 3.7e.

➤ You may select the print range and number of copies, then click **OK.**

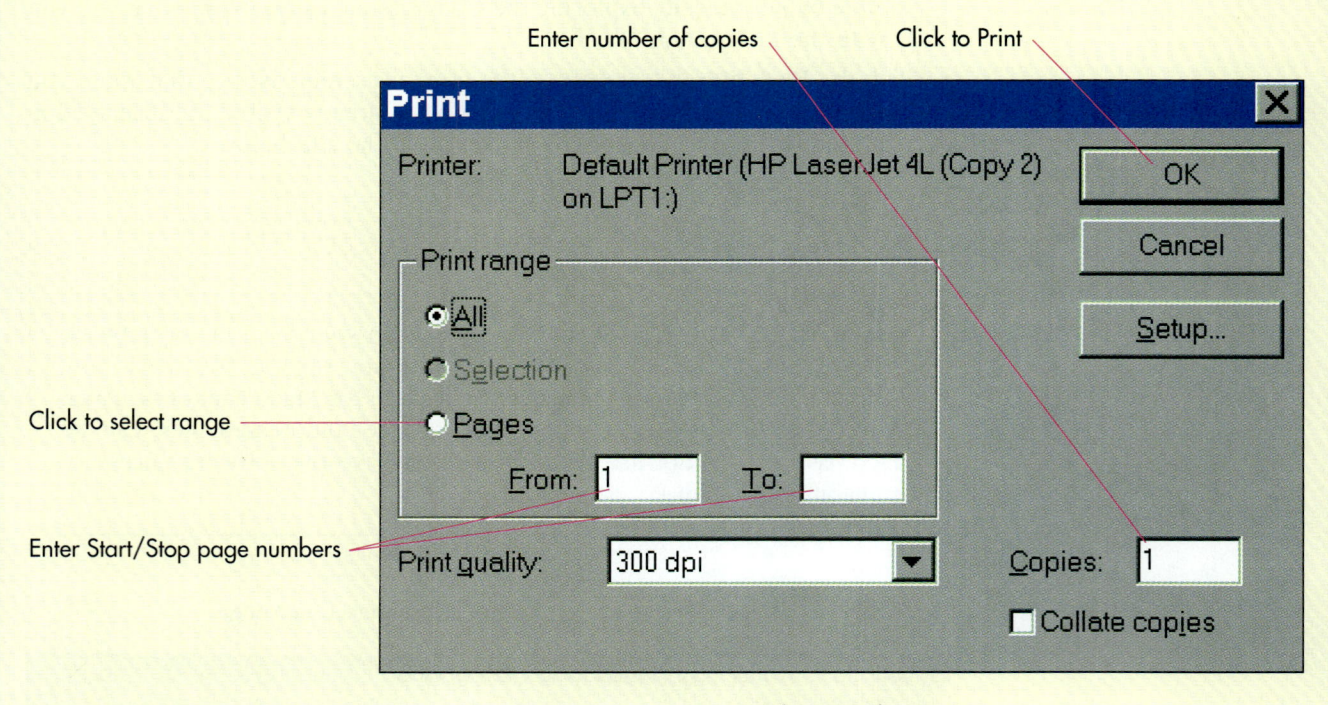

(e) The Print Dialog Box

FIGURE 3.7 Hands-on Exercise 1 (continued)

STEP 5: Link to a Web Site Using a Bookmark

➤ You will find many sites on the Web to which you want to return to explore again and again. You can do so without having to remember how to get there by creating a bookmark for the site.

- Pull down the **Go menu.** A list of sites you have recently visited is displayed, as shown in Figure 3.7f.
- Click the Thomas **Hot Legislation page** to return to it.
- Pull down the **Bookmarks menu.** The Bookmark dialog box is displayed.
- Click **Add Bookmark.** The Congressional home page will now be accessible from the bookmark list by a simple click.

THE GO AND VIEW HISTORY COMMANDS

You can return to a previously viewed Web page by clicking Go in the menu bar. The nine most recently visited sites are numbered. Simply click on or type the number of the site you want to go to. Selecting View History from the pull-down menu allows you to create a bookmark associated with one of the listed sites, without having to go back to the site.

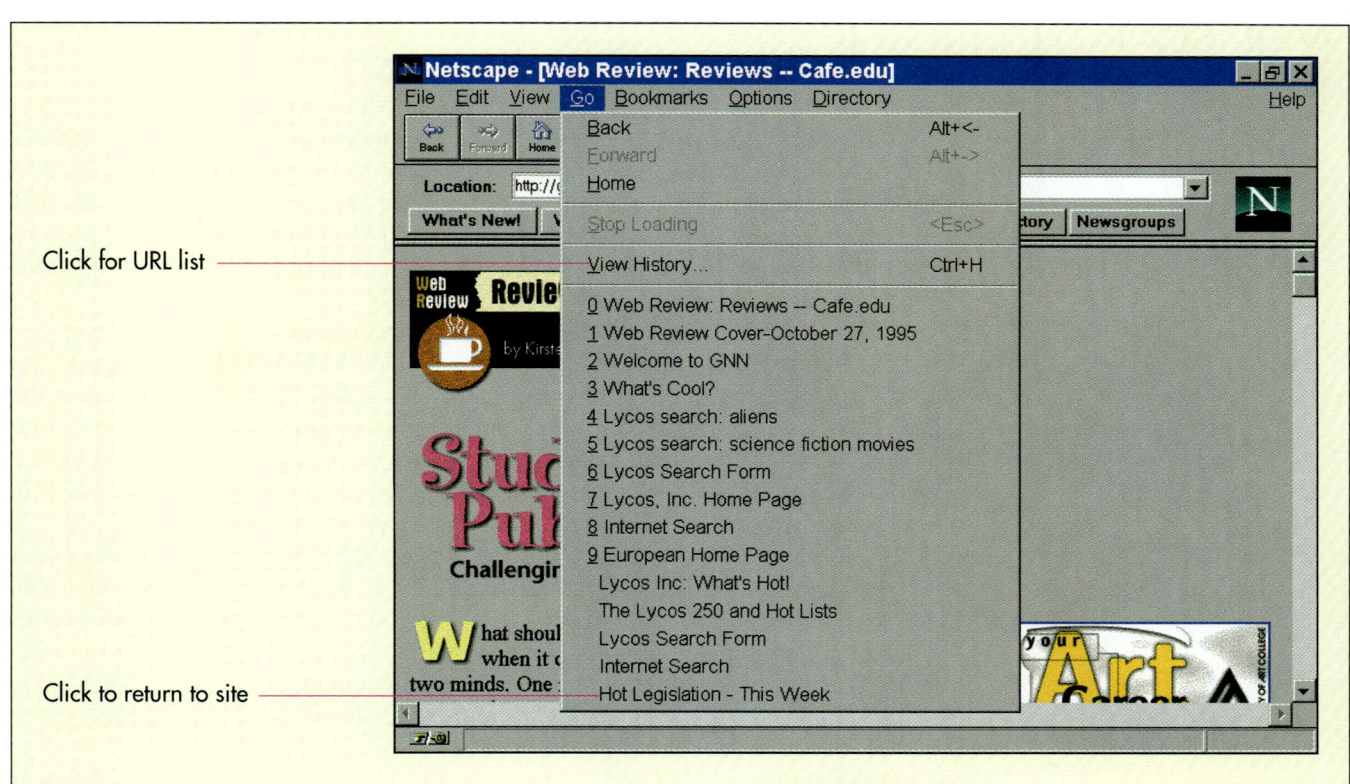

(f) The Go Pull-Down Menu

FIGURE 3.7 Hands-on Exercise 1 (continued)

- Click **Home** to return to your college's home page.
- Select the **View Bookmarks** on the **Bookmarks menu,** then click the Thomas URL, which you should now see in the bookmark list. You should link directly to the Thomas page you just bookmarked.

STEP 6: Surf the Net

➤ Choose different sites to explore:
  - Click the **What's Cool button** to explore the current cool sites. We don't know what you will find, but you can expect something interesting.
  - Choose a specific site and enter its URL.
➤ Click the hyperlinks that interest you, which in turn will take you to other documents at that site (or even at a different site). Save or print the documents that you find as you see fit.

SET A TIME LIMIT

We warn you that it's addictive, and that once you start "surfing the Net," it is difficult to stop. We suggest, therefore, that you set a time limit before you begin, and that you stick to it when the time has expired. Tomorrow is another day with new places to explore.

WEB SEARCH ENGINES

Browsing is fun, but as we warned you in the previous tip, it can be addictive and quite time consuming. Fortunately, a more productive way to search for specific topics on the Web is available. You can use one of many Web *search engines,* programs that handle queries, to enter search criteria and locate Web resources. The easiest way to access Web search engines is directly from your browser, or use one of the URLs shown in Table 3.1, which contains a list of some of the best search engines available at time of publication.

Clicking the Net Search button on the Netscape window brings up the screen shown in Figure 3.8a. This document contains links to several search engines but only the InfoSeek engine is visible in Figure 3.8a. Click the text box to enter the topic you are searching for (e.g., rock music hall of fame), click the Search button, then wait as the search takes place. Figure 3.8b displays the results of the search, which returns 100 documents. Click on any of the links and you move to the associated page. Research was never this easy!

If you scroll farther down in the Net Search window, you will see the **Lycos** search engine link, which you will use in the following hands-on exercise. The Lycos *search form,* shown in Figure 3.8c, allows you to specify the number of terms in your query, and how many **hits,** or documents, you want to see out of the total found. (Web queries can return thousands of documents, so it is a good idea to limit the number of hits you request.) Figure 3.8d shows the search results, which will vary if a different search engine is used.

Originally developed and operated by Carnegie-Mellon University, Lycos is now a commercial venture supported by advertising revenue generated by its site and licensing fees from its software. It maintains a catalog of Web sites; as of November 1995 it contained references to 7.98 million documents. Special programs called *spiders* automatically crawl the Web each day searching for new pages to add to the catalog, which indexes more than 91% of the Web. (The name Lycos comes from the first five letters of the Latin name for Wolf Spider.)

WHO IS PAYING THE PHONE BILL?

New users on the Web are frequently concerned about running up a huge phone charge on their Internet account as they link to all these far-off sites. Your college or university is indeed paying line charges. However, they are billed at a straight monthly rate, regardless of how many times you surf the Net, or where you link to. So relax, fasten your seat belt, and go!

TABLE 3.1 Web Search Engines

Site	URL
Yahoo	http://www.yahoo.com
Lycos	http://www.lycos.com
WebCrawler	http://webcrawler.com
World Wide Web Worm	http://wwww.cs.colorado.edu/wwww
InfoSeek	http://www.infoseek.com
OpenText	http://www.opentext.com

Search text

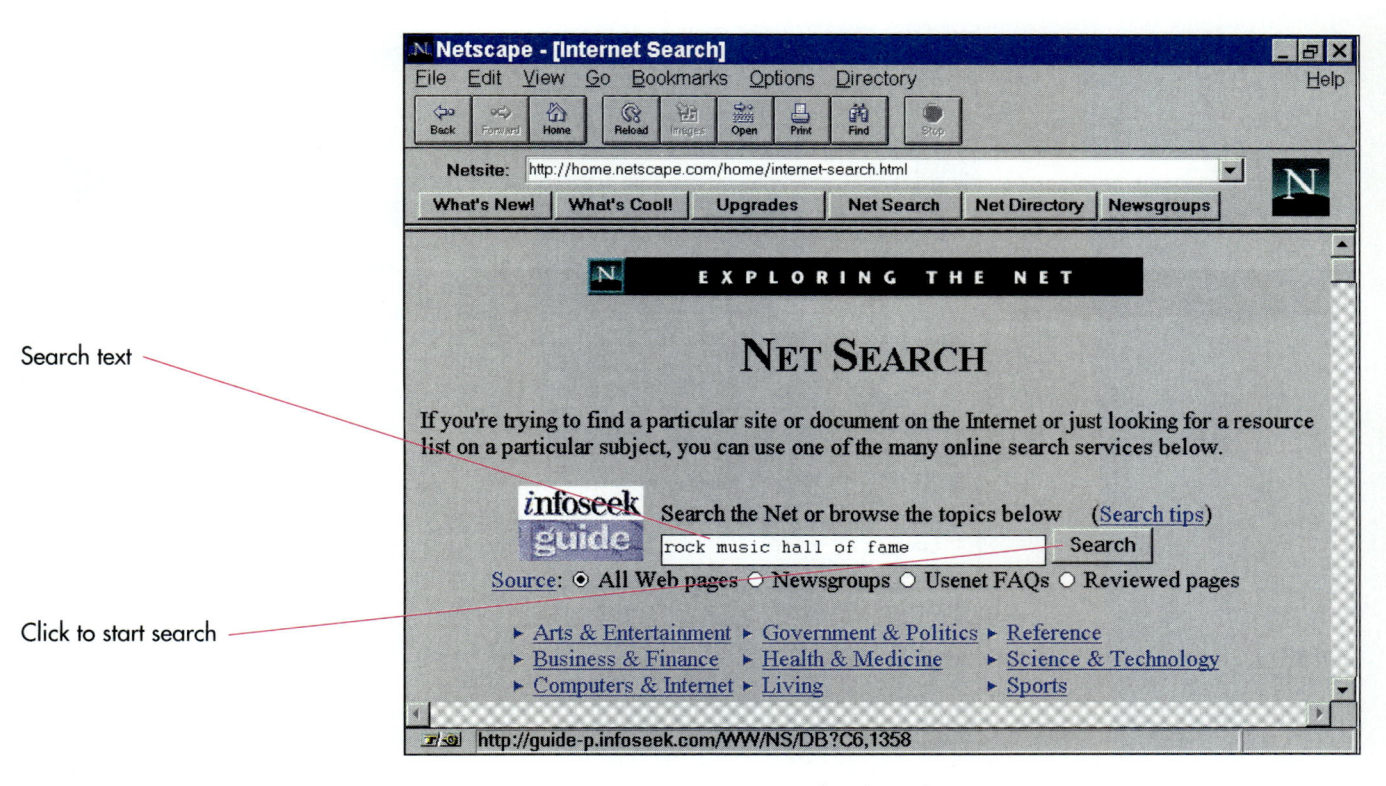

Click to start search

(a) InfoSeek Search Engine

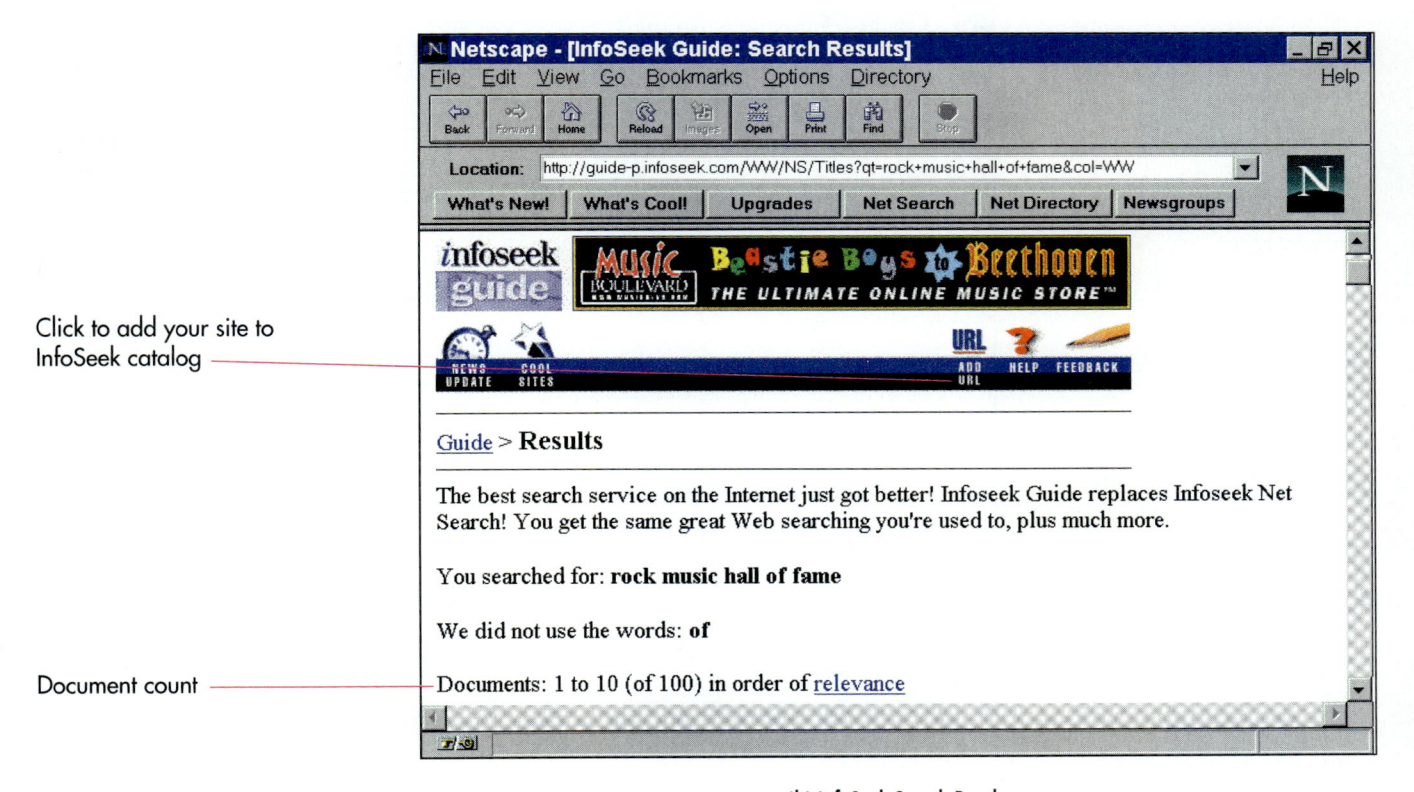

Click to add your site to InfoSeek catalog

Document count

(b) InfoSeek Search Results

FIGURE 3.8 Internet Search Engines

FINDING THINGS ON THE WORLD WIDE WEB

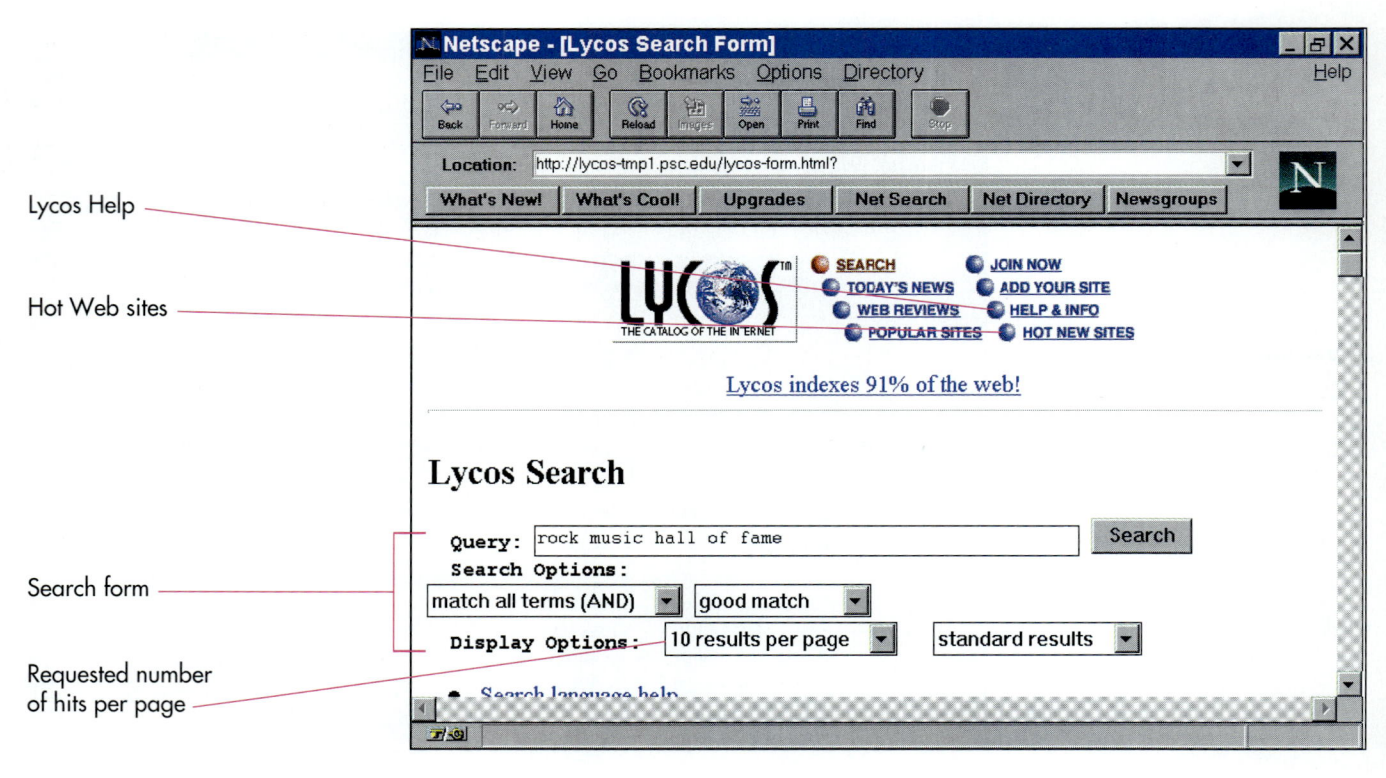

Lycos Help

Hot Web sites

Search form

Requested number of hits per page

(c) Lycos Search Form

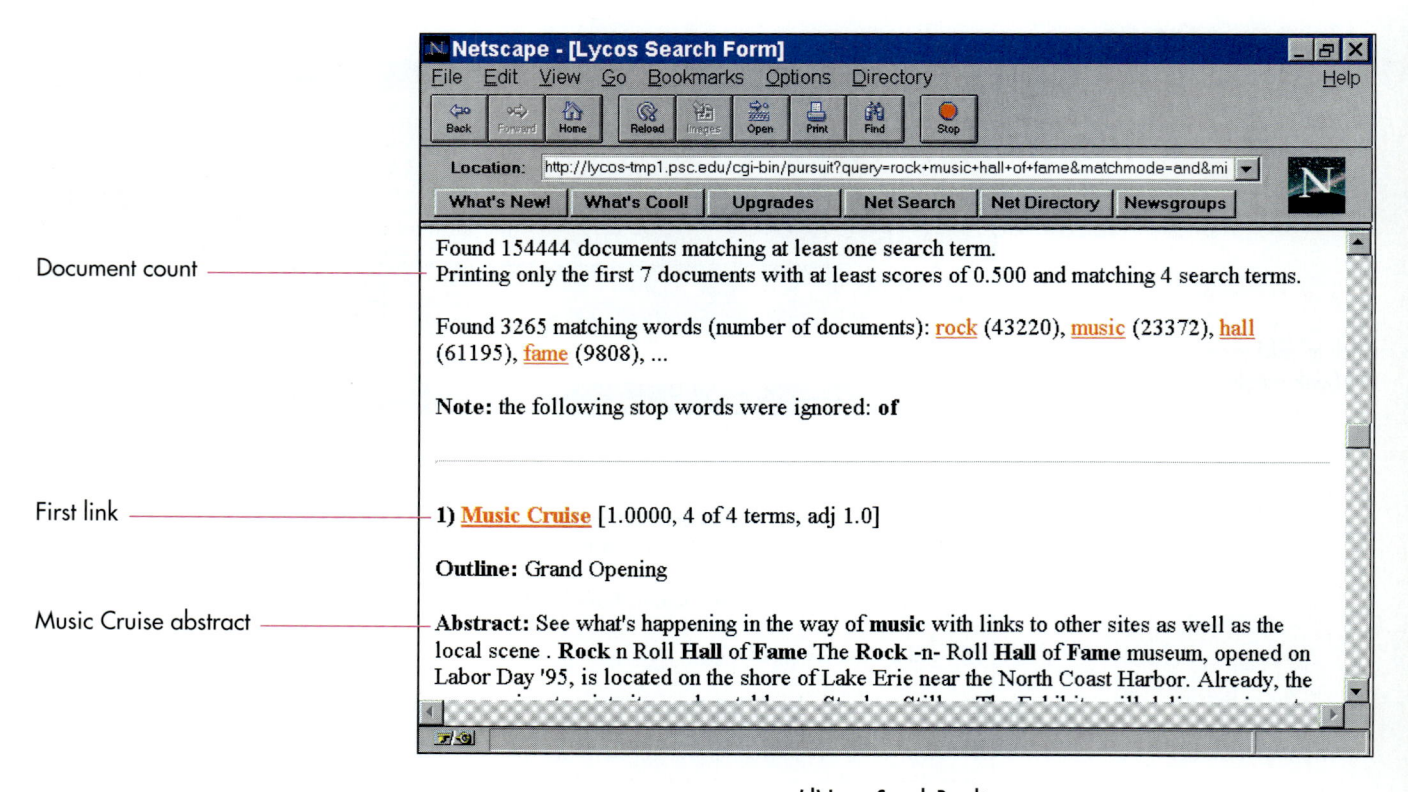

Document count

First link

Music Cruise abstract

Found 154444 documents matching at least one search term.
Printing only the first 7 documents with at least scores of 0.500 and matching 4 search terms.

Found 3265 matching words (number of documents): rock (43220), music (23372), hall (61195), fame (9808), ...

Note: the following stop words were ignored: of

1) **Music Cruise** [1.0000, 4 of 4 terms, adj 1.0]

Outline: Grand Opening

Abstract: See what's happening in the way of **music** with links to other sites as well as the local scene. **Rock** n Roll **Hall** of **Fame** The Rock -n- Roll **Hall** of **Fame** museum, opened on Labor Day '95, is located on the shore of Lake Erie near the North Coast Harbor. Already, the

(d) Lycos Search Results

FIGURE 3.8 Internet Search Engines (continued)

102 EXPLORING THE INTERNET

These spiders also measure the popularity of the Web sites in the catalog. Lycos has developed the Lycos 250 (hot spots on the Web grouped by category) based on its data. The lists are available from the Lycos home page, so after you have finished your search, you might want to return to browse!

The WebCrawler, developed at the University of Washington, is also available from the Net Search home page. It, too, uses programs to search the Web and periodically update its URL database.

ADD YOUR HOME PAGE TO THE LYCOS CATALOG

You can add your own home page to the Lycos catalog. Go to the URL http://lycos.cs.cmu.edu/register.html#add and fill out the form. Wait a week to 10 days, then try a search on your name. You should be cataloged on the Web!

Search Rules and Techniques

The Internet, as you are by now aware, is huge and expanding exponentially. (Lycos estimates 300,000 new pages are added each week to the Web.) Each search engine has rules to help you narrow your search so you are not inundated with thousands of documents you don't want. Generally, these rules are published and available in a link from the search engine home page.

In general, the more specific your query, the better. For instance, a search on "movies" would be very broad; better to request "science fiction movies" if that is your interest. Using the WebCrawler search engine, for example, a search on "movies" yielded 4,783 documents. Searching on "science fiction movies" resulted in 391 documents, a more manageable number. The "movie" search in Lycos yielded 28,253 hits, while "science fiction movies" returned 4 hits. These discrepancies reveal another guideline for Web searches: You may want to conduct a search with more than one search engine to get the best results.

It is important that you structure any query properly. When searching on multiple terms, Netscape's default is to use OR to concatenate the terms. In the previous example this would be the same as asking the question, "Can you find any documents with the word *science,* any with the word *fiction,* or any with the word *movies*?" Obviously that would not narrow the search at all, but rather increase it threefold! Instead you will request that Netscape use AND when combining terms. The query then becomes, "Find all documents containing the three words *science, fiction,* and *movies.* All three words must be present in each document found."

Figure 3.9 illustrates the results of a search for information on "President Thomas Jefferson." Figure 3.9a shows the query as it would be entered in the WebCrawler search engine. Figure 3.9b displays the results of the search in January 1996 that found a total of 126 documents ("hits"). Note, however, that only the first 25 documents were returned according to the query in Figure 3.9a. (Your results may be different, since the Web will change between the time we conducted our search and the time you do your research.)

Figures 3.9c and 3.9d show the same query and results for the Yahoo engine, which returns only four hits. The difference is due to the search techniques that are used by the various engines. It is important, therefore, to become familiar with multiple search engines if you intend to do serious research on the Web.

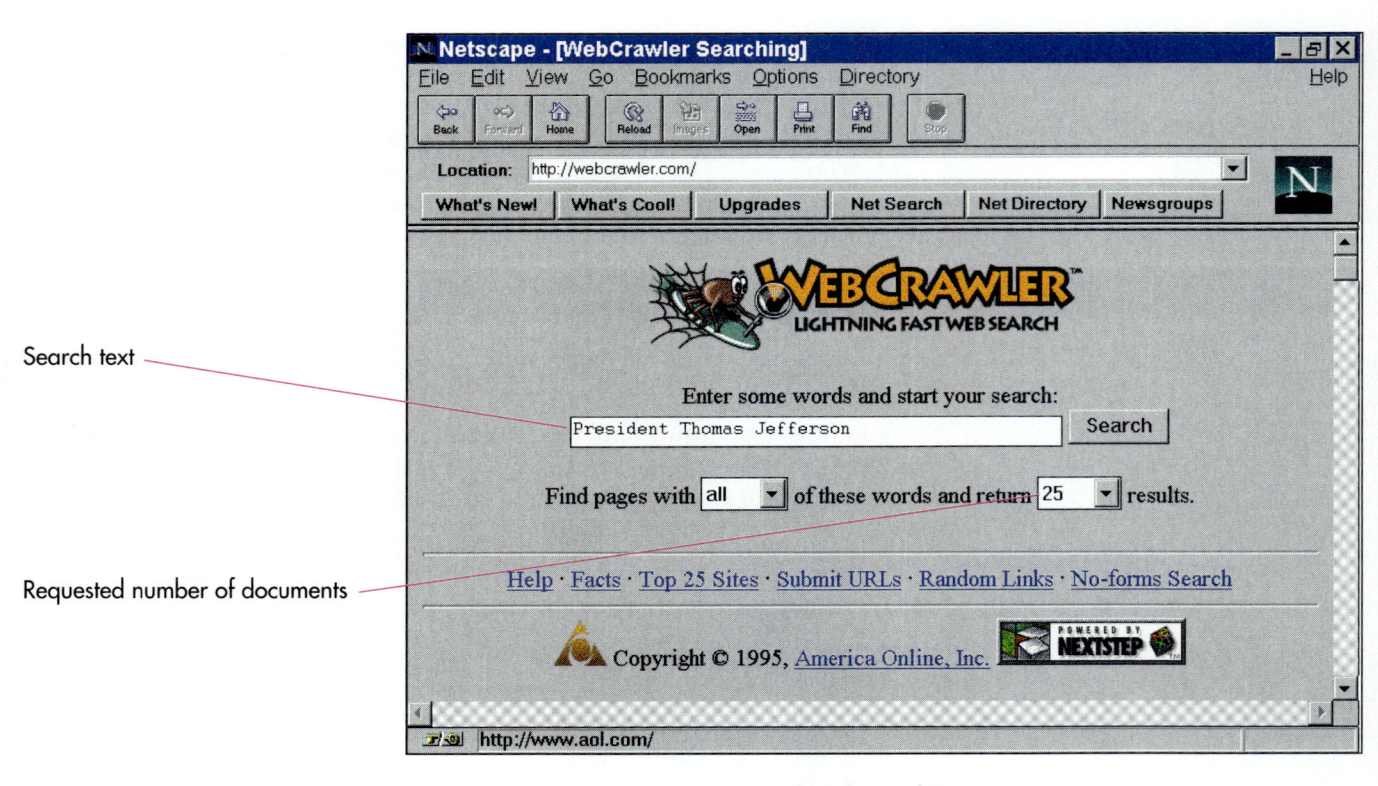

(a) WebCrawler Search Parameters

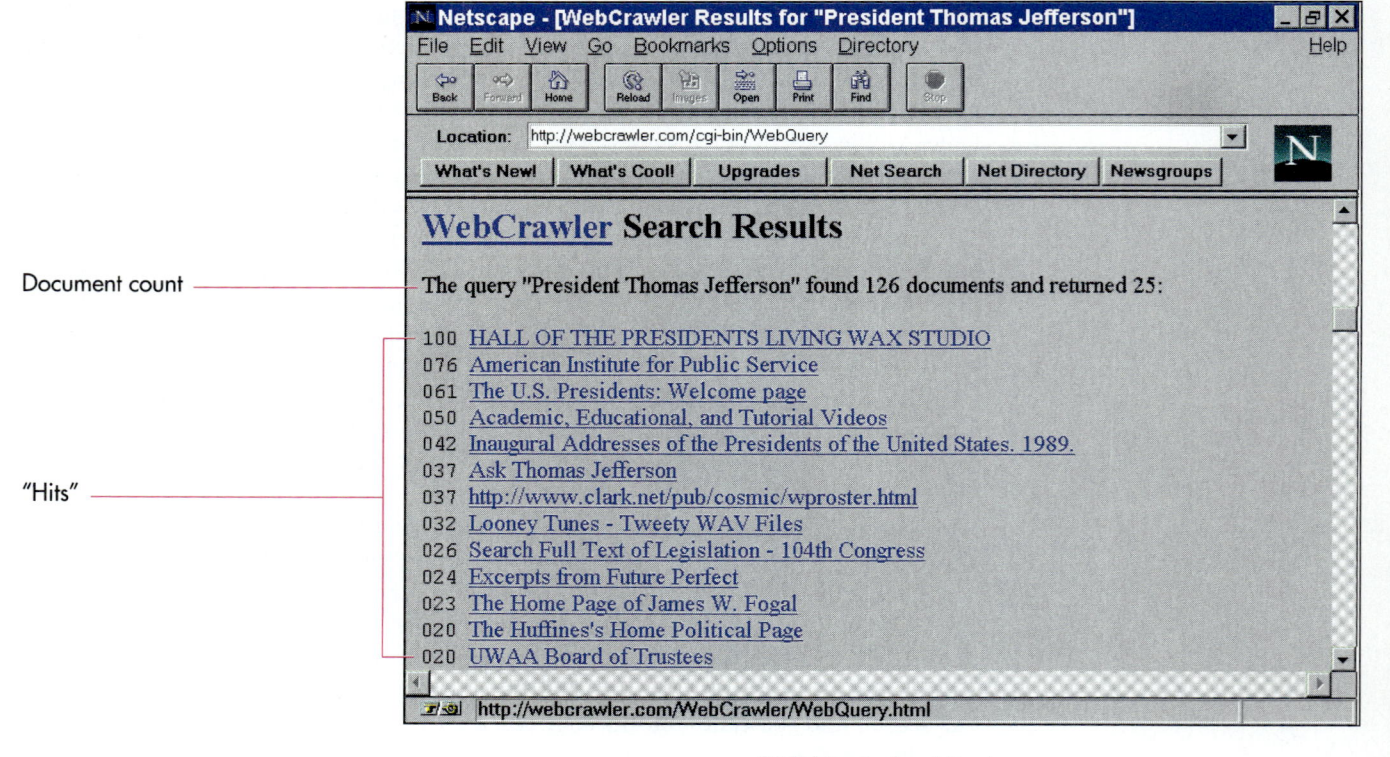

(b) WebCrawler Search Results

FIGURE 3.9 Search Engines (WebCrawler and Yahoo)

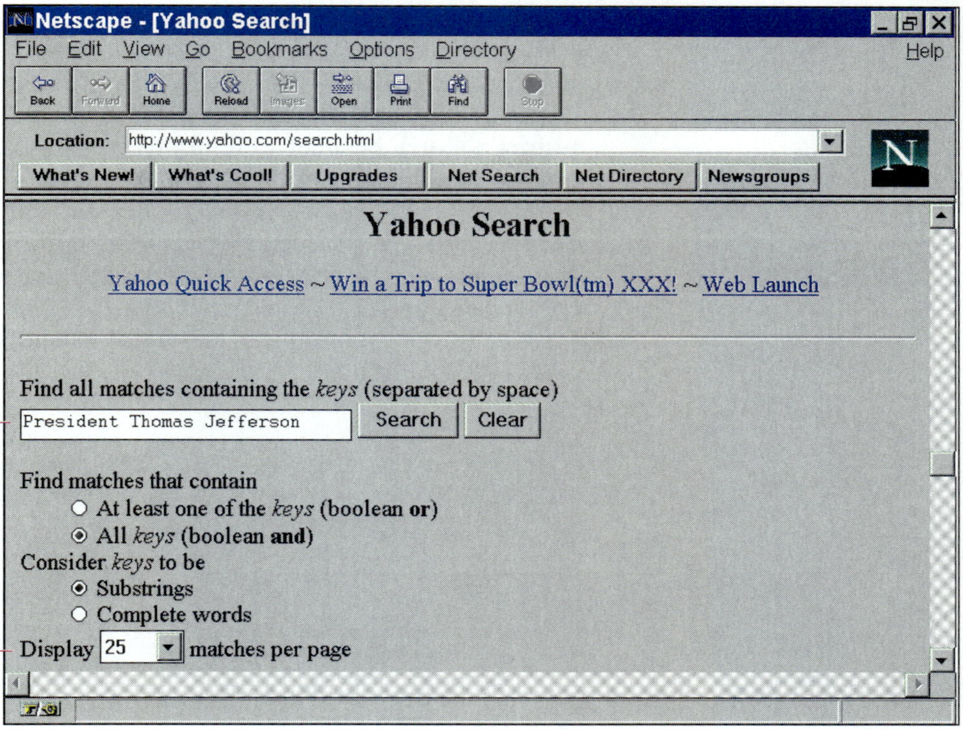
Search text
Requested number of hits
Netscape - [Yahoo Search]
File Edit View Go Bookmarks Options Directory Help
Location: http://www.yahoo.com/search.html
What's New! What's Cool! Upgrades Net Search Net Directory Newsgroups
Yahoo Search
Yahoo Quick Access ~ Win a Trip to Super Bowl(tm) XXX! ~ Web Launch
Find all matches containing the keys (separated by space)
President Thomas Jefferson
Search
Clear
Find matches that contain
At least one of the keys (boolean or)
All keys (boolean and)
Consider keys to be
Substrings
Complete words
Display 25 matches per page

(c) Yahoo Search Parameters

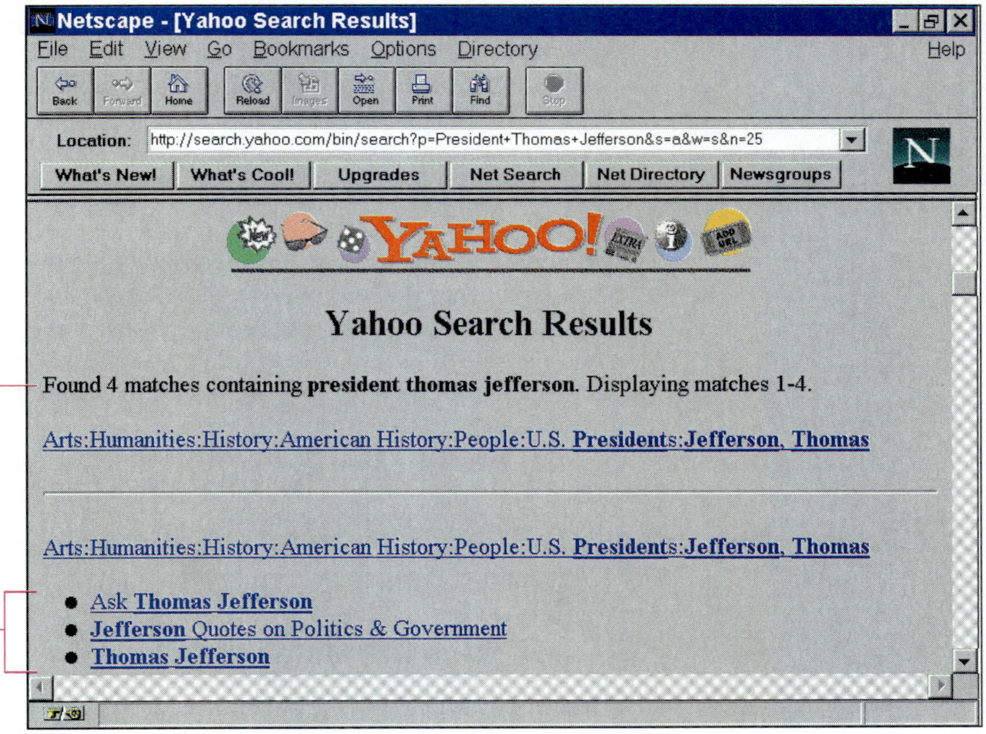
Document count
"Hits"
Netscape - [Yahoo Search Results]
File Edit View Go Bookmarks Options Directory Help
Location: http://search.yahoo.com/bin/search?p=President+Thomas+Jefferson&s=a&w=s&n=25
What's New! What's Cool! Upgrades Net Search Net Directory Newsgroups
YAHOO!
Yahoo Search Results
Found 4 matches containing president thomas jefferson. Displaying matches 1-4.
Arts:Humanities:History:American History:People:U.S. Presidents:Jefferson, Thomas
Arts:Humanities:History:American History:People:U.S. Presidents:Jefferson, Thomas
Ask Thomas Jefferson
Jefferson Quotes on Politics & Government
Thomas Jefferson

(d) Yahoo Search Results

FIGURE 3.9 Search Engines (WebCrawler and Yahoo) (continued)

And, Or, and Not

Each search engine has its specific syntax, which varies from one engine to the next. All engines, however, have the same basic capabilities that enable you to restrict a search in order to return relevant documents. All search queries are in essence combinations of the logical operations, And, Or, and Not. Using the And operation for "President Thomas Jefferson," for example, will return documents about Jefferson's presidency. Using Or, however, will return documents about presidents (any president) or Jefferson. The Not operation is useful to exclude certain documents; for example, searching on "Thomas Jefferson" but specifying Not "president" will return documents about other aspects of Jefferson's life.

> http://www.superbowl.com
>
> We don't know if this site will be around next year, but we truly enjoyed it for Super Bowl XXX.

OTHER BROWSER CAPABILITIES

As we mentioned several times above, the Web is changing continuously. The browsers used to access the Web are also undergoing constant revision, and it is probable that by the time you read this book, a new version of Netscape Navigator with new features will be available. Of the features in the current version as this book goes to press, the ones we think you will find most useful are Find, Autoload Images, and Mail.

To Load or Not to Load Images

Many of the graphics you have seen in the figures throughout this chapter and the hands-on exercise you just completed are called **in-line images.** This means that the data necessary to produce the graphic image on your screen is downloaded and displayed by the browser when you request the document. Because graphics add significantly to the file size, pages with in-line images may take considerable time to load.

If you don't want to experience this time lag, you can set Netscape to load only the text portion of the document. In-line images will be represented on the page by a small icon, as shown in Figure 3.10. If the image is set up as a link, you can click it even if you haven't loaded the graphic. In this case clicking the icon placeholder that Netscape displays in place of the graphic will let you jump to the linked page.

If, after retrieving a document, you decide you want to see the images after all, simply click the Images button and the document will be reloaded, this time with the graphics. (A word of warning, though: When loading images on demand this way, as compared to autoloading them, Netscape waits until the entire document is transferred before displaying it. It can seem like a very long wait, particularly if you are accustomed to Netscape's normal mode of operation, which is to overlay parts of a document received on top of earlier portions until the entire document is loaded.)

Click to reload current page with images

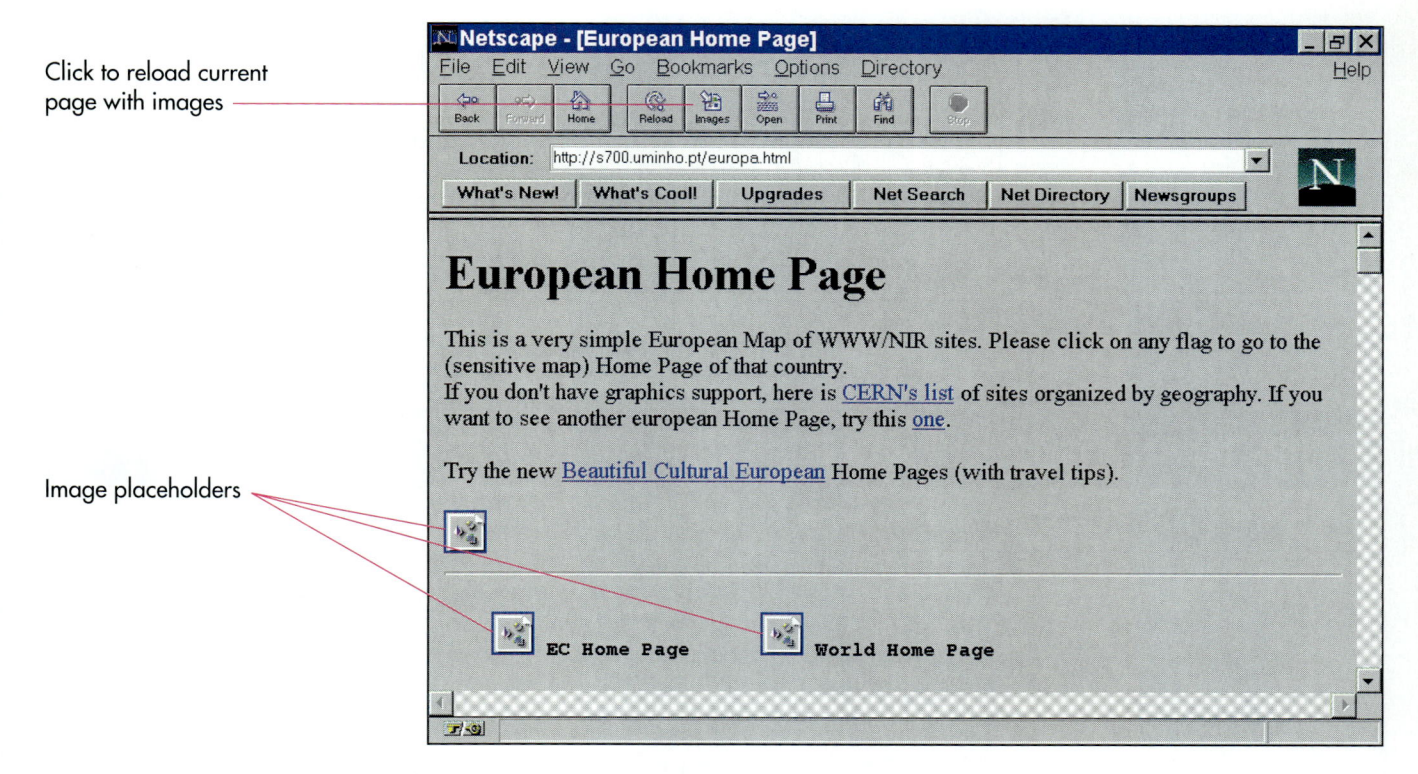

Image placeholders

FIGURE 3.10 A Web Page with Images Off

RETRIEVING IMAGES THAT ARE NOT EMBEDDED

A home page developer may want to include a large picture in a Web document, but not want visitors to have to wait for it to load each time they retrieve the page. Rather than include the entire image, he or she can reduce it significantly or choose a representative icon and enter this ***thumbnail sketch*** as a link in the document. Only those visitors who click on the thumbnail link will bring up the entire graphic. However, viewing the entire image when it is not embedded as an in-line image requires that the user have the appropriate software, or ***viewer,*** configured on his or her system to view the image.

Using E-mail in Netscape

Assume you have found a Web document describing a great ski location in Wyoming. You want to share the information with a friend at another campus. You could print the page and mail it, but you decide that is not the way to communicate on the Information Highway. You could write down the URL of the Web document, then log onto your e-mail server and send your friend a mail message containing the URL. But what if you copied it down wrong, or misspelled it? This method seems a bit cumbersome, too.

A better way uses a preference setting you may find helpful: Netscape can be configured to allow you to send e-mail. Netscape is certainly not a substitute for Eudora, Pine, or any other mail program. But it does provide a convenient way to e-mail a page you find of interest on the Web to someone else.

SETTING NETSCAPE PREFERENCES

You can set some of the Netscape preferences on your own, such as whether images will load with the document. For others, such as e-mail, you may need the assistance of your LAN administrator. It may be that in your environment some of the preferences and features in Netscape are not available. Check with your instructor and/or help desk to determine which features you can use.

HANDS-ON EXERCISE 2

Searching the Web

Objective: To use a Web search engine to find a specific resource on the Net, then locate a character string within it. To change Netscape settings and preferences, and to send e-mail using Netscape. Use Figure 3.11 as a guide in the exercise.

STEP 1: Choose a Search Engine
- Start Netscape or the browser you use in your campus computing environment.
- Click the **Net Search button** on the Netscape screen.
- Scroll or press **PageDown** until you see the InfoSeek and Lycos links.

THE RELOAD COMMAND

There are times when the requested document or resource is not returned, or is loaded incorrectly, particularly when graphics are included. You can request that Netscape reload the document simply by clicking the Reload button at the top of the screen.

STEP 2: Enter the Query Text
- Type **movies** in the Query text box under the InfoSeek link as shown in Figure 3.11a, then click the **Search button.** A short list of movie resources is displayed. (The version of InfoSeek you are using is a small version of a commercial search engine, to which you can subscribe if you wish to pay the fee.)
- Once the Netscape icon is still and the results are completed—downloaded to your PC (check the bottom line of the screen, the progress bar, for the *Document Done* message)—scroll down in the Query Results window to see more information.
- Click any of the listed movie links to browse the listed home pages.

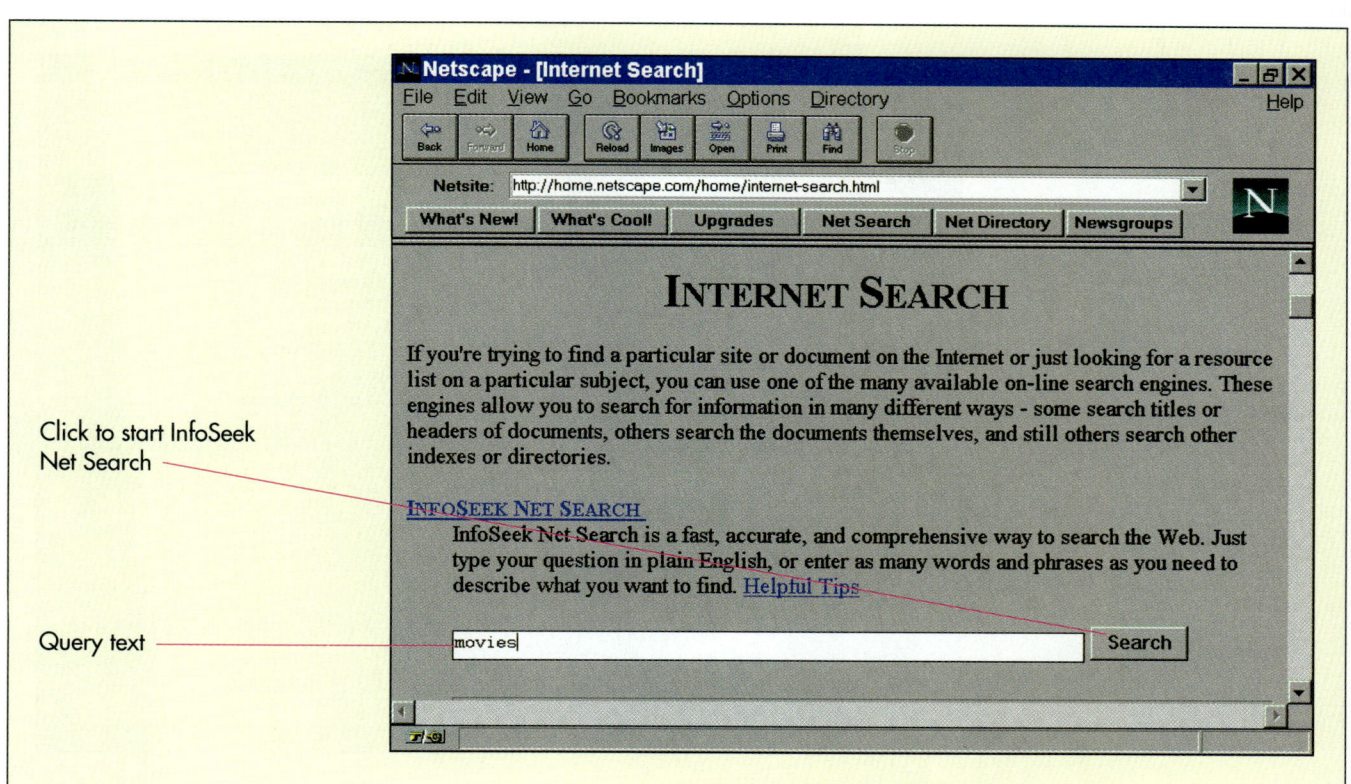

(a) The Query Text Box in InfoSeek

FIGURE 3.11 Hands-on Exercise 2

BOOKMARKING A QUERY

Running a query using a Web search engine actually creates a customized HTML page identified by the URL returned as a result of the search. You can return to the same query at a later time if you create a bookmark when the search is finished. However, be aware that the Web changes continuously, so the next time you visit the bookmarked query, the search results may be different.

STEP 3: Perform a Search on Multiple Terms

➤ Click the **Back button** until you return to the Net Search home page (or alternatively, click **Net Search**).

➤ Click on the **Lycos Home Page: Hunting WWW Information** link. You will see a screen similar to that shown in Figure 3.11b. However, the graphic will be different, as each time a browser accesses the Web server at Lycos, the server inserts a new advertisement in the graphics box.

- Type **movies** in the Query text box and click the **Search button.** The search finds a large number of documents containing the word *movies,* but displays only 10.
- Scroll or press **PageDown** to see abstracts of the 10 documents. The link for each document precedes the abstract.
- Click on any link in the list.

FINDING THINGS ON THE WORLD WIDE WEB — 109

Click to change Search Options

Enter query text here

Advertisement

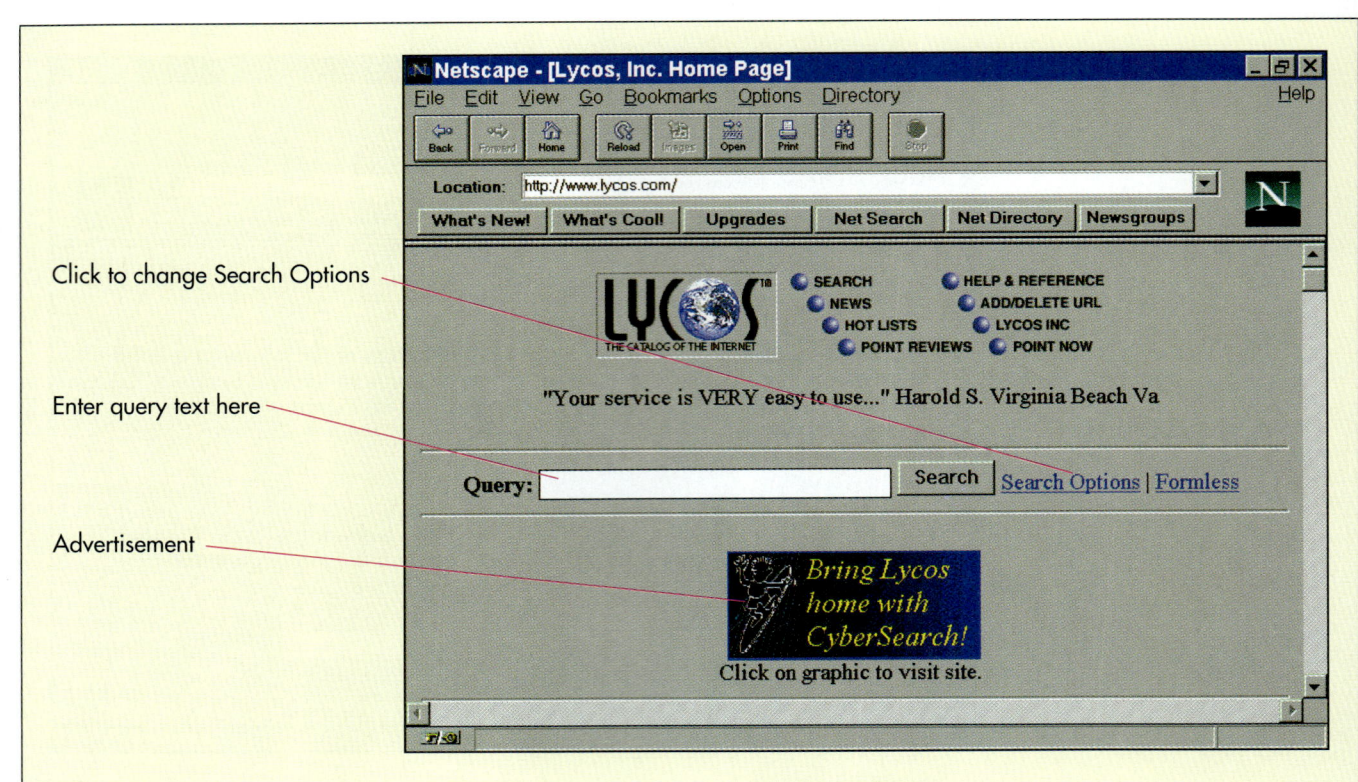

(b) The Lycos Home Page

FIGURE 3.11 Hands-on Exercise 2 (continued)

➤ Click **Back** until you return to the Lycos home page. Click on the **Search Options** link to display the search form shown in Figure 3.11c. A search form is a special feature of this and other search engines that will allow you to set the number of hits (the number of documents you want returned), and specify that you want to search on a phrase, such as *action movies,* instead of on a single word.

- Click in the **Query text box** and type **action movies.**
- Click on the **Down Arrow button** next to the Display Options text box that shows the number of results per page. Change the maximum number of hits to display to 20.
- The Lycos search engine as currently set will search for any documents containing the word *action* or the word *movies,* resulting in too many unrelated hits. You want to change the default search option from (OR) to (AND). Click the **Down Arrow button** next to the first Search Options text box, and select **match all terms (AND)** from the drop-down list.
- Lycos' default is to display a link followed by a short abstract from the document. You can change the form of the display of "hits" to show just a list of links, without the abstracts. Click the **Down Arrow** next to the Display Options text box that currently says **standard results**. Select **summary results** from the list. Your search form should look like the one shown in Figure 3.11c.
- Click on the **Search button** to display the results shown in Figure 3.11d. (Your results may vary.)

110 EXPLORING THE INTERNET

(c) The Completed Lycos Search Form

Callouts:
- Click to start search
- Enter search text
- Match all terms
- Display 20 hits
- Display hits as bulleted list

(d) Lycos Search Results

Callouts:
- Document count
- Summary list

FIGURE 3.11 Hands-on Exercise 2 (continued)

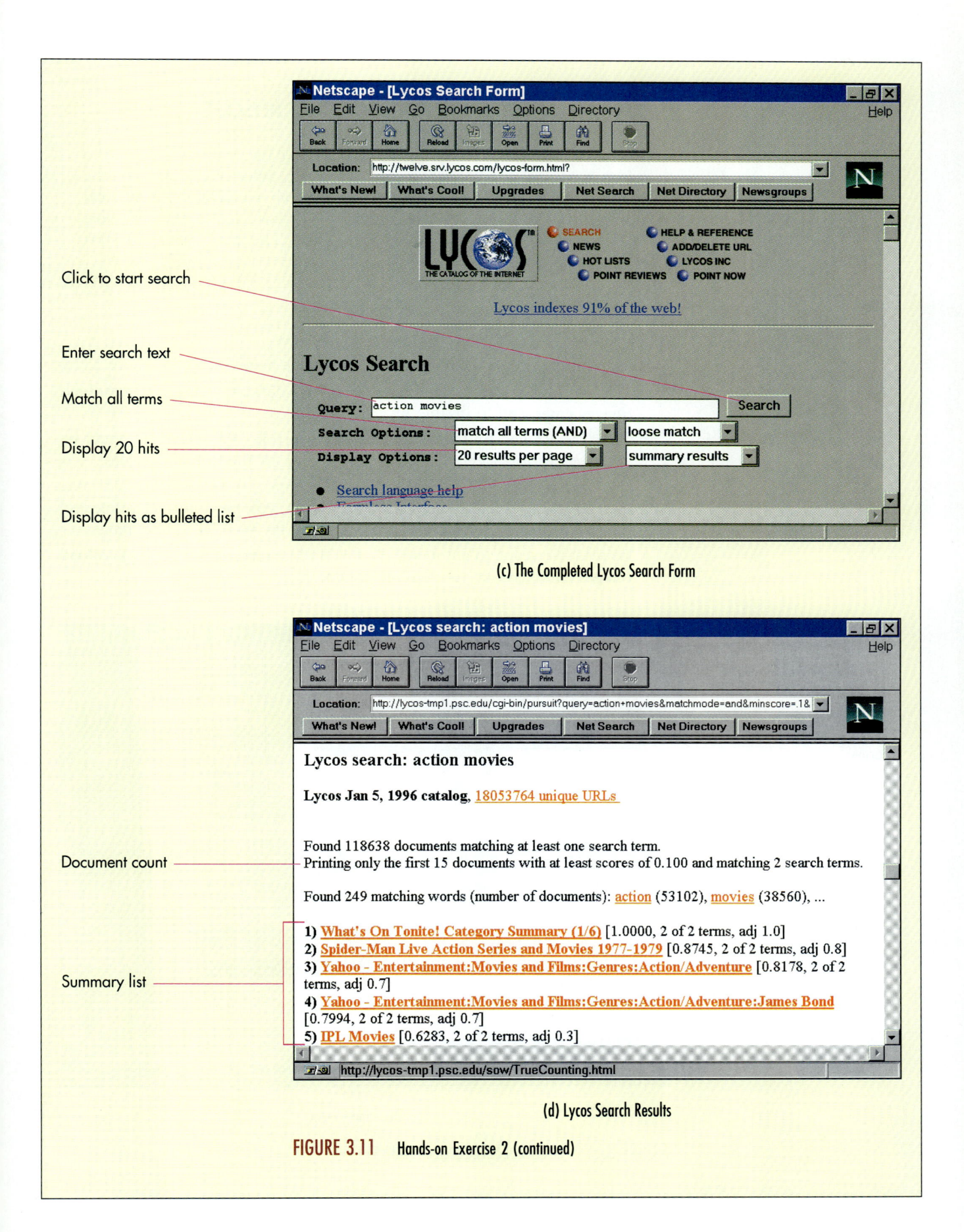

JUMP DIRECTLY TO LYCOS WHEN YOU START NETSCAPE

If you frequently search the Web, you can set Lycos up as the page to which Netscape automatically opens at start-up. Select Preferences on the Options menu. From there choose the Styles tab. Click Home Page location and enter the Lycos URL, http://www.lycos.com, in the text box. Select Save Options on the Options menu. The next time you start Netscape, you will link directly to Lycos.

STEP 4: Load a Web Page without In-line Images

➤ Select **Options** on the menu bar to pull down the menu shown in Figure 3.11e.

- The Autoload Images command is on by default. Click the **Autoload Images command** to disable it.
- Click the **Reload button** to redisplay the current Web page. It should be displayed with placeholder icons substituting for the in-line graphics.
- Click the **Images button.** Netscape will reconnect to the site and redisplay the page with in-line images. However, since you have not yet reselected Autoload Images, subsequent pages will display without in-line images.
- To reset Netscape to automatically load in-line images, select the **Autoload Images command** on the **Options menu.**

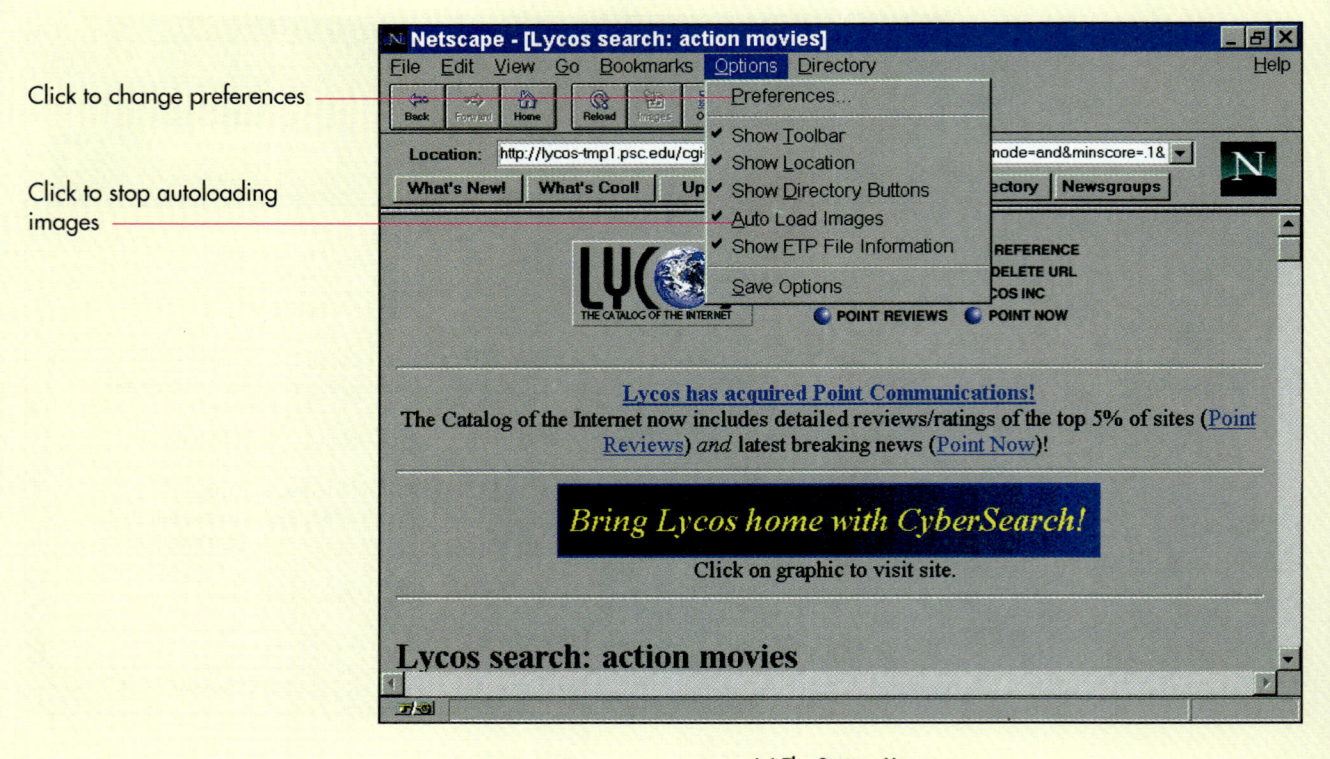

(e) The Options Menu

FIGURE 3.11   Hands-on Exercise 2 (continued)

112 EXPLORING THE INTERNET

STEP 5: Send E-mail with Netscape

➤ To send e-mail with Netscape, you must change settings in the Preferences dialog box. Select **Preferences** from the **Options menu.** Select the **Mail and News tab.** You will see a dialog box similar to Figure 3.11f.

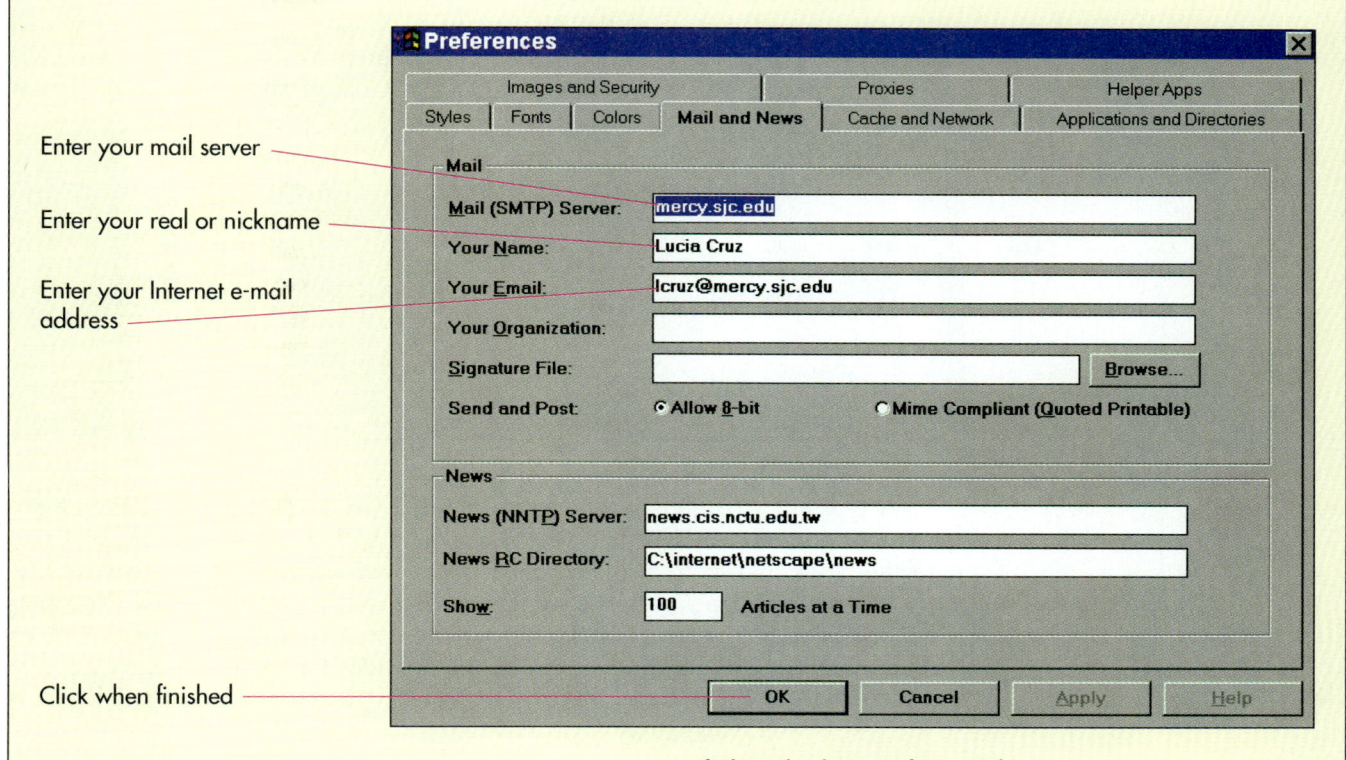

Enter your mail server

Enter your real or nickname

Enter your Internet e-mail address

Click when finished

(f) The Mail and News Preferences Tab

FIGURE 3.11 Hands-on Exercise 2 (continued)

- Enter the name of your mail server, your real name, and your Internet e-mail address, as shown in the example in Figure 3.11f. (See your instructor or help desk for specific information and instructions.) Click **OK.**
- Select **Save Options** on the **Options menu** to save your mail setup.

➤ Select **Mail Document** on the **File menu** to compose your e-mail message.

- Enter the name of the person to whom you wish to send the current page. We suggest that you send the page to yourself to test whether it works.
- Click to position the insertion point at the end of the URL in the message area and press **Enter** three times to insert three blank lines below the URL.
- Type some explanatory text to add to the information you are sending.
- Click the **Quote Document button** at the bottom of the screen to include the text of the current document in the message.
- Click **Send.** Your message is on its way.

FINDING THINGS ON THE WORLD WIDE WEB 113

LYNX

Netscape is a fun and exciting way to browse and search the Web, but not everyone has access to it. You must have a PC with lots of memory running Windows and TCP/IP, and a very fast connection to your Internet host, to be able to retrieve Web documents that include graphics. Because not all users have this type of equipment, programmers at the University of Kansas developed **Lynx,** a text-based Web browser that runs on a Unix Internet host. You can log on to the Unix machine with a telnet session, type Lynx at the Unix prompt, and use the arrow keys on your keyboard to scroll through the links in a Web document.

> http://www.usc.edu/dept/TommyCam/
>
> Visit the University of Southern California and get a live picture of campus, updated every minute!

A typical Lynx screen is shown in Figure 3.12a. It does not have the graphics or the formatted HTML text that is available with a graphical browser. Compare the "look and feel" of the White House home page, shown in Lynx in Figure 3.12b, with the types of pages you saw when browsing with Netscape. The links are there; what is missing are the graphics and text formatting that give the Web its visual appeal and impact. However, Lynx provides the same easy navigation of the Web as Netscape and other browsers. When you find and select a link that is of interest to you, you simply press the Enter key, and off you go.

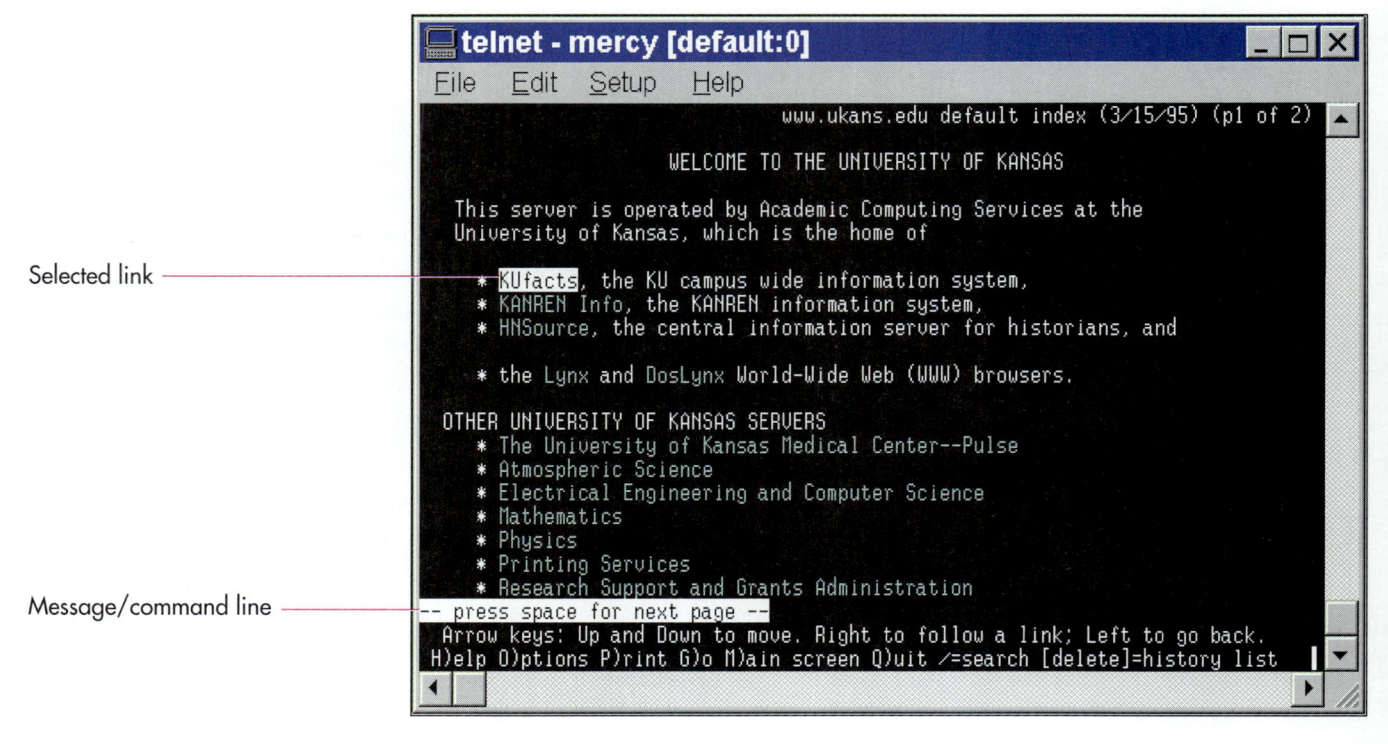

(a) The Lynx Main Page

FIGURE 3.12 Lynx

Press Enter to jump to selected link

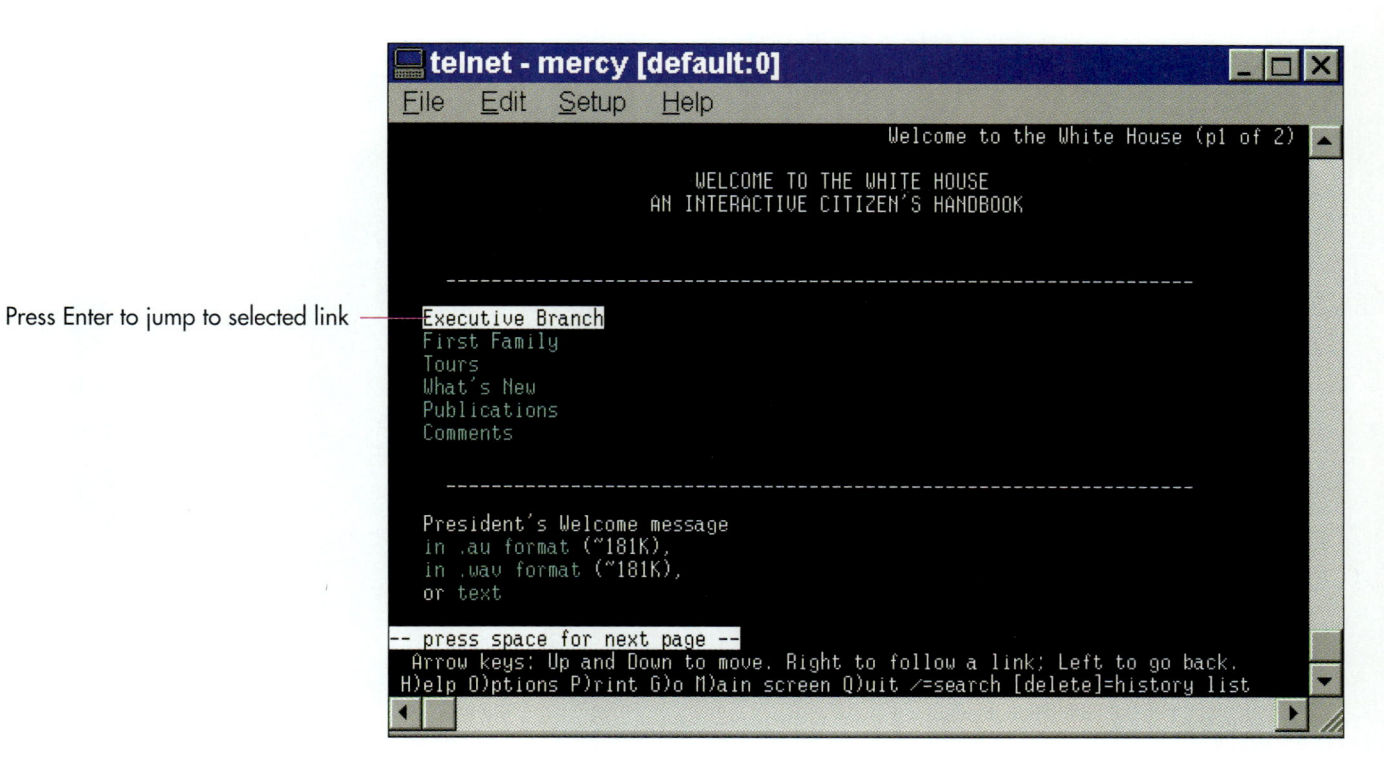

(b) The White House Home Page in Lynx

FIGURE 3.12 Lynx (continued)

HANDS-ON EXERCISE 3

Using Lynx on the World Wide Web

Objective: To use a text-based Web browser such as Lynx to surf the Net and search for documents. Use Figures 3.12 and 3.13 as guides in the exercise.

STEP 1: Log On and Start Lynx

▸ Log on to your network and telnet to your Unix system. (You did this in the hands-on exercise in Chapter 1. If you don't remember how, review those instructions; if you need help, see your instructor or help desk.)

▸ At the Unix prompt, type **lynx.** You will see a screen similar to Figure 3.12a. The hyperlinks are shown in blue or other contrasting color, while the static text is in white, and the background is black.

STEP 2: Navigate in Lynx and Select a Link

▸ Press the **Up/Down arrow keys** to move up and down the page to a desired link. Once you have selected a link, press **Enter** or **Right Arrow.** You will jump to the selected document. (If you go past the desired link, press the **PageUp key;** the cursor will jump back to the top of the previous page.)

▸ Press the **space bar** to display the next page of text; press **b** to display the previous page.

▸ Press the **Left Arrow** to go back to the most recent link.

FINDING THINGS ON THE WORLD WIDE WEB   **115**

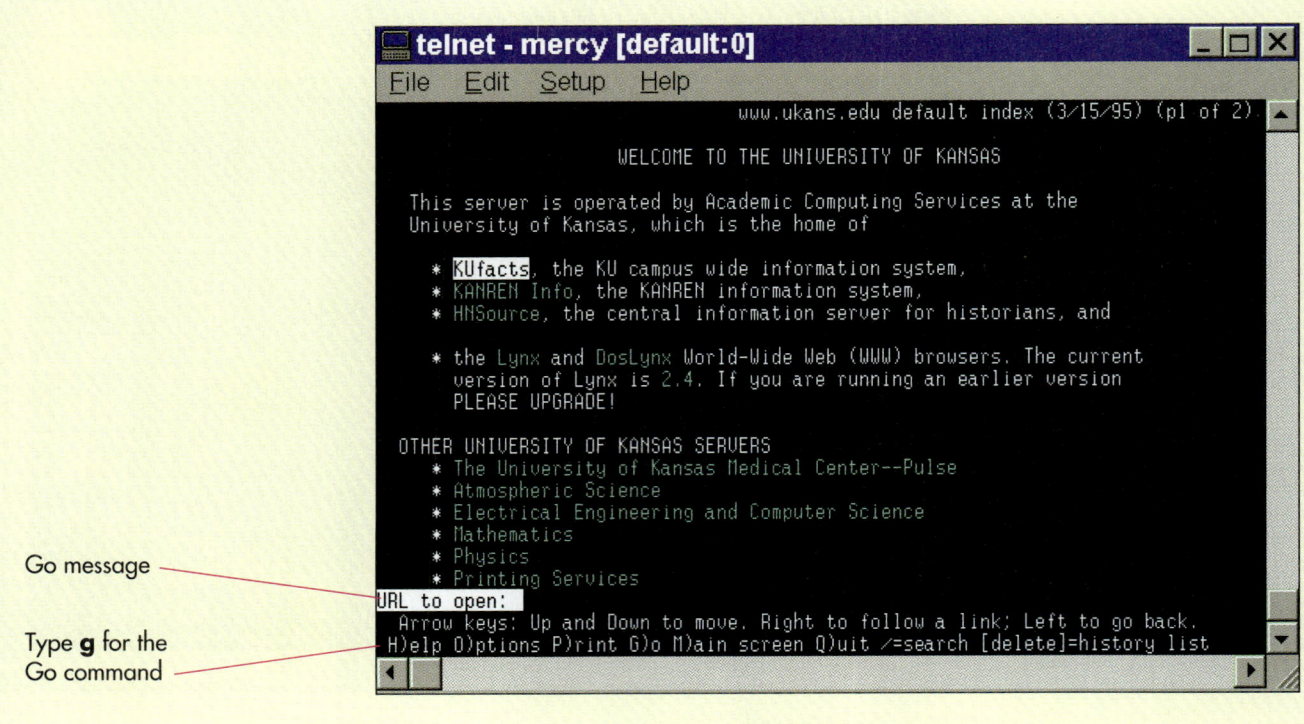

```
telnet - mercy [default:0]
File   Edit   Setup   Help
                    www.ukans.edu default index (3/15/95) (p1 of 2)
                          WELCOME TO THE UNIVERSITY OF KANSAS
    This server is operated by Academic Computing Services at the
    University of Kansas, which is the home of

       * KUfacts, the KU campus wide information system,
       * KANREN Info, the KANREN information system,
       * HNSource, the central information server for historians, and

       * the Lynx and DosLynx World-Wide Web (WWW) browsers. The current
         version of Lynx is 2.4. If you are running an earlier version
         PLEASE UPGRADE!
    OTHER UNIVERSITY OF KANSAS SERVERS
       * The University of Kansas Medical Center--Pulse
       * Atmospheric Science
       * Electrical Engineering and Computer Science
       * Mathematics
       * Physics
       * Printing Services
    URL to open:
    Arrow keys: Up and Down to move. Right to follow a link; Left to go back.
    H)elp O)ptions P)rint G)o M)ain screen Q)uit /=search [delete]=history list
```

Go message — (points to URL to open:)
*Type **g** for the Go command*

(a) The Lynx Go Command

FIGURE 3.13   Hands-on Exercise 3

STEP 3: Linking to a Specific URL

➤ You can link to a specific home page using Lynx. The menu at the bottom of the screen shows frequently used commands, one of which is Go.

  • Type the letter **g**; the command line shown in Figure 3.13a is displayed.
  • Fill in the URL of the site you want to visit: **http://www.whitehouse.gov**
  • When finished, press **Enter.** You will immediately link to the site.

YOUR KEYBOARD MAY ACT IN STRANGE WAYS IN LYNX

Because you get to Lynx by telnetting, the Unix system thinks it is communicating with a terminal. The keys on your PC keyboard may be sending signals that Unix interprets differently than does the PC. If you have problems with the arrow keys, backspace keys, and so on, check first to be certain the NumLock key is off. Then experiment to see if any other keys substitute for the ones that are not working properly. Finally, see your instructor or help desk for assistance.

STEP 4: Searching with Lynx

➤ You can jump to the Lycos search engine with Lynx just as you would with Netscape.

  • Type the letter **g** to invoke the Go command.

- Delete the existing URL, if any, by pressing **Backspace** or the **Left Arrow key.** (If neither key works properly, check with your instructor or help desk to find out which key will delete left when using telnet.)
- Enter the URL of the Lycos search engine, **http://www.lycos.com,** at the prompt.
- Press **Enter.**

➤ At the Lycos home page, shown in Figure 3.13b, press the **Down Arrow key** once to select the Query text field. There may be a short delay when selecting fields in Lynx. Pause before continuing so you will be sure the Query field is selected. The cursor will be blinking at the left edge of the text entry line.
- Type **movies.**
- Press the **Down Arrow key** once to select **Search.** Your screen should look like Figure 3.13c.
- With Search selected, press the **Right Arrow key** or **Enter.** Lycos performs the search and returns the results shown in Figure 3.13d.
- Press the **space bar** to see the second page. Press **b** to go back a page.
- The links to the documents shown in the abstracts are displayed in blue. Select any link using the **Up/Down Arrow keys.**
- Press **Enter** to jump to the document.

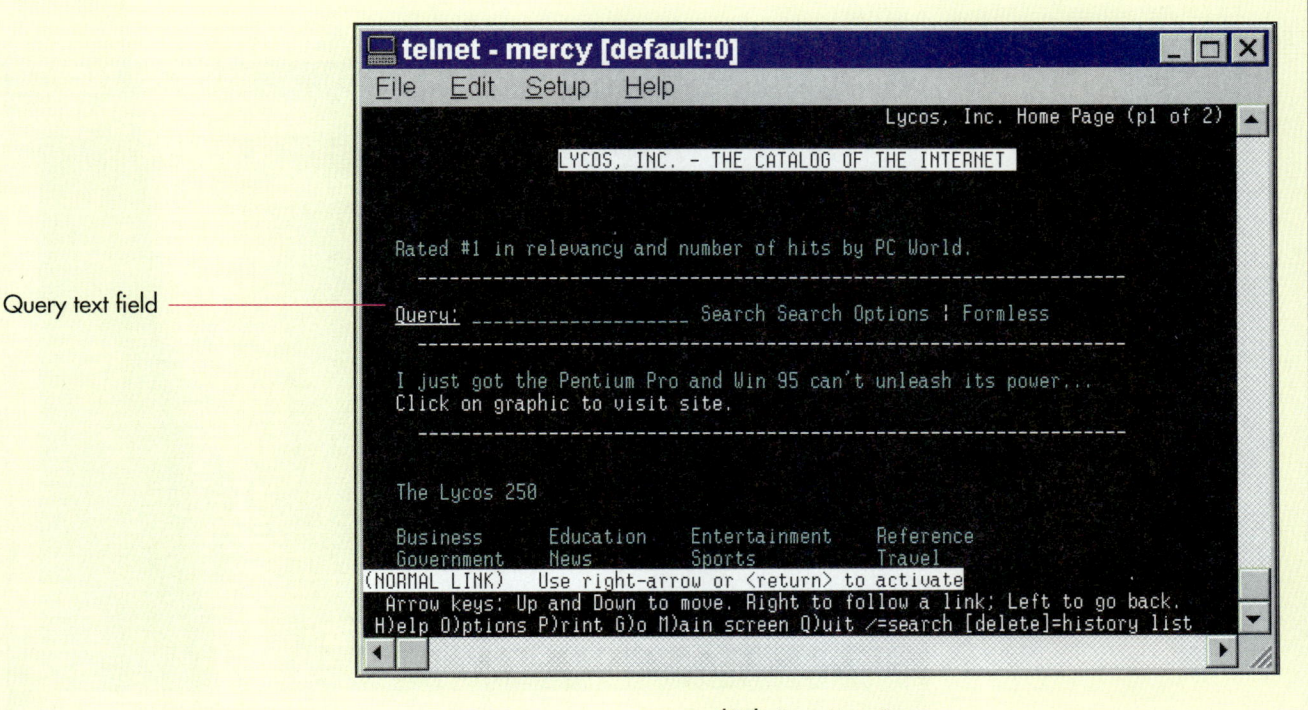

Query text field

(b) The Lycos Home Page

FIGURE 3.13   Hands-on Exercise 3 (continued)

STEP 5: Perform a Search Using Multiple Terms
➤ Go back to the Lycos home page by pressing the **Left Arrow key** until you are there (or press **g** and enter the Lycos URL).
- Press the **Down Arrow key** until you select the **Search Options link.**

FINDING THINGS ON THE WORLD WIDE WEB

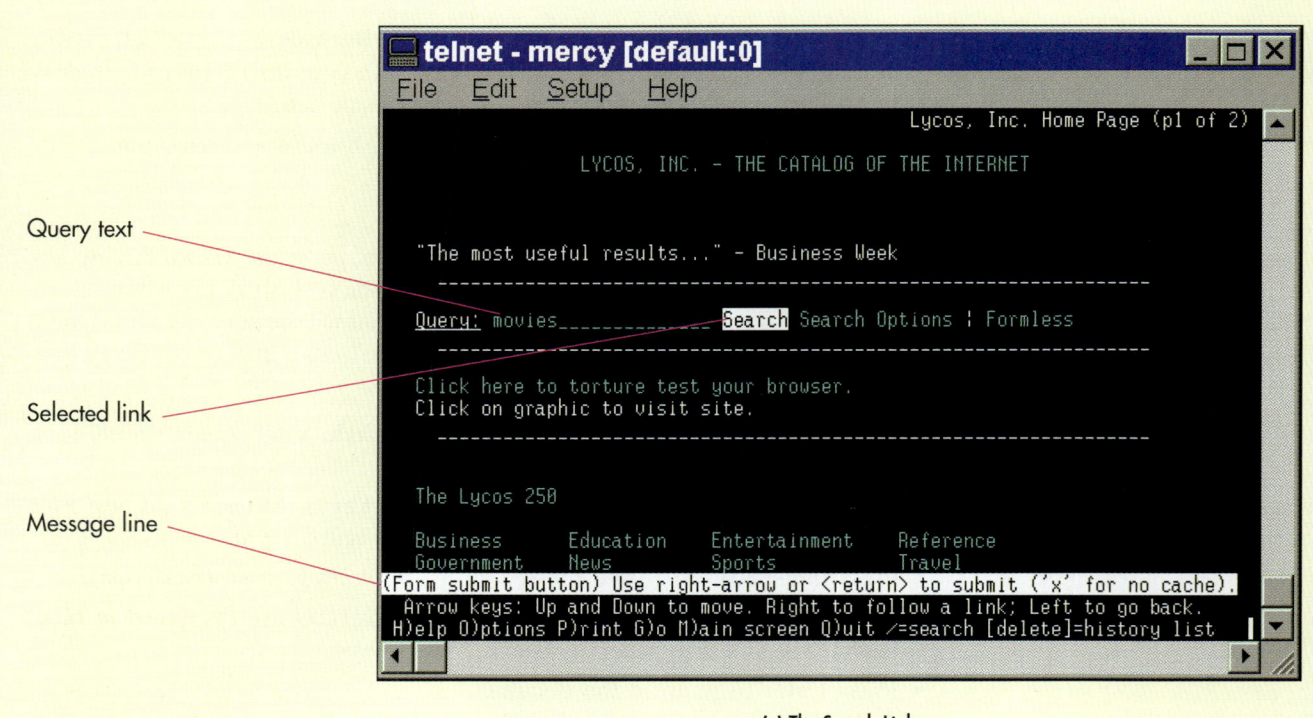

(c) The Search Link

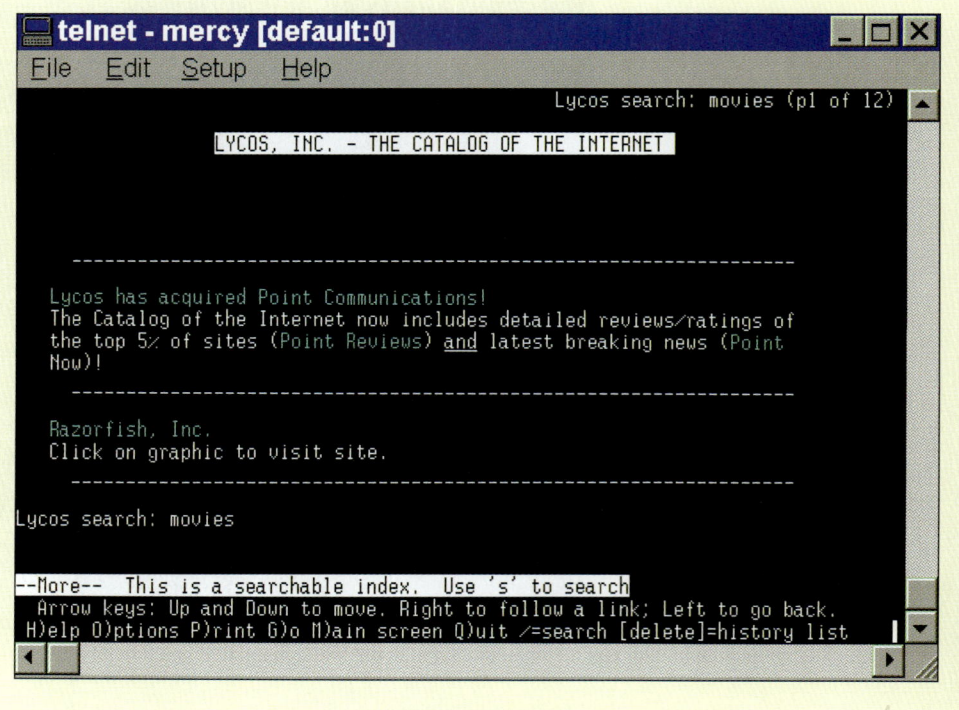

(d) Movie Search Results

FIGURE 3.13   Hands-on Exercise 3 (continued)

- Press **Enter**. The search options page shown in Figure 3.13e is displayed.
- Press the **Down Arrow key** until the cursor is in the **Query** text field. Enter the text of your query, **action movies**.

118   EXPLORING THE INTERNET

- Press the **Down Arrow key** until you select the **match any term (OR)** Search Options link below the query text. Your screen should match Figure 3.13f.

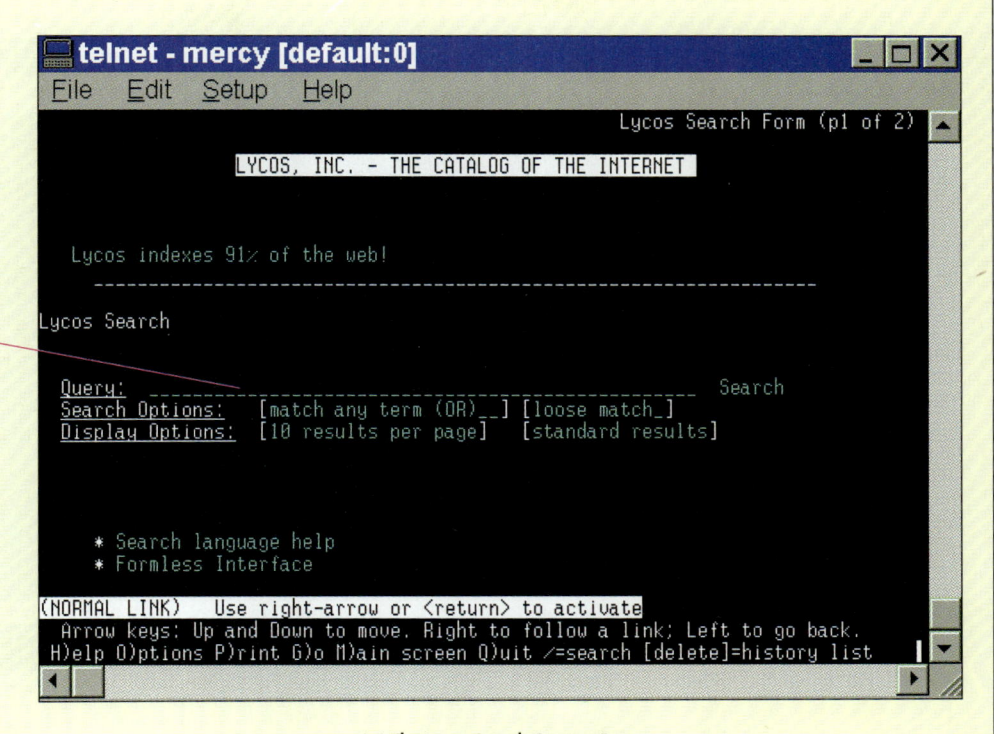

(e) The Lycos Search Options Page

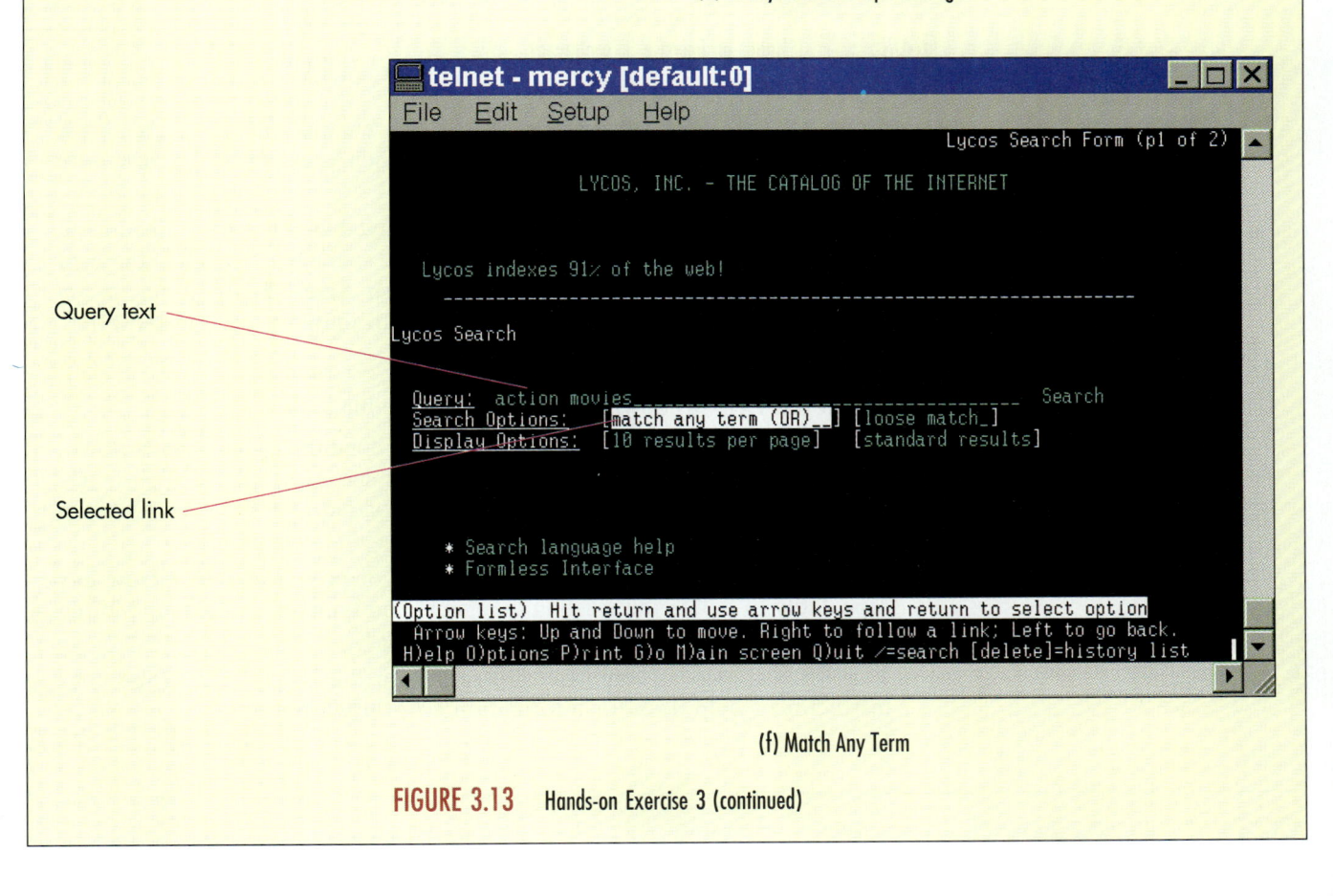

(f) Match Any Term

FIGURE 3.13 Hands-on Exercise 3 (continued)

- Press **Enter**. The menu shown in Figure 3.13g is displayed. Use the **Up/Down Arrow keys** to select the option you want. In this case select **match all terms (AND)**. Press **Enter**.

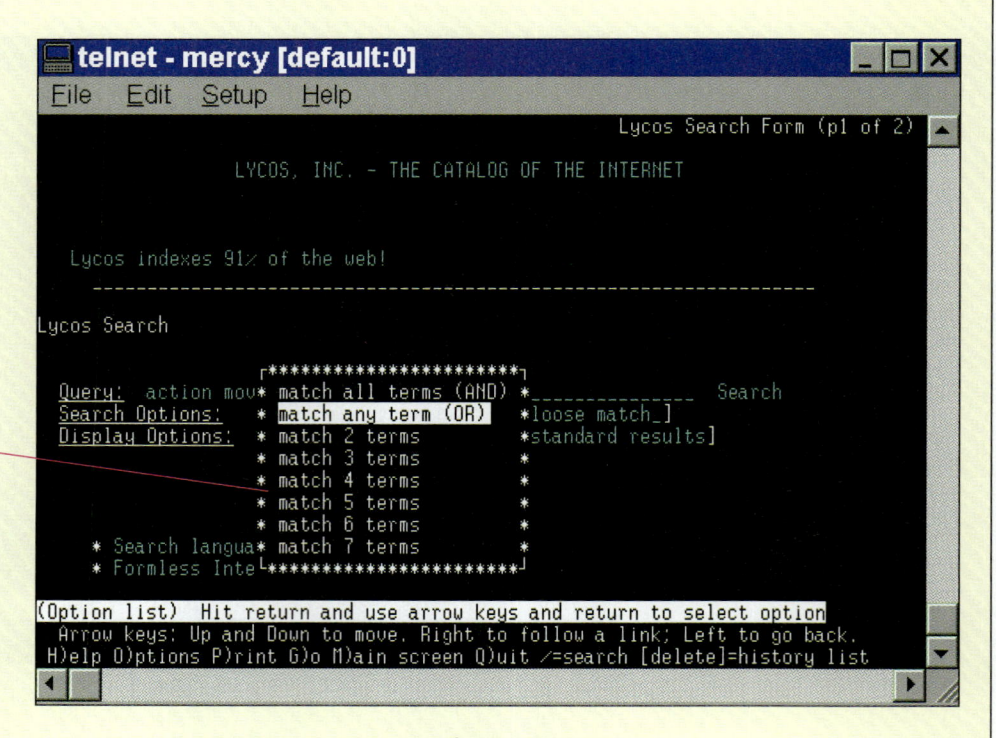

Match terms menu

(g) The Terms Menu

FIGURE 3.13 Hands-on Exercise 3 (continued)

- Since you have already gone past the Search link on this page, press **PageUp** to return to the top of the page, then press **Down Arrow** until **Search** is selected.
- Press **Enter**. Your query results will be displayed as a text-only document. You can see the search results by pressing the space bar to display the next page, shown in Figure 3.13h. Using the **Down Arrow key** you may select any hyperlink in the document. Press **Enter** to jump to the selected URL.

STEP 6: Download a File

➤ You can use Lynx to download a Web page or file.

- Use the arrow keys to select the URL of the document you want to download and press **d** (for download). A message shown in Figure 13.3i is displayed, indicating that the file will be downloaded to disk. Press **Enter** to save the file to disk.
- Press **Enter** to accept the existing file name or press the **Left Arrow key** repeatedly to delete the existing file name, and type a new file name in the command line.
- The file is copied to your home directory on the Unix server. (See your instructor or help desk for information on printing the file.)

120 EXPLORING THE INTERNET

First hit

(h) The Query Results

Press Enter to save current document to disk

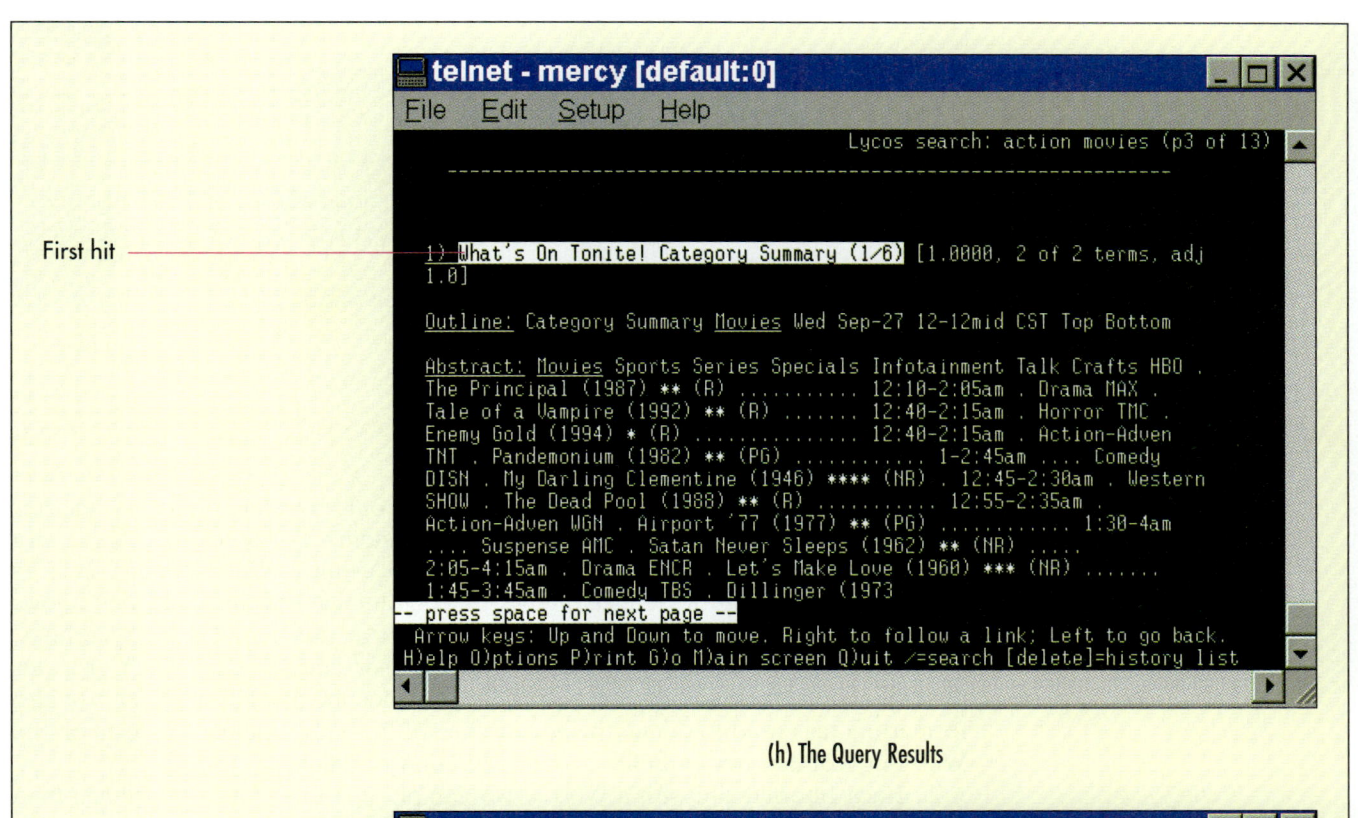

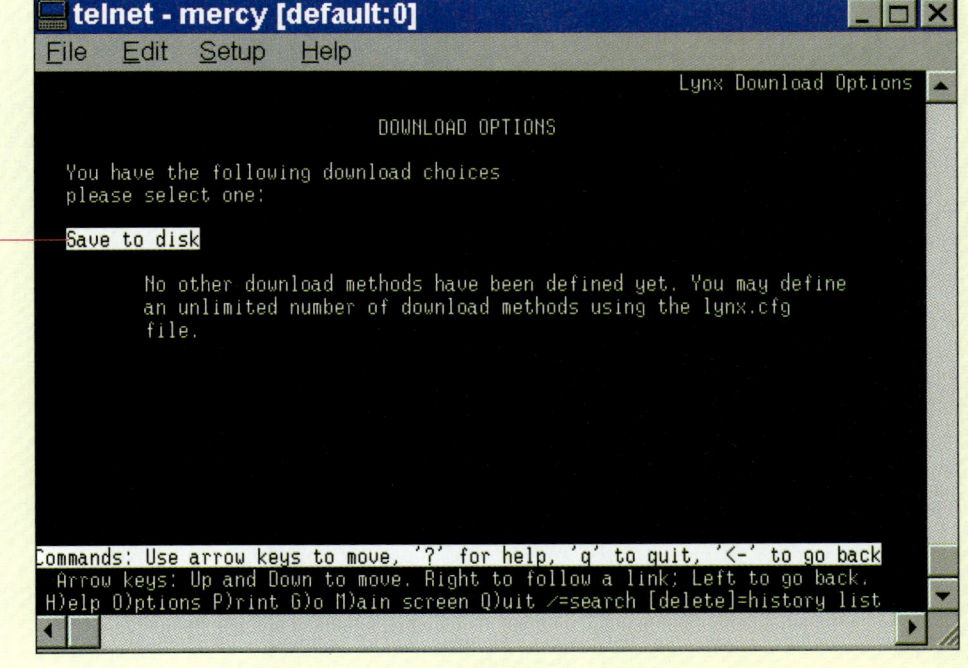

(i) The Save Message

FIGURE 3.13 Hands-on Exercise 3 (continued)

STEP 7: Exit Lynx and Log Off

- Press **q** to quit Lynx. At the prompt press **Enter** to confirm. (You can do a quick exit, without the confirmation, by typing an uppercase **Q**.)
- Type **exit** or whatever command you usually use to exit the Unix system. Press **Enter**. You are logged off.

> http://www.ajb.dni.us
>
> America's Job Bank is one of the largest job listings on the Net. Using this resource, thousands of Internet users find employment opportunities all over the United States.

SUMMARY

In the past, Internet resources could be obtained only by using difficult-to-master Unix-based commands and text-based retrieval systems. Today these resources are easily accessible through the World Wide Web using a Web browser such as Netscape. Netscape provides a Windows-based graphical user interface that allows users point-and-click access to millions of Web documents and files via hyperlinks. The documents are created using a word processor and HTML, which provides the tags that define each hypertext link to other documents. HTML also provides formatting tags used to define the appearance of Web documents. The files on the Web may contain text, graphics, sound, and/or video links.

Each Internet site with a Web server can put up home pages, which can then be accessed using a Web browser. Since the number of home pages on the Internet is currently in the millions and growing rapidly, browsing is a fun but inefficient way to search for information on the Web. Search engines provide a simple means of entering a query, to which the search engine will respond with a number of "hits," or Web documents that meet the search criteria. Users may bookmark the query or any frequently visited site to return to the same document at a later time. Browsers also provide the capability to print Web documents and save them to a local disk. For those users without a graphical Web browser, Lynx provides text-based browsing capability.

KEY WORDS AND CONCEPTS

Back button	In-line image	Spider
Bookmark	Link	Tag
Browser	Location text box	Thumbnail sketch
Client	Lycos	Uniform Resource
Hit	Lynx	Locator (URL)
Home page	Mosaic	Viewer
Hyperlink	Netscape Navigator	Web server
Hypermedia	Open Location	Web site
Hypertext	command	World Wide Web
Hypertext Markup	Reload button	(WWW)
Language (HTML)	Search engine	
Hypertext Transport	Search form	
Protocol (HTTP)		

Multiple Choice

1. Which of the following statements about the World Wide Web is true?
   (a) It has been in existence since the beginning of the Internet
   (b) Both graphics and text-based resources are linked on the Web
   (c) It can be accessed only by using a GUI-based browser
   (d) All of the above

2. When linking to a Web resource:
   (a) Your request must be routed through the Web server at the European Particle Physics Lab (the WWW developers)
   (b) You may link to a Web resource on the same computer or anywhere else on the Web
   (c) You must know the URL for the hyperlink to work
   (d) All of the above

3. Which of the following standard Windows elements are found in Netscape?
   (a) The Maximize button
   (b) A File menu
   (c) The title bar
   (d) All of the above

4. Which of the following defines the address of the current Web resource?
   (a) The title bar
   (b) The URL in the Location text box
   (c) Both (a) and (b)
   (d) Neither (a) nor (b)

5. Which part of the URL **http://www.microsoft.com/Windows/www.html** identifies the Internet address of the Web site?
   (a) http://
   (b) www.microsoft.com
   (c) Windows
   (d) www.html

6. Which of the following Netscape menus or buttons allows you to access a previously visited Web site without entering the URL?
   (a) File
   (b) Open
   (c) Go
   (d) None of the above

7. Which of the following is generally the first link at a Web site?
   (a) The home page
   (b) The root
   (c) The search form
   (d) The gopher server

8. When using Netscape, clicking on a link:
   (a) Brings up the Open URL dialog box so you can edit the link
   (b) Brings up a text-based menu for the site
   (c) Requires you to enter your username and password
   (d) None of the above

9. How does Netscape indicate it is in the process of transferring a Web document?
   (a) The Netscape logo flashes
   (b) A message is displayed in the URL text box
   (c) Both (a) and (b)
   (d) Neither (a) nor (b)

10. Which Netscape command allows you to create a bookmark for a previously visited site without returning to it?
    (a) View History
    (b) Bookmarks
    (c) Both (a) and (b)
    (d) Neither (a) nor (b)

11. If you are trying to limit the number of "hits" in a search on *space shuttle*, which of the following logical operations would you use?
    (a) And
    (b) Or
    (c) Both (a) and (b)
    (d) Neither (a) nor (b)

12. Which of the following is a text-based Web browser?
    (a) HTML
    (b) HTTP
    (c) Lynx
    (d) Netscape

13. Which of the following allows you to use hyperlinks to access World Wide Web resources?
    (a) Lynx
    (b) Netscape
    (c) Both (a) and (b)
    (d) Neither (a) nor (b)

14. A URL may be entered in:
    (a) The Location box on the Netscape screen
    (b) The Go dialog box
    (c) Both (a) and (b)
    (d) Neither (a) nor (b)

15. A hyperlink may point to:
    (a) A sound file
    (b) A text file
    (c) A video file
    (d) Any of the above

ANSWERS

1. b	6. c	11. a
2. b	7. a	12. c
3. d	8. d	13. c
4. b	9. a	14. c
5. b	10. a	15. d

Exploring the Internet

1. Using Figure 3.14, match each action with its result; a given action may be used more than once or not at all.

    Action
    a. Click at 1
    b. Click at 2
    c. Click at 3
    d. Click at 4
    e. Click at 5
    f. Click at 6
    g. Click at 7
    h. Click at 8

    Result
    ____ Return to the previous link
    ____ Print the current document
    ____ Enter a URL to link to a specific Web resource
    ____ Add the current link to a list of frequently visited Web sites
    ____ Browse a list of interesting Web sites
    ____ Display a list of the most recently visited Web sites
    ____ Find a Web resource using query criteria
    ____ Save the current document

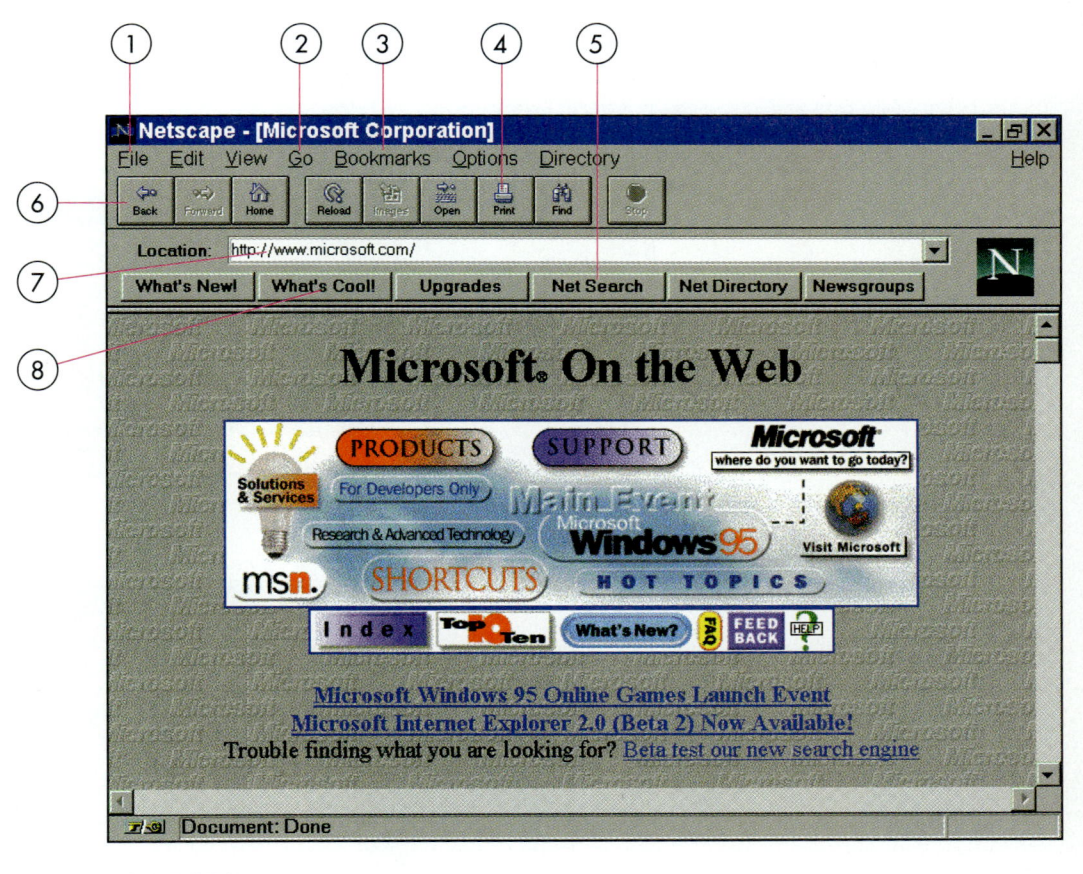

FIGURE 3.14   The Netscape Screen

2. Answer the following with respect to Web access at your college or university:
   a. What Web browser are you using?
   b. Does it provide a Windows GUI (graphical user interface)?
   c. What is the easiest way to access a search engine using your browser?
   d. Do you have Lynx or another text-based Web browser for access from the Unix prompt?
   e. What is your college or university's URL?
   f. Can you set up your own bookmarks on the system?
   g. Where do you go to get help?

3. The messages shown in Figure 3.15 appeared (or could have appeared) in conjunction with one of the hands-on exercises in this chapter. Explain the nature of each message and indicate the necessary corrective action (if any).

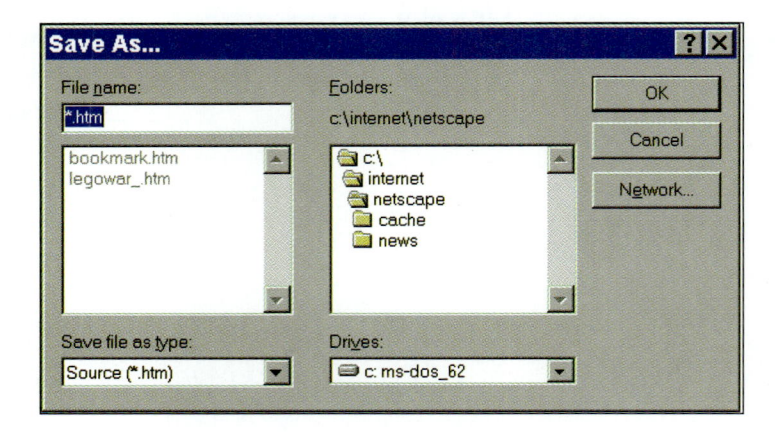

(a) Message 1

(b) Message 2

(c) Message 3

FIGURE 3.15   Messages for Problem 3

126   EXPLORING THE INTERNET

4. Describe in ordinary English what the Lycos search form shown in Figure 3.16 will search for and what results it will display when the search is completed. How could you reduce the number of "hits" found and displayed by the search?

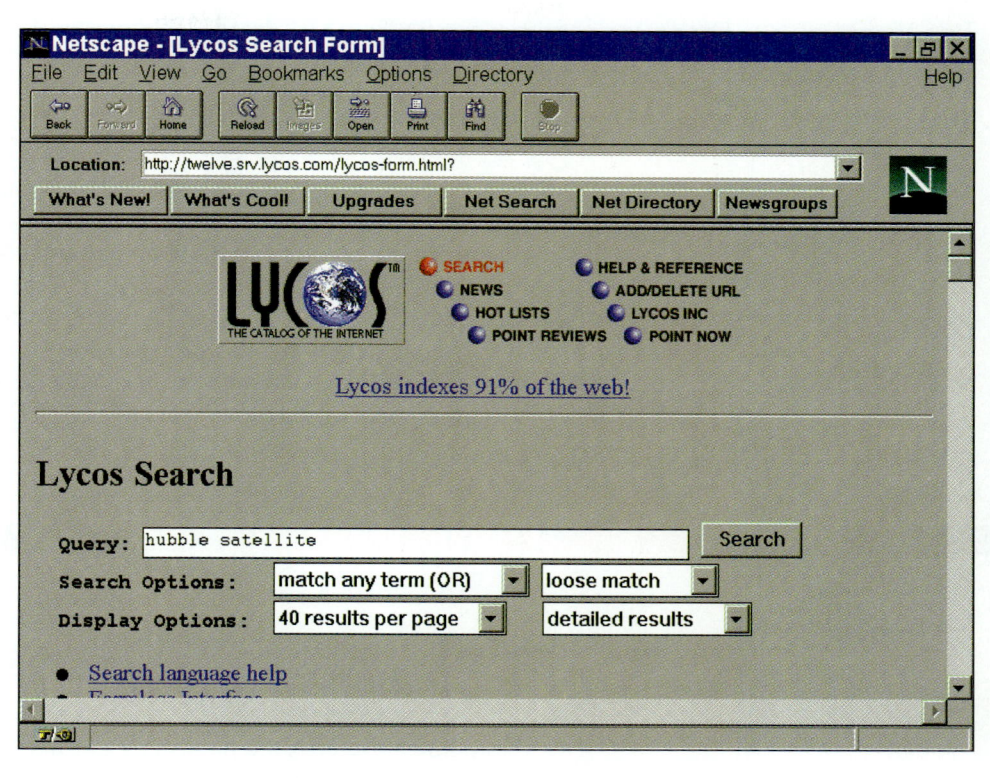

FIGURE 3.16　A Lycos Search Form

PRACTICE WITH THE WORLD WIDE WEB

1. **Get Help:** Online help in Netscape has a new meaning. It is not online on your system, it's online on the Internet. Netscape Communications Corporation, the company that markets Netscape, can update its help files instantly as the product changes or problems are noted. Get a look at online help by clicking the Help menu in Netscape, and notice the URL as you do so. Spend some time exploring the various links—there's lots of good stuff there.

2. **Learn about HTML:** Suppose you want to learn more about using HTML to create Web documents. Why go to a bookstore and spend $29.95 when the information is available online? The trick is to find it. Using whatever search engine is available to you, construct a search on the keywords *learning HTML*. Explore the sites that are "hits."

3. **Read a Zine:** Online publishing is becoming a hot, and very competitive, topic on the Net. TV news services, news magazines, and newspapers have Web sites. Visit the sites shown in Table 3.2, and compare the various offerings in terms of visual appeal, graphics quality, and so on. They all provide examples of the best (or most interesting) zines (electronic magazines) of the Net.

FINDING THINGS ON THE WORLD WIDE WEB　127

TABLE 3.2	Web Publishing Sites
Site	URL
MTV	http://mtv.com/MTVNEWS/index.html
Time Magazine	http://www.pathfinder.com/@@BnqVKTFCdgMAQDBT/time/timehomepage.html
ESPN	http://espnet.sportszone.com
Wired Magazine	http://www.wired.com/newform.html

4. **Just the FAQs, Please:** The Internet and the World Wide Web can be very intimidating to the newcomer. However, it doesn't have to be for long. All the information you need to understand the Net is on the Net! General information about popular subjects is often kept in files titled Frequently Asked Questions (FAQs). Compose a search to find out more about the World Wide Web; something like *WWW FAQs* should work. Follow the hyperlinks until you feel comfortable with the terms you're reading. Set up bookmarks to return to any interesting sites.

CASE STUDIES

Copyright Law in Cyberspace

The possibilities of electronic publishing are immense, as are the opportunities to plagiarize. How are authors' and artists' rights being protected in the online world? Research the latest information in cyberspace about cyberspace software and artistic piracy. Will the Internet be commercially viable for the publishing industry, given the ease with which anyone can retrieve and copy electronic information?

Cyberspace Education

The possible uses of online information sources are limited only by the imagination. Search the net for educational sites at all levels (K through 12th grade, university, postgraduate). What added value does the Net provide that learners cannot get from print media or from classroom instruction?

Here's to Your Health

Do you have a health-related question you've been wanting to ask? Try looking up an answer on the Internet. Using whatever search engine you have access to, enter the search words for your question and link to the sites that look promising. Keeping yourself informed about health issues can help you stay healthy!

It May Be Fun, but Is It Efficient?

You have a paper on Thomas Jefferson due on Monday. See what information you can find about Jefferson on the World Wide Web. You will discover that a search on Thomas Jefferson leads to many unrelated links (**Thomas Jefferson University,** for example). Try your search with different search parameters (*Thomas Jefferson constitution,* or *Thomas Jefferson President,* for instance. Is this an efficient way to get information?

OTHER INTERNET TOOLS: GOPHER, FTP, VERONICA, AND ARCHIE

OBJECTIVES

After reading this chapter you will be able to:

1. Explain what a gopher server is and its importance on the Internet.
2. Tunnel through gopherspace using a Web browser and/or your Unix shell account.
3. Explain what anonymous FTP is.
4. FTP a file from a remote host using a Web browser, a Windows-based FTP client, and FTP commands at the Unix prompt.
5. Explain how to find gopher and FTP resources.

OVERVIEW

HTML documents, with their hot graphics and hypertext links, define the World Wide Web, but they are not the entire Internet. Text-only documents, program files, graphic images, and audio and video files are also available. While HTML documents are transferred on the Internet using HTTP, other resources may use different cataloging and transport methods, two of which are gopher and FTP (File Transport Protocol).

At the time gopher and FTP were developed, you could access Internet sites only if you knew how to enter the proper commands at the Unix prompt, a task new users found daunting. Fortunately for us, travel on the Net has changed. If you have the location information, you can get to and navigate around gopher and FTP sites using your Web browser. You may have already seen URLs that point to gopher and FTP sites; gopher://info.umd.edu and ftp://ksuvxa.kent.edu are examples of these types of URLs.

In the hands-on exercises in this chapter you'll learn how to "tunnel" in gopherspace, and several ways to retrieve files using FTP. We discuss the limitations of Web searches, and describe Veronica and

Archie, two search tools that will help you find gopher and FTP sites that may not be cataloged on the World Wide Web.

GOPHER

You have already seen how easy it is to use a browser to jump from one Web document to another. Prior to the development of the World Wide Web, however, the primary method of organizing and locating documents on the Internet was through gopher.

Gopher was developed at the University of Minnesota in 1991 to organize text information stored on Internet hosts. Just as you store files in a filing cabinet in a series of folders within folders, documents at a gopher site are organized into menus within menus. Documents are accessed by *tunneling* downward through a series of menus that provide more specific choices at each level.

Imagine that you are doing research on the U.S. space program and that you open a file cabinet that contains a folder about space shuttle launches. When you reach into the cabinet, you are suddenly transported to the Kennedy Space Center in Florida and are looking through the file cabinet there.

As implied in our space shuttle analogy, the gopher menu you see on your screen may link to a gopher resource anywhere in the world. Using gopher you are not limited to the documents available on the *gopher server* that runs locally on your campus Internet host. You can quickly and easily navigate *gopherspace,* which consists of all the publicly accessible gopher servers in the world.

GOPHERING WITH A WEB BROWSER

Depending on your campus Internet environment, gopherspace may be accessed in several ways. If you have Mosaic, Netscape, or another browser, you may type a gopher address as a URL and link directly to the gopher server. Alternatively, your home page probably has a link to your campus gopher, or to All the Gophers in the World. Figure 4.1a shows the University of Miami Biomedical Gopher main menu, as displayed in Netscape. Clicking on any one of the listings automatically links to the next-level menu on the gopher server. Notice the URL in the Location text box. Instead of the http:// delimiter at the beginning that is used in HTML document links, you see gopher://. (The first part of the URL indicates the transport protocol being used, in this case gopher.)

Clicking on the **Exploring the Internet** link displays the menu shown in Figure 4.1b. Notice that all the listings are preceded by a folder icon. This indicates that the link is to another menu, rather than to a document. Clicking on **How to Use Gopher** brings you to the screen shown in Figure 4.1c. Notice that different icons are displayed on this screen. Text files are preceded by a document icon. By the way, look at the URL now. Without any fanfare, we've been linked to another gopher server at USC, the University of Southern California! Clicking on the first link, **Let's Go Gopherin'**, displays the screen shown in Figure 4.1d. Notice that the gopher document is text based, without any of the graphics, fonts, and other formatting that give HTML documents their visual appeal.

The document in Figure 4.1d contains a description of an online gopher course offered on the Internet in 1993. The memo (to someone in the Air Force) indicates that the course was offered free. Reading further to the end of the text, we find that the memo was forwarded by Richard Smith of the Carnegie Library of Pittsburgh and Jim Gerland of SUNY Buffalo. You never know what collaborations will develop on the Net—it is truly independent of time and space! Since this site contains an extensive online course in using gopher, our first hands-on exercise takes us there.

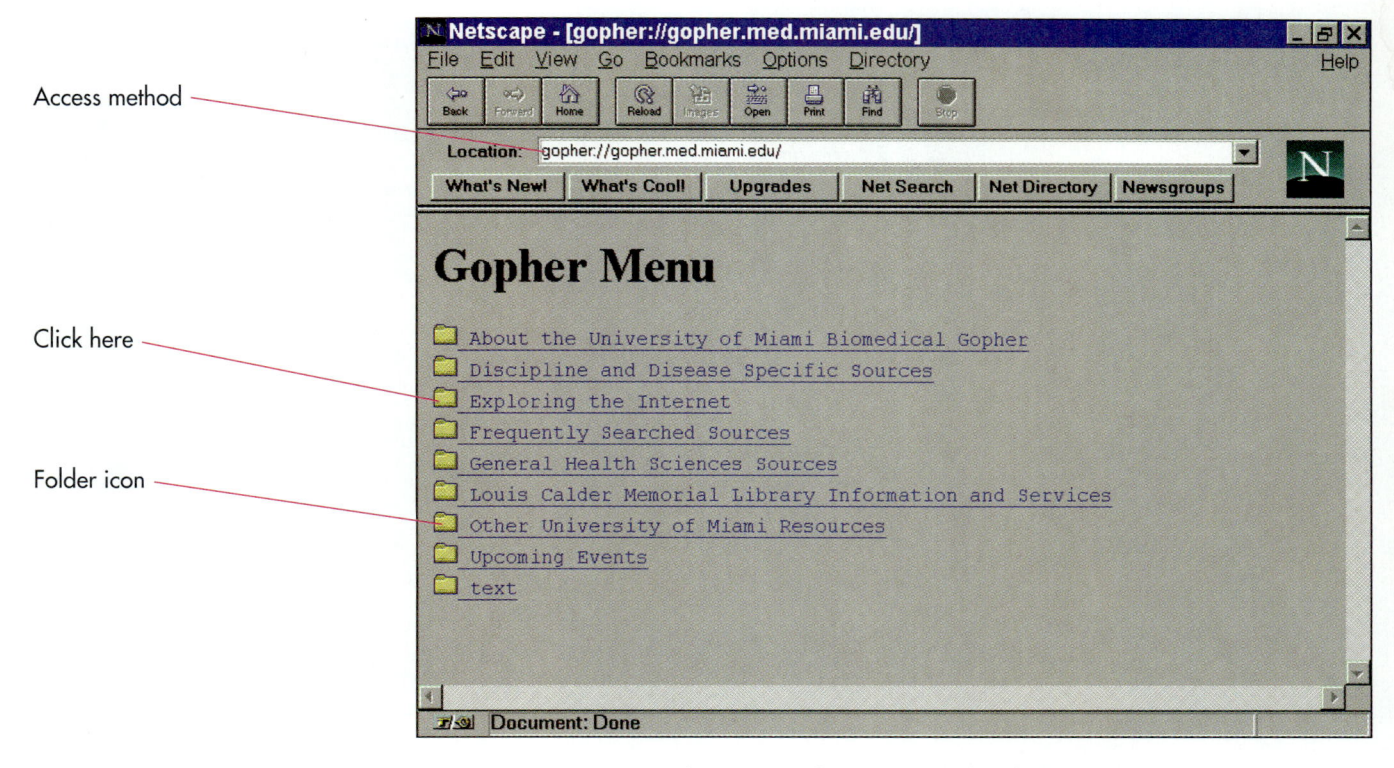

(a) The University of Miami Biomedical Gopher Main Menu

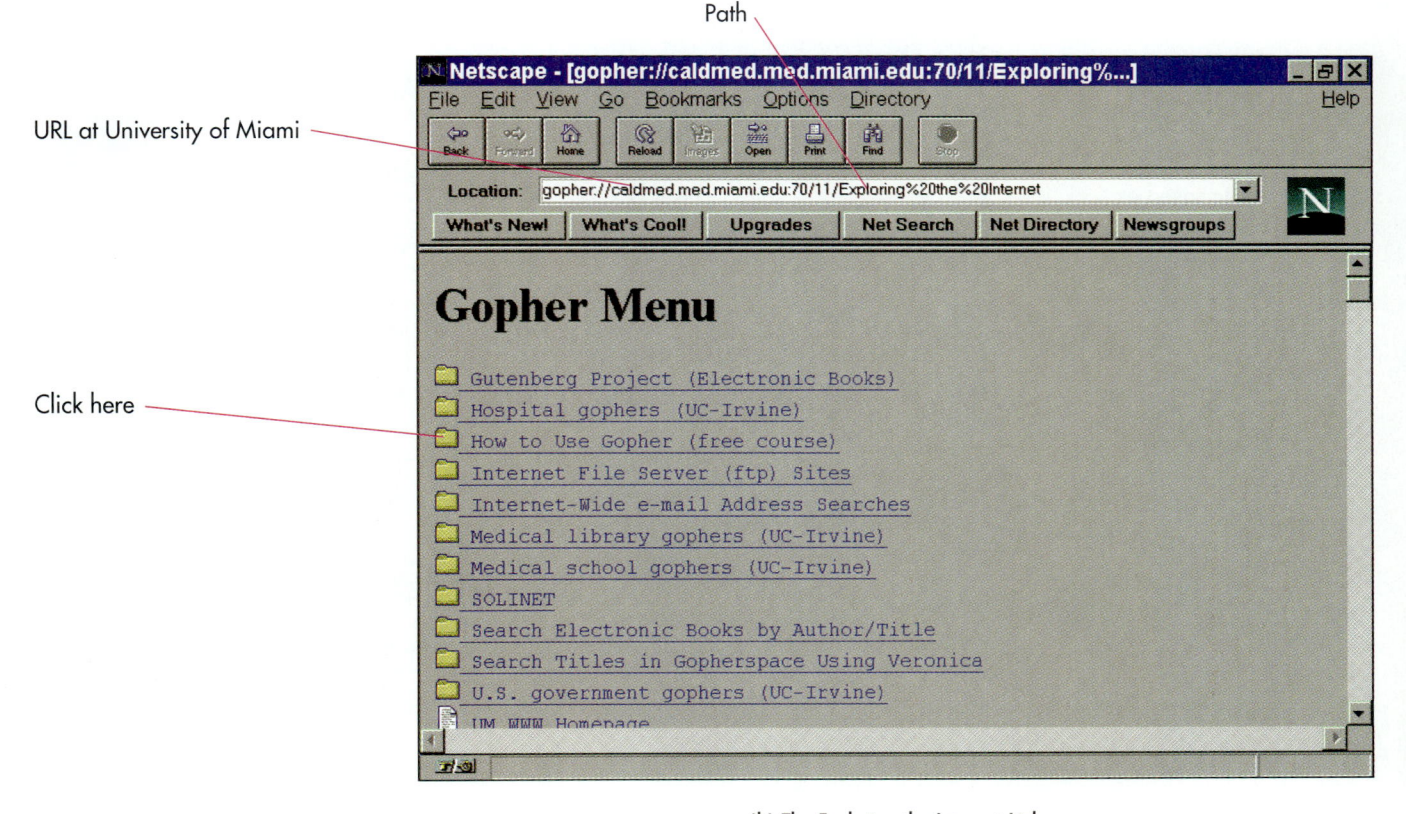

(b) The Exploring the Internet Link

FIGURE 4.1 Tunneling through Gopherspace

OTHER INTERNET TOOLS **131**

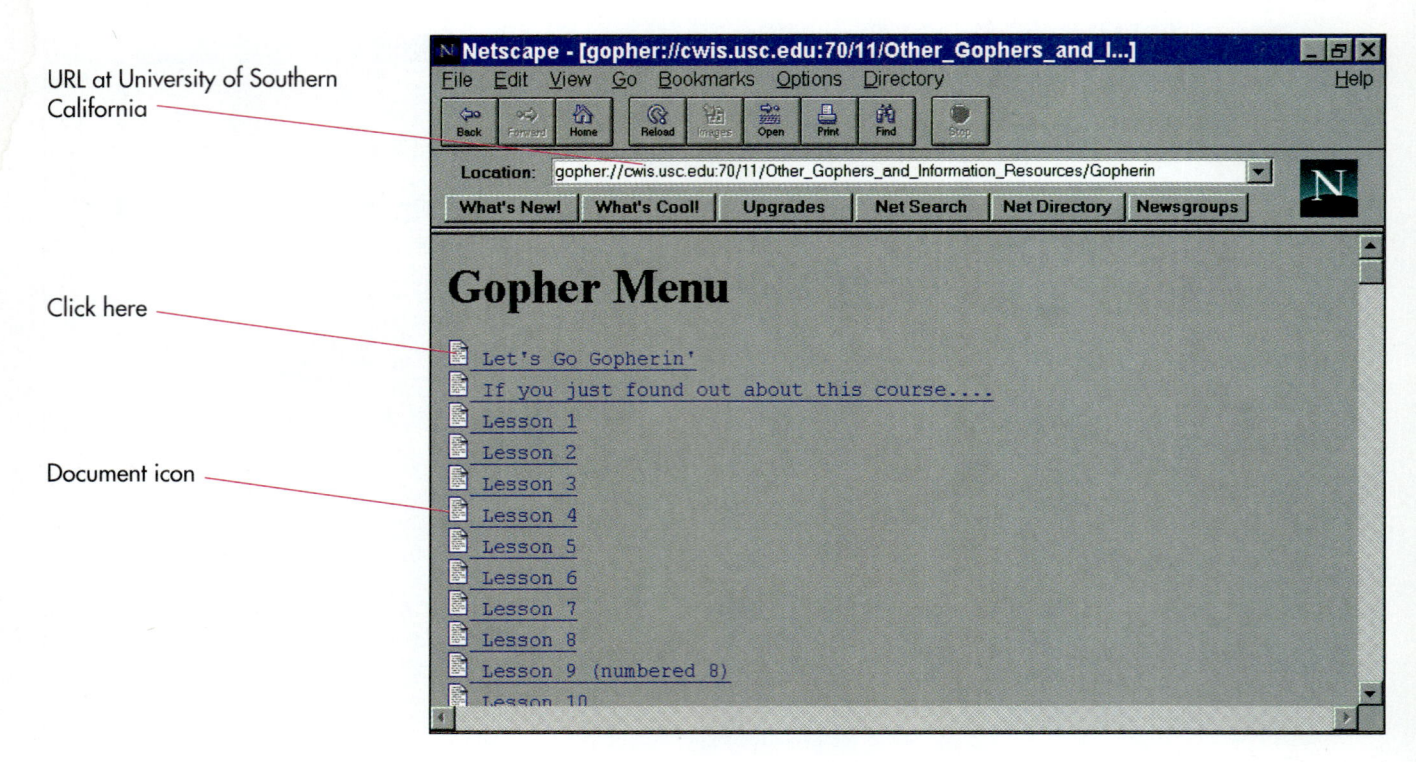

URL at University of Southern California

Click here

Document icon

(c) How to Use Gopher

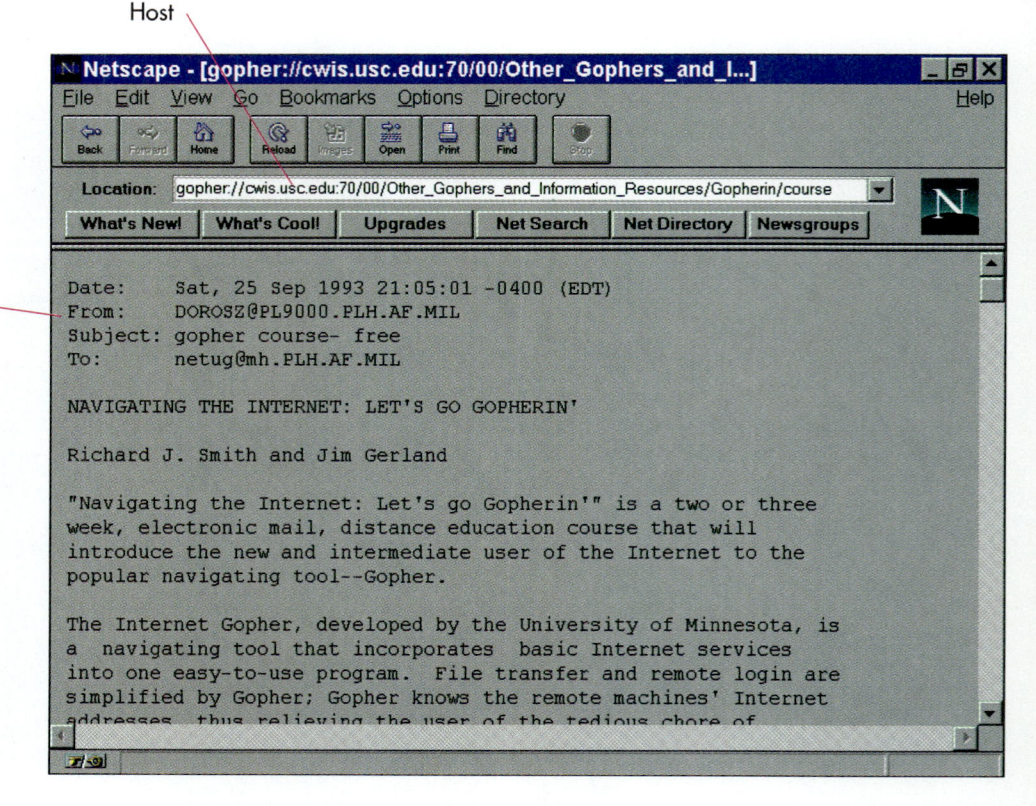

Host

E-mail message saved as gopher file

```
Date:    Sat, 25 Sep 1993 21:05:01 -0400 (EDT)
From:    DOROSZ@PL9000.PLH.AF.MIL
Subject: gopher course- free
To:      netug@mh.PLH.AF.MIL

NAVIGATING THE INTERNET: LET'S GO GOPHERIN'

Richard J. Smith and Jim Gerland

"Navigating the Internet: Let's go Gopherin'" is a two or three
week, electronic mail, distance education course that will
introduce the new and intermediate user of the Internet to the
popular navigating tool--Gopher.

The Internet Gopher, developed by the University of Minnesota, is
a navigating tool that incorporates basic Internet services
into one easy-to-use program. File transfer and remote login are
simplified by Gopher; Gopher knows the remote machines' Internet
```

(d) Let's Go Gopherin'

FIGURE 4.1 Tunneling through Gopherspace (continued)

132 EXPLORING THE INTERNET

LEARNING BY DOING

The Internet is so huge, is evolving so fast, and contains so many resources that it is hard to get a handle on it. Adding to your understanding of what it is and how to get around it will make your use of it more productive and, ultimately, more fun. In this exercise you will locate a specific gopher server through its URL, then take a more leisurely tour of gopherspace by tunneling through it, starting at the menu **All the Gophers in the World.** Most people think of the Internet entirely in terms of browsing Web documents. As you shall see in this exercise, gopher adds an entirely new dimension.

HANDS-ON EXERCISE 1

Tunneling through Gopherspace Using a Web Browser

Objective: To use a Web browser to tunnel through gopherspace. Use Figures 4.1 and 4.2 as guides in the exercise. The exercise is written using Netscape, but you can use any Web browser.

STEP 1: Enter the Gopher Site URL

➤ In Netscape, Mosaic, or whatever Web browser you use, enter the URL of the site you want to visit in the Location text box. In this case we'll visit the University of Miami gopher. Type the URL exactly as shown below:

   gopher://gopher.med.miami.edu

then press **Enter.** Your browser will pass the URL information to your Internet host, which will in turn make a request of the router, and so on, until the gopher site is located and the requested menu or document returned to your screen. It should look similar to the one shown in Figure 4.1a.

STEP 2: Select a Menu Item

➤ Click on the **Exploring the Internet** link to display the next set of gopher menus shown in Figure 4.1b.

➤ Click on **How to Use Gopher (free course).** You are linked to the list of documents shown in Figure 4.1c.

➤ Select **Add Bookmark** from the **Bookmark menu** to create a bookmark for this gopher site so you can return at any time to read the 25 short lessons on using gopher.

THE INTERNET IS ALWAYS CHANGING

Internet sites change all the time, depending on what the home page owners are doing. If you cannot reach the USC site by tunneling through the set of menus described above, try entering the URL to go directly to the gopher course: gopher://cwis.usc.edu/11/Other_Gophers_and_Information_Resources/Gopherin.

STEP 3: Tunnel Downward and Save the Document

➤ Click the first link, **Let's Go Gopherin'.** You will soon see a document describing the online gopher tutorial.

➤ Save this file locally so that you can read and refer to it without having to fight Internet traffic jams. Pull down the **File menu,** click **Save As,** and choose the appropriate drive and directory. Netscape contacts the gopher server, requests that the document be sent over the Net, and arranges for it to be stored in the directory you specified.

STEP 4: Browsing in Gopherspace

➤ Take a look at the URL for the *Let's Go Gopherin'* document. It should say

gopher://cwis.usc.edu/00/Other_Gophers_and_Information_Resources/Gopherin/course

➤ Click in the URL text box, then click again and drag to select the text

00/Other_Gophers_and_Information_Resources/Gopherin/course

➤ Press **Delete.** The URL should now point to

gopher://cwis.usc.edu

➤ Press **Enter.** You will link to the USC gopher menu shown in Figure 4.2. Click on **Other Gophers and Information Resources.**

➤ Click on **Gophers by Location.** Notice from the options that are displayed that you can tunnel down through gopherspace by geographic location. Clicking on North America would bring up a list of states in the U.S., any one of which you could click to locate a server.

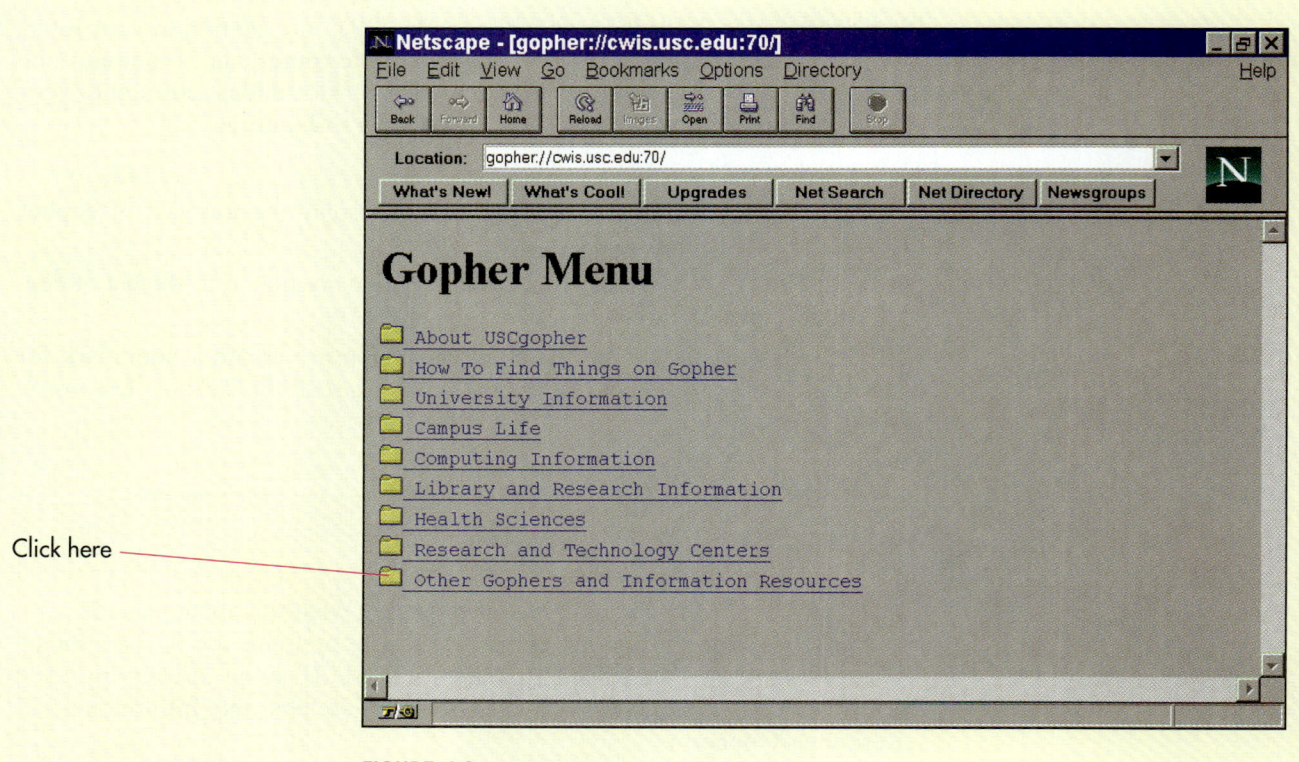

Click here →

FIGURE 4.2 Hands-on Exercise 1

134 EXPLORING THE INTERNET

> ► Click on **All the Gopher Servers in the World.** This document will take a while to load, as it is literally preparing a list of all the gopher resources around the world. Once it is done loading, click anywhere you want and go. Have fun!

GOPHERING USING YOUR SHELL ACCOUNT

You do not need Netscape or another Web browser to use gopher—you can access it from your Unix shell account. If your campus has a local gopher server (that is, a gopher program loaded on the Internet host at your site), you can simply type *gopher* at the Unix prompt, and your gopher main menu will appear on your screen. If you do not have a gopher server on your host, you can telnet to a public gopher server at another site.

In either case the menu you see will look something like the one shown in Figure 4.3. You will select menu items by using the Up/Down Arrow keys and pressing Enter, as you will practice in the following hands-on exercise. You will also discover how to set up a bookmark using gopher.

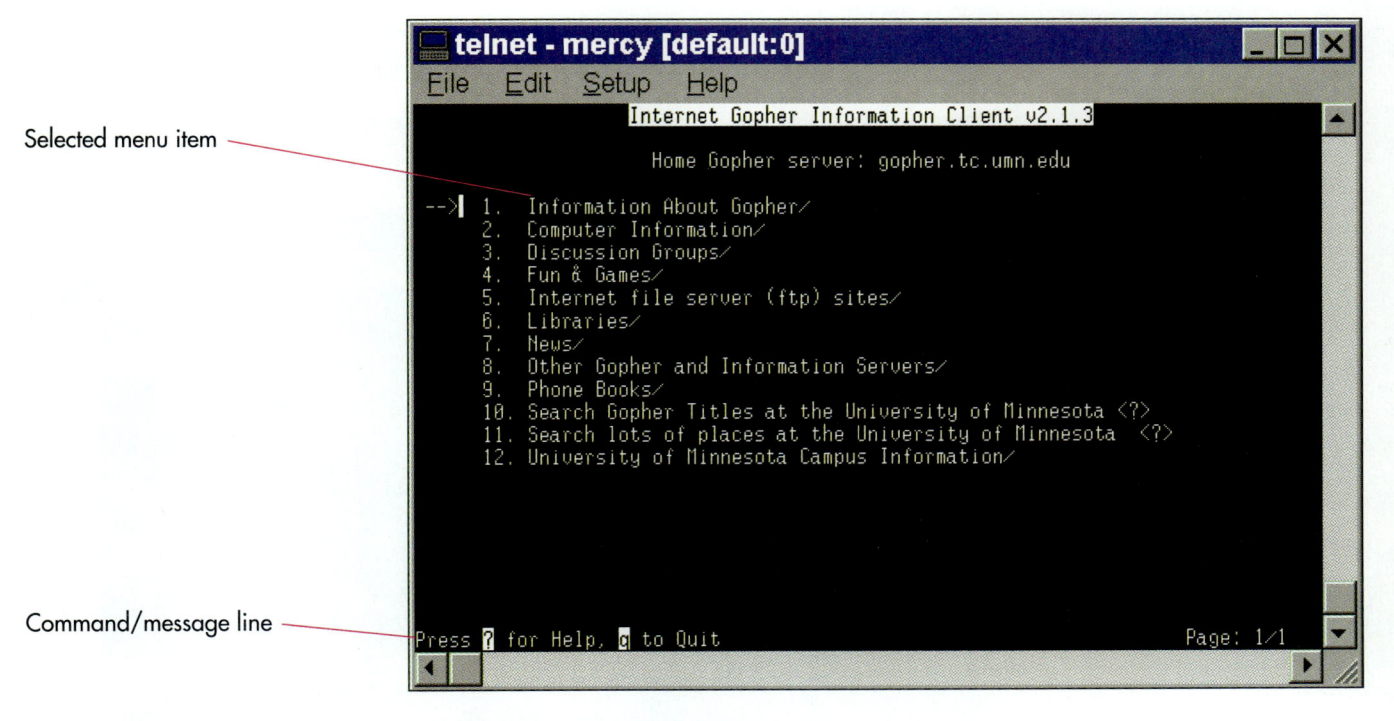

FIGURE 4.3 A Gopher Menu in Unix

HANDS-ON EXERCISE 2

Gophering Using Your Unix Shell Account

Objective: To use a gopher server to tunnel through gopherspace. Use Figures 4.3 and 4.4 as guides in the exercise.

OTHER INTERNET TOOLS

STEP 1: Log On to Your Unix Shell Account and Start Gopher

➤ Log onto your Unix shell account in the usual way. If you don't remember how, review the instructions in Chapter 1. Then see your instructor or help desk for assistance.

➤ At the Unix prompt, type **gopher** and press **Enter.**
- If your college or university main gopher menu is displayed, proceed to step 3.
- If you do not have a gopher server installed at your site, you will see an error message similar to that shown in Figure 4.4a. You will have to telnet to one of the public gopher sites listed in Table 4.1. Proceed to step 2.

TABLE 4.1

Gopher Site	Login ID	Location
University of Minnesota	gopher	consultant.micro.umn.edu
Michigan State University	gopher	gopher.msu.edu
UC Santa Cruz	gopher	infoslug.ucsc.edu
University of Iowa	panda	panda.uiowa.edu
Australia	info	info.anu.edu.au
South America	gopher	tolten.puc.cl
Japan	gopher	gan.ncc.go.jp

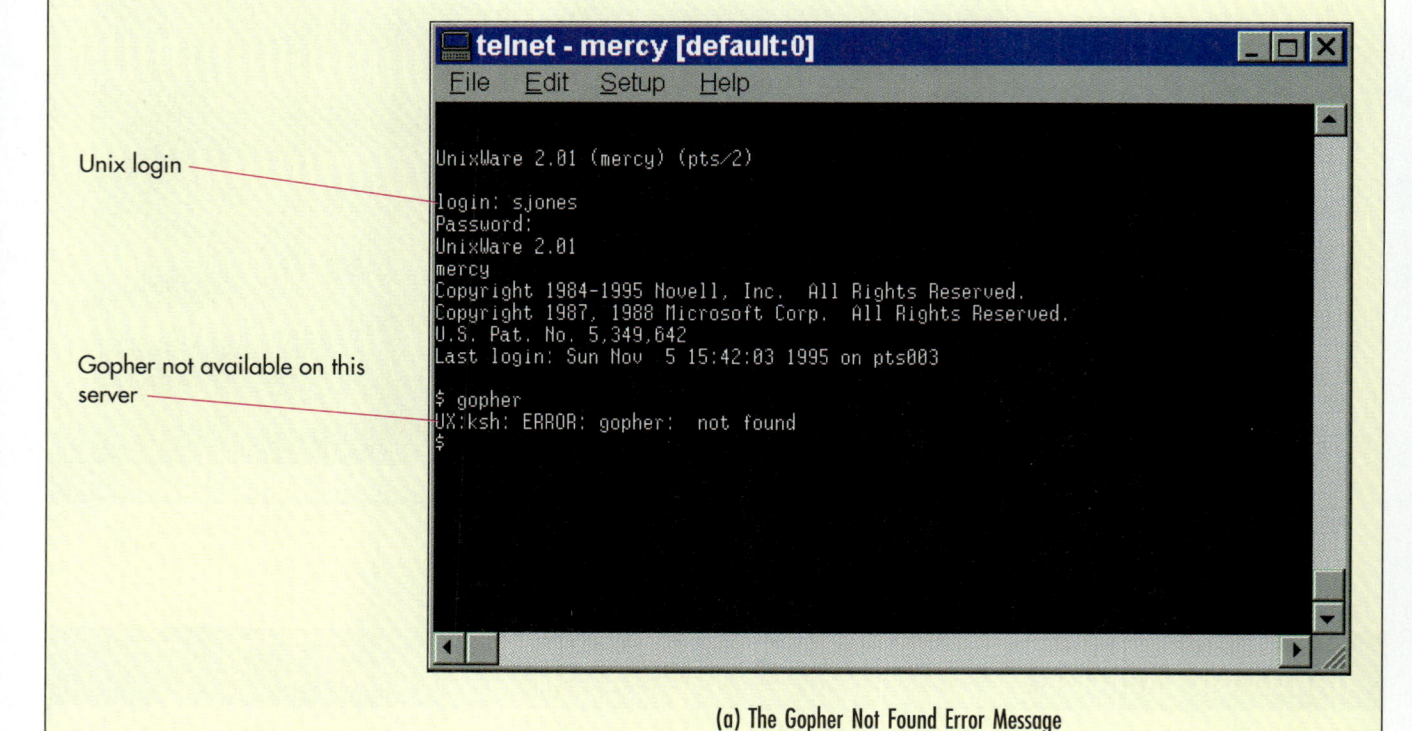

```
UnixWare 2.01 (mercy) (pts/2)

login: sjones
Password:
UnixWare 2.01
mercy
Copyright 1984-1995 Novell, Inc.  All Rights Reserved.
Copyright 1987, 1988 Microsoft Corp.  All Rights Reserved.
U.S. Pat. No. 5,349,642
Last login: Sun Nov  5 15:42:03 1995 on pts003

$ gopher
UX:ksh: ERROR: gopher:   not found
$
```

Unix login

Gopher not available on this server

(a) The Gopher Not Found Error Message

FIGURE 4.4   Hands-on Exercise 2

STEP 2: Telnet to a Public Gopher Server

Proceed with this step only if you do not have a gopher server at your location.

➤ At the Unix prompt, type **telnet consultant.micro.umn.edu,** substituting any of the public gopher addresses shown in Table 4.1 if the one at the University of Minnesota is busy. (You should attempt to use the one closest to you to avoid the overhead involved in transmitting the information from a distant site.)

➤ Press **Enter.** You will see a screen similar to that shown in Figure 4.4b.

➤ You will typically see instructions on the login screen explaining how to log on to the remote gopher server. Enter the guest login ID indicated in the instructions, which is usually a default of **gopher.**

➤ You must respond if the system you log on to asks for your terminal type. It will typically present you with a default of VT100 or VT220. Press **Enter** to accept the default, or type in your terminal type if different (check with your lab assistant or help desk to find out what terminal type you should use).

➤ Once you have successfully logged on, you can proceed with the rest of the exercise, starting at step 3.

STEP 3: Exploring Gopherspace

➤ Select a gopher menu to explore.
  • Use your **Up/Down Arrow keys** to move through the menu options until the menu you want is highlighted with reverse video (black on white).
  • Press **Enter.** The next-level menu is displayed.

➤ Continue tunneling through gopherspace as long as you wish.

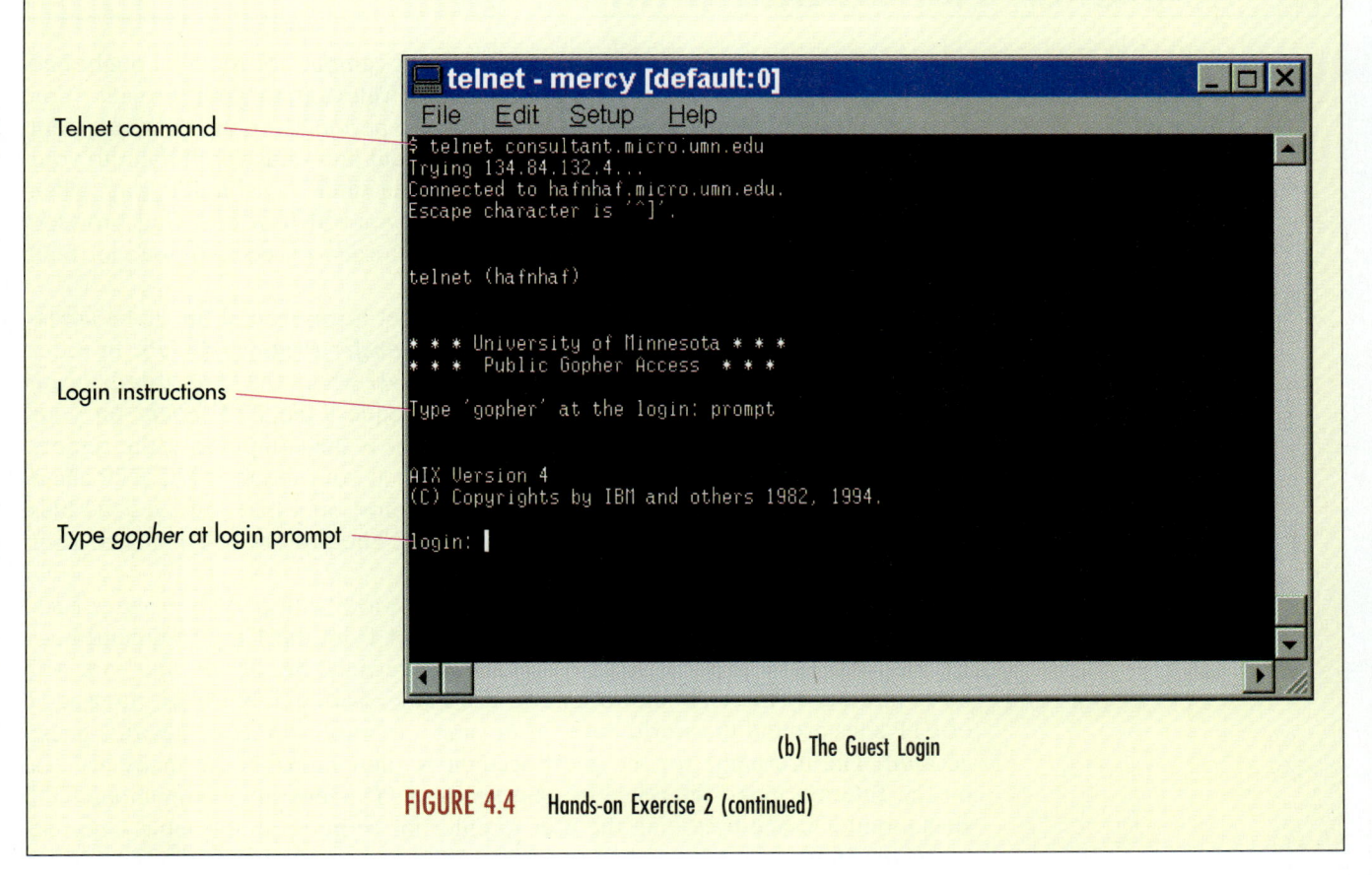

(b) The Guest Login

FIGURE 4.4 Hands-on Exercise 2 (continued)

STEP 4: Bookmark a Favorite Site

➤ Choose a site you want to return to, then type the letter **a** to add the gopher menu to your bookmark list.

➤ Type **v** to view the bookmark list. *Note: You will be able to view your bookmarks the next time you use gopher only if you are using a gopher server at your own site. If you are telnetting to a public gopher, your bookmarks will not be saved.*

STEP 5: Quit Gopher and Log Off

➤ When you are finished exploring gopherspace, press **q** to quit.

➤ Log off your Unix account in the usual manner.

---

gopher://una.hh.lib.umich.edu/11/inetdirs

The Internet Clearinghouse provides a searchable index of guides to using the Internet. This is a good place to start if you want more information about an Internet resource.

FILE TRANSFER PROTOCOL (FTP)

Imagine that you are researching a subject in your campus library. You might find several magazines and books with information relevant to your project. You browse quickly through the magazines while in the periodical room, but don't want to read the books in the library. You check them out and return with them to your residence hall where you will work on your paper later. In a similar way, when working with Web documents you may find some you will view with your browser, and others you will want to download and save locally on disk so you can read them at a later time.

There are literally millions of files on Internet hosts around the globe accessible through a special protocol known as *File Transfer Protocol (FTP).* In order to retrieve these files you must access the *FTP server* where they are stored, locate the specific directory where they reside, then request the *FTP client* on your machine to retrieve them for you. The FTP server is the computer at the remote site that houses the files and "serves" them to you at your request. The FTP client is the software that runs on your PC or Internet host, and that retrieves the files for you and stores them locally on your machine. The process of FTPing to your PC is diagrammed in Figure 4.5.

You may access an FTP server in multiple ways: with a Web browser such as Netscape, with a Windows-based FTP client, or from the Unix command line. Because you are logging into the remote site to retrieve the desired file, you will be requested by the FTP site to enter a username. Fortunately for us, thousands of FTP sites around the world have set up access to public directories with a guest account. The username for the guest account is anonymous, hence many articles on the Internet make reference to *anonymous FTP.* Generally, anonymous FTP sites monitor usage by asking the user to enter his or her real username—that is, *username@host.anyu.edu*—as the password. When accessing an FTP site via a Web browser, the software automatically enters the username and password for you.

138 EXPLORING THE INTERNET

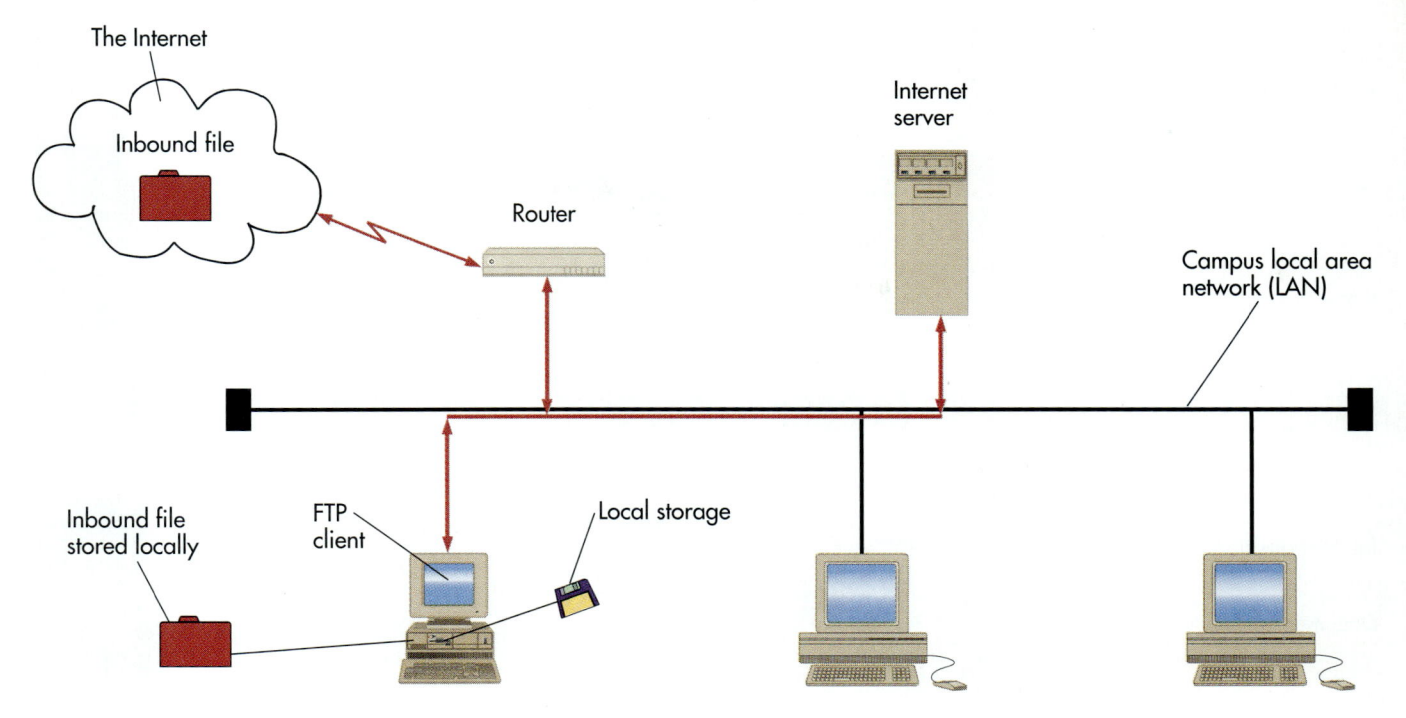

FIGURE 4.5 FTP with a PC Client

The following discussion first describes FTP using a Windows-based Web browser such as Netscape, which is very similar to browsing for any other type of Web document. Next you will learn about using a Windows-based FTP client to retrieve/download a file from a remote site to your PC. Some compressed files need to be retrieved and uncompressed using a Unix host, so we continue by discussing how you can download files using simple FTP commands from your Unix shell account. You will use these commands in the last hands-on exercise. There is generally a limit to the number of concurrent users at any site, so if you cannot reach a particular site, try again at a later time.

FTP with a Web Browser

Many FTP resources are cataloged on the World Wide Web, and will be included as links when you create a query using a search engine. Say, for instance, that you are researching genealogy. A Web search might yield the URL ftp://issl.cs.byu.edu/ as an FTP site at Brigham Young University, where information about genealogy resides. Netscape and other Web browsers make accessing the FTP server transparent to the user. You simply point to the FTP link and click as you would with any other Web hypertext document. Netscape takes care of contacting the FTP server at the remote site, logging in as anonymous, entering a password, and changing to the appropriate directory. You may also link to an FTP site by entering its address as a URL in the Location text box, preceded by the delimiter ftp://.

Clicking the BYU link brings up the screen shown in Figure 4.6, which displays the contents of the directory on the remote host. Icons indicate whether the item is a directory (folder icon) or file (document icon). If you click on a directory icon, you will tunnel down through the directory structure on the remote machine. If you click a file icon, Netscape will retrieve the file and display it on your screen. If you find a file you want to save locally, you can do so using the Save As command in the File menu.

OTHER INTERNET TOOLS

Click to save file

Compressed file

famHist directory

Documents

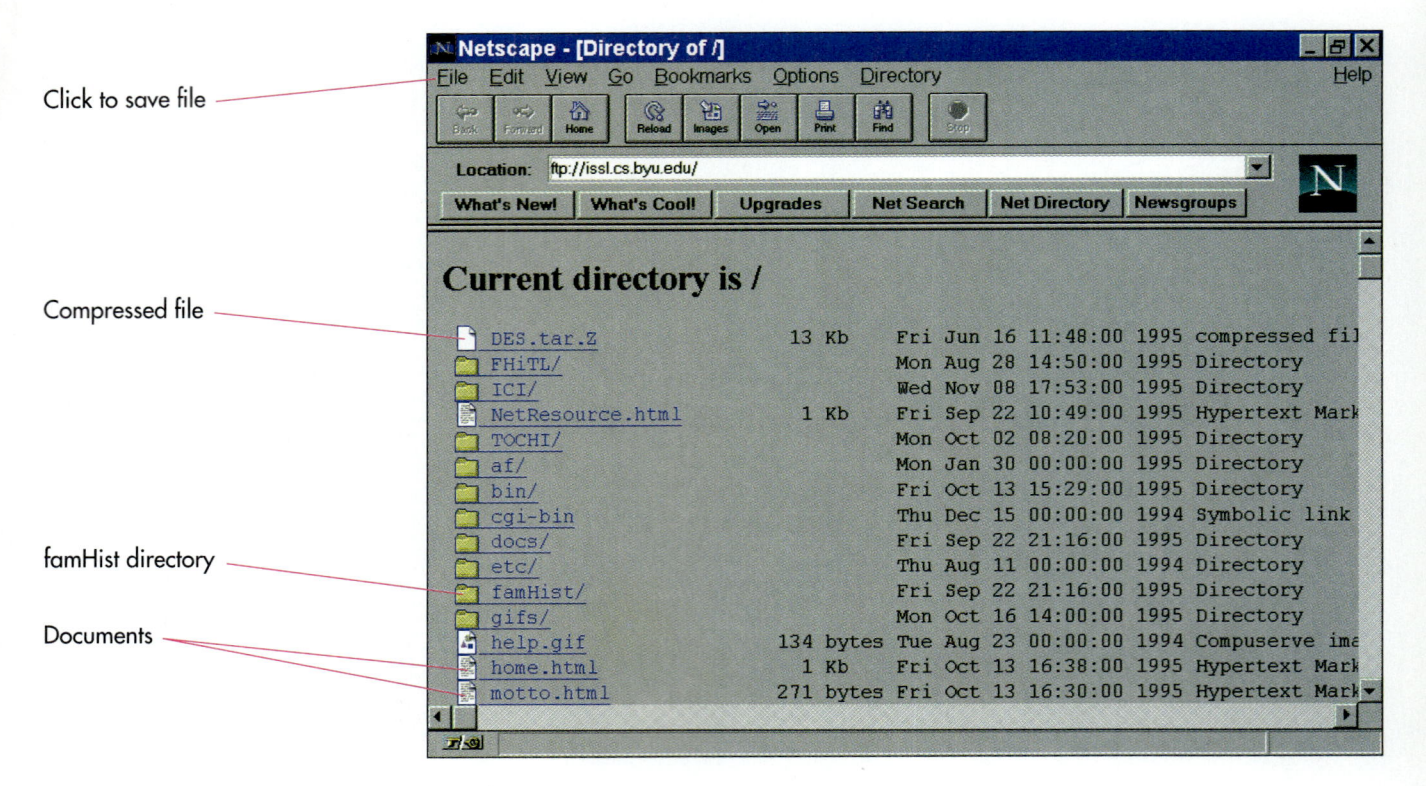

FIGURE 4.6 An FTP Directory

> ### DEALING WITH COMPRESSED FILES
>
> There are many program and graphics files at FTP sites that cannot be viewed with a Web browser because they are *compressed files.* Compression uses an algorithm to reduce the size of the file without losing any of the stored data. Common file extensions for compressed files are .Z, .ZR, .gz, and .zip. If you click on a compressed file while using a Web browser, you may see a message asking whether you want to save the file to disk. If you do, follow the instructions in the dialog box to do so. Occasionally, Netscape or your browser may retrieve and display a file format as "garbage." You should, in this case, retrieve the file again using a Windows-based FTP client that will download the file without trying to display it. See your campus system administrator for the appropriate software and commands to uncompress the compressed files once you have downloaded them.

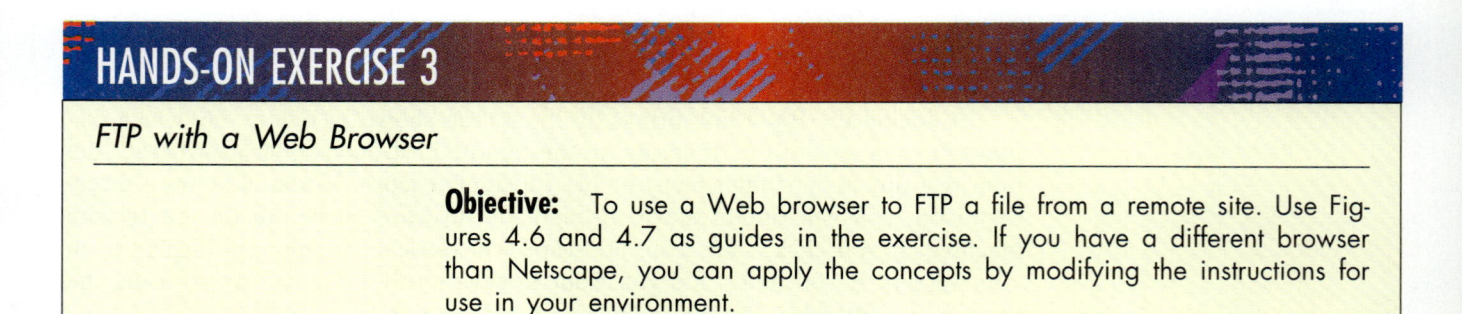

HANDS-ON EXERCISE 3

FTP with a Web Browser

Objective: To use a Web browser to FTP a file from a remote site. Use Figures 4.6 and 4.7 as guides in the exercise. If you have a different browser than Netscape, you can apply the concepts by modifying the instructions for use in your environment.

140 EXPLORING THE INTERNET

STEP 1: Access the FTP Site

➤ Open your Internet applications program group as you normally do and start your Web browser.

➤ Type the address of the FTP site you want to explore in the URL text box. In this case let's go to the site with information on genealogy, Brigham Young University. Type **ftp://issl.cs.byu.edu/** and press **Enter** to display the FTP directory at the site.

STEP 2: Select the Directory

➤ Click on the **famHist/** directory, which is preceded by the folder icon. A new screen full of documents and files is displayed.

STEP 3: Display the Document

➤ Click on **home.htm.** The document is downloaded and displayed on your screen. There is no need to close the FTP connection when retrieving files using a Web browser; the browser automatically closes the connection once the document is retrieved.

STEP 4: Save the File

➤ Select **Save As** on the **File menu.** The dialog box shown in Figure 4.7 is displayed.

➤ Select the appropriate drive and directory from those shown in the dialog box.

➤ Click **OK.** The document is now on your local or system hard drive.

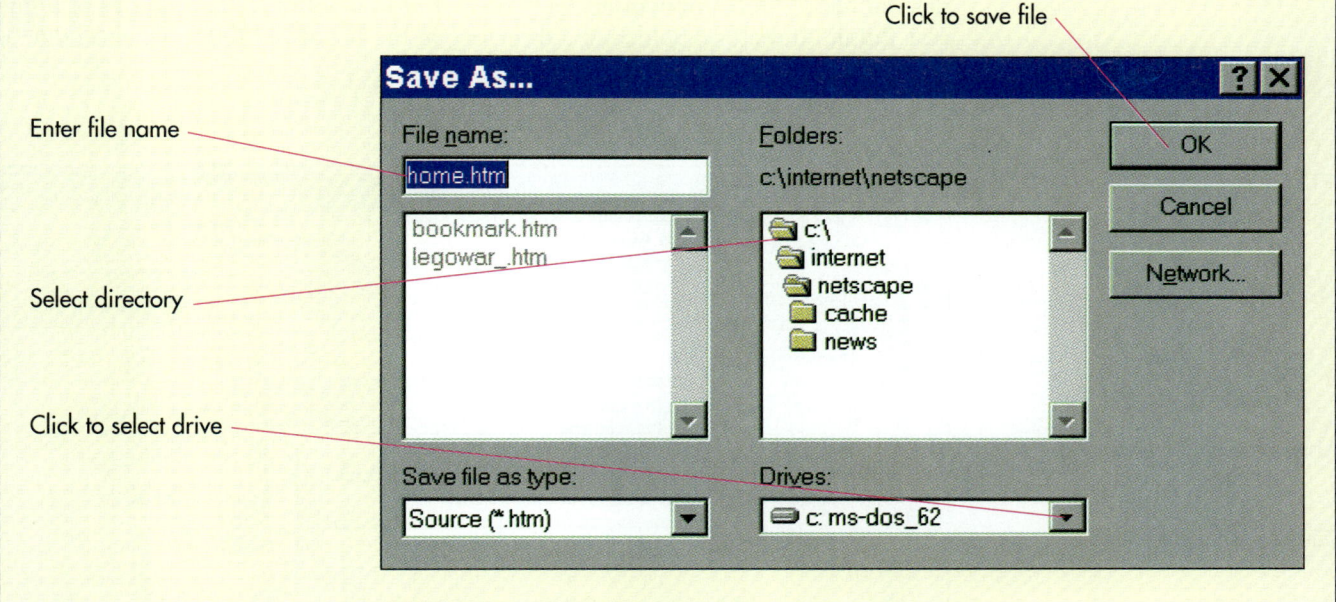

FIGURE 4.7   Hands-on Exercise 3

STEP 5: Exit Netscape

➤ Pull down the **File menu,** then click **Exit.** Log off the system.

OTHER INTERNET TOOLS   **141**

> **DOWNLOADER BEWARE!**
>
> The system administrator at an anonymous FTP site may not have checked all the files in his/her public directories for viruses. Be sure to scan all software you download *before* you install or execute it. Check with your system administrator or help desk for instructions on how to do this in your environment.

FTP with a Windows-based FTP Client

If for some reason you don't have access to a Web browser, you can easily connect to a remote system and retrieve files using a Windows-based FTP client.

In order to connect to the remote system, the FTP address is entered in the Host text box shown in Figure 4.8a. As we mentioned earlier, most public FTP servers on the Internet request that you log in as *anonymous,* with your username (e.g., *sjones@mercy.sjc.edu*) as the password. Once this information is entered, the user simply clicks OK, and the software will connect to the remote site and log on. (The host shown is an FTP site at MIT in Cambridge, Massachusetts. You might have found this host address in a magazine article or been told about it by a friend. It happens to contain a FAQ (Frequently Asked Questions) file about Greece, which you will retrieve in the next hands-on exercise.)

At the remote site you move through the directory structure to find the desired files. Often, anonymous FTP files are stored within subdirectories of a Pub (for Public) directory. Selecting a directory in the list at the right of the screen, as

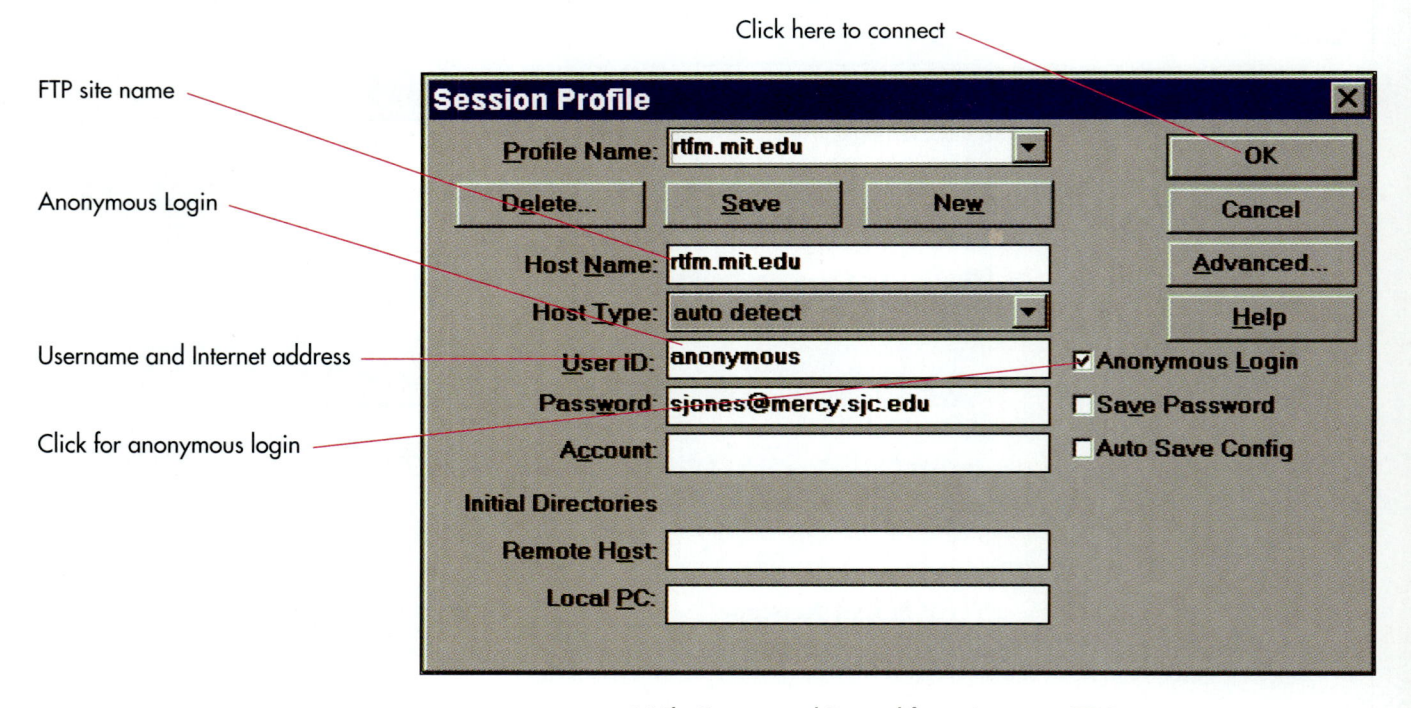

(a) The Username and Password for an Anonymous FTP Session

FIGURE 4.8 FTP with a Windows Client

142 EXPLORING THE INTERNET

(b) Selecting the Remote Directory

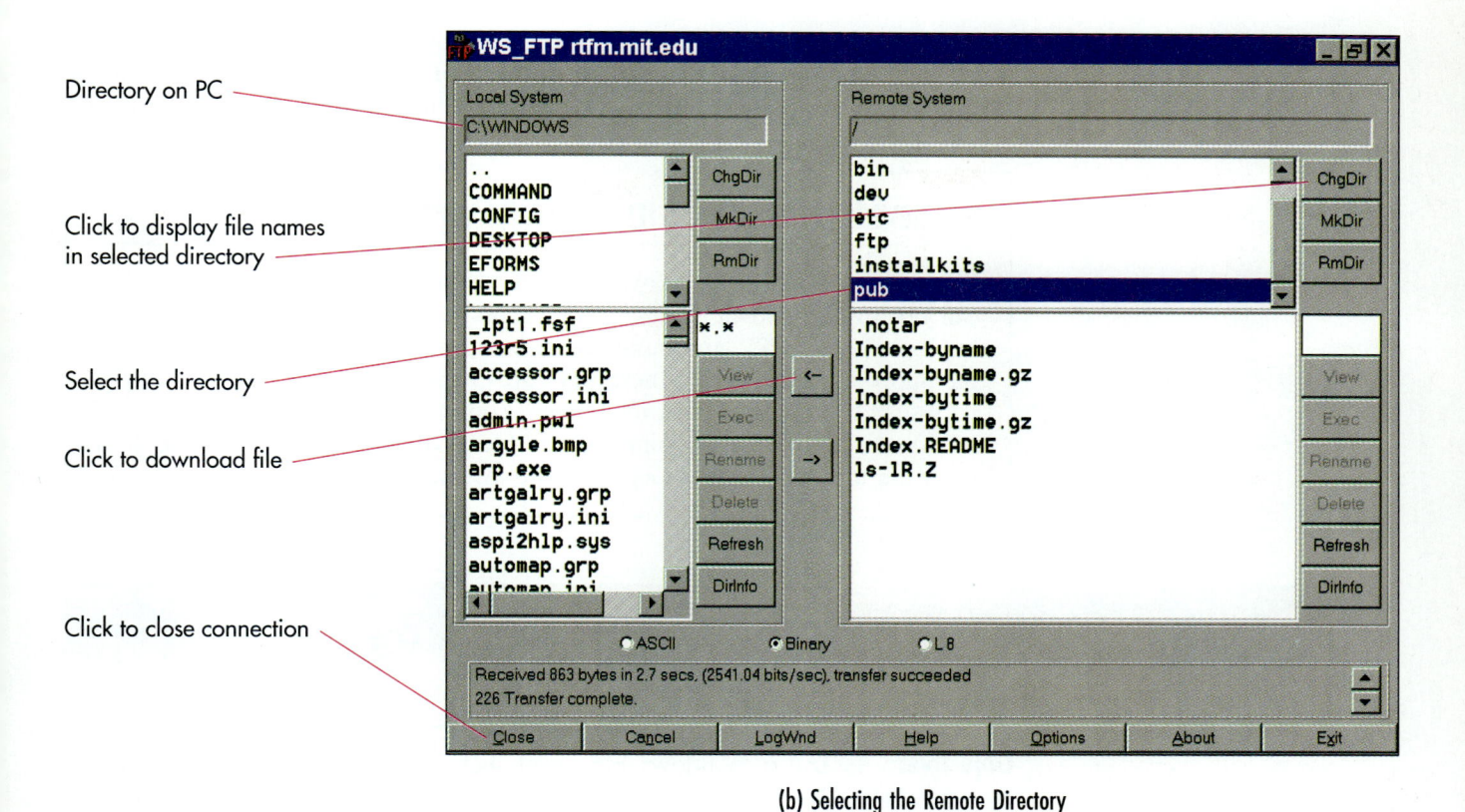

FIGURE 4.8 FTP with a Windows Client (continued)

BINARY VERSUS ASCII TRANSFER

You will notice in the middle of the WS_FTP screen the two options Binary and ASCII. These refer to the format in which the data is transmitted. *ASCII mode* will transmit text only, regardless of what's in the files. Any files that contain formatting (word processing documents, for instance) or graphics must be transmitted in *binary mode.* Therefore your best bet is to be sure that the Binary option is always selected prior to clicking Connect.

shown in Figure 4.8b, and clicking the ChgDir button will change to the requested directory. You can continue down through the directory structure this way until you locate the file you want, shown in the bottom half of the Remote Site list on the right of the screen in Figure 4.8b.

Once you find the file you want, select the target directory on the local host (your PC). Click the Left Arrow button in the middle of the screen to transfer the file from the remote host to the local directory. After downloading all desired files, click the Close button and the FTP client closes the connection.

When using an FTP client, you will observe that the file is not displayed when selected, as it is with a Web browser. It is simply transferred in its entirety to your computer. Once you retrieve it, if it is a document file, you can display it using whatever software was used to create it (Word, for instance, if it is a word processing document). If it is a program file, you should be able to load and execute

OTHER INTERNET TOOLS **143**

it on the appropriate machine (PC, Macintosh, and so on). If it is a compressed file, which many program files are, you will need to see your system administrator for the software and commands necessary to uncompress it on your system.

> **RETRIEVING INTERNET CLIENT SOFTWARE WITH FTP**
>
> FTP is how most of the software found on the Internet is transferred. You can retrieve your own copies of applications such as Netscape, Lynx, TurboGopher, WS_FTP, and hundreds of computer games using FTP. Perform the appropriate search on these keywords in your Web browser to find the FTP sites from which to retrieve them. You may also have to download the software necessary to decompress the files. Download all README files from the target FTP directory for more instructions.

HANDS-ON EXERCISE 4

FTP with a Windows FTP Client

Objective: To use a Windows FTP client such as WS_FTP to FTP a file from a remote site. Use Figure 4.8 as a guide in the exercise. Even if you have a different Windows client, you can still apply the concepts in your environment.

STEP 1: Open the Client Software

- Log onto your system and open your Internet applications program group.
- Double click the **FTP** client icon to display the Session Profile dialog box. Maximize the FTP window.

STEP 2. Connect to the Remote Site

- Click the **Anonymous Login** check box to fill in the user ID and password.
- Click **OK** in the Session Profile dialog box. Your PC will contact the remote location and set up the FTP connection.

STEP 3: Find the File

- Scroll down through the displayed directories on the right side of the screen until you see the directory in which the desired file is stored. In this case the file we want is located several levels down in a directory called **greek-faq**. (*FAQ* stands for Frequently Asked Questions. You will find FAQ directories about a myriad of subjects all over the Net.) You will tunnel down to the **greek-faq** directory. Click on **pub** to select it. Click the **ChgDir button** to change to the pub directory.
- Scroll down the directory structure on the right side of the screen, selecting **usenet** within the pub directory, then clicking **ChgDir**. This is a big directory, and it may take a while to load. Also note that the directory box at the top of the window will display Usenet-by-group.
- Once the list of newsgroups is displayed, select **news.answers** within usenet, and finally, **greek-faq** within news.answers. Click **ChgDir** each time you want to change to the next-level directory.

144 EXPLORING THE INTERNET

➤ Scroll down in the greek-faq directory in the bottom half of the Remote System directory window until the **culture** file is visible. Click the file to select it.

VIEWING FILES BEFORE RETRIEVING THEM

Your FTP client may let you look at a text file before you actually retrieve it and store it on your computer. In WS_FTP, with the file selected, click the View button on the same side as the Remote Host list box. It will take several seconds/minutes to display the file, which will be in its own window. After looking at the document, close the document window to return to FTP and continue with the transfer, or select a different file. *Note:* you will not be able to view compressed files (.Z, .ZR, .tar, .zip, .gz, and so on).

STEP 4. Change Directories on the Local Host
➤ On the left side of the screen select the drive and directory you want the file to be transferred to when it is downloaded.

STEP 5. FTP the File
➤ Click the **Left Arrow button** in the middle of the screen. The file will be FTPed to the directory you specified on the left side of the screen. The progress of the transfer is displayed in the bottom section of the screen.

FTP CAN TAKE "FOREVER"

Since each character in a file is sent over the Internet one bit at a time (and there are eight bits to each character), even small files can take a long time to transfer, especially if you're using a modem to FTP. Given that the Internet is already a crowded and busy place, you should confine your FTPing to very early in the morning or very late at night, or you may tie up significant resources at both your site and the remote host. Be considerate—Internet services such as FTP are built on the premise that we will all use the resources wisely.

STEP 6. Close the Connection
➤ You will see a message at the bottom of the screen when the file transfer is complete. Click **Close** to close the FTP session on the remote computer. Click **Exit** to exit the FTP client.

STEP 7. Read the File
➤ You can check that the file was indeed transferred by opening whatever word processor you use, then selecting **Open** from the **File menu.** Locate the document in the directory you selected in step 4.
➤ Select it and click **OK**. You should see a list of topics regarding Greek culture. Scroll down through the document—can you believe you just retrieved it from MIT? There's a world of FTP files out there waiting!

FTP Using the Unix Prompt

If you don't have the World Wide Web or a Windows-based FTP client to access FTP sites, or if you want to download compressed files that must be uncompressed in a Unix environment (.Z, .ZR, and .tar files), you will have to learn some simple FTP commands to retrieve files using your Unix shell account.

You will have to type in the command sequence to contact the remote computer, log in as anonymous, enter your username, change to the appropriate directory, and retrieve the file. Because the computer can do only what you tell it to do, and because it understands only a limited subset of commands, you must be sure to type each command correctly (spelling, punctuation, and capitalization are all very important). It is not as bad as it sounds, but you will surely appreciate the GUI interface available in the computer lab if you have one! The sequence of commands used to access an FTP site and retrieve a file, and what each command means, is shown in Table 4.1.

> **CASE MATTERS**
>
> URLs in the Internet are case sensitive, including FTP addresses. You must type the site, directory, and file names exactly as shown in whatever source you found them, or your attempts to retrieve the files will be unsuccessful. In particular, watch for 1(numeral) and l (letter), 0 (zero) and O (letter), and - (dash) and _ (underscore). They can be difficult to distinguish.

Occasionally, your FTP session may be interrupted, or you may not be able to find the file where you expected it to be. The commands shown in Table 4.2 may be useful as you navigate through another computer's directories.

TABLE 4.1 FTP Commands

Command	Description
ftp *hostaddress*	The command necessary to activate the FTP client and contact the remote site.
anonymous	Your login ID to use the remote system.
yourname@host.anyu.edu	Your username entered as the password on the remote system—helps the FTP site track users.
cd pub	Change to the public directory (substitute a different directory name if necessary).
cd /pub/*other_directory*	Use the full directory path given in the information where you found the FTP site reference if the desired file is down more than one level in the directory structure.
binary	The command necessary to ensure the correct transmission of files containing formatting (word processing documents) or graphic images.
get *filename*	Retrieve the file (substitute the file name of the file you wish to retrieve).
get *filename newfilename*	You may wish to rename the file locally. You can do so by specifying a different name for the file in the get command.
quit	To close the FTP connection to the remote host, return to the local Unix prompt.

TABLE 4.2 More FTP Commands

Command	Description
open *hostaddress*	If your command is not successful, you may have to try connecting to the site again from the ftp> prompt.
cdup	Allows you to move up one level in the directory structure on the host computer.
pwd	Displays the name of the current directory on the host.
dir	Displays the contents of the current directory, including files and subdirectories.
close	Closes the current connection, but keeps FTP running to access another site.
help	Displays a list of the available FTP commands.
help *command*	Displays help about the listed FTP command.

When you download a file using your Unix shell account, it resides on your college's Unix server, not your PC. This is shown in Figure 4.9. Contrast it with Figure 4.5, which shows the downloaded file residing on your PC. You will not be able to access the file you FTPed from the Unix prompt with your word processor, or uncompress it and run it on your PC. Contact your system administrator to find out how to uncompress the files in Unix, and how to transfer the uncompressed files, if possible, from your Unix host to a PC in your college computing environment. (You will probably use an FTP client to retrieve the uncompressed files from the Unix host, just as you did in Hands-on Exercise 4.)

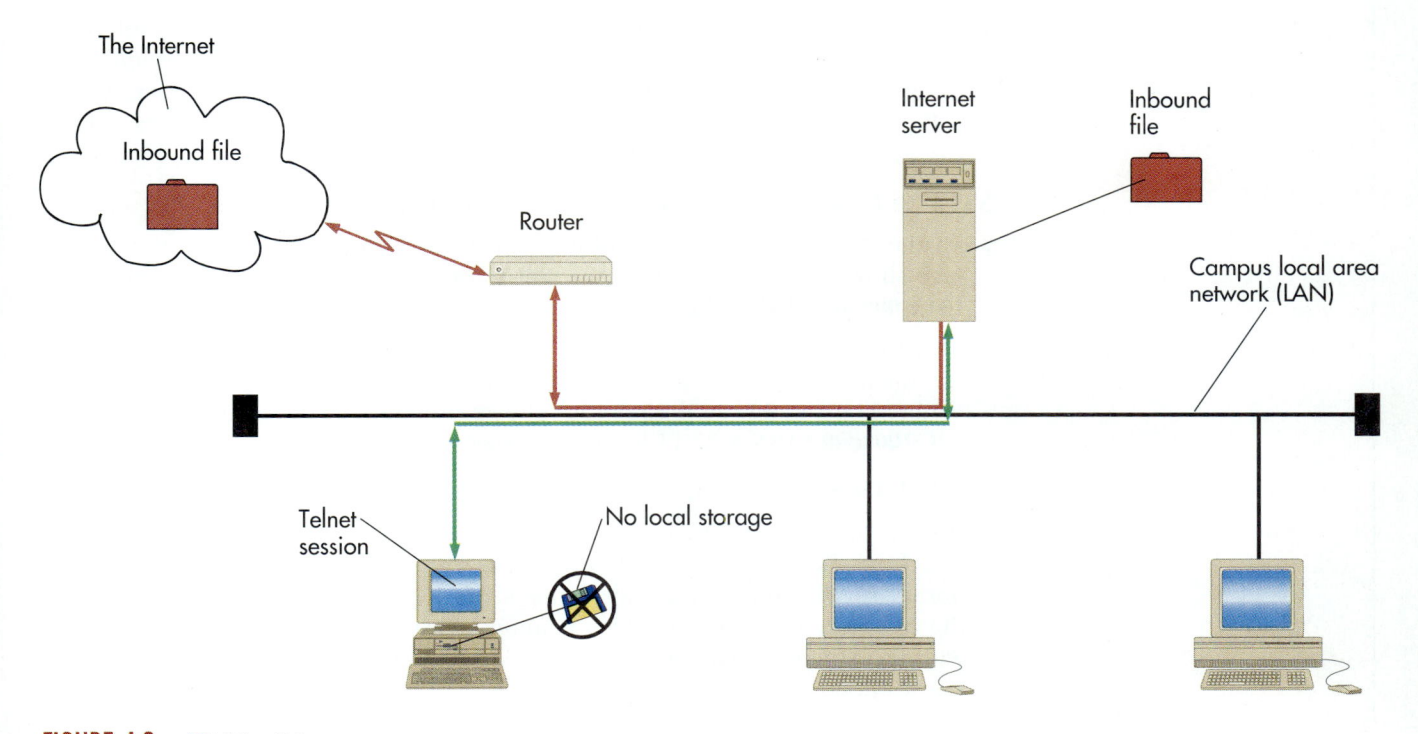

FIGURE 4.9 FTP Using Unix

OTHER INTERNET TOOLS   147

HANDS-ON EXERCISE 5

FTP from the Unix Prompt

Objective: To FTP a file from a remote site using FTP commands at the Unix prompt. Use Figure 4.10 as a guide in the exercise.

STEP 1: Start the FTP Session

➤ Open a session at the Unix command line. (See your instructor, lab assistant, or system administrator for instructions on how to do this in your campus computing environment.)

➤ Type the FTP command, followed by a space, then the name of the FTP site to which you want to connect. In this case type **ftp ksuvxa.kent.edu** to connect to Kent State, where you will find a directory full of academic mailing lists by subject, to which you can subscribe if you wish. Press **Enter.**

OPENING A SESSION FROM THE FTP> PROMPT

There are times when you do not connect to an FTP site on the first try. Your screen will display the ftp> prompt on your system. The syntax to open a session from the ftp> prompt instead of the Unix prompt is only slightly different: type the **open** command in front of the FTP address. Thus, typing **open ksuvxa.kent.edu** at the ftp> prompt would start an anonymous FTP session with that site.

STEP 2: Log On to the Remote Host

➤ You will be instructed by the remote host when it is ready for you to log on. Type **anonymous** as your username and press **Enter.** Type your username as the password—that is, **username@anyhost.anyu.edu**—and press **Enter.** You will get a message indicating that you have successfully connected to the FTP site, as shown in Figure 4.10a.

STEP 3: Change to the Directory Where the Desired File Resides

➤ At the ftp> prompt, type **cd library** and press **Enter.** You will see the message shown in Figure 4.10b saying **200 Working directory changed to "PUBLIC:[000000.LIBRARY]".**

➤ You can verify that you are in the right directory at any time using the pwd command. At the ftp> prompt, type **pwd** (print working directory) and press **Enter.** You should see the message shown in Figure 4.10a saying **257 "PUBLIC:[000000.LIBRARY]" is current directory.**

STEP 4: Display a List of All Files in the Current Directory

➤ Before you can retrieve the document, you must be sure it is in the current directory. Type **dir** and press **Enter.** You will see the long list of files in the library subdirectory, shown in Figure 4.10b. The file you want to retrieve is the bsn.investments;1 file, which contains a list of mailing lists having to do with investments. (The bsn is for *business*.) (You can scroll up and down in the window to see all the files in the directory.)

(a) Logging In and Changing Directories

- Anonymous login
- FTP command
- Enter username as password
- Change directory (cd) command
- Print working directory (pwd) command
- FTP prompt

```
UnixWare 2.01 (mercy) (pts/1)

login: sjones
Password:
UnixWare 2.01
mercy
Copyright 1984-1995 Novell, Inc.  All Rights Reserved.
Copyright 1987, 1988 Microsoft Corp.  All Rights Reserved.
U.S. Pat. No. 5,349,642
Last login: Sun Nov 12 16:37:00 1995 on pts002
$ ftp ksuvxa.kent.edu
Connected to Zeus.kent.edu.
220 FTP Service Ready
Name (ksuvxa.kent.edu:sjones): anonymous
331 ANONYMOUS user ok, send real identity as password.
Password:
230 ANONYMOUS logged in, directory PUBLIC:[000000], restrictions apply.
ftp> cd library
200 Working directory changed to "PUBLIC:[000000.LIBRARY]"
ftp> pwd
257 "PUBLIC:[000000.LIBRARY]" is current directory
ftp>
```

(b) The Directory Listing

- Scroll up to see additional files
- File name
- File size

```
BSN.INVESTMENTS;1       22-MAY-1995 07:59:22       7352/15       (RE,RE,,RE)
BSN.JOBS;1              13-JUL-1995 10:51:06      14162/28       (RE,RE,,RE)
BSN.LOCATION;1           1-JUN-1995 09:37:32      16914/34       (RE,RE,,RE)
BSN.MANAGEMENT;1        22-MAY-1995 07:59:22      12272/24       (RE,RE,,RE)
BSN.MARKETING;1          6-JUL-1995 11:45:21      80776/158      (RE,RE,,RE)
BSN.OPERATIONS;1         1-JUN-1995 09:44:10      24382/48       (RE,RE,,RE)
BSN.PERSONNEL;1          6-JUL-1995 11:45:03      21758/43       (RE,RE,,RE)
BSN.README;1            13-JUL-1995 10:51:05       5110/10       (RE,RE,,RE)
BSN.SMALL;1             22-MAY-1995 07:59:25      63466/124      (RE,RE,,RE)
LIBRES.LOG9207;1         8-APR-1994 15:54:14      12875/26       (RE,RE,,RE)
LIBRES.LOG9208;1         8-APR-1994 15:54:14      19464/39       (RE,RE,,RE)
LIBRES.LOG9209;1         8-APR-1994 15:54:14      32070/63       (RE,RE,,RE)
LIBRES.LOG9210;1         8-APR-1994 15:54:15      29566/58       (RE,RE,,RE)
LIBRES.LOG9212;1         8-APR-1994 15:54:16      66618/131      (RE,RE,,RE)
LIBRES.LOG9301;1         8-APR-1994 15:54:16     144999/284      (RE,RE,,RE)
LIBRES.LOG9302;1         8-APR-1994 15:54:16      49949/98       (RE,RE,,RE)
LIBRES.LOG9303;1         8-APR-1994 15:54:17      23974/47       (RE,RE,,RE)
LIBRES.LOG9304;1         8-APR-1994 15:54:17      34984/69       (RE,RE,,RE)
LIBRES.LOG9305;1         8-APR-1994 15:54:18     101457/199      (RE,RE,,RE)

Total of 30 files, 1921 blocks.

226 File transfer completed ok
ftp>
```

FIGURE 4.10 Hands-on Exercise 5 (continued)

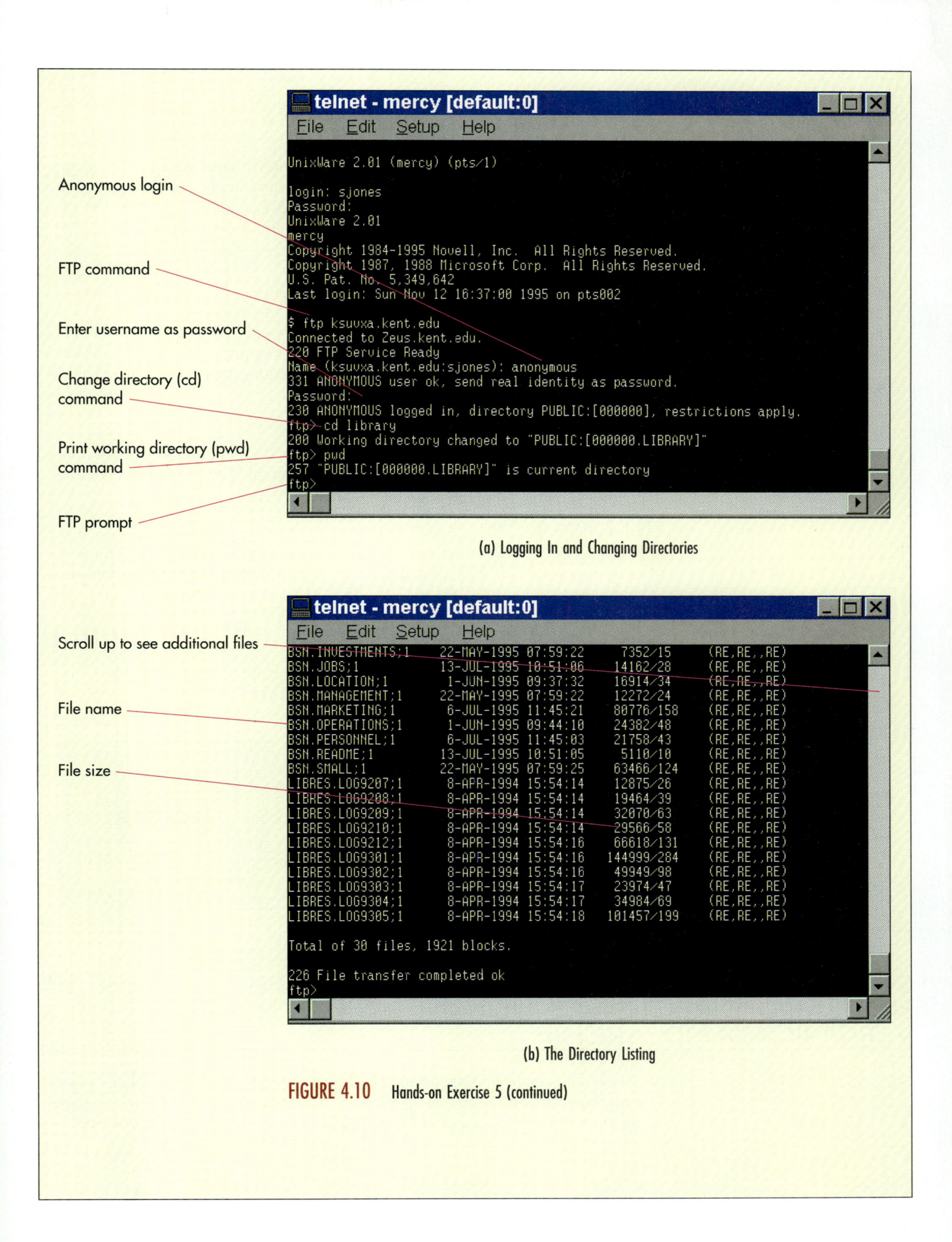

DOWNLOAD OUR DATA DISKS

You can download the data disks for the *Exploring Windows* series from the Prentice Hall FTP site. Connect to ftp://ftp.prenhall.com. Change to the **pub** directory, select **be** (for Business and Economics), then select **grauer.** Select **exploring.windows,** then choose the appropriate book.

STEP 5: FTP the File

➤ Type **get bsn.investments;1** (the file name ends with the number 1, not the letter l), and press **Enter.** (Case matters, so be sure your commands are typed exactly as shown.) You will see a message indicating that the document has been transferred successfully.

STEP 6: Quit the FTP Connection

➤ Type **quit** at the prompt. You will get a message saying **Goodbye,** and will be returned to the Unix prompt on your host system. The remote connection is closed.

STEP 7: Read the File

➤ The file you just retrieved will be on your Internet host machine. You can verify that it is there by typing **dir** and pressing **Enter** at the Unix prompt on your campus Unix host. See your campus help desk for information on how to read the file.

STEP 8: Log Off the Unix Host

➤ Type **exit** (or the command to quit Unix in your environment) at the Unix prompt and press **Enter.** You will be logged off the Unix host.

gopher://wiretap.spies.com:70/00/Library/Humor/Jokes/

Need a break from studying? Try visiting the humor archive at the Wiretap home page. Humor is the best medicine, as the saying goes.

SEARCHING FOR GOPHER AND FTP FILES AND DIRECTORIES USING VERONICA AND ARCHIE

As you are no doubt by now aware, the Internet is a huge and sprawling "place." The attempts to catalog its resources have barely begun, and the current search mechanisms are only as good as the means used to update the indexes or catalogs.

You will find that conducting a search with two search engines will give entirely different results, even when the search parameters are the same. This is because each search engine is searching a different Web index. In fact, because hosts change and/or go down, two searches using the same search engine and exactly the same parameters may yield different results. Doing an exhaustive search of the Internet can *be* exhausting!

Veronica and **Archie** are specialized search tools that were developed to deal specifically with gopher and FTP resources, respectively. Veronica (Very Easy Rodent-Oriented Netwide Index to Computerized Archives) is a database that indexes over 5,000 gopher servers worldwide, and contains 15 million items (as of November 1995). Since the advent of the World Wide Web, over 4,000 Web servers have been added to the Veronica database, which is updated monthly. Archie (short for *archives*) is a search tool designed specifically to find FTP resources. Developed by students and staff at McGill University in Toronto, Canada, Archie periodically searches anonymous FTP sites around the world and updates its databases.

You can access any of a number of public Archie servers around the world using an Archie client on your PC. Figure 4.11 shows WSARCHIE, an Archie client that allows you to enter a search string, set certain search variables (whether you want to search for a file or directory that matches the search string exactly, or whether the search string can be a portion of the directory name), and then search for matching files or directories. Check with your lab assistant to find out whether you have an Archie client available in your computer lab, and to get instructions for using it.

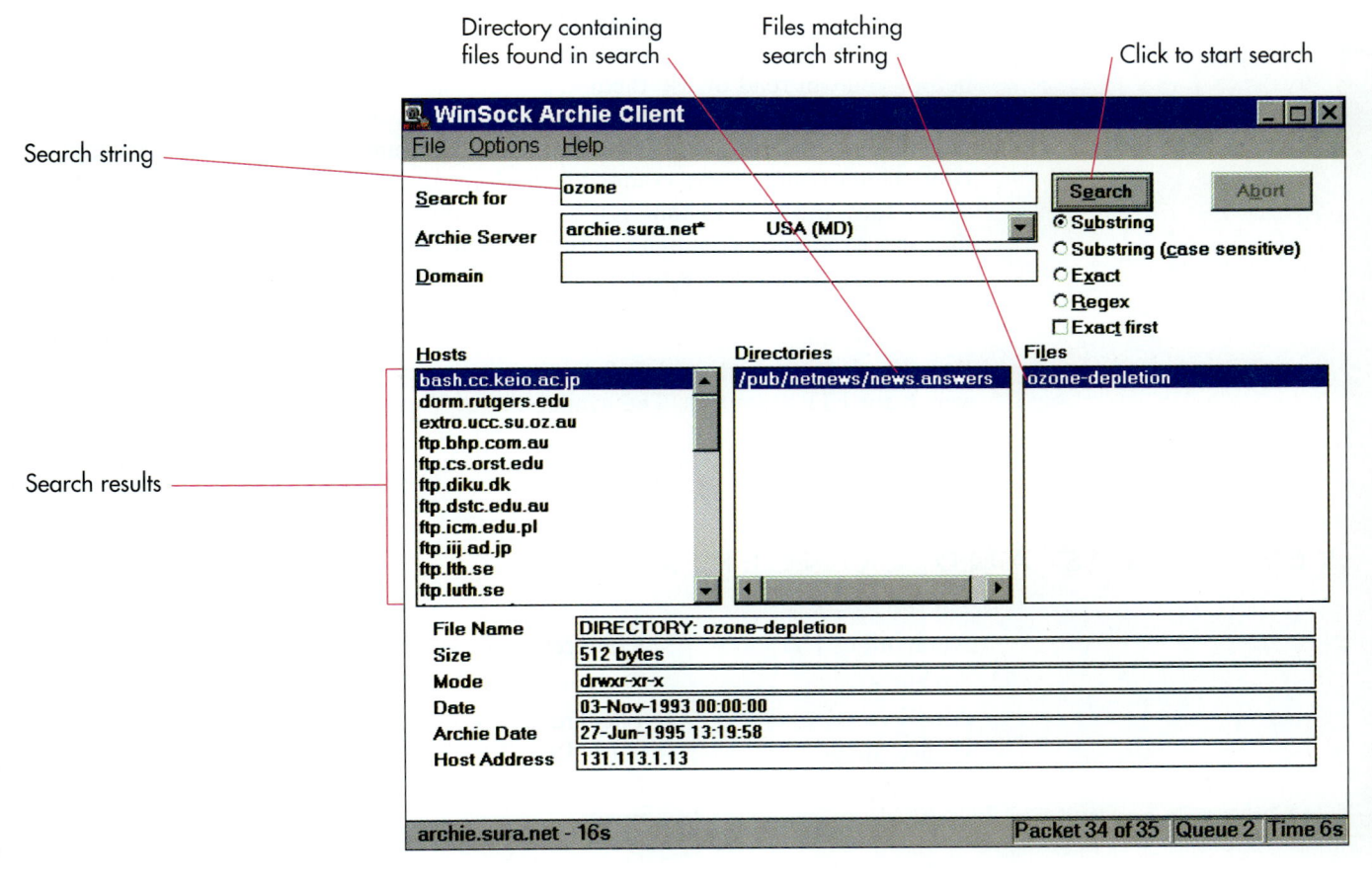

FIGURE 4.11   WSARCHIE

You can get more information about using Veronica by pointing your Web browser at the URL gopher://Veronica.scs.unr.edu:/70/11/Veronica. Look for the Veronica-FAQs menu, and tunnel down from there.

The development of the World Wide Web and the wide availability of Web browsers have made older Internet indexes and search tools, such as Veronica and Archie, obsolete virtually overnight. Few, if any, sites are allocating resources toward further enhancement of these products, or of the servers on which they run. You may find, as we did, that performing a Veronica or Archie search takes forever, if you get through to the public server at all (many have closed down altogether). Nevertheless, Archie and Veronica occupy a special place in the development of the Internet and are mentioned for that reason.

SUMMARY

Some Internet resources can be accessed via the older menu-based browsing system known as gopher. Internauts can tunnel through gopherspace using a Web browser, but will note that the documents retrieved generally are text only. Alternatively, if a Web browser is not available, users may access the gopher server using the Unix gopher command, or by telnetting to a public access gopher server.

Millions of files around the world are available to download to your PC or Internet host using the File Transfer Protocol (FTP). You may find the files using a Web search engine, then link to and retrieve the files using your Web browser. If the files are compressed files, as indicated by the file extension (.Z, .ZR, .zip, .gz), you may get better results FTPing the files with a Windows FTP client such as WS_FTP. Once you have retrieved compressed files, you must uncompress them before you can read or use them.

If you do not have an FTP client available, or if you want to retrieve files compressed in Unix, you will have to use FTP commands at the Unix prompt in your shell account. These commands perform the same FTP functions that a GUI client does, but require that you know the proper syntax of each command and that you type each command, directory, and file name exactly. For this reason, most users have switched to FTPing via a Web browser or FTP client when possible.

Web search engines do not find all the resources available on the Web. Veronica is the search tool to locate gopher sites and menus. Archie is a tool to search for FTP resources. The availability of Web browsers has made these tools virtually obsolete.

KEY WORDS AND CONCEPTS

Anonymous FTP
Archie
ASCII (text) mode
Binary mode
Cd command
Cdup command
Close command

Compressed files
Dir command
File Transfer Protocol (FTP)
FTP client
FTP server
Get command

Gopher
Gopher server
Gopherspace
Pwd command
Quit command
Tunneling
Veronica

Multiple Choice

1. Which of the following statements regarding FTP is true?
   (a) FTP files are not available on the World Wide Web
   (b) FTP files are available only on the World Wide Web
   (c) FTP files are available on the Web only in compressed format
   (d) None of the above

2. Which resource was designed as a text-based resource that allows you to "tunnel" down through a series of menus to find Internet documents?
   (a) Netscape
   (b) FTP
   (c) Gopher
   (d) None of the above

3. A gopher menu will display:
   (a) Additional gopher menus
   (b) Text files
   (c) Both (a) and (b)
   (d) Neither (a) nor (b)

4. All of the following are used to retrieve Internet resources except:
   (a) FTP
   (b) Netscape
   (c) Gopher
   (d) HTML

5. Which of the following allows you to FTP files to your PC?
   (a) A WWW browser
   (b) A Windows-based FTP client
   (c) Both (a) and (b)
   (d) Neither (a) nor (b)

6. Which file transfer mode is appropriate for transferring graphics files?
   (a) ASCII
   (b) Binary
   (c) Both (a) and (b)
   (d) Neither (a) nor (b)

7. In which method of FTPing files are the file contents generally displayed?
   (a) FTP using a WWW browser
   (b) FTP using a Windows-based FTP client
   (c) FTP using Unix commands
   (d) All of the above

8. Which of the following FTP methods allows you to "point and click" to locate desired directories on the remote host?
   (a) FTP using a WWW browser
   (b) FTP using a Windows-based FTP client
   (c) Both (a) and (b)
   (d) Neither (a) nor (b)

OTHER INTERNET TOOLS 153

9. When FTPing files:
   (a) You upload to your PC, which is considered the remote host
   (b) You download to your PC, which is considered the remote host
   (c) You download to your PC, which is considered the local host
   (d) You upload to your PC, which is considered the local host

10. Which of the following statements regarding FTP is true?
    (a) An unlimited number of concurrent users can access most FTP sites
    (b) Because it is anonymous, the FTP host does not know who is accessing the site
    (c) You can generally retrieve files only from the public directory on the FTP host
    (d) None of the above

11. Which of the following resources will Archie locate?
    (a) Gopher sites
    (b) FTP files and directories
    (c) HTTP resources
    (d) All of the above

12. Archie searches can be conducted using:
    (a) A Windows-based Archie client
    (b) Unix commands
    (c) Both (a) and (b)
    (d) Neither (a) nor (b)

13. FTP files may be uncompressed using:
    (a) PC compression software
    (b) Mac compression software
    (c) Unix compression software
    (d) Any of the above

14. What is the login ID at most FTP sites from which anyone may download files?
    (a) FTP
    (b) Anonymous
    (c) Your username
    (d) Info

15. Which of the following are generally found at gopher sites?
    (a) Text-only documents and other gopher menus
    (b) HTML pages
    (c) Both (a) and (b)
    (d) Neither (a) nor (b)

ANSWERS

1. d	6. b	11. b
2. c	7. a	12. c
3. c	8. c	13. d
4. d	9. c	14. b
5. c	10. d	15. a

Exploring the Internet

1. Using Figure 4.12, match each action with its result; a given action may be used more than once or not at all.

Action

a. Click at 1
b. Click at 2
c. Click at 3
d. Click at 4
e. Click at 5
f. Click at 6
g. Click at 7

Result

____ Change directories on the local host

____ Quit the FTP session with the remote host

____ Look at the file before transferring

____ Change directories on the remote host

____ Select a file for transfer

____ Select the mode for transfer of graphic files

____ Transfer a selected file

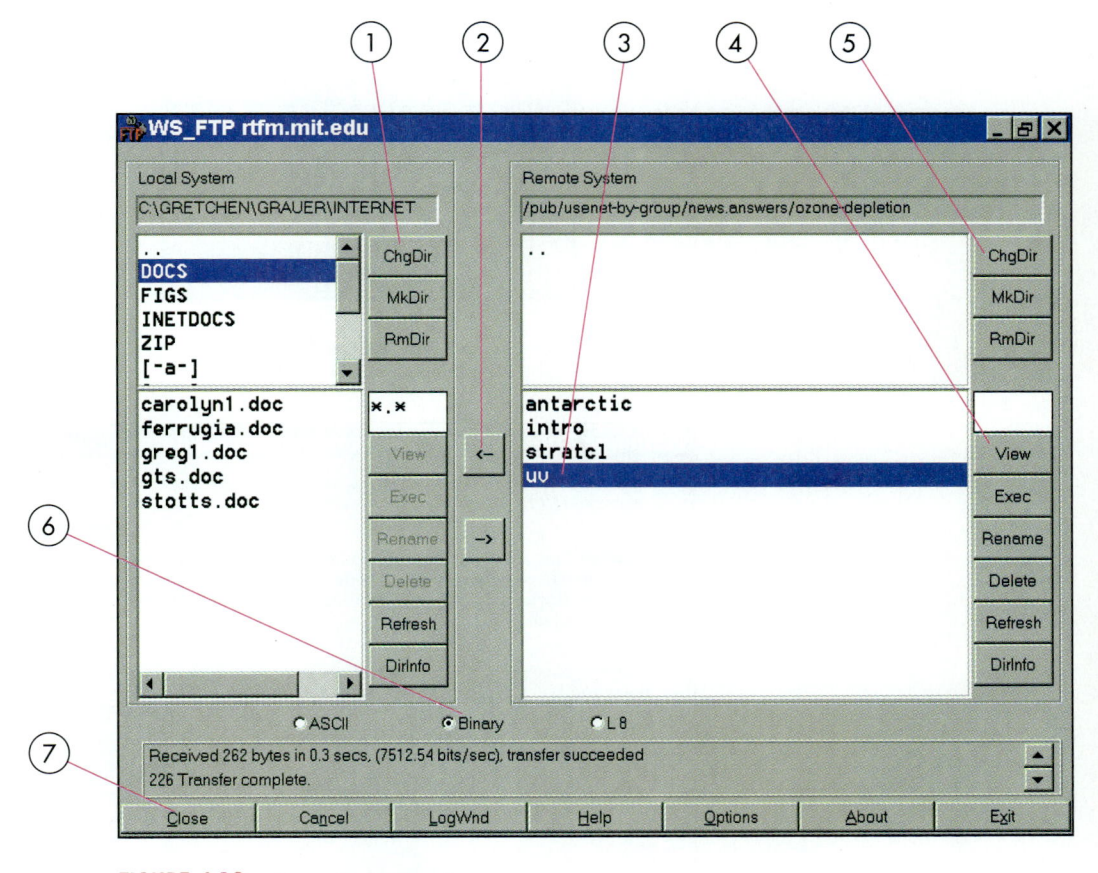

FIGURE 4.12 Screen for Problem 1

2. Answer the following with respect to gopher and FTP at your college or university:

  a. Do you have a gopher server running locally on your Unix host?

  b. Does your college or university have a gopher menu?

  c. Do you have an FTP client on the PCs in your computer lab? If so, which one? How do you access it?

  d. Can you FTP from your Unix shell account?

3. The messages shown in Figure 4.13 could have appeared while you were exploring the Web. Explain the nature of each message and indicate the necessary corrective action (if any).

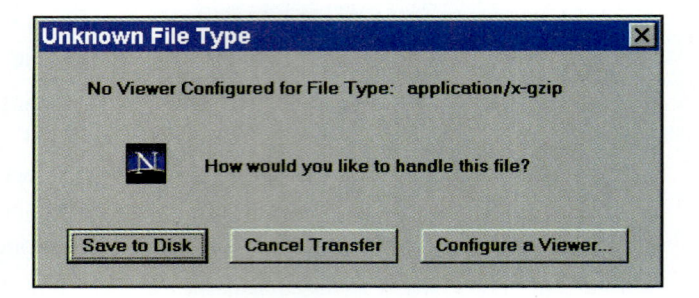

(a) Message 1

(b) Message 2

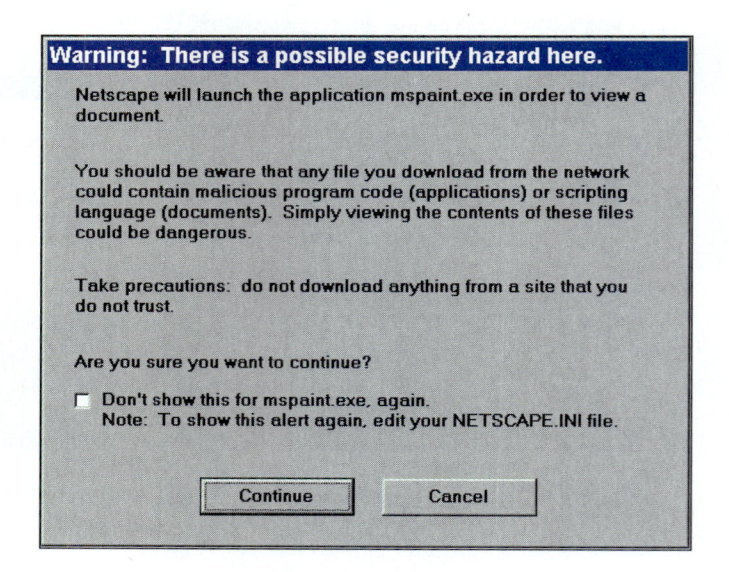

(c) Message 3

FIGURE 4.13 Messages for Problem 3

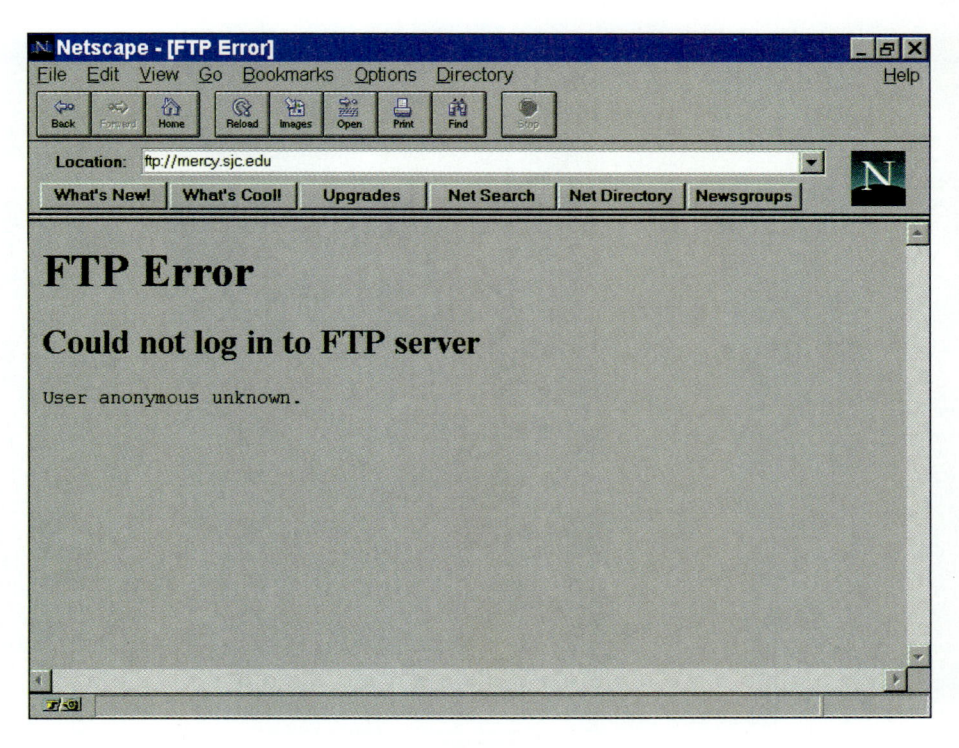

![Netscape FTP Error window showing "Could not log in to FTP server — User anonymous unknown."]

(d) Message 4

FIGURE 4.13   Messages for Problem 3 (continued)

4. Learn more about FTP and gopher online. Connect your Web browser to the URL http://www.vcn.com/server/help.html and from there jump to the FTP and gopher links. If you want to find additional information about either topic, search on *FTP primer* and/or *Gopher primer* using your Web browser.

Practice with Gopher and FTP

1. Find Gopher Jewels: Gopherspace, like the World Wide Web, is a very big "place." Tunneling down through menu after menu to find something can certainly be time consuming. However, the University of Southern California maintains a subject index of gopher sites called Gopher Jewels, which many other sites mirror (copy or maintain links to). Enter the URL http://galaxy.einet.net/TexasONE/gopher-jewels.html in Netscape. You will find the menu shown in Figure 4.14. Explore any of the choices. Note that one option is Employment Opportunities and Resume Postings. It might be an interesting menu to explore!

2. Explore Genealogy at the Library of Congress: Assume you are interested in learning more about your family history and want to know more about genealogical research resources on the Internet. Begin your search at gopher://marvel.loc.gov/11/research/reading.room/genealogy. This is the Library of Congress gopher server, and it contains a wealth of material and links to many other interesting sites.

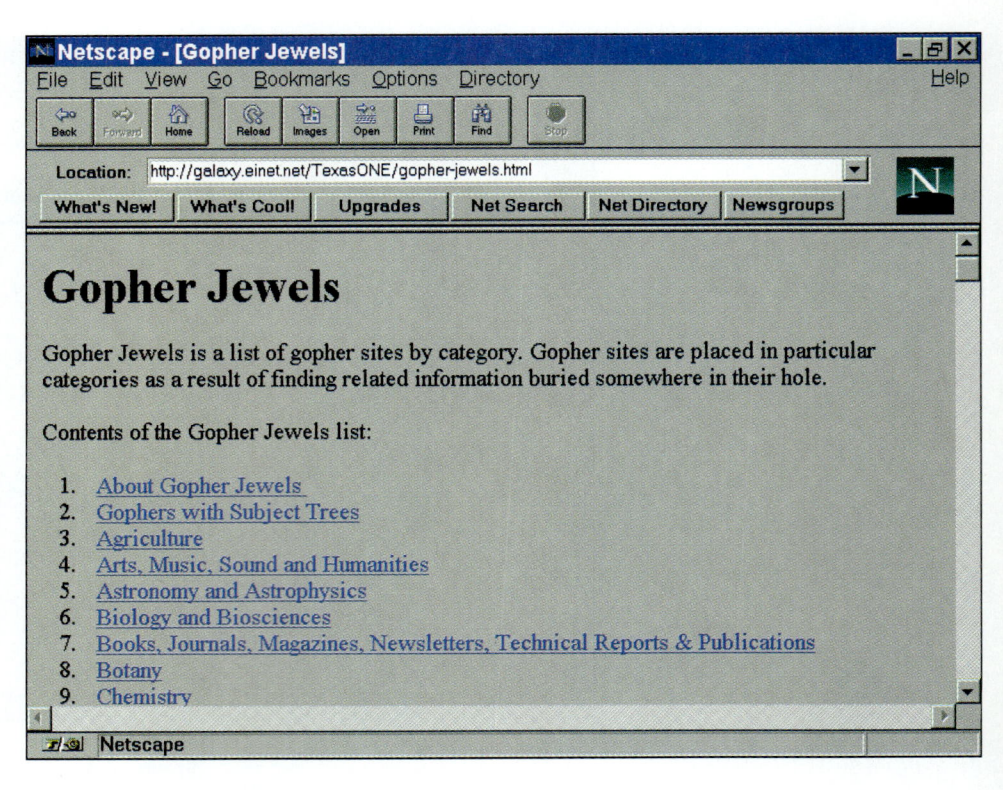

FIGURE 4.14 Practice Exercise 1

3. **Download an Image and Embed It in a Word Document:** Suppose you are doing a report on the scientific progress made with the repaired Hubble telescope. You would like to find out more about it and perhaps include some images from the space program in your presentation. You are browsing through the Aeronautics subject listing at the WWW Virtual Library at the URL (http://www.w4.org/hypertext/DataSources/bySubject/Overview.html), and you find a reference to student work in this area. Finding this intriguing, you click on the link and retrieve a long list of interesting sites, one of which is ftp://seds.lpl.arizona.edu/pub/images.

    The instructions below will help you download an image file and include it in a document.

    a. Using your WWW browser or FTP client, download an image of the Hubble mission from this FTP site, and save the file.
    b. While the image is displayed on your screen, press Print Screen to capture the image to the Windows clipboard.
    c. Open a new document in whatever word processor you are using, and press Enter several times to move the insertion point down the page.
    d. Press Ctrl+V or click Paste to paste the image in the document.
    e. Press Alt+Tab to go back to the FTP site.
    f. Retrieve and save to your local hard drive a text file describing the Hubble mission.
    g. Insert the text file into the current document (using the Insert File command) and format it as you wish. A sample picture is shown in Figure 4.15.

FIGURE 4.15 Practice Exercise 3

4. Download Pkzip: Perhaps the most common use of FTP is to download software. Because program files may be very large and time consuming to download, they are often compressed before being put up at the FTP site. You will need Pkzip if you plan to FTP many files. Pkzip is a DOS file compression program commonly used on FTP files. Any programs with the extension .zip have been compressed, and must be inflated using pkzip.

   Enter the URL ftp://efn.org/pub/download/DOS/ in your Web browser. When you see the list of FTP files, click on pkzip204.exe to download the file. Be sure to read any README.TXT files that go with the program. You must check with your system administrator to determine whether you can actually install and run the program in the computer lab.

CASE STUDIES

Comparing Search Results

Say you are doing a report on Maya Angelou, the poet who read her work at President Clinton's inauguration in 1992. Complete two searches using different Web search engines, and note the number of "hits" your searches yield. Now try the same search using Veronica. How do the results compare?

The Threat of Virus Infection

A computer virus is an actively infectious program that attaches itself to other programs and alters the way a computer works. Some viruses do nothing more than display an annoying message at an inopportune time. Many, however, are more harmful, and, in the worst cases, erase all the files on the disk. When is a computer subject to infection by a virus? Certainly downloading software from the Internet can be a risky experience. What precautions does your school or university take against the threat of virus infection in its computer lab? What will be the consequences for you and the college if you FTP and execute an infected file?

The Global Labor Market

The U.S. economy has been characterized by repeated layoffs, restructuring, downsizing, reengineering, and other strategies to reduce costs and increase profits. Do a Web search to find online employment listings. Would the listings you found really be helpful to someone looking for work? Where are the jobs being advertised? How will U.S. workers be affected by a truly global labor market?

Expand Your Horizons

The Internet certainly has the capacity to help us all learn more about the world in which we live—if we take advantage of it. Most of us browse through topics of interest to us, without a second glance at subjects about which we know little. You can increase your knowledge just by changing this strategy, by browsing through parts of gopherspace you have never considered before. Using your Web browser, enter the URL to go to the Gopher Jewels subject index, http://galaxy.einet.net/TexasONE/gopher-jewels.html, and tunnel down through an area you *would not normally visit*. We think you will find some very fascinating information, and expand your horizons!

5

CONVERSATIONS ON THE INTERNET: IRC, WEBCHAT, AND USENET

OBJECTIVES

After reading this chapter you will be able to:

1. Define Internet Relay Chat (IRC).
2. Join an IRC channel and exchange messages with other people.
3. Converse with other people on the Internet using WebChat.
4. Describe Usenet and find Usenet archives.
5. Use your Web browser to read and reply to Usenet postings.

OVERVIEW

As you have seen, e-mail, mailing lists, the Web, gopher servers, and FTP sites provide a vast array of worldwide information resources. Yet some people view the ability to communicate with all types of people, on all types of subjects, to be the most important function of the Internet. In this chapter we will explore additional Internet resources—Internet Relay Chat (IRC), WebChat, and Usenet—that allow you to participate in wide-ranging discussions of every conceivable topic, from the profound to the mundane.

You may not have access to some or all of the resources discussed in this chapter. Students have been known to tie up lab PCs for hours while participating in an online discussion using IRC. As a result some schools have banned IRC. Many colleges and universities do not want to devote hardware to providing Usenet access, which requires considerable memory and disk drive space on the Internet server.

Whether you can use these resources in your computing lab is not critical to your understanding of the material in the chapter. You should be aware that the Internet goes beyond search and retrieval of mail and other documents. After reading this chapter you will understand what those other services are and how they can be used.

INTERNET RELAY CHAT (IRC)

E-mail, as you have learned from your own messaging, is an asynchronous means of communication. That is, when you send a message, the recipient reads it some time in the future (or not at all, depending on whether he or she has embraced this new medium). **Internet Relay Chat (IRC),** on the other hand, allows anyone with Internet access to strike up an electronic, written conversation with anyone else in real time; that is, both parties are sending and receiving messages during the same period of time. Both can read the messages on their computer screens and respond as though they were having a written telephone conversation. IRC, however, goes beyond communication between two people, as any number of people can participate.

Imagine an international coffee house, where people come and go, strike up conversations with friends and strangers alike, on subjects from the profound to the frivolous, and you have a picture of Internet Relay Chat. However, in the cyberspace version of our coffee house, you will have to type all your communications, you can't see the people in the café with you, and of course, there isn't any coffee!

If you are visiting a real coffee house, you open the door, step in, and find the room abuzz with conversation. You pause for a few minutes to let your eyes adjust to the light, and to see if anyone you know is there. Imagine that each table in the coffee house has a sign on it, announcing, more or less, what the group at that table is all about. Some of the labels are indecipherable because they are in another language, some don't give you much clue to the topic, and some have signs indicating they are talking about topics that appear to be obscene or offensive. You listen to various conversations going on at the tables around you to decide if you want to join a discussion in progress, or find an empty table and start your own group (you assume someone will eventually join you).

Similar to reading the signs on the tables in our imaginary coffee shop, once you start an IRC session, you can get a list of which **channels** are in operation, join one, or start your own. A channel, an electronic conversation between participants, is analogous to a table in our cafe.

Anyone on IRC can start a channel on any topic, and anyone else may join at anytime. Anywhere from one to an unlimited number of people may be conversing on the channel, and they can be from anywhere around the world. And just as at the coffee shop you may find people at two or more tables discussing something that interests you, you may join more than one channel at a time, and "hop" back and forth between the conversations on the channels you have joined. (You will not actually be able to see the messages being sent back and forth between people who have joined a channel unless you first join it yourself.)

Just as you might be reluctant to give out your real name to a stranger in a bar or coffee shop, you might want to protect yourself from future unsolicited and unwanted contact with someone you "meet" on IRC. You use a **nickname** in IRC to provide a measure of anonymity to your messages. When you establish your IRC session, you will also establish your nickname, which cannot be in use by anyone else on IRC (anywhere in the world) at that time. When you finish your session, or change your nickname, someone else can use your former nickname.

You can get a list of all the open channels and decide whether to join a conversation in progress or start your own. Once you have joined a channel, the server will announce that you have joined (using your nickname), and your PC will display the messages being exchanged by the people already on the channel, as shown in Figure 5.1. The nickname of everyone participating on the channel is displayed on the right side of the screen in this IRC client, **mIRC,** developed by Khaled Mardam-Bay and made available by him free of charge on the Internet.

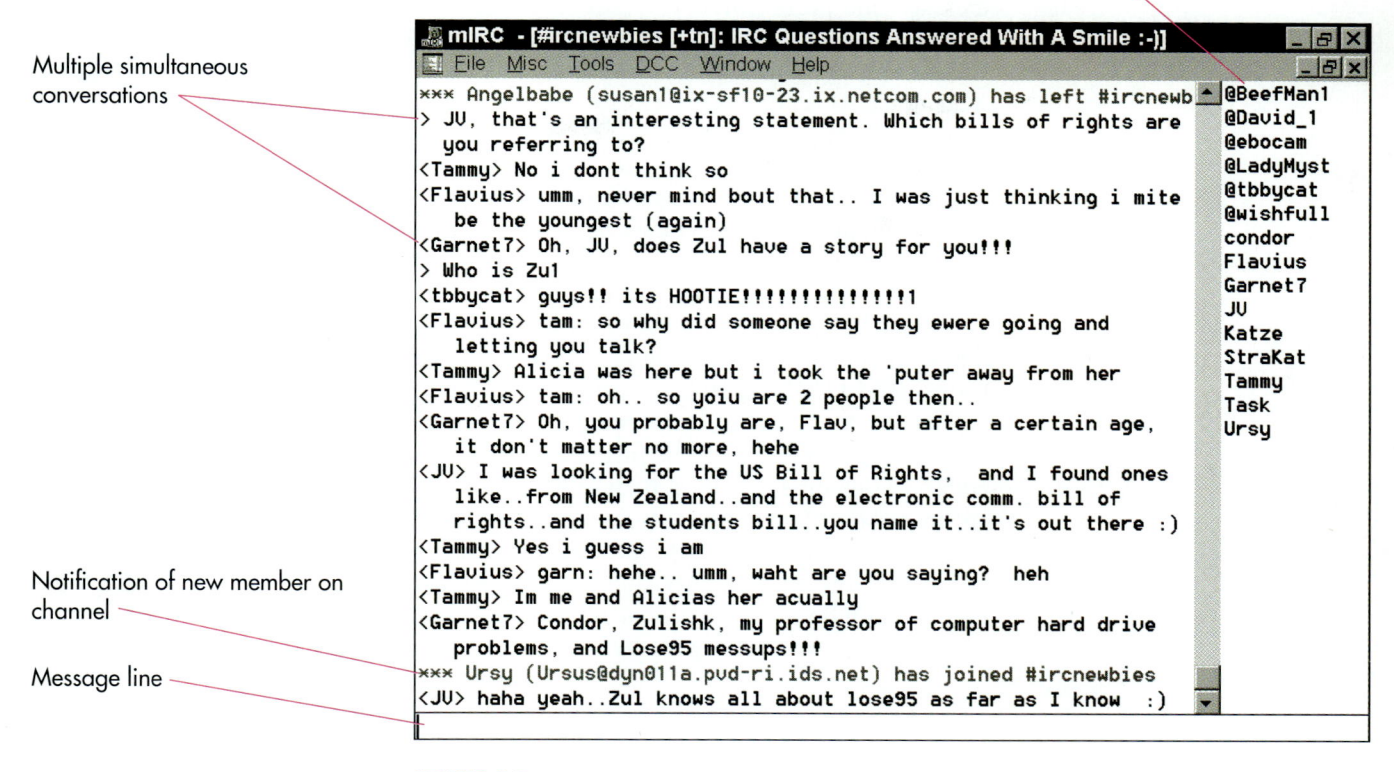

FIGURE 5.1 The mIRC Client

Callouts:
- People on the channel
- Multiple simultaneous conversations
- Notification of new member on channel
- Message line

> **PROTECTING YOURSELF ON THE NET**
>
> You should be aware that the IRC server will display both your nickname and your real username when you join a channel. The anonymity provided by your nickname is illusory. You should be sure that the messages you exchange are not going to cause you embarrassment (or worse), should someone contact you by your real username, or should you decide to run for office some day!

Once you have joined a channel, you may want to pause a bit to watch the flow of messages before adding your own messages. Simply sit and watch, and the conversation will flow by on your screen; just as at our coffee house, multiple conversations can be going on at our "table," which everyone can "hear." SuzyQ will type something: *JoeyD: How did your exam go on Friday?* She is directing the message at JoeyD, although everyone on the channel can read it. Chatty to LaLaLucy: *LaLaLucy: I'm devastated—I can't go to Ft. Lauderdale this spring!* Speechless to everyone: *Can anyone tell me what this channel is discussing?!?* JoeyD may respond to SuzyQ, then to Speechless, or he may not respond at all. The conversation scrolls along, sometimes aimlessly, sometimes intensely, until everyone leaves the channel. You may, of course, leave at any time—but think what you will be missing!

When you want to respond to someone or something, you simply type your message and press Enter. It is instantly sent onto the Internet by the IRC server. Anyone who is signed onto the channel (regardless of where in the world he or she is) will see the message, with your nickname, displayed on his or her screen. You can also send a private message to someone on the channel. This is analogous to leaning over and whispering something to someone at the table in our coffee house, except that no one on the channel can see you do it. Two or more people can strike up a side conversation while still connected to the channel.

As with other Internet services, IRC is implemented using client/server software. An IRC client on your PC will set up a session with an IRC server on your campus Internet host or on one of a dozen publicly accessible IRC servers around the world. The IRC server you are connected to is in turn connected to one or more other IRC servers around the world. Therefore the messages you send are propagated to all the IRC servers at once. This process, illustrated in Figure 5.2, is what enables you to join a channel with people from any other location.

The possibilities of this instantaneous communication are staggering. People collaborating on a project can establish meeting times, and communicate regularly, getting instant feedback from colleagues worldwide. News events about disasters such as earthquakes, floods, and terrorist attacks are transmitted as they are happening by the participants themselves—without the involvement of the news media. Members of the global village can communicate about whatever topics interest them without regard to nationality, color, or place of origin.

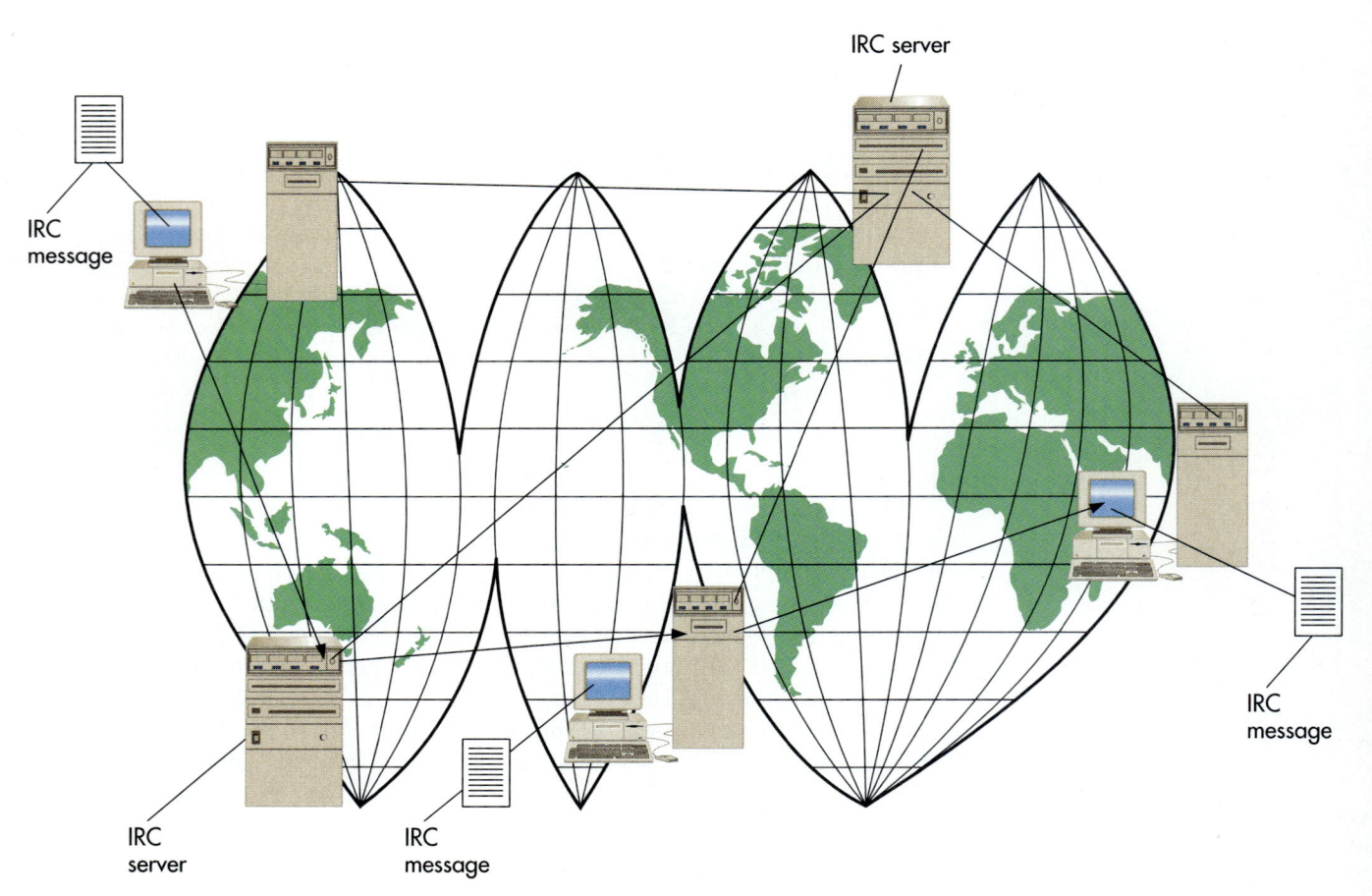

FIGURE 5.2 An IRC Message Travels the Internet

EXPLORING THE INTERNET

> ### THE POSSIBILITIES OF IRC
>
> The possibilities of IRC are as broad as human nature. Will it succumb to the worst, most base instincts of the human animal, and end up an instantaneous global bar scene that people use to "hit" on each other? Certainly many of the conversations on IRC at any given time make it appear that it will. Or will it promote new links between people, regardless of color, disabilities, age, gender? Since no one can see anyone else, it appears that IRC (and other forms of online communication) has made the Net truly nondiscriminatory. Cyrano de Bergerac would approve. (Don't know this famous Frenchman? Look him up on the Web!)

IRC Commands

Before trying out IRC, it is helpful to know a few simple commands. Table 5.1 shows the commands you will need most frequently. All commands are preceded by the forward slash (/). *Note that after joining a channel, anything you type without a slash will be interpreted as a message and broadcast to the entire channel.*

TABLE 5.1   IRC Commands

Command	Description
/list	Displays a list of all the channels in operation at the time you issue the command. (This can be a very long list, as it is common for over 1,500 channels to be in operation at any time.)
/list -min *nn*	Displays a list of all channels with a minimum number of users as specified in the command line. /list -min 15 would display all channels with 15 or more users. (The "table" at the coffee house is full of people, and it will be noisy!)
/list -max *nn*	Displays a list of all channels with less than or equal to the specified number of participants. (Allows you to find a channel where you actually have a chance of getting a word in edgewise. However, this command will list hundreds of channels, as many people open a channel by themselves.)
/join #*channelname*	Adds you to the specified channel. The # sign is required in front of the channel name, and don't forget the / in front of the command.
/part #*channelname*, or, /leave #*channelname*	End your visit on the channel. IRC will announce on the channel that you are leaving.
/msg *nickname messagetext*	Allows you to send a private message to whomever you name in the command. No one else on the channel will see the message.
/msg , *messagetext*	Sends the message to the last person who sent you a private message.
/msg . *messagetext*	Sends the message to the last person to whom you sent a private message.
/query *nickname*	Establishes a private conversation with the person, so that all your messages will now go to the person specified in the command.
/query	Entering the query command without a nickname turns the query capability off, so all messages will again be sent to the entire channel.

Additional IRC commands govern what the channel *operator,* the person who initialized the channel, can do. He or she has control of the channel and can set it up to exclude certain people, include only certain people, kick people off the channel during a chat, and so on. (Channel operators will be designated with a @ in front of their names, such as @StealthMan. Check the online Help available with your IRC client to find all the appropriate commands.)

AUDIO CHAT

If you could participate in a real (as in audio) conversation with others around the world, and not have to type your messages or pay a phone bill, would you join in? This is what Internet Voice Chat (IVC) and Internet Phone, two new products on the Net, let you do. You must have client software, and have a 486 PC (or better), equipped with sound card, microphone, and speakers to use the new system. Search the Web for more information if you are interested. These two services will certainly provide long distance phone companies with something to think about!

LEARNING BY DOING

IRC, like a good cup of coffee, is best appreciated with someone else. Since it is hard to have a discussion by yourself, and since there are no permanent IRC channels that we know will be live when you are ready to try IRC, we suggest this hands-on exercise be done with a group of your classmates. You should agree on a time to be online together, on either one or several channels. Choose the channel name(s), so you know on which channel to find each other. Then, at the appointed time, start up your IRC client. You will log on to an IRC server using a specific **port** number, which defines to the host which Internet service you are using. IRC has one port number, gopher another, telnet a third, and so on. See whether you can be the first one on, thus becoming the channel operator!

HANDS-ON EXERCISE 1

IRC Chat

Objective: To establish a chat session and converse with others on the Internet. Use Figures 5.1 and 5.3 as guides in the exercise.

STEP 1: Log On to IRC
- Log on to your system in the usual way.
- Find the IRC client and start it. Get specific instructions for doing this from your instructor, lab assistant, or system administrator.

STEP 2: Set Up mIRC and Connect to a Server
The instructions that follow are specifically for setting up mIRC. If you have a different IRC client, see your instructor for information about what to do in your environment.

➤ Customize mIRC.
  • Select **Set Up** from the **File menu.** The dialog box shown in Figure 5.3a appears.

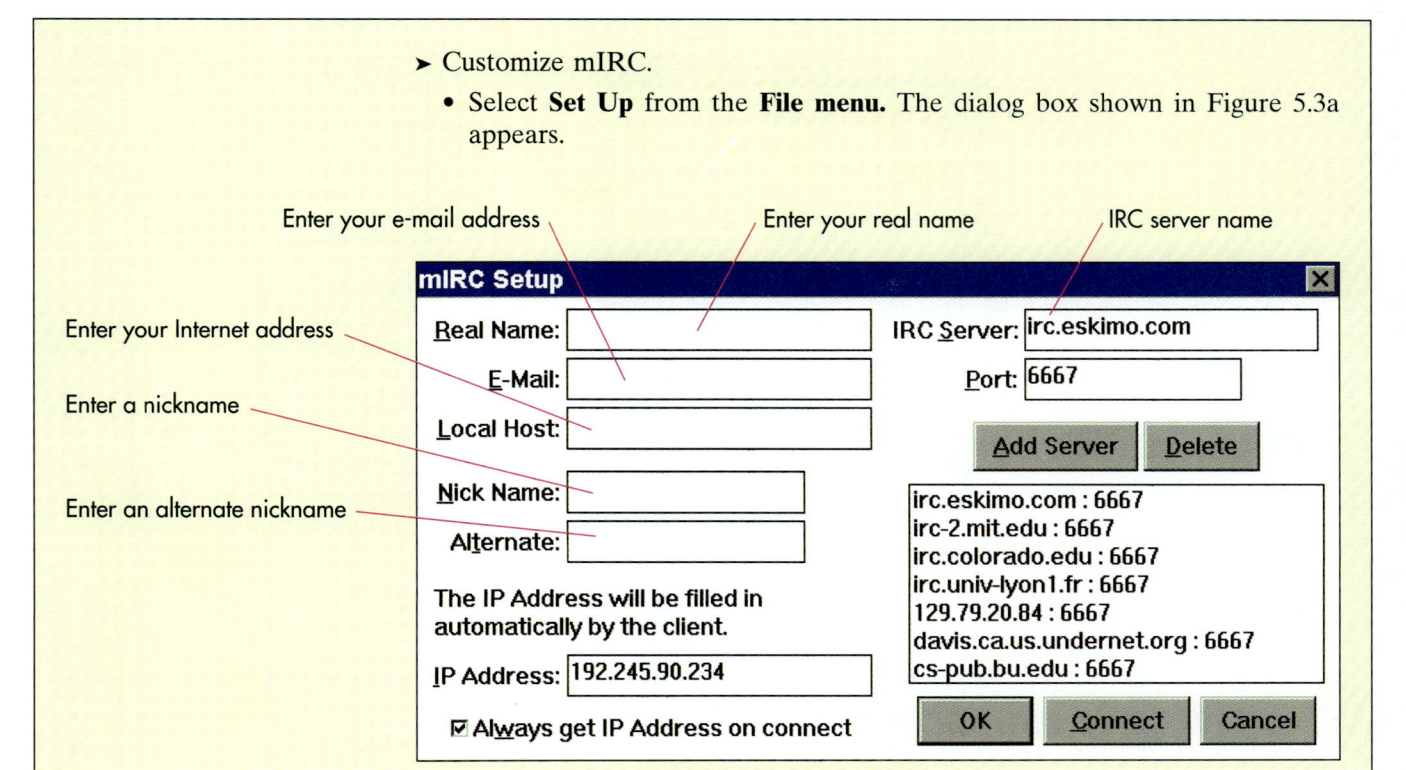

mIRC Setup

- Enter your Internet address → Real Name:
- Enter your e-mail address → E-Mail:
- Local Host:
- Enter a nickname → Nick Name:
- Enter an alternate nickname → Alternate:
- Enter your real name (Real Name field)
- IRC server name → IRC Server: irc.eskimo.com
- Port: 6667

Add Server | Delete

irc.eskimo.com : 6667
irc-2.mit.edu : 6667
irc.colorado.edu : 6667
irc.univ-lyon1.fr : 6667
129.79.20.84 : 6667
davis.ca.us.undernet.org : 6667
cs-pub.bu.edu : 6667

The IP Address will be filled in automatically by the client.

IP Address: 192.245.90.234

☑ Always get IP Address on connect

OK | Connect | Cancel

(a) The mIRC Setup Dialog Box

FIGURE 5.3 Hands-on Exercise 1

- Enter your first and last name in the Real Name text box.
- Enter your e-mail address in the E-Mail text box.
- Enter a nickname and alternate in the appropriate boxes. (mIRC will attempt to use your nickname first. If someone else is using it, it will automatically try your alternate.)
- Select one of the preconfigured public IRC servers from the list at the right of the screen. (If you do not have any IRC servers listed, add one from the list shown in Table 5.2.) Leave the port number set at the default.
- Your dialog box should now look similar to the one shown in Figure 5.3b. Go back and add any information you left out before proceeding.

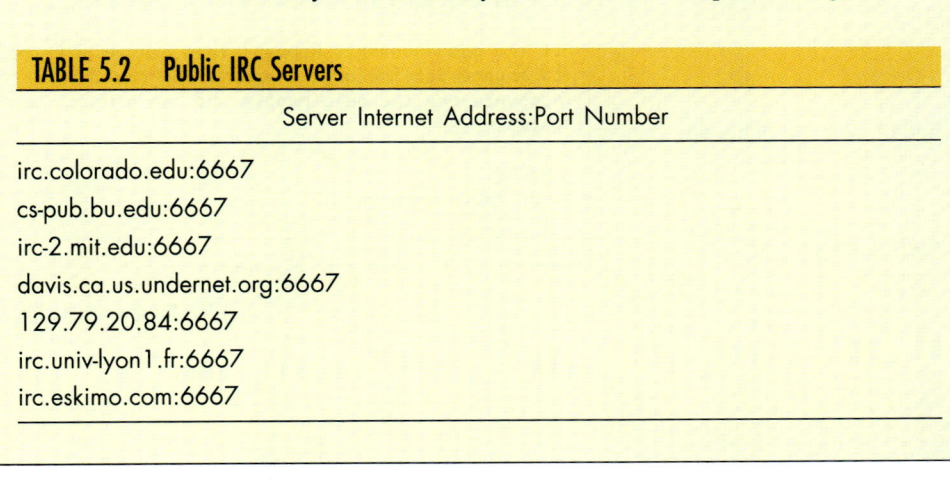

TABLE 5.2   Public IRC Servers

Server Internet Address:Port Number

irc.colorado.edu:6667
cs-pub.bu.edu:6667
irc-2.mit.edu:6667
davis.ca.us.undernet.org:6667
129.79.20.84:6667
irc.univ-lyon1.fr:6667
irc.eskimo.com:6667

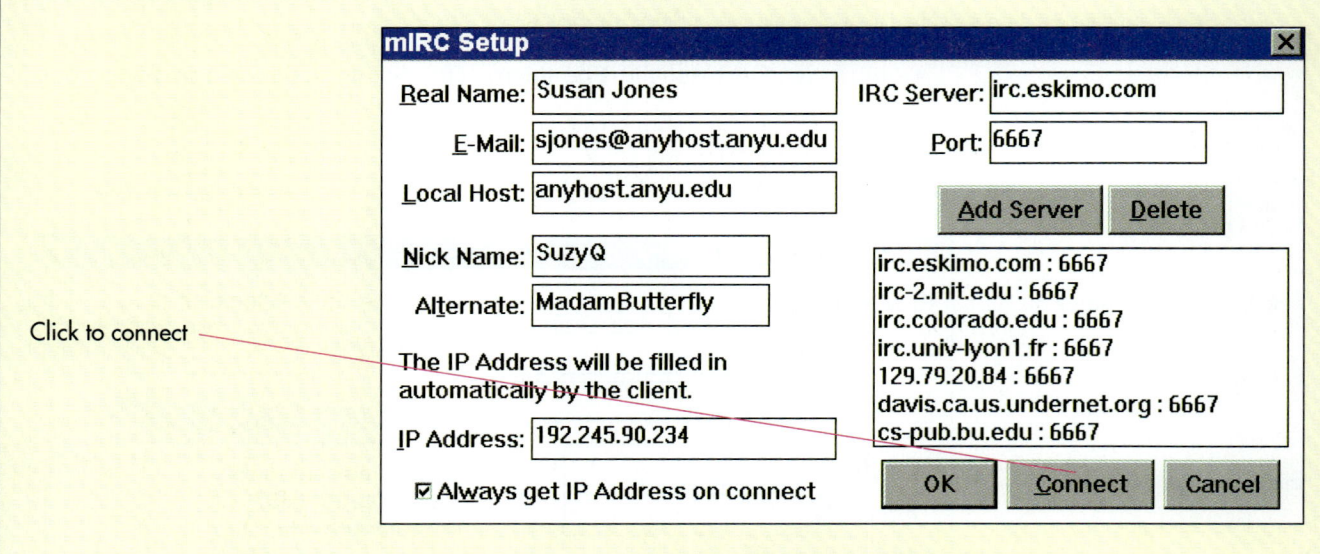

mIRC Setup

Real Name:	Susan Jones	IRC Server:	irc.eskimo.com
E-Mail:	sjones@anyhost.anyu.edu	Port:	6667
Local Host:	anyhost.anyu.edu		Add Server Delete
Nick Name:	SuzyQ		irc.eskimo.com : 6667
Alternate:	MadamButterfly		irc-2.mit.edu : 6667

The IP Address will be filled in automatically by the client.

IP Address: 192.245.90.234

irc.eskimo.com : 6667
irc-2.mit.edu : 6667
irc.colorado.edu : 6667
irc.univ-lyon1.fr : 6667
129.79.20.84 : 6667
davis.ca.us.undernet.org : 6667
cs-pub.bu.edu : 6667

☑ Always get IP Address on connect   OK   Connect   Cancel

Click to connect → Connect

(b) The Completed Setup Dialog Box

▶ Click **Connect**. You will see a message while the mIRC client is attempting to connect to the IRC server. Once connected you will see the message of the day scroll by. Your screen will look similar to the one shown in Figure 5.3c.

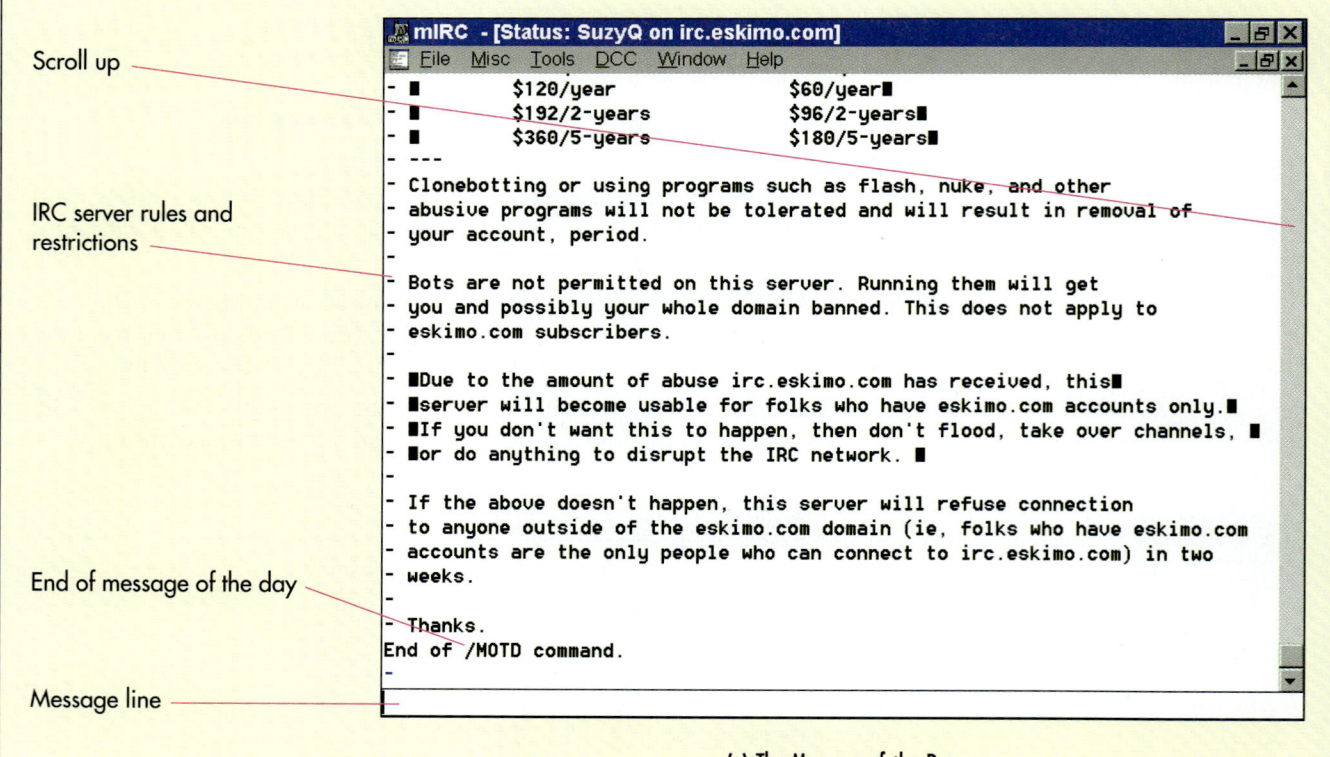

mIRC - [Status: SuzyQ on irc.eskimo.com]

File   Misc   Tools   DCC   Window   Help

```
-       $120/year              $60/year
-       $192/2-years           $96/2-years
-       $360/5-years           $180/5-years
- ---
- Clonebotting or using programs such as flash, nuke, and other
- abusive programs will not be tolerated and will result in removal of
- your account, period.
-
- Bots are not permitted on this server. Running them will get
- you and possibly your whole domain banned. This does not apply to
- eskimo.com subscribers.
-
- Due to the amount of abuse irc.eskimo.com has received, this
- server will become usable for folks who have eskimo.com accounts only.
- If you don't want this to happen, then don't flood, take over channels,
- or do anything to disrupt the IRC network.
-
- If the above doesn't happen, this server will refuse connection
- to anyone outside of the eskimo.com domain (ie, folks who have eskimo.com
- accounts are the only people who can connect to irc.eskimo.com) in two
- weeks.
-
- Thanks.
End of /MOTD command.
-
```

Labels: Scroll up; IRC server rules and restrictions; End of message of the day; Message line

(c) The Message of the Day

FIGURE 5.3   Hands-on Exercise 1 (continued)

168 EXPLORING THE INTERNET

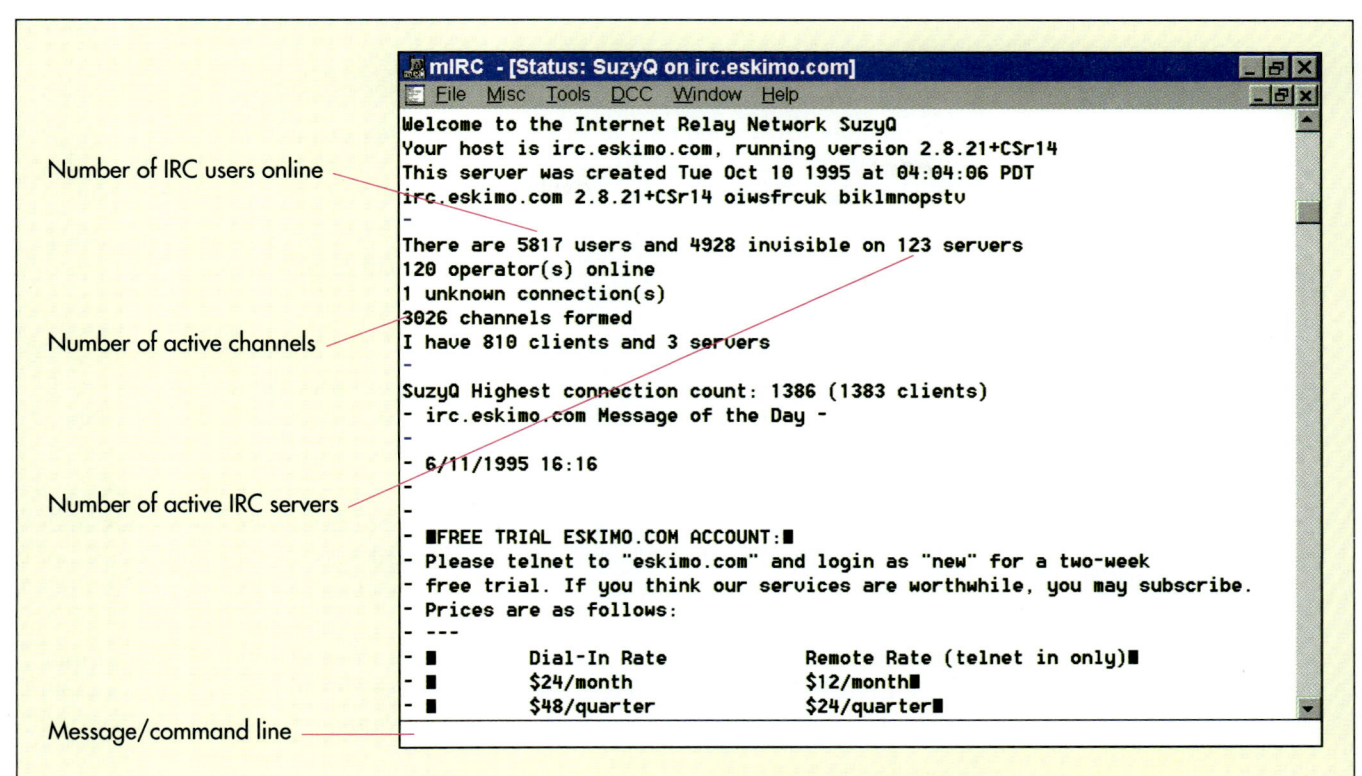

```
mIRC  - [Status: SuzyQ on irc.eskimo.com]
File  Misc  Tools  DCC  Window  Help
Welcome to the Internet Relay Network SuzyQ
Your host is irc.eskimo.com, running version 2.8.21+CSr14
This server was created Tue Oct 10 1995 at 04:04:06 PDT
irc.eskimo.com 2.8.21+CSr14 oiwsfrcuk biklmnopstv
-
There are 5817 users and 4928 invisible on 123 servers
120 operator(s) online
1 unknown connection(s)
3026 channels formed
I have 810 clients and 3 servers

SuzyQ Highest connection count: 1386 (1383 clients)
- irc.eskimo.com Message of the Day -
-
- 6/11/1995 16:16
-
-
- ■FREE TRIAL ESKIMO.COM ACCOUNT:■
- Please telnet to "eskimo.com" and login as "new" for a two-week
- free trial. If you think our services are worthwhile, you may subscribe.
- Prices are as follows:
- ---
- ■         Dial-In Rate            Remote Rate (telnet in only)■
- ■         $24/month               $12/month■
- ■         $48/quarter             $24/quarter■
```

- Number of IRC users online
- Number of active channels
- Number of active IRC servers
- Message/command line

(d) The Top of the Status Window

FIGURE 5.3 Hands-on Exercise 1 (continued)

STEP 3: Join the Class Channel

▶ Scroll up in the status window until you see the top of the message of the day, which will be similar to Figure 5.3d.

▶ The very last line of the status window is the message/command line. Type the command **/join #*channelname*** in the message/command line, using the channel name you agreed upon with your classmates.

▶ Press **Enter.** If you are the first one using the channel, you will become the channel operator. Otherwise you will be joined as a member. You should be able to see a list of everyone on the channel. In mIRC, this list is displayed in a separate box at the right of the window. The channel name will appear in the title bar at the top of the window. (If no one joins you at the appropriate time, check to make sure you joined the right channel!)

STEP 4: Send a Message

▶ Type any message you want in the message line at the bottom of the window, then press **Enter.** The message is broadcast to the entire channel, and will be displayed on everyone's screen. Remember, your nickname will appear next to the message, so everyone on the channel will know from whom the message was sent.

▶ Send a private message to someone on the channel using the **/msg *nickname messagetext*** command, substituting someone's nickname and a message in your command. (Of course, this works only if the person is already on the channel. Check the list of participants before sending the message.)

▶ Watch the conversation scrolling by, and add a comment when you want to.

STEP 5: Leave the Class Channel

➤ When you are ready to leave the channel, type **/part #*channelname*** (your client may use the command **/leave #*channelname***), then press **Enter.** You will exit the channel. (mIRC is configured with aliases, or shortcuts for the commands. Try leaving the channel with **/p** next time.)

➤ Quitting a channel does not mean you have left IRC (any more than getting up from the table means you have left the coffee house). You can continue to explore IRC.

STEP 6: Get a List of Other Open Channels

➤ Type **/list -min 15** in the message line, and press **Enter.** You will soon see a list of all channels having a minimum of 15 participants, as shown in Figure 5.3e. The list may be quite long, depending on the time of day. Scroll through the list.

➤ You can join another channel without leaving the first, then jump back and forth between the channels and the private chat session. You can scroll up and down in the window to follow the conversation you missed while you were gone.

➤ Double click another channel to join it. (If that does not work, select **Status** from the **Window menu.** Type the join command in the command/message line at the bottom of the screen: **/join #*channelname.*** Press **Enter.**)

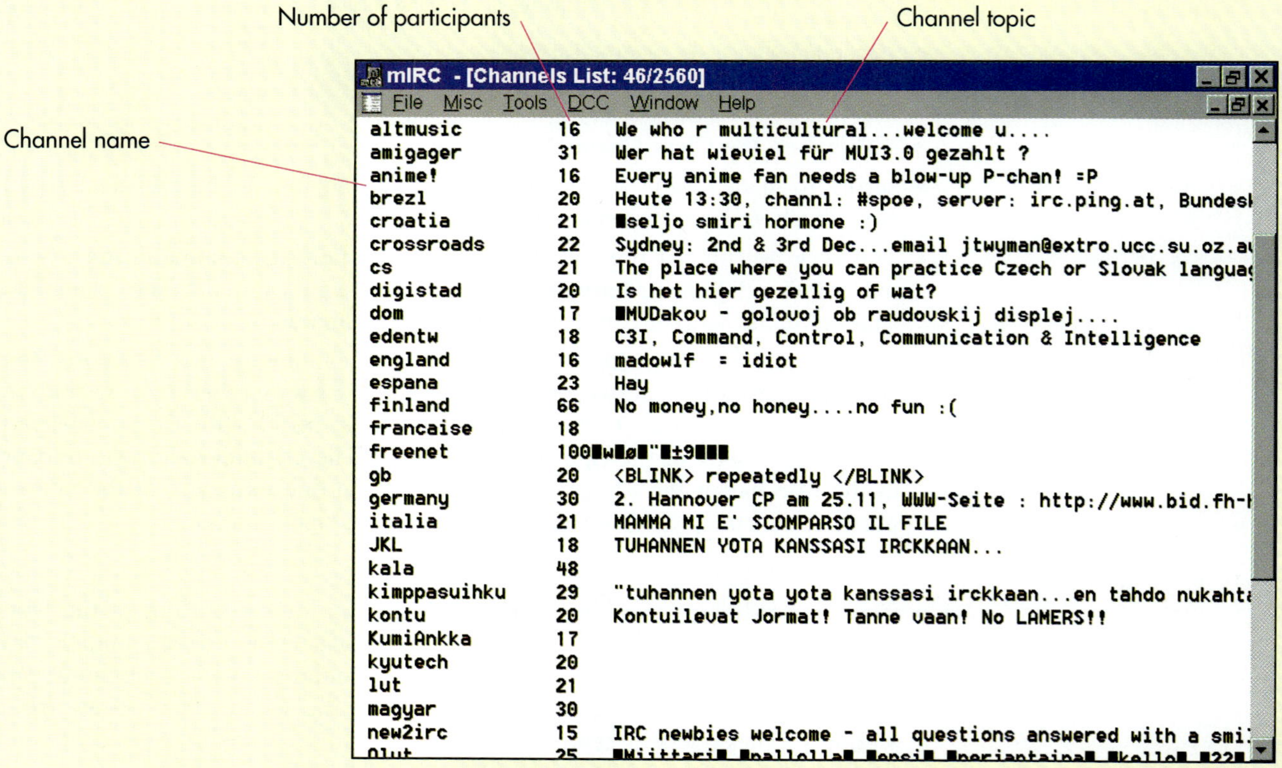

Number of participants — Channel topic

Channel name

(e) The Channel List

FIGURE 5.3 Hands-on Exercise 1 (continued)

170 EXPLORING THE INTERNET

STEP 7: Send a Private Message

➤ Select the **DCC pull-down menu,** then click **Chat.**

➤ Type the nickname of the person with whom you want to have a private conversation and press **Enter.** The IRC server will notify you once the person is located and the private chat session is established. The messages you type in the DCC chat window will be seen only by him or her.

STEP 8: See Where You Are

➤ Pull down the **Window menu** as shown in Figure 5.3f to display the windows in IRC.

➤ The check mark (√) next to the pound or number sign (#) indicates the current IRC window.

➤ To change to another IRC window—for example, the private chat with Joe—click the window.

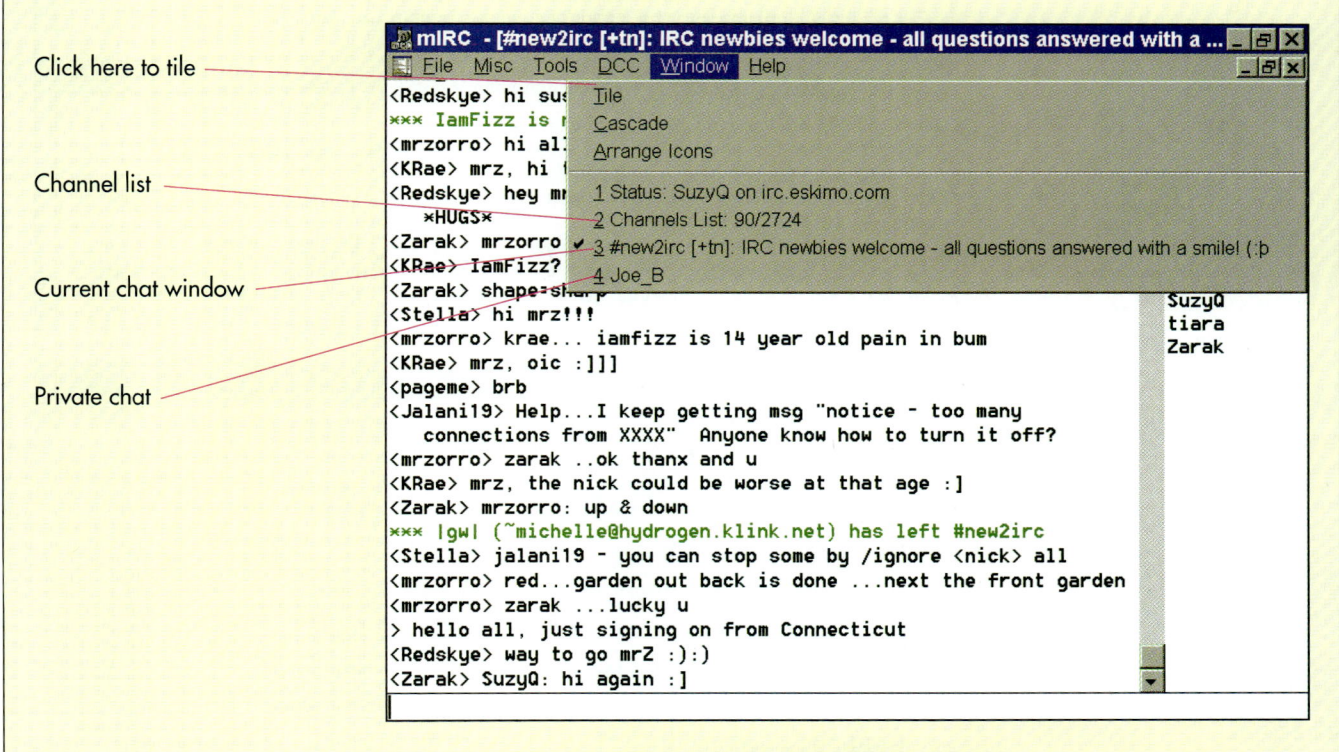

- Click here to tile
- Channel list
- Current chat window
- Private chat

(f) The Window Pull-down Menu

FIGURE 5.3   Hands-on Exercise 1 (continued)

---

http://www.iag.net/mgoetz/win95.html#Windows 95 Software - Internet

Download lots of Internet software from this site, including the latest version of mIRC.

CONVERSATIONS ON THE INTERNET   **171**

▶ If you want to watch the conversation in several channels/chat sessions at once, select **Tile** on the **Window menu.** Tiled chat and channel sessions are shown in Figure 5.3g.

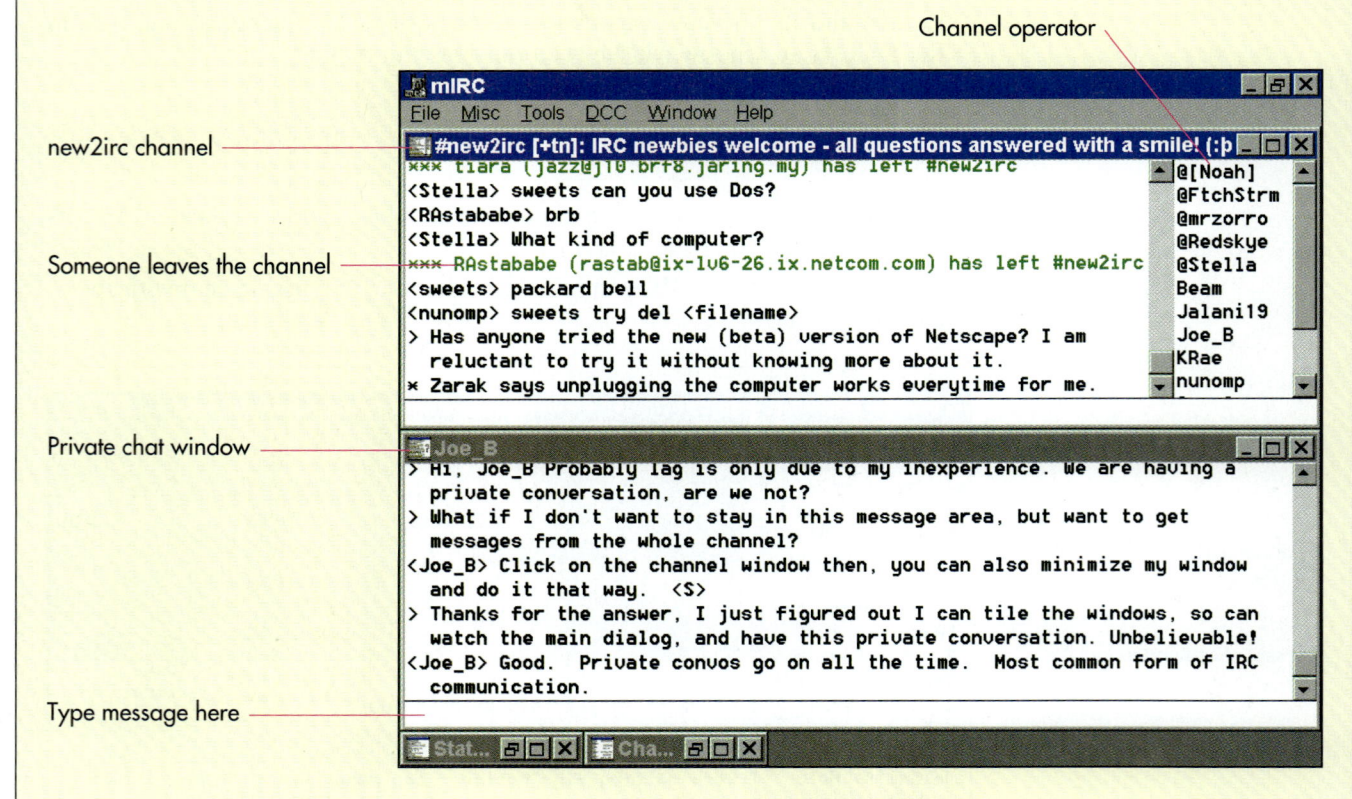

(screenshot of mIRC tiled windows with labels: Channel operator, new2irc channel, Someone leaves the channel, Private chat window, Type message here)

(g) The Tiled Windows

FIGURE 5.3 Hands-on Exercise 1 (continued)

STEP 9: Leave All Channels and Log Off IRC

▶ When you are ready to leave the channel, type **/p.**
  - Pull down the **Window menu** and select any other open channel you may have joined. Part from this channel with the **/p** command.
  - Continue selecting open channels from the **Window menu** and using the **/p** command to leave them until you have closed all open channels.

▶ Select **File** then **Exit** to exit your mIRC session.

BLOCKING ANNOYING MESSAGES

As at any public gathering place, you meet all types on the Internet. There are some unusual people and conversations on IRC, and you may occasionally run into someone you just don't want to deal with. You can send an IRC command, **/ignore nickname all,** and all communication to you from the person with the nickname will be blocked by the IRC server. It would be nice if blocking incoming prank calls were so easy on the telephone!

172 EXPLORING THE INTERNET

WEBCHAT

Similar to IRC in concept, **WebChat** allows you to send messages to other people surfing the Net at the same time you are. You can use your Web browser to link to any of a number of WebChat sites. Digital Equipment Corporation's (DEC) Global Chat home page is shown in Figure 5.4. A 1995 Best of the Web nominee, at time of publication this site was receiving *16.5 million* visitors per month!

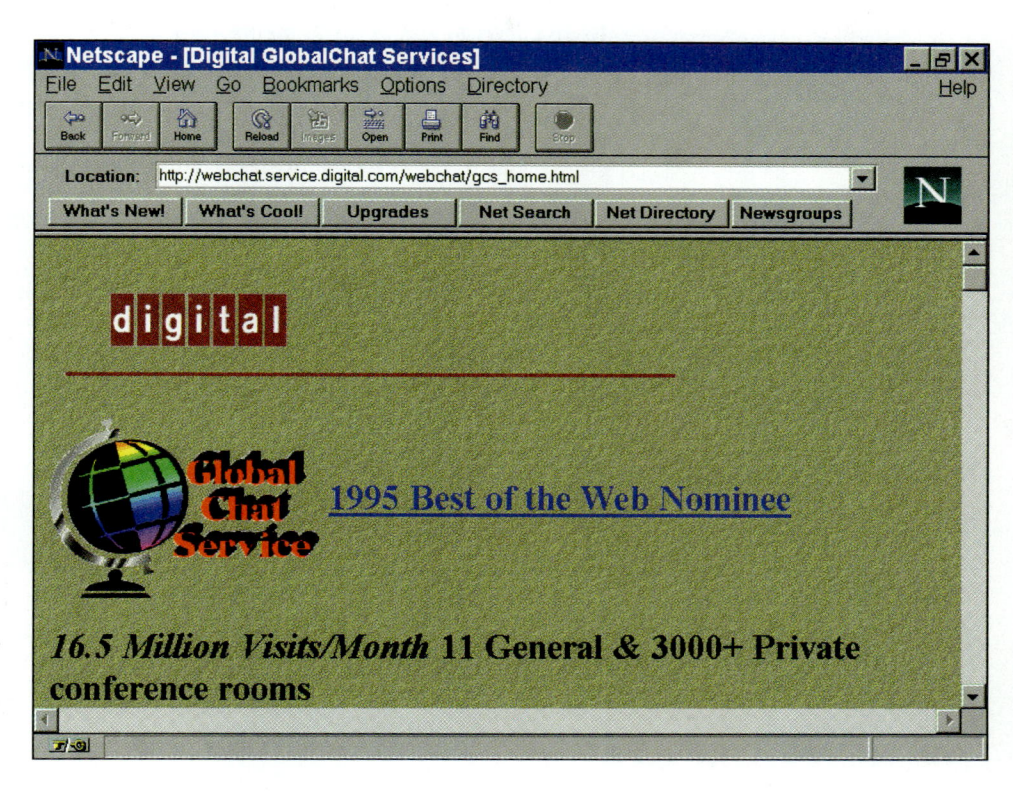

FIGURE 5.4   The Global Chat Home Page

Using this site, you can enter 11 different predefined **chat rooms** devoted to specific topics, or establish your own private conference room and invite someone into it. A chat room is analogous to an IRC channel. Anyone who links to the same chat room sees the same messages, just as everyone on the same channel in IRC does. Just as in IRC, you establish a nickname, or **handle,** for yourself before you enter a chat room. A conceptual map of the site is shown in Figure 5.5.

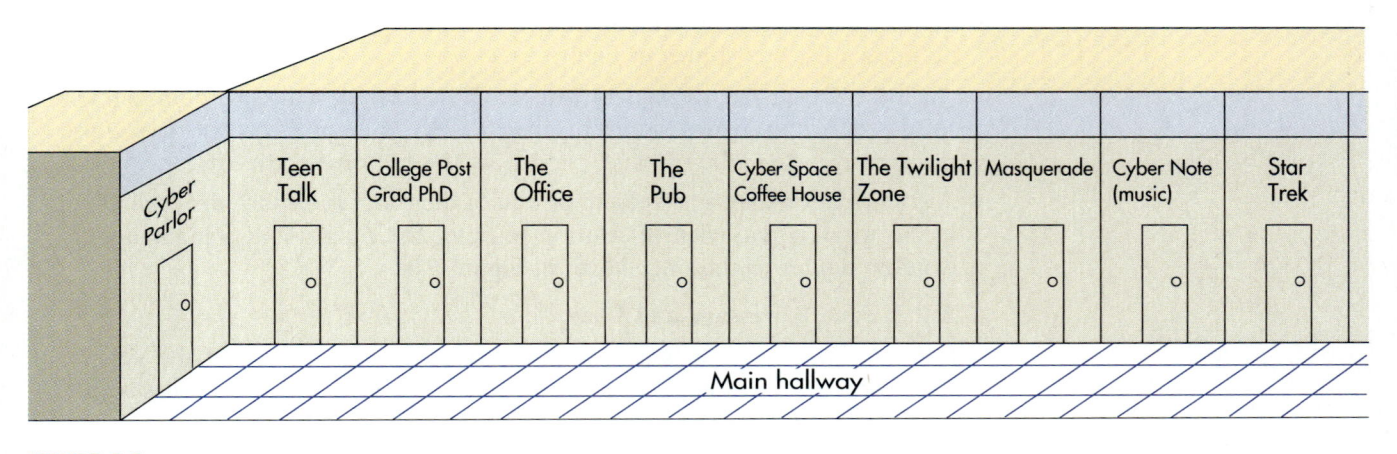

FIGURE 5.5   The Global Chat Map

While similar to IRC, WebChat has one major difference. Your Web browser establishes a connection with the chat site just long enough to download the current page, which includes the most recent messages posted to it. However, unlike IRC, it does not maintain the connection, so you will not see messages scrolling by on your screen. WebChat, while allowing conversations, is an asynchronous medium, meaning that you post, then refresh with an updated page, then post again, and so on. To anyone accustomed to the instantaneous nature of IRC, WebChat seems painstakingly slow. On the other hand, if you don't have access to IRC, WebChat is an amazing tool.

---

http://www.cco.caltech.edu/~cbrown/BL/

Do you think advertising on the Net should be banned? Are you annoyed when you see Usenet postings that are obvious hucksterism at work? Check out the Black List of Internet Advertisers to get the latest information on the advertising scourges of cyberspace.

HANDS-ON EXERCISE 2

Using WebChat

Objective: To enter a WebChat room and send a message. To set up a private conference room. Use Figures 5.4 and 5.6 as guides in the exercise.

STEP 1: Open Your Web Browser and Jump to a WebChat Site

- Log on to your system and open your browser.
- Enter the URL **http://webchat.service.digital.com/webchat/gcs_home.html** in the Location text box. Press **Enter.** You will see the DEC WebChat home page previously shown in Figure 5.4. (If this site is not available, try connecting to the WebChat page of the Internet Roundtable Society at **http://www.irsociety.com/webchat.html.** Modify the rest of the instructions accordingly.)

STEP 2: Enter a Chat Room

- Scroll down in DEC's **Global Chat home page** until you see the icons and pull-down list box shown in Figure 5.6a.
- Click the **Down Arrow** next to **Select a Room Here.** A list of rooms similar to that shown in Figure 5.6b is displayed. Select one of the rooms (we chose the CyberSpace Coffee House), and click the button to enter it.
- A confirmation message welcoming you to the room is displayed. Scroll down in the window and click the button to enter the room. You will see a **Chat** window similar to the one shown in Figure 5.6c.

STEP 3: Send a Message and Chat

- Before composing a message, drag the scroll box to the top of the vertical scroll bar to read the most recently sent messages. The ones we saw are shown in Figure 5.6d.

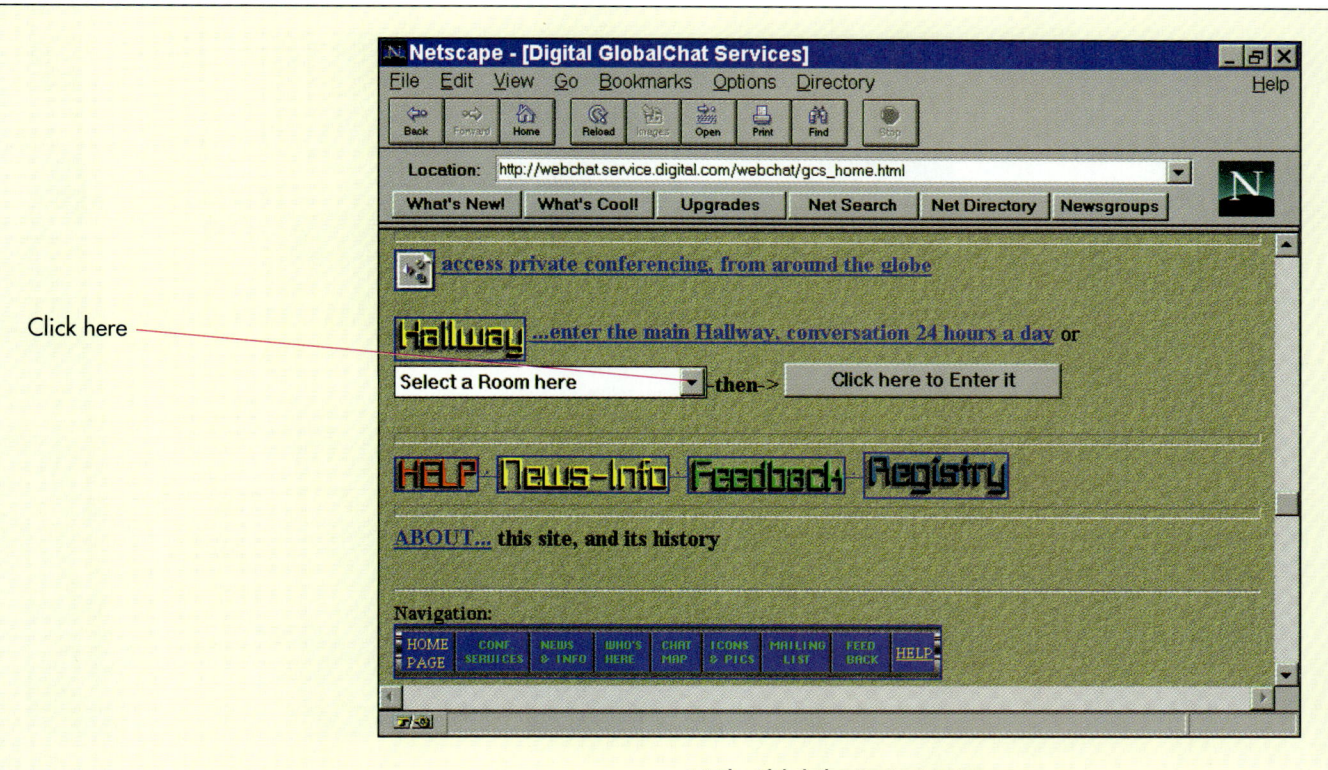

(a) The Global Chat Navigation Area

(b) The List of Chat Rooms

FIGURE 5.6 Hands-on Exercise 2

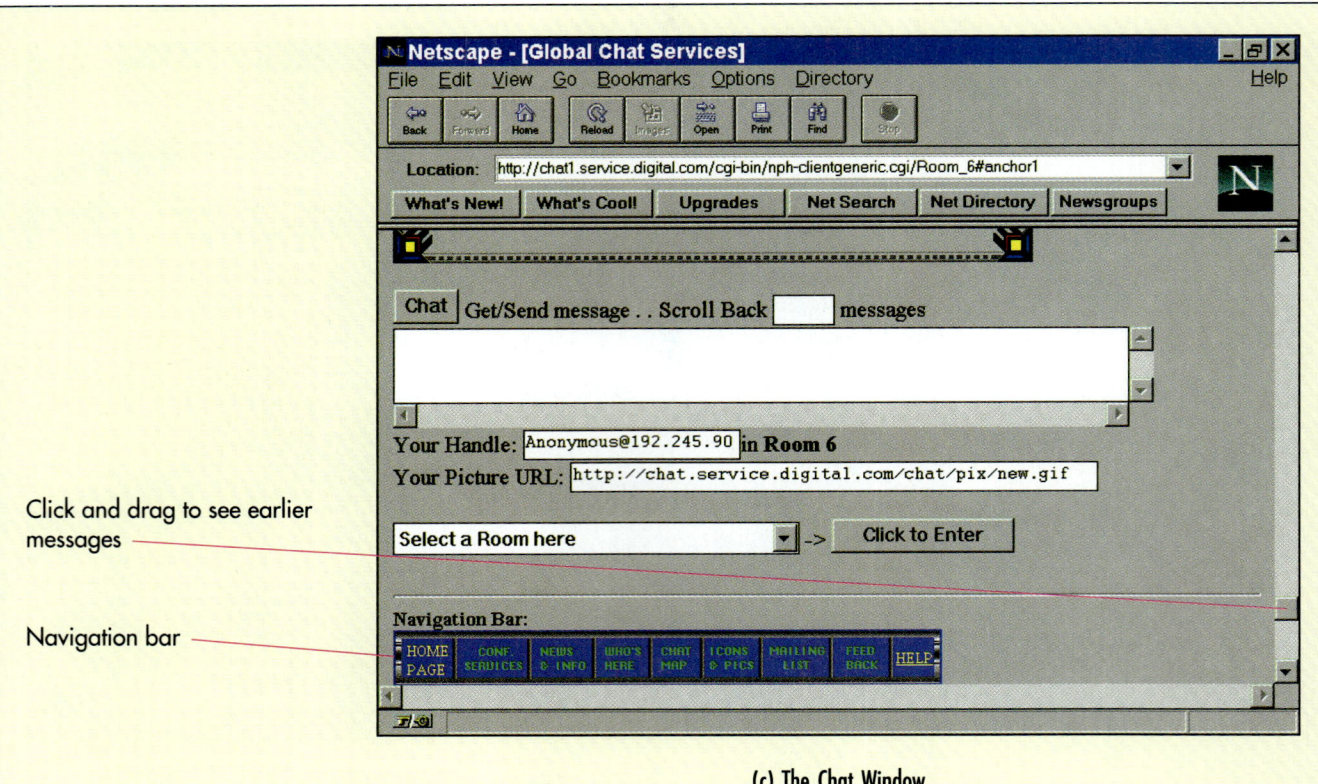

Click and drag to see earlier messages

Navigation bar

(c) The Chat Window

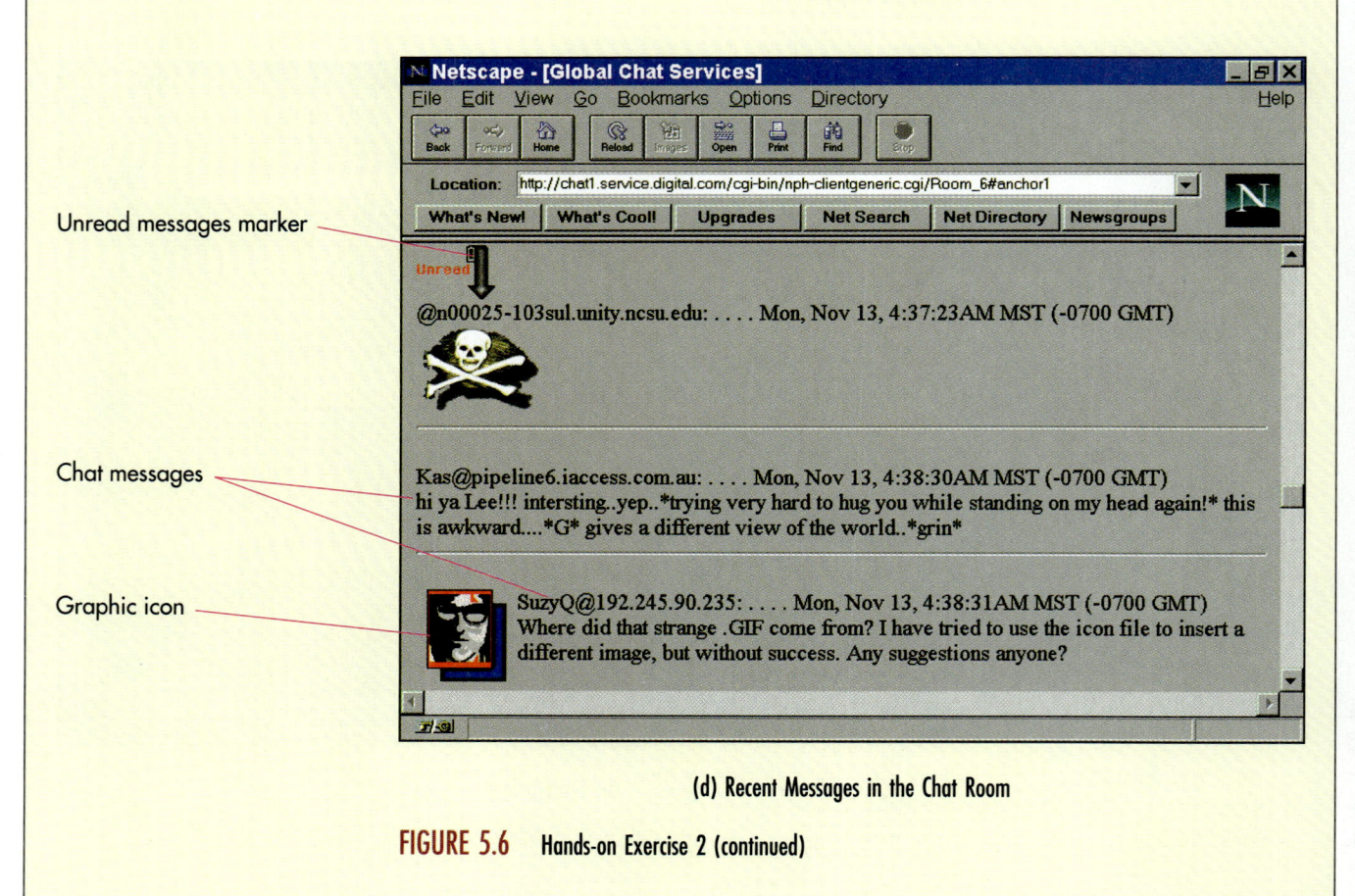

Unread messages marker

Chat messages

Graphic icon

(d) Recent Messages in the Chat Room

FIGURE 5.6 Hands-on Exercise 2 (continued)

➤ Send a chat message.
- Scroll back down to the bottom of the chat window.
- Enter a nickname in the **Handle** text box as shown in Figure 5.6e. (You can enter whatever you want. Just remember, it's not a good idea to use your real name, and keep it clean.) If you don't enter a nickname, Global Chat will use the default, *anonymous,* and it will be difficult for you and others to follow your messages in the conversation.
- Click in the message box and type a message.
- Click **Chat.** Your message is sent to the Web server and added to the collection of messages in the chat room you selected.
- Scroll down, if necessary, until you see your message. The graphic image displayed next to your message is a default image from the Global Chat image library. You will change the graphic in the next message you send.
- After a minute or two click **Chat** again. Any messages received at the Web server after yours was sent are now displayed.

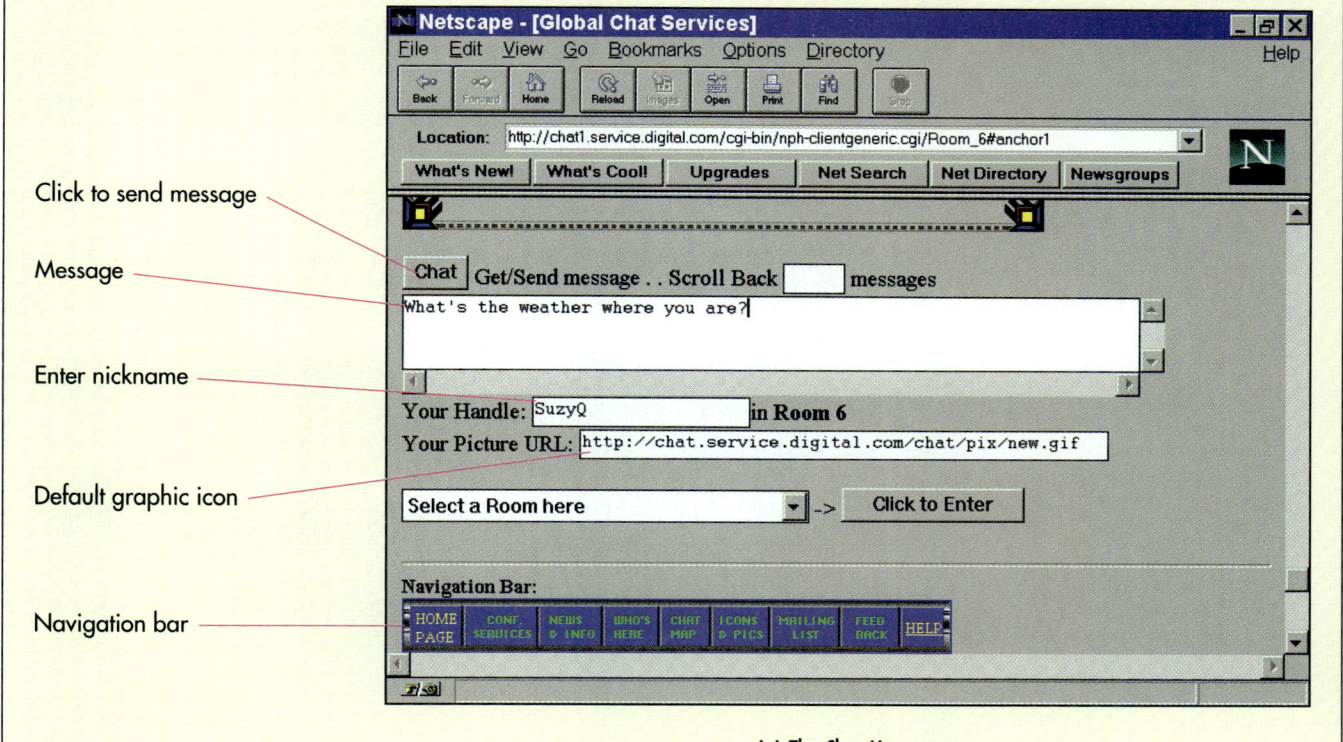

(e) The Chat Message

FIGURE 5.6 Hands-on Exercise 2 (continued)

STEP 4: Explore Global Chat

➤ Add a graphic to your message. First you choose the graphic, then you enter the URL for the graphic in the message itself.
- Scroll down in the **Chat window** until you reach the navigation bar at the bottom of the screen.
- Click the **Icons & Pics button.** Scroll down in the window until you see the image categories shown in Figure 5.6f.

Click to select a category

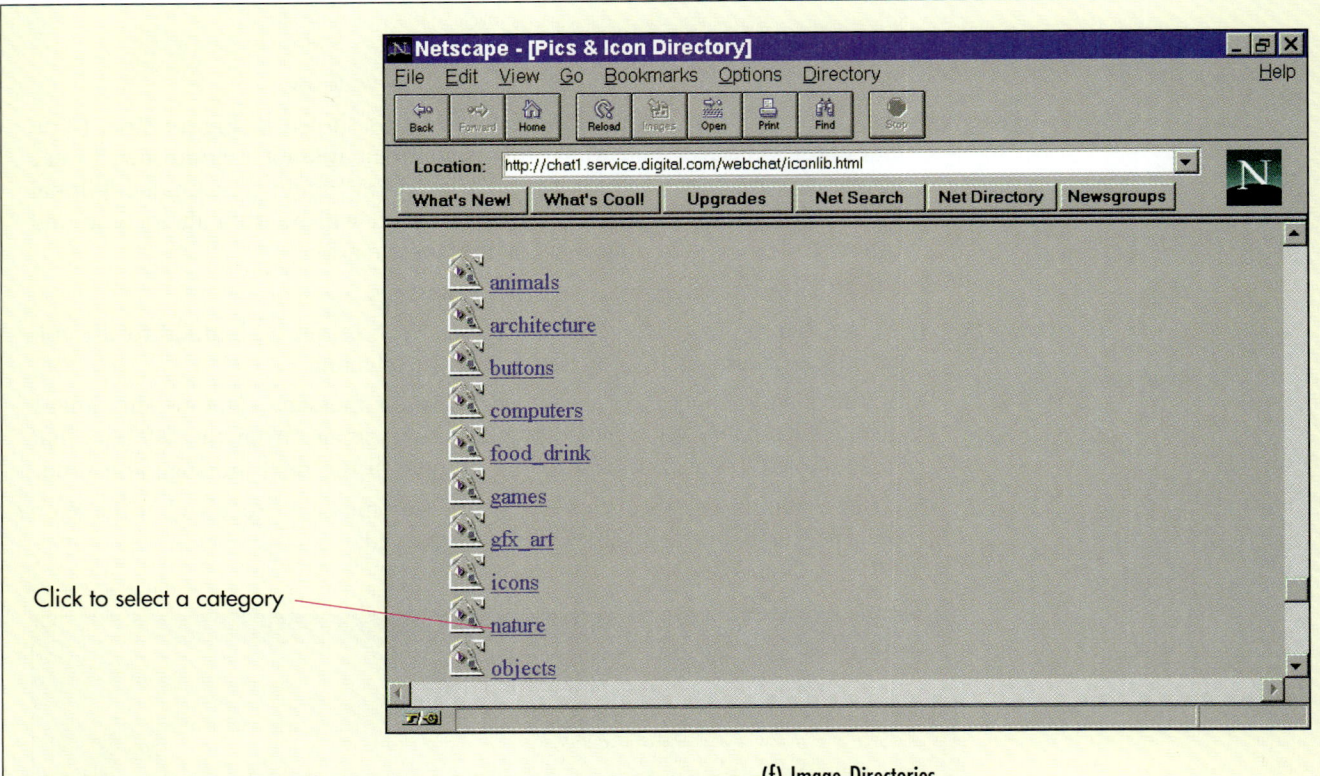

(f) Image Directories

- Select a category by clicking the link. A list of icons on DEC's chat server is displayed, as shown in Figure 5.6g.

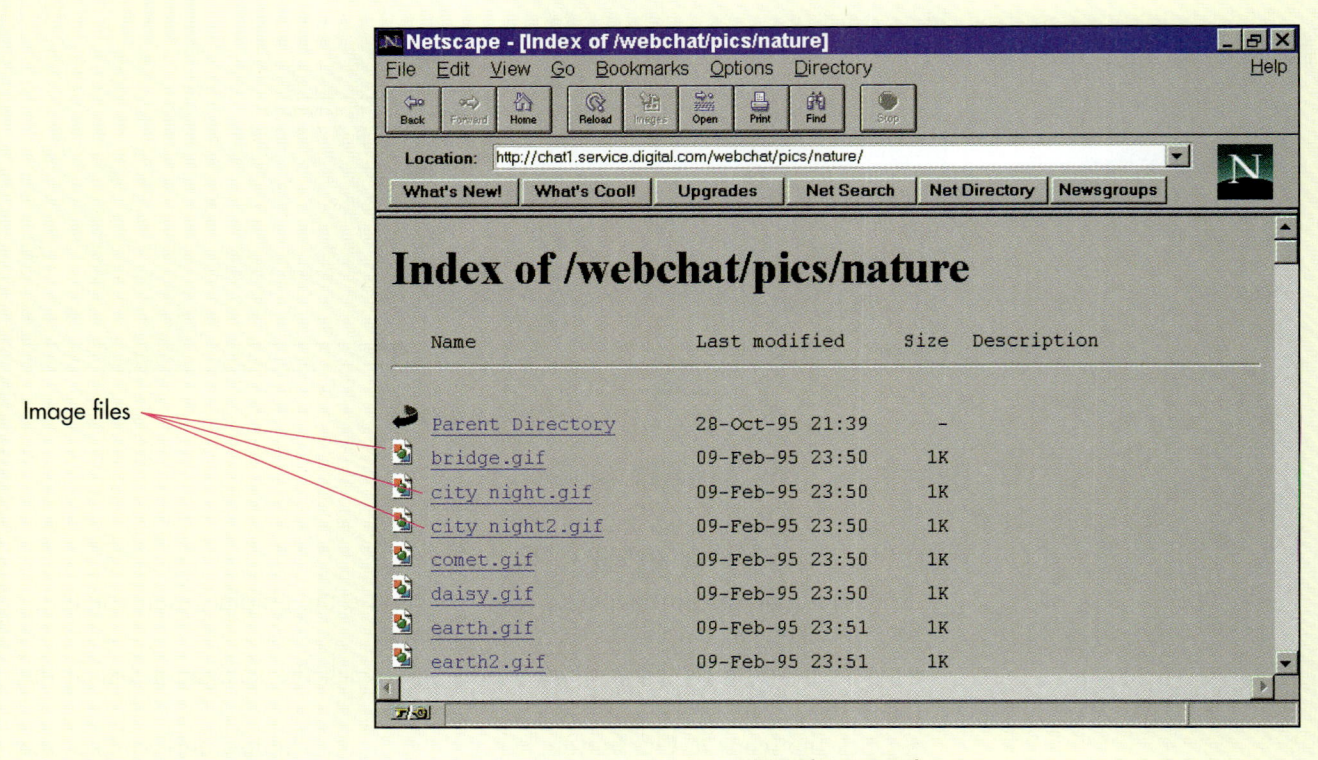

Image files

(g) Graphic Image Files

FIGURE 5.6　Hands-on Exercise 2 (continued)

178　EXPLORING THE INTERNET

- Select an icon from the list.
- When the icon is displayed on your screen, select the URL in the Location text box and press **Ctrl+C**. This will copy the icon's URL to the Windows clipboard.
- Click **Go** or press **Alt+G** to display the Go pull-down menu. Select **Global Chat Services** to return to your chat room.
- Enter a new message in the chat message box. Press **Ctrl+V** to paste the URL of the graphic icon anywhere you choose in the message. Click **Chat.** When the screen has finished loading, you should see your message with the icon embedded in it.

➤ Return to the main hallway to see what is being discussed there.
- Scroll to the bottom of the **Chat window** and click on the **Main Hallway icon.**

---

http://www.acmeweb.com/webchat/webstation.html

The Acmeweb Webstation contains links to dozens of chat rooms on the Web about a wide variety of topics. Visit anytime to strike up an interesting conversation.

STEP 5: Set Up a Private Conference Room

➤ Agree upon a time to meet a classmate or two in the lab and create a private conference room in which to "talk."
- Scroll down to the bottom of the **Chat window** and click on the **Conference Services button** in the navigation bar.
- Scroll down in the **Conference Services window** and click in the conference room text box. Enter the name of the conference room upon which you have agreed with your group. Press **Enter** or click the **Create button.** You will enter a private conference room. Remember the name as there is no way to get a list of private rooms (then they wouldn't be private!).
- You can verify that you are in the room by the message on the screen, as shown in Figure 5.6h. Anyone else who knows the name of the room can enter it with you and carry on a private conversation. Just be advised that almost nothing on the Internet is really private, and someone could be lurking without your knowing. (Do not enter any text that you would be embarrassed about later.)
- When you are ready to leave, scroll down in the window to find the navigation bar at the bottom, and click on any option, or change the URL in the Location text box to go to another Web site.

Conference room name

in--> MIS201Chat

(h) A Private Conference Room

FIGURE 5.6   Hands-on Exercise 2 (continued)

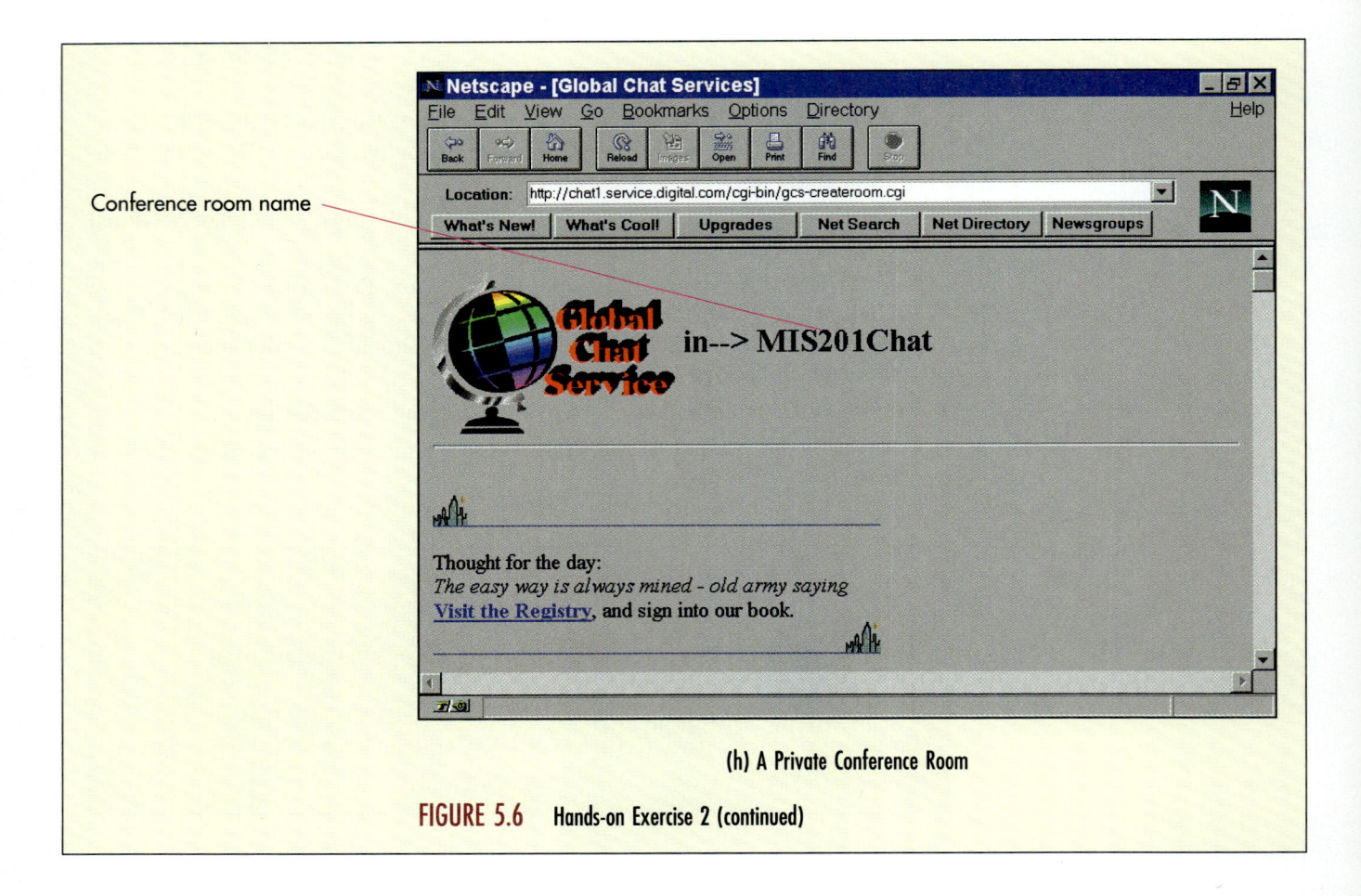

USENET

We used the analogy earlier of IRC and WebChat being similar to an international online coffee house, and you have now experienced it, *sans* coffee. You can equate **Usenet** to a combination of classified ads, the editorial section in your local newspaper, and a bulletin board at your local student center or student union. Except Usenet, like IRC and everything else on the Internet, is international in scope.

Similar to mailing lists, Usenet is an Internet news service that was developed to allow ongoing discussions among an unlimited number of people about a multitude of diverse topics. Individuals subscribe to one or more Usenet ***newsgroups,*** as these discussions are called, and receive daily messages posted to the groups by other subscribers. Anyone interested in a particular topic can request delivery of all the messages relating to the topic, which are automatically forwarded to all subscribers, much like the newspaper is delivered each day. At time of publication, millions of people were participating in well over 6,000 newsgroups, with more being added every day.

To help users find newsgroups of interest to them, Usenet is divided into **hierarchies,** or nominally related categories of topics. The big eight of the mainstream hierarchies (which are approved by international consensus) are *news, soc, talk, misc, sci, comp, rec,* and *humanities.* They cover the topics shown in Table 5.3. Dozens of discussion groups carry on ongoing "conversations" within each hierarchy.

The names of the groups are identified by the hierarchy name and additional modifiers, each separated by a period. Should you be interested in comic books, for instance, rec.arts.comics.marketplace is concerned with the buying and selling of superhero magazines. On a more serious note, sci.bio.ethnology is devoted to animal behavior and behavioral ethnology.

Many hierarchies do not go through the formal Internet screening process that those shown in Table 5.3 went through prior to being accepted as newsgroup hierarchies. Chief among these are *alt, biz,* and *info,* although there are many others *(k12, vmsnet, ieee,* and *bionet* to name a few). In addition, there are hundreds of local and regional newsgroups that are not distributed worldwide. (Think of it as the difference between the local, regional, national, and international editions of a newspaper, if there were such a thing.)

Alt is the newsgroup that has received the most media attention, primarily for some of its X-rated content. However, the alt hierarchy is also home to hundreds of discussions on serious topics having to do with politics, office management, culture, religion, society, support groups—the list goes on. Biz is devoted to business topics, including product announcements, technical specifications, and discussions about business.

USENET NETIQUETTE, OR ASK EMILY POSTNEWS

Although there is no regulatory body or central organization controlling the Internet, there are all sorts of simple do's and don'ts that are generally agreed to by the millions of people who use it daily. These are collectively referred to as **netiquette,** about which you will hear more in Chapter 6. Usenet participants generally have little tolerance for a **newbie's** (new user's) questions. You can find answers to frequently asked questions (FAQs) in multiple archives, or in the newsgroups news.answers.newusers and news.emily.postnews. Read these postings for a few weeks, then post any questions you may have to the news.answers.newusers group. It is there to keep newbies from flooding other groups with inappropriate questions—and to protect you from getting flamed by irate news groupies. Forewarned is forearmed.

TABLE 5.3 Usenet Mainstream Hierarchies

Hierarchy	Description
news	News is used to talk about all kinds of news, including Internet and Usenet news. You can find a list of all Usenet discussion groups in news.lists, for instance.
soc	Society encompasses discussions about all types of social issues, including women's issues, AIDS, public policy, and more. The topics, of course, are international, such as soc.culture.ukrainian.
talk	Talk is just that. As in any conversation on controversial topics, discussions can get pretty heated on talk.politics.guns.
misc	Discussions that don't fit elsewhere. Misc.jobs.misc contains job postings, for instance.
sci	Science is wide ranging. Check out sci.space.shuttle to learn about space shuttle missions and see reviews of space movies.
comp	If you want to find out the latest about computers, from Unix systems to PCs, the computer hierarchy will have a discussion for you. An interesting group is comp.graphics.animation.
rec	The recreation hierarchy covers a myriad of hobbies from antiques (rec.antiques) to woodworking (rec.woodworking).
humanities	Humanities, added in April 1995, is the newest hierarchy. As the book went to press, there were few newsgroups, one of which was humanities.misc.

> http://www.yahoo.com/Entertainment/
> Humor_Jokes_and_Fun/Internet_Humor
>
> Do you need a break from studying? Check out Yahoo's Humor site.

When someone wants to start or contribute to a conversation in a newsgroup, he/she composes a message and *posts* it to the group. The message is sent by the *newsreader,* software on the sender's Internet host, which forwards it to a *news server* on the Internet. That system forwards it to all other regional or worldwide Internet news servers, depending on the requested distribution, thus propagating the message worldwide (assuming the distribution is to the entire world). This process is illustrated in Figure 5.7.

The news servers compile the daily postings to all the newsgroups and periodically download them to Internet hosts around the world. These distributions are known as *newsfeeds.* The receiving organization can select which newsgroup hierarchy newsfeeds to receive, and will often limit the number due to the volume of traffic each hierarchy generates. Newsfeeds are illustrated in Figure 5.8.

A user who subscribes to the newsgroup may read the original posting and respond to it. The response will become part of the next newsfeed. Other readers will also respond to the original posting, or respond to the responder. The collection of messages about one topic, including those from the original sender and multiple respondents, is called a *thread.* The newsreader you use will be able to provide you with a list of current threads in a particular newsgroup, as shown in

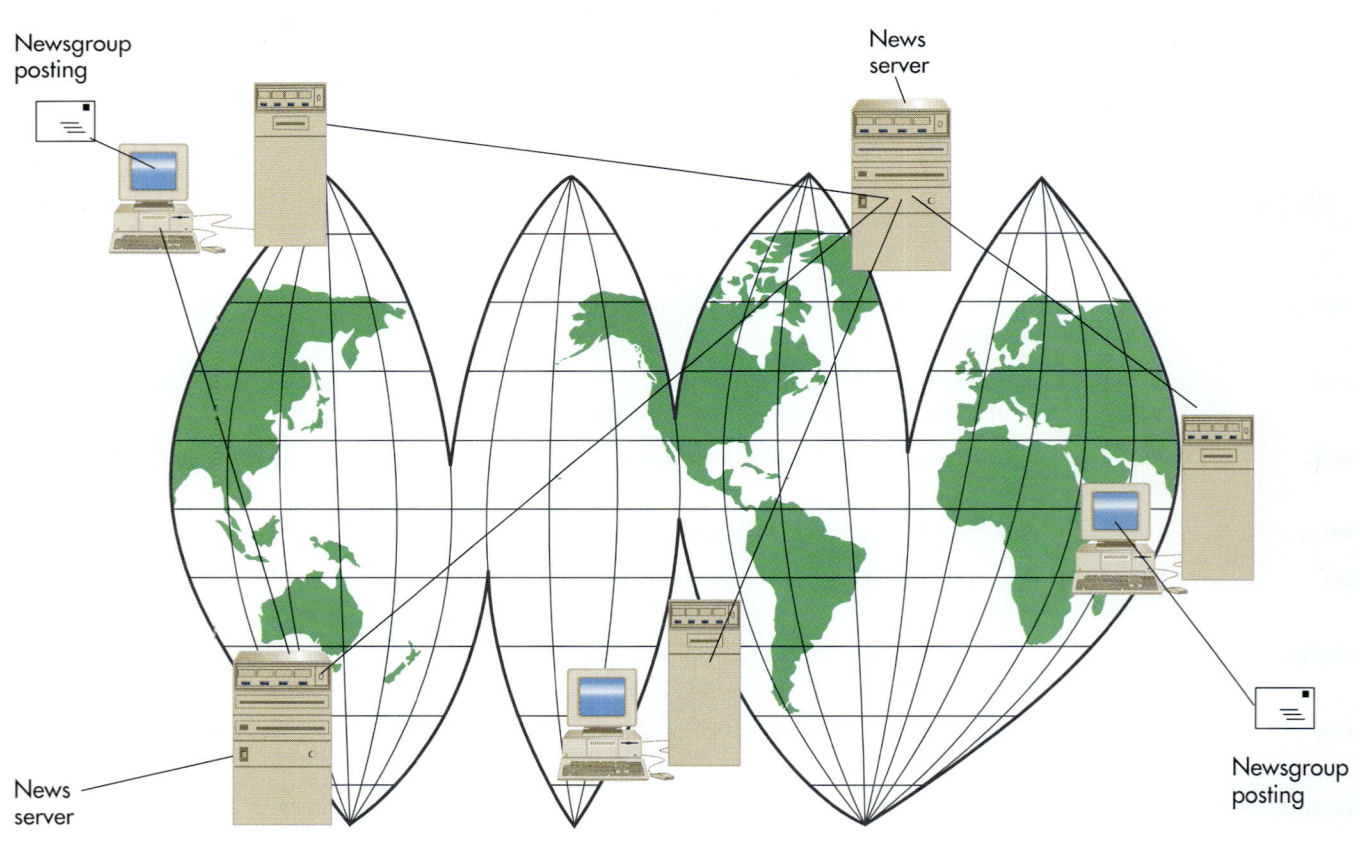

FIGURE 5.7 Usenet

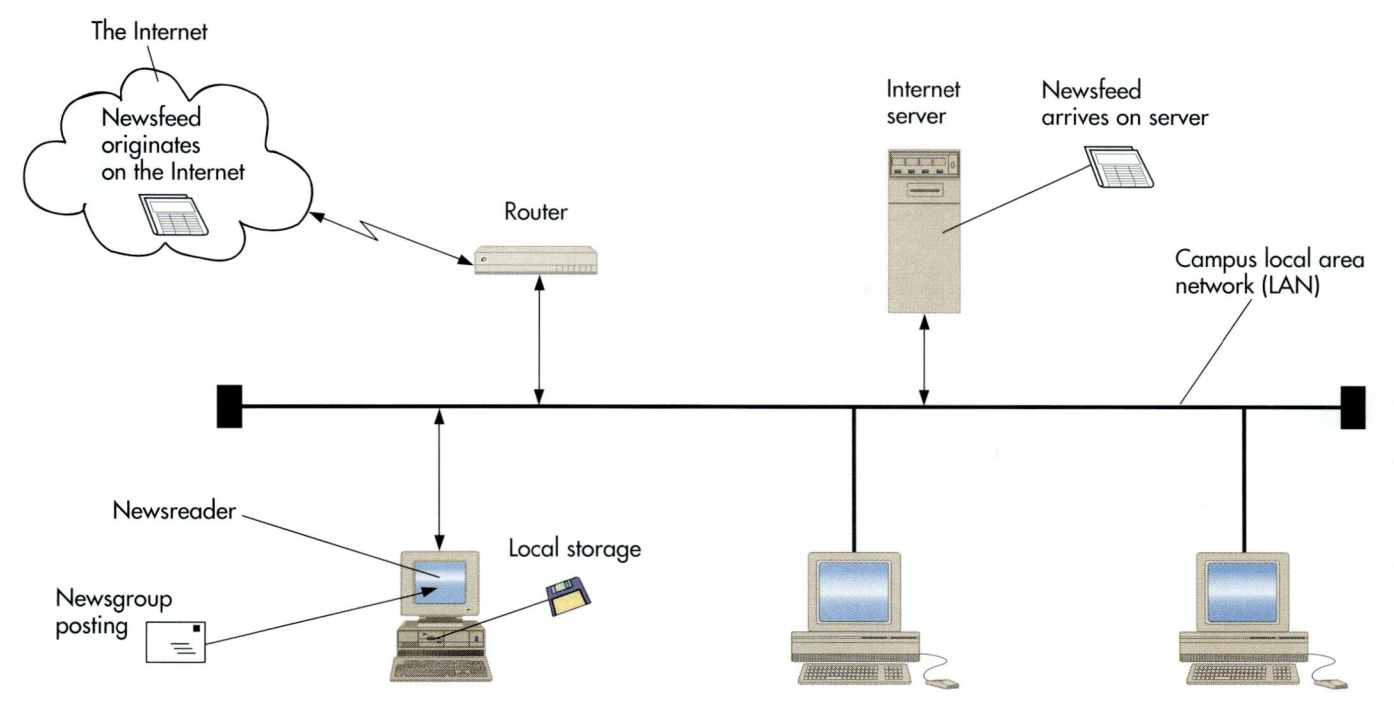

FIGURE 5.8 Newsfeeds

Figure 5.9. You can select a posting within a thread and read it. A message posted to the news.test newsgroup is shown in Figure 5.10.

You can use your newsreader to subscribe to specific newsgroups of interest to you. The newsreader available at your campus computing center may be able to organize your incoming news into threads and allow you to select which threads you want to follow so you don't have to receive all the postings to a newsgroup. Newsreaders can also keep track of which postings or threads you have already read, so you won't repeatedly receive them each time you access the newsgroup.

The news server at your local Internet host sets a news expiration date, so incoming news is automatically purged after some period of time, much as you stack your newspapers and recycle them weekly. Once the message has been purged from your system, you cannot recall it. However, many newsgroups are *archived* at various sites on the Web. You can visit the archives with your Web browser to find and read threads you missed or messages from hierarchies you do not receive.

Each newsreader, and there are many, has different features and commands to activate those features. See your campus computing staff for information about the newsreader you will use in your environment.

DON'T LET THE NEWS GET YOU DOWN

Reading the news can be an interesting and enlightening experience. However, the *signal-to-noise ratio* of various hierarchies and newsgroups can be quite low, meaning that most of what passes as information is really unsubstantiated opinion. Students have been known to spend hour upon hour in the lab, reading furiously, trying not to miss out on their favorite threads. Now, think about it. Would you spend this many hours reading the daily newspaper or the bulletin board at the local supermarket? As in all things, moderation is recommended.

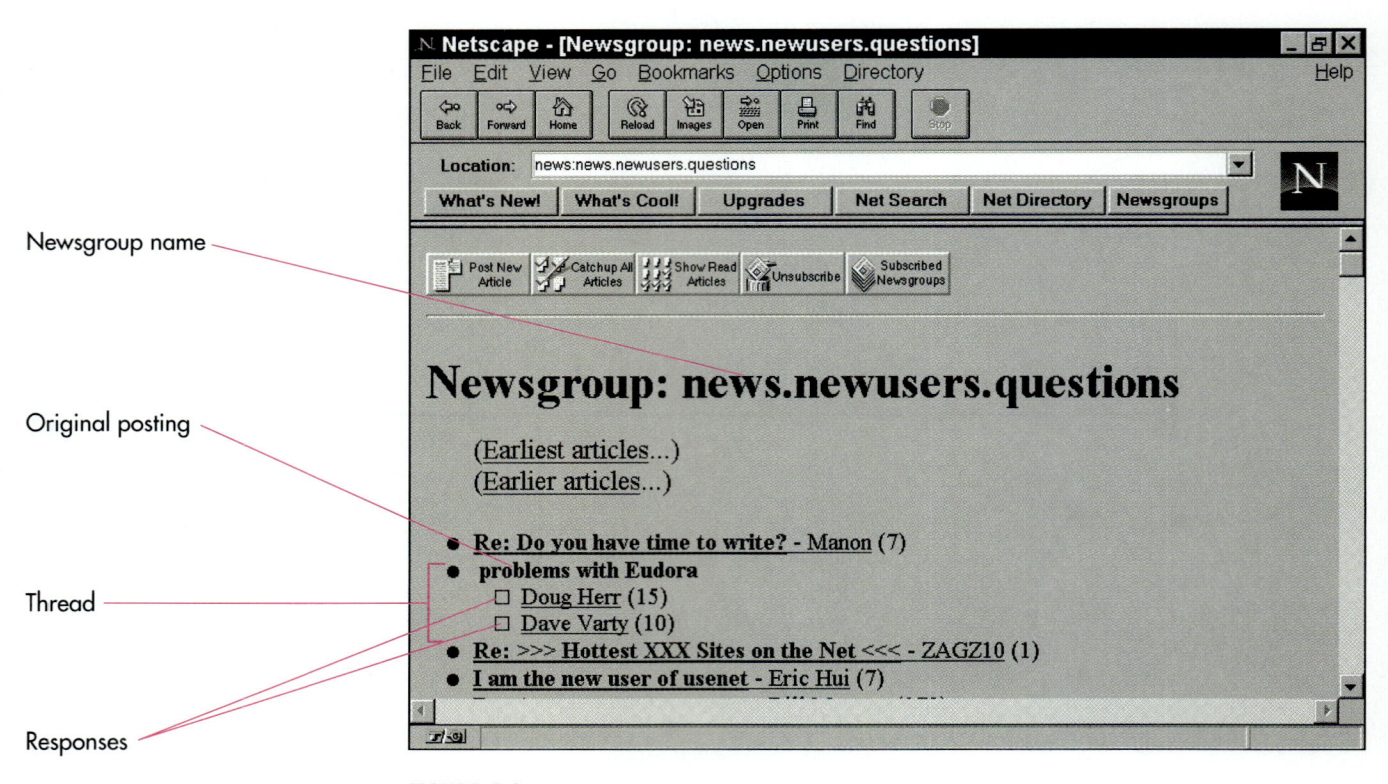

FIGURE 5.9 A News Thread

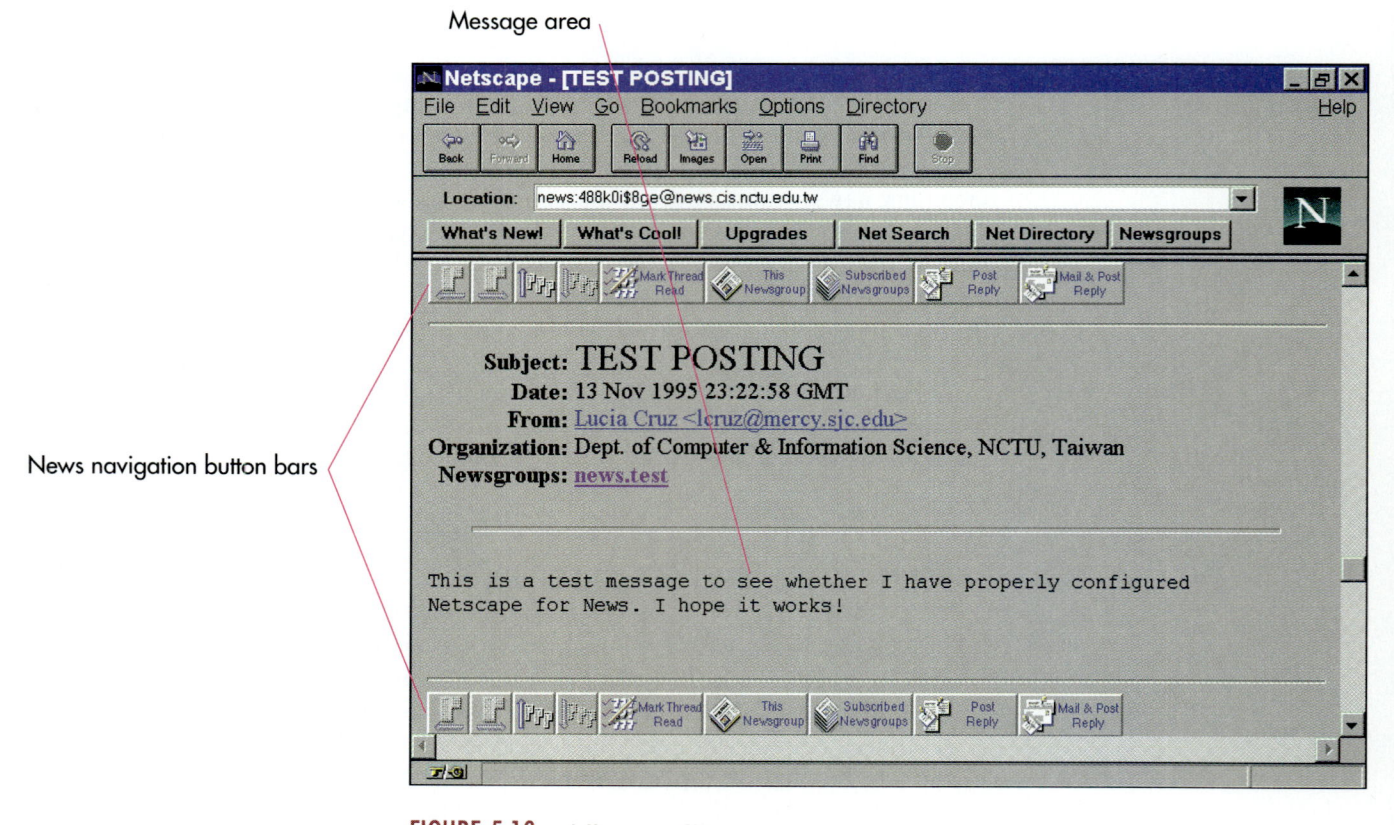

FIGURE 5.10 A Newsgroup Message

184 EXPLORING THE INTERNET

LEARNING BY DOING

As in many of our previous examples in this book, not everyone will be using the same newsreader—that is, client software—to access the newsgroups available in their campus computing environment. As mentioned earlier, some colleges and universities have chosen to limit newsfeeds or not provide them at all due to their exorbitant use of system resources.

You can complete the first three steps in the exercise even if you do not have news. You will explore your campus news environment and learn how to access news postings through FTP archives. In the second half of the exercise you will read threads and post a message using Netscape. Because the manner in which you read news and post to a newsgroup is highly dependent on the type of newsreader or browser that you have on your campus, you should check with your instructor or system administrator if you do not have Netscape or if it is not configured for news.

In addition, as mentioned in the tip earlier in the chapter, you should read the postings on a newsgroup for several weeks before considering adding your two cents to the discussion. Newbies are definitely given little slack on Usenet. You can learn more about Usenet on the Web, of course, and by reading the appropriate archives, which you will search in the next hands-on exercise.

HANDS-ON EXERCISE 3

Usenet

Objective: To learn about the Usenet environment on your campus, and use various Internet tools to explore newsgroup postings and archives. To use the Netscape news reader to follow a thread. Use Figure 5.11 as a guide in the exercise.

STEP 1: What News Options Do You Have?

▶ Learn about the Usenet environment at your college or university. Get answers to the following questions:
- What newsfeeds do you receive?
- How do you set up your Web browser to read the news?
- How do you subscribe to specific newsgroups?
- Can you post to a newsgroup using your Web browser?
- If you do not have a Web browser that allows you to read news, which Unix-based newsreader do you have, if any, and how do you use it?

STEP 2: Get a List of Newsgroups

▶ Log on to your system and open your Web browser.
- Type the URL **ftp://rtfm.mit.edu/pub/usenet/news.lists** in the Location text box and press **Enter**. At the resulting screen, click on the **List of Active New...** link. This will bring up a list of all current newsgroups, as shown in Figure 5.11a, which will take a few minutes given the size of the file.
- Scroll through the list (use **PageDown** to move a little faster), scanning the newsgroup names. Notice that every topic under the sun seems to have its own newsgroup!

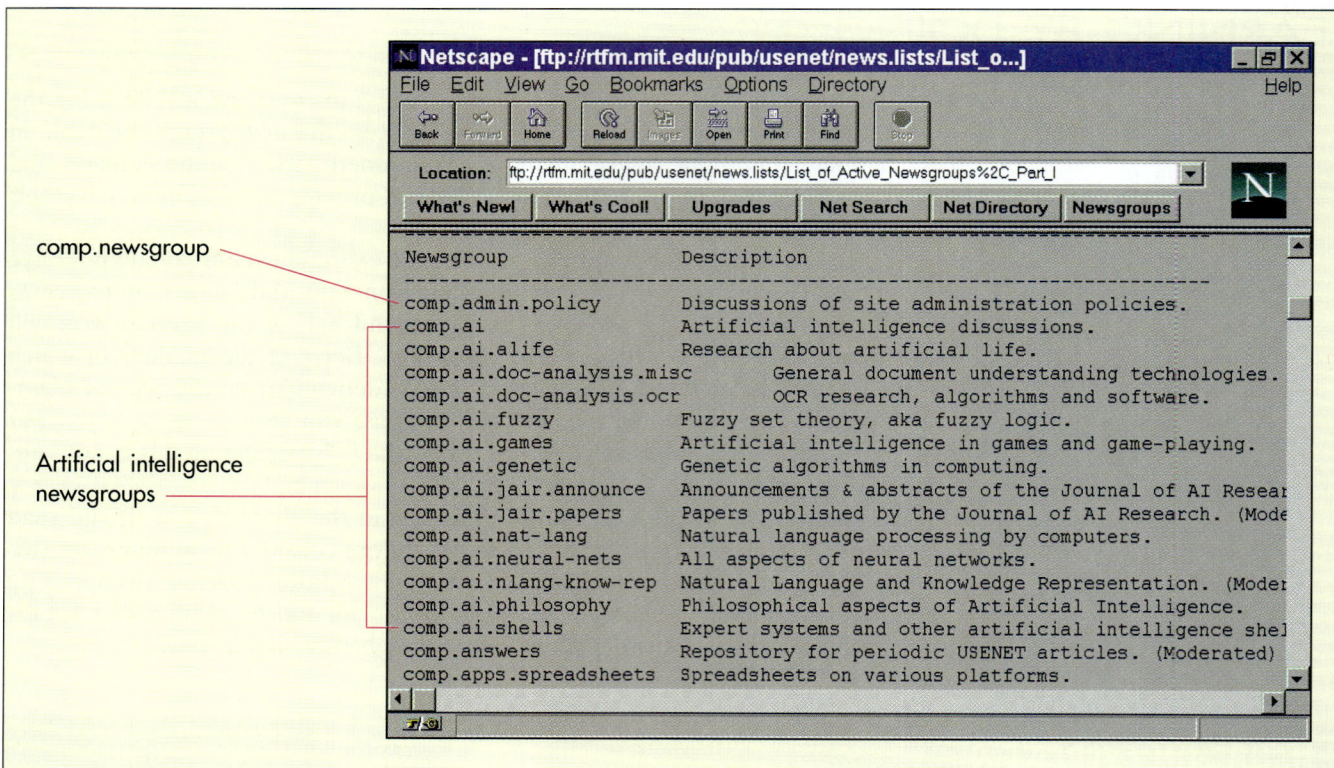

```
Netscape - [ftp://rtfm.mit.edu/pub/usenet/news.lists/List_o...]
File  Edit  View  Go  Bookmarks  Options  Directory                                    Help

Location: ftp://rtfm.mit.edu/pub/usenet/news.lists/List_of_Active_Newsgroups%2C_Part_I

What's New!   What's Cool!   Upgrades   Net Search   Net Directory   Newsgroups

Newsgroup                    Description
----------------------------------------------------------------
comp.admin.policy            Discussions of site administration policies.
comp.ai                      Artificial intelligence discussions.
comp.ai.alife                Research about artificial life.
comp.ai.doc-analysis.misc    General document understanding technologies.
comp.ai.doc-analysis.ocr     OCR research, algorithms and software.
comp.ai.fuzzy                Fuzzy set theory, aka fuzzy logic.
comp.ai.games                Artificial intelligence in games and game-playing.
comp.ai.genetic              Genetic algorithms in computing.
comp.ai.jair.announce        Announcements & abstracts of the Journal of AI Resear
comp.ai.jair.papers          Papers published by the Journal of AI Research. (Mode
comp.ai.nat-lang             Natural language processing by computers.
comp.ai.neural-nets          All aspects of neural networks.
comp.ai.nlang-know-rep       Natural Language and Knowledge Representation. (Moder
comp.ai.philosophy           Philosophical aspects of Artificial Intelligence.
comp.ai.shells               Expert systems and other artificial intelligence shel
comp.answers                 Repository for periodic USENET articles. (Moderated)
comp.apps.spreadsheets       Spreadsheets on various platforms.
```

comp.newsgroup — points to `comp.ai`

Artificial intelligence newsgroups — points to `comp.ai` through `comp.ai.shells`

(a) The List of Active Newsgroups

FIGURE 5.11   Hands-on Exercise 3

▶ Your instructor may prefer that only one person in the class print the list, as it is quite long, or it may already be available in your lab. If so, do not complete this step. Select **Print** from the **File menu** to print the file, then select **Save As** from the **File menu** to save the file for later reference.

STEP 3: Use the Web to Learn about Usenet

▶ Type the URL **ftp://rtfm.mit.edu/pub/usenet/news.newusers.questions** in the Location text box and press **Enter.** If you click on the **Welcome to news.ne...** link, you should see a screen similar to Figure 5.11b. Browse through this document for a while, then click **Back** to browse through the site to get a sense of what is possible with Usenet.

▶ Type the URL **ftp://rtfm.mit.edu/pub/usenet/news.announce.newusers** in the Location text box and press **Enter.** You will jump to the site shown in Figure 5.11c. Spend some time reading the information in this archive, or save the file on your hard drive and read it later.

---

http://www.yahoo.com/News/Usenet/Public_Access_Usenet_Sites/

Even if you don't have Usenet at your campus, you can read Usenet postings. Try one of the public access Usenet sites listed by Yahoo.

news.newusers.questions document —

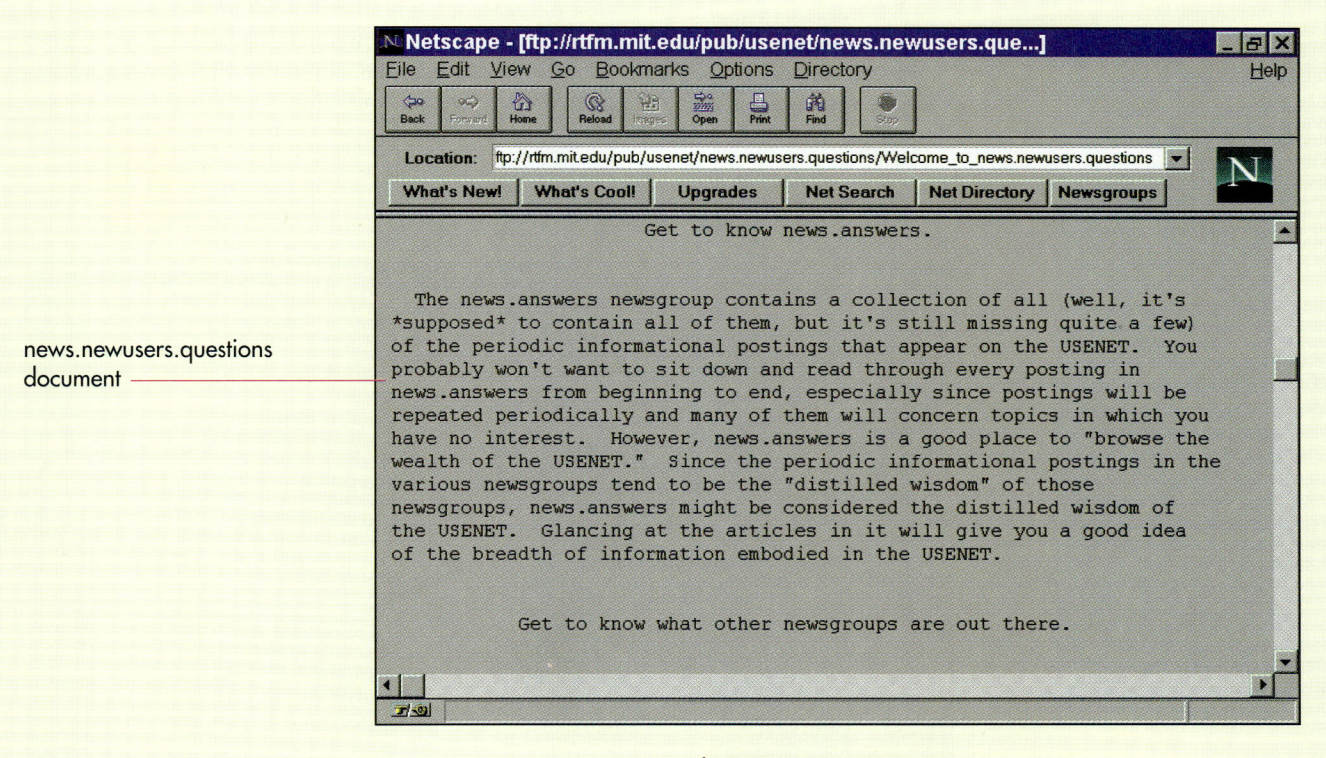

(b) Getting to Know News.answers

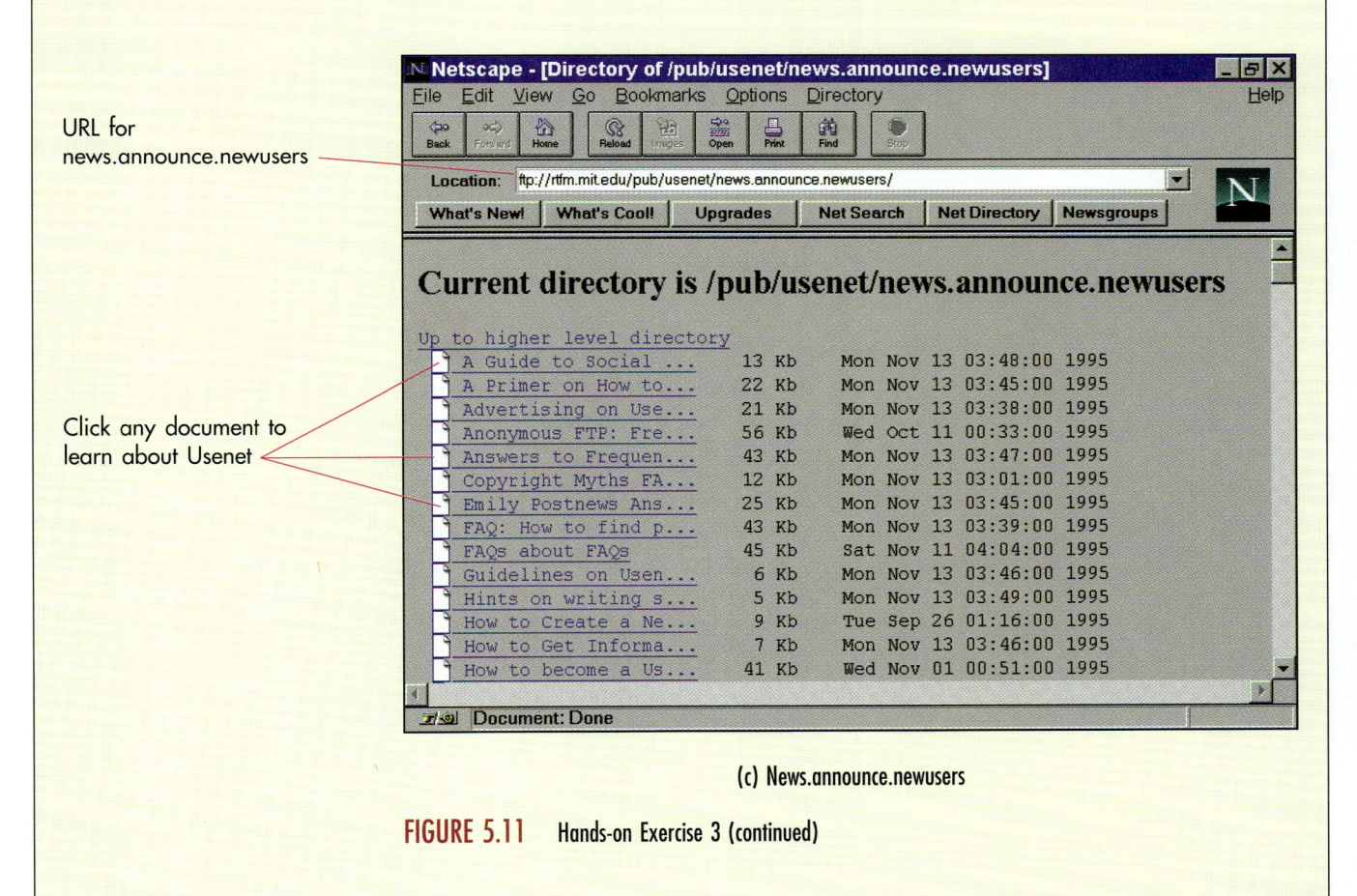

URL for news.announce.newusers —

Click any document to learn about Usenet —

(c) News.announce.newusers

FIGURE 5.11 Hands-on Exercise 3 (continued)

CONVERSATIONS ON THE INTERNET 187

➤ Type the URL **ftp://rtfm.mit.edu/pub/usenet/news.answers/usenet/emily-postnews/part1** in the Location text box. The archive, shown in Figure 5.11d, contains a tongue-in-cheek message of the do's and don'ts of posting to newsgroups. Don't skip this one!

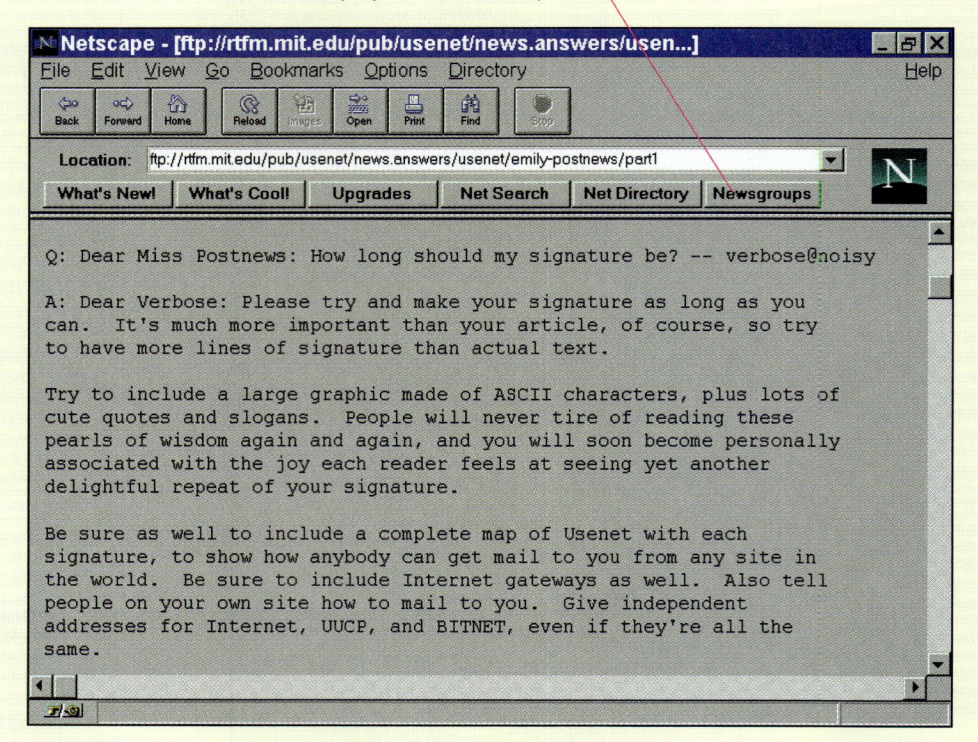

Click to display current subscriptions

```
Q: Dear Miss Postnews: How long should my signature be? -- verbose@noisy

A: Dear Verbose: Please try and make your signature as long as you
can.  It's much more important than your article, of course, so try
to have more lines of signature than actual text.

Try to include a large graphic made of ASCII characters, plus lots of
cute quotes and slogans.  People will never tire of reading these
pearls of wisdom again and again, and you will soon become personally
associated with the joy each reader feels at seeing yet another
delightful repeat of your signature.

Be sure as well to include a complete map of Usenet with each
signature, to show how anybody can get mail to you from any site in
the world.  Be sure to include Internet gateways as well.  Also tell
people on your own site how to mail to you.  Give independent
addresses for Internet, UUCP, and BITNET, even if they're all the
same.
```

(d) Emily-postnews (part 1)

FIGURE 5.11 Hands-on Exercise 3 (continued)

STEP 4: Subscribe to a Newsgroup

➤ Complete the following steps if Netscape is configured for news. See your instructor for alternate instructions if you have a different newsreader.

➤ Click on the **Newsgroups button** in the Netscape window.

- If you have never used your newsreader, Netscape briefly displays a message indicating it must build a file for you containing information about your news subscriptions. After a few moments a list of newsgroups to which you are currently subscribed is displayed, as shown in Figure 5.11e. (Your newsreader may automatically subscribe to one or more newsgroups for you.)

- Scroll down in the window until you see the text box to subscribe to a newsgroup. Enter **news.test** in the box, as shown in Figure 5.11f. Press **Enter**. Your subscription list should be updated to reflect the new subscription.

- In case you are not already a subscriber to news.announce.newusers, news.newusers.questions, and news.answers, subscribe now, following the same procedure as you used to subscribe to news.test.

(e) Current Subscriptions

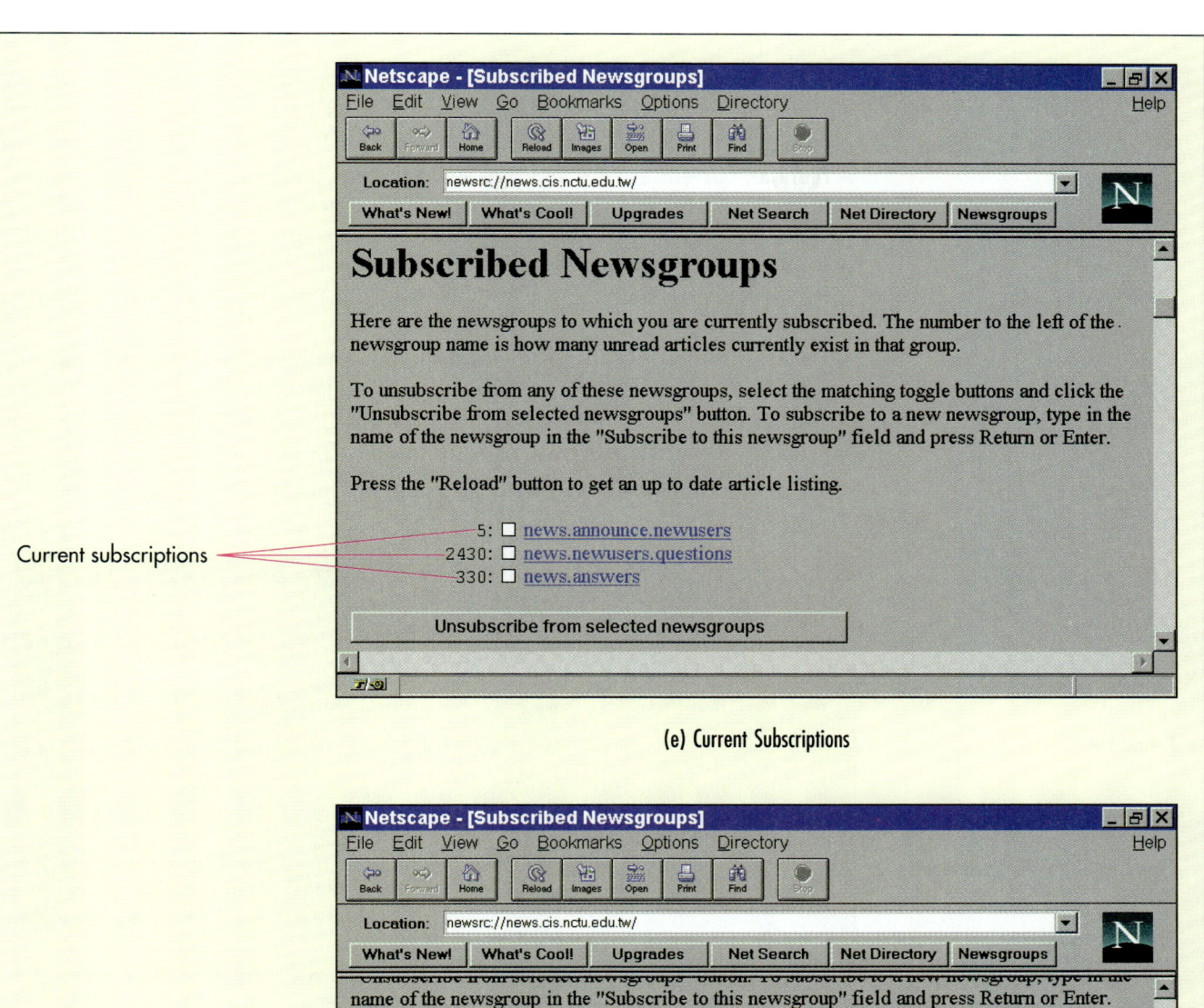

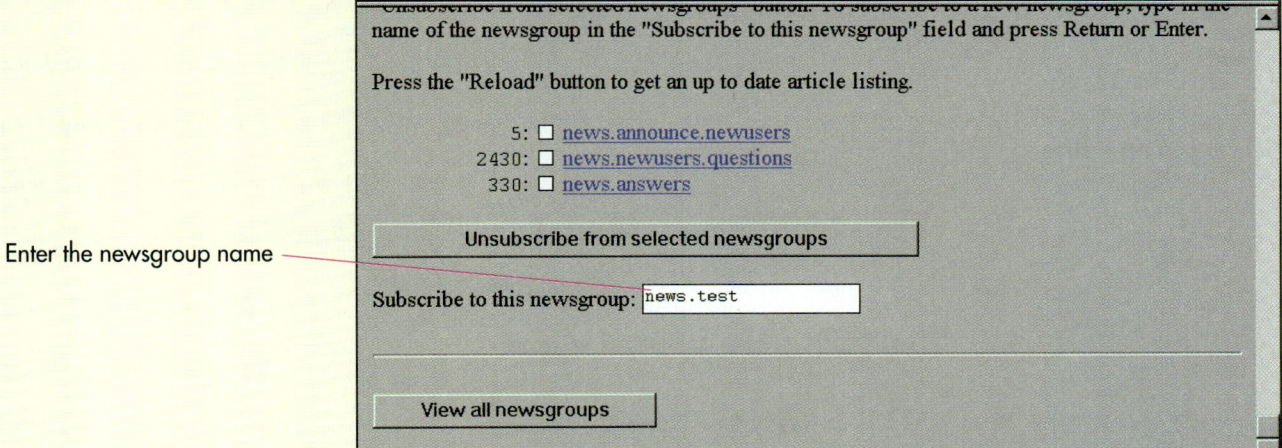

(f) Subscribing to a New Newsgroup

FIGURE 5.11   Hands-on Exercise 3 (continued)

STEP 5: Read the Postings in a Newsgroup

➤ Scroll up in the window if necessary and click on the news.test newsgroup link.

➤ A list of current articles and threads in the newsgroup is displayed, as shown in Figure 5.11g. The figure also shows several new buttons that Netscape displays. The original posting in a thread is shown with a black bullet. Articles in the same thread are shown indented below the bulleted posting, and are set off with a square box. The number to the right of the posting indicates the number of lines in the message.

- Click on the original posting in a thread. The message is displayed, along with additional Netscape buttons used to navigate through the thread, shown in Figure 5.11h. Read the posting.
- Click on the **Right Arrow** to go to the next posting in the thread.
- Click on the **Down Arrow** to go to the first posting in the next thread.

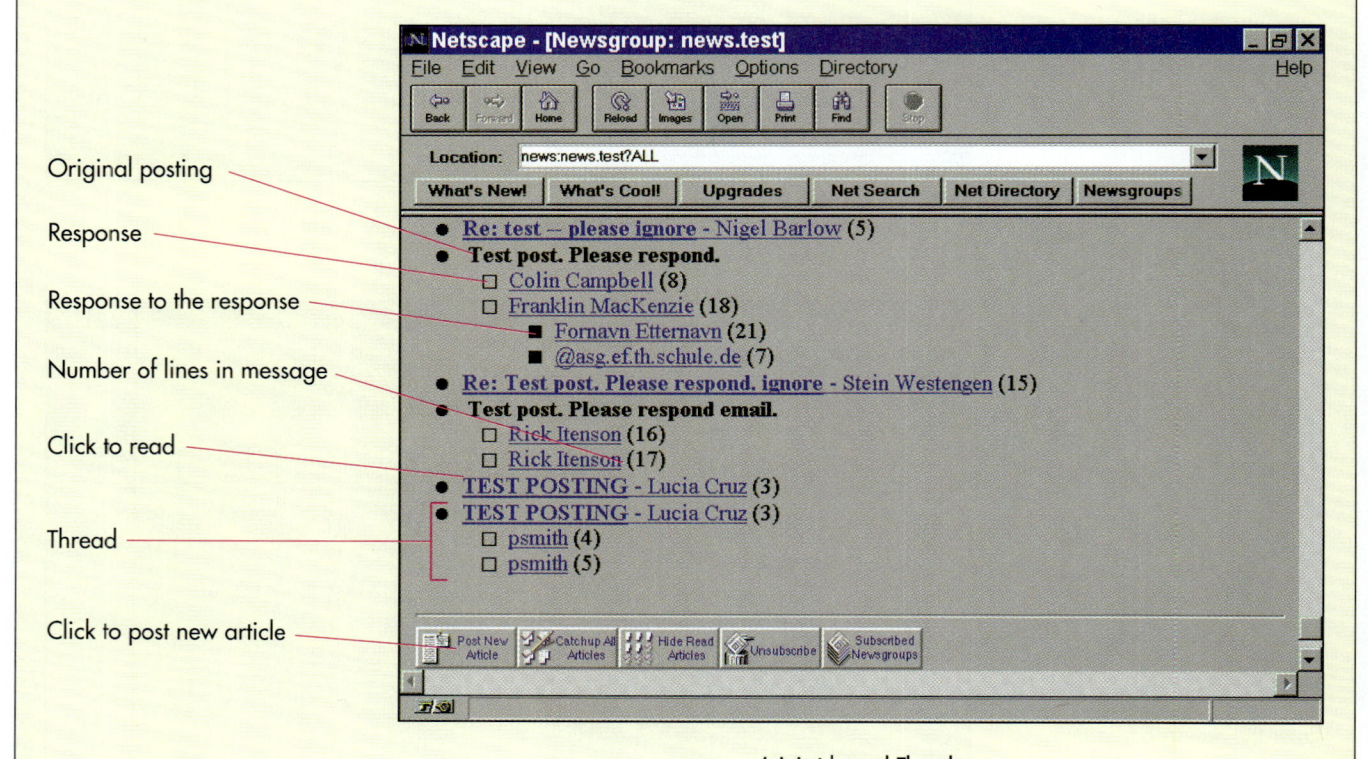

(g) Articles and Threads

FIGURE 5.11   Hands-on Exercise 3 (continued)

STEP 6: Reply to a Posting

➤ Select the posting to which you want to reply and click the **Post Reply button.** The Send Mail/Post News window shown in Figure 5.11i is displayed.

- Leave the Mail To text box blank. (It is used to send e-mail directly to the person who sent the posting to which you are replying.) Tab down to the message area. Click the **Quote Document button** at the bottom of the screen to include the text of the original message so other readers will understand your response.
- Type your reply and click **Send.** Your posting will appear in the list of articles the next time your news server updates your news.

Click to move up to previous thread

Click to post reply to newsgroup

Click to send e-mail to originator and post reply to newsgroup

Return to newsgroup

Click to view next message in thread

Netscape - [TEST POSTING]

Location: news:488k0i$8ge@news.cis.nctu.edu.tw

Subject: **TEST POSTING**
Date: 13 Nov 1995 23:22:58 GMT
From: Lucia Cruz <lcruz@mercy.sjc.edu>
Organization: Dept. of Computer & Information Science, NCTU, Taiwan
Newsgroups: news.test

This is a test message to see whether I have properly configured Netscape for News. I hope it works!

(h) A Usenet Posting

Send Mail / Post News

From: Lucia Cruz <lcruz@mercy.sjc.edu>
Mail To:
Post: news.newusers.questions
Subject: Re: Help
Attachment:

Click to quote original posting in reply

Click to send posting

Send   Quote Document   Cancel

(i) Post News

FIGURE 5.11 Hands-on Exercise 3 (continued)

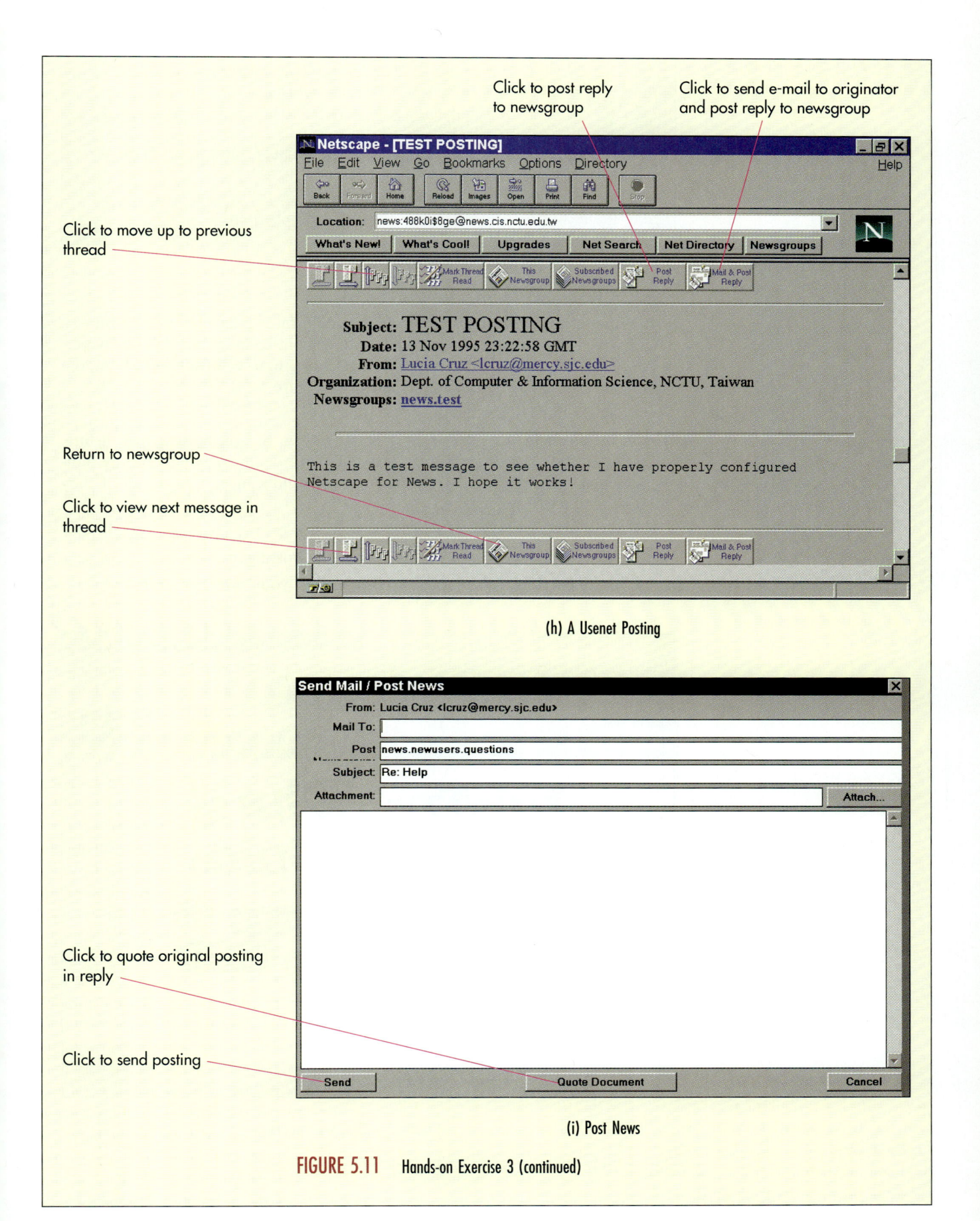

CONVERSATIONS ON THE INTERNET   **191**

> http://www.yahoo.com/News/Usenet/Newsgroup_Listings/
>
> Not sure what newsgroups you want to subscribe to? Yahoo's site is probably the easiest and fastest way to find a group to join.

STEP 7: Read the Postings from a Hyperlink

➤ Assume you are writing a paper on the cultural significance of rock music, and you want to find a newsgroup to add current commentary to your paper. Point your Web browser at **http://www.teleport.com/~celinec/music.shtml,** the Internet Music Resource Guide, shown in Figure 5.11j.

- Click on the **Usenet** link.
- Scroll down in the resulting list until you see the **rec.music.gdead** listing. (The outpouring of grief over Jerry Garcia's death in 1995 certainly indicated that the Grateful Dead have social significance. You decide if they have cultural significance.)
- If your browser is configured for news, click on the **rec.music.gdead** link.
- Read several threads to get a sense of the postings.
- Click **Subscribe.** The newsgroup is added to your subscription list.

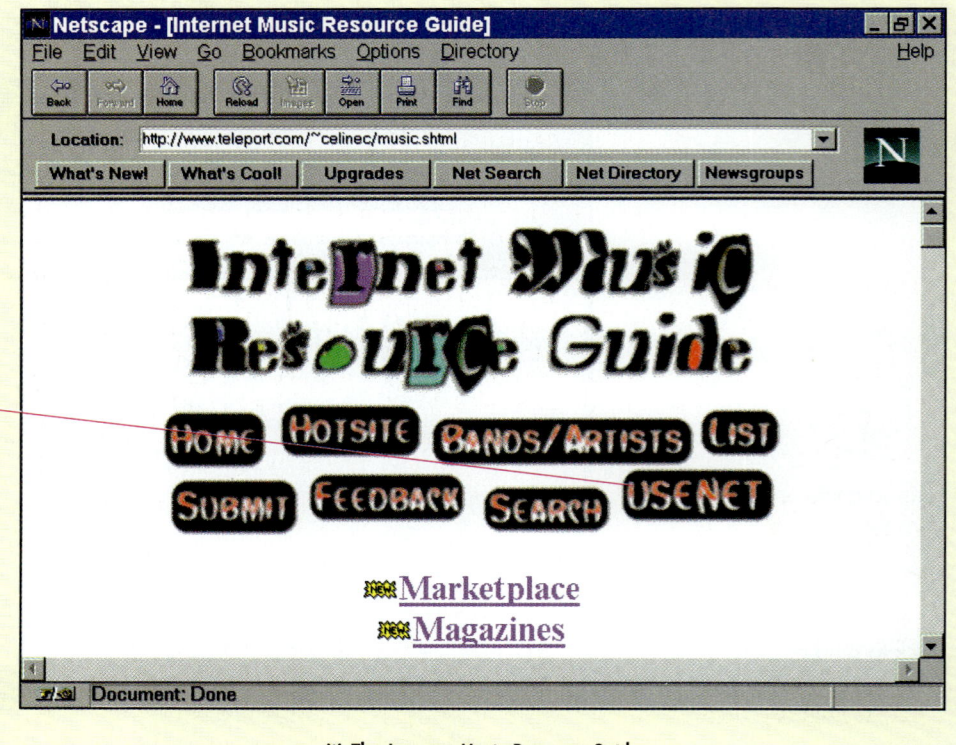

Click here to jump to Usenet resources

(j) The Internet Music Resource Guide

FIGURE 5.11 Hands-on Exercise 3 (continued)

192 EXPLORING THE INTERNET

READING ARCHIVED USENET POSTINGS

Many, but by no means all, newsgroups are archived, as you saw when you retrieved the emily-postnews FAQ in step 3 of this exercise. You have already visited the archives at the FTP server at MIT several times. You can find many newsgroup archives by pointing at the following URLs:

ftp://rtfm.mit.edu/pub/usenet/*newsgroup.name* or
ftp://rtfm.mit.edu/pub/usenet/news.answers/usenet/*newsgroup.name*

where you substitute the name of the newsgroup archives you are trying to locate. If you can't find the newsgroup archives in either of these two directories, try a net search with three terms: *newsgroup.name, newsgroup,* and *archives*. You may find the archives as a link from a home page listed in the results of your search.

SUMMARY

The Internet is much more than a network for browsing, searching, and e-mail. Services such as IRC, WebChat, and Usenet let vast numbers of people converse with each other about virtually every topic imaginable. In order to participate in them, you must have access to an IRC server, a Web browser configured for Chat, and newsfeeds/newsreader, respectively. However, because of the demand these services place on computing resources, you may not be able to use them at your site.

    Both IRC and WebChat allow users to send and receive messages while they are logged on to the computer. IRC will display the messages as soon as they are received. WebChat, however, is based on a constantly updated Web page, and the user must reload the WebChat screen to see new messages. Both services allow users to carry on private "conversations" with other chat partners.

    Usenet is similar to mailing lists in that people post and respond to messages sent to the list. Usenet topics are organized in newsgroups within hierarchies, and the user subscribes to desired newsgroups. A newsreader is used to read the threads that are contained in the newsfeeds.

KEY WORDS AND CONCEPTS

Archive	Netiquette	Port
Channel	Newbie	Post
Chat room	Newsfeed	Signal-to-noise ratio
Handle	Newsgroup	Thread
Hierarchy	Newsreader	Usenet
Internet Relay Chat (IRC)	News server	WebChat
mIRC	Nickname	
	Operator	

Multiple Choice

1. Which of the following statements about Internet Relay Chat is true?
   (a) IRC allows online communication between only two people at a time
   (b) IRC allows online communication among multiple people at a time
   (c) IRC allows asynchronous communication only
   (d) IRC threads are typically archived on an FTP server

2. A group of people discussing the same subject in the same area of IRC is called a:
   (a) Newsgroup
   (b) Chat room
   (c) Forum
   (d) Channel

3. Which of the following statements is false?
   (a) IRC allows "side" conversations between two or more people that others on the same channel cannot see on their screens
   (b) IRC is regulated by the International Internet Commission
   (c) Some IRC channels "talk" about X-rated subjects
   (d) A channel operator can "kick you off" the channel

4. Which of the following is used to provide at least a measure of anonymity on an IRC channel?
   (a) Your user ID
   (b) A user-defined nickname
   (c) A system-assigned nickname
   (d) None of the above

5. Who controls an IRC channel?
   (a) The channel operator
   (b) The last person who joined
   (c) All people on the channel
   (d) No one on the channel

6. Which of the following allows you access to the postings in Usenet newsgroup hierarchies?
   (a) A newsreader
   (b) Usenet archives
   (c) Both (a) and (b)
   (d) Neither (a) nor (b)

7. How many newsgroups exist?
   (a) Less than 100
   (b) Between 100 and 500
   (c) Between 1,000 and 2,000
   (d) Over 6,000

8. Which of the following is required to post to a newsgroup?
    (a) A newsreader
    (b) A news server
    (c) Both (a) and (b)
    (d) Neither (a) nor (b)

9. Which of the following are considered part of a thread?
    (a) The original posting on a subject to a newsgroup
    (b) The response to the original posting
    (c) The response to the response
    (d) All of the above

10. Which of the following requires you to use a nickname?
    (a) WebChat
    (b) IRC
    (c) Both (a) and (b)
    (d) Neither (a) nor (b)

11. Which of the following statements about IRC is true?
    (a) You may join more than one channel at a time
    (b) The first person on a channel is the channel operator
    (c) Your username and address are published when you initially join an IRC channel
    (d) All of the above

12. Which character precedes IRC commands?
    (a) *
    (b) #
    (c) /
    (d) ?

13. Which service allows you to conference privately with another user?
    (a) WebChat
    (b) IRC
    (c) Both (a) and (b)
    (d) Neither (a) nor (b)

14. Which of the following is automatically updated with new messages as you watch the screen?
    (a) IRC
    (b) WebChat
    (c) Usenet
    (d) All of the above

15. Which of the following is not considered a mainstream Usenet hierarchy?
    (a) Alt
    (b) Soc
    (c) Rec
    (d) News

ANSWERS

1. b	6. c	11. d
2. d	7. d	12. c
3. b	8. c	13. c
4. b	9. d	14. a
5. c	10. d	15. a

Exploring the Internet

1. Use Figure 5.12 to match each action with its result; a given action may be used more than once or not at all.

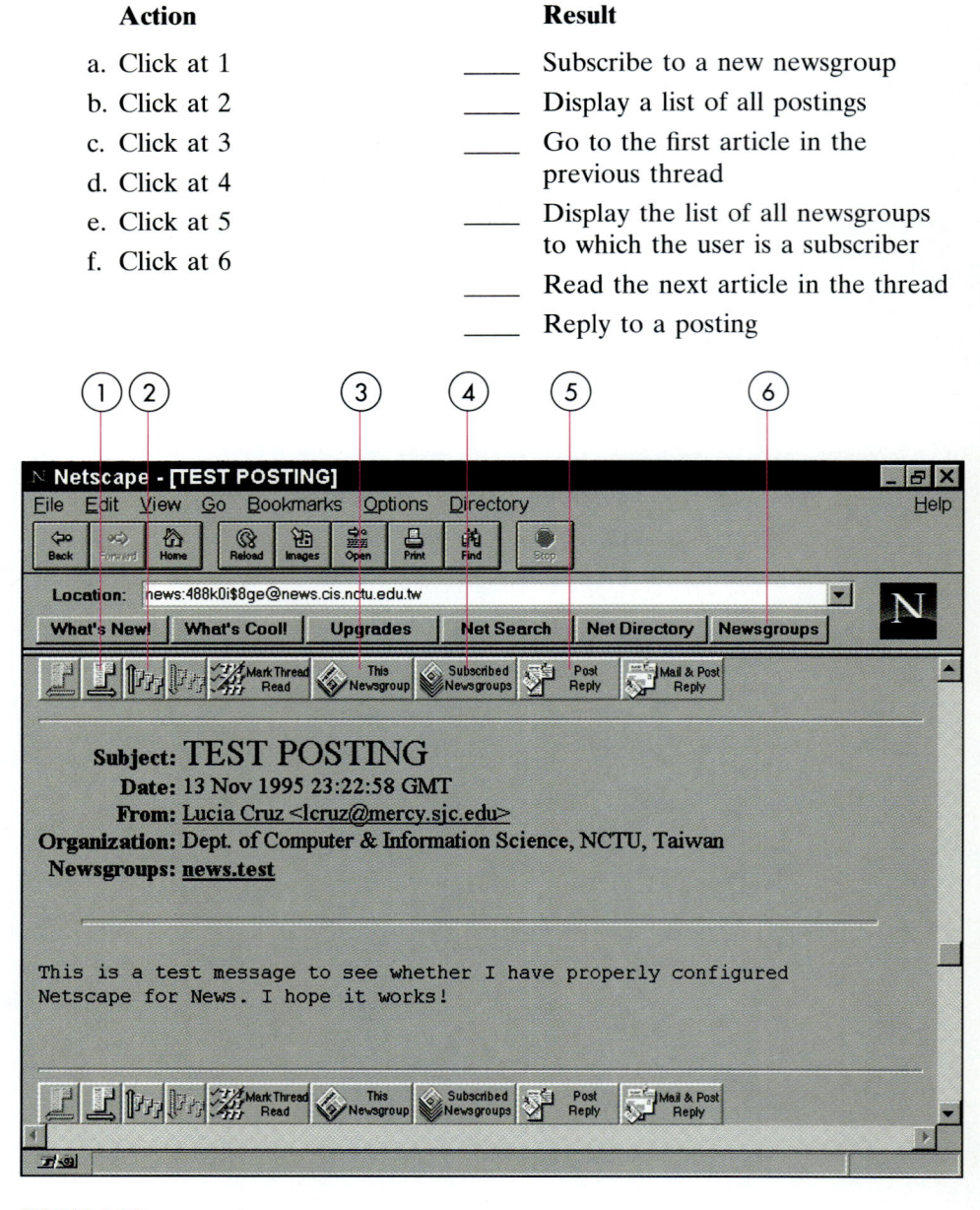

   Action

   a. Click at 1
   b. Click at 2
   c. Click at 3
   d. Click at 4
   e. Click at 5
   f. Click at 6

   Result

   ____ Subscribe to a new newsgroup
   ____ Display a list of all postings
   ____ Go to the first article in the previous thread
   ____ Display the list of all newsgroups to which the user is a subscriber
   ____ Read the next article in the thread
   ____ Reply to a posting

FIGURE 5.12   Screen for Exercise 1

196 EXPLORING THE INTERNET

2. Compare IRC, WebChat, and Usenet: Answer the following questions about communicating on the Internet with IRC, WebChat, and Usenet.
   (a) Which methods are asynchronous (that is, the message you send may be received at a later time by the recipient)?
   (b) What are the advantages of either type of chat over Usenet?
   (c) What are the advantages of Usenet over either type of chat?
   (d) Describe several examples of business and/or personal situations where you would use one or the other service, and explain the reasons for your choice.

3. Exploring Usenet: Search the Web for information and FAQs about Usenet hierarchies. Answer the following questions.
   (a) How many newsgroups are there?
   (b) How are new newsgroups approved and created?
   (c) Which newsgroups are the most popular (have the greatest number of postings)?
   (d) Of the newsgroups you identified in part c, how many are sexual in nature? What, if anything, does this indicate about the Usenet user population?

4. Exploring IRC: Search for information on the Web to answer the following questions about IRC.
   (a) When was IRC first developed, where, and by whom?
   (b) Where can you find a copy of mIRC? How big is the file?
   (c) What can a channel operator do?
   (d) What are *bots,* and why are they forbidden on many IRC sites?

PRACTICE WITH IRC, WEBCHAT, AND USENET

1. Use the Help feature in your IRC client to look up the commands available to the channel operator. Set up a time to work with a group of your classmates, setting up and joining each others' channels, and using the channel operator commands.

2. Read several threads in the *sci.space.shuttle* newsgroup for a while to find out the latest about the space program. If you don't have access to newsgroups, check the FTP server at MIT, rtfm.mit.edu/pub/usenet, and read the FAQ in the sci.space.shuttle directory for further information about NASA's calendar.

3. Scroll through the listings at ftp://rtfm.mit.edu/pub/usenet/news.answers to see the variety of topics covered. Read the information about IRC and Usenet.

4. Starting at Digital Equipment Corporation's Global Chat home page at http://webchat.service.digital.com/webchat/gcs_home.html, click on the Chat Map icon at the bottom of the window to find other chat sites. Visit several, lurk, and join a conversation or two. How do the sites compare?

Case Studies

Limited Resources

IRC and Usenet require significant resources. Which of these resources does your college provide? What are the pros and cons of offering them? Can and should a college or university control access to the sexually explicit content found in both resources?

Controversy in the News

The print news media are no strangers to controversy, publishing articles every day about such contentious topics as gun control, abortion, and the O.J. Simpson verdict. The media purport to print facts, and the larger newspapers have editorial personnel devoted to checking reporters' work for errors and omissions. Opinion is supposed to be limited to the editorial, commentary, and news analysis sections of the paper. Read through the postings in the newsgroups alt.abortion.inequity and alt.politics.correct. How do newsgroups compare to news and editorials found in a newspaper?

Chatters Anonymous

WebChat and IRC have the potential to be important, even life-saving communications media. Like many other powerful tools, chat has its dark side. Explore the psychological implications of the seeming anonymity of chat sessions using nicknames. Do people take on different persona when they chat? Is chat dangerous? Is chat addicting? Conduct some of your research on the Web, and some of it in print journals such as *Psychology Today*. Write a report on your discoveries about the workings of the human psyche in cyberspace.

CU-SeeMe

IRC, WebChat, and Usenet facilities are based on the written word. The telephone and cable TV industries are developing new transmission technologies (ATM, ISDN, and others) that will provide greater bandwidth and allow the transmission of audio and video signals. Cornell University has developed CU-SeeMe, which allows two-way video communication between two or more viewers. Search for information on CU-SeeMe on the Web, and arrange to use it or see it demonstrated on your campus if possible. What are the implications of this and other new technologies such as audio IRC?

THE INTERNET AND SOCIETY: NETIQUETTE, SAFE SURFING, AND OTHER ISSUES IN CYBERSPACE

OBJECTIVES

After reading this chapter you will be able to:

1. Understand the educational and other societal concerns associated with the Internet.
2. Explain the debate between those opposing cyberporn and those defending freedom of the Net.
3. Understand security issues on the Internet, and find online resources to keep up to date on solutions.
4. Explain what netiquette is, including some of its more common rules; use smilies in your e-mail and Usenet postings.
5. Understand the offerings of the various commercial online services.
6. Browse through shopping, banking, and other services on the Internet.

OVERVIEW

The advent of the online age is not without its dangers, as movies and other popular media continue to point out. Pornography is rampant on the Net, and criminals of all sorts have found easy marks on its byways. Besides the obvious threat from people intent on using the Internet for devious purposes, however, there are less obvious but equally compelling issues in cyberspace.

Educators are struggling to provide equal access in a world of shrinking budgets. How does a free society prepare all of its citizens for life and work in the new digital age? The task is daunting when school systems are without computers, let alone network connectivity. Are girls and women underrepresented on the Net, and if so, what effect will this have on their employability? How can users protect their privacy as well as their pocketbooks? Copyright infringement is illegal;

how do you avoid it on the Net? We will discuss these and other social, ethical, and legal dilemmas in this chapter, and point you toward several resources that can help you formulate your own answers to the questions we should all be asking ourselves.

We describe some of the rules of the road on the Information Highway. Our intention is not to stifle anyone's natural curiosity about this exciting and ever-expanding medium. It is to help users learn to navigate it creatively and responsibly, and have fun doing so. New users are often eager to jump in and start surfing without testing the water first. This can be an unpleasant experience on the Internet (and other online networks as well), as experienced users often don't have the patience to explain mistakes to these newbies.

We also want you to realize that the online community is not limited to the Internet. Millions of people use commercial providers such as America Online and Prodigy, and we will briefly discuss these services. Finally, we explore the advertising and merchandising potential of the Internet, and send you on a cyberspace shopping expedition.

LEGAL ISSUES

The world of online networks is new and evolving, and existing laws have not always been able to rectify problems involved in their use. In particular, lawmakers, software publishers, artists, authors, and others have been concerned with protection of their works under current copyright laws. E-mail and Usenet users want to know what privacy rights they have. Network providers are concerned about limiting their liability for the content of network traffic. The answers to these questions are still being formed, and you will have an opportunity to research the latest information on the Web in the first hands-on exercise.

Copyright Infringement

Copyright provides legal protection to written and artistic work, published or unpublished, as soon as it is created. A *copyright* means the author has exclusive rights to its use and reproduction, except as governed under the fair use exclusion. Copyright laws are undergoing constant review in the digital age, as lawmakers try to cope with the changing means of production of written and artistic work. It seems clear from both the current legislation, and the results of litigation, that anything on the Internet must be considered copyrighted, unless it specifically says it is in the *public domain.* If the author states in the work that he or she is putting the work in the public domain, then he/she loses all rights to its reproduction or distribution.

Does this mean you cannot quote in your term papers statistics and other facts you find while browsing the Web? Does this mean you cannot download an image to include in your report? The answer to both questions depends on your intent and use of the information. It is considered *fair use,* and thus not an infringement of copyright, to use a portion of the work for educational, nonprofit purposes, or for the purpose of critical review or commentary. This exclusion would seem to cover your use of a quote from a Usenet newsgroup, a downloaded image, or other information from the Web. Just be sure to cite the work in your footnotes and/or bibliography. Facts themselves are not covered by copyright, so you can use statistical and other data without fear of infringement. (However, you should still cite the original source in your bibliography.)

Fair use, however, does not extend to software, even if you intend whatever you copy to be for your use only, and even if it is for educational purposes. The Software Publishers Association (SPA) estimates that *software piracy*—that is, the unlicensed and unauthorized copying of software—cost the U.S. software industry

$8 billion in 1994. The association suspects that 25% of software in use in the United States is pirated, while in Asia the number is over 90%. The economic impact on the software industry of these crimes is such that law enforcement efforts have stepped up in recent years. (You can visit the SPA home page at http://www.spa.org, shown in Figure 6.1.)

You cannot legally copy any licensed software, except to create an archive copy to use in case your licensed original is damaged. You cannot make a copy of a program to run on a second machine you own—you must buy a second copy. How, then, can all these people be downloading software from the Internet? If the author has expressly given up his or her rights, with a statement such as "The author releases all copyright on this software and places it in the public domain," you are free to copy it. If the program is *shareware*—software that the user may evaluate prior to purchase (usually for a nominal fee)—you may download it. Just be sure to send a check to the author if you decide to keep the copy.

DON'T BREAK THE LAW!

If you are in the habit of sharing software with friends, you are most likely breaking the law, and may be subject to disciplinary action by your college or university at best, and to fines and/or imprisonment at worst. You are also at increased risk of infecting your computer with a virus. The best policy is honesty: do not copy other people's software.

Do copyright laws extend to Usenet postings and e-mail? The courts have yet to decide. An e-mail message or Usenet posting is certainly a written work. However, the whole purpose of these two media is to exchange information and

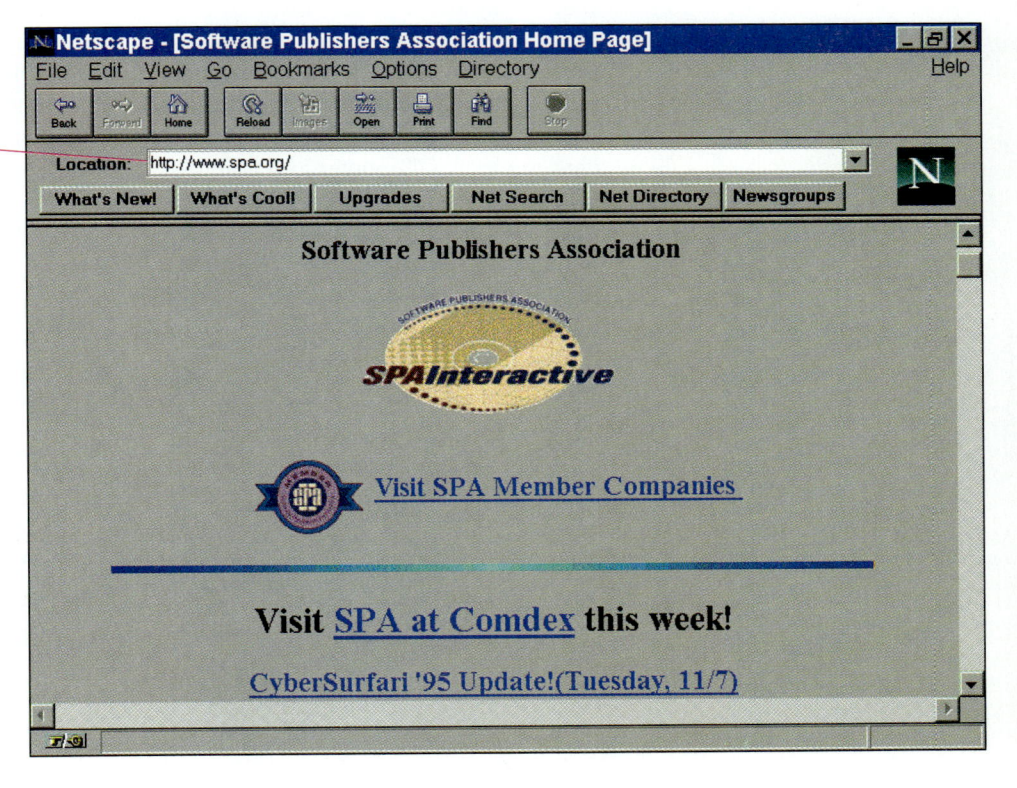

FIGURE 6.1   The Software Publishers Association Home Page

ideas. The response or reply to a posting, using the original message in the reply, would seem to be covered under the fair use exclusion, in that the quote is being used for critical review or comment. However, could you use a clever mailing list or Usenet posting in an advertisement? Maybe not, but no one knows for sure. Watch for continued legislative activity in this area.

Freedom of Speech and the Right to Privacy

Is someone's desire to download pornographic images from a Usenet newsgroup or archive protected by freedom of speech and privacy laws? Does an employer or your college or university have the right to look at your e-mail without your permission? Can someone post critical comments about a product or service to a newsgroup? Can a network provider be held liable for the content of the traffic on the network? These and other thorny questions are being raised as the Internet expands geometrically, and as the general public becomes more aware of what occurs on the Net.

At the time of this writing the legality of the dissemination of pornography on the online world, and who should be liable for it if it is illegal, was still very much an open question. President Clinton was pushing for legislation that would require providers to create filters to allow adults to keep children from accessing inappropriate material. In fact, the commercial online providers have largely done so. The Internet, however, remains entirely accessible for anyone with a direct connection. Legislators do not seem anxious to suggest that providers be responsible for the content of messages or files, any more than the post office is responsible for what is sent in envelopes and packages. (They would, presumably, be responsible for programming content over which they do have control.)

The courts have ruled that corporations have the right to read an employee's e-mail without his or her permission. This means that e-mail within a company is not considered private, and does not belong to the employee. Does this extend to the educational/nonprofit use of e-mail? It is not clear. Users should be aware that the system administrator of any network has access to any and all directories on the system, so no one's e-mail is ever completely private in any case. One simple guideline is to never put anything in an e-mail message that you would be uncomfortable seeing on the front page of tomorrow's newspaper.

And what about libel or defamation of character? Suppose you have just purchased a new CD player and amplifier, and are dissatisfied with their performance. Does this give you the right to complain about the company on the Internet? It depends on what you say and how you say it. When the news broke about the defects in the Intel Pentium chip a few years ago, the information was first reported in a newsgroup. Because it was factual information, and it was accurate, there was little Intel could do to stop the spread of the reports. However, if someone were to make a highly inflammatory, unsubstantiated claim about someone or something on the Net, it seems fairly likely that the laws covering libel would apply.

SOCIAL ISSUES

According to an online survey conducted by the Georgia Institute of Technology in 1995[1], 15% of Internet users are female, up from 10% the year before. Of those who accessed the survey from Prodigy, females constituted 19% of the users. The survey, results of which are shown in Figure 6.2, found that 82% of users were

---

[1]Georgia Institute of Technology On-line Survey, http://www.cc.gatech.edu/gvu/user_surveys/survey-04-1995

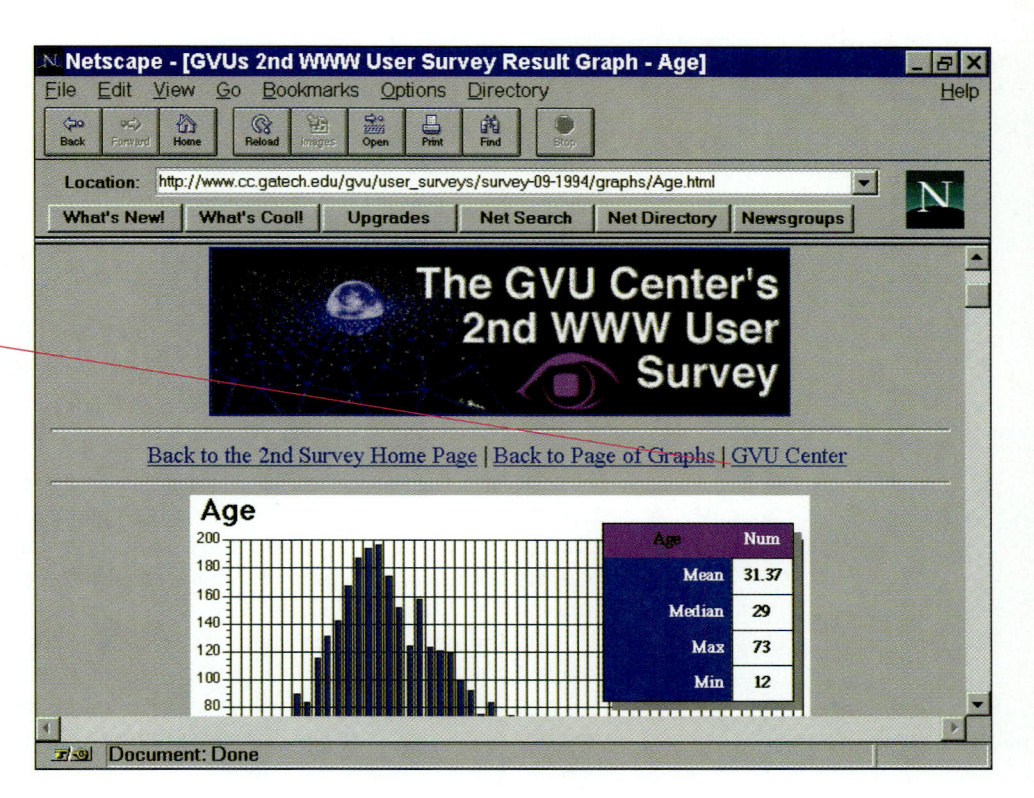

FIGURE 6.2 Georgia Institute of Technology's Internet Survey Results

white, and that the average income of users was $69,000. With statistics like these, some people are beginning to wonder whether the Internet is reserved for middle- and upper-middle class white males. If it is, what can and should be done about it?

The 21st century will complete the transition of the U.S. from an industrial/manufacturing economy to an information-based economy where the majority of jobs go to computer-literate information workers. How will those without computers find an onramp to the information highway? How will schools prepare children for adulthood without computers? Are we becoming a nation of information access haves and have-nots? Does it matter?

Because school budgets are largely funded by property taxes, wealthier schools and school districts generally have more computers per student than less wealthy districts. The division between rich and poor districts is certainly nothing new. Even today there are school districts without enough money to buy new books, let alone computers.

The National Science Foundation (NSF) and other government agencies have funded several million dollars in proposals over the last few years aimed at bringing the Internet to both rural and disadvantaged urban populations. Libraries, schools, shopping malls, and other public areas have been funded to connect to the Internet. Many corporations are funding computers and other technology for local school systems.

These initiatives are a step toward insuring that all citizens of the new information age have access. However, for educators trying to integrate new technologies and new ways of teaching in the classroom, this approach can be frustrating indeed. As you have no doubt experienced, the best way to learn about computers is to use them. That will be a difficult task if there are only a few PCs for an entire school district. And, with the rapid change in technology, one-time funding is no guarantee that communities will be able to keep current once they are connected. With the difficult economic realities many communities are facing in the 1990s, it seems this issue will not be solved easily or any time soon.

> ### THE U-DO-IT INTERNET ESTIMATOR
>
> Various Web sites carry statistics showing the Internet is doubling every 12 months. From 213 hosts in 1981 to over 6.5 million in July 1995, the growth is truly astronomical. To get a sense of what that means, point your Web browser at http://www.gnn.com/gnn/news/feature/inet-demo/web.size.html

Another problem to resolve is who walks up the onramp once it is provided. By their nature online services are self-selecting, and not everyone is interested in using them. If most women do not want to use the Internet, can anyone force them to? Of course not. The broader question is not really usage, it is one of effect. Will the young girls of today be hampered in the job market of tomorrow because they have not acquired skills necessary to navigate their world?

Preliminary research seems to suggest that young girls do well with online computer activities if they are interested in them. While uninterested in search-and-destroy games, they excel at logic games, puzzles, mysteries, and nonviolent adventures. An unscientific observation of an elementary school room showed that girls were very enthusiastic about games such as *Where in the World Is Carmen San Diego?* and *The Oregon Trail*.

If the Internet consisted solely of downloadable games, the percentage of women using the Net might remain static. However, the Web and easy-to-use mail packages have opened the Internet up to millions outside of the scientific research and defense communities it was originally designed to serve, which are still largely populated by men. Internet statistics showing a gender gap are likely to continue to change.

Should the Internet and/or other online services be used for national referenda on political issues? There is no doubt about the power of the media to influence elections. Ever since the first televised presidential debate between Kennedy and Nixon, it has been clear to politicians that they could not win at the polls without winning the air waves.

Candidates have unprecedented opportunity to disseminate their political views directly to the electorate via the Web, e-mail, and other online services. It seems that the effect on democracy should be positive. The more informed the voter, the more informed the vote. However, the same opportunity to provide misinformation, opinion presented as fact, and outright lies exists with Internet communication as with television and news media. Having the electorate make direct decisions about the country's laws and its citizens' rights based on what may be little more than propaganda is a chilling proposition. Responsible citizens and legislators should be very wary of the possibility of electronic mob rule replacing democratically elected representation.

LEARNING BY DOING

Laws related to electronic commerce, copyright, privacy, pornography, and so on are undergoing constant change. Internet usage is growing exponentially. The best way to find out the current status of both topics is to search the Web. In the following exercise you will explore some of the topics discussed in the chapter.

HANDS-ON EXERCISE 1

Exploring Legal and Social Issues on the Internet

Objective: To research the latest information about legal and social issues in the online world. Use Figures 6.2 and 6.3 as a guide in the exercise.

STEP 1: Log On

➤ Log on and start your Web browser as usual.

STEP 2: Visit the Library of Congress

➤ Enter the URL **gopher://marvel.loc.gov/11/copyright** in the Location text box to visit the Library of Congress copyright gopher. The site, shown in Figure 6.3, contains the text of copyright legislation and lots of other useful copyright information.

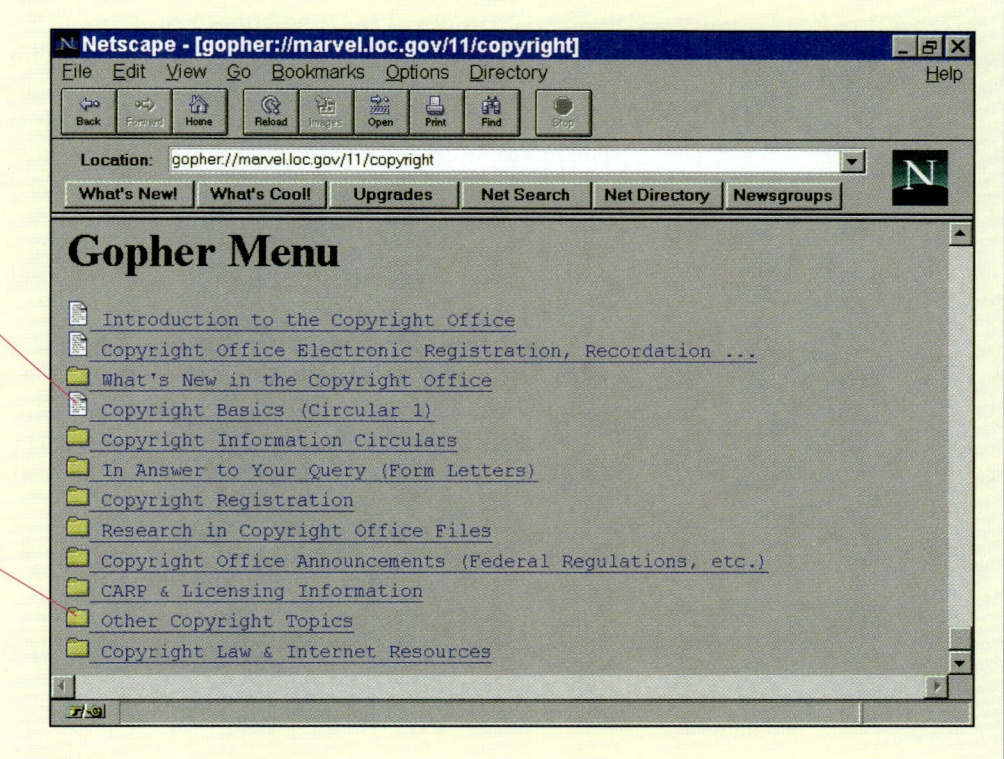

Click here for document on copyright information

Click here for other copyright documents and/or folders

FIGURE 6.3 Hands-on Exercise 1

STEP 3: Explore Copyright Issues

➤ Use Lycos or your favorite Web search engine to do a Web search on the term *copyright law*.

➤ Visit a copyright FAQ location, and review the exclusions for fair use.

STEP 4: Explore Privacy Issues

➤ Do a Web search on the term *Internet privacy*. Find and read several references dealing with this topic.

> **STEP 5: Explore an Internet Usage Survey**
> ➤ Enter the URL **http://www.cc.gatech.edu/gvu/user_surveys** in the Location text box. You can browse through the latest survey information, shown previously in Figure 6.2. Read the information provided by the latest Internet use survey and determine how it compares to earlier statistics.
>
> **STEP 6: Explore the Internet Gender Gap**
> ➤ Conduct a Web search using the search term *Internet gender gap.* You should find several sites providing useful information about trends in online usage.

SECURITY

The Internet is by definition an open network, allowing users from all over the globe to access resources on remote computers that they would not otherwise be authorized to use. The vast majority of these users follow the implicit rules governing the Internet, and use systems and services for which they have a username and password. On the other hand, there is a population of hackers who will go after the security holes on any and every system they can. A **hacker** (originally referred to as crackers on Usenet and other Internet services) is an individual who attempts to gain unauthorized access to a computer system, from which he or she can steal information such as telephone or credit card numbers, or cause malicious damage by infecting the system with a virus or other damaging program. (Not all hackers seek to do damage. Some are motivated solely by the possibility that they may be successful in breaking in.)

Information flowing back and forth in unencrypted files can easily be intercepted at any of the multiple computers forwarding the packets to their intended destinations. The person intercepting the information can then use it in a manner for which it was not intended, such as selling it to a firm's competitors. Internet providers are pursuing various strategies to reduce the risk of unauthorized access; chief among these is encryption.

Encryption and the Clipper Chip

Electronic commerce on the Internet will be of limited use until secure transactions can be ensured, so there is considerable pressure to establish some reasonable—that is, inexpensive and easy-to-implement—encryption standard. *Encryption* is the process of encoding data so that it is no longer in its original form and can be understood only by decoding it. Various encryption algorithms exist to transpose data using an **encryption key,** and then restore it to the original, also using the key. Obviously both the sender and the recipient must know the key, or the recipient will not be able to decipher the message. Multiple nonprofit and commercial organizations (IBM and HP, among others) have proposed encryption algorithms, but none has currently been selected as a standard.

While the standards issue is being reviewed from a technical perspective, others are busy debating the practical result of the capability of all users to encrypt all transactions. Imagine every criminal cartel in the world having access to super-secure communications that a law enforcement agency could not tap even with a court order.

That prospect has prompted the U.S. government to restrict the distribution of encryption technology abroad. All software must be approved for export by both the Department of Commerce and the Department of State. The Clinton administration also proposed what was dubbed the **Clipper Chip**—a hardware device that, when installed in a computer, would allow the government, presumably with proper legal safeguards, to decipher encrypted communications. Given this proposal, now imagine any government with the power to invade the privacy of your electronic transactions.

Many people find that a chilling thought, including Mitch Kapor, founder of Lotus Development Corporation, and others. In 1990 they joined together to found the Electronic Frontier Foundation (EFF), which has been involved since its inception in the debate about privacy versus the need for the ability to find and prosecute criminals. The notes on its home page, shown in Figure 6.4, describe it as: *"A non-profit civil liberties organization working in the public interest to protect privacy, free expression, and access to online resources and information."* EFF led the fight against the Clipper Chip, claiming its use was an invasion of privacy. The debate about the appropriate way to safeguard the public, its transactions, and free access to information from government intrusion continues.

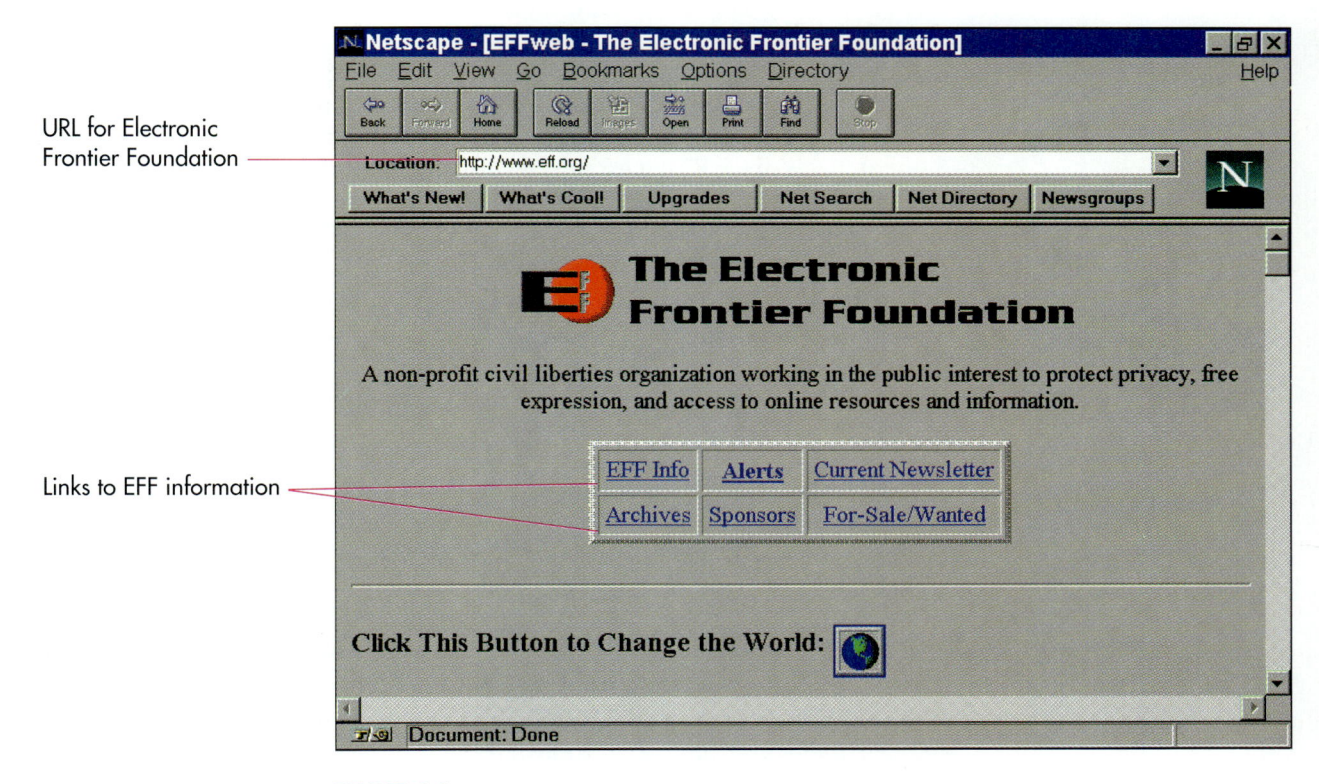

FIGURE 6.4   The Electronic Frontier Foundation Home Page

Viruses

Nearly 2,000 *viruses* and other types of malicious software have been reported worldwide, and many if not all of them have found their way onto the Internet at one time or another. They have generally been classified into four types of programs: viruses, worms, logic bombs, and trojan horses. Viruses often infect the command files that launch the computer's operating system, which subsequently affects the user's ability to boot and run the computer. They may also infect memory or the File Allocation Table, which helps the operating system find data on disk. Any of these effects will generally be fatal to the system. What makes viruses even more dangerous is that they can copy themselves to other disks and infect other programs.

Worms are designed to corrupt the data on a computer's hard drive, and like viruses they can replicate themselves. A worm let loose on the Internet in 1988, called the Internet Worm, caused thousands of computers worldwide to crash. ***Logic bombs*** are generally hidden inside an existing, valid application, and are set to go off at a given time, wreaking damage and destruction inside the computer of the unfortunate, unsuspecting user who may have used the program hundreds of times before without mishap. Logic bombs cannot replicate themselves, but of course can be copied to other systems if the application containing them is copied. A ***trojan horse,*** like a time bomb, exists inside another program and causes its intended damage when the valid application is executed. Trojan horses are also not self-replicating.

THE COMPUTER EMERGENCY RESPONSE TEAM TO THE RESCUE

The Computer Emergency Response Team (CERT) was founded in 1988 to assist the online community in responding to Internet security challenges. It offers 24-hour technical assistance, seminars on security, a mailing list, archives of CERT advisories, security analysis of software products, and other services to Internet host systems operators. The Usenet newsgroup comp.security.announce was created for CERT to post security advisories, which are also sent to the mailing list valert-l. You can find out more about CERT by pointing your Web browser at http://www.cs.ruu.nl/cert-uu.

Safeguards

Given the inconvenience and outright damage viruses can cause, it is important that you observe proper procedures to prevent infecting your computer and/or network. It is recommended that you follow the measures listed below to practice safe surfing.

- Never run pirated (illegally copied) software. Obtain the original from the vendor or an authorized FTP site.
- Write-protect the master disks of any programs you purchase and then copy them. Use the copies to install the program. (The write-protection will keep a virus from copying itself from your computer to the originals during the setup procedure.)
- Run virus scanning software to check a floppy before copying its contents to the hard drive or executing a program on the floppy.
- Periodically scan the hard drive for viruses.
- Virus-check all software downloaded from the Internet before running it.
- Back up your work frequently.
- Notify your lab assistant or network administrator if you notice any software or computer acting in a suspicious manner.

Authentication

One of the key safeguards any system has is user authentication. This is why you are assigned a username and password, which must be verified by the system before you are allowed to use it. The username and password files, however, are a weak link in the system, and if they can be hacked and stolen, anyone possessing them can use them to gain access to one system, and from there, possibly others. Other security loopholes have been discovered in popular Unix software.

One way to avoid some of these loopholes is to encrypt the password file. Other, more complicated authentication systems grant tickets to the user after he or she has signed on to the system. Only users with authenticated tickets may have access to services on the system. The tickets are time-stamped and are valid only for a specific time period. Someone "listening" on the network may be able to grab the unsuspecting user's username and password as it is entered at login. However, without the resulting ticket and means to decipher it, they cannot use services on the system. One such authentication method is known as **Kerberos,** named after the dog in Greek mythology that guards the gates to the underworld.

Authentication systems can be expensive to install and maintain, and are by no means widespread. This makes the Internet a nonsecure environment. Your first weapon against unauthorized entry is to observe standard safety precautions:

- Change your password frequently.
- Do not use simple English words as your password; add other characters or numbers so password sniffers cannot use automated programs to find your password.
- Do not give your password to anyone.

SATAN

If you were a network administrator, wouldn't you want to know if someone could break into your system? Wouldn't it be good to have software that would check it for weaknesses and back doors that hackers could sneak into? This was precisely the reasoning of Dan Farmer and Wietse Venema, two young programmers who wrote Satan, a program designed to conduct a security check and attempt to break into Unix systems. It was a great idea, except they decided to distribute it free on the Internet, after which every hacker in the world could busily use it to find systems to break into. This engendered much discussion about security on the Internet, which may also have been one of their motives.

HANDS-ON EXERCISE 2

Internet Security and Privacy

Objective: To learn more about Internet security and privacy issues. Use Figures 6.4 and 6.5 as a guide in the exercise.

STEP 1: Log On
- Log on to your system and start Netscape in the usual manner.

STEP 2: Explore Internet Security
- Using your favorite search engine, conduct a Web search on the keyword *kerberos;* then another on *internet security.*
- Explore some of the links to learn more about both of these topics.

STEP 3: Explore the Electronic Frontier Foundation

➤ Visit the Electronic Frontier Foundation (EFF) at **http://www.eff.org,** shown previously in Figure 6.4, to read the latest press release and other information about EFF's activities.

STEP 4: Explore CERT

➤ Enter the URL of the CERT pages at **http://www.cs.ruu.nl/cert-uu,** shown in Figure 6.5, to see the latest virus advisories.

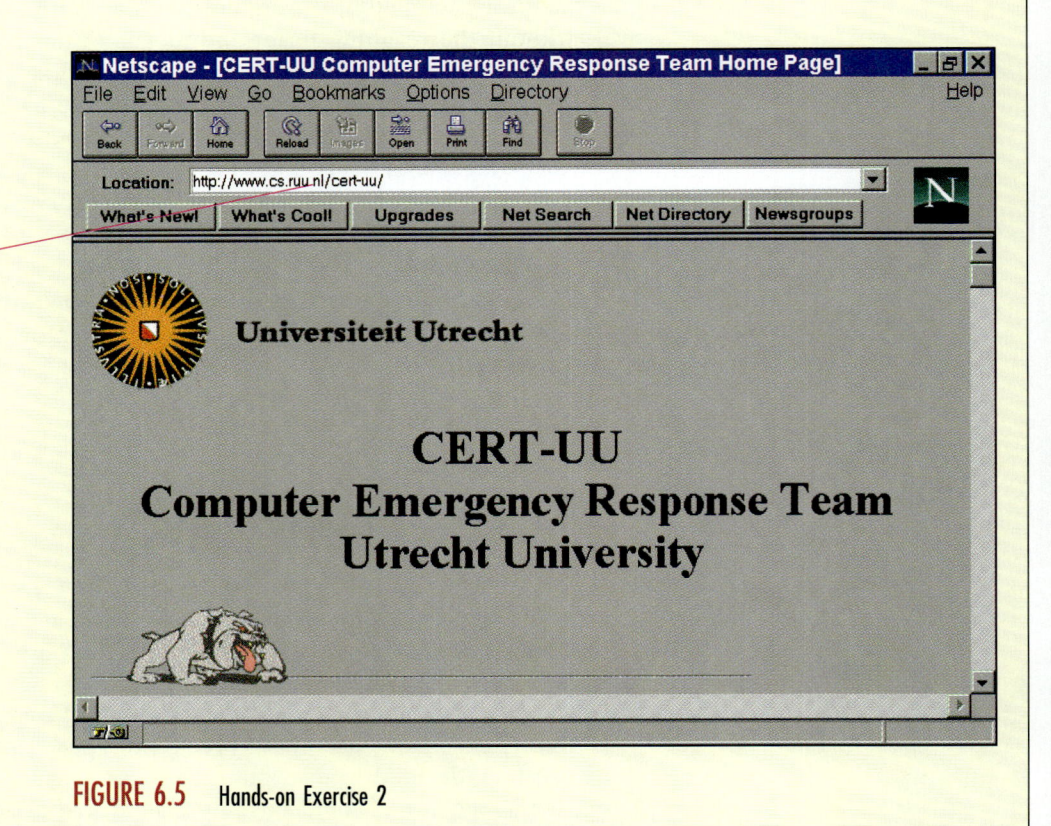

URL contains **nl** as country code for the Netherlands

FIGURE 6.5 Hands-on Exercise 2

NETIQUETTE

Do's and Don'ts

The Internet is an amazing "place," an international community in a sense. Any community has rules by which it operates, and it pays to know and understand them before you venture forth in foreign territory. We offer a short list of commonly understood rules of the Net, called *netiquette,* that you ought to observe. You can find more information about netiquette on the Web.

Do: Read as much information as you can about a service before you try it. Use the FAQ files available from FTP servers such as rtfm.mit.edu to answer your own questions. Experienced users will not appreciate questions such as "How do I post to this newsgroup?" from newbies, and you will get flooded with nasty messages telling you your questions are inappropriate. This is one kind of *flame,* or e-mail harassment, you can easily avoid.

210 EXPLORING THE INTERNET

Do: Read the newsgroup or mailing list postings for several weeks before you actually post anything. (During this time, when you are watching but not participating, you will be known as a *lurker,* which in this case is considered a positive character trait!) You will not be forgiven for posting a question or response to a thread that is old and long since discarded. Consider this transgression an open invitation to get flamed.

Do: Post to a mailing list the responses you receive in your own, personal e-mail to a question you send to the list. Others probably had the same question, but were lurking and waiting for someone else to ask it, so the answers will be much appreciated.

Do: Remember that your words will last a long time in print, and it is difficult to take them back. Think before you write or post.

Do: Try to convey your meaning clearly. Someone may read your words in a different way than you intended, so if you are making a joke or being sarcastic, indicate it to your recipient by using words, <just kidding>, for example, or smilies (see page 213).

Do: Remember that the Internet does cost money, even if you are not paying a charge each time you use it. Use the resources wisely, so we will all continue to have access to them.

Don't: Cross-post the same message to multiple newsgroups and mailing lists. Flooding the Internet with your lucid and insightful thoughts, called *spamming,* will only bring on a flame of international proportions.

Don't: Post an advertisement to a newsgroup or mailing list; it is decidedly against the rules, and you will be flamed for a long time to come if you try it. Advertising on the Net is allowed, as long as you create a home page and let people come to you.

HOW TO MAKE A NAME FOR YOURSELF ON THE INTERNET

If you want to achieve international ignominy, cross-post an advertisement to multiple newsgroups. That is what Laurence Canter and Martha Siegel, two attorneys in Phoenix, did in 1994, violating one of the sacred tenets of the Internet. Many long-time denizens of the Net are opposed to any commercialization of the network, and they reacted quickly to the infraction. The lawyers were flooded with millions of angry messages decrying their base, self-serving use of free resources, and they lost their Internet account. They sued the provider, and got it back, only to have their service terminated again when they continued to spam, and were repeatedly flamed. The saga continues.

NetSpeak—The Language of the Internet

You will discover in your travels that many people use acronyms to speed up their data entry/typing time. These are used in the body of an e-mail message, in the salutation or close, as part of a chat session—virtually any place where written communication is exchanged on the Internet. There are possibly hundreds of these shortcuts, collectively called **NetSpeak.** We reproduce only a few in Table 6.1. It may seem strange, at first, sending a long string of capitalized alphabet soup, but you will soon find your favorites, and they will save you time.

TABLE 6.1	Commonly Used NetSpeak Acronyms
BCNU	Be Seeing You! Ciao! Arrivederci!
BOF	Birds Of a Feather. People interested in the same topic; they flock together.
BTW	By The Way.
FAQ	Frequently Asked Question.
FOF	Friend Of a Friend. A rather distant, and possibly unreliable, source.
FWIW	For What It's Worth
<G>	Grin.
GIGO	Garbage In, Garbage Out. From general computer usage, if your input data is inaccurate, you will not get good results from your program.
HHOK	Ha Ha Only Kidding. Just a joke, man.
HHOS	Ha Ha Only Serious. Whatever was said was funny, but at least half serious too.
IMHO	In My Humble Opinion. If it really was so humble, you wouldn't use this!
IMO	In My Opinion. IMO, this sounds more humble than IMHO.
IWBNI	It Would Be Nice If.
IYFEG	Insert Your Favorite Ethnic Group. Used in humor newsgroups to allow the user to insert whatever ethnic group he/she desires, to avoid offending anyone on the joke list.
LOL	Laughing Out Loud.
LTNS	Long Time No See.
MEGO	My Eyes Glaze Over. Used to indicate being overrun by technical or boring detail.
MOTAS	Member Of The Appropriate Sex.
MOTOS	Member Of The Other Sex.
MOTSS	Member Of The Same Sex.
PMJI	Pardon My Jumping In.
POMKIF	Pounding On My Keyboard In Frustration. Learn how to type!
ROTFL	Rolling On The Floor Laughing. It was that funny, really...or was it?
RTFAQ	Read The Frequently Asked Questions. Read the FAQ archive instead of posting stupid questions to the newsgroup.
RTM	Read The Manual. A polite way of suggesting that you should try to find the information in online Help or a manual before posting the question.
<S>	Smile.
SO	Significant Other.
TIA	Thanks In Advance. Nice to add to the end of an e-mail posting in which you ask for reader response or assistance.
TTFN	TaTa For Now!
WOMBAT	Waste Of Money, Brains, And Time.
WRT	With Respect To.
YMMV	Your Mileage May Vary. You won't necessarily get the same results.

Smilies and Emoticons

This chapter has raised some very heavy and demanding issues and has warned you about proper behavior. (We are beginning to sound like your Great-Aunt Mildred!) Well, the Net is there to learn on, to explore, to get lost on, then found, to have fun. To ensure the latter, we introduce one of our favorite topics—how to enrich your text with silly symbols, called **emoticons** (emotional icons) by very proper surfers, **smilies** by those of us who just want to have fun.

Since the Internet is currently based primarily on written, not oral, communication, the nuances of inflection, facial expression, and body language are lost on the recipient of your message. Therefore it is important that you relay to the person, particularly one that you do not know well if at all, the emotional subtext of your message. Newbies often **PUT EVERYTHING IN UPPERCASE,** but this implies you are yelling, and it is not recommended. An alternative is to add an explanatory statement in your text, highlighted in some way: <hehehe>, <giggle>, <just kidding>.

Some people prefer a more graphic approach, and have devised smilies to help broadcast their meaning. Table 6.2 shows some of the more popular and/or clever emoticons, which are created from various combinations of letters and symbols in the character set. (Tip your head to the left, or rotate the book to the right, to decipher their meaning more clearly.) Use them freely, invent your own, and spread cheer and good tidings on the Net.

TABLE 6.2 Smilies and Other Emoticons

:-) or :)	Smilie face	C=]:-)	I am a chef
;-) or ;)	Winky; just kidding	:X	My lips are sealed
:-(	Oh, so sad	{_}>	Java brew
:'-(	So sad I'm crying	C|_|	A mug of coffee
:'-)	So happy I'm crying	:-&	I'm tongue-tied
>;-)>	Little devil	X-(	That comment killed me
8-{)	Dude with shades and mustache	%-)	User has been looking at the screen too long!
8-)	Cool dude with shades	:-o	Surprise!

THE COMMERCIALIZATION OF CYBERSPACE

The topic of commercialization of the Internet has emerged several times throughout this book, and it is an ongoing issue for many long-time Internet gurus. Because the Internet was developed without the involvement of advertisers and major vendors, it should remain a pure, commercial-free zone of communication, goes the argument. That is not a likely prospect, and indeed as we have discussed, many commercial organizations already have Web pages and are advertising all types of products and services on the Internet.

The **backbone,** or main network links between Internet providers around the country, is no longer provided or maintained by either Department of Defense or National Science Foundation funding. Since April 1995 it has been operated by telecommunications companies such as Sprint and MCI. The Internet service providers, which formerly were NSF-funded and located on major campuses such as MIT and Princeton, have spun off as for-profit providers. Netscape, developed as a follow-on to Mosaic, is now a publicly traded company on the New York Stock Exchange, and debuted as one of the most successful initial public offerings in history.

Is this commercialization good? Does it mean there will be more government regulation, particularly if the Federal Communications Commission (FCC) and Interstate Commerce Commission (ICC) are concerned with the transmission of sexually explicit materials? Will there be further government attempts to control encryption on the Net? All of these questions remain to be answered. One thing is certain: there will be continued controversy about the Internet over the next decade.

While long-time internauts are dismayed at the sudden traffic on the Net, others just venturing on are delighted by the capabilities it represents. We finish the chapter by exploring commercial on-line services and how they are affecting the Internet, and by discussing the newest of electronic pastimes, cybershopping.

Commercial Online Network Providers

While the intent of this book is to allow you to use your campus Internet access productively, we also hope to give you as broad a picture of the online world as possible. The public and media interest in the Net has been spurred, in part, by the millions of people already online on commercial services such as America Online (AOL), CompuServe, Delphi, Microsoft Network (MSN), and Prodigy. We will explore, briefly, what online services some of these companies offer, and how they differ from the Internet.

Figure 6.6 shows the interface to user services offered by four leading commercial networks: AOL, CompuServe, MSN, and Prodigy. All offer an easy-to-use Windows interface with buttons and menu bars for skipping to different services. They each offer frequent online conferences, or chats, with technical specialists; rock, TV, and movie stars; health experts; and many others. They also provide forums (Windows NT forum, or O.J. forum, for example) for ongoing discussions of topics of interest to members, similar to newsgroups in Usenet.

Each carries daily news synopses, while some provide detailed reports from the major wire services, CNN, foreign journals and newspapers, network news services, and more. Daily stock quotations and personal portfolio management are common, as are entertainment areas where members can preview and download shareware games. Hobbies, health and lifestyle, travel, and weather are additional popular topics.

The commercial services differ from the Internet in some important ways. They are private networks, and thus may be able to assure their members a better degree of security for transmitting online banking and credit card information. Because they control their own programming, they have been able to offer software controls to keep children from getting into age-inappropriate material. Their user interfaces organize services into categories, enabling users to navigate the resources more directly than they can when searching the Web.

Commercial online providers are also able to offer value-added services that have not yet achieved much success on the Internet, which is still resisting the commercialization inherent in fee-based services. Portfolio management and news consolidation are two examples of these services.

Portfolio management lets the user define the names of the stocks he or she wants to track in order to keep a day-to-day record of the performance of the portfolio. The value of the portfolio is updated automatically, based on the stock price retrieved daily by the online service. In addition, various services track the performance of mutual funds. *Money* magazine's FundWatch Online provides the

(a) America Online

(b) CompuServe

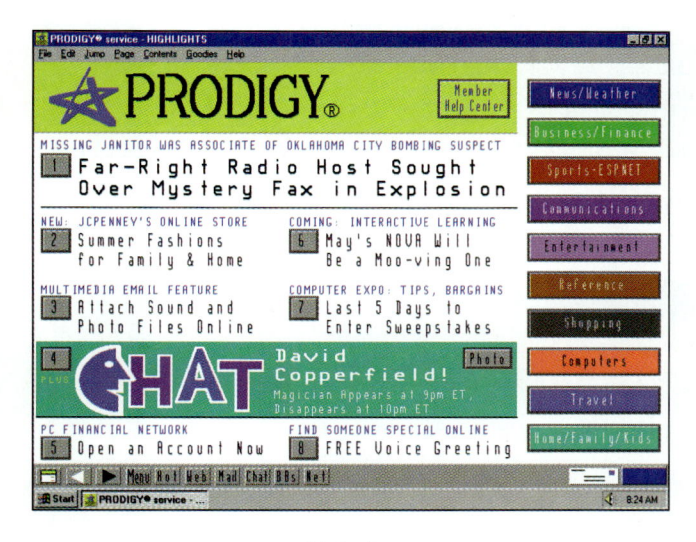

(c) Prodigy

(d) Microsoft Network

FIGURE 6.6 Online Information Services

annualized return of funds from various management companies, as shown in Figure 6.7.

News consolidators use hundreds of news sources—such as newspapers, news services, magazines, and newsletters—and abstract the news according to user-specified topics. The abstracted articles are presented to the subscriber each day as an e-mail message or as a fax. Other organizations allow online searches of worldwide databases of up-to-the-minute news. These services are not free. ADP's Global Report service rates, for example, are shown in Figure 6.8.

All of the major commercial online services now offer access to selected Internet resources, such as World Wide Web. Some offer access to Usenet as well. For the millions of people who do not have a direct Internet connection through their college, university, or work environment, commercial online services provide a low-cost way to get online and start surfing. You might want to consider subscribing during the summer if your Internet account at your computer lab is deactivated. You will need a computer, modem, and valid credit card to sign up. See Appendix A for more information about requirements for dial-up access.

THE INTERNET AND SOCIETY

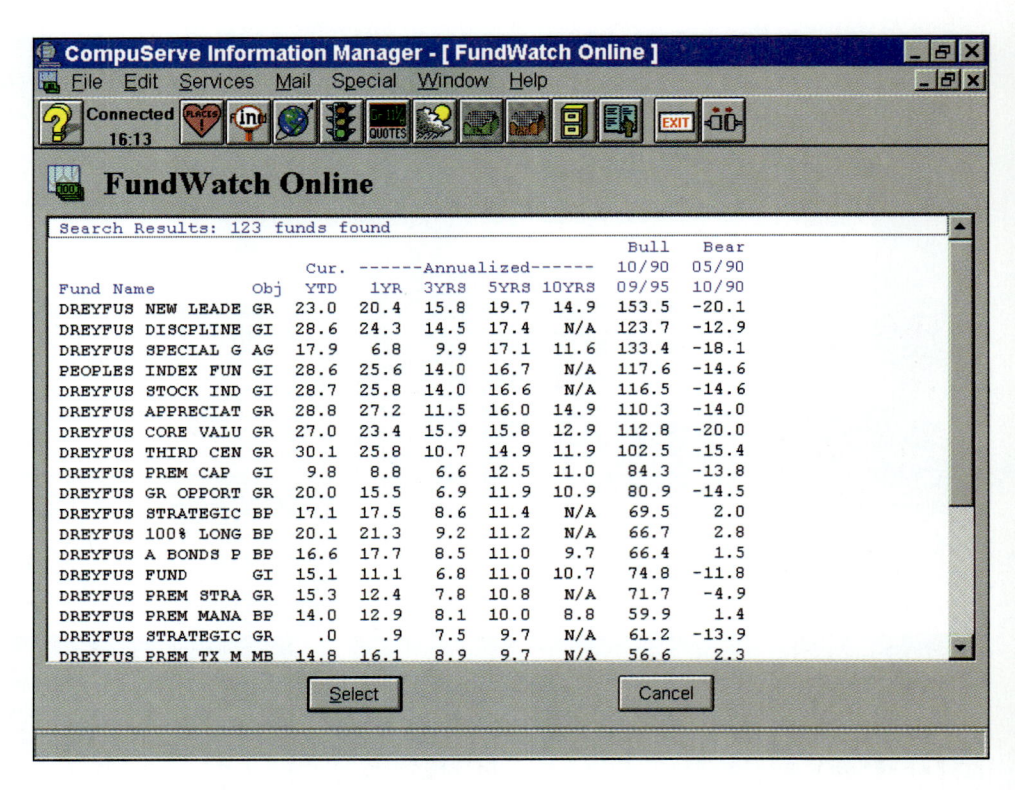

FIGURE 6.7 *Money* Magazine's FundWatch Online

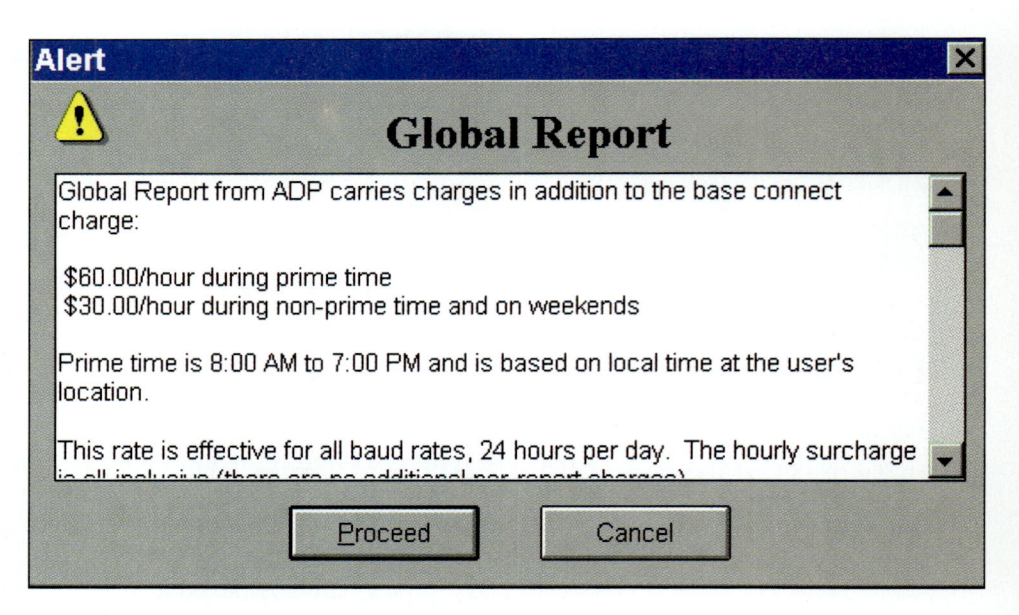

FIGURE 6.8 ADP's Global Report News Gathering Service

Shopping In Cyberspace

You have learned about gophers, browsers, home pages, newsgroups, and much more. But even that is not all there is to the Internet, which changes as you read this. The Internet by design and legislation was originally off-limits to commercial services. That changed with a ruling by the National Science Foundation in 1991, which lifted its own prohibition on commercial use and advertising on the Net.

216 EXPLORING THE INTERNET

With the advent of digital telecommunications, low-cost modems and PCs, and friendlier software, online uses of all kinds have grown geometrically. Corporations from computer vendors to insurance companies have home pages, and consumers are starting to venture into online shopping malls to make quick and easy catalog purchases. In our last hands-on exercise, you will explore a few of these cybermalls, and be among the new breed of consumers shopping with a mouse in hand.

HANDS-ON EXERCISE 3

Shopping on the Internet

Objective: To explore several Internet shopping sites to learn the types of goods and services offered there, and to understand methods of payment, delivery, and so forth. Use Figure 6.9 as a guide in the exercise.

STEP 1: Log On
- Log on to your system and start your Web browser as you usually do.

STEP 2: Start Your Cyberspace Shopping Expedition
- Explore several of the Internet sites shown in Table 6.3. Note the variety of goods and services offered, the method of payment and delivery, and the graphics.

TABLE 6.3   Shopping Sites on the Internet

URL	Site
http://www.mastercard.com	MasterCard International
http://update.wsj.com	Business news and hourly updates of stock prices from the *Wall Street Journal*
http://www.discovery.com	The Discovery Channel online
http://www.wellsfargo.com	Wells Fargo Bank's secure place to do banking
http://www.ups.com	A place to check out the company that ships millions of packages each year
http://www.fedex.com	The overnight air carrier; you can check the delivery of your product here.
http://www.mig29.com/mig29/Welcome.html	Fly with Us, for the man or woman who has everything except flight training aboard a Russian fighter
http://www.spiegel.com	The shopping site for Spiegel, the famous catalog department store
http://www.isurf.com	The Internet Surf Shop; quick, visit the site and catch a wave
http://community.net/~csamir/aisshop.html	A huge list of many Internet shopping services
http://www.mecklerweb.com:80/imall/	Online department store with eight floors of great merchandise, from surfboards to lingerie
http://www.lenox.com/baz	Bazilians, discounters of name brand sportswear
http://isms.com/index-e.html	The Internet Shopping Mall
http://www.catalogsite.com/Gen/CatalogBigBoard.html	The mother of all catalog lists; if you like catalog shopping, this is a must

STEP 3: Analyze the Effectiveness of the Cybermall Experience

> Compare notes with your classmates to see which sites have the best merchandise, the best graphics, the best response time, and so on. You will find that few of the sites contain actual images of the merchandise. Instead, you will see information on how to mail away or call for a catalog.

> One site that does include images and diagrams of products and prices is Bazilians, a discounter of men's and women's sportswear. A page from their site is shown in Figure 6.9.

> Exit Netscape. Window shopping is permitted.

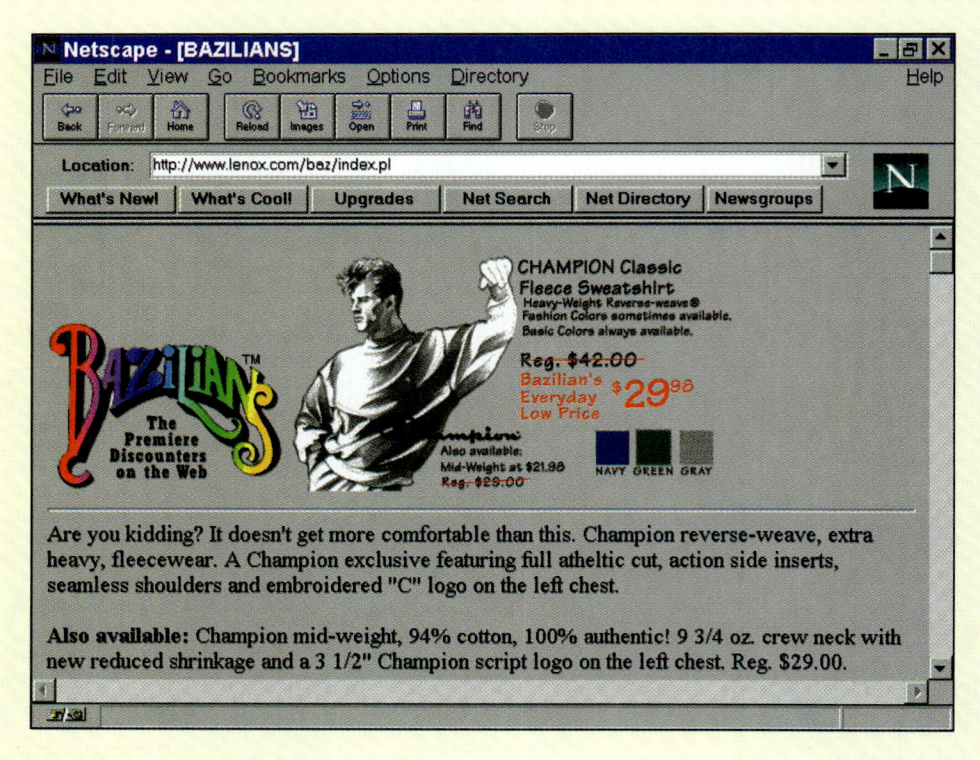

FIGURE 6.9   Hands-on Exercise 3

INTERNET SECURITY

As this book went to press, there was no Internet encryption standard. You should be very aware of this before sending a credit card number, social security number, phone number, or other personal information over the Net. *Never, ever* send your username and password over e-mail or any other transmission, other than to log on. Read carefully any vendor's claim to provide a secure environment. If it sounds too good to be true, it probably is. The most secure way at this time is still to pay for an order using your credit card and the telephone. Just be sure not to use your portable or cellular phone—anyone could be listening in and intercept your credit card number. You can, of course, keep abreast of Internet security issues by reading about them on the Web.

SUMMARY

The Internet is a rich and diverse network, full of potential, and of potential harm. Travelers should not be naive about the dangers that lurk there, and should understand how to avoid some of the risks from hackers, viruses, and antiprivacy legislation. In addition, we as a society will face challenges over the next decade—challenges such as how to provide equal access to the Information Superhighway.

The argument will continue about how best to ensure that the gap between information haves and have-nots is bridged, and that the existing gender gap on the Internet closes, or that it doesn't have a negative impact on women's employability. Users should be aware of copyright law when copying or downloading material from the Internet, and ensure that they don't infringe on an artist's or author's copyright.

KEY WORDS AND CONCEPTS

Backbone	Hacker	Smily
Clipper Chip	Kerberos	Software piracy
Copyright	Logic bomb	Spamming
Emoticon	Lurker	Trojan horse
Encryption	Netiquette	Virus
Encryption key	NetSpeak	Worm
Fair use	Public domain	
Flame	Shareware	

MULTIPLE CHOICE

1. Which of the following statements about copyrights on the Internet is true?
   (a) All work published on the Internet is copyrighted unless otherwise noted
   (b) Works in the public domain are not copyrighted
   (c) You may cite copyrighted Internet documents in assignments
   (d) All of the above

2. All of the following actions are considered fair use and not copyright infringement *except:*
   (a) Copying commercial software for a friend
   (b) Copying an e-mail message in your reply
   (c) Using a line from a poem in a term paper, with the reference cited in a footnote
   (d) Quoting a statistic from a Web home page

3. Which of the following may be legally downloaded from an Internet site?
   (a) Shareware
   (b) Public domain software
   (c) Both (a) and (b)
   (d) Neither (a) nor (b)

4. Which term is used to describe a person who attempts an unauthorized break-in to a computer?
   (a) Hacker
   (b) Computer nerd
   (c) Sysop
   (d) None of the above

5. Which of the following is required to send encrypted messages?
   (a) An encryption algorithm
   (b) An encryption key
   (c) Both (a) and (b)
   (d) Neither (a) nor (b)

6. When text is encrypted, who possesses the key?
   (a) The sender
   (b) The recipient
   (c) Both (a) and (b)
   (d) Neither (a) nor (b)

7. The U.S. government proposed the Clipper Chip to:
   (a) Keep track of Internet traffic
   (b) Allow federal agencies access to encrypted data
   (c) Keep children from seeing adult-oriented information on commercial network services
   (d) Keep children from seeing adult-oriented information on the Internet

8. Which of the following can be affected by viruses and other malicious programs?
   (a) Memory
   (b) The hard drive
   (c) A network
   (d) All of the above

9. Which of the following types of programs can replicate themselves and spread to other disks?
   (a) Logic bombs
   (b) Trojan horses
   (c) Both (a) and (b)
   (d) Neither (a) nor (b)

10. What is CERT's mission?
    (a) Providing commercial online services
    (b) Protecting privacy and free speech on the Internet
    (c) Helping network operators respond to security threats on the Internet
    (d) None of the above

11. Which of the following is considered spamming?
    (a) Sending an advertisement for a tax preparation service to multiple newsgroups
    (b) Including an icon to link to a product or service from a home page
    (c) Both (a) and (b)
    (d) Neither (a) nor (b)

12. Which of the following is a program designed to check and analyze a system's security loopholes?
    (a) CERT
    (b) Satan
    (c) Clipper Chip
    (d) Kerberos

13. Which of the following are required to use Internet services on a system when Kerberos is used?
    (a) A username
    (b) A password
    (c) An authenticated ticket
    (d) All of the above

14. Which of the following are new Internet users encouraged to do?
    (a) Flame
    (b) Spam
    (c) Lurk
    (d) All of the above

15. Why were no commercial organizations found on the Internet when it was originally developed?
    (a) It was not technically feasible for them to gain access
    (b) Legislation prohibited commercialization of the Internet
    (c) Both (a) and (b)
    (d) Neither (a) nor (b)

ANSWERS

1. d	**6.** c	**11.** a
2. a	**7.** b	**12.** b
3. c	**8.** d	**13.** d
4. a	**9.** d	**14.** c
5. c	**10.** c	**15.** b

EXPLORING THE INTERNET

1. Shop Some More: Visit more of the Internet shopping malls listed previously in Table 6.3. Answer the following questions:
    (a) What, if any, advertising is present at these sites?
    (b) Is the merchandise presented in an effective manner?
    (c) What types of costs are incurred by the advertisers/stores?
    (d) What is required to make the Internet a cost-effective medium in which to advertise/do business?

2. Practice NetSpeak: Decipher the following messages:
    (a) PMJI, but IWBNI the BOF in this newsgroup would not be so hard on newbies.
    (b) IMHO it appears that WRT many newsgroups the GIGO principal reigns.

(c) TIA for your replies. I know they will be pearls I won't find in any FAQ archive.

(d) After many hours in this chat room, I wish I could say I was ROTFL. Instead, I'm sure it was a WOMBAT.

3. The Computing Gender Gap: Observe the computer labs at your college or university for several days and survey users to answer the following questions:

   (a) What were the proportions of men and women during the times you visited?

   (b) What percentage of the men had used the Web? IRC or WebChat? Usenet?

   (c) Answer the preceding question for the women.

   (d) What percentage of the men/women had downloaded software from the Web?

   (e) What percentage of men/women could define the terms gopher, FTP, IRC, and Usenet?

   (f) What percentage of the men/women had downloaded sexually explicit material from the Internet?

4. Games on the Internet: Visit FTP archives, review the mailing list and Usenet list of lists, and conduct Web searches to answer the following questions about game playing on the Internet:

   (a) What is a MUD? How do you join one?

   (b) What percentage of the alt and rec news hierarchies are devoted to games?

   (c) What game software can be downloaded from the Net? Are there any particularly good sites? (E-mail the author with your answers to this question, and the URLs may be published in the next edition!)

   (d) From what types of organizations and from what domains are the games available?

   (e) How would you estimate the total Internet resources devoted to game playing? Is this a good/valid use of the investment the government and corporations have made in the Internet?

Practice with the Internet

1. Find Out about Spamming: Check out the Black List of Usenet Advertisers, set up to identify and punish people who are posting advertisements to inappropriate newsgroups and to those that don't allow advertising, at http://www.cco.caltech.edu/~Cbrown/BL. Read about the continuing Usenet flame warfare that caused Laurence Canter and Martha Siegel, the Phoenix attorneys who spammed the Net, to lose their accounts, at gopher://gopher.well.sf.ca.us:70//00/Publications/online_zines/Canter_and_Siegel.

2. Learn More Netiquette: Visit the netiquette home page at http://rs6000.adm.fau.edu/rinaldi/netiquette.html and read emily-postnews at the ftp://rtfm.mit.edu/pub/usenet site.

3. Talk the Talk: Visit two incredible jargon indices, and learn about hacker lore and other interesting subjects, at http://www.phil.uni-sb.de/fun/jargon/index.html and http://www.eps.mcgill.ca/jargon.

4. Explore Satan. Find out what has happened to the Satan program since its introduction by conducting a search on the keywords *Satan, internet,* and *security.*

Case Studies

Computers, Freedom, and Privacy

Many colleges and universities have restricted access to Usenet newsgroups, particularly those in the alt hierarchies. Carnegie Mellon University's decision to do so generated a great deal of controversy. You can obtain more information by doing a search on the keywords *computers, freedom,* and *privacy,* and by visiting the site, http://www.cs.cmu.edu/afs/cs/user/jeanc/www/cfp/cfp.html. Write a report on your findings.

Pornography on the Net

Determine how many newsgroups are devoted to sexually explicit topics, and look up the latest information on restrictions on pornography on the Internet. (You can get a complete list of newsgroups at the RTFM server at MIT. See Chapter 3 for details.) Write a short report on your findings.

Advertising on the Internet

Assume you are consulting with a small retailer that wants to set up business on the Web. Advertisers on the Internet are flamed and blacklisted if they conduct their advertising in what many on the Net consider to be inappropriate ways. Research what is considered inappropriate, and write a short report for your client recommending an advertising strategy. You can get all the information you need on the Web.

Internet Security

Watch the movies *The Net* and *War Games.* Could the events portrayed in the movies happen? What kind of safeguards can be put in place to avoid the situations illustrated in the films?

PUBLISHING ON THE NET: GETTING STARTED WITH HTML

OBJECTIVES

After reading this chapter you will be able to:

1. Define HTML; explain what HTML markup tags are and what they do.
2. Use Notepad to create a home page with bookmarks, ordered and unordered lists, in-line images, and hyperlinks to other Web resources.
3. Add formatting tags to create headings; bold, italicized, and underlined text; horizontal lines; and other design elements.
4. Use an HTML editor to modify your home page.
5. View the source of other HTML documents and copy useful elements to your own page.

OVERVIEW

Hypertext Markup Language (HTML) is the language used to create a Web page. In essence, HTML consists of a set of codes that allows you to format a document for display on the World Wide Web and that marks links to other Web sites. Since the inception of the World Wide Web, millions of people and organizations have created home pages. You can too.

It is easy to learn and use the basic HTML commands. In this chapter you will set up a simple home page that displays your name, a few lines of information about you, and your e-mail address.

This chapter is just a beginning. You can learn more about HTML on the Web, by conducting a search on the keywords *HTML guide* or *HTML primer*. Several excellent primers are available.

Before starting your home page, you should check with your system administrator to determine how he or she wants you to submit your material when it is complete. You also need to find out any site-specific information about using HTML in your campus computing environment.

INTRODUCTION TO HTML

Figure 7.1 displays a home page similar to the one you will create in this chapter. It has the look and feel of various Web pages you have visited throughout the text. Our page contains different types of formatting, such as lists, underlined links, a horizontal rule across the page, and enlarged headings. These effects are created by inserting codes, or **HTML tags,** in the document to identify the formatting that should be applied.

There are two ways to insert HTML tags in your document. One is to simply type them in, using a text editor such as Notepad. Another is to use an **HTML front end** or **HTML editor,** which is software that partially automates the process of HTML tags. One such editor is Microsoft's **Internet Assistant,** which works with the current version of Microsoft Word. This chapter contains two hands-on exercises so that you can practice both techniques.

http://www2.best.com/~dsiegel/tips/tips_home.html

After you have had some time to experiment with HTML, get help from experienced Web designer David Siegel. This site is fascinating, and well worth the trip. And by the way, Mr. Siegel is looking for a paid intern to help him with his next book, and is hiring experienced Web designers to help him with his many projects.

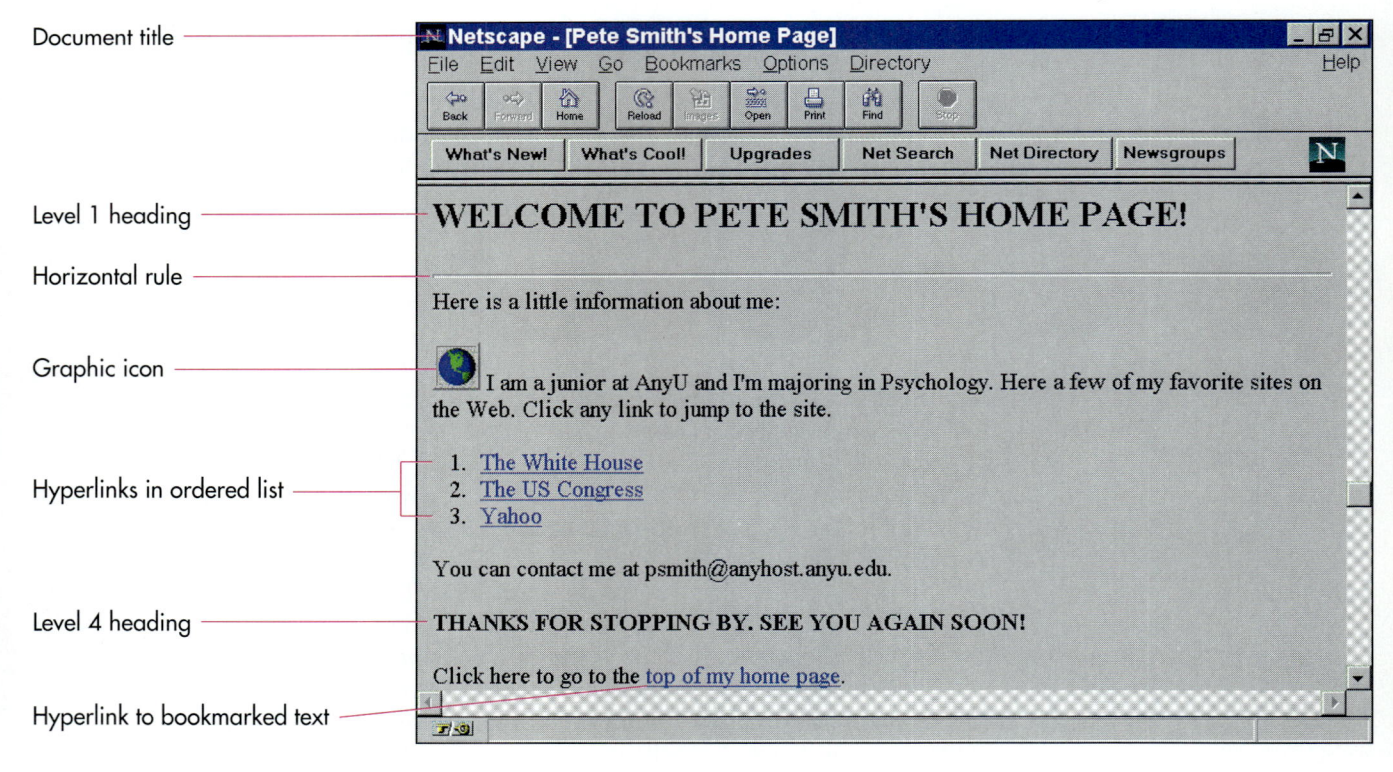

FIGURE 7.1   Sample Student Home Page

HTML CODES

Most HTML codes follow the same basic format. An HTML tag is inserted at the beginning of the text to be formatted, and a matching tag is placed at the end of the text. The first tag represents a begin-formatting command; the second is the end-formatting command. For example, text may be centered by preceding it with the <center> tag, and following it with the </center> tag. The tags around the text <h1>THIS IS A HEADING</h1> indicate that the enclosed text is a level 1 heading, that is, the largest in the document. You can see from these examples that the tags are very similar to styles in your word processor.

Unfortunately, not all browsers adhere to the same standards, and some tags, such as the center tag, will be ignored by some browsers. However, the tags you will use in this chapter are standard tags, and you should have no problem setting up a simple home page using them. The next several pages describe various types of tags.

Titles

You can create a title for your Web page that will be displayed in the title bar at the top of the document window (but not in the document itself). This is done with the <title> tag of Figure 7.2a (you may use upper- or lowercase for HTML tags), the effects of which are shown in Figure 7.2b.

<title>DOCUMENT TITLE</title>

The title is used by Web spiders and crawlers to update Web search engine catalogs. It is important to choose a title that best represents the contents of the page. *Suzie Jones's Home Page* is more indicative of the page content than simply *My Home Page.*

Headings and Lists

In the past you may have inserted word processing codes in a document to produce a larger font size and/or style (such as bold or italics) for headings. Web browsers will generally not recognize these word processing codes. HTML heading text must be preceded with an HTML heading tag, which indicates the general size of the font (large to small), and the appearance (bold). The largest heading in the document is designated as <h1>, the smallest as <h6>.

Each browser is set to display a default font for each heading type, so the actual appearance of the heading may differ from site to site. However, the relative size of the headings will stay the same, largest to smallest. You will see your text in whatever font and size you type it, as shown in Figure 7.3a. As displayed by the browser it will appear as shown in Figure 7.3b.

<h1>THIS IS A FIRST LEVEL (LARGEST) HEADING</h1>

Many home pages consist of information in a list, called an **unordered list** when the items have bullets, or an **ordered list** when they are preceded by numbers. Each item in the list will be surrounded by the appropriate tags, <ul> and </ul> for an unordered list, or <li> and </li> for an ordered list. Figure 7.3 shows the original document and the effects of ordered and numbered lists in the finished home page.

Title tag

```
<html>
<title>DOCUMENT TITLE</title>
<body>

</body>
</html>
```

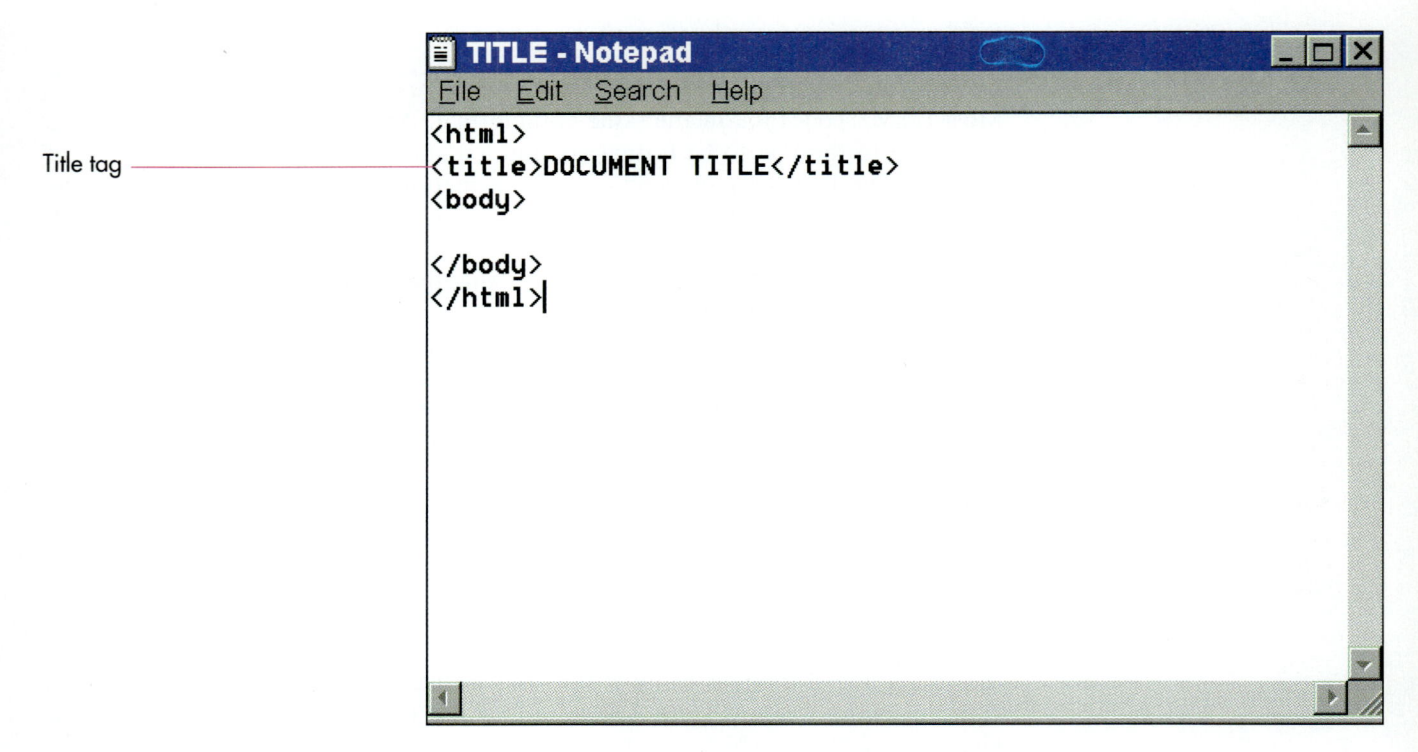

(a) The Title Tag in HTML Source

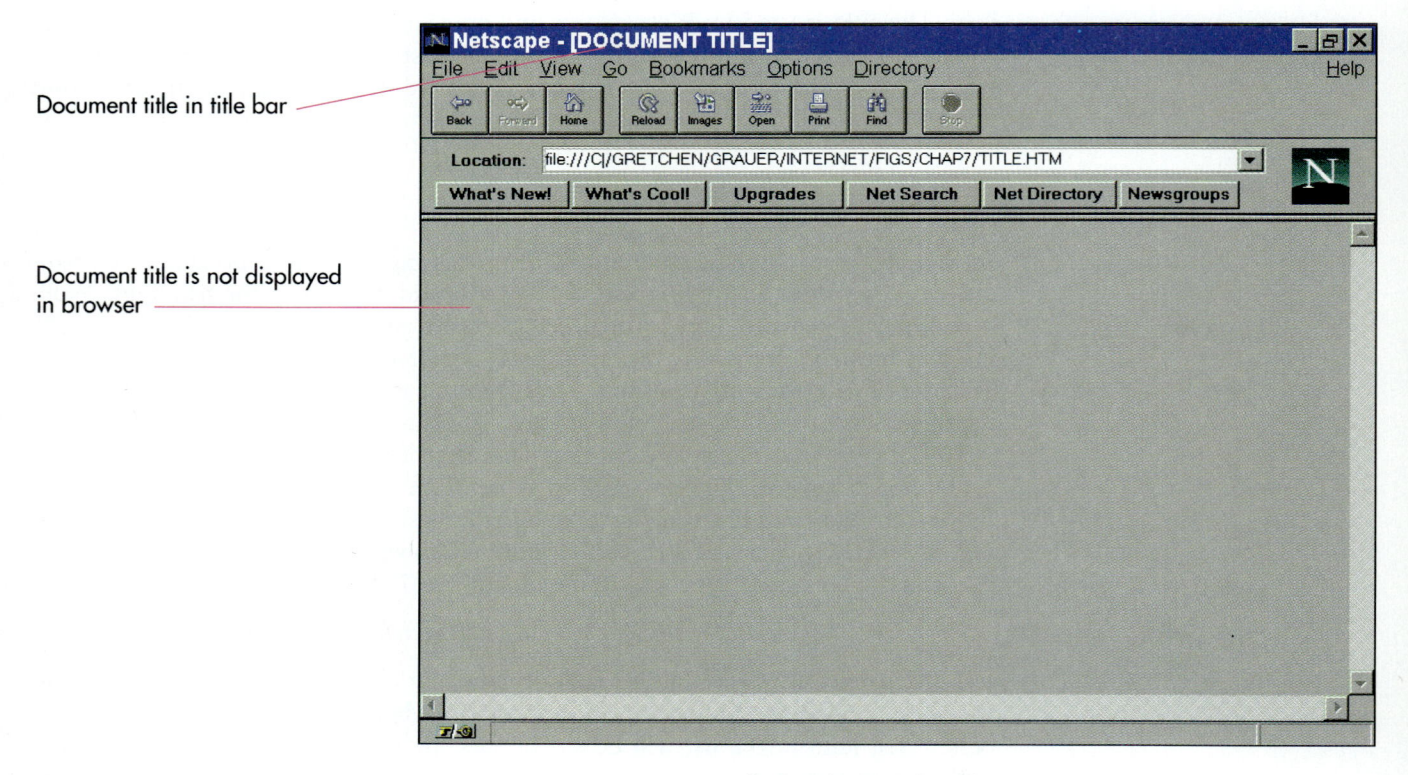

Document title in title bar

Document title is not displayed in browser

(b) The Title Tag in the Web Browser

FIGURE 7.2   The HTML Document Title

228 EXPLORING THE INTERNET

List elements

Level 1 heading tag

Unordered list

Ordered list

```
<html>
<title>DOCUMENT TITLE</title>
<body>
<h1>THIS IS A FIRST LEVEL (LARGEST) HEADING</h1>
<ul>
<li>This is the first bullet in the unordered list.
<li>This is the second bullet in the unordered list.
</ul>
<ol>
<li>This is the first item in the ordered list.
<li>This is the second item in the ordered list.
</ol>
</body>
</html>
```

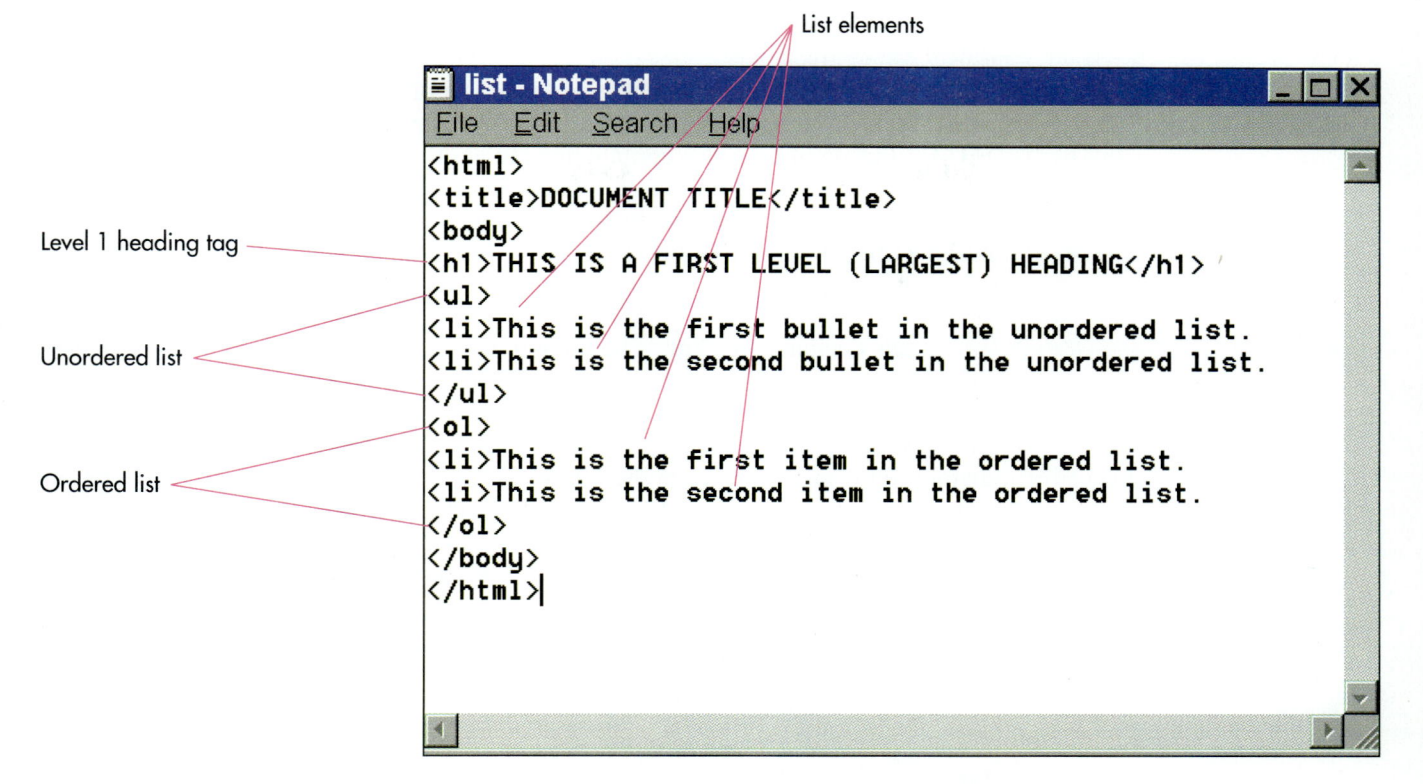

(a) Heading and Lists in HTML

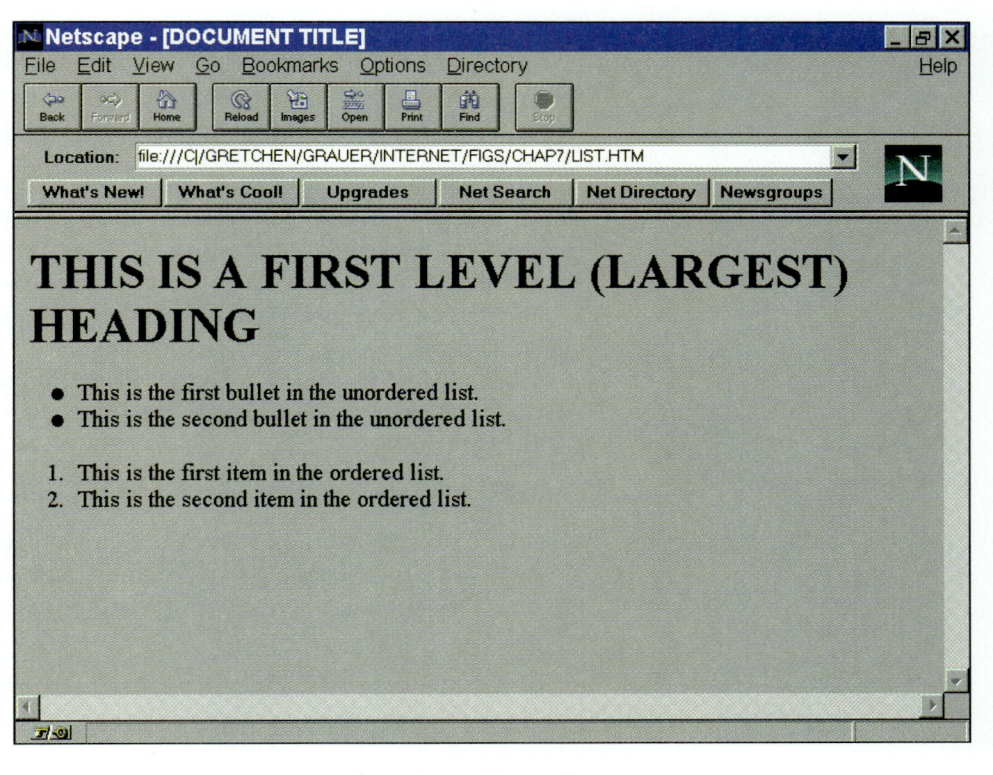

THIS IS A FIRST LEVEL (LARGEST) HEADING

- This is the first bullet in the unordered list.
- This is the second bullet in the unordered list.

1. This is the first item in the ordered list.
2. This is the second item in the ordered list.

(b) Heading and Lists in Netscape

FIGURE 7.3   Headings and Lists

PUBLISHING ON THE NET   229

Links to URLs and Local Files

The World Wide Web is composed of millions of home pages, each with links to other Web documents, both on the local Web server and at other Web sites. An HTML document may also contain links to another section of the same document, so readers can quickly jump to a topic of interest. These links, or *anchors,* are set up using the <a HREF= command. A sample link to the Prentice Hall home page is shown below and in Figure 7.4a:

<a HREF="http://www.prenhall.com/">Prentice Hall Home Page</a>

Let's decipher this link. The <a and </a> are the begin and end anchor tags. (There is a space after the leading <a.) HREF= is the hypertext reference parameter, which is followed by the Uniform Resource Locator (URL) of the Web site to which the tag is linking. The URL must be surrounded by quotes. Immediately following the URL is the text to be displayed as the link, preceded by the right angle bracket (greater than sign, >), which is followed by the end anchor tag.

Links are often nested within an ordered or unordered list, especially when multiple links appear one after another. For example:

<ul><li><a HREF="http://www.whitehouse.gov/">The White House</a></ul>

The <ul> tag preceding the White House link indicates an unordered list and displays a bullet on the page as shown in Figure 7.4b.

Linked Documents

Links can also be established to another document on the local Web server. If the document to which you are creating a link is in the same directory as the Web page you are working on, you will simply include the document name in the anchor:

<a HREF="univhome.html">Click here to link to the AnyU home page.</a>

This anchor will display the text shown after the right angle bracket (>), as shown in Figure 7.4b. The text will be underlined and displayed in a different color so it is easy to distinguish it as a link. You would, of course, have to know the correct file name of the college or university's home page to set up such a link. When creating your own HTML document, you will substitute the appropriate file name, *filename.html,* in the HREF parameter.

If you want to link to a document in a different directory on the same computer, the anchor must include the path to get to the other document from the current directory:

<a HREF="AnyU/homepage.html">Click here for the AnyU homepage.</a>

This reference indicates that the AnyU home page is in a directory called AnyU. You will need to see your system administrator or help desk to learn more about the directory structure at your school and how to set up the appropriate links.

LINKING TO NON-HTML DOCUMENTS

You are not limited to creating links to HTML documents. You may link to graphics, audio, video, and compressed files as well. However, the person using the link will not be able to hear, view, or decompress these files unless he or she has the proper helper software configured in his or her browser.

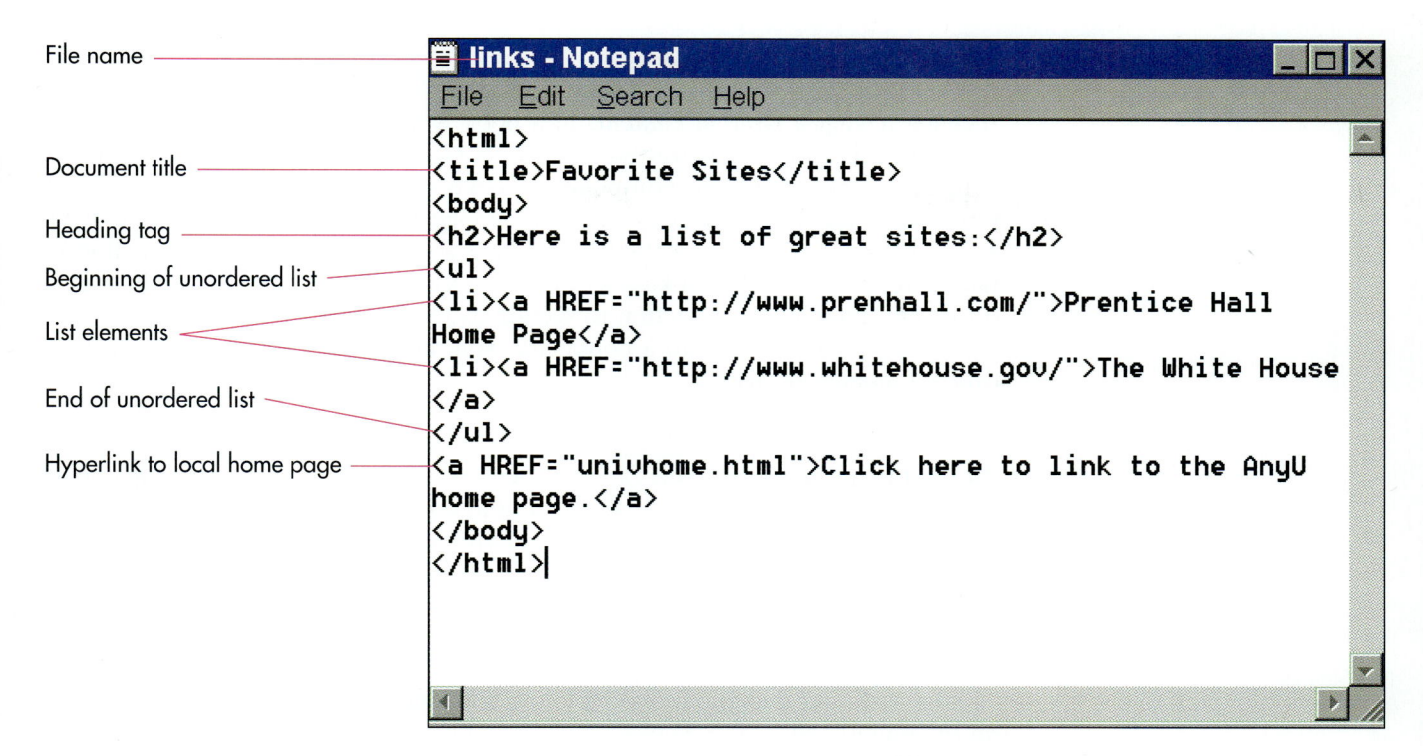

Annotations (left column, figure a):
- File name
- Document title
- Heading tag
- Beginning of unordered list
- List elements
- End of unordered list
- Hyperlink to local home page

Notepad window — links - Notepad:

```
<html>
<title>Favorite Sites</title>
<body>
<h2>Here is a list of great sites:</h2>
<ul>
<li><a HREF="http://www.prenhall.com/">Prentice Hall Home Page</a>
<li><a HREF="http://www.whitehouse.gov/">The White House</a>
</ul>
<a HREF="univhome.html">Click here to link to the AnyU home page.</a>
</body>
</html>
```

(a) Hyperlinks in HTML

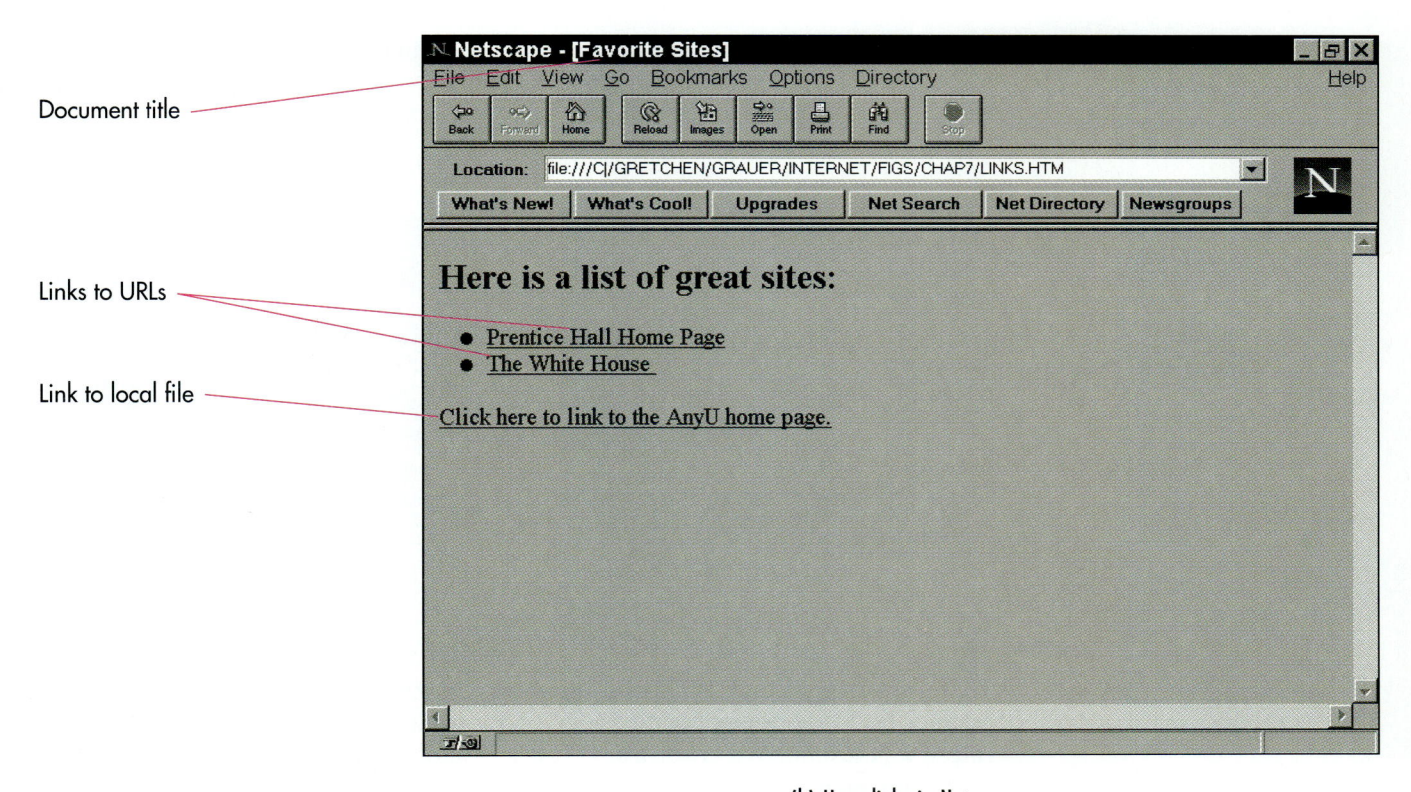

Annotations (left column, figure b):
- Document title
- Links to URLs
- Link to local file

Netscape - [Favorite Sites]:

Location: file:///C|/GRETCHEN/GRAUER/INTERNET/FIGS/CHAP7/LINKS.HTM

Here is a list of great sites:

- Prentice Hall Home Page
- The White House

Click here to link to the AnyU home page.

(b) Hyperlinks in Netscape

FIGURE 7.4 Hyperlinks

PUBLISHING ON THE NET   231

Links to Bookmarks

Imagine having a table of contents in a book where you can simply point to the topic in which you are interested, and the book would automatically open to the page (even the paragraph) you pointed to. You have probably seen examples of this using online Help in many Windows applications, or while surfing the Web. In order to do this, you create a link, called a **bookmark,** to another section of the current document. Bookmarks make it easy for readers to scroll through a document, jumping from section to section as they desire.

Before you can link to a bookmark, you must create the bookmarked text, called a **named anchor:**

<a name="Copyrights">Section I: Software Copyrights</a>

The text in quotes is the name of the bookmark. The text following the right angle bracket (>) is the text that will appear in the document, as shown in Figure 7.5b. As you can see, the bookmark itself is not visible in the document. You can place a link to the copyright section elsewhere in the document, as shown in Figure 7.5a. The HTML tag that creates the link is:

<a HREF="#Copyrights">Click here to learn about software copyrights</a>

This tag indicates that you will jump to the bookmark "Copyrights" when you click on the underlined text. You can also create a link to a bookmark in another document:

<a HREF="AnyU/homepage.htm#LabHours">Computer Lab Hours</a>

This assumes that the bookmark, in this case LabHours, has already been set up in the AnyU homepage document. When the person browsing the home page clicks on the underlined text, *Computer Lab Hours,* he or she will link to the LabHours bookmark in the AnyU home page.

---

http://www.loc.gov/global/html.html

Maintained by the Library of Congress, this site contains lots of useful information about creating HTML documents, as well as information about the latest HTML standards. This is a good place to visit if you want to know what's coming next in the world of Web publishing.

Other HTML Tags

There are many other HTML tags, which you can learn about by locating and reading HTML primers on the Web, or by using an HTML editor, such as the Internet Assistant. We cover a few you will find useful.

You may leave blank lines in your word processed document, but your browser will ignore them. To insert a blank line, use the <p> tag, which is an exception to the paired tags rule. Simply use one <p> wherever you want a blank line, much as you press the Enter key while typing in your word processor. You can add a horizontal line using the <hr> tag. Like the <p> tag, it does not require a matching end-of-horizontal-rule tag.

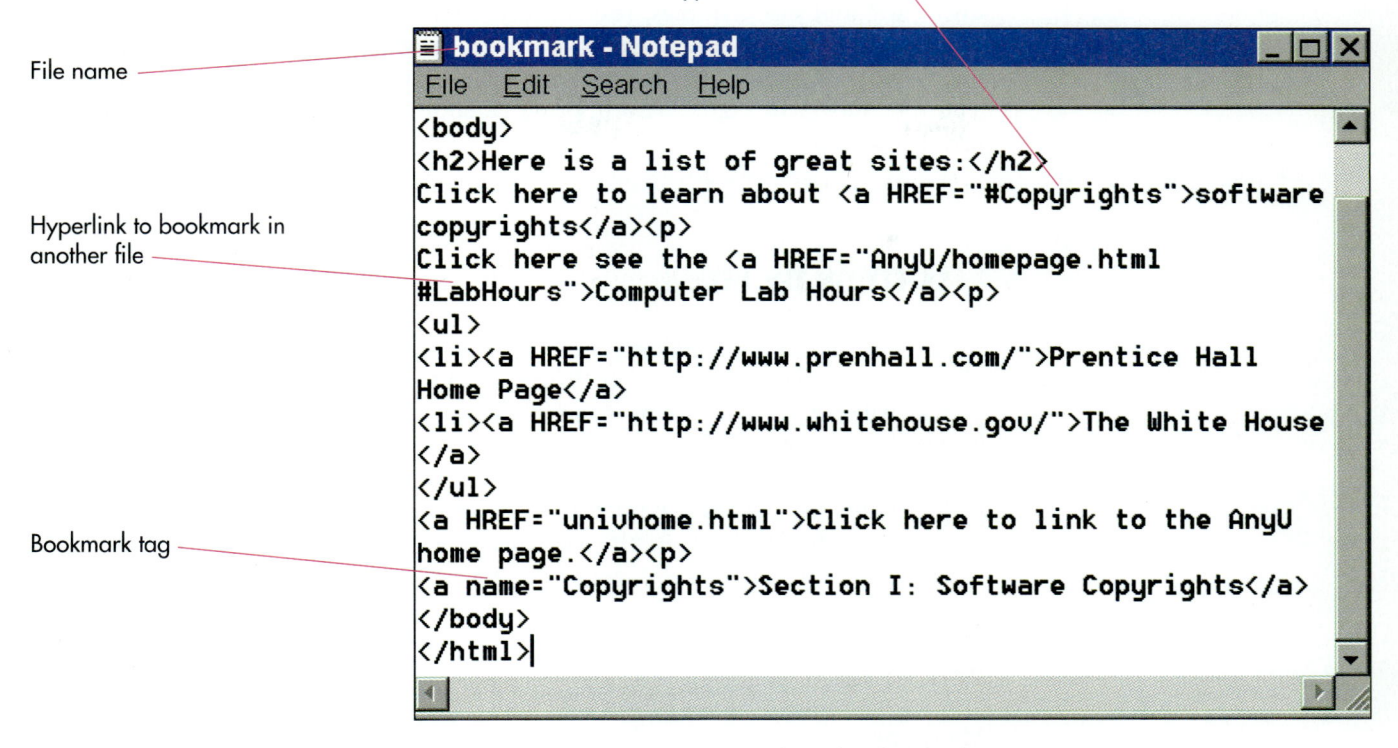

File name — Hyperlink to bookmark

```
<body>
<h2>Here is a list of great sites:</h2>
Click here to learn about <a HREF="#Copyrights">software
copyrights</a><p>
Click here see the <a HREF="AnyU/homepage.html
#LabHours">Computer Lab Hours</a><p>
<ul>
<li><a HREF="http://www.prenhall.com/">Prentice Hall
Home Page</a>
<li><a HREF="http://www.whitehouse.gov/">The White House
</a>
</ul>
<a HREF="univhome.html">Click here to link to the AnyU
home page.</a><p>
<a name="Copyrights">Section I: Software Copyrights</a>
</body>
</html>
```

Hyperlink to bookmark in another file

Bookmark tag

(a) The Bookmark and Link in HTML

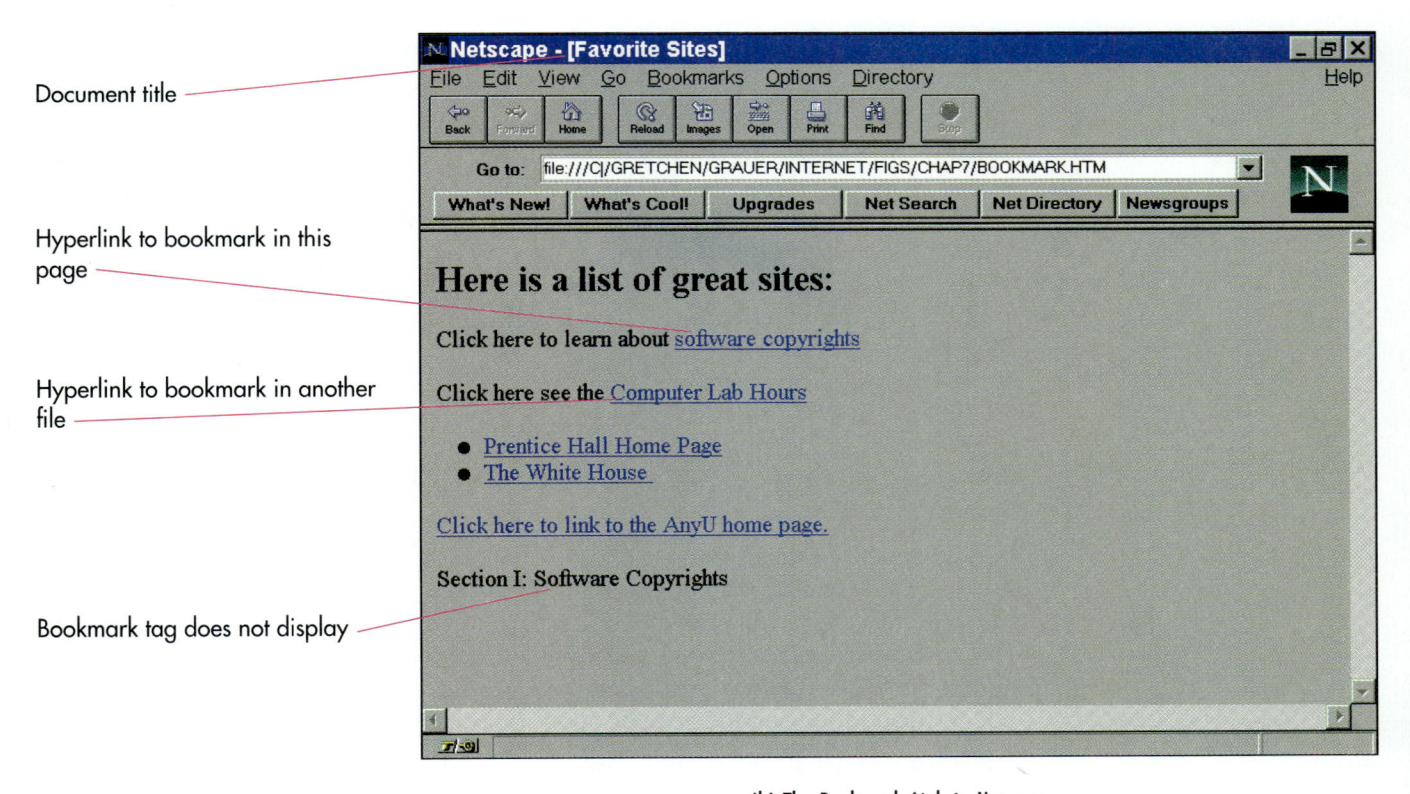

Document title — Netscape - [Favorite Sites]

Hyperlink to bookmark in this page

Here is a list of great sites:

Click here to learn about software copyrights

Click here see the Computer Lab Hours

- Prentice Hall Home Page
- The White House

Click here to link to the AnyU home page.

Section I: Software Copyrights

Hyperlink to bookmark in another file

Bookmark tag does not display

(b) The Bookmark Link in Netscape

FIGURE 7.5 Bookmarks

PUBLISHING ON THE NET

You can format text to be bold, underlined, or italicized using the <b> </b>, <u> </u>, and <i> </i> tags, respectively. (You may find that your browser recognizes the bold and italics tags in your word processor, but another browser may not, so you should insert these tags to ensure that you achieve the desired effect.) The text shown in Figure 7.6a appears as shown in Figure 7.6b when displayed using your browser.

> ### SAFETY ON THE NET
>
> As with any other medium, there is always the potential for misuse, even criminal activity, on the Web. You should think very carefully about what you will put on your home page. You should not put any identifying personal information on it, such as your address or phone number. You may want to think twice about putting a picture of yourself on it. Millions of people, however, put their e-mail address on their home pages, so others can get in touch with them easily. The rule is, let common sense prevail.

Inserting Images

Many pages you see while surfing the Web include a small graphic next to a hyperlink or a larger graphic element elsewhere on the page. You can include one of these *in-line images* in your document using the IMG tag, as shown in Figure 7.7a.

<img src="AnyU/picture.gif">

The reference above is to a **GIF,** or graphics *file,* stored in the AnyU directory on the Web server. The image will be displayed in the page when it is viewed with a Web browser, as shown in Figure 7.7b.

You must store the GIF images in the appropriate directory before you can create such a link. GIF images are located at many sites on the Web, and a little browsing will help you locate some and download them (provided they are not copyrighted). Once you have downloaded them and saved them as a file, consult with your system administrator on how to get them to the appropriate directory on your Web server.

> ### WHEN PICTURES ARE TOO MUCH OF A GOOD THING
>
> *In-line images* (graphics that load automatically with the page) help make a Web document visually interesting. However, image files are generally considerably larger than text files, and take a long time to download. Use icons and other images sparingly in your home page, or visitors will not want to come back. One way you can avoid long delays is to place a link to an image instead of placing the graphic in the home page. For example:
>
> <a HREF="GrCanyon.gif">Click here to see my vacation picture of the Grand Canyon.</a>.
>
> That way, only the people who really want to see the picture will have to wait while it loads.

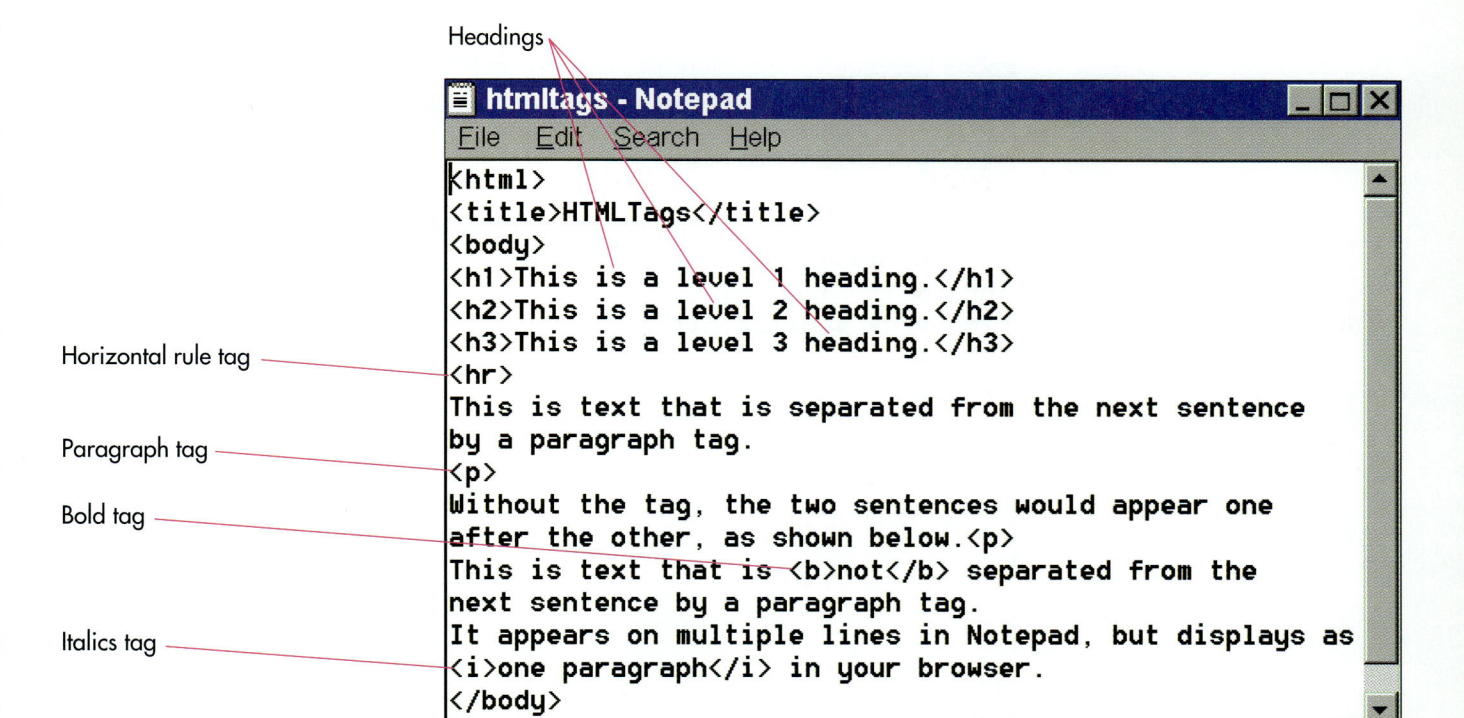

(a) Formatting Tags in HTML

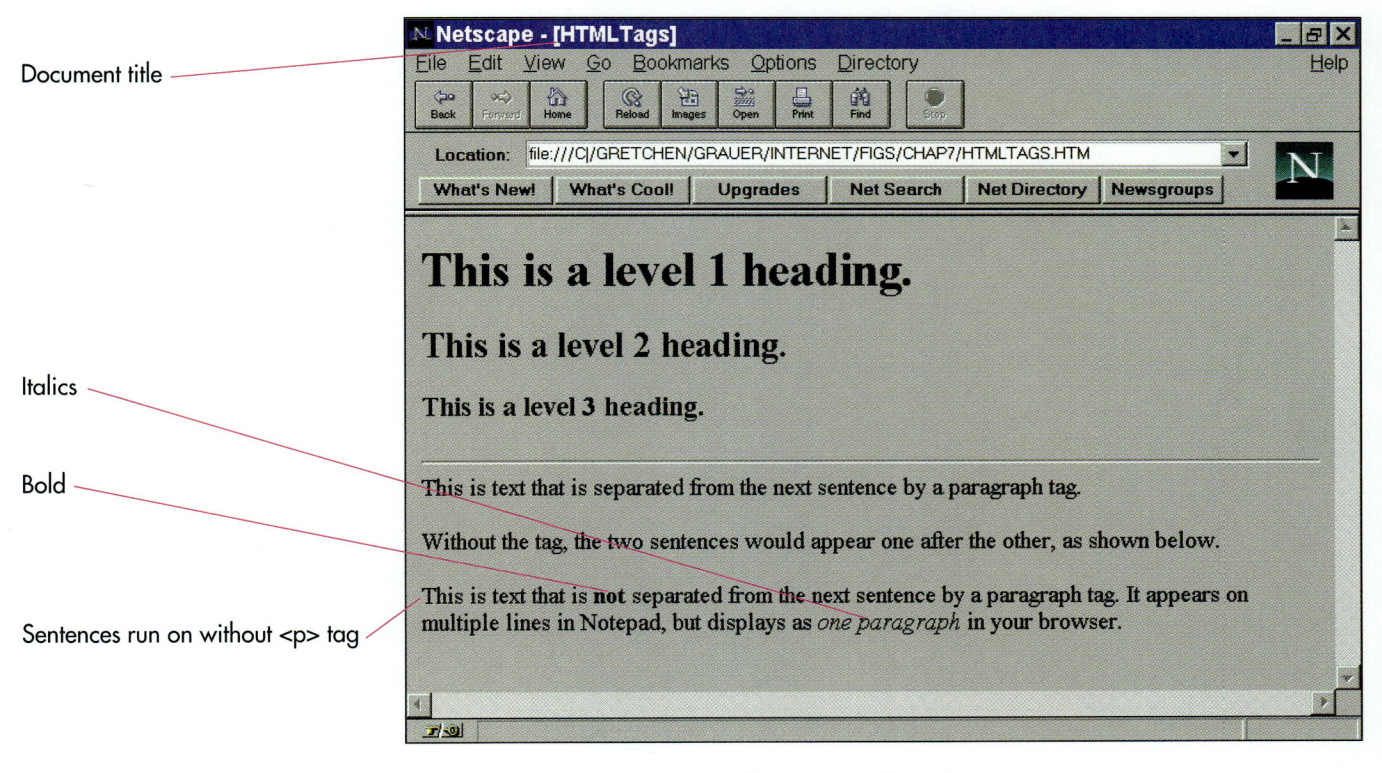

Headings → `<h1>`, `<h2>`, `<h3>` lines

Notepad contents:

```
<html>
<title>HTMLTags</title>
<body>
<h1>This is a level 1 heading.</h1>
<h2>This is a level 2 heading.</h2>
<h3>This is a level 3 heading.</h3>
<hr>
This is text that is separated from the next sentence
by a paragraph tag.
<p>
Without the tag, the two sentences would appear one
after the other, as shown below.<p>
This is text that is <b>not</b> separated from the
next sentence by a paragraph tag.
It appears on multiple lines in Notepad, but displays as
<i>one paragraph</i> in your browser.
</body>
```

- Horizontal rule tag → `<hr>`
- Paragraph tag → `<p>`
- Bold tag → `<b>`
- Italics tag → `<i>`

(b) Formatting Effects in Netscape

Document title: Netscape - [HTMLTags]

This is a level 1 heading.

This is a level 2 heading.

This is a level 3 heading.

This is text that is separated from the next sentence by a paragraph tag.

Without the tag, the two sentences would appear one after the other, as shown below.

This is text that is **not** separated from the next sentence by a paragraph tag. It appears on multiple lines in Notepad, but displays as *one paragraph* in your browser.

- Italics
- Bold
- Sentences run on without `<p>` tag

FIGURE 7.6 Formatting Tags

Document title ──

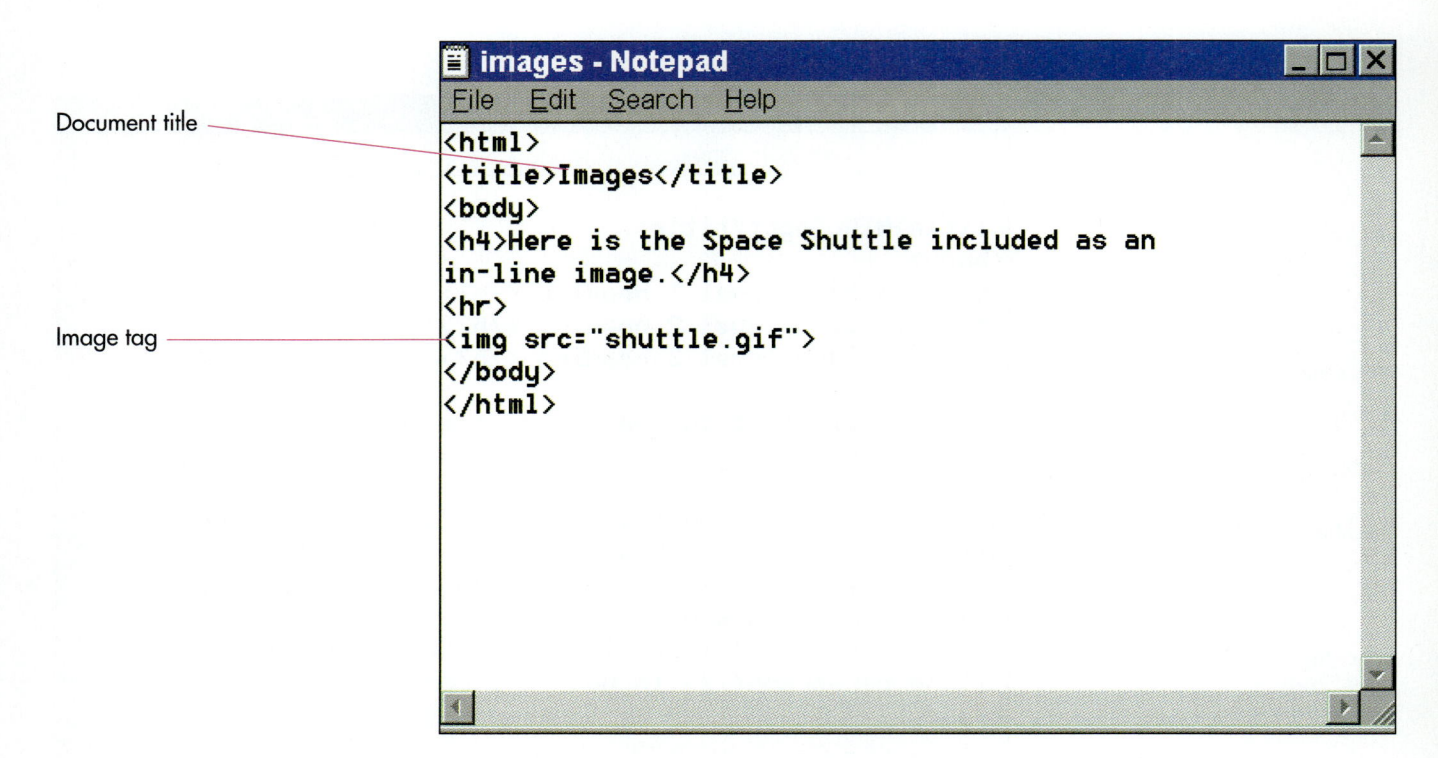

Image tag ──

```
<html>
<title>Images</title>
<body>
<h4>Here is the Space Shuttle included as an
in-line image.</h4>
<hr>
<img src="shuttle.gif">
</body>
</html>
```

(a) The HTML Image Tag

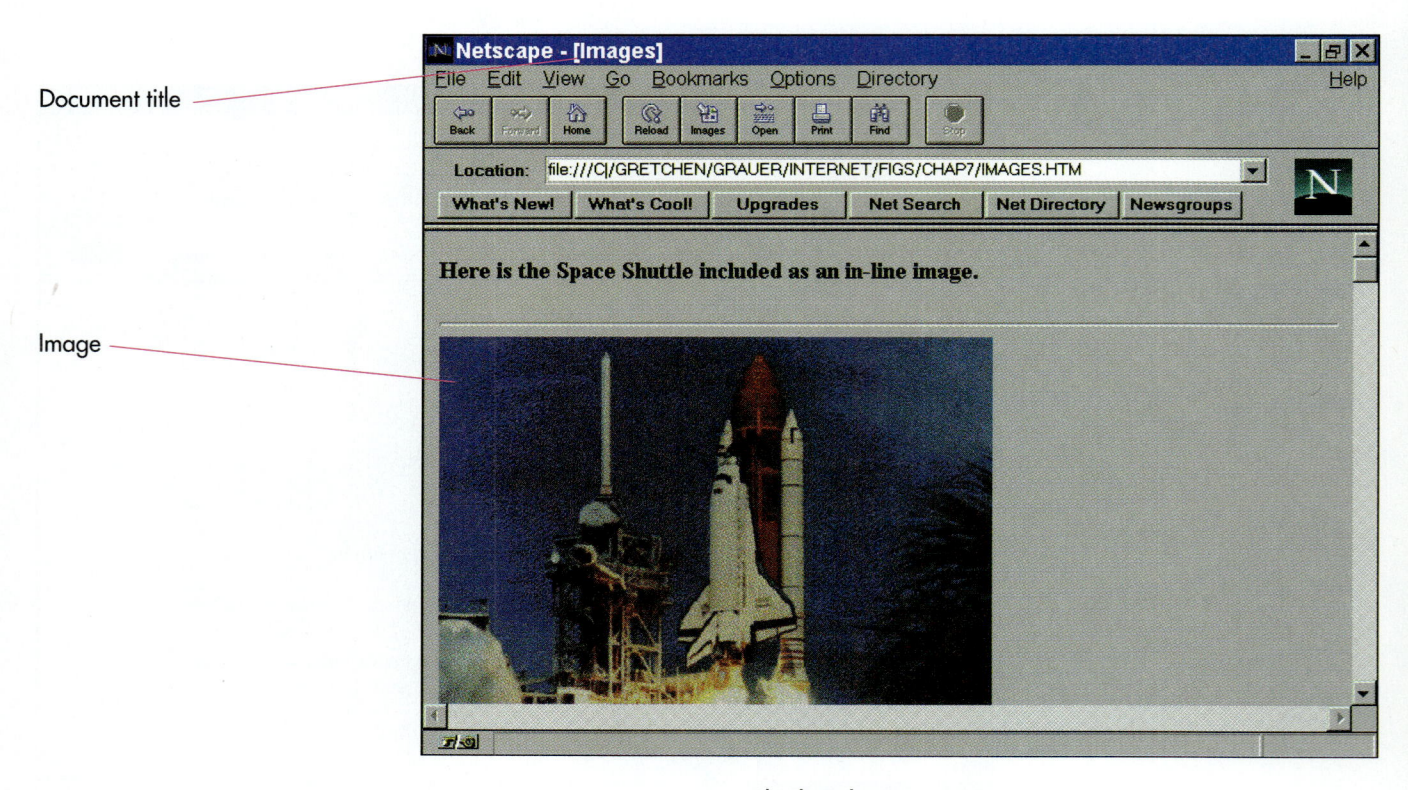

Document title ──

Image ──

(b) The In-line Image in Netscape

FIGURE 7.7 Inserting Images

236 EXPLORING THE INTERNET

LEARNING BY DOING

HTML is the means by which you, too, can have a place on the Web (think of it—millions of people worldwide can visit you!). The following exercise will walk you through the process of setting up a simple home page.

We encourage you to use the home page you develop in the exercises in this chapter as a sample, and then to learn more about HTML on your own from resources you find on the Net. You can then modify your home page to add any special features and tags you desire. You will, of course, have to consult with your system administrator or lab assistant for instructions on how to load your home page on the Web server at your school.

HANDS-ON EXERCISE 1

Entering HTML Tags in Notepad

Objective: To create a WWW home page using basic HTML tags and Windows Notepad. Use Figure 7.8 as a guide in the exercise.

STEP 1: Create the Unformatted Document

➤ Log on to your system as you always do and start Windows Notepad. (You can generally find it in the Accessories icon or program list.)

➤ Type the text as shown in Figure 7.8a, substituting your name, headings, and other information where appropriate.

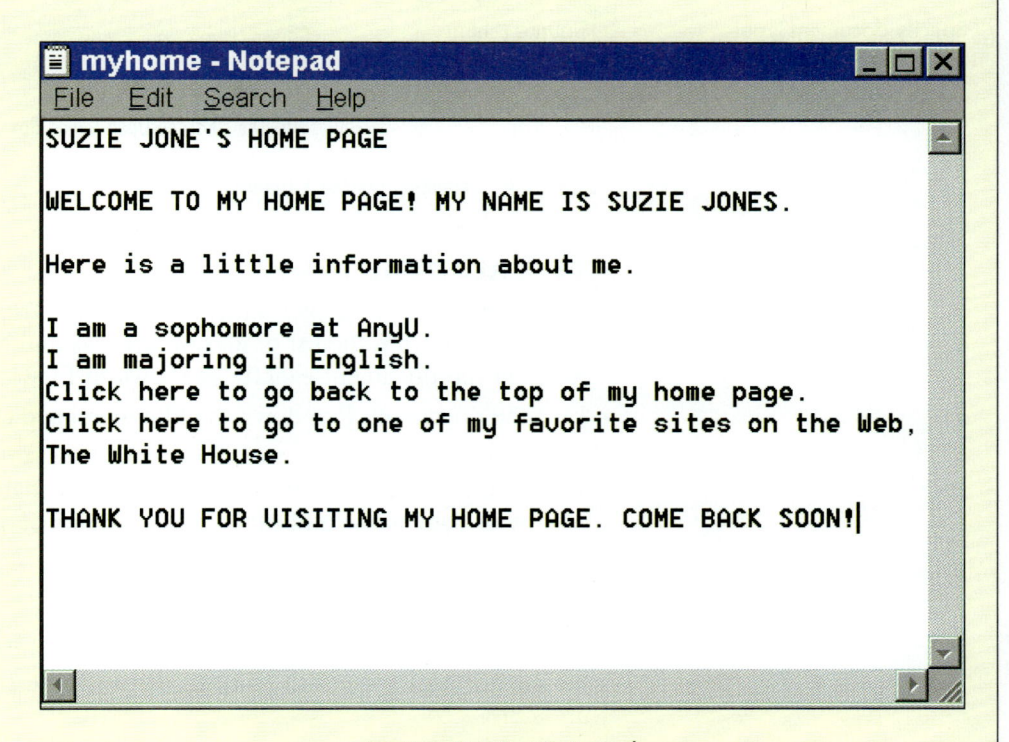

```
myhome - Notepad
File  Edit  Search  Help

SUZIE JONE'S HOME PAGE

WELCOME TO MY HOME PAGE! MY NAME IS SUZIE JONES.

Here is a little information about me.

I am a sophomore at AnyU.
I am majoring in English.
Click here to go back to the top of my home page.
Click here to go to one of my favorite sites on the Web,
The White House.

THANK YOU FOR VISITING MY HOME PAGE. COME BACK SOON!
```

(a) Home Page Text in Notepad

FIGURE 7.8 Hands-on Exercise 1

➤ Select **Save** from the **File menu,** and save the document as **myhome.htm** on a disk in drive A:.

➤ Pull down the **File menu** a second time and click **Exit.** (You must exit from Notepad before you can look at it with your browser.)

➤ To see the document, start Netscape (or your browser) and select **Open File** from the **File menu.** The standard File Open dialog box shown in Figure 7.8b is displayed.

➤ Select the appropriate drive letter (drive A if you saved the HTML document on a floppy), and then select **myhome.htm** from whatever directory it is in. You will see your document in plain text as shown in Figure 7.8c. At this point it does not contain any bulleted lists, bookmarks, or links.

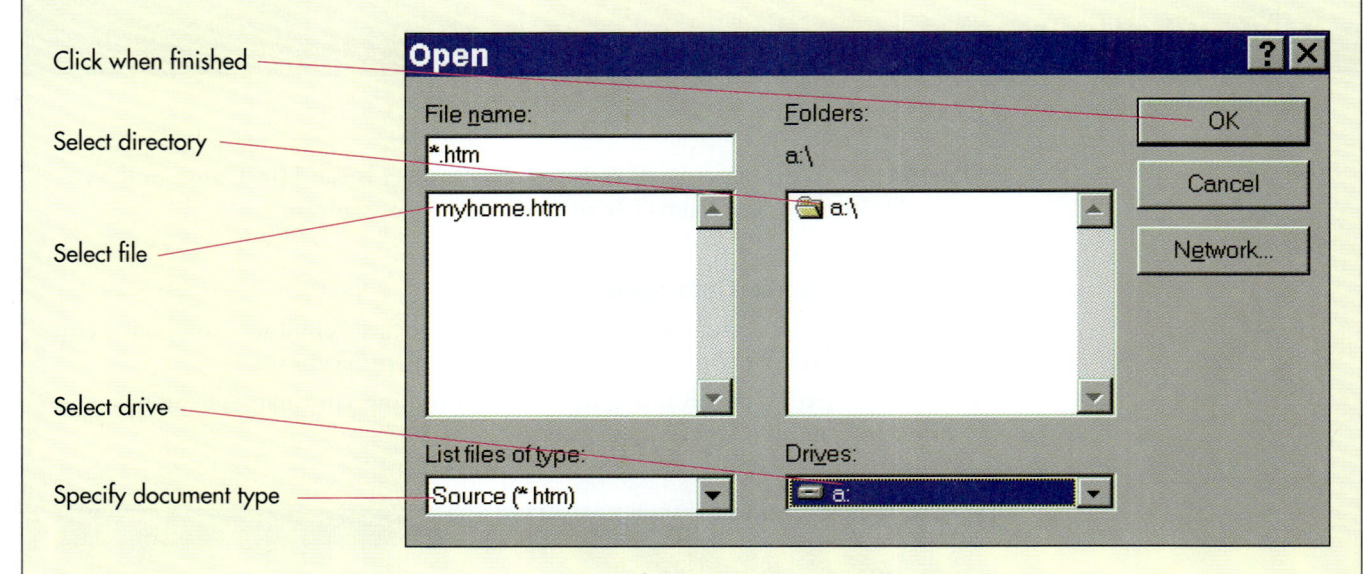

Click when finished
Select directory
Select file
Select drive
Specify document type

(b) The Netscape Open Dialog Box

FIGURE 7.8 Hands-on Exercise 1 (continued)

STEP 2: Add HTML Tags

➤ Switch back to Notepad and select **Open** from the **File menu.** Select **myhome.htm** from the list of files on drive A and click **OK.** Insert the HTML codes in the document exactly as shown in Figure 7.8d.

➤ Save the document. Pull down the **File menu** and click **Exit** to leave Notepad.

➤ Open the document in Netscape (or your browser) using the **Open File command** from the **File menu,** and verify that it matches that shown in Figure 7.8e, with your name and other information inserted.

STEP 3: Enhance the Home Page

➤ Using Notepad, open the file **myhome.htm.**

➤ Insert the named anchor (bookmark) tags around the welcome heading, and the anchor tags around the link to the welcome bookmark as shown in Figure 7.8f.

➤ Insert the horizontal rule tag below the first heading.

EXPLORING THE INTERNET

No document title; Netscape displays file name

Unformatted text

SUZIE JONE'S HOME PAGE WELCOME TO MY HOME PAGE! MY NAME IS SUZIE JONES. Here is a little information about me. I am a sophomore at AnyU. I am majoring in English. Click here to go back to the top of my home page. Click here to go to one of my favorite sites on the Web, The White House. THANK YOU FOR VISITING MY HOME PAGE. COME BACK SOON!

(c) Unformatted Document in Netscape

File name

Document title

Heading tags

Bulleted list

Numbered list

Heading tags

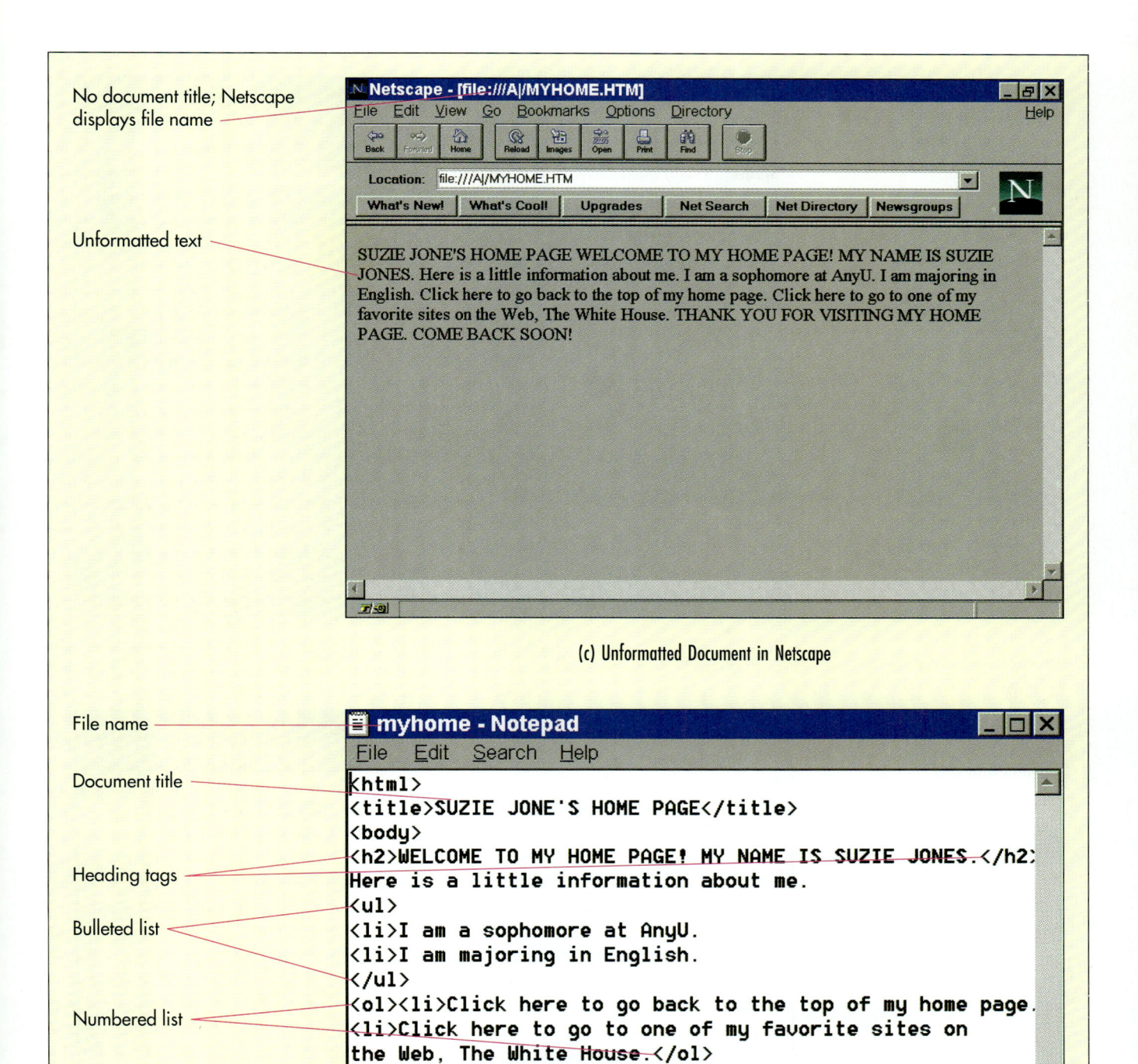

```
<html>
<title>SUZIE JONE'S HOME PAGE</title>
<body>
<h2>WELCOME TO MY HOME PAGE! MY NAME IS SUZIE JONES.</h2>
Here is a little information about me.
<ul>
<li>I am a sophomore at AnyU.
<li>I am majoring in English.
</ul>
<ol><li>Click here to go back to the top of my home page.
<li>Click here to go to one of my favorite sites on
the Web, The White House.</ol>
<h3>THANK YOU FOR VISITING MY HOME PAGE.
COME BACK SOON!</h3>
</body>
</html>
```

(d) Heading and List Tags

FIGURE 7.8 Hands-on Exercise 1 (continued)

PUBLISHING ON THE NET **239**

Document title

WELCOME TO MY HOME PAGE! MY NAME IS SUZIE JONES.

Here is a little information about me.

- I am a sophomore at AnyU.
- I am majoring in English.

1. Click here to go back to the top of my home page.
2. Click here to go to one of my favorite sites on the Web, The White House.

THANK YOU FOR VISITING MY HOME PAGE. COME BACK SOON!

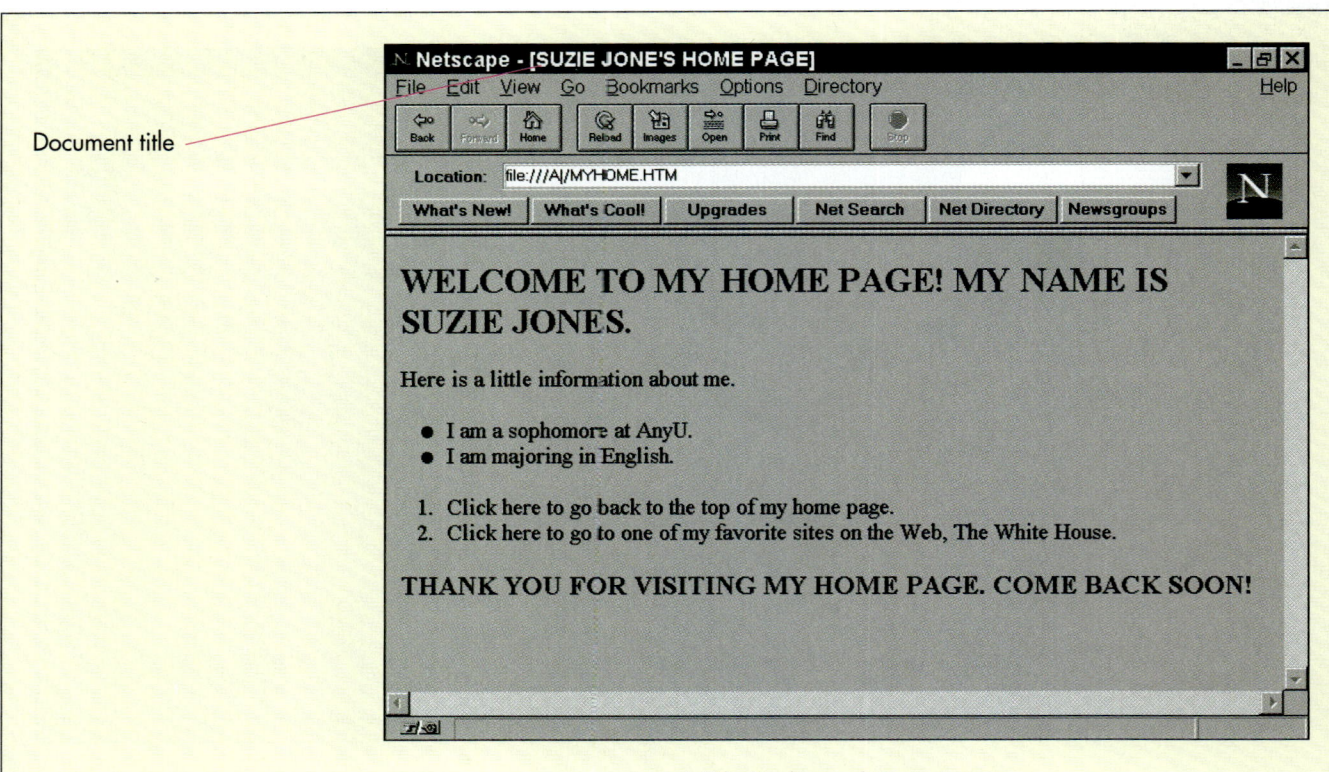

(e) The Headings and Lists in Netscape

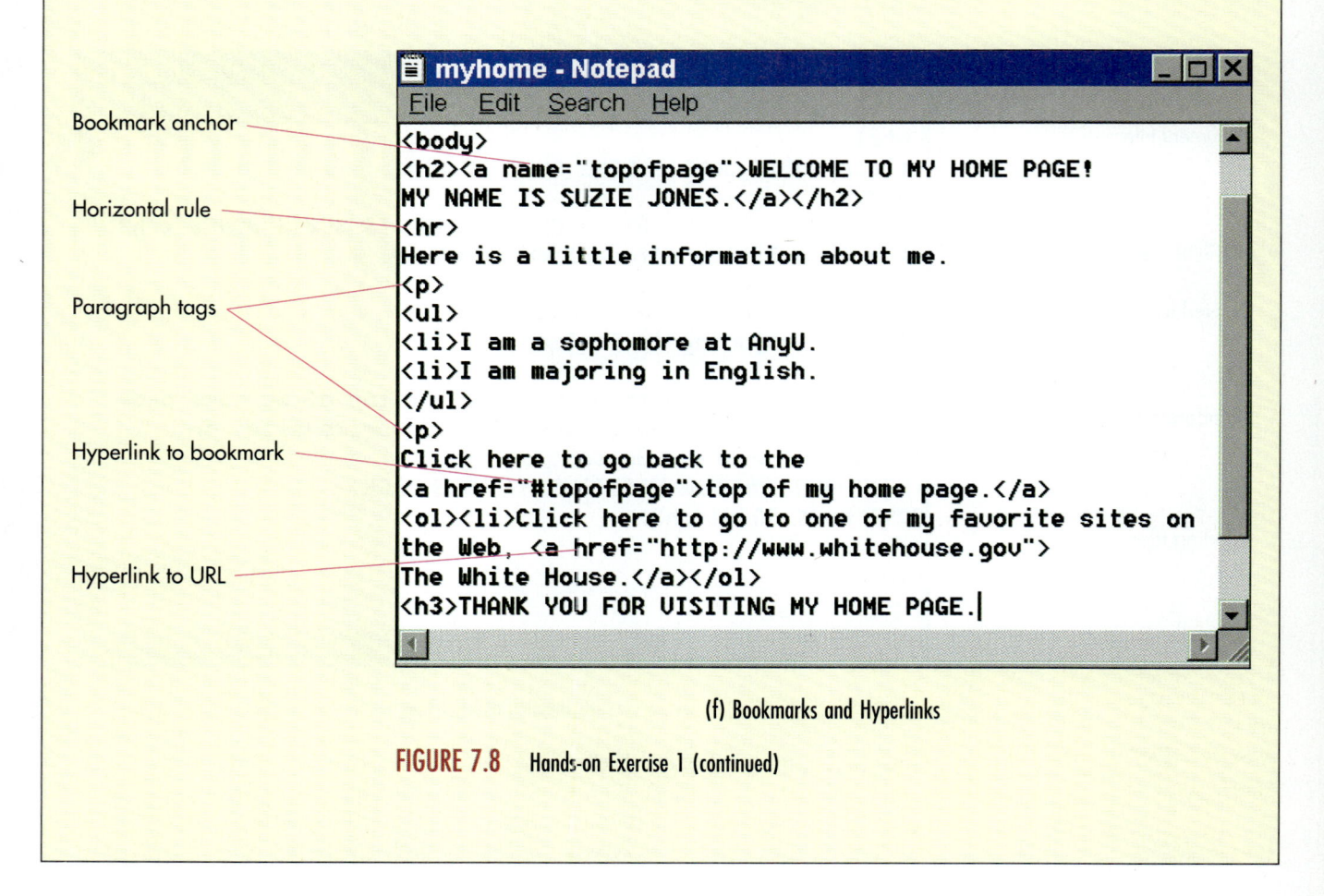

Bookmark anchor

Horizontal rule

Paragraph tags

Hyperlink to bookmark

Hyperlink to URL

```
<body>
<h2><a name="topofpage">WELCOME TO MY HOME PAGE!
MY NAME IS SUZIE JONES.</a></h2>
<hr>
Here is a little information about me.
<p>
<ul>
<li>I am a sophomore at AnyU.
<li>I am majoring in English.
</ul>
<p>
Click here to go back to the
<a href="#topofpage">top of my home page.</a>
<ol><li>Click here to go to one of my favorite sites on
the Web, <a href="http://www.whitehouse.gov">
The White House.</a></ol>
<h3>THANK YOU FOR VISITING MY HOME PAGE.
```

(f) Bookmarks and Hyperlinks

FIGURE 7.8   Hands-on Exercise 1 (continued)

> Add the anchor tag to the ordered list to link to one of your favorite sites. We linked to the White House home page, as shown in Figure 7.8f. Save and close the document.

> Open the document in Netscape (or your browser) using the **Open File command** from the **File menu**. It should look similar to Figure 7.8g.

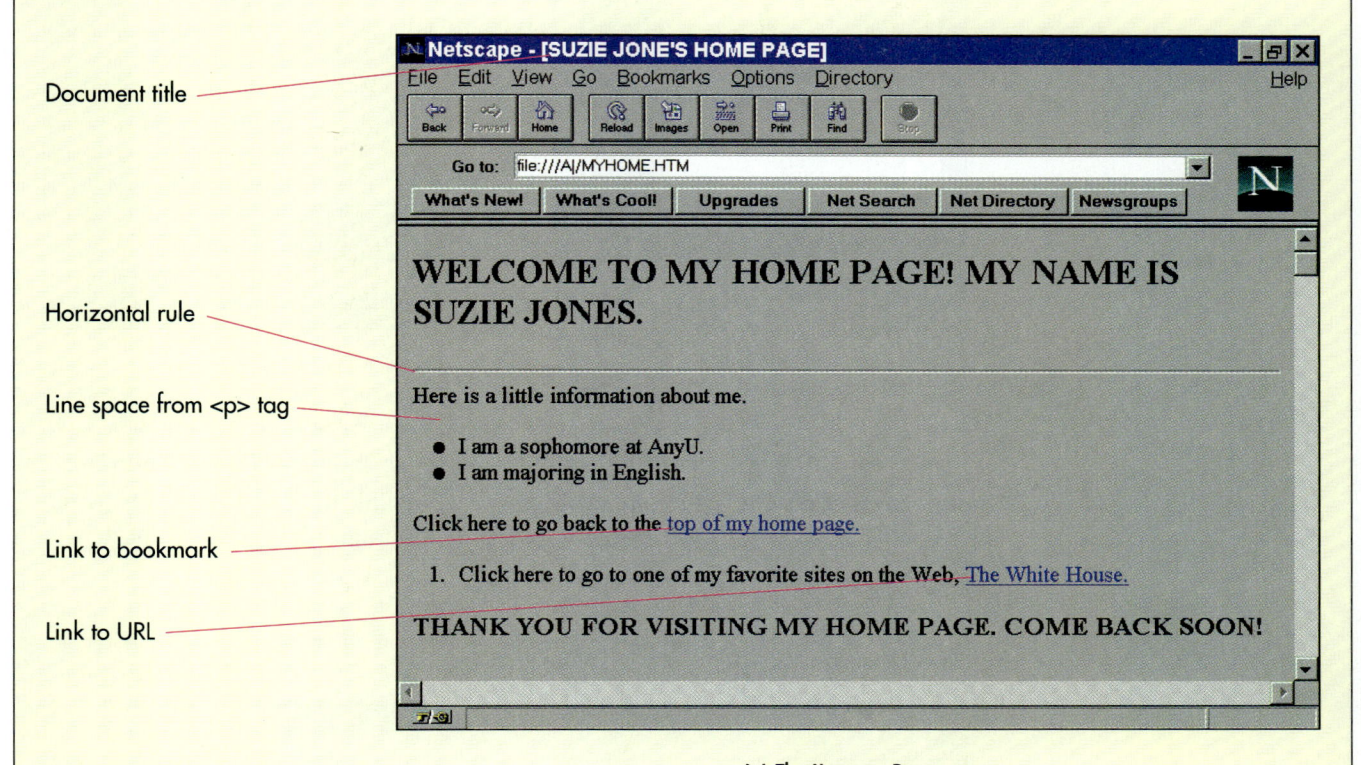

Labels on figure:
- Document title
- Horizontal rule
- Line space from <p> tag
- Link to bookmark
- Link to URL

(g) The Netscape Document

FIGURE 7.8   Hands-on Exercise 1 (continued)

STEP 4: Add a Graphic Image

> Before you can insert a GIF in your home page, you must download one from the Web.
> • Using Netscape or another browser, go to the URL **http://www.efn.org/images**.
> • Select one of the image files, then select the **Save As command** in the **File menu**. The Save As dialog box shown in Figure 7.8h is displayed.

> Select the same drive and directory on which you have saved the HTML home page file (in this case, drive A). Click **OK**. The graphic is downloaded to the directory.

> Open **myhome.htm** using Notepad.
> • Remove the tags you used to create the bulleted list of information about you. Separate the list items with the
 (for line break) tag as shown in Figure 7.8i.
> • Insert the HTML image tags as shown in Figure 7.8i, substituting the appropriate file name for your GIF images.

PUBLISHING ON THE NET   **241**

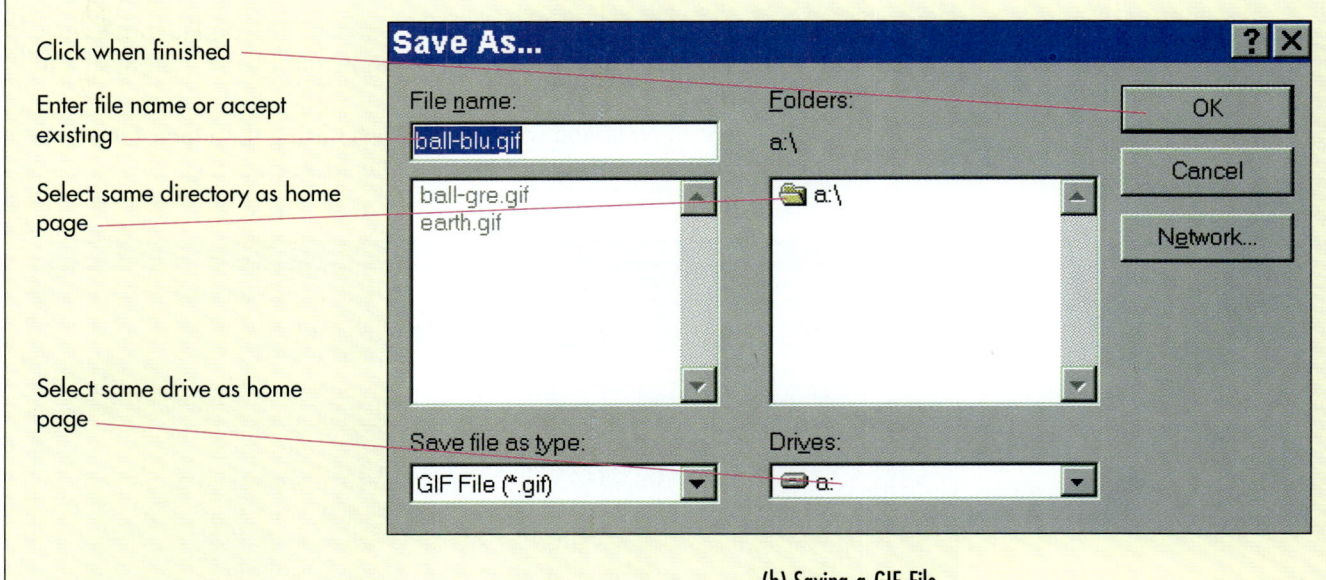

Click when finished
Enter file name or accept existing
Select same directory as home page
Select same drive as home page

(h) Saving a GIF File

- Create a bookmark at the top of the page as shown in Figure 7.8i.
- Using **Edit Cut** and **Edit Paste,** move your link to your bookmark to the bottom of your home page. Insert several paragraph tags ahead of it.
- Save the file and exit Notepad.

Line break tag

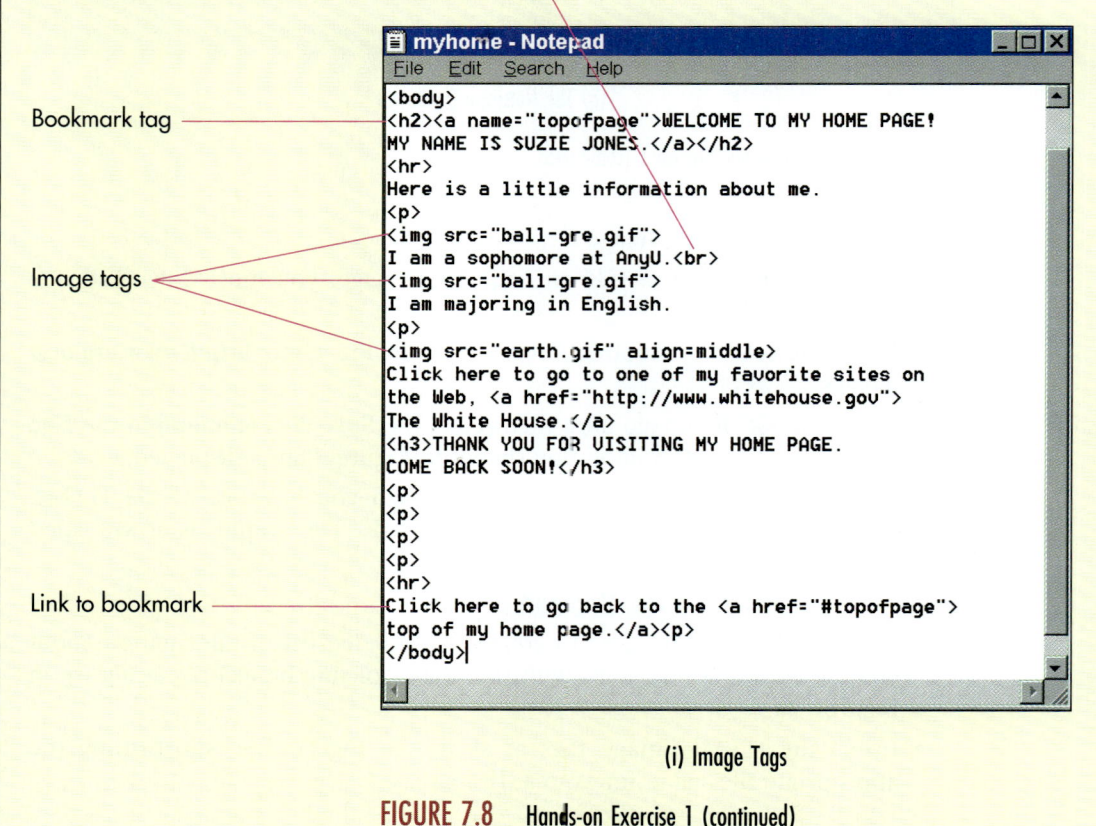

Bookmark tag

Image tags

Link to bookmark

```
<body>
<h2><a name="topofpage">WELCOME TO MY HOME PAGE!
MY NAME IS SUZIE JONES.</a></h2>
<hr>
Here is a little information about me.
<p>
<img src="ball-gre.gif">
I am a sophomore at AnyU.<br>
<img src="ball-gre.gif">
I am majoring in English.
<p>
<img src="earth.gif" align=middle>
Click here to go to one of my favorite sites on
the Web, <a href="http://www.whitehouse.gov">
The White House.</a>
<h3>THANK YOU FOR VISITING MY HOME PAGE.
COME BACK SOON!</h3>
<p>
<p>
<p>
<p>
<hr>
Click here to go back to the <a href="#topofpage">
top of my home page.</a><p>
</body>
```

(i) Image Tags

FIGURE 7.8 Hands-on Exercise 1 (continued)

242 EXPLORING THE INTERNET

STEP 5: Test Your Home Page

- Open the document in your browser with the **Open File command** from the **File Menu.** It should look like Figure 7.8j.
- Scroll down to the bottom of your home page, then click on the bookmark link. You should jump back to the top of the page.
- Click the **White House link.** You should jump to the White House.
- Make note of any links that do not work as anticipated. Return to Notepad and open the **myhome.htm** file. Make any necessary changes in the file, then save it. Test it again using your Web browser.
- See your instructor, lab assistant, or system administrator for information on how to load your home page on your Web server. (Be sure to save the home page file and the GIF files in the same directory.)

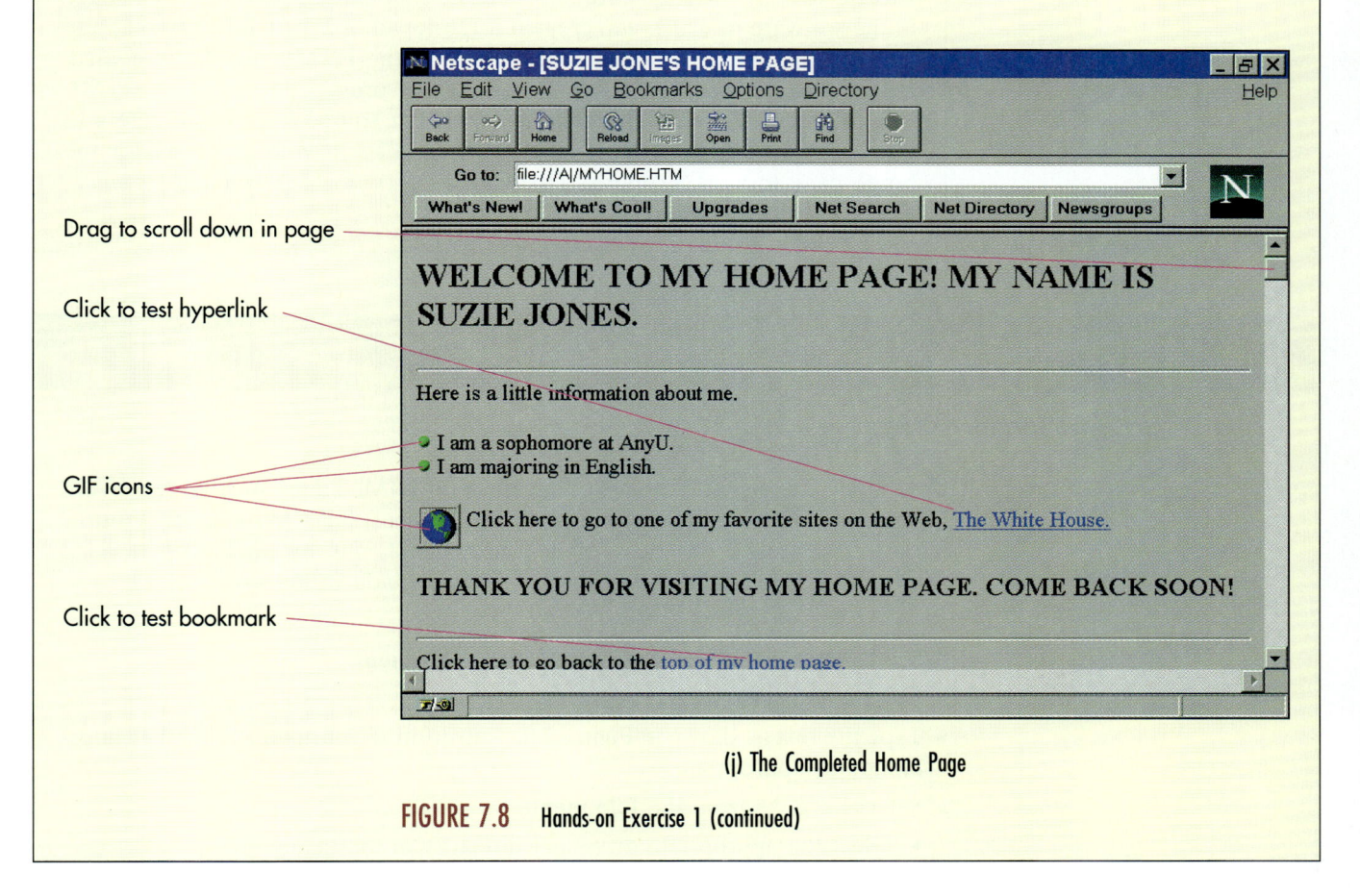

(j) The Completed Home Page

FIGURE 7.8   Hands-on Exercise 1 (continued)

USING AN HTML EDITOR

The process you just went through to create your home page using Notepad and inserting HTML tags was not difficult, just tedious. It requires you to check your work thoroughly to ensure that you have matching beginning and ending tags, and that you have added quotation marks and anchors in the right places.

There are, however, several HTML editors available to automate the process. These editors allow you to add HTML tags much as you select text and format it with a named style in your word processor. Word and WordPerfect each provide a companion product to help prepare home pages. You can also buy a package such as HotDog, which allows you to easily add special features, such as transparent images, to your home page. The following exercise demonstrates the process of creating a home page with the Internet Assistant, an add-on product to Microsoft Word. The concepts can be applied to any HTML editor.

USE WHAT'S AVAILABLE

Much of the work of designing great home pages has already been done, so why should you reinvent the wheel? As you cruise the Internet, make note of pages you consider particularly interesting. If there are design elements you think might be useful, select **Source** from the Netscape **View** menu to view the underlying code. Select the source of the effects you like, then press **Ctrl+C** to copy the source to the Windows clipboard. Open your home page in the software in which you created it (Notepad or Word, for example) and position the insertion point where you want the HTML tags to be copied. Select **Paste** from the Standard toolbar (or press **Ctrl+V**). The HTML source is copied into your home page. (If the source you copied refers to GIF or other files, you must have the same files in your directory for the home page to work properly. *Do not use other people's copyrighted material in your home page.*)

HANDS-ON EXERCISE 2

Using Microsoft Internet Assistant for Word

Objective: To create a home page using an HTML editor such as MS Word Internet Assistant. To perform the exercise, you must have MS Internet Assistant and Word installed on your system. The concepts can be applied to working with other HTML editors. Use Figure 7.9 as a guide in the exercise.

STEP 1: Create the Unformatted HTML Document.

➤ Log on and start Word.

➤ Type the text as shown in Figure 7.9a, substituting your name and other information as appropriate.

➤ Select **Save As** from the **File menu**.
- Select the appropriate drive and directory in the dialog box.
- Then select **HTML** in the **Save File as Type** drop-down list, shown in Figure 7.9b.
- Enter an appropriate file name in the **File Name text box** (we used **Pete-Home**).
- Click **OK**. The file is saved in HTML format, and new buttons appear on the Standard and Formatting toolbars, as shown in Figure 7.9c.

➤ Figures 7.9d and 7.9e indicate the functions of the various buttons on the Standard and Formatting toolbars. You will use several of these buttons as we progress through the exercise.

➤ Click on the **Switch to Web Browse button** (the eyeglasses) at the left end of the Formatting toolbar to look at the document using the Web Browse

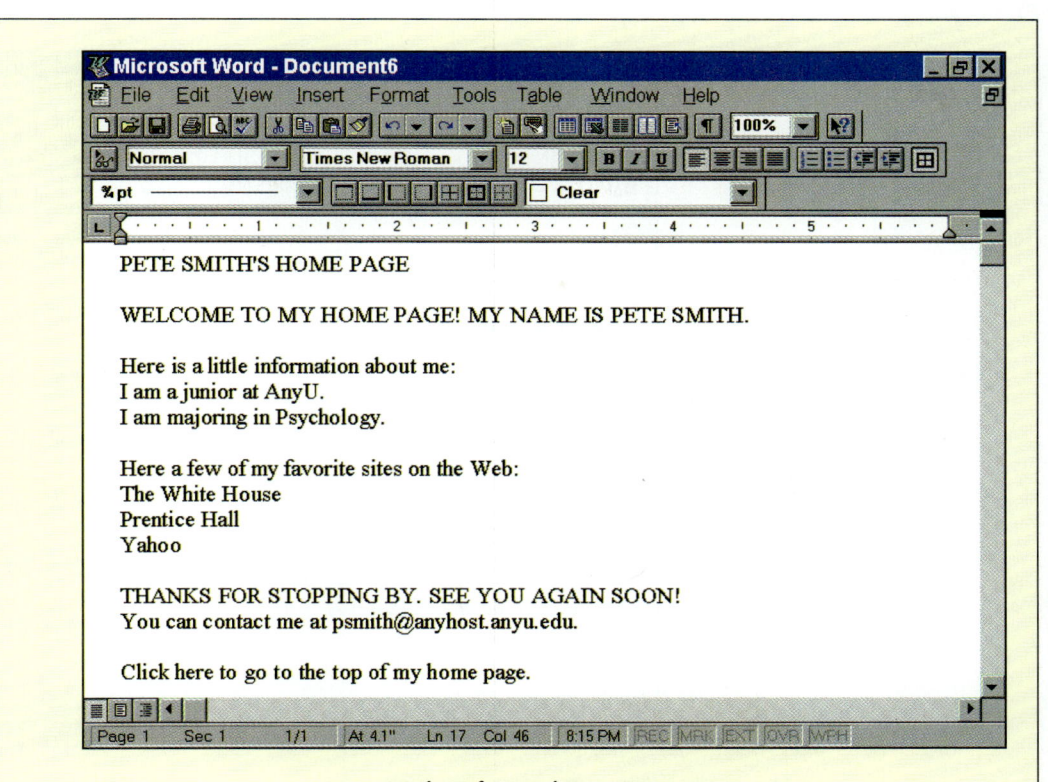

(a) The Unformatted Home Page Text

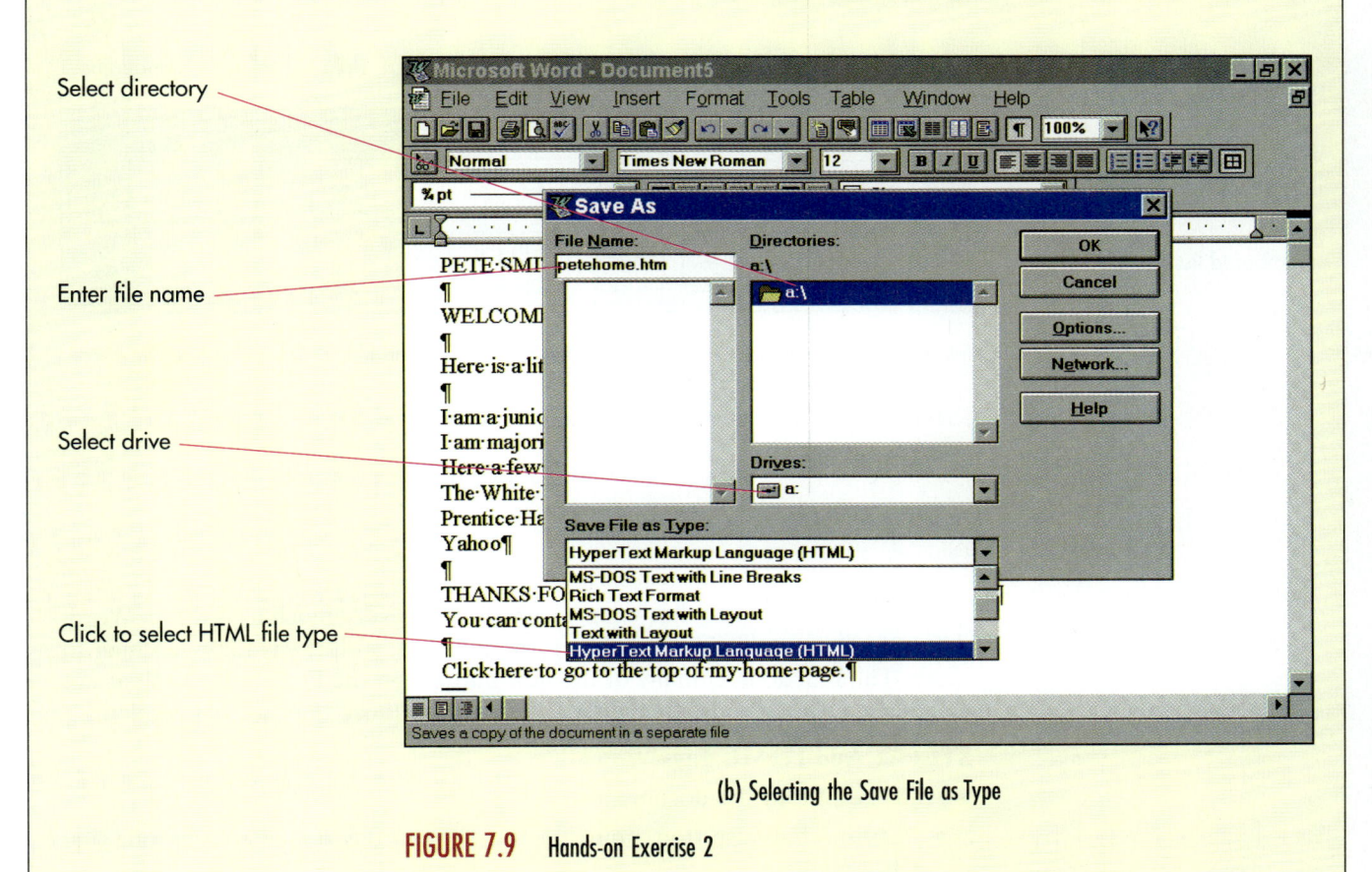

(b) Selecting the Save File as Type

FIGURE 7.9 Hands-on Exercise 2

PUBLISHING ON THE NET 245

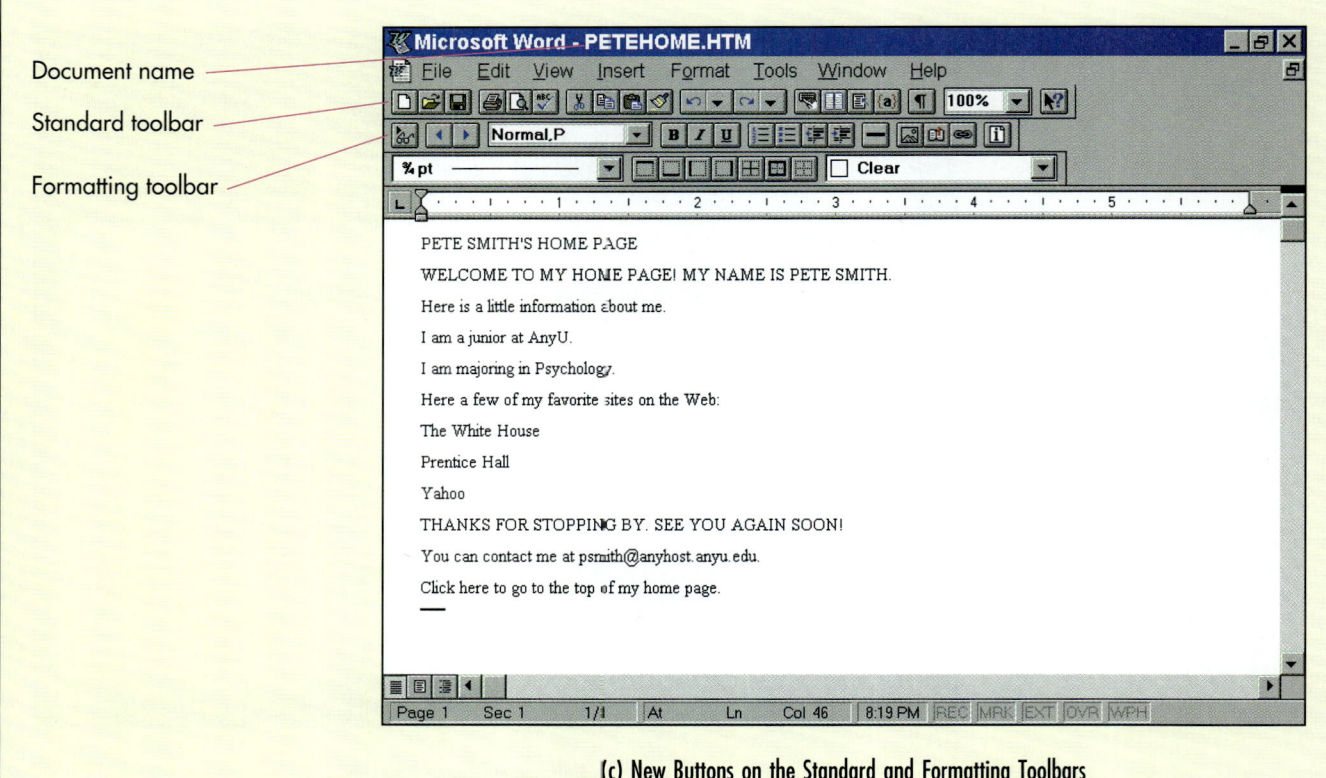

Document name
Standard toolbar
Formatting toolbar

PETE SMITH'S HOME PAGE
WELCOME TO MY HOME PAGE! MY NAME IS PETE SMITH.
Here is a little information about me.
I am a junior at AnyU.
I am majoring in Psychology.
Here a few of my favorite sites on the Web:
The White House
Prentice Hall
Yahoo
THANKS FOR STOPPING BY. SEE YOU AGAIN SOON!
You can contact me at psmith@anyhost.anyu.edu.
Click here to go to the top of my home page.

(c) New Buttons on the Standard and Formatting Toolbars

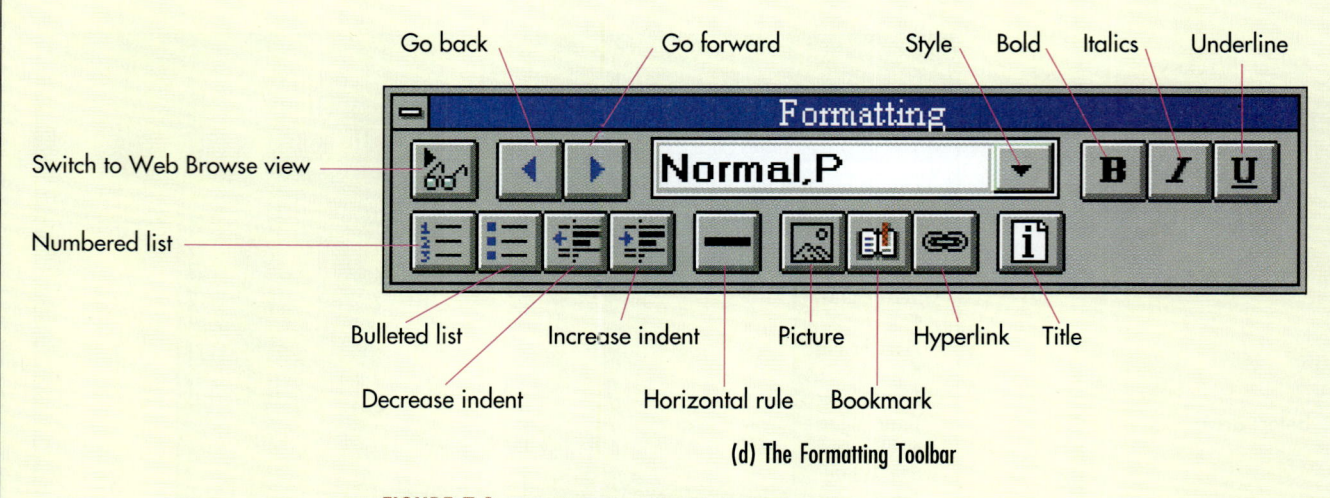

Go back — Go forward — Style — Bold — Italics — Underline
Switch to Web Browse view
Numbered list
Bulleted list — Increase indent — Picture — Hyperlink — Title
Decrease indent — Horizontal rule — Bookmark

(d) The Formatting Toolbar

FIGURE 7.9 Hands-on Exercise 2 (continued)

view. You will notice that your document looks very much as it did in Word. You have not added any HTML formatting yet, so there is really nothing to see. The functions of many of the new buttons on the Formatting toolbar are indicated on the buttons. Figure 7.9f identifies those that are not labeled.

STEP 2: Add HTML Tags

➤ Add the title to the document.
- Position the insertion point at the top of the document by pressing **Ctrl+Home.**
- Click the **Title button** on the Formatting toolbar to display the title dialog box shown in Figure 7.9g.

246 EXPLORING THE INTERNET

New Open Save Print Preview Find

Copy hyperlink | Para keep w/next | Para keep lines together | HTML hidden | Show/Hide | Zoom control | Help

(e) The Standard Toolbar

Switch to Edit view | Go back | Go forward | Stop

(f) The Formatting Toolbar in Web Browse View

Enter title | Click when finished

HTML Document Head Information

Title: Pete Smith's Home Page

OK Cancel Advanced... Help

(g) The Title Dialog Box

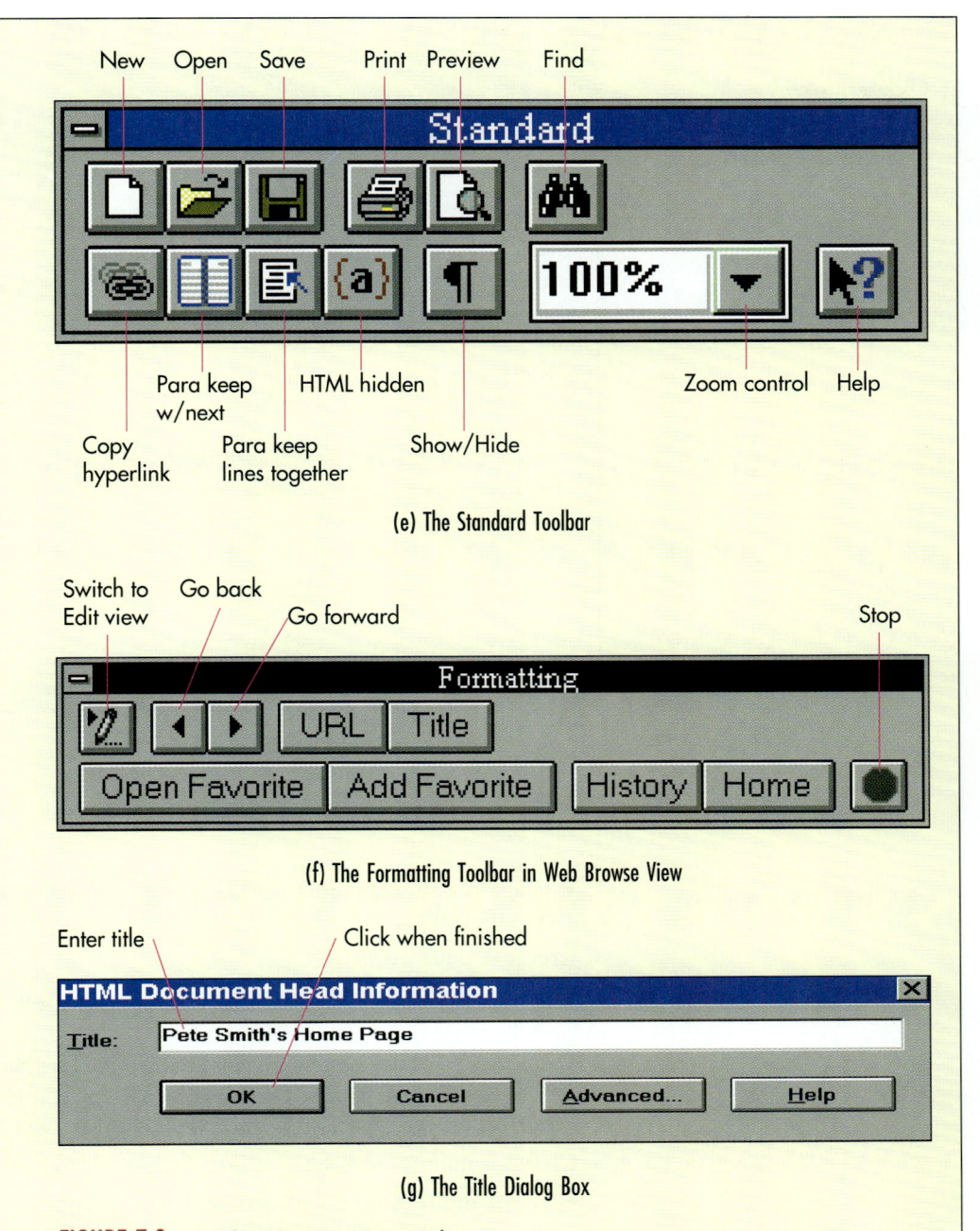

FIGURE 7.9 Hands-on Exercise 2 (continued)

- Enter the text you want to appear in the title bar of the home page window.
- Click **OK.** You will not see anything displayed on the screen, but the title will be added to the HTML source code for this home page. When you display the page with your browser, the title will appear in the title bar of the window.

➤ Add the heading tag.
  - Select the welcome text.
  - Click the **Down Arrow** next to the **Styles box** on the Formatting toolbar.
  - Scroll up in the list until you see the heading styles, as shown in Figure 7.9h.

PUBLISHING ON THE NET **247**

Click to display style list

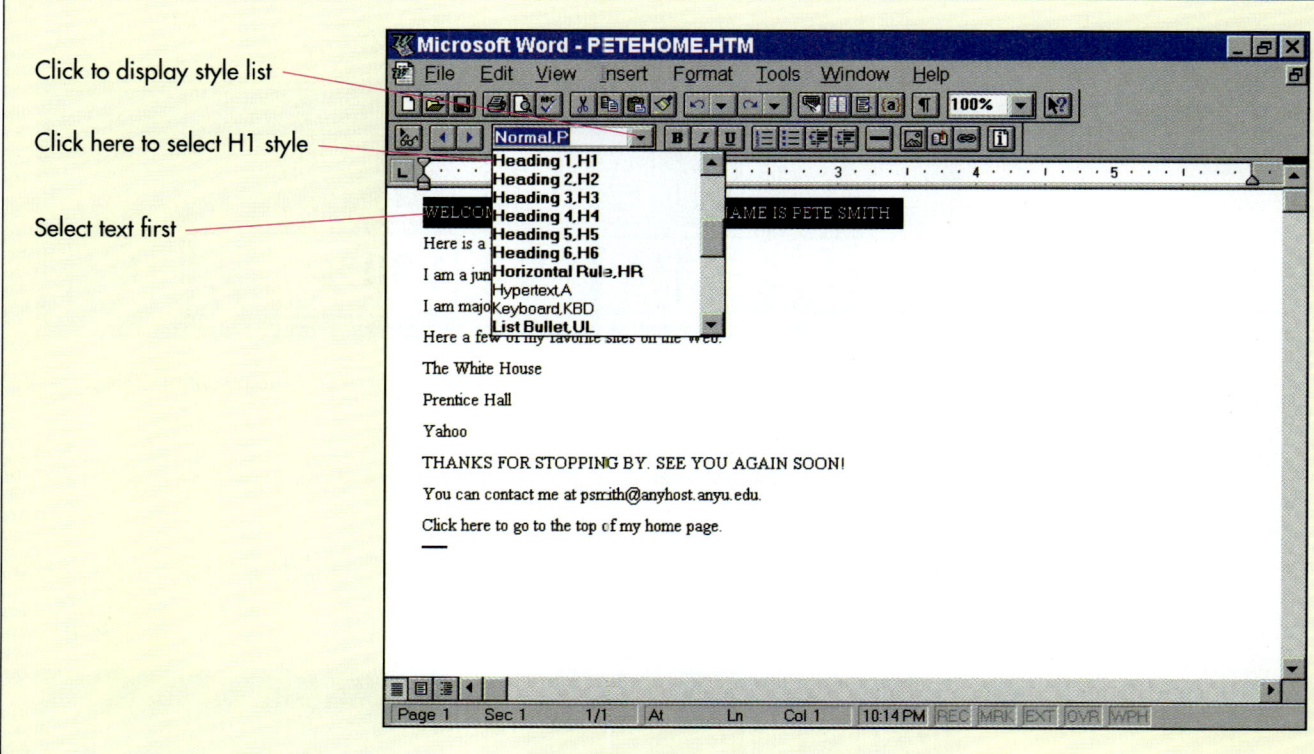

Click here to select H1 style

Select text first

(h) The Styles Drop-down List

FIGURE 7.9 Hands-on Exercise 2 (continued)

- Click on the **Heading 1, H1** option. Your welcome will be shown in enlarged type.
➤ Create a bulleted list.
  - Select the two lines of information about your year in school and your major.
  - Click the **Down Arrow** next to the **Styles box** on the Formatting toolbar, then select **List Bullet, UL** from the Styles list. (Or click the **Bulleted List button** on the Formatting toolbar.) The text will be shown with bullets.
➤ Create a numbered list.
  - Select the three lines of text that will be hyperlinks to your favorite Web sites.
  - Click the **Down Arrow** next to the **Styles box,** then select **List Number, OL** from the Styles list. (Or click the **Numbered List button** on the Formatting toolbar.) The text will be shown as a numbered list.
  - Click the **Save button** to save the file.

STEP 3: Set Up the Hyperlinks

➤ Now you are ready to set up the links to the Web sites.
  - Select the text for the **White House** link (or the first site in your favorite Web sites list). Click the **HyperLink button** to display the HyperLink <A> dialog box shown in Figure 7.9i.
  - Enter the URL for the site you selected, as shown in Figure 7.9j.
  - Click **OK.**

248 EXPLORING THE INTERNET

Selected text displayed here

(i) The HyperLink Dialog Box

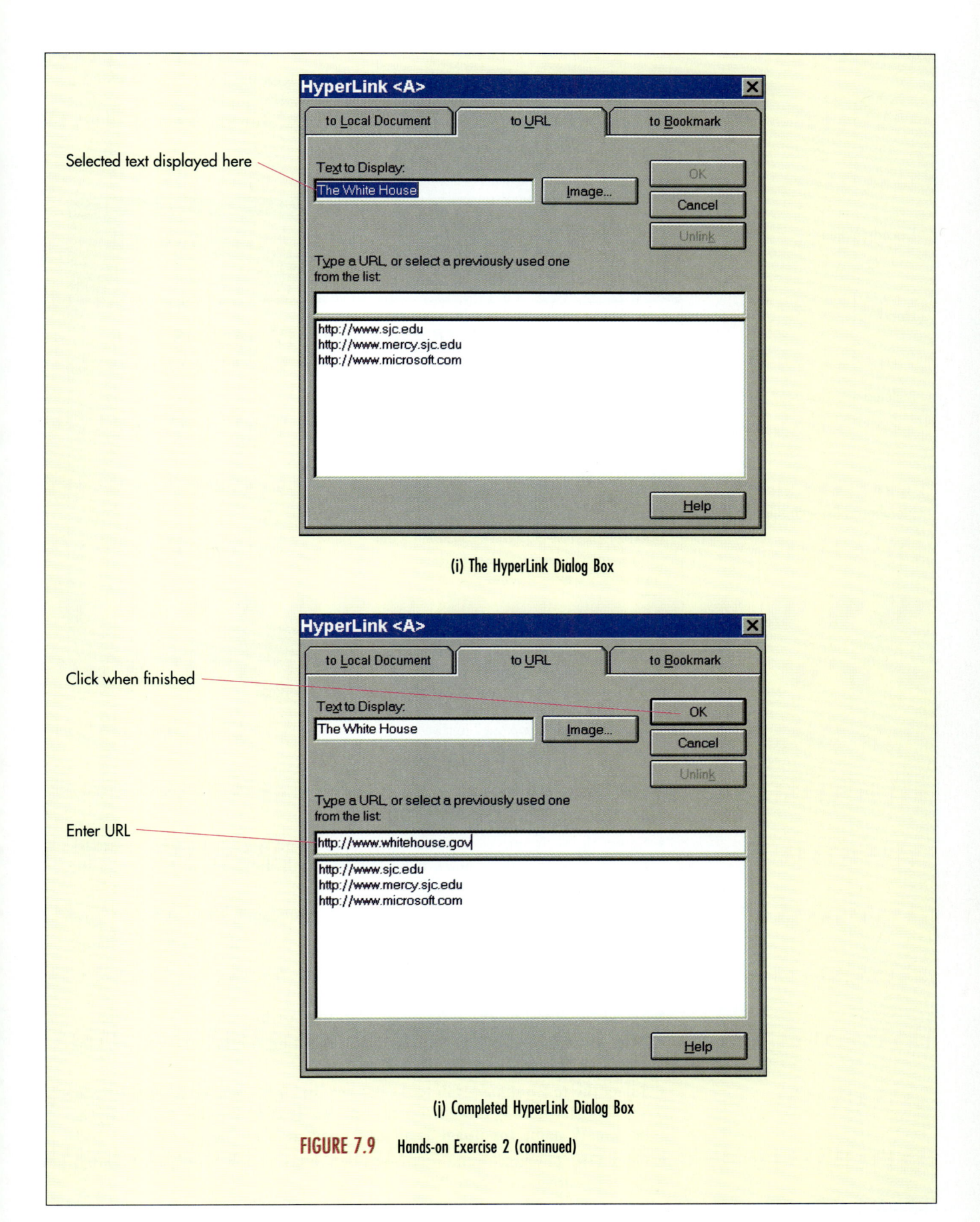

Click when finished

Enter URL

(j) Completed HyperLink Dialog Box

FIGURE 7.9 Hands-on Exercise 2 (continued)

- Continue selecting sites and entering their URLs until you have created a hyperlink for each of your favorite sites. When complete, your document should be similar to that shown in Figure 7.9k, with your customized list.

➤ Save your file.

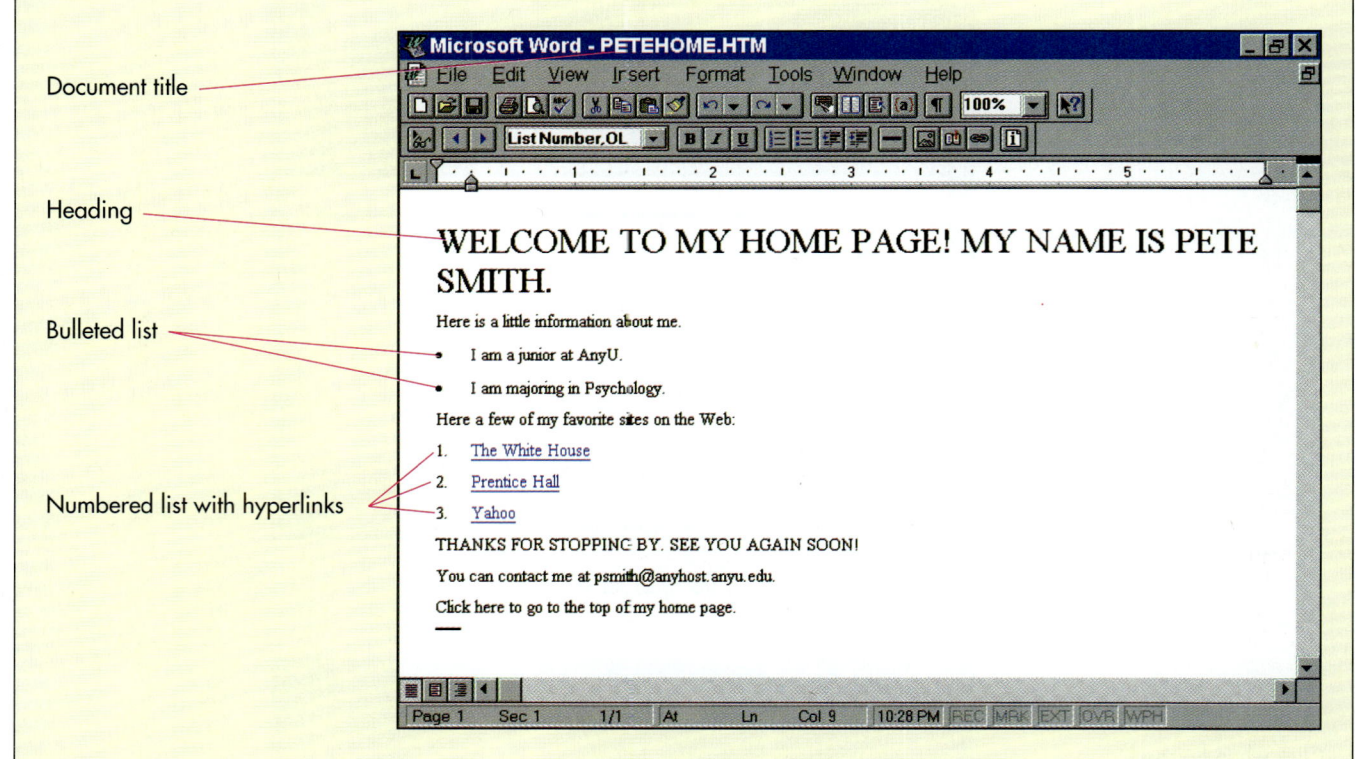

Document title — *Microsoft Word - PETEHOME.HTM* (title bar)

Heading — **WELCOME TO MY HOME PAGE! MY NAME IS PETE SMITH.**

Here is a little information about me.

Bulleted list
- I am a junior at AnyU.
- I am majoring in Psychology.

Here a few of my favorite sites on the Web:

Numbered list with hyperlinks
1. The White House
2. Prentice Hall
3. Yahoo

THANKS FOR STOPPING BY. SEE YOU AGAIN SOON!

You can contact me at psmith@anyhost.anyu.edu.

Click here to go to the top of my home page.

(k) The Completed Home Page in Netscape

FIGURE 7.9 Hands-on Exercise 2 (continued)

STEP 4: Create a Bookmark

➤ Mark the bookmarked text.
- Select the welcome text at the top of your home page. Click the **Bookmark button** or select **Bookmark** from the **Edit pull down menu** to display the dialog box shown in Figure 7.9l.
- Enter the bookmark name, in this case **topofpage,** in the text box.
- Click **Add.** The selected text is bookmarked. You will not see any change on the screen.

➤ Create the link to the bookmarked text.
- Select the text **top of my home page** in the last line of the home page.
- Click the **HyperLink button** on the Formatting toolbar. The HyperLink <A> dialog box appears.
- Select the **to Bookmark tab** to display the dialog box shown in Figure 7.9m. The selected text is already entered in the **Text to Display** text box. The bookmark name **topofpage** is already selected in the bookmark list.
- Click **OK.** The link to the topofpage bookmark is now visible in the home page, as shown in Figure 7.9n.

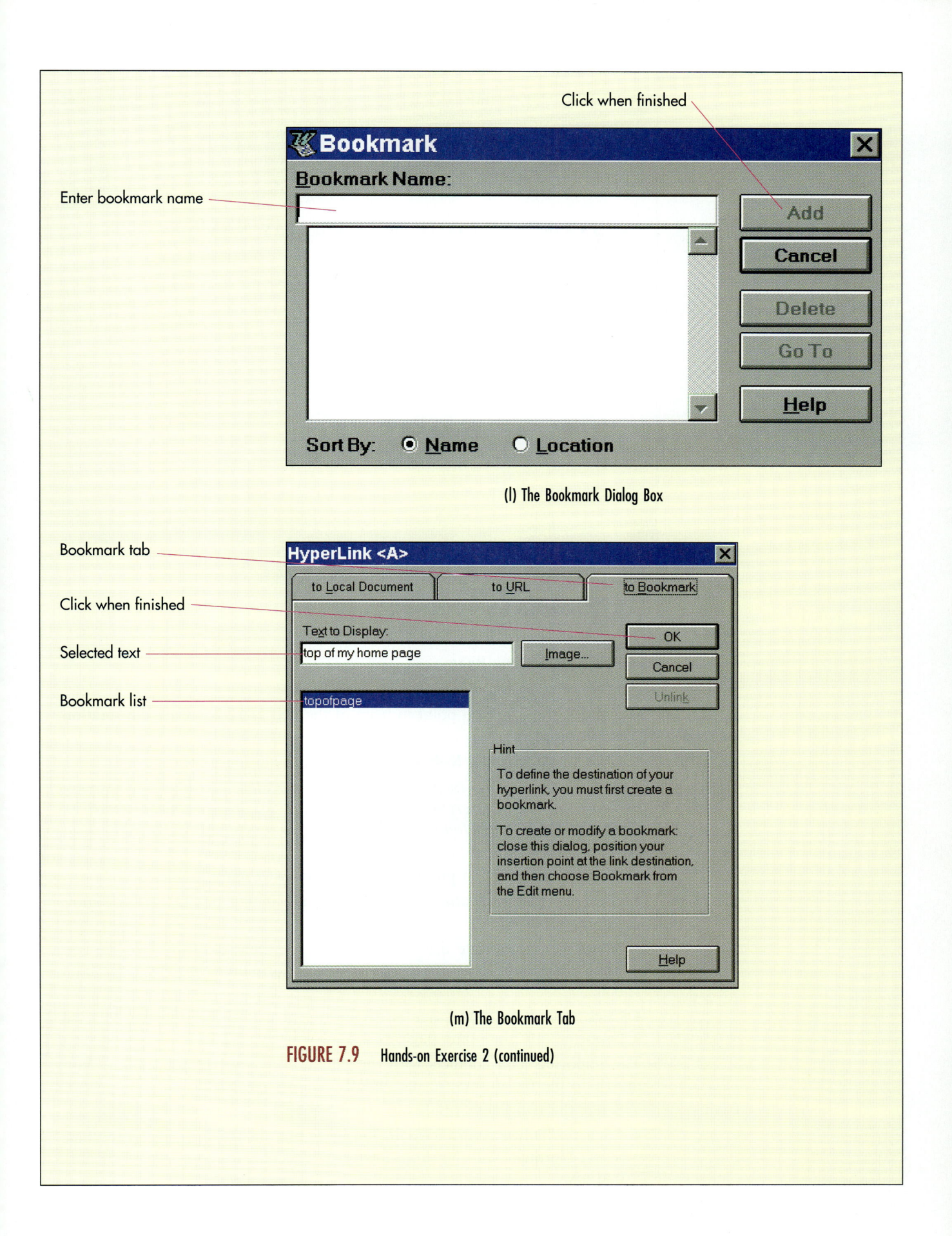

Enter bookmark name

Click when finished

(l) The Bookmark Dialog Box

Bookmark tab

Click when finished

Selected text

Bookmark list

(m) The Bookmark Tab

FIGURE 7.9 Hands-on Exercise 2 (continued)

Document title

Bookmark link

WELCOME TO MY HOME PAGE! MY NAME IS PETE SMITH.

Here is a little information about me.

- I am a junior at AnyU.
- I am majoring in Psychology.

Here a few of my favorite sites on the Web:

1. The White House
2. Prentice Hall
3. Yahoo

THANKS FOR STOPPING BY. SEE YOU AGAIN SOON!

You can contact me at psmith@anyhost.anyu.edu.

Click here to go to the top of my home page.

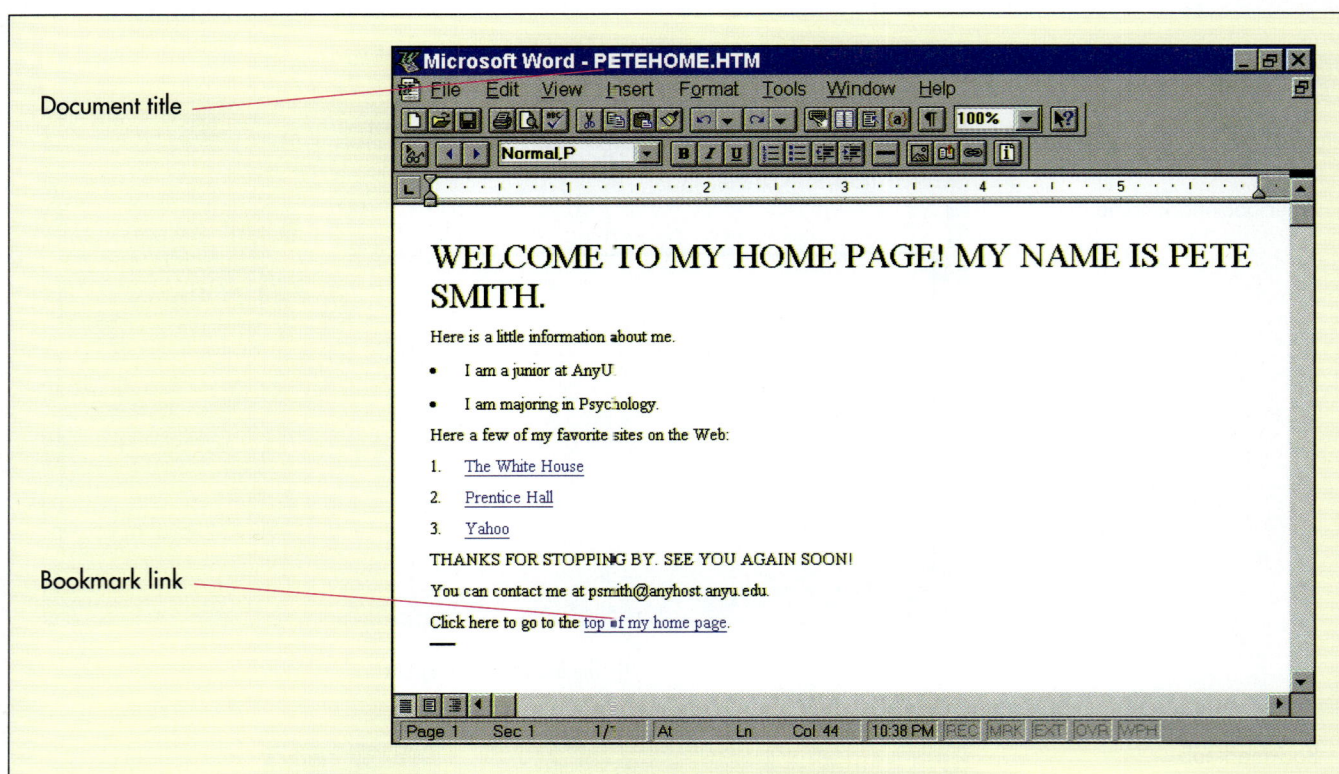

(n) The Bookmark Link in Netscape

FIGURE 7.9   Hands-on Exercise 2 (continued)

STEP 5: Enhance the Page

➤ Add a horizontal rule.
- Position the insertion point in front of the text **Here is a little information about me.**
- Click the **Horizontal Rule button** on the Formatting toolbar.

➤ Add GIF icons. *Note: In order to complete this step, you must have downloaded GIF files in Exercise 1. If you have not yet done so, please return to Exercise 1, step 4 and follow the instructions to download two or more icon files.*
- Position the insertion point in front of the text **I am a junior.**
- Click the **Picture button.** The Insert Picture dialog box shown in Figure 7.9o is displayed.
- Select the appropriate drive letter (Drive A), then select the GIF file you want to insert in front of your descriptive information. We chose the blue ball.
- Click **OK.** A brief message is displayed, indicating that the file is being imported into the home page.

➤ The imported icon conflicts with the bulleted list you created earlier. You must edit the file to remove the bullets.
- Select the two lines of bulleted text.
- Click the **Down Arrow** next to the **Style box** on the Formatting toolbar. Select **Normal** from the drop-down list. The bulleted lines return to normal text.

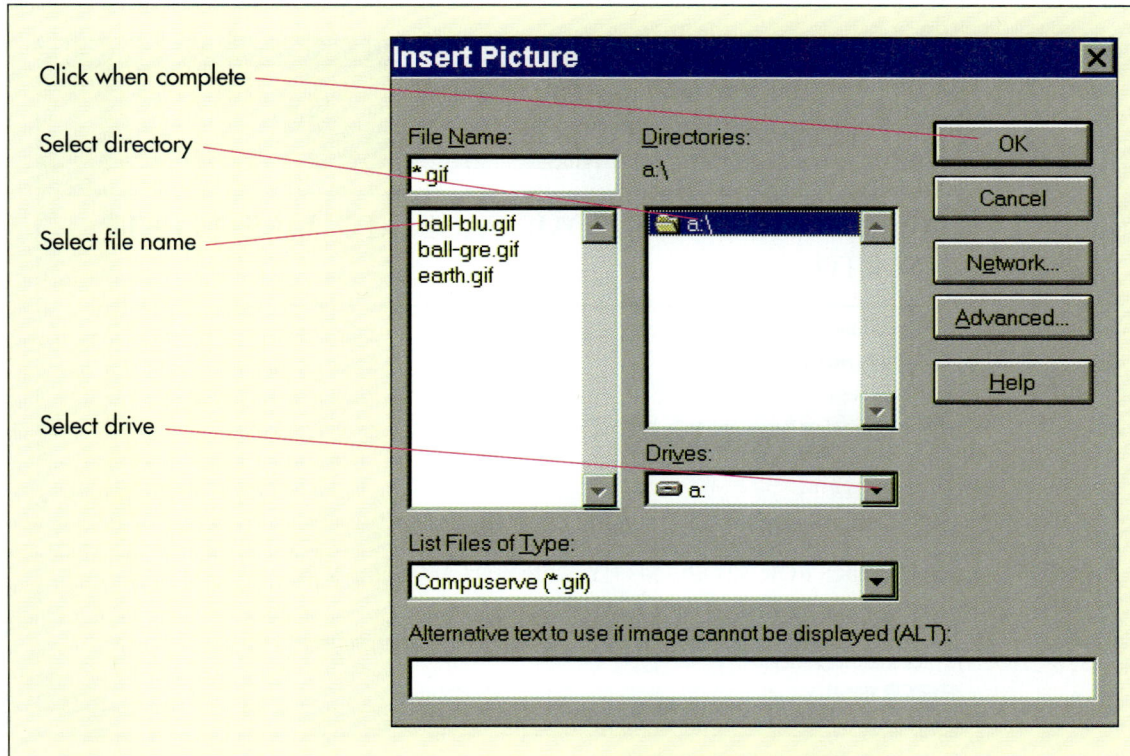

Click when complete
Select directory
Select file name
Select drive

(o) The Insert Picture Dialog Box

FIGURE 7.9 Hands-on Exercise 2 (continued)

- Position the insertion point between the GIF icon and the first character of the text describing your year in school. Press the **space bar** twice to insert a bit of white space between the icon and the text.
- Position the insertion point at the beginning of the text describing your major. Repeat the process to add another GIF icon in front of that line. Add white space as necessary.

➤ Create a new heading.
- Select the text **THANKS FOR STOPPING BY. SEE YOU AGAIN SOON!**
- Select the **Heading 3, H3** option from the list in the **Style pull-down menu** on the Formatting toolbar.
- Position the insertion point in front of the last line of text on the page.
- Click the **Horizontal Rule button** on the Formatting toolbar. Your home page should now look like the one shown in Figure 7.9p.

➤ Save and close the file.

STEP 6: Test Your Home Page in Netscape

➤ Open Netscape.
- Select **Open File** from the **File menu,** and select the **myhome2.htm** file from the dialog box (or the file name you used).
- Click **OK.** Your home page should resemble Figure 7.9q.
- Scroll down in the home page until you can see the link to return to the top of the page.

Horizontal rule

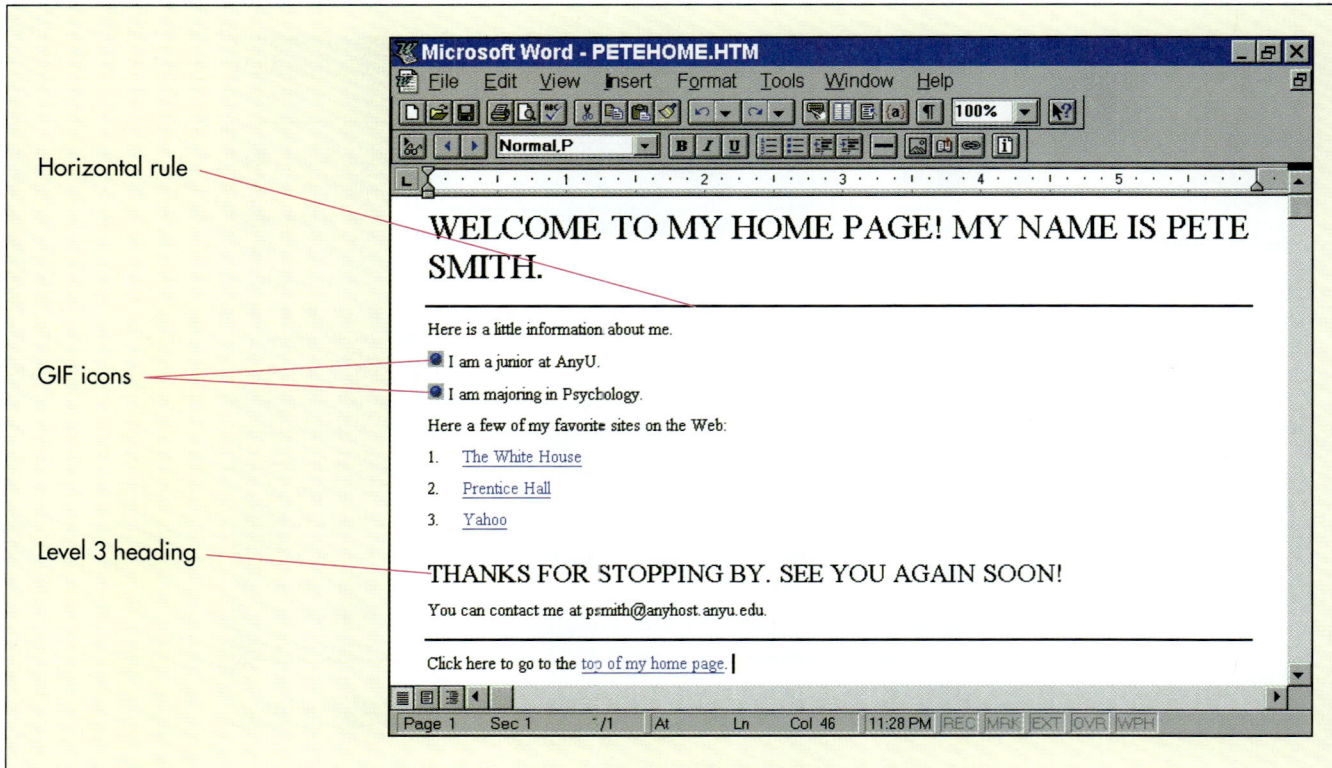

GIF icons

Level 3 heading

(p) Completed Home Page in Word

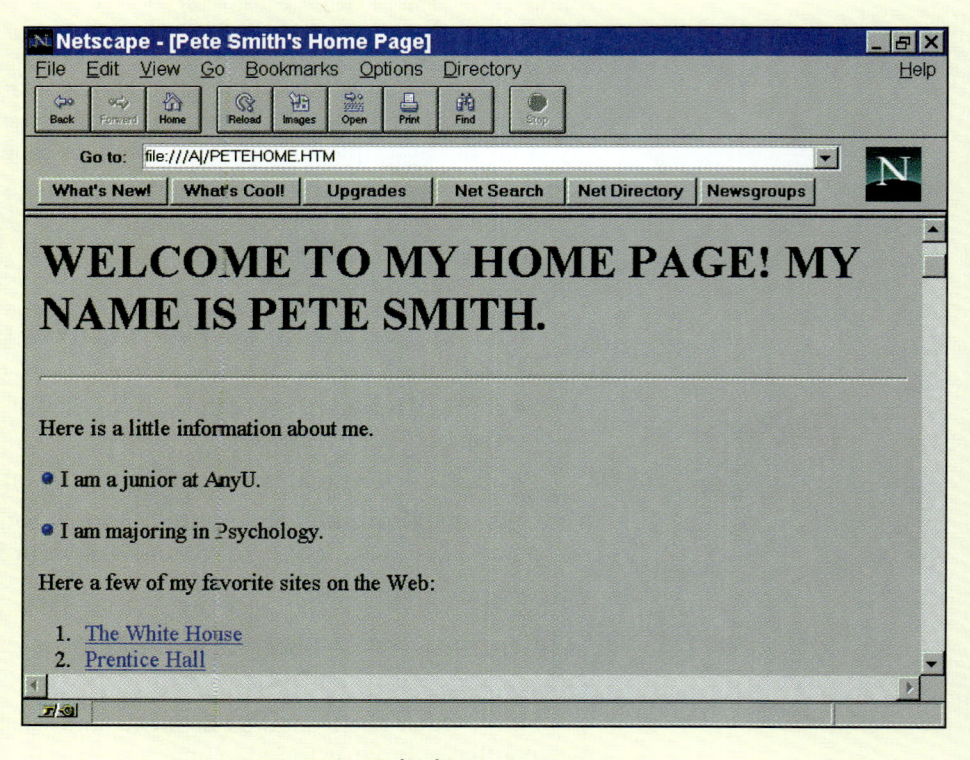

(q) Completed Home Page in Netscape

FIGURE 7.9 Hands-on Exercise 2 (continued)

254 EXPLORING THE INTERNET

> - Click the link. You should see the home page jump back to the top of the page. (The URL text box also shows the bookmark name.)
> - Click any of your links to other Web sites to determine if the links are working properly.
>
> ➤ Open the home page file in Word and make any necessary changes to fix links that are not working properly.
>
> ➤ Save and close the file.
>
> ➤ Return to Netscape and select the file again using the **Open File command** from the **File menu.** Repeat this process until your home page is satisfactory.
>
> ➤ See your instructor or lab assistant for instructions on how to add your home page to your college server. Be sure to copy the GIF files to the same directory as your home page.

SUMMARY

HTML files are the heart of the World Wide Web. Embedded HTML tags are used to format a document to display various effects when viewed with a Web browser. These tags can be manually inserted into a file using a text editor such as Notepad, or they can be created using an HTML editor such as the Internet Assistant for Word. The latter offers the ease of use associated with word processing styles.

In addition to formatting codes such as bold, italics, and underlining, HTML codes are used to establish links to other hypermedia resources, and to bookmarks within HTML files. Images can be included in a home page so they load with the home page, or they can be linked with an HTML reference tag. Design elements from various home pages can be copied to any other home page using the View Source and Copy/Paste commands.

KEY WORDS AND CONCEPTS

Anchor	HTML front end	Line break
Bookmark	HTML tags	Named anchor
GIF file	In-line image	Ordered list
HTML editor	Internet Assistant	Unordered list

MULTIPLE CHOICE

1. Which of the following programs automates the creation of HTML documents?
   (a) Notepad
   (b) Internet Assistant
   (c) Both (a) and (b)
   (d) Neither (a) nor (b)

2. All of the following tags require a matching code except:
   (a) <hr>
   (b) <h1>
   (c) <ul>
   (d) <a>

3. Which of the following is a valid bookmark?
   (a) <a HREF="AnyU/homepage.html">Click here for the AnyU home page<a/>
   (b) <a <img src="AnyU/picture.gif"</a>
   (c) <a name="Music Links">My Favorite Music Web Pages</a>
   (d) All of the above

4. Links may be created to:
   (a) A section of the current document
   (b) A bookmark in another document
   (c) A graphic file
   (d) All of the above

5. Which of the following file extensions denotes a graphics file?
   (a) .HTML
   (b) .DOC
   (c) .GIF
   (d) None of the above

6. You can create a link to a file:
   (a) In the same directory as the home page
   (b) In a different directory on the same computer as the home page
   (c) On a different computer
   (d) All of the above

7. In which program are the effects of the HTML formatting codes in a document visible?
   (a) Notepad
   (b) Netscape
   (c) Both (a) and (b)
   (d) Neither (a) nor (b)

8. Which of the following codes creates a horizontal line across a page in an HTML document?
   (a) <hr>
   (b) <hl>
   (c) <p>
   (d) <ul>

9. Which of the following HTML tags would you most likely use for the highest-level heading an a document?
   (a) <hr>
   (b) <h1>
   (c) <h6>
   (d) <ul>

10. Which of the following menu options allows you to see the HTML tags in a Web document?
    (a) File Open
    (b) Options View Tags
    (c) View Source
    (d) Go HTML

11. If you do not include a path in an anchor, where does Netscape assume the referenced document is?
    (a) In the root of the Internet server on which your document is stored
    (b) In the /pub directory of your Internet server
    (c) In the same directory as the current document
    (d) It is not possible to determine

12. Which of the following is required to jump to another section of an HTML document?
    (a) A bookmark
    (b) An ordered list of the document's contents
    (c) An anchored graphic image
    (d) All of the above

13. Suppose you are creating a Web page and include the HTML phrase <TITLE>MY FAVORITE WEB SITES<TITLE/> in the document. Where will the text enclosed in the <TITLE> </TITLE> tags appear when the page is displayed using a Web browser?
    (a) In the title bar
    (b) At the top of the document
    (c) Both (a) and (b)
    (d) Neither (a) nor (b)

14. Which of the following statements regarding HTML tags is true?
    (a) They can be inserted only by using an HTML editor
    (b) They cannot be nested
    (c) They cannot be viewed while using a Web browser
    (d) None of the above

15. Which HTML tag(s) is(are) required to create an unordered list?
    (a) <ul>
    (b) <ol>
    (c) <hr>
    (d) All of the above

ANSWERS

1. b	6. d	11. c
2. a	7. b	12. a
3. c	8. a	13. a
4. d	9. b	14. d
5. c	10. c	15. a

EXPLORING THE INTERNET

1. Use Figure 7.10 to match each HTML tag with its description; a given resource may be used more than once or not at all.

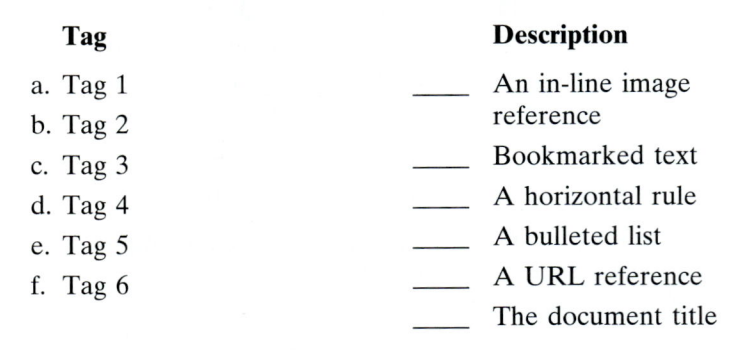

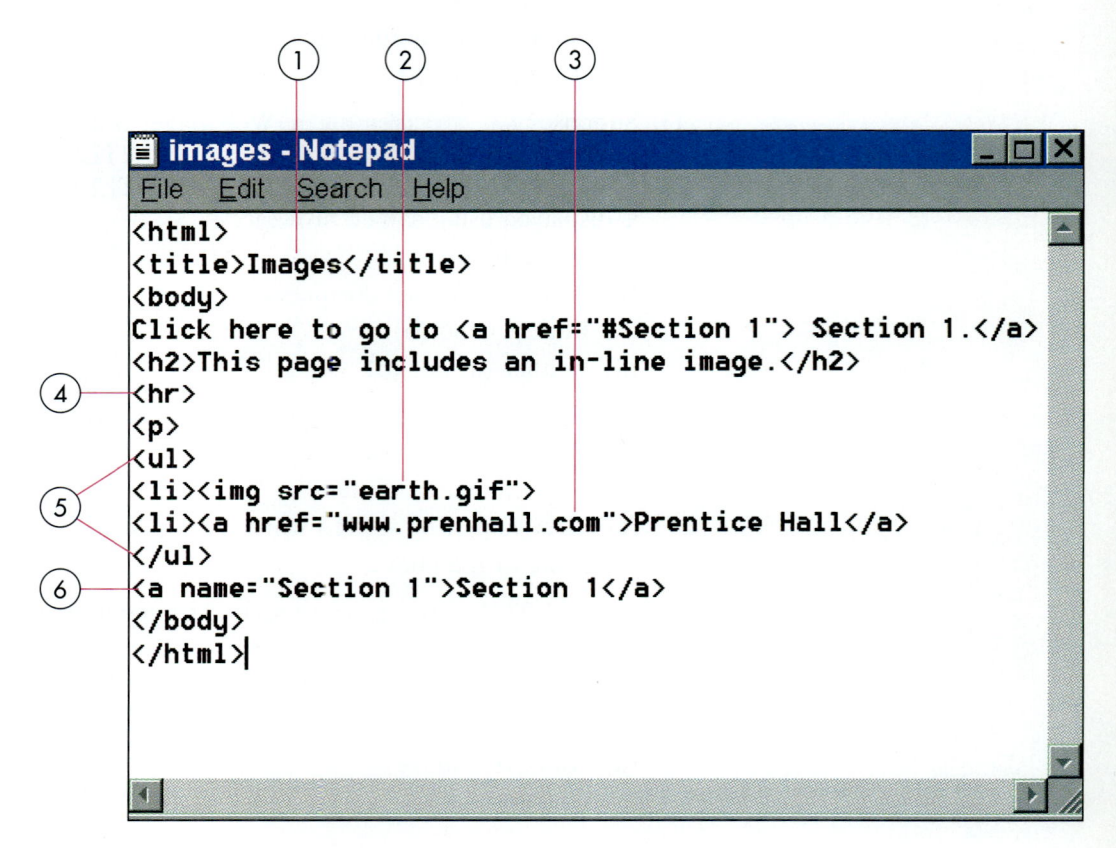

   Tag
   a. Tag 1
   b. Tag 2
   c. Tag 3
   d. Tag 4
   e. Tag 5
   f. Tag 6

   Description
   ____ An in-line image reference
   ____ Bookmarked text
   ____ A horizontal rule
   ____ A bulleted list
   ____ A URL reference
   ____ The document title

   ```
   <html>
   <title>Images</title>
   <body>
   Click here to go to <a href="#Section 1"> Section 1.</a>
   <h2>This page includes an in-line image.</h2>
   <hr>
   <p>
   <ul>
   <li><img src="earth.gif">
   <li><a href="www.prenhall.com">Prentice Hall</a>
   </ul>
   <a name="Section 1">Section 1</a>
   </body>
   </html>
   ```

   FIGURE 7.10   Screen for Exercise 1

2. **Get Help:** Read the online Help manual in your HTML editor. You will learn about additional HTML features and capabilities you can easily incorporate into your home page. Write a short report describing a feature not covered in the chapter.

3. The messages shown in Figure 7.11 appeared (or could have appeared) in conjunction with one of the hands-on exercises in this chapter. Explain the nature of each message and indicate the necessary corrective action (if any).

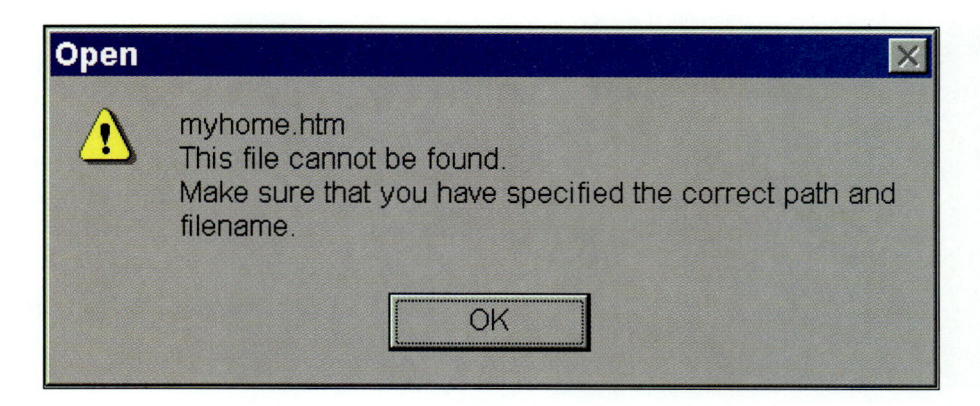

```
┌─────────────────────────────────────────────┐
│ Open                                    [X] │
├─────────────────────────────────────────────┤
│                                             │
│  ⚠  myhome.htm                              │
│     This file cannot be found.              │
│     Make sure that you have specified the   │
│     correct path and filename.              │
│                                             │
│              ┌────────┐                     │
│              │   OK   │                     │
│              └────────┘                     │
└─────────────────────────────────────────────┘
```

(a) Message 1

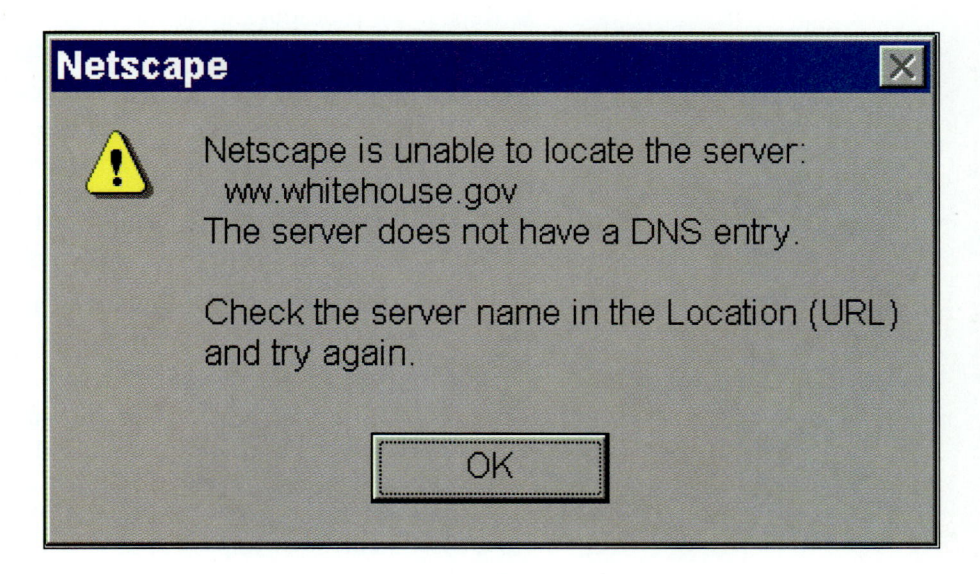

```
┌─────────────────────────────────────────────┐
│ Netscape                                [X] │
├─────────────────────────────────────────────┤
│                                             │
│  ⚠  Netscape is unable to locate the server:│
│     ww.whitehouse.gov                       │
│     The server does not have a DNS entry.   │
│                                             │
│     Check the server name in the Location   │
│     (URL) and try again.                    │
│                                             │
│              ┌────────┐                     │
│              │   OK   │                     │
│              └────────┘                     │
└─────────────────────────────────────────────┘
```

(b) Message 2

FIGURE 7.11 Messages for Exploring the Internet Exercise 3

4. **Discover HTML 3:** The current standard for HTML software is HTML 2. This standard specifies for software developers what HTML features and functions they should incorporate in their products. As discussed in the chapter, not all features are fully implemented by all browsers, and some browsers incorporate features not included in the standard, such as the <center> code. Search the Web for information about the HTML 3 standard, and learn how it extends HTML capabilities. Does the current release of Netscape incorporate these new features? Write a report on your findings.

Practice with HTML

1. **Change the Background Color:** You can change the background color of your home page by adding a color parameter to the <BODY> tag. The parameter takes the form: <BODY BGCOLOR="#rrggbb" where *rr* is the

amount of red in the background, *gg* is the amount of green, and *bb* is the amount of blue. Each color may range from 00 to HH, with each higher number representing a greater amount of the color. Adding color to the background may cause some of the text in the page to be unreadable (because it may not display well against the new background color.)

Research backgrounds on the Web. Use the following procedure to experiment with your home page:

- Open your home page file in Notepad.
- Edit the <BODY> tag to show the command <body bgcolor= "FFFFFF">.
- Save and close the file.
- Open the file in Netscape using the Open File command from the File menu. Your background should show as white.
- Repeat the procedure using the color tag <body bgcolor="CCFFFF">. This should show your background as light blue.

2. Forms in HTML Documents: You may have come across Web pages that allow you to enter information in a text box and submit that information to a Web server. Every time you use a Web search engine, for instance, you complete this step, entering your query in a *form*. Research how to include forms in Web pages by querying with a Web search engine, and by examining the HTML source at sites that use forms.

3. Search for GIF Icons: Use a Web search engine to find GIF icons. Use the Save As command in the File menu to download any you want to use into the same directory as your home page.

4. Explore HTML Editors: In the chapter we introduced the Internet Assistant for Word. However, there are many HTML editors available. Search the Web for information about other editors. Download one and evaluate it. What additional features does it offer? How easy is it to use? How much does it cost? Remember to pay for it, or delete it from your computer if you do not choose to purchase it.

Case Studies

Employment Opportunities

The Internet abounds with employment opportunities, help-wanted listings, and places to post your resume. Your home page reflects your skills and experience to the entire world, and represents an incredible opportunity never before available to college students. You can encourage prospective employers to visit your home page, and make contact with hundreds more companies than would otherwise be possible. Update your home page to include a link to your resume, and then surf the Net to find places to register it.

Personal Security

As in the real world, the virtual world of cyberspace harbors some strange people. For this reason, many experienced Internauts recommend against putting personal information on your home page. Write a short report indicating the pros and cons of placing personal information on your home page. Describe what you are willing to share on your home page, and indicate why you have made these choices.

Designer Home Pages

The earliest HTML standard, HTML 1, was concerned with getting the pages' contents displayed regardless of what platform (Mac or PC, for example) the browser was installed on. With advancements in the standards, and with the exploding popularity of the Web, more emphasis is being placed on designing hot Web sites. Develop some criteria you think make a Web site visually interesting. Search the Web for HTML design guidelines and incorporate them in your list. Write a report on your findings.

Home Pages off the Web

Many companies are discovering HTML documents for internal use. Pick two companies in two industries (hotel and toy manufacturing, for instance), and think of some uses they might have for hypertext documents. Write a two-page memo justifying to management why you should be given a summer internship to develop these documents.

APPENDIX A: REMOTE ACCESS TO THE INTERNET

OVERVIEW

The emergence of local area networks in no way eliminates the need for communication with remote computers or information services from PCs outside the network. Indeed, remote communication was common well before the advent of the PC and is growing exponentially in the era of the Information Superhighway.

When you are in your computer lab or using a networked PC elsewhere on campus, you are directly attached to a LAN, and from there to the campus backbone and your Internet host. The computer you use in the lab must have a network card that attaches the PC to the LAN and sends/receives signals to/from it. If you are running a GUI-based Web browser such as Netscape or Mosaic, your PC must have a version of TCP/IP on it in order to operate as a node on the Internet.

Communicating from home, however, requires you to purchase a modem in order to connect your PC over the telephone system to a remote computer. You also need the necessary software.

DIALING IN TO THE INTERNET

When you dial in from outside your campus LAN, your PC will attach to the telephone network and send signals over telephone lines to the campus network. Special hardware is required to make this connection. A modem connects your computer to the outside world, be it a remote computer thousands of miles away or your friend's computer a few blocks away. It is the interface between your computer and the telephone system. If you can dial a phone number, your modem can access the computer on the other end of that number, provided you have an authorized user ID and valid password, and provided the remote computer allows remote log on.

Once connected, you can enter commands on your computer and have them executed on the remote machine. You can generally download a file from the remote computer, and you may be able to upload a file to the remote computer. All data transmission goes through the modems of both the sending and receiving computers. Data passes from your computer to your modem, through the phone line to a modem on the other end, and finally to the remote computer. The process works in reverse when you receive data from the other computer. The process is depicted in Figure A-1.

The word modem is derived from two words, *modulate* and *demodulate*. Modulation is the process of converting the digital data processed by a computer to an analog signal that is used by the telephone. Demodulation is the opposite. On the transmitting end, a modem converts the binary data (1s and 0s) produced by the sending computer to a sound wave, which is sent over the telephone line. On the receiving end, the modem converts the sound wave from the telephone back to a digital signal, which is then forwarded to the receiving computer.

WHEN YOU USE A MODEM

1. The communication software in your computer sends a command to your modem to dial the phone number of the remote computer. The modem dials the number.

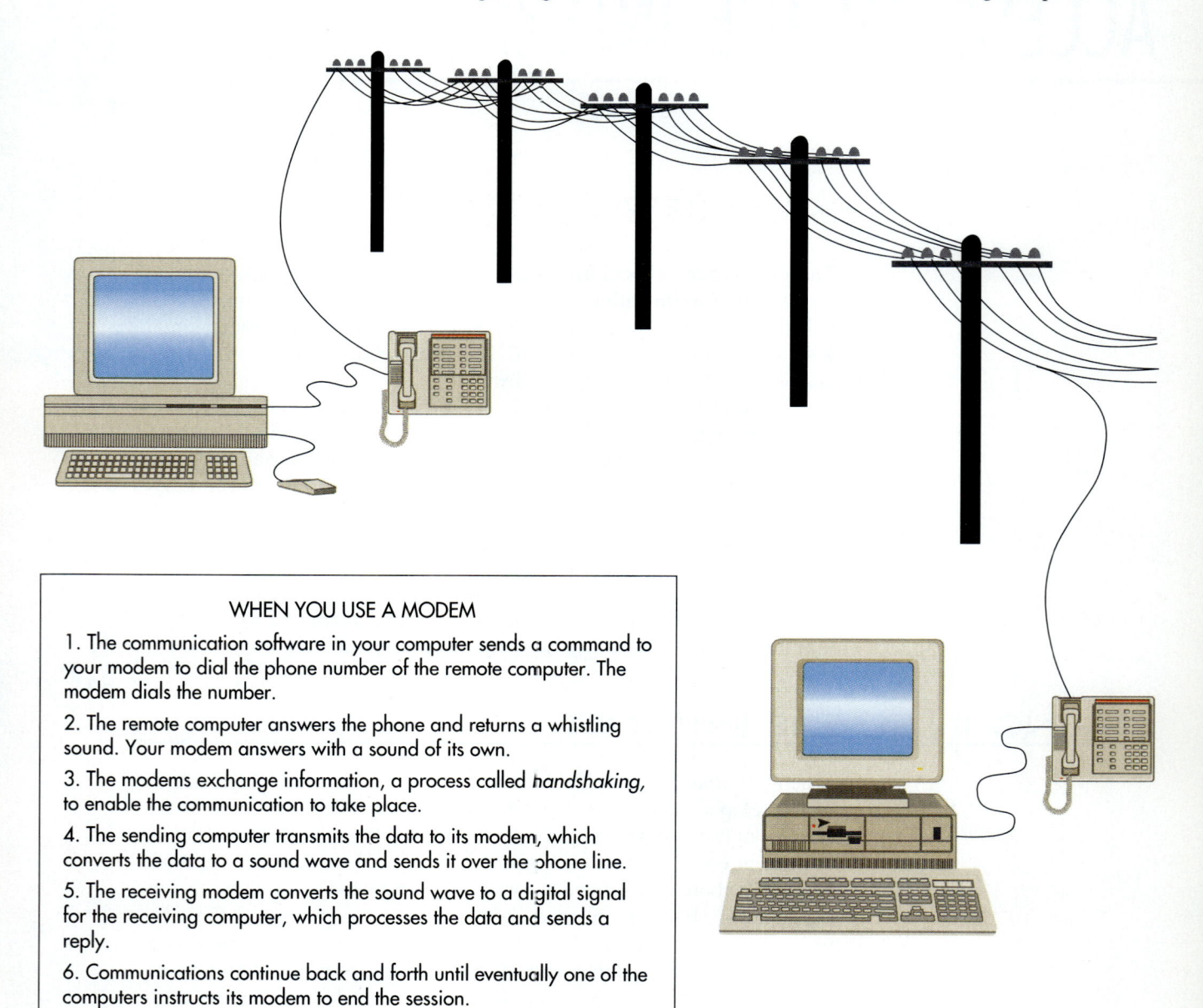

2. The remote computer answers the phone and returns a whistling sound. Your modem answers with a sound of its own.

3. The modems exchange information, a process called *handshaking*, to enable the communication to take place.

4. The sending computer transmits the data to its modem, which converts the data to a sound wave and sends it over the phone line.

5. The receiving modem converts the sound wave to a digital signal for the receiving computer, which processes the data and sends a reply.

6. Communications continue back and forth until eventually one of the computers instructs its modem to end the session.

FIGURE A.1   The Essence of Communication

You can purchase an internal modem that plugs directly into a slot on the system board of your PC, or you can purchase an external modem that attaches to the serial port on your computer. In either case you will want to purchase the fastest modem you can afford. A 14,400 bps (or 14.4 Kbps) modem (request a "14-dot-4" modem at the store) is the minimum standard in today's environment. We recommend, however, that you spend the additional money to purchase a 28.8 Kbps modem to use a graphic browser such as Netscape.

The HyperTerminal Accessory

A communications program is required in addition to a modem in order to connect to another computer. The communications software establishes the protocol that will be in effect between the two communicating devices. The HyperTerminal accessory is the communication program included in Windows 95 and is illustrated in Figure A-2.

The Connection Description dialog box in Figure A-2a appears the first time you use HyperTerminal. You enter a name for the connection (e.g., My School), choose an appropriate icon, then click the OK command button. Next you enter the phone number in the Phone Number properties sheet of Figure A-2b, then you dial the number in Figure A-2c. (The *70 that appears prior to the phone number is used to block call waiting so no one can call you and interrupt your HyperTerminal session.) Finally, you complete the connection and log on to the remote computer as shown in Figure A-2d.

The HyperTerminal accessory establishes a telnet session that lets you access Lynx, Pine, FTP, and other Unix programs as described in this book. Because the protocol does not support a graphics interface, you will not be able to use Netscape, Eudora, and other PC-based clients when you dial in with HyperTerminal or other similar communications software.

(a) Connection Dialog Box

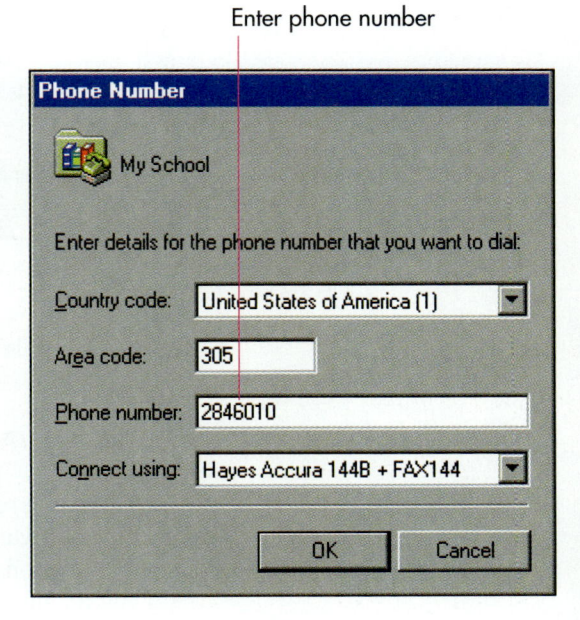

(b) Phone Number Properties Sheet

FIGURE A.2   The HyperTerminal Accessory

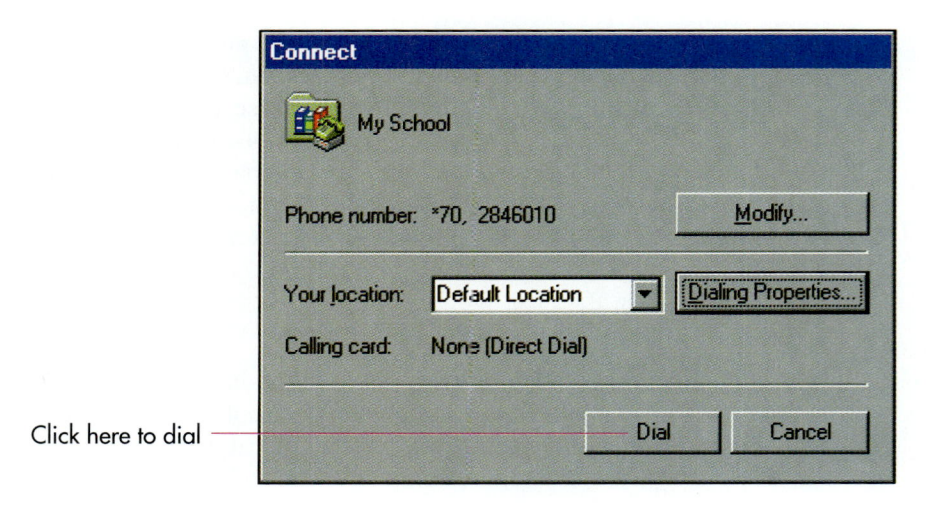

Click here to dial

(c) Dial the Number

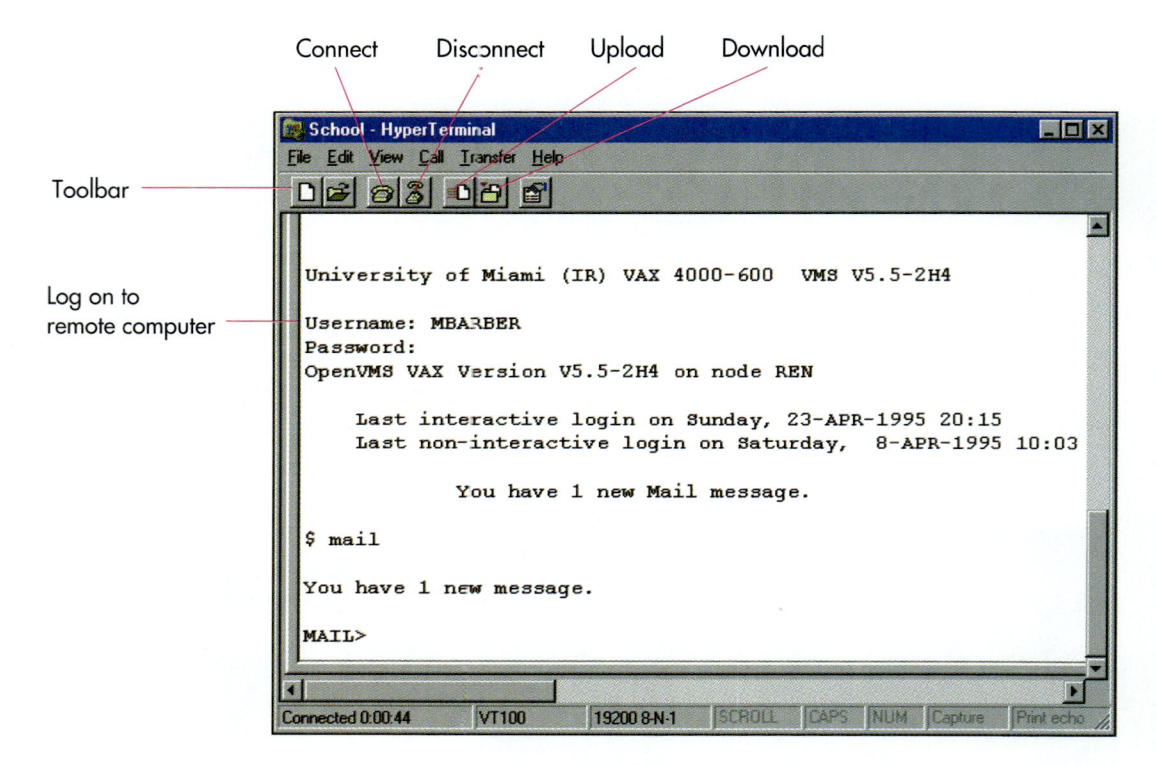

Connect   Disconnect   Upload   Download

Toolbar

Log on to remote computer

(d) Complete the Connection

FIGURE A.2   The HyperTerminal Accessory (continued)

Logging in with SLIP/PPP

The HyperTerminal accessory establishes a telnet session but does not let you run graphic software such as Netscape or Eudora. To do so you will have to install a special version of TCP/IP, known as SLIP or PPP on your PC. You will have to download the applications (Netscape, Eudora, and so on) and a SLIP/PPP program, such as Trumpet Winsock, from the Internet, then install and configure them to run properly on your PC. As a final step your LAN administrator must assign your PC an IP address in order to connect to your Internet host using SLIP/PPP.

All of this software is available on the Internet. Some of the sites you might try are shown in Table A-1. On the other hand, you can purchase the software as a complete Internet installation kit from several software vendors. Check your favorite software catalog or retailer for more information. Read the licensing information carefully on any software you download, and pay any fees to the software publisher.

TABLE A-1

Software	Description	Download Site/URL
Eudora	E-mail	ftp://ftp.qualcomm.com/quest/windows/eudora/1.5
HotDog	HTML Editor	http://www.sausage.com
mIRC	IRC Client	ftp://papa.indstate.edu/winsock-l/winirc
Netscape	Web Browser	ftp://papa.indstate.edu/winsock-l/WWW-Browsers/NetScape
Trumpet Winsock	PPP/SLIP	ftp://b-box.trumpet.com/au/pub/winsock
WS_FTP	FTP Client	ftp://papa.indstate.edu/winsock-l/ftp

USING A COMMERCIAL ONLINE PROVIDER

You can access most Internet resources through an online commercial provider, as was discussed in Chapter 6. You will be billed a monthly access fee, and additional charges for special services if you use them.

Any of the providers will send you a free disk with the software required to log on to their networks. Look for the free disks in many computer magazines, or call one of the numbers listed in Table A-2. Good luck, and happy surfing!

TABLE A-2

Provider	Telephone Number	URL
America Online (AOL)	800-827-6364	http://www.aol.com
CompuServe	800-848-8990	http://compuserve.com
Delphi	800-695-4005	http://www.delphi.com
Microsoft Network	800-936-4200	http://www.msn.com
Prodigy	800-776-3449	http://www.prodigy.com

APPENDIX B: HOT SITES ON THE INTERNET

Searchable Lists and Directories

Site Name	URL	Description
Clearinghouse for Subject-oriented Internet Resource Guides	http://www.lib.umich.edu/chhome.html	A list of educational Web sites by category
EINet Galaxy	http://www.einet.net/galaxy.html	A searchable directory of Internet resources
Gopher Jewels	gopher://gopher.csv.warwick.ac.uk:70/11/remote/other-gopher/Gopher_Jewels	The ultimate list of gophers by subject
InterNIC Directory	http://ds.internic.net	A searchable directory of Internet resources
List of American Universities	http://www.clas.ufl.edu/CLAS/american-universities.html	Contains links to over 150 college and university home pages
Lycos	http://lycos.cs.cmu.edu/	Carnegie Mellon University home page—has links to search tools
Open Market's Commercial Sites Index	http://www.directory.net	An alphabetical list of commercial, government, and nonprofit sites on the Net
Internet Services List	http://www.uwm.edu/Mirror/inet.services.html	40 categories of links to thousands of other sites
WebCrawler	http://webcrawler.com	A Web search engine
WWW Worm	http://www.cs.colorado.edu/home/mcbryan/WWWW.html	A Web search engine called the Worm (hence, WWWW)
Yahoo	http://www.yahoo.com/	Searchable index of Web resources by category
Ziff-Davis Publishing	http://www.ziff.com/~pcmag	*PC Magazine's* home page with links to 100 other interesting Web sites

Internet Information/Web News

Site Name	URL	Description
Georgia Institute of Technology	http://www.gatech.edu/gvu/user_surveys	Survey of Web users
Global Network Navigator	http://nearnet.gnn.com/gnn/index.html	Best of the Net, the Whole Internet Catalog, with lots of info about the Net, and a catalog of resource books
InfoGuide[SM]	http://www.internic.net/ds/dspg0pubdbs.html	Databases on many interesting topics
Internet by E-mail	listserv@ubvm.cc.buffalo.edu	Send the following message to the listserv to find out how to access many Internet resources via e-mail: GET INTERNET BY-EMAIL NETTRAIN F=MAIL
Internet Mail Guide	ftp://csd.uwm.edu/pub/	The ultimate guide on e-mail, written by the expert, Scott Yanoff
Netsurfer Digest	http://www.netsurf.com/nsd/index.html	Free weekly magazine of Web news
Online World Resources Handbook	http://login.eunet.no/~presno	Online guide to international Web resources
Publicly Accessible Mailing Lists	http://www.NeoSoft.com:80/internet/paml/bysubj.html	Find lots of mailing lists on lots of interesting topics.
The Internet Group	http://tig.com/IBC	Want to know about commercial use of the Internet? Here's one site.
The Scout Report	http://rs.internic.net/scout_report-index.html	The Scout Report provides information on what's new and interesting on the Net.
Virus FAQ	ftp://rtfm.mit.edu//pub/usenet-by-hierarchy/comp/virus	Get all the information you need on viruses.
W3 Consortium	http://www.w3.org	In Switzerland, the point of origin of the World Wide Web
WWW Frequently Asked Questions	http://sunsite.unc.edu/boutell/faq/www_faq.html	Provides answers to frequently asked questions about the Web

Software Sites

Site Name	URL	Description
Cybersource	http://software.net	Lots of software. Check it out.
HTML Kit	http://www.halcyon.com/webwizard/welcome.htm	HTML kit allows you to easily create your own home page.
Internet Phone	ftp://ftp.vocaltec.com/pub/iphone13.exe	The voice version of IRC
IRC Client	ftp://cs.bu.edu/irc/clients	Download an IRC client and start chatting.

Software Sites (continued)

Site Name	URL	Description
RealAudio	http://www.realaudio.com	Audio over the Internet: uses compression methods to reduce audio files to 8% of original size
VMPEG Software	ftp://ftp.netcom.com/pub/cf/cfogg/vmpeg/	Download video software so you can see motion pictures from the Internet on your PC (vmpeg17.exe or latest version).

Commercial Sites

Site Name	URL	Description
AT&T	http://www.tollfree.att.net/dir800/	AT&T 800 number directory
CBS	http://www.cbs.com	What's David Letterman up to these days? (Did you miss yesterday's Top 10 list?) Find out here.
CompuServe	http://www.compuserve.com	Information about the largest commercial online service in the U.S.
Dow Jones Quote Server	http://www.secapl.com/cgi-bin/qs	Find out the latest stock prices.
Dun & Bradstreet	http://www.dbisna.com	The D&B home page
Fidelity Investment Co.	http://www.fid-inv.com	Investment information about Fidelity Investment Co.
Godiva On-line	http://www.godiva.com/	Chocolate, anyone?
IBM	http://www.ibm.com	Find out about OS2 Warp and other IBM products.
InfoPost	http://www.infopost.com	The place to go if you want someone to create and maintain a home page for you
Intel	http://www.intel.com	Get a technology briefing and find out about Intel's PC plans.
Internet Yellow Pages	http://www.yellow.com	The Internet yellow pages
Microsoft	http://www.microsoft.com/	Find out all about Windows 95 and other Microsoft news.
PC Computing	http://www.pccomputing.ziff.com/~pccomp	*PC Computing* magazine online
Prodigy	http://www.astranet.com	Home page for online commercial service provider
Promus Hotel	http://stargate.promus.com/public/magazines.html	Online magazine directory

APPENDIX B 271

Government, Political, and Nonprofit Organization Sites

Site Name	URL	Description
CIA	http://www.idci.gov/cia/publications/pubs.html	A worldwide factbook published by the CIA
Concord Coalition	http://sunsite.unc.edu/concord	Find out about the Concord Coalition, and what they are doing to fight the federal deficit. Find out more about the deficit—what you don't know could hurt you.
EPA	http://www.epa.gov/	A searchable guide to the Environmental Protection Agency
FBI	http://www.fbi.gov	Contains the FBI's 10 most-wanted list and other law enforcement information
Fed'l Info Exchange List of U.S. Gov't WWW servers	http://www.fie.com/www/us_gov.htm	Links to hundreds of other government sites
Fedworld	http://www.fedworld.gov	Links to 120 government agencies
IRS	http://www.ustreas.gov/treasury/bureaus/irs/irs.html	Review the latest changes in the tax law before filing your income taxes.
Legislate Gopher	gopher://gopher.legislate.com	Information about legislation affecting higher education
Library of Congress	http://lcweb.loc.gov/homepage/lchp.html	Start with the American History Project, and browse for hours—a fantastic site.
NASA	http://www.gsfc.nasa.gov	Find out about the latest space shuttle launch and other vital NASA information.
National Park Service	http://www.nps.gov/nps/	A list of more than 350 sites in the National Park System
Right Side of Web	http://www.clark.net/pub/jeffd/index.html	Find out more about Newt Gingrich's Contract with America, Whitewater, and other conservative hot topics.
Social Security Administration	http://www.ssa.gov/SSA_Home.html	Everything you need to know about the Social Security Administration
Space Shuttle Site	http://liftoff.msfc.nasa.gov	Daily schedule of mission events, including video and virtual reality clips
Thomas (Congress' site)	http://thomas.loc.gov	Searchable information from the last two congressional sessions
U.S. Geological Survey	http://edcwww.cr.usgs.gov/dclass/dclass.html	The USGS declassified satellite photos. Find your home or college from 50,000 feet!
U.S. House of Representatives	http://www.house.gov	Send a message to wired House members.
U.S. Patent and Trademark Office	http://www.uspto.gov/	Check here to see if someone already has a patent on your invention.
White House	http://www.whitehouse.gov	Get the text of President Clinton's speeches; take a tour of the White House; see pictures of the First Family.

Fun, Education, Entertainment, Shopping

Site Name	URL	Description
America's Cup	http://www.ac95.org/	For those who like the yachting life
Biology Image Archive	gopher://muse.bio.cornell.edu:70/11/images	Biology images and JPEG image viewers available for downloading
Branch Mall	http://branch.com	Shop without leaving your house.
Clark Network	http://www.clark.net/	Interesting sites including Campaign Central and Atomic Books
CyberMall	http://199.171.5.200.CyberMall.html	Links to other Web malls
Cyspacemalls	http://chili.rt66.com/cyspacemalls	"The Internet Santa Fe Style"
Financial Links at Yahoo	http://mtmis1:mis.semi.harris.com/financial.html	Stocks and market information
Find A Friend	http://www.ais.net:80/findafriend	Haven't seen your high school teammate in years? Want to find an old buddy? Try this site.
Games Domain	http://gamesdomain.co.uk	Contains links to computer and online games
Grand Canyon National Park	http://www.kbt.com/gc/gc_home.html	Pictures and information about this national treasure
Guide to the Stars and Galaxies	http://www.telescope.org/btl/	And you thought roaming cyberspace was fun—try traveling through the universe!
Hang Gliders' Home Page	http://cougar.stanford.edu:7878/HGMPSHomePage.html	Lots of interesting links related to hang gliding and flying
Homeopathy Home Page	http://www.dungeon.com/home/cam/homeo.html	Find out about treating many ailments without a prescription—the alternative to mainstream medicine.
Hostel's Europe Pages	http://www.tardis.ed.ac.uk/~og/hostels.html	How to find good, and stay away from the bad, hostels in Europe
Interactive Frog Dissection	http://curry.edschool.virginia.edu/~insttech/frog/	Biology without the formaldahyde!
Interactive Geometry	http://www.geom.umn.edu/apps/gallery.html	Math on the Net
International Tutors	http://www.iamot.org/it/index.html	Help is available from around the world in a wide variety of academic disciplines.
Internet Shopping Network	http://www.internet.net/	Free membership required to shop and order here
Joke of the Day	http://www.ddv.com/Jokes/jokeoftheday.html	Get a laugh!
Lego Home Page	http://legowww.homepages.com	Provides news on what's up in Legoland
Linguistics Resources	http://writing.samford.edu/ling.htm	Need help with your writing? Start here.
Medical Matrix (Internet Clinical Medicine Resource Guide)	http://www.kumc.edu:80/inmatrix	A database of Internet clinical medicine resources

APPENDIX B 273

Fun, Education, Entertainment, Shopping (continued)

Site Name	URL	Description
MTV Online	http://www.mtv.com	MTV online with lots of movie information
National Organization for Women	http://now.org/now/home.html	Women's rights are still an issue. Check out this page to see why.
Perdue Weather Server	http://thunder.atms.purdue.edu/	Get up-to-the-minute weather forecasts.
Roulette	http://www.uroulette.com:8000	Spin the page, and who knows where on the Web you will end up? Random links to cyberspace
San Jose *Mercury News*	http://www.sjmercury.com	The San Jose *Mercury News* online
SkiWeb	http://diamond.sierra.net/SkiWeb	The latest ski conditions; *Alpine World* magazine and more
Social Studies Education	http://www.indiana.edu/~ssdc/eric-chess.html	Are you an education major, and do you want to know more about social studies? Try this site.
Star Trek Stuff	http://generations.viacom.com/	"...a galaxy of unique Star Trek pictures, sounds, and a movie preview"
Tennis Server	http://www.tennisserver.com/Tennis.html	Tennis, anyone?
The Internet Movie Database	http://www.yahoo.com/Entertainment/Movies_and_Films/	Searchable guide to all the movies there ever were; provides links to filmography on actors
The Internet Plaza	http://plaza.xor.com/	Some vendors let you browse, others let you place online orders.
The Internet Shopkeeper	http://shops.net/cgi-bin/	Another great place to shop
The Jason Project	http://seawifs.gsfc.nasa.gov/scripts/JASON.html	Descriptions of various scientific expeditions; provides fascinating information about everything from volcanoes to Mayan ruins.
The Keirsey Temperament Sorter	http://www.sunsite.unc.edu/jembin/mb.pl	Find out your personality type, based on the Meyers-Briggs Personality Type Indicator test.
The Louvre	http://www.paris.org/musees/Louvre/Treasures	Online museum; visit the Louvre in Paris (but expect to wait for the graphics files to download to your computer).
The Virtual World Tourist Guide	http://wings.buffalo.edu/world	An online map with links around the world
Time magazine	http://www.timeinc.com/time/universe.html	*Time* magazine online
Tower Records	http://www.shopping2000.com/shopping2000/tower	Order records through this online catalog.
TV Listings	listserv@netcom.com	Can't wait to see a *Cheers* rerun? Want to know when it's on? Subscribe to this list, using the message below, and get daily e-mail with the latest TV shows. **subscribe tv2nite-1**

Fun, Education, Entertainment, Shopping (continued)

Site Name	URL	Description
Ultimate Band List	http://american.recordings.com/WWWoM/ubl.html	Alphabetical listing of bands
Ultimate TV List	http://tvnet.com/UTVL/utvl.html	Just what it says, the ultimate TV listing
Warner Bros. Records	http://www.wbr.com/Warner/	Information on Warner Bros. artists
Women on the Net	http://www.cybergrrl.com	Links to many online resources for women, including information about domestic violence
Woodstock Redux	http://www.well.com/woodstock	See all the sights and sounds of the Woodstock '94 reunion.
WWW of Sports	http://tns-www.lcs.mit.edu/cgi-bin/sports	Sports home page, with links to many other sports sites

APPENDIX C: INTERNET ACRONYM LIST

ARPAnet	Advanced Research Projects Agency Network	The precursor to the Internet; started by the Department of Defense
ASCII	American Standard Code for Information Interchange	A coding scheme used in PCs and other computers that defines a specific sequence of bits for each character in a character set
AUP	Acceptable Use Policy	A definition of what is acceptable online behavior, and what is not
BBS	Bulletin Board Service	A computer that allows you to log on and post messages to and receive information from other subscribers of the service
DNS	Domain Name System	The system of addresses devised to ensure that every site and host on the Internet is assigned a unique address
FAQ	Frequently Asked Question	What you always wanted to know, but were afraid to ask; many FAQs are available by FTP.
FQDN	Fully Qualified Domain Name	A complete Internet address, including the complete host and domain name, such as rtfm.mit.edu
FTP	File Transfer Protocol	The protocol that defines how files are transferred over the Internet
GIF	Graphics Interchange Format	A type of compressed graphics format
GUI	Graphical User Interface	Software that allows the user to interact with the computer and execute commands by pointing at icons and pull-down menus with a mouse or other selection device
HTML	Hypertext Markup Language	The specialized language used to insert formatting commands and links in a hypertext document
HTTP	Hypertext Transport Protocol	The protocol used to transport hypertext files across the Internet

IP	Internet Protocol	The standards and software that define how packets are addressed and passed to the network access layer for routing on the Internet
IRC	Internet Relay Chat	A program that allows multiple users worldwide to carry on typed "conversations" online
ISP	Internet Service Provider	An organization that provides direct access to the Internet, such as the provider that links your college or university to the Net
Kbps	Kilobits per second	The speed at which a modem can transmit a signal over a line
LAN	Local Area Network	A group of computers, printers, and other computing resources in close physical proximity and cabled together so that users can share programs, data, printers, memory, and other computing resources
POP	Post Office Protocol	The standard for exchange of e-mail when a user mailbox is created on a PC
PPP	Point-to-Point Protocol	The specifications for a dial-up connection to an Internet host
RFC	Request for Comments	Documents defining the specifications of Internet protocols and other technical topics
SLIP	Serial Line Internet Protocol	The specifications for dial-up connection to an Internet host
SMTP	Simple Mail Transfer Protocol	The protocol used to route e-mail on the Internet
TCP	Transmission Control Protocol	The standards and software that divide a file into packets and forward the packets to the IP protocol layers
URL	Uniform Resource Locator	The primary means of navigating the Web, consisting of the means of access, the Web site, the path, and the document name of a web resource, such as http://www.whitehouse.gov
WWW	World Wide Web	A subset of the Internet that provides archives of information accessible via browsers and search engines

APPENDIX D: INTERNET GLOSSARY

Acceptable Use Policy (AUP)	A definition of what is acceptable online behavior, and what is not
Address book	A list of usernames and Internet addresses used to create a distribution list for e-mail messages
Advanced Research Projects Agency Network (ARPAnet)	The precursor to the Internet; started by the Department of Defense
Alias	A nickname used in sending e-mail or participating in online discussions
Anonymous FTP	A type of FTP that allows a user to log on to a remote host, which the user would otherwise not have access to, to download files
Application layer	The TCP/IP protocol stack with which the user applications interact, and which forwards user messages/requests to lower TCP/IP layers
Archie	A search tool used to find FTP resources
Archive	Information about a specific topic stored at an Internet site
ASCII (text) mode	A type of data transfer mode used for sending text files; formatting characters and images will be lost if transmitted in ASCII mode.
Backbone	The main network links between Internet providers
Bandwidth	The volume of traffic a communications channel can support
Binary mode	A type of data transfer mode that allows images and formatted text to be sent over the Internet
Blind carbon copy	A copy of a mail message that is sent without the original recipient's knowledge
Bookmark	A saved hypertext link (URL) that you can visit later simply by clicking the bookmark
Browser	Software that lets you roam and retrieve documents and files from the Web
Browsing	Reading hypertext or gopher documents, and jumping to other sites as you find links that are of interest
Bulletin Board Service (BBS)	A computer that allows you to log on and post messages to other subscribers to the service

Carbon copy	A copy of a mail message
Cd command	The FTP command that changes directories on an FTP server
Cdup command	The FTP command that moves up one level in the directory structure on an FTP server
Channel	A group of people communicating on IRC; equivalent to a chat room in WebChat
Channel operator	A person who controls an IRC channel
Chat room	An area of a WebChat service that people can "enter" with their Web browsers where the conversations are devoted to a specific topic; equivalent to a channel in IRC
Client	PC software that interacts with a server
Clipper Chip	A hardware device that can allow government agencies to decode encrypted messages
Close command	The FTP command that discontinues an FTP session
Command line interface	A method of interacting with a program in which the user must know and enter commands using specific programming syntax
Compressed file	A file that has been reduced in size by a special compression program; it must be decompressed before it can be used.
Copyright	The author's or artist's right to control the copying of his or her work
Cyberspace	A term coined to denote the online world of the Internet
Digest	A form of receiving mail messages in which all the messages from a mailing list are delivered as one daily message
Dir command	The FTP command that displays the contents of a directory
Direct Internet connection	A connection to the Internet that allows access to the full range of Internet services available at that site
Distribution list	The list of all the people you want to get an e-mail message
Domain	A subset of hosts on the Internet, divided by type, such as education (.edu), network support (.net), and so on
Domain name	The name used to identify an Internet host
Domain name server	An Internet host that checks the address of incoming and outgoing Internet messages
Domain Name System (DNS)	The system of addresses devised to ensure that every site and host on the Internet is assigned a unique address
Domain root server	A computer on the Internet that keeps information about the IP addresses in its domain
Download	To retrieve a file from another computer or remote host
E-mail	Electronic messages sent from one computer user to another over a network
Emoticon	A small symbol used to express emotions in a written message—for example, :=)
Encryption	The process of encoding a message so it can be read only by another party holding an encryption key
Encryption key	A special mathematical code that allows encryption hardware/software to encode and then decipher an encrypted message
Fair use	A set of exclusions/exceptions to copyrights that allows you to use quotes, images, and other sources in commentary, educational, and other nonprofit ways
File server	A shared computer on a local area network that users on attached PCs can access to retrieve documents and run programs
File Transfer Protocol (FTP)	The protocol that defines how files are transferred over the Internet
Flame	To send angry e-mail messages in response to someone else's posting on the Net
Folder	A directory where mail is stored

Folder index	A list of mail folders in Pine
Frequently Asked Question (FAQ)	What you always wanted to know, but were afraid to ask; many FAQs are available by FTP
FTP client	Software that allows the user to locate FTP servers and directories, and download the desired files
FTP server	An Internet host program that allows users to access FTP directories on the server
FTP site	An Internet host that allows remote access to files on certain directories
Fully Qualified Domain Name (FQDN)	A complete Internet address, including the complete host and domain name
Get command	An FTP command used to retrieve a file from an FTP site
Gopher	A software client that lets you "tunnel" through layers of menus to find information on a gopher server
Gopher server	An Internet host running gopher software that provides an archive of hierarchical menus that contain information or additional menus
Gopherspace	The collection of gopher servers and archives around the world
Graphical User Interface (GUI)	Software that allows the user to interact with the computer and execute commands by pointing at icons and pull-down menus with a mouse or other selection device
Graphics Interchange Format (GIF)	A type of compressed graphics format
Hacker	A person who attempts to break into computers that he or she is not authorized to use
Handle	A nickname used when sending a WebChat message
Header	The beginning of a message sent over the Internet; typically contains addressing information to route the message or packet to its destination
Hierarchy	A group of related Usenet newsgroups
Hit	The result of a successful search by a Web browser
Home page	The top HTML document, to which someone can link in a group of related HTML pages
Host	A remote computer that provides a variety of services, typically to multiple users concurrently
Hyperlink	An electronic link between one or more documents, such that when the user selects the link, the linked document is automatically loaded to the user's workstation
Hypermedia	A combination of text, graphics, sound, and video files that allows the user to proceed through the document in nonlinear fashion
Hypertext	A type of text that allows the user to proceed through it in a nonlinear fashion, by linking to topics of interest within the text
Hypertext Markup Language (HTML)	The specialized language used to insert formatting commands and links in a hypertext document
Hypertext Transport Protocol (HTTP)	The protocol used to transport hypertext files across the Internet
In-line image	A graphic image or icon that is encoded and embedded in a hypertext document; in-line images will be displayed by the browser as it loads the rest of the home page.
Information Superhighway	A term used to describe the Internet and other online information resources
Internaut	An intrepid soul who uses the Internet
Internet	A worldwide network of networks encompassing more than 140 countries and millions of connected computers

Internet address	The address of a resource on the Internet; may be a mailing address or a Web URL
Internet host	A computer that is attached to the Internet and on which mail, Web, gopher, and other servers are installed
Internet layer	The stack in the TCP/IP protocols that addresses a packet and sends the packets to the network access layer
Internet Relay Chat (IRC)	A program that allows multiple users worldwide to carry on typed "conversations" online
Internet Service Provider (ISP)	An organization that provides direct access to the Internet, such as the provider that links your college or university to the Net
IP	Internet Protocol; the software stack that sets up the physical connection for an Internet session
IP address	A unique number assigned to each computer on the Internet, consisting of four numbers, each less than 256, and each separated by a period, such as 129.16.255.0
Kerberos	An authentication algorithm that involves sending the user a ticket, which is then required for access to services
Kilobits per second (Kbps)	The speed at which a modem can transmit a signal over a line; Kbps represents 1,024 bits per second.
Link	A line of text or a graphic icon in a hypertext document that contains an embedded Internet address and that allows you to jump to that address by selecting the link
List owner	The person who manages a mailing list
Listproc	A program that provides mailing list services
Listserv	A program that provides mailing list services
Local Area Network (LAN)	A group of computers, printers, and other computing resources in close physical proximity and cabled together so that users can share programs, data, printers, memory, and other computing resources
Location text box	The area in a Web browser window in which you enter the URL of the Web home page you want to retrieve
Logic bomb	A type of malicious software that is activated based on some defined condition, often a date
Lurker	A person who reads mailing lists, newsgroup postings, or chat messages without participating in the discussion
Lurking	Reading postings to a list or newsgroup without posting anything yourself
Lycos	A Web search engine
Lynx	A text-based Web browser
Mail client	The software that lets a PC download mail from a mail server
Mail folder	A directory where incoming mail is stored
Mail server	A program on an Internet host that serves mail to users
Mailbox	A directory where incoming mail is stored
Mailing list	A list of subscribers who post and reply to comments or questions about a specific topic
Majordomo	A mailing list server
mIRC	A windows-based IRC client
Mirror site	Another location on the Internet that has the same files as the originating site; if the first site is busy, try the mirror.
Moderator	A person who reads postings to mailing lists or newsgroups to determine their appropriateness for the forum prior to directing them to the subscribers
Mosaic	A graphical Web browsing program from NCSA
Netiquette	Manners on the Net

Netscape Navigator	A graphical Web browsing program from Netscape Communications Corporation
NetSpeak	The jargon used by Internauts
Network access layer	The layer of the TCP/IP protocol stacks that sends the message out through the physical network onto the Internet
Network administrator	The person who maintains user accounts, password files, and system software on your campus network
Newbie	Someone new to the Net
News	Another name for Usenet
News server	A program on an Internet host that passes the Usenet news to news clients
Newsfeed	The set of Usenet hierarchies served to a location by an Internet news server
Newsgroup	A forum for discussion of a specific topic in Usenet
Newsreader	A program that allows the user to access, read, and post messages to Usenet newsgroups
Nickname	An alternate username used to preserve anonymity when using IRC and some other Internet services
Nickname list	A list of users and Internet addresses to which you wish to deliver e-mail
Node	A device attached to a network
Offline	A device on a network that is not currently communicating with the network
Open Location command	The Netscape command used to point the browser at a particular Web page
Packet	A portion of a message sent over the Internet
Password	A secret combination of numbers and letters used to identify and authenticate a user
Ping	A command that can be used to test the status of an Internet node
Port	A service such as gopher or FTP on an Internet host
Post	To send a message to a mailing list, Usenet newsgroup, or other online forum
Post Office Protocol (POP)	The standard for exchange of e-mail when a user mailbox is created on a PC using client software
Point-to-Point Protocol (PPP)	The specifications for a dial-up connection to an Internet host
Protocol	A standard for exchange of information or data
Public domain	Software, documents, and other forms of expression for which the copyright has expired, or to which the creator specifically revokes his or her copyright
Pwd command	The FTP command that will display the name of the current directory
Reload	To request a Web browser to reload an image or Web page
RFCs—Request for Comments	Documents defining the specifications of Internet protocols and other technical topics
Router	A hardware device that reads a packet's destination address and sends it to another Internet host on its way to its final destination
Search engine	A program written to allow users to search the Web for sites that match user-specified parameters
Search form	A form used to enter search parameters when looking up information on the Web
Server	A computer that provides a service to another computer, such as a mail server, a file server, or a news server
Session	A completed connection to an Internet service, and the ensuing connect time
Shareware	Software available on the Internet that may be downloaded to your machine for evaluation and for which you are generally expected to pay a fee to the originator of the software if you decide to keep it
Shell account	The Unix account you use to log in to the Internet

Signal-to-noise ratio	The amount of information relative to talk and blarney passed around a newsgroup or mailing list
Signature	An e-mail sender's unique salutation
Simple Mail Transfer Protocol (SMTP)	The protocol used to transport mail from one Internet mail server to another
SLIP connection	The specifications for a dial-up connection to an Internet host
Smiley	A small symbol such as :-) used to convey the writer's intent in the text-only environments of e-mail and news
Software piracy	The illegal copying of software
Spam	A Usenet posting that violates news etiquette by indiscriminately sending to multiple newsgroups
Spider	A program that crawls the Web searching for new pages
Stack	A software program or driver such as TCP/IP used to connect a computer to the Internet
Surfing	To cruise the Internet, in particular the Web, going from site to site looking for information
Suspend	To put an e-mail subscription to a mailing list on hold; to suspend mail delivery
Tag	An HTML code inserted in a Web document; used to control the formatting of Web pages
Telnet	Software that allows the user to log in to a remote computer
Telnet session	A connection to a host computer using the telnet program that allows the remote computer to appear as a directly attached terminal
Terminal	A device having a CRT and keyboard, but without memory or disk storage, used to interact with a computer
Terminal session	A connection to a computer using or emulating a terminal
Thread	A related series of postings to a Usenet newsgroup, including the original posting, responses, and responses to the responses
Thumbnail sketch	A representative icon, reduced in size and embedded in a Web document; clicking on the icon will jump to the full-size image.
Transmission Control Protocol (TCP)	The standards and software that divide a file into packets and forward the packets to the IP protocol layers
Transport layer	The protocol stacks that divide a message/file into packets and number them so the packets can be reassembled at the receiving end of an Internet transmission
Trojan horse	A type of malicious software that is generally hidden inside another, harmless application. The trojan horse starts up when the other program is executed. A trojan horse cannot replicate itself, thus is not classified as a virus. Nevertheless, one can do severe, often fatal, damage to a system
Tunnel	To work your way down through a series of menus or directories to find what you are looking for
Uniform Resource Locator (URL)	The primary means of navigating the Web, consisting of the means of access, the Web site, the path, and the document name of a Web resource
Unix	An operating system frequently found on Internet hosts
Upload	To send a file to another computer or remote host
URL—Uniform Resource Locator	The address of a node, server, or document on the Internet
Usenet	A facility of the Internet, also called the news, that allows users to read and post messages to over 6,000 discussion groups on various topics
User ID	An account access code that allows you to log on to a computer network
Username	The name you use to log on to your system
Veronica	A search tool for locating gopherspace resources

Viewer	Special software that allows the user to view image files
Virus	A type of malicious software that can destroy the computer's hard drive, files, and programs in memory, and that replicates itself to other disks
Web server	An Internet host that runs software to allow clients on the server to surf the World Wide Web
Web site	A location on the World Wide Web to which you can link using a URL
WebChat	A program on the World Wide Web that allows users to exchange messages, or chat, online
Workstation	A PC attached to a network
World Wide Web (WWW)	A subset of the Internet that provides archives of information accessible via browsers and search engines. The data is presented in hypertext format, with links to other Internet sites. Graphics, video, and audio can be included in the hypertext document, or as a linked document
Worm	A type of malicious software that typically affects the hard drive, eventually corrupting it so the files and programs on it can no longer be used

INDEX

Advance Research Projects Agency (ARPAnet), 2
Alias. *See* Nicknames
Anchor, 230, 238
Anonymous FTP. *See* File Transfer Protocol, anonymous
Application layer, 22
Archie, 12, 13, 151–152
Archives
 for mailing lists, 64
 Usenet, 181, 183, 193
ASCII (text) mode, 142
Audio chat, 166
Authentication, for security, 208–209

Backbone, 213
Back button, in Netscape, 86, 97
Binary data, 264
Binary mode, in FTP, 142
Blind carbon copy, 40, 50
Bookmarks
 in Gopher, 138
 in HTML documents, 232, 238, 242, 243, 250
 in Netscape, 93, 98, 109, 133
Browser. *See* Web browser
Bulleted list, 248

Carbon copy, 40, 50, 57
Channel, 12, 162
Chat program, 12, 13, 30
Chat room, 173, 174
Client, 19, 86
Client software, 44
Clipper Chip, 207
Command line interface, 55
Commercial service providers, 14, 15, 214–216
Compressed files, 139, 140, 147
Computer Emergency Response Team (CERT), 208
Concord Coalition, 86–87
Copyright, 200–202
Cyberspace, 3, 91
 commercialization of, 213–214
 shopping in, 214–216, 267

Demodulation, 264
Digest command, in mailing lists, 64
Directories, in FTP, 141, 143, 144
Distribution list, 60, 65–66, 71–73
Domain, 24, 25

Domain Name System (DNS), 24, 30
Domain root server, 25
Downloading
 files, 10, 264
 with Lynx, 120
 mail messages from Internet server, 44

E-mail, 3–5, 30, 39–77
 addresses, 46, 48, 50
 attaching documents to, 40, 62
 composing, 42
 deleting, 54, 59
 editing messages in, 50
 forwarding, 42, 54
 mailboxes for, 40, 54, 61–62, 68, 73–74
 rejected messages, 53
 replying to, 42, 53, 59
 retrieving, 51, 58
 sending, 42, 50, 57
 structure of messages in, 40–42
 subscribing to mailing lists using, 63–64, 68, 70, 75–76
 using Netscape for, 107–108, 113
Emoticon, 213
Encryption, 206–207
Eudora, 3, 4, 43
 configuring, 46
 deleting messages in, 51
 distribution lists, 65–66
 editing messages in, 50, 51
 mailboxes in, 43, 54–55, 68
 nicknames, 65–66
 passwords, 49
 sending e-mail with, 49–51
 signatures in, 66

Fair use, 200
FAQs. *See* Frequently Asked Questions
File server, 17
File Transfer Protocol (FTP), 10–12, 129
 anonymous, 138, 139, 143, 144, 148
 and Archie, 151
 client, 138, 143, 144–145
 commands, 146–147, 148
 compression software, 140
 directory structures in, 141, 143, 144, 148
 downloading software with, 144
 FAQs, 143, 144, 210
 files, 10
 server, 138
 sites, 10, 30
 viewing files with, 145

Flaming, 63, 210, 211
Folder index, 44, 58
Folders, e-mail, 58, 61–62, 73–74
Freedom, of speech, 202
Frequently Asked Questions (FAQs), 143, 144, 181, 193, 210
Fully Qualified Domain Name (FQDN), 24

Gender gap, on the Internet, 204
GIF file, 234, 241, 252
Gopher, 7–10, 30, 129, 130–138
 bookmarks in, 133, 138
 logging in to remotely, 136
 telenetting to, 136
 using with Unix, 135
Gopherspace, 12, 130
 searching using Veronica, 151–152
Graphical User Interface (GUI), 3, 30, 44, 86
Graphics, including in HTML documents, 106–107, 234–236, 241, 252–253

Hacker, 206
Handle, 173, 177
Header, 23, 40
Hierarchy, Usenet. *See* Usenet, hierarchies in
Hits, 100
 changing the number of, 110
Home page, 86
Hyperlink, 89, 95, 230, 248, 250
Hypermedia, 86
HyperTerminal, 265–266
Hypertext, 16, 86
Hypertext Markup Language (HTML), 16, 30, 91, 225–255
 anchor tag, 230, 238
 bookmarks, 232, 238, 242, 250
 editor, 226
 formatted text, 234
 front end, 226
 heading tag, 227, 247, 253
 horizontal rule, 232, 238, 252, 253
 line break, 241
 lists, 227, 229
 paragraph tag, 232
 tags, 16, 227–236
 title tag, 227, 228
Hypertext Transport Protocol (HTTP), 89, 91

In-line image, in Web pages, 106, 112, 234
Information Superhighway, 16, 107

INDEX **11**

Internaut, 3
Internet, 1, 2, 20, 30, 103
    architecture, 22–24
    backbone, 213
    defined, 2
    evolution of 2, 3, 30
    gender gap, 204
    logging on to, 26–28
    security on, 218
    server, 17
Internet address, 24, 25, 46, 50, 88
Internet Assistant, 226
Internet host, 12, 40, 263
Internet layer, 22, 23, 24
Internet Protocol (IP), 21
Internet Relay Chat (IRC), 161, 162–172, 274
    channels, 162
    clients, 164
    commands, 165
    operators, 166
    public servers, 167
    sending a private message with, 171
    servers, 164
IP address, 22, 23, 25, 30

Java, 93
Jumping, between Web documents, 85, 86

Kerberos, 209

Libel, on the Internet, 202
Link, 7, 86, 91, 130, 230, 248
List owner, 63
Listproc, 63
Listserv, 63
Local Area Network (LAN), 17, 163
Location text box, 88
Logging on
    remotely, 263
    to a Telnet session, 28
Logic bomb, 208
Login ID, 19
Lurker, 211
Lurking, 63
Lycos, 100, 102, 103, 109, 112, 116–117
Lynx, 5, 6, 86, 114–121

Mailboxes, 40, 42, 44, 54, 61, 62, 68
Mail client, 44
Mail folder, 61, 73–74
Mailing list, 4–5, 62–64
    archives, 64
    digest option for, 64
    etiquette of, 63
    finding, 63
    moderated lists, 63
    subscribing to, 63–64, 68, 70, 75–76
    suspending mail from, 64
Mail server, 44
Majordomo, 63
Mardam-Bay, Khaled, 162
mIRC, 162
Moderator, 63
Modem, 263–265
Mosaic, 5, 86

Named anchor. *See* Anchor
Netiquette, 181, 210–213
Netscape, 5, 6, 85, 88–89
    bookmarks, 98
    e-mail in, 107, 113
    Go menu, 98

Home button, 99
Images, 106
Preferences menu, 108, 113
Print command, 98
Query Results window, 108
Reload button, 108
Save command, 97
Usenet in, 185–192
View History command, 98
Netscape Navigator. *See* Netscape
NetSpeak, 211–212
Network access layer, 22–23
Newbie, 181
News, 12
Newsfeed, 181
Newsgroup, 12, 14
    archives, 183, 193
    defined, 180
    FAQs for, 193
    finding, 185
    posting a reply to, 190–191
    subscribing to, 188, 192
    threads in, 190
Newsreader, 12, 182–183
News server, 182, 183
Nickname, 44, 46, 65–66, 162, 173, 177
Nickname list, 60, 65–66
Node, 263

Offline, mail retrieval, 12
Open Location command, 89
Operator, in IRC, 166
Ordered list, 227, 241, 248

Packet, 21, 22, 30
Password, 19, 30, 42, 55
    choosing, 42, 209
Path, within URL, 88–89
Pine, 3, 4, 57–60
    deleting messages in, 59
    distribution lists in, 71–73
    exiting, 60
    folders in, 44, 45, 58, 73
    menus in, 57, 58
    replying to messages in, 59
    retrieving and reading mail in, 58
    subscribing to a mailing list using, 75–76
    using to send e-mail, 57–58
Pornography, on the Internet, 202
Port number, 166,
Posting, to newsgroups, 12, 182
Post Office Protocol (POP), 44, 46
Privacy, on the Internet, 202
Progress bar, in Netscape, 108
Protocol, 10
Public domain, 200

Query Results window, in Netscape, 108
Queries
    using FTP, 139
    using Lynx, 117–119
    using a Web browser, 100–106, 108–111

Reload button, 108
Remote log on, 263
Router, 21, 23, 44, 50
Routing table, 23

Satan, 209
Search button, 100
Search engine, WWW, 7, 30, 86, 100–111
    search criteria, 100
Search form, 100, 110

Shareware, 201
Shell account, 55, 135
Signal-to-noise ratio, 183
Signature, 60, 66–68
Simple Mail Transfer Protocol (SMTP), 44, 46
Smilie, 213
Software
    downloading, 201
    piracy, 200
    sites on the Internet, 267
Software Publishers Association, 200
Spamming, 211
Spider, 100
Stack, 22, 23, 30
Stop button, 96
Subscribing. *See* Mailing lists, Newsgroups
Sun Microsystems, 93
Surfing, 3, 94, 99
Suspend, 62, 64

Tag, in HTML. *See* Hypertext Markup Language, tags
TCP/IP protocol, 21–22, 23, 30, 263
Telnet, 20, 115, 135, 136, 265
Terminal, 19
Terminal session, 19
Thomas, U.S. Congress home page, 94–97
Thread, in newsgroup, 182, 184
Thumbnail sketch, 107
Transmission Control Protocol (TCP), 21
Transport layer, 22, 24
Trojan horse, 208
Tunnel, 130, 137, 139

Uncompressing files, 147
Uniform Resource Locator (URL), 88–89, 91, 130, 133, 146
Unix, 17, 19, 55, 265
Unordered list, 227, 248
Upload, 44
Usenet, 12, 30, 161, 180–191
    FAQs, 181, 193
    hierarchies in, 180
UserID, 42, 57
Username, 30, 31

Veronica, 12, 151–152
Viewer, 107
Virtual, 14
Virus, 142, 201, 207–208
    safeguards against, 208

Web browser, 5, 30, 86, 234, 243, 263, 265
WebChat, 161, 173–180
WebCrawler, 103
Web documents, saving and printing, 92
Web server, 86, 234
Web site, 7, 88
Whats Cool, in Netscape, 95
Workstation, 17
World Wide Web (WWW), 5, 30, 85–122
Worm, 208

Yahoo, 89–92

12 INDEX